Communication in a Changing World

An Introduction to Theory and Practice

Fourth Edition

Dr. Bethami A. Dobkin
St. Mary's College

Dr. Roger Pace
University of San Diego

Boston Burr Ridge, IL Dubuque, IA New York San Francisco St. Louis
Bangkok Bogotá Caracas Lisbon London Madrid
Mexico City Milan New Delhi Seoul Singapore Sydney Taipei Toronto

The McGraw-Hill Companies

Communication In A Changing World
An Introduction To Theory And Practice, Fourth Edition

1 2 3 4 5 6 7 8 9 0 WDD WDD 12 11 10

ISBN-13: 978-0-07-803911-9
ISBN-10: 0-07-803911-8

Learning Solutions Representative: James Doepke
Production Editor: Kelly Heinrichs
Printer/Binder: Quad/Graphics
Cover Design: Felicia Cornish

ABOUT THE AUTHORS

Bethami A. Dobkin is Provost and Vice President for Academic Affairs at Saint Mary's College of California. In addition to teaching the basic course since 1985, she has taught courses in public speaking, communication theory, media criticism, and gender and communication. Dr. Dobkin has received several awards, including the National Communication Association Award for Excellence in Teaching from the Mass Communication Division. Since completing her Ph.D. at the University of Massachusetts at Amherst in 1990, she has written extensively about media and political violence. Her research has focused on the role media play in shaping political debate about race, class, and gender, and the relationship between television news and foreign policy formation. Dr. Dobkin's work can be found in journals such as the *Quarterly Journal of Speech, Western Journal of Communication, Cinema Studies,* and *Legal Studies Forum.* Dr. Dobkin lives with her husband, Randy Chiotti, and her children, Alexandra and Randall.

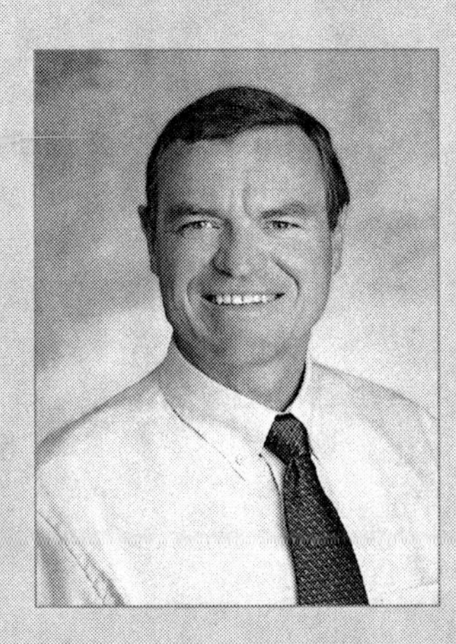

Roger C. Pace is a Professor of Communication Studies at the University of San Diego. He received his Ph.D. from Pennsylvania State University in 1984. He is the director of the basic course and teaches introduction to communication, public speaking, small group communication, communication theory, interviewing, and organizational communication. Dr. Pace's research interests are group and organizational decision making and the effects of emerging and developing technologies on communication patterns and outcomes. His research has appeared in *Communication Monographs, Southern Journal of Speech Communication, Human Communication, Western Journal of Communication,* and *Small Group Research.* Dr. Pace is also former Associate Dean of the College of Arts and Sciences and Chair of the Faculty Senate at the University of San Diego. Dr. Pace's family includes his wife, Diane Williams Pace, and their children Thomas, Kimberly, Steven, and Jessica.

BRIEF CONTENTS

TABLE OF CONTENTS

PART TWO Communication in Context

PREFACE

Communication is the social glue that bonds people together in relationships, groups, communities, and countries. The strength and quality of those bonds depends on our ability to understand and use communication well. Our belief in the transforming possibilities of communication and education drew us to positions in an institution that prioritizes teaching undergraduate students, and to write *Communication in a Changing World.* The better our students can think and communicate, the more likely they will be to effectively and ethically guide the ways that the world is changing.

We continue to work on this text because of our excitement about the field of communication and our commitment to helping students become responsible citizens of a multicultural world. To us, this responsibility means promoting thoughtful consideration of others and improving the efficiency and competency of students as communicators. Our goal is to cultivate good communicators who are both skilled in their construction, presentation, understanding, and evaluation of messages, and who have the knowledge and willingness to take responsibility for their communication behaviors.

Content and Organization

Communication in a Changing World is divided into three parts, 15 chapters and an appendix. Part One, "Foundations of Communication," includes six chapters that establish basic communication theories and skills.

Chapter 1, Understanding the Process of Communication, defines communication, presents a model of basic communication elements, and discusses the importance of civility, diversity, and ethics in the study of communication. *Highlights:* Discussions of shared meaning and co-constructed messages; the variety of communication channels and their influence on meaning; the prominence of culture as a fundamental element of the communication context; and ways to communicate civilly, value diversity, and behave ethically.

Chapter 2, Constructing the Self through Communication, examines the importance of communication in the development of a self-concept, the cultural influences on this development, and communicating about identity. *Highlights:* Discussions of the relationship between identity and the development of the self; the role of the media in developing one's identity; and communicating an authentic self.

Chapter 3, Perceiving and Communicating with Others, defines and illustrates each stage of the perception process and identifies potential problems for communication in this process. *Highlights:* Discussions of overcoming attribution bias, perception checking, and practicing perspective taking.

Chapter 4, Listening and Responding to Others, explains the stages of the listening process, identifies obstacles to successful listening, and suggests guidelines for becoming a more effective listener. *Highlights:* Discussions of the importance of responsible and effective listening in the communication process; listening critically to media messages; and responding to messages as part of the listening process.

Chapter 5, Understanding and Shaping the World through Verbal Communication, explains the power of language, explores the influence of words on thoughts and perceptions, and discusses relationships between meaning and symbols. *Highlights:* Discussions of the power of language in the formation of identity; the importance of codes in verbal communication; communicating culture through language; deception and gossip; and speaking with cultural sensitivity.

Chapter 6, Appreciating and Using Nonverbal Communication, examines various ways of communicating beyond words such as through facial expressions, body movement, hand gestures, and touching. *Highlights:* Discussions of the impact of culture on the meaning and variance of nonverbal messages; gender and nonverbal communication; nonverbal symbols in computer-mediated communication; cultural differences in display rules; and the ethics of intrusive nonverbal messages.

Part Two, "Communication in Context," has four chapters that look at specific communication situations.

Chapter 7, Communicating in Interpersonal Relationships, defines interpersonal communication and presents a model of relational development and dissolution. *Highlights:* Discussions of the influence of culture on interpersonal communication; gender differences in interpersonal communication; contemporary patterns of relationship development; and the benefits and risks of self-disclosure.

Chapter 8, Building Common Ground in Interpersonal Relationships, examines the types of conflict that occur in relationships and how communication can build common ground between people who have different attitudes and backgrounds. *Highlights:* Discussions of dialectical tensions in interpersonal relationships; high- and low-context cultures; communicating across cultures in business relationships; handling conflict constructively; and creating common ground from conflict.

Chapter 9, Communicating in Groups, examines the importance of communication in small groups and presents a model, the Problem Solving Agenda, for effective group decision making. *Highlights:* Discussions of virtual groups that communicate through the Internet; the power of civic and community-based groups; cultural influences on group norms including collectivism/individualism, power distance, uncertainty avoidance, and masculinity/femininity; and advice for leading a community-based group.

Chapter 10, Exploring Mediated Communication, examines the differences between mediated communication and mass media, the evolution of communication technologies, and the importance of media literacy. *Highlights:* Discussions of the role of media in everyday communication; technological convergence; using television to promote positive social change; and developing media literacy.

Part Three, "Public Communication," the final part of the text, contains five chapters on public speaking.

Chapter 11, Planning Public Presentations, teaches students how to analyze a speaking situation, select appropriate speech goals, and research a topic. *Highlights:* Discussions of the dangers of relying solely on demographics to analyze an audience; finding and evaluating information on the Internet; selecting appropriate topics according to the audience and occasion; presenting a balanced perspective; and avoiding plagiarism.

Chapter 12, Organizing and Outlining Public Presentations, explains how to structure a speech, develop main points, and construct effective introductions and conclusions. *Highlights:* Discussion of the use of narrative as a speech structure and the appropriate use of attention steps in speech introductions.

Chapter 13, Delivering a Confident Presentation, discusses various types of delivery, the use of nonverbal gestures in presentation of the speech, and managing speech anxiety. *Highlights:* Discussions of speech anxiety; civility and appropriate words and gestures; using technology such as PowerPoint to support a speech; and advice on avoiding sexist language.

Chapter 14, Speaking to Inform and Inspire, examines the importance of credibility in public speaking, various types of informative speaking, and special occasion speeches such as those of introduction and tribute. *Highlights:* Discussions of cultivating and assessing credibility in speaking situations; speeches of narration as a form of informative speaking; using appropriate humor in speaking situations; inspirational speaking; and responsible speaking.

Chapter 15, Speaking to Persuade, explains how to build a persuasive argument and organize a persuasive speech. *Highlights:* Discussions of the relationship between informative and persuasive speaking; building persuasive arguments with statements of fact, value, and policy; using emotional appeals effectively and ethically; advice for speaking to a "tough crowd"; avoiding fallacies, and the importance of integrity in persuasive speaking.

Appendix, A Brief Guide to Interviewing, explains how to conduct an interview and answer questions effectively.

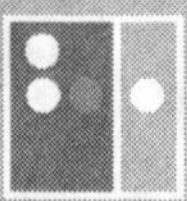

Acknowledgments

Our work on *Communication in a Changing World* has benefited from the contributions of the many reviewers whose names appear on page xxi.

Several members of the McGraw-Hill team contributed to the development of the manuscript and the eventual design of the book. Nanette Giles offered substantial support and wisdom. Rhona Robbin provided thorough, helpful, and compassionate editorial direction. We are also grateful to Phil Butcher for his support. Leslie Carr and Glenn Turner contributed their expertise as freelance editors, and we are indebted to Jessica Bodie for the originality of our CD and Online Learning Center. Cathy Iammartino guided the text through production, offering clear direction and helping us stay on schedule. Jennie Katsaros provided guidance for the 2006 edition. Brian Pecko did a superb job of researching photographs, and we are confident in the expertise Leslie Oberhuber brings in generating excitement about the book.

We also wish to thank our students and colleagues at the University of San Diego. Our students have inspired us, and our colleagues have generously provided advice, support, and expertise at every stage in the writing of this book. Patrick Drinan, Dean of the College of Arts and Sciences, provided the institutional resources that make writing a textbook possible while also enabling us to teach and maintain our research programs.

Finally, our greatest debt is owed to our families. They have heard about our plans and progress on the book for longer than we care to admit. We have dedicated *Communication in a Changing World* to them for their support, patience, and love.

REVIEWERS

Richard Abel
South Texas Community College

Marcee Andersen
Anoka Ramsey Community College

Marco Benassi
College of DuPage

Peter J. Bicak
Rockhurst University

Vince Bloom
California State University, Fresno

Steve Braden
Georgia State University

Scott Britten
Bowling Green State University

Ann Burnett
Southwest Texas State University

Lori Carrell
University of Wisconsin, Oshkosh

April Chatham-Carpenter
University of Northern Iowa

Christina B. Coons
Valdosta State University

Dawn Craner
Boise State University

Roberta A. Davilla
University of Northern Iowa

Dale Davis
University of Texas, San Antonio

Marcia Dixson
Indiana University–Purdue University Fort Wayne

Kelly Dorgan
East Tennessee State University

Dennis Dufer
St. Louis Community College, Meramec

Tony Gattis
University of Kansas

John Gilgun
California State University, Sacramento

Bethany Girton
Indiana State University

Jonathan Gray
Southern Illinois University

Ernest Hakanen
Drexel University

Valerie Hennen
Gateway Technical College–Racine

Susan Holton
Bridgewater State College

Ron Howell
Illinois Central College

Lawrence Hugenberg
Youngstown State University

Diana Hutchinson
Scottsdale Community College

Barbara Imboden
University of Texas at San Antonio

Deborah A. Kernisky-Worley
Indiana State University

Bobbie Klopp
Kirkwood Community College

Betty Jane Lawrence
Bradley University

Mary Jane Leary
Kirkwood Community College

Carole Lewandowski
Oral Roberts University

Ronna Liggett
University of Nevada, Reno

Elizabeth Lindsey
New Mexico State University

Hazel A. Lundy
Bowie State University

Shirley Maase
Chesapeake College

Ritchard M'Bayo
Bowie State University

William C. McConkey
University of Wisconsin, Oshkosh

James B. McOmber
Valdosta State University

Gail Medford
Bowie State University

Susan J. Messman
Arizona State University

Bernadette Mink
University of Arkansas

Becky Mostyn
Southwest Texas State University

Kay Neal
University of Wisconsin, Oshkosh

James F. Nolan
Eastern Kentucky University

Doug Parry
University of Alaska, Anchorage

Nan Peck
Northern Virginia Community College

Charlotte Pillar
College of DuPage

Craig Rickett
Spokane Falls Community College

Karen Rudick
Eastern Kentucky University

David E. Schneider
Saginaw Valley State University

Pam L. Secklin
St. Cloud State University

Deborah Shelley
University of Houston–Downtown

Julie Simanski
Des Moines Area Community College

Eric W. Trumbell
Northern Virginia Community College

Jennifer Waldeck
University of Kansas

David Worley
Indiana State University

Jane Wypiszynski
University of Wisconsin, Oshkosh

Ray Young
Valdosta State University

LIST OF BOXES

Think It Over

Exploring Communication Concepts

Applying Communication Concepts

SIX-STEP GUIDE

Diversity of Human Experience

University of San Diego's "D" requirement

All sections of Introduction to Communication (COMM 101) are identified as "D" courses. The "D" designation identifies a course which focuses, in part or in whole, on the "variety of experiences and contributions of individuals and social groups in the United States, especially of those traditionally denied rights and privileges" (University of San Diego Bulletin, p. 60). The course text, *Communication in a Changing World* (Dobkin & Pace, 2010) provides a strong foundation for such a focus. From the opening chapter, the text identifies the need to understand multiple perspectives and communicate effectively with diverse populations as a central reason to study communication. Indeed the study of communication and diversity are not only compatible but inseparable. Communication occurs only when people understand and respect each other and bridge the differences that inevitably separate them and it is through communication that those bridges are built. The authors believe that the need for understanding, tolerance, and inclusion is woven implicitly and explicitly into every chapter of the text. In the introductory discussion of culture as influencing the communication process, the text discusses culture as dynamic, including co-cultures, rituals, and traditions. The text also discusses responsible communication throughout the course, highlighting "valuing diversity" as one of the guiding principles. The integration of multiculturalism continues in learning objectives, contemporary examples, end-of-chapter exercises, boxes, and summary tables which all reflect attention to diversity. The goals of a "D" course are to:

1) Analyze and appreciate the variety of experiences and contributions of different individuals and social groups in U.S. society.
2) Understand and appreciate the needs for inclusion of groups traditionally underrepresented.
3) Identify issues, opportunities, challenges, and contending world views associated with living in a diverse society.

The following table identifies and introduces concepts which will help students achieve these goals. It will also serve as a reference and resource for course activities and assignments which deal with the diversity of human experience.

CHAPTER	SECTION	DESCRIPTION
1	Culture	Culture and co-cultures influence the communication process in many ways and inclusion is an important part of effective communication
	Communicating with Civility	Accepting others as equal partners in reaching common goals
	Valuing Diversity	Developing the competence to live, learn, and work within many cultures
	Communicating Ethically	Perspective taking is the ability to consider behavior from someone else's point of view and respond in appropriate ways
2	Seeing Ourselves as Others See Us	Communicators evaluate themselves based on their view of how others are responding to them
	Gender and Identity	People often choose how to talk to others based on their gender
	Social Identity	Identification with social groups is important in the development of a self-concept
	Cultural Identity	Cultural beliefs and assumptions guide how communicators view the world
	Communicating Assumptions about Identity	Communication barriers such as stereotypes and identity tags are discussed
	Interacting with the Media	Communicators form part of their self-concepts through comparisons with images in the media
	Maintaining an Authentic Self	Authentic communication involves presenting an image that is appropriate both for the situation and the outcome you desire and is consistent with your self-concept
3	Factors that Influence Perception	Communicators process perceptions through cultural filters
	Stereotypes	When perceptual constructs are simplistic, communicators have difficulty recognizing and appreciating people's individual qualities.
	Perception Shifts	Strategies for managing different perspectives

CHAPTER	SECTION	DESCRIPTION
	Biases in Attributions	The assignment of meaning to the actions of others is often influenced by inaccurate perceptions
	Use Perception Checks	Tools that gauge the accuracy of perceptions by engaging in conversations with others
	Practice Perspective Taking	Empathy is the ability to accurately perceive the experience and behavior of another person
4	Think It Over: Do Deaf People Listen?	The blending of visual and auditory cues is particularly relevant to hearing-impaired and deaf communicators
	Overcoming Attitudinal Obstacles to Listening	Attitudes pose the single biggest challenge to effective listening
	Empathy in Listening	Empathetic listening establishes common ground between people by acknowledging the legitimacy of feelings and giving support to others
	Using Perception Checks in Listening	Use perception checks to assess the speaker's intentions
5	Words Influence the Way We Think	Human thought is influenced by cultural patterns of language usage
	Connotation	The meaning of words is based on cultural experiences and values
	Codes	Codes are sets of conventions or rules shared by members of a culture
	Communicating Culture through Language	Collected and repeated use of signs and symbols form the basis of communicator's culture
	Including Others	Inclusive language is verbal communication that demonstrates respect for others by using language that values them as individuals
	Practicing Civility in Language	Use language that empowers rather than disparages, builds trust rather than deceives, and helps others rather than hurts them

CHAPTER	SECTION	DESCRIPTION
	Speaking with Cultural Sensitivity	Possessing the knowledge, awareness, and skills to communicate effectively and appropriately with diverse people
6	Nonverbal Communication is Influenced by C ulture and Gender	Nonverbal messages are dependent on cultural knowledge and values
	Exploring Communication Concepts: Gender Differences in Nonverbal Communication	Although men and women have many similarities in their use of nonverbal cues, there are some persistent differences between the genders
	Facial Expressions	Display rules are cultural expectations about the public display of emotions
	Emblematic Greetings	Nonverbal greetings vary from country to country
	Remember the Cultural Context of Nonverbal Cues	Being sensitive to and tolerating differences between cultures is an important communication skill
7	Interpersonal Communication is Influenced by Culture and Gender	Recognizing cultural and gendered expectations in interpersonal communication can help people meet their communication goals
8	Conflict	Differences in perspective and experience sometimes create disagreement
	The Value of Conflict	Conflict can provide opportunities for growth and change when managed appropriately
	Differences in Beliefs and Values	Communicators sometimes come into conflict because they have different sources of knowledge, different perceptions of events, or different values
	Exploring Communication Concepts: Communicating Across Cultures	Communicating across cultures is essential in a global economy
	Building Common Ground with Responsible Communication	Specific strategies for managing conflict and building common ground in ways that maintain personal integrity, show respect for others, and build lasting and productive relationships

CHAPTER	SECTION	DESCRIPTION
	Communicating Across Differences	Steps in valuing differences
	Think It Over: Communication, Community, and Responses to Racial Conflict	Ground rules for communicating in a difficult situation
9	Community Based Groups	Nongovernmental Groups (NGO) often provide an alternative voice to official government positions
	Group Norms are Influenced by Culture	Group norms and expectations about communication often differ from culture to culture or from co-culture to co-culture
	Cultural Influences and Group Roles	Culture influences the formation and selection of group roles
	Leading a Community Based Group	Leading a community based group poses many unique challenges and opportunities
10	Defining Public Agenda	Media executives often set a public agenda which is exclusive rather than inclusive
	Cultivating Worldviews	Under represented groups are often unfairly portrayed or ignored in media programming
	Using Media Responsibly	Media literacy can help audiences uncover patterns of discrimination and exclusion
	Create Responsible Media	Media should create and distribute programming which empower and edify
11	Audience Analysis	Speakers should adapt their speech to the audience's needs, level of knowledge, and background
	Difficulties with Demographics	Niche marketing plays on some of our worst cultural stereotypes
	Select an Appropriate Topic for the Audience and Occasion	Select a speech topic that is not offensive or does not exclude audience members

CHAPTER	SECTION	DESCRIPTION
12	Gain and Maintain Appropriate Audience Attention	Speakers should not insult the audience or tell offensive jokes
13	Delivering a Responsible Presentation	Speakers should choose appropriate language and gestures
14	What Constitutes Desirable Humor	The appropriateness of humor is based on culture
	Treat Your Audience with Care and Respect	Think about ways to inspire others
	Use Humor Appropriately	Humor should be relevant, brief, and enjoyable
15	Persuasion Based on Cultural Myths	Mythos is the use of myths, legends, and folktales from a culture as persuasive appeals

Six-Step Guide to Preparing and Delivering Your First Speech

This concise six-step tutorial will lead you through the process of building a speech. A more comprehensive discussion of public speaking is contained in Chapters 11 through 15 of this text, and you will want to read those chapters as you progress through the course. In the meantime, this tutorial will help you prepare and deliver your first speech. There are six steps in the tutorial. Be sure to complete the worksheet at the end of each step before moving on to the next one. Good luck!

Steps in Building Your First Speech

Step 1 Analyze the Audience and Situation
Step 2 Select a Topic for Your Speech
Step 3 Gather Speech Materials for Your Speech
Step 4 Build a Structure for Your Speech
Step 5 Make a Key Word Outline of Your Speech
Step 6 Rehearse and Deliver Your Speech

Step 1: Analyze the Audience and Situation

Your goal in giving a presentation will be to receive a positive response from your listeners. The more you know about them and the speaking situation, the more successful your speech will be. Begin analyzing the audience and situation by asking three basic questions: Who, What, and Why? First, **who** is your audience? Understanding your audience will allow you to adapt your speech to their needs, level of knowledge, background, and interests. Successful speeches are centered on the audience (not on the speaker), and the more you find out about your audience, the more audience centered you will make your speech. Find out how many audience members will attend, their age range, and what interests they have. Finally, find out how much your audience knows about your topic and how they feel about your topic. Good communication occurs when speakers and listeners develop shared understanding, so you will need to be aware of your listeners' points of view and level of interest in your topic.

Second, **what** is the occasion? The occasion influences what the audience is likely to expect from your speech. A toast at a wedding is very different than a business briefing at work, and a speech to introduce yourself at the beginning of the semester is very different than informing students about the dangers of food poisoning at the end of the semester. There are several aspects of the occasion that you need to discover to help you prepare your speech. What is the mood of the occasion? Respectful, celebratory, mournful, or joyous celebrations call for very different speeches. How much time do you have to speak? Audiences usually criticize presentations that are too long, and instructors who grade speeches want to see that you can make wise choices in your use of time. Last, what is the physical setting of the speech? Ask about the size of the room and available media, such as projectors, microphones, and boards/flip charts.

Finally, ask yourself **why** am I speaking? The truth might very well be, "Because I want to pass the course!" Look beyond the immediate course requirements and think about the general purpose or goal of your speech. There are three general purposes to any occasion: to inform, persuade, or entertain. Speeches to inform try to explain a concept, idea, or process to the audience. Speeches to persuade attempt to influence audiences to accept a belief, agree with a value, or take an action. The goal of a speech to entertain is to amuse, enthrall, cheer, charm, or otherwise please the audience.

Step One Worksheet: Analyzing the Audience and Situation

1. Approximately how many people will be in the audience? ____________________
2. What is the average age of the audience? ____________________
3. What are some interests of the audience? ____________________
____
____
____
____
4. Describe the mood of the audience in one sentence. ____________________
____
____
____
____
5. How much time do I have to speak? ____________________

6. Which of the following media are available? (check all that apply)
   ____ black or white board
   ____ slide or computer projector
   ____ microphone
   ____ DVD or VHS player
   ____ tape or CD player
   ____ flip chart
7. What is the purpose of the speech?
   ____ To Inform
   ____ To Persuade
   ____ To Entertain

Step 2: Select a Topic for Your Speech

For your first speech, you might be asked to give a speech that introduces yourself or a classmate. However, if you are asked to choose your own topic, you should probably pick one that interests you and which you either know something about or would like to investigate. Your natural enthusiasm for such a topic will enhance your credibility with the audience, make speech preparation much easier, and enliven your delivery. Look for a topic by analyzing your interests and making an inventory of things that appeal to you—often the best speech topics come from your day-to-day experiences, such as classes you have enjoyed, things you do for fun, books or magazines you have read recently, interesting occupations in your family, or places you have traveled.

Next, you need to narrow your topic by writing a specific purpose. A specific purpose states your objective for the speech and should be stated in the form of a speech goal for your audience. A specific purpose should look something like this: "I want my audience to (know, do, or believe)": ______________________________

Here are some examples of possible specific purposes:

1. I want my audience to understand the difference between the North American Grizzly Bear and the American Black Bear.
2. I want my audience to believe that herbal medicines are a viable complement to prescription drugs.
3. I want my audience to stop buying campus apparel made in overseas sweatshops.

As you develop your specific purpose, keep your audience's interests in mind. Why should they listen to you? Will they benefit in some way from the information you are giving them? Is there some reason that your specific purpose fits well for this particular group rather than another?

Step Two Worksheet: Selecting a Topic

1. My topic is: ______________________________
2. Complete the following specific purpose: I want my audience to (choose one: understand, believe, or do) ______________________________

Step 3: Gather Speech Materials for Your Speech

Gather interesting and informative material by searching books, magazines, newspapers, journals, and websites. Sometimes interviewing people, such as your classmate for a speech of introduction, is the best way to start. If you use the Internet for research, be sure that you are visiting credible websites that have accurate and up-to-date information. Look for sources that are clearly identified, writers who are experts and have firsthand knowledge of a topic, and information that has been published in other formats. Evaluate the information you find carefully, because your audience will quickly tune out if they think that your information is out-dated, unreliable, or biased. Remember to note reference information as you research so that you can reference your materials in your speech and provide a bibliography if your instructor asks you for one. The most important reference information are authors, publication dates, book and periodical titles and web addresses.

One key to success in your first speech is to use a variety of supporting materials. Sometimes you can get a good start on developing your topic by turning to your own experience or talking to friends and family members. Perhaps you want to give a speech on mandatory bike helmets for riders of all ages, and you had a friend whose life was saved because she was wearing a helmet. Her story is a good start. Then, you might think about the kind of medical care she received and decide to do some research on helmets and head injuries. Or, if you are speaking to 18–22-year-old college students, you might adapt your topic to them by finding out how many people in that age group avoid wearing helmets. As you research your topic, look for information such as testimony that supports an idea, examples or stories, analogies (like comparing the size of a tumor to a baseball), statistics, definitions (vegans do not consume any animal products), and explanations (one method of stopping hiccups is to plug both ears with the thumbs of your hands, pinch the nostrils of your nose with your pointer fingers, and drink water through a straw).

Step 3 Worksheet: Gathering Materials

1. List three sources or references that you are going to use in your speech.
   1. Source #1 ______________________________
   2. Source #2 ______________________________
   3. Source #3 ______________________________
2. Check each type of information that you have gathered to use in your speech.

____ Testimony	____ Example	____ Analogy
____ Statistic	____ Explanation	____ Definition

Step 4: Building a Structure for your Speech

Speeches typically begin with an introduction, develop the specific purpose in the body of the speech, and end with a conclusion. In general, the introduction and conclusion should take up no more than 10 to 15 percent of your time, with the remaining

85–90 percent of your speech devoted to the body. This would mean for a three minute speech you would spend just 10–15 seconds on the introduction and conclusion. The easiest way to build your speech is to start with the body, then the introduction, and finally the conclusion, because sometimes your ideas about the best way to begin and end your speech change as you develop ideas in the body.

Divide the body into three main points or topic areas. Main points are the most important ideas to be communicated to the audience. The three main points should be divided around a common logic, such as three types of something, three periods of time, three keys to success, three reasons to believe or to do something, or three problems. Next, construct at least two sub points for each main point. Sub points amplify or develop the main points and often include the types of information you gathered such as testimony, statistics, or examples. If you cannot think of at least two sub points, then your main point is too narrow. If you have more than four sub points, then your main point is too broad.

Next, decide how you will begin the speech. Start your introduction by getting the audience's attention and showing them that you have developed your ideas with them in mind. For instance, you might share a common experience, read a clever and relevant quote, narrate a short story, present a surprising statistic, or tell an appropriate joke. Your introduction should also give the audience reasons to listen. Let them know what they will gain from the speech and what expertise you have with the topic. Finally, state your specific purpose and preview your main points. By doing this, you let the audience know what topics to expect as they listen to the speech.

Your last step should be to construct a brief and compelling conclusion. Summarize the key ideas of the speech by repeating the main points, and then end with a clincher. A clincher is a vivid ending that motivates the audience to embrace the purpose of the speech. Let the audience know you are finished by reminding them of the story or statistic you gave in the introduction, or wrap up with another interesting quote, statistic, or anecdote. You might also challenge the audience to accept some belief or perform some action based on the information you have presented in your speech.

Step 4 Worksheet: Building a Structure

1. Complete the following outline of your three main points and the related sub points.
    1. Main Point #1:

       Sub point:

       Sub point:
    2. Main Point #2:

       Sub point:

       Sub point:
    3. Main Point #3:

       Sub point:

       Sub point:

2. Complete the following statements about your introduction:
   1. Write your attention step. ____________________

   ____

   ____

   ____
   2. Write your reason for listening. ____________________

   ____

   ____

   ____
   3. Write your central idea and preview. ____________________

   ____

   ____

   ____
3. Complete the following statements about your conclusion:
   1. Write a concise summary of your main points. ____________________

   ____

   ____

   ____
   2. Write a convincing clincher. ____________________

   ____

   ____

   ____

Step 5: Make a Keyword Outline of Your Speech

The next step in building your speech is to make a key word outline. A typical outline presents a clear order of ideas to show how those ideas relate to one another and support the specific purpose. Full outlines are crucial to developing a clear and substantial presentation, but they are generally too cumbersome to use while speaking. Like standard outlines, the keyword outline should use a consistent set of indentations and symbols to identify all levels of your speech. The first level headings should be Roman numerals and used for the: I. Introduction; II. Body; and III. Conclusion. The second level should be capital letters and used for the main points of your speech. The third level should be Arabic numbers and used for the sub points.

By abbreviating the outline into key words and phrases, keyword outlines can aid your memory while you speak. A keyword outline uses only a few important words for each main point and sub point, making the outline readable at a quick glance. It should be brief enough for you to find your place in the speech quickly, but detailed enough to remind you what to say.

Step 5 Worksheet: Keyword Outlines

Fill in the following keyword outline for your speech. Remember to use as few words as possible.

I. Introduction

  A. Attention Step: ______________________________

  B. Reason for Listening: ______________________________

  C. Specific Purpose and Preview: ______________________________

II. Body

  A. Main Point #1: ______________________________

    1. Subpoint #1: ______________________________

    2. Sub point #2: ______________________________

  B. Main point #2: ______________________________

    1. Subpoint #1: ______________________________

    2. Sub point #2: ______________________________

  C. Main Point #3: ______________________________

    1. Subpoint #1: ______________________________

    2. Sub point #2: ______________________________

III. Conclusion

  A. Summary: ______________________________

  B. Clincher: ______________________________

Step 6: Rehearse and Deliver Your Speech

After all of the work that you have put into preparing your speech, you might feel as though you know it well enough to simply stand up and deliver it. However, reading notes aloud or talking to friends about your speech topic cannot substitute for practicing the speech the way that you plan to give it for an audience. Rehearse the speech several times until you are comfortable with phrases and words that you will use in your presentation. As you rehearse, be sure to say the speech out loud so that you can practice using your voice to convey the meaning of your words. Keep the following in mind as you rehearse, and ultimately deliver, the speech.

1. Use as much vocal variety as possible. Vary the rate, volume, and inflection of your voice to add meaning to your words, communicate enthusiasm for the topic, and to gain and maintain the audience's attention.
2. Look at the audience. You should look at the audience 80 to 90 percent of your speaking time. Looking at the audience can be difficult, especially if you are anxious about delivering your speech, but with efforts and practice, even the shyest speakers learn to establish good eye contact.

3. Use your hands for gestures. Use the same hand gestures in public speaking that you use in your private conversations, only make them larger. Practice using gestures in your rehearsal so that they become a natural part of your delivery.

Step 6 Worksheet: Rehearsing and Delivering Your Speech

Rehearse your speech three times and record the dates and times of the rehearsal. Try to have a friend or family member listen to your speech at least once; note their comments below your record.

1. ____________________ 2. ____________________ 3. ____________________

Comments from listener(s):

____

____

____

____

____

Checklist for Responsible Speaking

Now that you have completed the preparation for your first speech, how do you feel about it? Look at the checklist below to see if you have followed some basic principles for crafting an effective and ethical presentation.

1. Did you choose a topic that is appropriate for the audience and occasion?
2. Have you presented an evenhanded perspective?
3. Did you identify the sources you used for your information?
4. Are the main points of your speech clear and balanced?
5. Have you rehearsed your speech using appropriate language and gestures?
6. Does your speech fall within the expected time limits?

If you can answer "yes" to the above questions, you are well on the way to presenting your first successful speech.

Communication in a Changing World

Fourth Edition

Understanding the Process of Communication

CHAPTER 1

It was Craig's first day of work at a large department store, and he was feeling self-conscious. He was excited about his job, but the other employees seemed to be ignoring him and he was unsure exactly what he was supposed to be doing. Eventually, he wandered over to a table of clothes and began to fold and straighten some women's sweaters. Katherine, a fellow employee, had worked at this same store for several months. This day, her supervisors had left her in charge of the women's department while they attended a staff meeting. Soon afterwards, she noticed that many "sale" signs had been placed on the wrong racks of clothes. Several customers were already trying to purchase the items at incorrect prices, and the lines at the register were getting long. The signs needed to be taken down immediately. Anxiously, Katherine looked around for help and spotted Craig unfolding and refolding merchandise. She rushed over to him and asked in a demanding voice, "Are you doing anything?" Startled and somewhat defensive, Craig replied, "Of course." "Well, what are you doing?" Katherine asked incredulously. Craig smiled as he remembered a specific phrase from his orientation and said, "Merchandise display."

Katherine thought Craig's smile was a sarcastic smirk, and asked sharply, "Do you want to do something important?"

QUESTIONS TO FOCUS YOUR READING

1. How is communication defined?
2. How has the study of communication evolved?
3. What are the basic elements of the communication process?
4. What is the difference between verbal and nonverbal communication?
5. What are the dynamic dimensions of the communication process?
6. Why are civility, diversity, and ethics important for communicators?

"My trainer said this was important."
"Who is your trainer?"
"I don't remember his name. Who are you?"
"I am in charge."
"Of what?"
"Never mind. I will find somebody else to do it."
"To do what?"
"To do something more important than 'merchandise display,'" said Katherine in a mocking voice as she rushed away.

What went wrong? Katherine needed help and Craig was willing to assist, but they were incapable of communicating their intentions clearly. Although it seems simple to ask "Will you help me?", sometimes a simple message can become complicated. In Katherine and Craig's exchange, several factors contributed to the miscommunication. Craig's employers failed to clearly explain job expectations and responsibilities. Neither Craig nor Katherine knew each other nor their communication styles. In her hurry to solve a problem, Katherine's "Are you doing anything?" sounded like an accusation instead of an invitation to help. Feeling attacked, Craig tried to respond in generalities so that he would not incriminate himself. Katherine misinterpreted Craig's nonverbal expressions, and both communicators felt anxious because of the circumstances.

Like Katherine and Craig, becoming a knowledgeable, skilled, and responsible communicator will help you in many everyday situations. In addition to improving the quality of your personal and social life, effective communication skills are among the most highly sought qualifications of employers (Job Outlook 2010). Effective and responsible communicators can think analytically, make sound decisions, appreciate diverse perspectives, listen effectively, present ideas clearly, motivate others, use a range of communication technologies, represent their companies well in small group and public settings, and work well with others who are different from themselves.

Despite the many benefits of becoming a more knowledgeable and skilled communicator, you may feel a little nervous about taking an introductory course in communication. For example, the prospect of giving a presentation before a group of people may provoke anxiety, even if you think of yourself as a smooth social talker who has already mastered basic communication skills. This text will certainly discuss different types of communication anxiety and offer some strategies to alleviate it.

Our introduction to communication begins with a brief discussion of why it's worthwhile to study communication. The chapter proceeds with a definition of "communication." Then, the chapter discusses the elements of the communication process and the dynamic way they interact to produce effective and ineffective communication. We spend a good portion of our lives talking and listening to others, yet few of us ever think about this process in which we engage so frequently. Precisely because we do it so often, we assume that it just happens. Understanding the basic process will increase your awareness of potential problems and challenges and lay the foundation for improving your ability to communicate effectively (National Communication Association [NCA] 2010). By the end of this chapter, you should be able to:

- Define communication,
- Understand a model of communication and identify basic elements of communication,
- Explain characteristics of the communication process,
- Consider the guiding principles of communicators.

Why Study Communication?

The power and possibilities of communication have drawn people to the study and practice of it for centuries. Communication has the potential to shape identities, relationships, environments, and cultures. It includes talking informally with friends, family, and peers; using communication tools such as telephones, e-mail, and faxes; providing leadership in group and organizational settings; preparing, presenting, and evaluating public presentations; and becoming a critical consumer of advertisements, television programs, and films.

Communication in Relationships

Humans are social animals. From the time we are born, we need contact with other people to grow and thrive. We rely on communication as the basis of our relationships. More than one study has concluded that poor communication is a leading cause of divorce (Stanley, Markman, and Whitton 2002). Infants who are held and spoken to, children who receive generous praise and support, and adults who have close and satisfying relationships all tend to lead longer, healthier, and more productive lives (Interpersonal Relationships 2000). Our satisfaction with relationships, living arrangements, classroom performance, and working environments all hinge on our ability to communicate. We also use communication to learn more about the people we interact with by asking questions and debating answers, and we use it as a tool to achieve specific results, such as expressing ourselves and instructing, inspiring, and motivating others.

Communication and Society

At a broader level, communication is the key to establishing identities, communities, and systems of shared governance. We use communication to signal to others our sense of self through clothing, possessions, and style of speech. Through communication, we come together with others and share ideas, beliefs, and values. Many advances in the understanding and practice of communication have come from religious leaders who recognize the power of language and symbols to instruct and inspire. Indeed, your first exposure to a public presentation may have been a religious sermon. Communication is also necessary for a healthy democracy, serving as the process by which people express ideas and make informed evaluations of others.

Communication and Changing Technology

Mastering communication is becoming increasingly important in our changing world. Information can now be conveyed quickly around the globe, and messages

Dunagin's People

"Are we there yet?"

Source: Tribune Media Services, Inc. All rights reserved. Reprinted with permission.

are becoming increasingly complex. In the past, someone with excellent technical skills might survive and even succeed in the workplace without mastering personal and professional communication. Computer whizzes, car mechanics, and carpenters could hone the skills of their profession and hire someone else to do the talking to clients. For example, entire careers were made by people who could effectively translate the work of physical scientists and computer programmers into messages that could be understood by clients and fellow employees in an organization.

Increasingly, new technologies and the demands of global markets create the expectation that everyone has good interpersonal and presentational skills. Technology specialists increasingly have to interact with a wider range of people, executives must communicate with shareholders and staff, and staff input is increasingly expected at a variety of levels. Employees of all types are expected to create, transmit, and interpret messages almost simultaneously. Employees who are the most talented communicators compete more effectively than others for managerial positions (Rich 1998).

Communication in a Diverse Workplace

As our population becomes increasingly diverse, so does the need to understand multiple perspectives in order to work well with team members of different ages, cultures, races, and religions. Working with diverse groups of people requires skills in collaboration and relationship building. Although individual companies can provide technical training that fits a job requirement, they are not always prepared to teach their employees how to communicate with each other. This helps to explain why top executives and faculty members across disciplines rank communication skills as a basic competency for all college graduates (Diamond 1997; Murane and Levy 1996). Some studies even identify oral communication as the *most important competency* for graduates entering the workforce.

The study and practice of communication means taking all aspects of communication seriously, from the unconscious nod to a passerby to formal presentations in professional settings, and from conversations with intimate partners to the television programming we watch at night. The purpose of this text is to help you become a better communicator—one who is skilled in the construction, presentation, understanding, and evaluation of messages. It will also help you acquire the knowledge and develop the ability to take responsibility for your behavior, from building ethical, productive relationships with friends and family members to influencing others in ways that meet their needs.

Defining Communication

Communication means many different things to different people, making it difficult to define. Nonetheless, a few central concepts underlie most definitions. **Communication** can be defined as the process of creating and sharing meaning through the use of symbols. It includes a set of skills to be mastered such that everyone from the most awkward to the most gifted communicator can improve. Communication is partly an art and a form of expression. Communication is also a science, open for study and rigorous examination. Many contemporary professions depend on both the art and science of communication for success. For example, think about the marketer who uses certain words, phrases, and images to produce pleasant feelings regardless of the item being promoted. Campaign consultants often test carefully the words a candidate or political leader will speak before the words are uttered in public. Survey research, focus group interviews, and test marketing are all part of the research effort behind many communication strategies to promote both people and products. But no matter how carefully words are pretested or audience reactions measured, there is always a human element of expression and unpredictability.

communication
The process of creating and sharing meaning through the use of symbols.

The mystery, power, and science of communication make it complex and multifaceted. The following discussion highlights the basic facets of communication: It is a process, it involves the creation and sharing of meaning, it is largely intentional, and it relies on the use of symbols.

Communication Is a Process

Our definition emphasizes communication as a process. We are always engaged in some form of communication; it is an ongoing activity that continues even as we stop to think about what might be happening. For instance, think about an argument between Ruben and Ed. Ruben might recall an insult or comment that Ed made days or weeks before. For Ruben, the conflict is still continuing, while Ed might have long forgotten the insult. Once the process of communication is set in motion, it can't be taken back or frozen in time. The way this process unfolds affects everyone involved. For example, if Sarah's supervisor pays her a compliment during a business meeting, then those who are present are likely to pay more attention to what Sarah says and to treat her differently than they did before.

Our shared experiences become more meaningful through communication.
© Elizabeth Crews/The Image Works

We Create and Share Meaning through Communication

Our definition of communication also emphasizes the creation and sharing of meaning. We create meaning whenever we think about our actions, interact with others, or even engage in an internal dialogue with ourselves. Once we decide what to say or do, we begin the act of sharing.

Most of the time, we move through life fairly confident that others understand the words we use in the ways we intend. We assume that if we say something clearly enough, several different times, or in many different ways, we have conveyed or shared meaning with others. Unfortunately, our attempts at sharing meaning can fall short of creating mutual understanding. Sometimes we try talking more loudly or slowly to someone who does not share our native language or know it well, as though this will help the listener understand unfamiliar words. Other times, we may share a common language but take different meanings from the same words. Suppose two friends are having dinner together. Sue begins clearing dishes from the table while Marla watches. As Sue rinses the dishes and puts them in the dishwasher, Marla, still seated, says:

Marla: Oh, don't do that; I can do the dishes.

Sue: [continuing her work] That's OK. I'm almost done. Would you like some cake?

Marla: I'll take a piece of cake, but do you have any paper plates? I don't want to get another dish dirty.

The statements made by Sue and Marla can be interpreted in many different ways. Is Sue ignoring Marla's offer to help? Does Marla really want to help with the dishes? Communication has certainly occurred between Sue and Marla, and they have shared an experience that influences each of their thoughts and behaviors. They understand each other well enough to enjoy a meal and maintain a friendship, even if they don't always have complete agreement about the meaning of what was said.

Communication Is Largely Intentional

Our emphasis on creating and sharing meaning also places particular importance on those behaviors that are intentional. Certainly, we all have engaged in unintentional communication, or the inadvertent sending of messages. Actions that we take unintentionally or are unaware of can communicate many things about us. For example, the person whose cell phone starts ringing during a movie may not intend to disrupt the viewing of other audience members, but nonetheless, members of the audience are likely to feel that person has communicated self-absorption and carelessness. Although intent can be difficult to determine, we make assumptions about it all the time.

Instances of communicating unintentionally are part of the communication process, but they happen inadvertently, often by chance. Throughout this text we will focus on intentional communication, messages that are consciously constructed to be shared with a person or audience, such as conversations, speeches, e-mail, and advertisements, for they comprise most overt acts of communication. We can make conscious choices about intentional communication and work to improve our skills as communicators.

Communication Is Symbolic

To communicate with others, we must come to some agreement about the language we will use and the rules that will govern its use. Communication depends on the use of **symbols,** which include all the words, images, gestures, and expressions that we use to represent our thoughts, ideas, beliefs, and feelings. We don't always agree about which words are the best to use or what symbols mean; saying, "Get outta here!" to a friend can be a request to leave or a statement of disbelief. Serious conflict can erupt over how to label events, from decisions about calling an evening out with someone a "date" to labeling a pause in peace talks a "breakdown."

symbols
The words, images, gestures, and expressions that we use to represent our thoughts, ideas, beliefs, and feelings.

The beauty of human communication lies in our ability to negotiate enough shared understanding about words, gestures, and other kinds of symbols to interact with others who are very different from us. We possess this ability because we can use words to talk about things that aren't immediately present. From being able to read directions on a map to go to places we have never been, to recounting the emotions we have felt during embarrassing incidents, we use communication to recall different places, situations, and times. Furthermore, even when we don't completely understand or agree with what someone else is saying or doing, we can coordinate our behavior. For example, we can agree to let another person pause before we enter a conversation, to place certain topics off limits for discussion, even to raise our hands before speaking in a group or public forum. Our ability to use symbols and coordinate our behavior with others is the means by which communication occurs.

Our definition of communication emphasizes the process of creating and sharing meaning through interaction with other people. As you read the "Think It Over" box, think about whether this definition can be applied to nonhuman animals.

Think It Over

CAN ANIMALS COMMUNICATE?

The question of whether animals communicate fascinates many people. Certainly, animals coordinate their behavior by sending messages, such as indicating where food might be found or warning others of danger. The distinct roles that ants play and the highly specialized signals they use, the mating rituals of reptiles and birds, and the songs of marine mammals all invite comparisons to human communication. David Givens (1999) reported that in the United States, 90 percent of pet owners speak to their dogs, cats, and birds, and, according to a Utah State University study, 73 percent think their pets talk back.

But given our discussion of sharing and creating meaning, animals may not communicate in the same sense that humans do. When we communicate, we do more than use abstract symbols and coordinate behavior; we also make assumptions about the internal states of others—their emotions, moods, beliefs—and communicate based on those assumptions. In a series of experiments with chimpanzees, Dr. Daniel Povinelli determined that although they can use many human symbols and coordinate behaviors, chimpanzees probably do not empathize in the same ways that humans do (Wheeler 1999). Think about stories of brave dogs that recognize the distress of their owners. Although they have learned to respond to a facial expression and sounds of distress, we don't know if they have the capacity to understand what caused the distress or to develop new responses to it.

How far can you take the comparison between human and animal communication?

How important is interpreting the intent of others to the process of communication?

Do animals use symbols to communicate?
© Bill Losh/Getty Images/FPG

Basic Elements in the Communication Process

Communication is the most universal human activity, but it is also one of the most idiosyncratic. We all do it, but we all do it differently. Explaining something so universal, yet personal, is a challenge. To help explain the elements in the communication situation, scholars construct theoretical models. Models often provide a simplified visual explanation of complex processes. They are similar to the picture on the box of a jigsaw puzzle. The picture allows you to see where each individual piece fits into the completed puzzle. Similarly, a model allows theorists to isolate and define individual elements of the communication process and show their relationship to the whole. A contemporary model of the communication process is depicted in Figure 1-1.

Check out the Connections CD-ROM for a series of animations that illustrate an interactive model of the communication process.

Every communication situation, no matter how unique and singular, contains the following elements: (1) two or more communicators, (2) one or more messages, (3) one or more communication channels, (4) a certain amount of noise or interference in the communication process, (5) feedback exchange between communicators, and (6) a communication setting or context (NCA 1998). While the number of basic elements is small, the process itself is rich. Each time we communicate, the elements interrelate differently and produce unique outcomes. To more fully explain the model, we begin with a discussion of each element in the communication process.

FIGURE 1-1 A CONTEMPORARY MODEL OF THE COMMUNICATION PROCESS

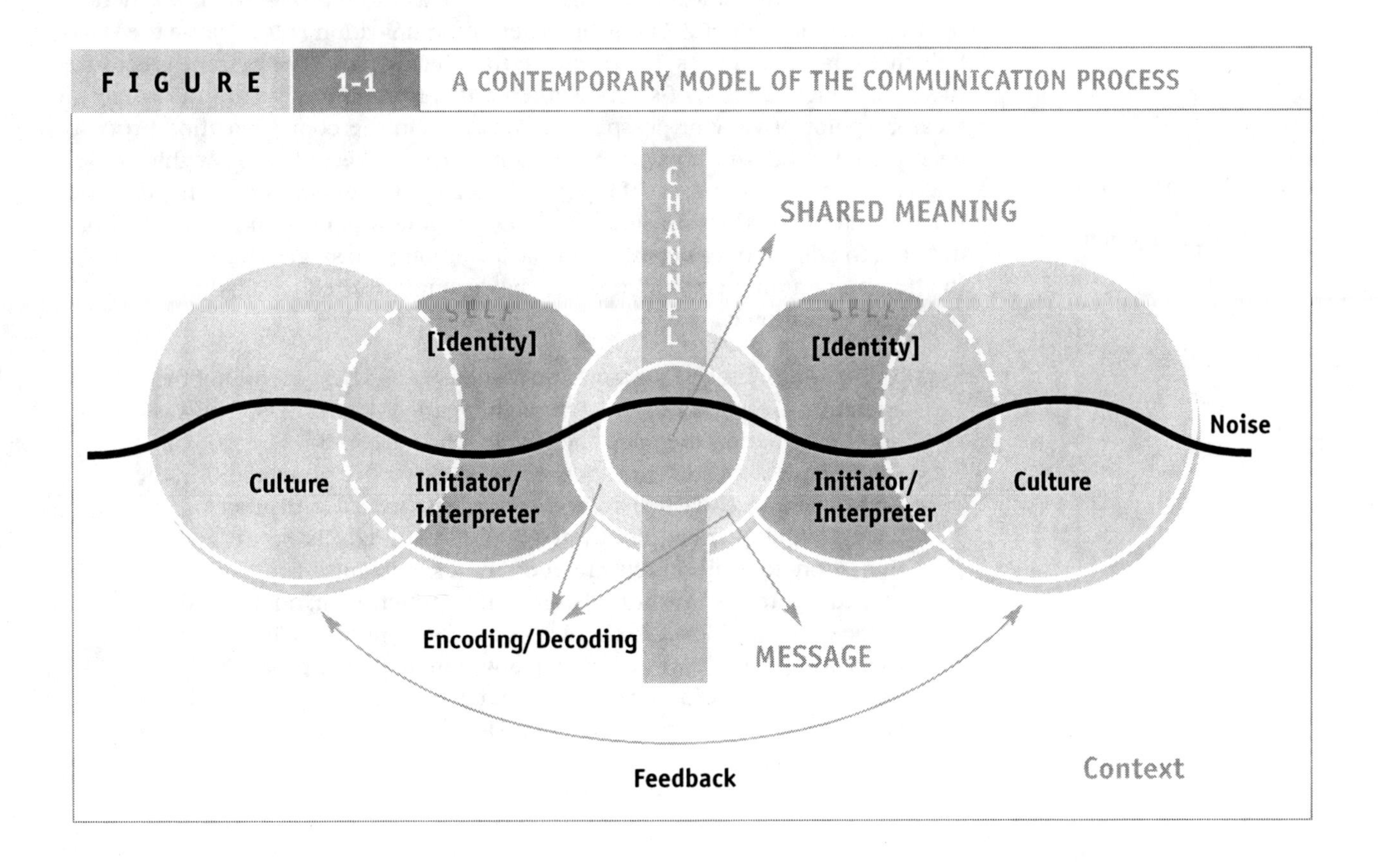

Communicators

Communication is a shared experience between humans who simultaneously initiate and interpret messages through the processes of encoding and decoding.

initiator
One who begins or advances the communication process by generating a message.

interpreter
One who perceives and attempts to understand a message.

encoding
The initiation and creation of a message as a communicator translates ideas, thoughts, and feelings into symbols.

decoding
The interpretation of a message by deciphering symbols into understandable and meaningful ideas, thoughts, and feelings.

Initiators and Interpreters.

The communication process begins with the perception or establishment of a relationship between communicators. It requires an **initiator,** one who starts or advances the communication process by generating a message ("How's your family?") and an **interpreter,** one who perceives and attempts to understand a message ("Everyone's doing great, thanks"), who exist in some kind of relationship with each other, whether they be strangers at a bus station or friends talking on the telephone.

Encoding and Decoding.

Encoding occurs with the initiation and creation of a message as a communicator translates ideas, thoughts, and feelings into symbols. **Decoding** is the reverse of encoding and occurs as a communicator interprets a message by deciphering the symbols into understandable and meaningful ideas, thoughts, and feelings. Suppose that you want to ask a question during your communication class. You need to translate this desire into a meaningful message. You encode your desire into a symbolic gesture by raising your hand. The professor sees your raised hand, decodes it as a request to ask a question, and calls on you. In this way, communicators create shared meaning by encoding and decoding thoughts, feelings, ideas, desires, and goals.

self
The total composite of a person's personality, experiences, and identity.

The Self.

Communication succeeds as long as the symbols are mutually recognizable and meaningful. Often, however, communication fails because the symbols that one person uses do not match the meaning another person assigns to them. Misunderstanding of symbols often arises from differences in the communicator's point of view or perspective. Messages in the communication process must pass through the "self" of each communicator. This **self** can roughly be defined as the total composite of a person's personality, experiences, and identity. No two selves are identical, and this makes common understanding of symbols difficult. The differences between people are among the single biggest challenges to effective communication. Consider this example related by a father in one of our communication classes:

> A few summers ago I took my son Steven and his best friend Robby to a church social. Both boys were eight years old and the social was a potluck buffet on the back lawn of the chapel. The boys eagerly filled their plates with food and poured large glasses of punch. Robby, the first one in line, dashed to where we had spread a blanket on the lawn. Half way there, Robby tripped and spilled his entire glass of punch on several church members in a spectacular fall. Horrified, I looked up to see my son also running, punch in hand, toward the scene of the accident. Anxiously I yelled, "Steven!!! Stop!" Steven came to an abrupt halt without spilling any punch. As I approached him, I chided, "Steven, didn't you see what happened to Robby?" "Don't worry Dad," my son reassured me, "There is plenty of punch—Robby can get more."

While Steven's father was worried about the church members and the mess of another accident, Steven was worried about his friend Robby. Communicators all encode and decode symbols by drawing upon their unique experiences and personalities, and some amount of common experience is necessary for effective communication to occur.

The greater the common experiences, the more resources communicators have to create meanings. If there are few common experiences between people, communication is more difficult. In these instances, communicators must first establish some mutually understood symbols. For example, if you were a computer novice, you might find it difficult to understand a computer expert until you gained at least some minimal experience. Even the act of purchasing your first computer would require you to know a few basic terms, such as the parts of a computer, in order to understand a salesperson and the various options available. Similarly, the more experiences people have in common, the easier it is to communicate.

Messages

Messages are symbolic expressions of ideas, thoughts, and feelings. Messages can be either verbal or nonverbal, or both. Many people think of verbal messages as vocal, or spoken communication, and nonverbal as unspoken. This popular misconception presents definitional problems for communication scholars who believe that much verbal communication is unspoken and some nonverbal messages are voiced. For example, how would you classify written English? Is it nonverbal because it is unspoken? Another source of possible confusion is sign language, which is surely verbal but not necessarily vocal. Similarly, nonverbal communication can be vocalized. Consider this first person account of a near-accident.

message
A symbolic expression of ideas, thoughts, and feelings.

> I was standing on a street corner waiting to cross a four-lane road. I could hear a skateboard rider approaching the same crosswalk down a steep hill. Almost instantaneously, I also noticed a car, in the nearest lane, speeding toward the intersection. Neither the skateboarder nor the car appeared to be slowing down and I could see a horrible accident in the making. It all happened so quickly that I only had enough time to turn to the skateboarder and blurt out, "AAAAAAA." Remarkably, the skateboarder understood my warning and stopped just as the car sped by without incident.

"AAAAAAA" was clearly a vocal and effective warning. But was it verbal? Communication scholars clarify these definitional questions with a linguistic distinction between verbal and nonverbal messages.

verbal communication
Messages expressed through a formal language, using oral, written, or signed words.

nonverbal communication
Messages expressed through symbols other than words, including hand gestures, facial expressions, touching, vocal inflection, and clothing.

Verbal and Nonverbal Communication.

Verbal communication consists of messages expressed through a formal language. Under this definition, communication can be oral, written, or even signed and still be verbal as long as it involves the use of words. **Nonverbal communication** consists of messages expressed through symbols other than words. They are "extralinguistic," or outside of language (Anderson 1999). Nonverbal messages include hand gestures, facial expressions, touching, the inflection of your voice, the clothes you wear, and even silence.

Written and Oral Communication. Although verbal communication can be either written or oral, significant differences exist between the two. First, oral communication is usually less formal and more personal than written communication. Speakers frequently use slang and other colloquial sayings that would be inappropriate in written communication. For instance, speakers sometimes use personal pronouns like "I," "me," and "you" more liberally than writers and are less precise when talking about facts and figures. A writer might state, "The price of the airline ticket was $619," while a speaker might simply say, "The ticket cost more than $600."

"A word is dead/When it is said/ Some say. I say it just/Begins to live/ That day."
—Emily Dickinson, poet

Oral communication is also more interactive than writing. The physical presence of other people makes speaking a spontaneous and fluid style of communication, whereas written messages are more stable and less flexible. In oral communication, sentences are often shorter, thoughts are interrupted before they are completed, and speakers sometimes shift topics midsentence based on the reactions they are getting from other communicators.

Finally, oral communication is more transient than writing; that is, oral communication is not recorded on paper or other media. The only recollection of most oral communication is the memory of the communicators. Because oral communication is transient, communicators often repeat words and phrases as they talk. By contrast, if readers do not understand a particular part of a written message, they can reread the passage or stop to contemplate the author's meaning—as you may do from time to time when reading this text! Repetition in an oral message serves the same function and allows listeners to comprehend the message more fully.

Messages are the substance of shared meaning. They are complex combinations of verbal and nonverbal symbols. As communicators initiate and interpret these symbols, they hope to establish mutual understanding. But communicators rarely, if ever, understand messages in their entirety. Shared meaning is the portion of messages that is mutually understood by the communicators in the situation. The difference between shared meaning and the total sum of messages is represented in Figure 1-2.

Channels

Messages cannot be exchanged without some means of delivery or transportation. **Channels** are the mediums that carry messages between communicators. There are an amazing number of channels to choose from when sending a message, ranging from traditional forms like speaking and writing to more contemporary ones such as text messaging and sending email. Creative communicators inscribe messages in the sand at the beach, write comments in the dust of dirty cars, post notes on refrigerators, or tattoo messages on their bodies.

channels
The mediums that carry messages between communicators.

The choice of a channel is an important part of the communication situation. The communication channel influences the message you send by intervening in the communication process and altering the intent, substance, or result of the message. For example, suppose your supervisor at work wants to clarify a com-

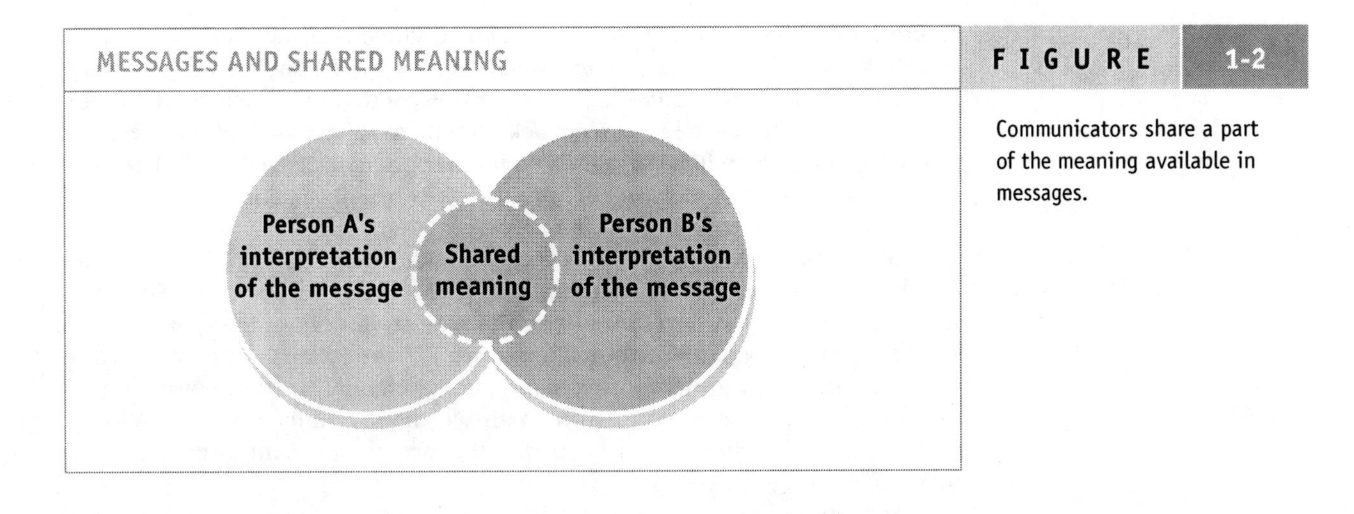

FIGURE 1-2

Communicators share a part of the meaning available in messages.

pany policy about employee parking. If she takes the time to talk to you about the policy in person, you might infer that her concerns are important. On the other hand, if she writes an impersonal memo to everyone in the office about the policy, you might think the message is less important and even routine. There are three dimensions of mediation that can alter a message: specificity, richness, and interactivity.

Specificity. Audience specificity refers to the ability of a channel to focus or customize the message for particular individuals. A channel with much specificity delivers a unique message to each communicator while a more "audience general" channel sends the same message to all receivers. An e-mail you write to a friend has much specificity because the message is directed at a particular person and filled with idiosyncratic references to shared experiences and situations. Furthermore, you expect only one person, your friend, to read the message. By contrast, a "Help Wanted" sign in the window of a business would be much more "audience general" because it could be read by anyone who walks past.

Richness. The second dimension of mediation is richness. Richness refers to the number of verbal and nonverbal cues or modes of communication that the channel carries. A rich channel carries multiple communication cues and a lean channel carries a limited number. For instance, face-to-face communication allows a full range of communication cues including words, vocal inflection, touch, eye contact, hand gestures, and even smell. But voice mail is a less rich channel and carries only two communication cues, words and vocal inflection. An even leaner channel would be a text message that allows only a limited number of words or numbers.

Interactivity. A final dimension of mediation is the interactive quality of the channel. Interactive channels facilitate rapid feedback of a message and allow the communicator to respond immediately to the message. A static channel has either no response capabilities or significantly delayed feedback. Communication in computer chat rooms can be very interactive, allowing instant and continuous feedback. Radio broadcasts, in comparison, are very static and are characterized by indirect or delayed feedback. If you dislike something you hear on the radio, you cannot communicate your feedback directly to the initiator of the message. Instead, you simply switch the station to another program. Even if you call the station to complain, your message will probably be taken by an answering machine rather than by the originator of the message.

People who communicate effectively consider the range of available channels and select the best alternatives to reach their desired outcome. Suppose, for instance, that you have a friend graduating from college and you want to send a message of congratulations. You could tell your friend in person at commencement, send a greeting card, send a dozen helium balloons, write a message on a cake, leave a message on an answering machine, or send an e-mail. The channel you choose will influence the way your friend interprets your message of congratulations.

Specificity, richness, and interactivity are not discrete channel characteristics, but rather points on a continuum from high to low. For instance, the telephone is less rich than face-to-face interaction but certainly not as lean as a fax machine, and an e-mail is more interactive than a billboard message but not as interactive as computer chat. Table 1-1 lists some channels of communication and possible ways to mediate a message.

Noise

noise
Anything that interferes with the creation of shared meaning between or among communicators.

Despite our best efforts, various aspects of the communication situation get in the way of mutual understanding. **Noise** is anything that interferes with the creation of shared meaning between or among communicators. Noise can occur at any stage of the communication process and is depicted in the model in Figure 1-1 with a line that extends through all elements of the situation.

Internal Noise. Internal noise happens when physiological need or psychological characteristics interfere in the communication process. For example, you might daydream in class and miss part of your professor's lecture, or you may be hungry and unable to concentrate on the message. One common form of internal noise is confusion over the meaning of words; two people may have different meanings for the same word or phrase. Consider this statement from an experienced college student to a new, first-year student: "One thing to remember about college is that *you can't study too much*." This statement has two opposite meanings: (1) study as much as you can because there is always more to learn or (2) limit how much you study, because there are other things to do in college. The English language has many such ambiguous words and phrases that lead to internal noise as communicators try to figure out which meanings are intended.

Another form of internal noise is the preconceived notion you have about a communication situation. Suppose you want to return a purchase to a store for a refund but cannot find the receipt. You are aware that the sales associate might deny your request. You might even imagine a hostile conversation in which the associate rebukes you for trying to return the purchase. How is this preconceived notion about the situation likely to affect your role in the interaction? If your fears are strong enough, they might deter you from asking for the refund, or you might

TABLE 1-1

Communication Channels Influence How Messages Are Interpreted

CHANNEL	SPECIFICITY	RICHNESS	INTER-ACTIVITY	COMMENT
Physical Presence				
Face-to-face	High	High	High	The most audience-specific, rich, and interactive channel.
Written/Printed				
Personal letter	High	Medium	Medium	Very audience specific, but restricts the communication cues to verbal expression and inferences from writing style and handwriting. Delayed feedback gives it the nickname "snail-mail."
Newspaper	Low/medium	Medium	Low	Many large newspapers publish different editions for different parts of a city. Readers can further customize the message by selecting which articles they read. Feedback is limited to letters from readers and market research.
Electronic/Computer				
Telephone	High	Medium	Medium/ high	Very interactive with instantaneous feedback. Communication cues limited to voice and vocal characteristics.
Texting/ Chatting	High	Low/ medium	High	Very interactive but a somewhat lean medium. Emphasizes written verbal skills, although regular users develop codes for nonverbal communication. Emphasizes "keyboard" skills, but new technology continues to add other communication cues such as sound and graphics.
Mass Media				
Television	Low	Medium/ high	Low	Television reaches a mass audience with a rich message. Primary feedback consists of television ratings, critical reviews, and sale of advertising "spots."

be more defensive or unpleasant than usual. In this way, our expectations about the situation are a form of internal noise that can shape the interaction and sometimes interfere with effective communication.

Self-interest also creates internal noise. As we communicate with others, we often begin to form responses to their messages or think of our own experiences. If this self-interest is particularly strong, it can significantly interfere with our ability to pay attention to and understand others. For example, suppose a classmate says to you, "I just took the hardest exam." Almost instantly you might begin to think of difficult exams you have taken and reply with, "Well, it couldn't be any harder than my economics exam." By focusing on your own response, you have neglected to offer the consolation that your friend was probably seeking.

"Egotism: The art of seeing in yourself what others cannot see."
—George Higgins, author

External Noise. In contrast to internal noise, which is interference within the communicator, external noise is interference in the environment, such as sounds that compete for your attention. Have you ever tried to converse with someone while an air conditioner runs nearby or fans cheer at a ball game? External noise can also be caused by interference in the communication channel. Handwriting that is difficult to read or cellular phones that "break up" are examples of external noise. There are many types of noise that are particular to the situation. Effective communicators minimize both internal and external noise and focus on the intent and substance of the message.

Feedback

feedback
A response or reaction to a message.

We can often detect the presence of noise or interference in the communication situation through feedback. **Feedback** is a response or reaction to a message. It tells us if our messages are being interpreted as intended. We then use the feedback to adjust and clarify messages. For example, if other people look confused as we talk, we can repeat part of the message or simply ask what needs clarifying. Conversations are full of verbal clarifications, questions, and extensions that serve as feedback to help communicators build understanding. Consider the simple act of giving directions.

Alexia: Do you know how to get to my place?

Shannon: No. Do you live by Zach?

Alexia: Sort of. Go down Second Street a little further and turn at the video store. Do you know where I mean?

Shannon: Is that the one with a big bag of popcorn in the window?

Alexia: That's the place. You can't miss the popcorn. Turn there.

Shannon: Right or left?

Alexia: Where you coming from?

Shannon: From Bayside.

Alexia: Then turn right, go about two blocks. Brown building called Kelly's Terrace. You can't miss it. A big green sign out front. You have probably seen it before.

Shannon: I know exactly where you mean. I will be there at eight.

Alexia: A.M.?

Shannon: [Laughs] Hardly. See you tonight.

Through a series of questions and reactions, both communicators were able to clarify simple directions and verbally talk through potential misunderstandings. Much feedback is also nonverbal. Preachers delivering a sermon, for instance, rely on the congregation's facial gestures, body posture, and other nonverbal cues to understand how the message is being received. Similarly, professors always know when the end of class is approaching because students engage in nonverbal feedback such as looking at the clock, glancing at the door, and even closing their books.

Context

Context is the environment surrounding the communication process. Communication never occurs in a vacuum apart from the environment, but always emerges out of and is influenced by the surrounding context. Three important aspects of context are (1) physical setting, (2) communicative setting, and (3) culture.

> "Not a sentence or a word is independent of the circumstances under which it is uttered."
>
> —Alfred North Whitehead, English philosopher

Physical Setting. The physical setting can have a profound impact on the communication situation. Consider this example. Several years ago our university hosted a presidential debate, and two of our students had the opportunity to attend the televised event in person. One student was seated near the front of the auditorium and one was seated in the rear. The student in front was able to hear the debate clearly as well as see the facial reactions of the candidates. The other student was sitting behind a taller member of the audience and continually had to look from side to side to see the speakers. The speakers appeared as small figures on a large stage, and this student could not detect any facial expressions. In addition, the auditorium's acoustics were not very good and the "far" student could not hear the debate very well. The near student enjoyed the debate and was excited about casting a vote in the election. The far student was disappointed in both candidates and regretted attending the debate. Thus, two communicators who heard the same message formed very different meanings based on the physical context of the situation. There are many important aspects of the physical setting including the time of day, the proximity of communicators, and the occasion. We will discuss the physical setting in greater detail in Chapters 11–15 on public speaking.

Communicative Settings. Communicative setting is a broad term that refers to the number of communicators, the type of relationship, and the nature of the interaction. Communication varies greatly from one setting to the next. You have probably noticed this difference in your own college classrooms. There is a substantial difference between a small class of a few students and a large lecture section. In the small class, students usually participate more in the discussion and interact more with the professor. In a large lecture course, the students do not participate much, if at all, in discussions. On the other hand, they may talk more among themselves than they would in a small class. Communicative settings are also one way to organize the study of communication because they divide the

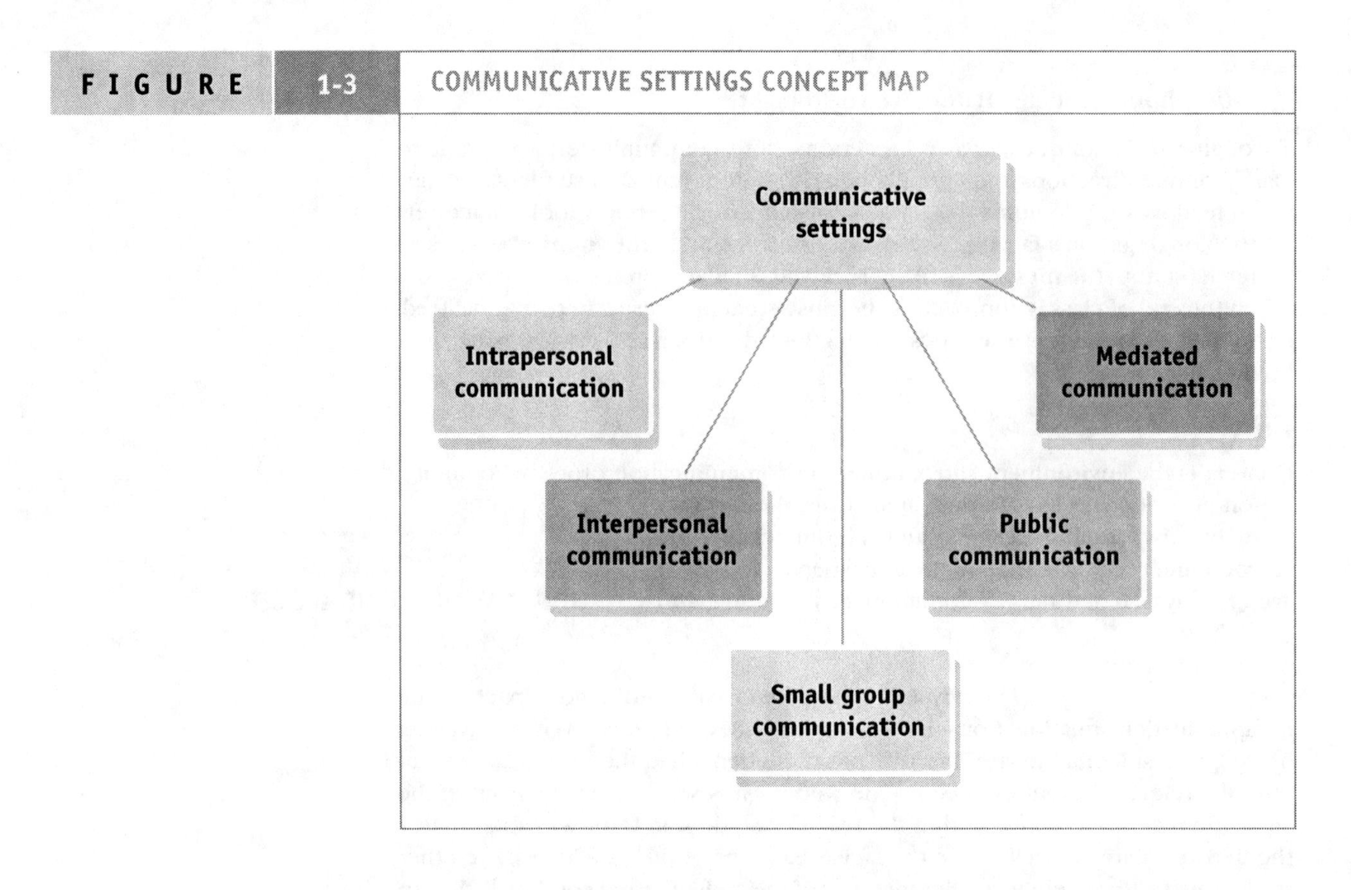

discipline into subfields based on the situation. Dividing the study of communication into categories based on communicative groupings highlights the notion that each setting has particular qualities that distinguish it from other situations. These categories include intrapersonal, interpersonal, small group, public communication, and mediated communication. The following is a brief introduction to each communicative setting.

intrapersonal communication An internal dialogue with ourselves; self-talk.

Intrapersonal communication is communication within oneself. Talking to yourself is quite normal—we all do it in some fashion. Even disagreeing with yourself is a basic cognitive process that enables you to make choices about communication. Important scholars such as Sigmund Freud and George Herbert Mead theorized that you are able to "take different sides" in your own mind and debate the advantages and disadvantages of particular behaviors. Intrapersonal communication is an important prelude to other forms of interaction when we talk to ourselves about the initiation of messages by others and our interpretation of those messages. The box, "Exploring Communication Concepts: Self-Talk" discusses some of the important functions of intrapersonal communication.

interpersonal communication Interaction among a small number of people.

Interpersonal communication is interaction among a small number of people and is characterized by more personal and individualized communication than that which takes place in larger groups. A common form of interpersonal communication is *dyads,* or interaction between two people, which is often called dyadic communication. We spend much of our communication time in dyads; even some large groups, like social gatherings, are composed mostly of people talking in dyads. Dyadic communication is also the foundation of our personal

Exploring Communication Concepts

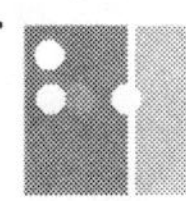

SELF-TALK

Research shows that talking to ourselves in not only normal, but also healthy. Researchers use many different terms for self-talk, including self-statements, private speech, inner dialogue, self-monologue, and self-cognition (Lawrence and Valsiner 2003, Burnett 1996; Cauchon 1994). Self-talk is either silent inner speech or "mutterings" that are voiced but not intended for anyone else to hear.

We use self-talk to regulate our behavior. For instance, we often remind ourselves, through self-talk, to return a library book, e-mail or call home, or run an errand. We talk ourselves through difficult situations, like the student who silently repeats "slow down" while delivering a public speech. We also use self-talk to mitigate against the comments of others. We can talk ourselves through an insult, for example, by remembering other more positive comments. Similarly, recent research also reveals that we use self-talk to make sense of our experiences. One study found that women with high self-esteem used self-talk to gain a perspective on challenging experiences, develop individual maturity, and solidify a strong core of personal values (Chathan-Carpenter and De Francisco 1997).

Self-talk can build or lower self-esteem. Positive self-talk can build confidence and improve skills. For example, one study found that children who repeated phrases such as "Don't worry," "Remember to use your plan," and "Take it one step at a time" performed better on a math exam than students who engaged in negative self-talk such as "I can't do this" (Kamann and Wong 1993). Other researchers have discovered positive self-talk improves many other skills including learning a foreign language, writing, and even sports performance (Tice 1992; Van Raalte and Brewer 1995). Finally, one study reviewing research on positive self-talk found that it helped students overcome deficits in math computation, served as a way for impulsive children to control their behavior, and generally helped students' ability to listen, solve problems, and read information (Solley and Payne 1992).

ASK YOURSELF:

1. When are you most likely to engage in self-talk?
2. How might self-talk help you prepare for future interactions with others?

relationships, which are most often created and maintained by talking one-on-one with another individual, whether about world politics or the best place to buy pizza. Interpersonal communication is often characterized by a quick and continuous exchange of messages and rapidly changing roles of the initiator and interpreter. It is usually informal and spontaneous, as communicators rarely prepare their messages in advance of the interaction. Finally, there is constant and instantaneous feedback in interpersonal conversations. Rapid feedback helps communicators adapt messages to the situation and makes interpersonal communication the most intimate and personal form of communication. We will discuss interpersonal communication in more detail in Chapters 7 and 8.

Small group communication takes place among three to seven people who communicate over time to accomplish some goal or purpose, such as a school committee that is raising money for a field trip. Small groups are interactive, and all members can actively participate in the initiation and interpretation of messages. When some or most members of the group are limited to passive roles

small group communication
Interaction among three to seven people who communicate over time to accomplish some goal or purpose.

such as listening while others talk, group interaction has been replaced by public communication.

Small group communication is similar to interpersonal communication, but there are some important differences. As the number of communicators increases, so does the chance of interpersonal conflict. Small groups also increase pressure on members to conform to group expectations. However, small groups also provide communicators with support and resources as members draw on the talents and experiences of others. Perhaps, for example, you are working with a small group on a class project. Each group member will bring unique talents to the project such as artistic abilities, computer expertise, public speaking experience, or writing skills. The group can draw from these talents to produce a class project that no individuals in the group could do by themselves. The added resources often make small groups innovative and creative. Small group communication is usually more formal than interpersonal communication, members often must wait their turn to participate, and groups often have a specific purpose or task to perform. Finally, groups are greatly influenced by a leader who directs the communication. Leadership is a unique role in small groups and often determines the success of the group. We will discuss group communication and leadership in Chapter 9.

public communication
Interaction with large numbers of people.

Public communication, as its name implies, refers to interaction with large numbers of people. Often, public communication consists of one communicator interacting with a large audience, as in public speaking. Public communication is more formal than either interpersonal or small group communication. Speakers usually prepare and rehearse their messages prior to the event, and feedback is often limited to the nonverbal behaviors of an audience. Many people feel anxious about public communication. A survey in 2000 found that only 24 percent of Americans said they felt "very comfortable" speaking in public whereas 65 percent reported feeling very comfortable speaking to another person face-to-face (Roper-Starch). More recent surveys indicate that the fear of speaking in public is a still common emotion (Associated Press, 2008; National Public Radio, 2010). These surveys also showed that people who where comfortable speaking in public felt more successful in their careers. We will discuss public speaking, including ways to reduce anxiety, in Chapters 11 through 15.

mediated communication
Occurs when communicators use some form of technology, including television, radio, film, newspapers, and the Internet.

Mediated communication refers to communication using some form of technology and includes communication by means of television, radio, film, printed books, newspapers, and the Internet. In mediated communication, communicators are rarely in the same place at the same time. When messages are produced for a large audience, they are often structured and edited carefully before the interaction, and feedback is very limited or delayed. Much mediated communication is commercial in nature and has sponsors who pay to present a particular point of view. We will discuss mediated communication at various points throughout this text as well as in Chapter 10.

culture
Everything that makes up our way of life, including shared values, knowledge, behaviors, and symbolic expression.

co-culture
Cultures within a culture.

Culture

Culture permeates communication situations and significantly influences the process. **Culture** is everything that makes up one's way of life, including shared values, knowledge, behaviors, and symbolic expression. Communication situations also contain a number of **co-cultures,** which are cultures within a culture. Co-cultures reflect both their connection to and distinction from the dominant culture. For example, you might be a Philadelphia-born woman whose parents emigrated from

Puerto Rico. Or you might be a Catholic man from Ohio. Or you might be a foreign student from Morocco who lived in New York for five years before moving to California. Which of these various cultures is your true culture? Obviously, the answer is none of them. We are all products of various cultures and co-cultures.

Cultures and co-cultures influence the communication context in many ways. Culture is often the link that provides communicators with similar perspectives, attitudes, and expectations. Commonly held beliefs, such as the belief in free speech, make it easier for communicators to understand the situation, share meaning, and understand feedback. Cultural values are frequently celebrated in the traditions and rituals of a society. Immigrants who are sworn into the United States as citizens, couples who participate in a marriage ceremony, and mourners at funerals all participate in rituals that rely on communication to give meaning to the most significant events in their lives.

These rituals and traditions provide a sense of continuity for communicators and supply them with commonly understood symbols. For example, the Fourth of July has many symbols that are easily recognized by most U.S. citizens, including the national flag, picnics, parades, and fireworks. These symbols reflect cultural values like freedom, citizenship, and patriotism. Common values and traditions provide us with familiar communication situations, and typically we are most comfortable communicating within a culture we understand.

Because the United States includes an increasingly diverse mix of co-cultures, most communication situations now include numerous and often conflicting values and beliefs. While traditions can provide a sense of continuity for many communicators, they can also become inflexible barriers to change and acceptance. Consider the effects of a dominant culture and traditions on members of co-cultures in the following situations.

- A non-Christian on Christmas Day.
- A person of color on a mostly white college campus.
- A woman executive in an office full of male colleagues.
- A gay member of the military.
- A U.S. citizen who does not speak fluent English.
- A physically disabled person trying to attend a sporting event
- A Native American on Thanksgiving.

Each of these communicators is likely to feel like an outsider and excluded from full participation in many interactions. Communicating within and between different cultures requires acknowledgement of diverse cultures and beliefs, a willingness to create shared understanding, and the ability to adapt one's style of communication. Throughout the text, we will discuss the role of culture in the communication process and offer suggestions for communicating effectively and responsibly in a changing world.

Dynamic Characteristics of the Communication Process

The model of communication, as we have described it so far, is static and motionless. Just as a doll is not dynamic like a real person, our model does not look much like real communication. Communication, as we all know it, is full of back-and-forth verbal and nonverbal cues informed by one's culture, perception, background, and personal experience. No two interactions, no matter how similar, are identical, and each communication event combines the elements of the situation in a unique manner. Understanding the model of communication described in this chapter requires an appreciation of the dynamic qualities of the process. When we say that communication is dynamic, we mean that it is transactional, irreversible, inevitable, and multidimensional.

Communication Is Transactional

Transactional communication implies that communicators initiate and interpret messages simultaneously. As you initiate a message, you are also looking for feedback from the other communicators. You use that feedback to adapt your message to the situation. You encode your message and decode feedback from others at the same time they are decoding your message and encoding feedback. The transactional nature of communication makes the process very fluid. In any given situation, some elements of the model are more stable than others, but all elements can change from moment to moment. Whether changes are large or small, communication is in a constant state of movement.

Consider your classroom. How does the communication situation change during just one class period? At the beginning of class, students are sometimes unsettled and preoccupied with other things. The professor might start the period by leisurely calling the roll and carefully introducing the topic for discussion. Once the class is under way, most students begin to pay attention to the material, contribute to the discussion, and actively take notes. Toward the end of the period, the students become tired and anxious to leave. The professor, on the other hand, may have a large amount of material still to cover and lecture even more vigorously, ignoring raised hands and nonverbal feedback indicating that time is running out.

Transactional communication also implies that each element of the situation is connected or interrelated. Recall the exchange between Katherine and Craig at the beginning of the chapter. How might Craig's nonverbal behavior have changed when Katherine asked him, "Are you doing anything?" The defensiveness and dissatisfaction was produced as each communicator built on the frustration of the other. If a customer had approached them or a supervisor had begun to observe them, the dynamic of the situation would have changed yet again.

Communication Is Irreversible

You have probably said something you regretted and wished that you could "take back" the statement. Unfortunately, communication is mostly irreversible. There are some exceptions. You can write a letter and not send it, for example. But most forms of communication move forward and cannot be erased. Consider the following personal ad that appeared in a college newspaper:

> To the sorority member who wore "a hell of a blouse" last spring, from the guy who was rude to you. I wish I could tell you how sorry I am. I wish you could know how uncharacteristic that was for me, how little

> I intended to say that to you and how surprised I was myself after it was done. Most of all I wish I could erase the words so that we could once again be strangers and you wouldn't hate me anymore.
>
> Truly Sorry Would-be Stranger

You can regret, repair, apologize for, or even forget communication, but you cannot erase it. Once someone knows you, you can never truly be a stranger again. Because communication is irreversible, it builds on previous transactions and occurrences and establishes a history between the communicators. Future communication is shaped by that history. If a friend has repeatedly failed to return your phone calls in a reasonable amount of time, you are likely to call someone else if you want to go out to eat on the spur of the moment.

> "Every once in a while, you let a word or a phrase out and you want to catch it and bring it back. You can't do that. It's gone, gone forever."
>
> —Dan Quayle, former Vice President of the United States

The irreversible nature of communication makes it powerful. Throughout our lives, the words that people use and the interactions that we've had with others shape us and make a lasting impact. The power of communication is evident in everything from words of support from someone you respect to the speeches of influential leaders. Think about a time when someone said something to you that changed how you think about yourself. For some high school graduates, hearing their name at graduation can have a powerful impact.

The lasting impact of communication creates a considerable responsibility for communicators. We often like to think that saying "I didn't mean it" or "I'm just being honest" will soften or erase whatever negative impact our words have had on others. Sometimes clarifying our intent can be helpful, but it cannot erase what has been said. We can ask others to forgive; forgetting is more difficult, if not impossible. Think about the lawyer who makes a comment that violates a rule of courtroom procedure before a jury. Although an objection might be sustained, the comment has already been made and the effect on the jury has likely been achieved. The lasting impact of communication might be the reason that some people are hesitant to leave messages on answering machines. The intrusion of a recording device calls attention to this misconception, because the words can literally be called back. Although we can't always remember the exact words that others use, our communication behaviors often have a lasting impact that can't be reversed.

Communication Is Inevitable

Influential communication theorists Paul Watzlawick, Janet Bavelas, and Don Jackson (1962) pointed to the inevitability of communication when they stated, "You cannot not communicate." Even attempts to avoid communicating are often interpreted as meaningful by others. When public figures such as politicians or athletes become dissatisfied with the stories the newspapers and magazines are running about them, they sometimes decide to stop talking with reporters. They hope that by not talking to sports writers, newspapers will stop running negative stories. Just the reverse often happens, however; for example, the press might write in great detail about the "arrogant" player who wouldn't even talk with them.

Communication is inevitable when at least one of the communicators perceives an attempt by another person to communicate. For instance, suppose you cross the street just as some friends are approaching, but you don't see them. They might suppose that you avoided them on purpose. In this case, your act communicated something to them whether you meant to or not. If your friends did not see you cross the street, no communication would have occurred.

Not all behavior is communication (Motley 1990). Still, it is important to realize people attribute meaning to many of your behaviors. Knowing that communication is mostly inevitable should highlight the importance of monitoring your communication.

Communication Is Multidimensional

Since communication is something we do all the time, most of us feel fairly comfortable doing it. However, even the most familiar exchanges between people typically have many purposes and levels of meaning. For instance, you might playfully joke about your roommate's or partner's piles of dirty laundry. The playful banter serves to both "keep the discussion light" and remind him or her to clean up the mess. Similarly, all messages have at least two dimensions of meaning, a content level and a relationship level (Watzlawick et al. 1962). The content level of a message is the substance of or the overt purpose for the communication. The relationship level establishes the nature of the connection between communicators. For example, suppose Gilbert playfully says to his friend Ophelia, "Sister, you're always full of yourself." Gilbert's content tells Ophelia that he thinks she is confident (perhaps overly so). At a relationship level, Gilbert could be telling Ophelia that he considers them to be close enough for him to tease her and call her "sister."

Sometimes, communicators might agree on the content of a message but disagree about the relationship dimension. Parents often say, "Don't talk to me that way" in an attempt to remind children who is in charge of the family. Relationships are established and maintained through interaction, and the quality of the relationship is linked with the quality of the communication. It is also important to realize that "what you say" and "how you say it" are two dimensions of the same message.

As with all aspects of communication, the culture of the communicators influences the two dimensions within a message. Different cultures often emphasize or privilege one dimension of the message over the other. Scholars explain these differences by talking about high- and low-context cultures. High-context cultures emphasize the relationship dimension of a message and use the relational context to covey much of the meaning in a communication situation. For example, Japanese, Chinese, and Korean cultures are generally believed to be high-context cultures. Low-context cultures focus on the content level of a message. The United States and the Scandinavian countries are usually thought to be low-context cultures. Low-context cultures emphasize the explicit symbols within the message and words to covey much of the meaning (Hall 1977). For instance, suppose you receive an invitation to a social gathering or party. In a low-context culture, the invitation would explicitly describe many of the details, including the appropriate dress ("black tie optional"). In a high-context culture, the invitation would probably not contain as much information. Instead, the nature of the situation, who invited you, and the occasion, would serve to imply the nature of dress and other particulars.

Guiding Principles for Communicators

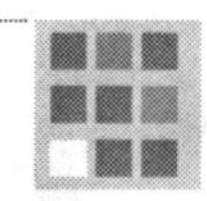

Thus far, we have taken an initial look at how communication is defined and the tradition from which the study of communication was drawn. Our definition has emphasized communication as a process of creating and sharing meaning that occurs between at least two people and which can have broad social implications. As we move into the 21st century, the importance of communication in our personal, professional, and public lives has never been greater. Increasingly, people are turning to communication as a way to improve their personal and *communal* lives. For communication to improve lives, it must be civil, it must value diversity, and it must be ethical.

Communicating with Civility

Most of us were raised to observe basic rules of etiquette, such as saying "please" and "thank you." Although **civility** can be reduced to simple politeness, it also means accepting others as equal partners in reaching common goals. In the context of your text, civility refers to faith in the power of argument, the celebration and protection of individual freedom of speech, and the recognition of the importance of community standards (Benson 1996). This definition is based on the assumption that a vibrant and responsive democracy requires the participation of its citizens (Elshtain 1998). The civil communicator cares about the world at large, is willing to participate in it, and understands the delicate balance between individual rights and the welfare of others. This balance is essential to preserve the liberty of individuals to do what they believe is right while acknowledging the effect that their actions may have on others and the possibility that different points of view may be valid.

civility
Accepting others as equal partners in reaching common goals.

One way to think about civility is to consider its opposite—incivility. Think about the effect of hate speech on the Internet, *trash talk* by sports fans, *shock talk* by radio hosts, humiliation of guests on daytime television, and deceitful political advertising. These examples have in common the use of communication to humiliate, anger, insult, or otherwise bring harm to a perceived opponent. Some people find these forms of incivility entertaining, but this entertainment comes at the expense of others. Other people justify incivility as a choice made by communicators. In some cultures, for example, verbal aggression might be valued as a skill or badge of social status. Nonetheless, incivility is designed to harm others. It closes discussion, discourages equal participation, undermines critical thinking, destroys trust, and can make hurting others seem normal and acceptable.

The choice to be a civil communicator might feel like a constraint, and it can become stifling if used as a way to silence people with deep disagreements (McKerrow 2001). Civil communication alone cannot always solve deep conflicts

Public conversations and debates are good opportunities for civil communication.

of interests and values. For example, two men can communicate clearly and with civility to each other about their love for the same woman, but understanding the feelings of their rival may intensify their conflict rather than reduce it. They might understand each other perfectly well but disagree about what to do. Or suppose that a person, group, or country has criminally abused its power. A clear, verbal apology might be a good start at repairing the damage, but civil words will not be enough.

Civility need not be reduced to politeness, used as an argument for closing off discussion, or misunderstood as the answer to all communication problems. Rather, civility is the starting place for good communication. It calls for communicating clearly, effectively, and appropriately with your family, friends, neighbors, club members, and political groups. It means participating in society in many ways, from engaging in spirited discussions on Internet chat rooms, to organizing group activities, to presenting public speeches. Finally, although civil communication cannot solve all problems, it can help build and sustain decent institutions based on ties of trust, reciprocity, and accountability (Elshtain 1998).

"To the extent that we protect other people's religion, speech, freedom to learn and participate in the political process, we preserve our own."

—John Frohnmayer, Chair, National Endowment for the Arts

Valuing Diversity

The people with whom we associate and communicate often come from different social circles, backgrounds, or cultures, making the valuing of diversity a second key principle of effective communication. Many people equate diversity with demographics, such as race, sex, age, and economic class, or with the tolerance of perspectives different from one's own. Although these are first steps in valuing diversity, rather than counting divisions among people or merely putting up with different points of view, we would like you to think of **diversity** as the value of

diversity
Valuing the process by which difference becomes meaningful and developing the competence to live, learn, and work within many cultures.

distinct perspectives that membership in various groups can bring. Diversity means understanding the process by which difference becomes meaningful and developing the ability to live, learn, and work within many cultures. It requires taking the risk of subjecting your values and beliefs to scrutiny and respecting the right of others to disagree.

Embracing diversity doesn't mean that you abandon your core principles or evaluate all perspectives as equal. But the communicator who values diversity is willing to include others and acknowledge the participation of those who are different. This can be difficult. Most of us prefer to be around those who are like us. It is easier to talk to, understand, and predict the behavior of people with similar backgrounds and beliefs. The effort required to communicate with those who may challenge our messages or beliefs may seem uncomfortable, like a distraction, or a waste of time. Although valuing diversity can be difficult, it makes us more effective communicators and helps us develop productive and satisfying relationships. Throughout this text, we will look at ways to both understand and practice communication skills that value diversity.

Communicating Ethically

With civility and diversity as core values, we also need ethics to guide our behavior in ways that are consistent with those values. **Ethics** refers to the principles that guide our decisions about what is good or bad, right or wrong. These principles aid us in determining whether our actions are consistent with our values. For religious institutions, ethics appears in the form of rules that guide behavior in accordance with sacred teachings. For professional organizations, ethics is often expressed as codes of conduct. For every group to which you belong, there are expectations about appropriate behavior that are part of the culture of that group. Each expectation is based on agreement about what is good, right, and just.

ethics
The principles that guide our decisions about what is good or bad, right or wrong.

You are undoubtedly familiar with some basic principles of ethical communication. For instance, deception is rarely wise or just; taking credit for someone else's work, falsifying material, or sharing confidential information all constitute unethical behavior. Ethical behavior includes not only actions to be avoided, but also active steps to create good communication. In this spirit, we emphasize appropriateness, perspective-taking, and self-monitoring throughout the text.

"Ethical communication enhances human worth and dignity by fostering truthfulness, fairness, responsibility, personal integrity, and respect for self and others."
—National Communication Association Credo

Appropriateness means responding in ways that fit the communication context. It requires addressing the expectations and needs of others. Sometimes figuring out appropriate behavior seems easy. We know to avoid profanity in professional and formal gatherings, and to begin casual conversations with personal greetings. More often, however, appropriateness involves more complex judgments about the nature of your relationship with others, the immediate situation, and the broader cultural context. For example, when you are introduced to the parent of a friend, how do you address him or her? Do you use "Mr." or "Ms."? Do you establish eye contact? Shake hands? Bow? Use her or his first name? The age, culture, gender, past history, and nature of your relationship with your friend all might play a role in determining appropriateness. The ethical communicator is willing to take responsibility for her or his behavior in ways that respect the expectations of others.

appropriateness
Responding in ways that fit the communication context.

perspective taking
The ability to consider behavior from someone else's point of view.

Perspective taking is the ability to consider behavior from someone else's point of view. We often assume that we know the motivations behind the actions of others. The ethical communicator is willing to take the time to find out what others think and feel, and to act based on this understanding of different perspectives. Perspective taking begins with the assumption that you may not understand others well enough to speak for them. For example, suppose Donna is leading a group meeting during which Warren objects to a proposal that the group subsequently adopts. Warren leans back, arms folded, and remains quiet for the rest of the meeting. Donna could assume that Warren isn't a "team player" and ignore him, or she could ask Warren how he feels about the way the decision was handled and invite him to speak.

To practice perspective taking, create opportunities to learn about others. Ask questions, and be willing to let others speak first. Consider the many possible reasons why people communicate the way they do, and be willing to participate in conversations that help you see the world from their point of view.

self-monitoring
The ability to see, think about, and act based on the consequences of your behavior.

Finally, ethical communication requires responsible **self-monitoring,** the ability to see, think about, and act based on the consequences of your behavior. Self-monitoring requires a level of detachment as you interact with others and a willingness to consider why others might see you the way that they do. This can be as simple as the professor who knows when to pause during a lecture or the person who knows when to enter a conversation. In both cases, the communicator is aware of the impression she or he is making and is able to control the presentation of self in social situations. People who lack the ability to self-monitor are often awkward in social situations and become confused or angry about the responses others make toward them. For instance, if Saluna regularly slams the front door of her house and walks to her room without speaking to her housemates, they might think that Saluna is angry and either avoid or confront her. But if Saluna doesn't monitor her own behavior—that is, if she is unaware that she is communicating hostility—she might think that her housemates are overly sensitive. At the other extreme, self-monitoring can become a form of "pretending," such as imitating the behaviors of others, displaying insincere emotions, or acting under false pretense for personal gain. Ethical, skilled self-monitors tend to be appreciated because they know how to take responsibility for the effects they have on the communication process.

The practices of appropriateness, perspective taking, and self-monitoring are beginning steps in ethical communication. With these goals in mind, consider the following situation:

> You are tired and stressed about trying to get the courses you need to graduate into your schedule, fitting your school schedule around the demands of your part-time job, and helping a friend move into a new apartment. You really want some support from your partner, and you tell your partner that you are feeling overwhelmed. Your partner advises you that you need to do a better job of managing your time. How do you react to this comment?

As you think about the scenario above, consider what would be appropriate given the relationships between the participants and the context of the interaction, the perspective that guides your response and whether you know enough about the other person, and the self-monitoring you are willing to do once you respond. As

Applying Communication Concepts

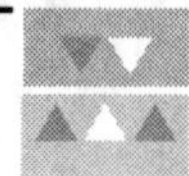

ETHICAL GUIDELINES FOR COMMUNICATORS

Each chapter in your text will offer suggestions for ethical communication in a variety of contexts. Although situations vary, some general guidelines are worth remembering during any interaction (Frohnmayer 1994). Ask yourself the following questions:

Am I communicating in ways that are consistent with what I believe?
Am I showing respect for others, even if they are different?
Am I speaking from a position of knowledge?
Did I fulfill both my own right to speak and my duty to listen?
Can I fairly restate the argument of one with whom I disagree?
Am I prepared not only to admit my mistakes, but also to undo the damage?
When I am in a position of power, am I willing to give something up?
Can I make the distinction between passionate support and hostility?
Do my actions bring people together or pit them against each other?

ASK YOURSELF:

1. On the basis of these questions, can you devise a code of conduct for your communication classroom?
2. How might participants demonstrate their respect for others?
3. What kind of behaviors will ensure that everyone gets to participate?

you develop these skills, you will build a communication *repertoire,* or a range of effective and ethical communication behaviors from which to choose. No one can tell you the ideal behavior for every situation, but the greater your repertoire, the more effective and principled communicator you will become. The box on "Ethical Guidelines for Communicators" should help you develop and refine your own communication repertoire in ways consistent with your personal values.

Some students enroll in communication courses with the belief that good communication will solve all of their personal, academic, and professional problems. The challenge lies in knowing when improving communication can help solve problems and when other kinds of change are needed as well. Often, misunderstanding *is* the source of conflict. Communicators need to use good, clear, ethical communication to reach shared understanding about everything from simple requests, such as "Would you please take out the garbage?" to the meaning of terms such as "best friend," "joint custody," and "excellent work." Conflicts ranging from marital dissatisfaction to civil wars have been blamed on the failure to communicate, and learning about and practicing good communication is the first, and often most important, step in resolving these conflicts. In this way, effective, ethical communication contributes to a better quality of life.

Communication is the basis of our relationships with others. Through communication, we develop our identities, form relationships, try out roles, explore the world, and accomplish goals. Communication is also central to maintaining a vibrant and responsive democracy. Understanding communication is the first step to mastering it. Becoming a skilled communicator can help you develop stronger relationships, increase your workplace effectiveness, and achieve your personal goals.

Resources for Review and Skill Building

Many of these resources are supported by the Connections CD-ROM and free Online Learning Center website.

SUMMARY

This summary is organized around the questions found at the beginning of the chapter. See if you can answer them before reading the summary paragraphs.

1. How is communication defined?

   Communication is the process of creating and sharing meaning through the use of symbols. It is an ongoing activity of producing meaning through messages primarily intended to be shared with others.

2. How has the study of communication evolved?

   The study of communication can be traced back at least to ancient Greece with the study of rhetoric. More recently, scholars have adopted social scientific approaches to communication, leading to a diverse field that focuses on the initiation and interpretation of messages in a variety of contexts.

3. What are the basic elements of the communication process?

   The basic elements of the communication process are initiators and interpreters, messages, noise, channels, feedback, context, and culture. Communication relies on symbols used by initiators and interpreters who create messages by encoding and decoding ideas, feelings, and thoughts into symbols. Noise is anything that interferes with the creation of shared meaning. Channel refers to the medium that carries a message. Feedback is the reaction to a message; it consists of verbal and nonverbal reactions to a message. Context is the environment surrounding the interaction and includes physical setting, communicative settings, culture, and rules. Culture is everything that makes up our way of life, including shared values, knowledge, behaviors, and symbolic expression. Co-cultures exist within the prevailing beliefs of the dominant culture.

4. What is the difference between verbal and nonverbal communication?

   Verbal communication is expressed through the use of formal languages. Nonverbal communication uses hand gestures, facial expressions, touch, voice inflection, and other extralinguistic symbols.

5. What are the dynamic dimensions of the communication process?

   The communication process is transactional, irreversible, inevitable, and multidimensional. Transaction means that communicators initiate and interpret messages simultaneously. Communication is irreversible because it moves forward and creates a history between communicators. Inevitable means that communicators are continuously initiating and interpreting messages, including some that are unintentional. Finally, communication is multidimensional because there is a content and relationship aspect to all messages.

6. **Why are civility, diversity, and ethics important for communicators?**

   The civil communicator cares about and participates in the world at large in ways that balance individual rights with the welfare of others. Attention to diversity aids the communicator's ability to account for differences and include others in the communication process. Both civility and diversity are important principles for contemporary communicators. Ethical guidelines that help communicators practice civility and diversity include appropriateness, perspective taking, and self-monitoring.

KEY TERMS

Test your understanding of these key terms by visiting the Connections CD-ROM and Online Learning Center website at www.mhhe.com/dobkinpace.

FOR FURTHER REFLECTION

1. Some people use the Internet to create or enhance personal relationships. Do you think the connections created online with others are as satisfying as those developed in face-to-face situations? What might be the advantages and limitations of communicating online?
2. Coaches often advise athletes to "listen to your body." Can you listen to your body? In what way is pain, pleasure, or hunger intrapersonal communication? Is pain, pleasure, or hunger purely a physical response, or is it also symbolic expression?
3. One type of noise we discussed in this chapter is confusion over the meaning of words. Purportedly, the word *set* has the most number of meanings of any word in the English language. The *Oxford English Dictionary* has more than 25 pages devoted to this single word. How many of these definitions can you identify? How does the communication context (setting, communicative grouping, culture, and rules) help communicators clarify which of these many meanings they are using?

Join a conversation about chapter concepts by visiting the Online Learning Center website at www.mhhe.com/dobkinpace

BUILDING COMMUNICATION SKILLS

1. Discuss the same topic with three different people. Select people who are from different co-cultures, age groups, or majors. Choose a topic that all three would be comfortable discussing. How does the conversation with each communicator differ? How did the context, messages, channels, or feedback change from one situation to the next?
2. Look at the directory of student organizations on your campus or check bulletin boards and kiosks for event listings. Attend a meeting or event. What are some of the different forms of communication, such as conversations with outside members, e-mail lists, or newsletters, that might contribute to the success of the group?

NET WORK

/dobkinpace

Note: While all the URLs listed were current as of the printing of this book, these sites often change. Please check our website (www.mhhe.com/dobkinpace) for updates and hyperlinks to these exercises.

1. Take a look at the NCA Credo for Ethical Communication posted at http://www.natcom.org/policies/External/Ethical/Comm.htm. After reading the credo, provide one example from your personal experience of both ethical and unethical communication for each of the listed concerns. Which ones are more important to you, and which ones might be overstated? Why?
2. The Michigan State University library has one of the largest "voice libraries" in the country. The website http://www.lib.msu.edu/vincent/ contains several short speech selections from presidents of the United States. Listen to one or more of these speeches and analyze the communication situation. Identify the communicators, channels, messages, and context. What aspects of nonverbal communication are expressed through the use of the voice?

MEDIA MOMENTS

1. Listen to a popular radio or television talk show host, such as Dr. Laura Schlesinger, Sean Hannity, or Bill O'Reilly. Do they practice appropriateness, perspective taking, and/or self-monitoring? Do you expect them to engage in these behaviors? Why or why not?
2. The film, *Into the Wild* (2007) tells the story of a college graduate named Chris McCandiess (Emile Hirsch) who gives away all of his money and possessions and moves to the Alaskan wilderness. During the film, Chris undergoes a transformation and develops a new sense of self.
   - Identify examples of intrapersonal, interpersonal, group, public, and mediated communication. How do each of these situations differ depending on the context?
   - What types of nonverbal communication can you identify in the film?
   - What are some examples of perspective taking in the film?

Constructing the Self through Communication

2

CHAPTER

Sometimes a word or phrase can change the image we have of ourselves and help us achieve a goal. One of those moments came early in Simon Thompson's college career, when he learned he would need to pass a course in statistics. Simon had failed algebra three times in high school and considered himself "mathematically impaired." He recounts the story this way:

> *One day I was called into my professor's office. Professor Fine . . . read my transcript and held up his hands over his head. . . . "This is indeed your lucky day. This is where all of your tenacity pays off. You're going to be great in stats. . . . You have the second kind of mind. Listen. First kind of minds are the kids who do well in algebra but don't get stats. They struggle like crazy in stats. It's a different kind of math that takes a different kind of mind. Second kind of minds like yours. . . .*
>
> *"Kids who don't get algebra understand statistics with no problem. If you failed algebra once, I'd guess you'd get an A or B in stats. Think about it, son. You flunked three times. You're gonna be a genius."*

Professor Fine's prediction made Simon ecstatic. Each time they saw each other on campus, Professor Fine would hold up two fingers for "second kind of mind," and

QUESTIONS TO FOCUS YOUR READING

1. How does communication contribute to the development of the self?
2. How do identity and culture influence our self-concept?
3. What are some of the challenges in communicating identity?
4. How do we present our selves to others?
5. Why might communicating an authentic self be important, and what are ways to do so?

Simon would hold up three fingers for "flunked three times." As Professor Fine provided encouragement, Simon began to tell his friends how well he expected to do in statistics. He wrote, "This singular change in attitude affected all my grades. With the awareness of my new 'second kind of mind,' I received the best grades of my life in college." Two years later, when he finally took statistics, Simon sat in the front row, asked questions, studied hard, and enlisted the aid of an occasional tutor. He received one of the few A's given in statistics that semester (Thompson 1990).

Simon's story illustrates the influence that communication can have on our understanding of ourselves, our self-confidence, and our ability to act. Gaining knowledge of who we are begins early and continues throughout life, as we interact with parents, friends, teachers, and others. Think about how you describe yourself to others. Do you see yourself as cheerful, industrious, or energetic? Do you consider yourself to be a good friend, athlete, or parent? Can you identify people who have had a significant impact on how you view yourself? Communication with others, from the language we use to describe ourselves to the reactions others have to us, is perhaps the single most powerful influence in the development of our sense of self.

This chapter explores the relationship between our sense of self and how we communicate. The title of this chapter, "Constructing the Self through Communication," suggests that the self evolves and changes over time based on our interactions with others, and that we can play an active role in shaping our identities, abilities, and esteem. As we communicate with those around us, we begin to see aspects of ourselves in others, we come to understand ourselves based on how people respond to us, and sometimes we come to see ourselves as others do. This chapter will help you to:

- Appreciate the role of communication in the development of the self.
- Understand how your conception of yourself influences your interactions with others.
- Know how people present themselves to others.
- Be able to present an authentic self.

Developing the Self through Communication

A television commercial shows a mother coming home to her children after a long day at work. She is harried and cross with her children, and her harsh words make one of them cry. A voiceover begins: "Do you feel like you're not yourself any more?" and suggests that an antidepressant drug would restore her sense of self. The commercial ends with the mother, rested and smiling, pushing her child on a swing. Through suggestive words and imagery, the commercial attempts to define a tired woman's self-concept for her.

The Emergence of a Self-Concept

We all begin the journey of discovering who we are when we develop **self-awareness,** the consciousness of our existence and an understanding of our selves. As infants, we have no knowledge that we exist independently of our parents. Our world is made up largely of eating, sleeping, and reacting to the people and events around us. As we acquire language, we begin to understand that we are separate beings. Language enables us to think about our "self" as an object that can be named, defined and discussed. As we put names such as "Mama" and "Dada" to our parents, we also attach a name to our "self" and we become self-aware. From that point forward, we develop images, perceptions, and beliefs that define who we are.

self-awareness
The consciousness of our existence and degree to which we understand ourselves.

How you see yourself affects how and what you communicate to others. The impressions that you form about yourself constitute your **self-concept,** a relatively consistent image or set of perceptions that you have about your self. Your self-concept is a more or less stable *construct* that serves as a basis of comparison when you reflect on your behaviors and their consequences (Kollack and O'Brien 1994). Some perceptions of the self remain relatively constant, such as core beliefs about whether you are a good, intelligent, or kind person. Other perceptions change or evolve throughout your life as you encounter people and events. For example, an influential teacher might have convinced you that you really do have artistic ability.

self-concept
A relatively consistent image or set of perceptions that you have about yourself.

Seeing Ourselves as Others See Us

As we interact with others, we begin to evaluate ourselves based on our view of how others are responding to us. Scholars call this phenomenon the "looking-glass self" because our self-concept is reflected back to us through our interactions with others and the broader society in which we live (Mead 1934; Cooley 1964). We imagine how others see and judge us, and we develop impressions of what we are like based on what we imagine others think of us. For example, suppose Rebecca is preparing for an important job interview. She rehearses possible questions and answers with Leila, who tells Rebecca when to expand her answers, what additional information she might need to get about the employer, and what to wear for the interview. Based on Leila's comments, Rebecca evaluates her own performance. Rebecca decides that she is better prepared than she thought, and that she really is poised, competent, and ready for the interview. By evaluating Leila's statements, Rebecca uses Leila as a mirror on herself, refining her self-concept and developing a better understanding of herself.

Comments that come from specific individuals whom you trust and respect, such as family members, friends, teachers, and even adversaries, are most likely to shape your self-concept and help you sort through numerous and often contradictory encounters. For example, a compliment from your professor about a speech you have given will most likely have more credibility than one from a student you hardly know. Or, you might tell a trusted friend what a particular professor wrote about a section of your term paper and ask her or him to read it and give you a "second opinion. "Your self-concept is refined and altered as you change groups and associate with different people. When you entered college and began to interact with new friends and professors, your impression of how these people reacted to you may have led you to see yourself in a new way. Perhaps you developed increasing self-confidence in your ability to make new friends or doubts about your study skills. When you graduate from college and enter or change careers, you may discover your self-concept changing once again in response to your interactions with new people. In this manner, your self-concept grows and develops through communication with others.

generalized other
A composite view of society's reflection of yourself.

In addition to the important people that shape your self-concept throughout your life, you learn and carry with you an idea about who society thinks you should be. This overall impression takes the form of a "generalized other." The **generalized other** represents a composite of society's norms and values. Throughout your life, you have become aware of general social rules about communication behaviors, such as how to tell whose turn it is to talk in a conversation. You also share expectations with others about the kind of person you should be and how people, in general, will respond to you. For example, your parents, high school teachers, and friends may have all encouraged you to go to college. From their frequent discussion of your college plans, you probably developed a generalized notion that "everyone expects me to go to college." Other students may have had the opposite experience. Their friends and family may have discouraged their college plans. These students probably developed an overall, or generalized, expectation that "no one thinks I should go to college." This composite view of what "people" might think or say is always with you, and sometimes you might even carry on an internal dialogue with the generalized other just as you might a real person. For example, you might say to yourself, "They think I am taking too many easy classes" without attaching specific people to "they."

Our self-concept grows and develops through interaction with others. The conclusions we draw affect whether we feel good or bad about ourselves. Communication, then, is more than a method of exchanging messages—it is central to the development of our self.

The Power of Self-Fulfilling Prophecies

self-fulfilling prophecy
The tendency to live up to the expectations created for us.

One particularly powerful way that communication with others helps define our self-concept is through the **self-fulfilling prophecy,** the tendency to live up to the expectations created for us. Although we don't always internalize the judgments that other people make about us, they often affect how we feel and behave. The story at the beginning of the chapter about Simon's success in his statistics course shows that self-fulfilling prophecies can have positive outcomes. Unfortunately, they can also work to place some individuals at an advantage over others. For example, a considerable body of research suggests that the ways many teachers communicate to students create self-fulfilling prophecies that empower some students while discouraging others. When teachers expect students to succeed, those expectations contribute to student self-concepts that include competence and intelligence. Sometimes, these expectations are communicated more often to male than to female students. Boys are called on more often, coached in their answers, given more time to formulate answers, asked questions that require critical thinking, and given more extensive comments in response to their answers (Cooper 1993). For instance, if Dr. Jensen only asks Tanya closed (yes or no) questions, gives her little time to respond, and offers few or no comments when she speaks in class, Tanya might feel that her opinions are not interesting and her contributions to class are not valued. Tanya is then less likely to participate in class discussions, which will confirm Dr. Jensen's low expectations of her.

Self-fulfilling prophecies are good examples of the powerful influence that communication can have on an individual's self-concept. Once a negative prediction seems to come true, others follow more easily. Similarly, we can use self-

FIGURE 2-1 COMMUNICATION AND SELF-FULFILLING PROPHECIES

Chris: "I'm no good at giving speeches. I get so nervous, I'm sure I'll forget my speech."

Chris focuses on his nervousness and forgets his speech.

Professor Jalisco tells Chris that he needs to be less nervous and more familiar with his speech.

Chris hears the Professor and thinks, "I'll never be good at public speaking."

Josie: "I'm someone who can grab an audience's attention easily."

Josie forgets part of her speech and focuses on winning back her audience's attention.

Professor Jalisco tells Josie that she has a good command of the audience.

Josie hears the Professor and thinks, "I did a good job."

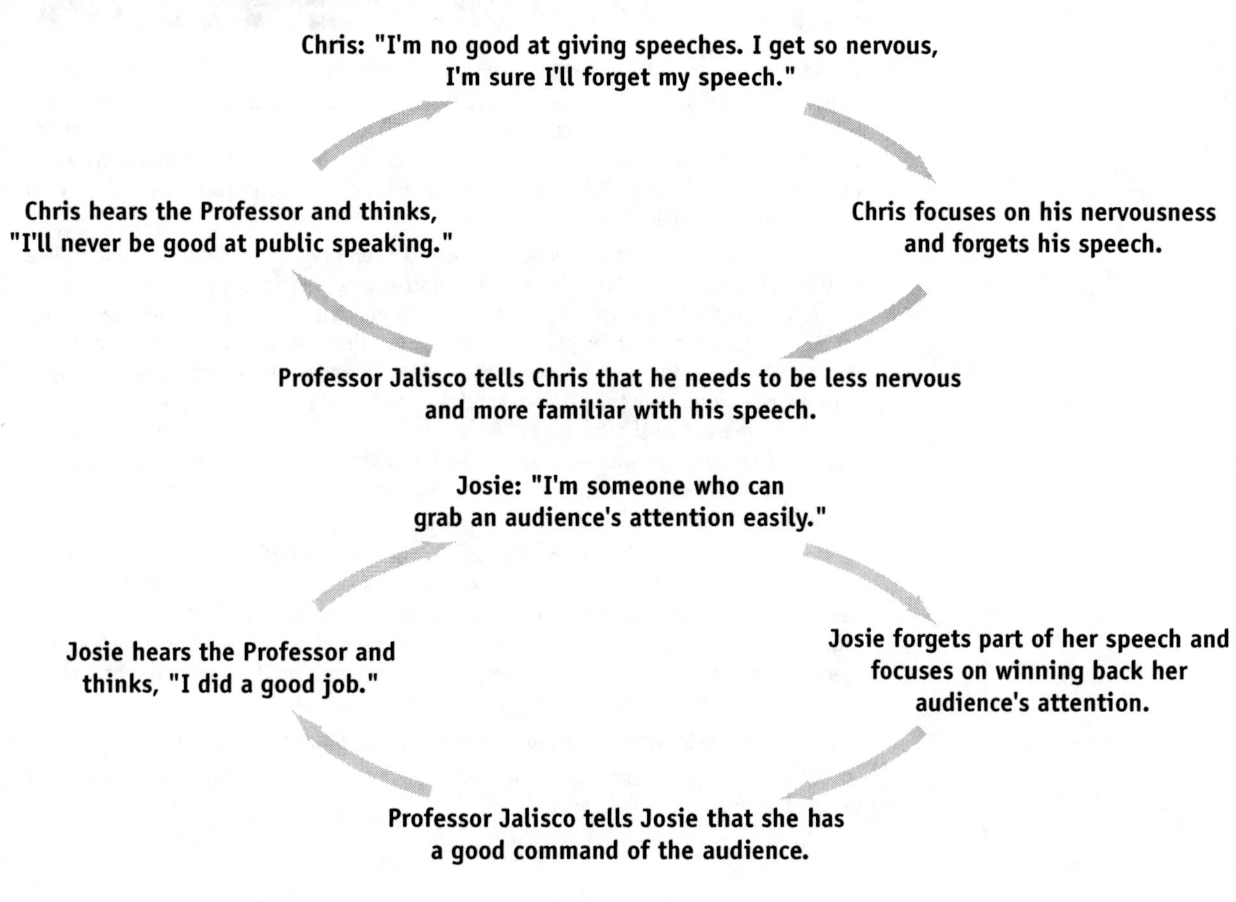

Communication can have a powerful influence on self-concept by creating self-fulfilling prophecies.

fulfilling prophecies to motivate others and inspire success. For example, if you are Ben's manager and you describe him as "assertive," you are likely to have a positive impact on his identity as an employee. He might, for example, be emboldened to offer a controversial opinion about a work-related issue. On the other hand, if you called him "bossy," Ben might reconsider talking at all. Look at Figure 2-1 for an image of how self-fulfilling prophecies can work.

Our discussion of the self has emphasized the changing nature of one's self-concept and the ways that communication influences those changes. The box, "Do You Have a 'True Self'?" asks you to think about how independent and unchanging you consider yourself to be.

Once we acknowledge the potential role of communication in defining our self-concept, we can begin to understand and take responsibility for our behaviors. As we evaluate and refine our view of ourselves, we become increasingly aware of our connections to others and how those connections influence us. The next section explains how communication about identity and culture influence how we think about ourselves and interact with others.

Think It Over

DO YOU HAVE A "TRUE SELF"?

The idea of a "true self" is most common in cultures in which individualism is emphasized. The focus on individualism is particularly strong for Americans of European descent who have grown up in a culture that values independence and resistance to social pressure. As more than one student has remarked, "I want you to know who I *really* am. No one tells me who to be." But if the "self" is produced through your interactions with others, how independent are you?

Social psychologists Peter Kollock and Jodi O'Brien (1994) wrote that many of us like to think that we have a "true" self that is unchanging and *resilient*. The idea that the self is constructed through interaction with others makes people uncomfortable, because it suggests that other people have an incredible amount of influence in determining who we think we are. However, as Kollock and O'Brien noted, our ability to consider whether we are truly free or controlled by society is made possible by that very process of interaction that produced our self in the first place. After all, how would you know that you existed without asking others and seeking their opinion? (Is this really happening? Was I dreaming?). Furthermore, our ability to think about ourselves happens in the form of internal dialogue, or self-talk.

Many of us take comfort in thinking about our self as a stable, consistent entity and like to think that we have a "true" self underneath a social one. There might be a "true" self that exists independently of our interactions with others, a self that is either biologically determined or constitutes the soul and spirit of a person. Even if such a *transcendent* soul exists, its role in our everyday lives depends on the knowledge we have of it, and our perceptions are the product of social interaction.

Can a "true self" exist independently of the words you have to define it?

In what ways have the evaluations made by others influenced who you understand yourself to be?

Communication and Identity

In our discussion of the self thus far, we have emphasized communication behaviors that help to shape our self-concept, such as whether we think of ourselves as smart, honest, funny, or ambitious, and the degree to which interactions with others support or challenge our views. Our self-concept is also informed by our identity. **Identity** refers to the conception of oneself as a member of a group or category. Figure 2-2, the Identity Wheel, illustrates a few of the common groups and categories that individuals often recognize as contributing to their identity. Some of these categories are probably more significant to you than others. As you look at the diagram, think about the spokes that are most relevant to you. Have the groups and categories that are most important to you changed over time?

identity
The conception of yourself as a member of a group or category.

Some aspects of identity are freely chosen, as in the case of the decision to join a group or participate in a leisure activity. For instance, you might be a member of a commuter student group, a fraternity or sorority, an outdoor adventure club, a political organization, or a church, synagogue, or mosque. At other times, membership in a particular group, and therefore certain aspects of identity, are *socially ascribed* or assumed by others based on our physical characteristics, such as race,

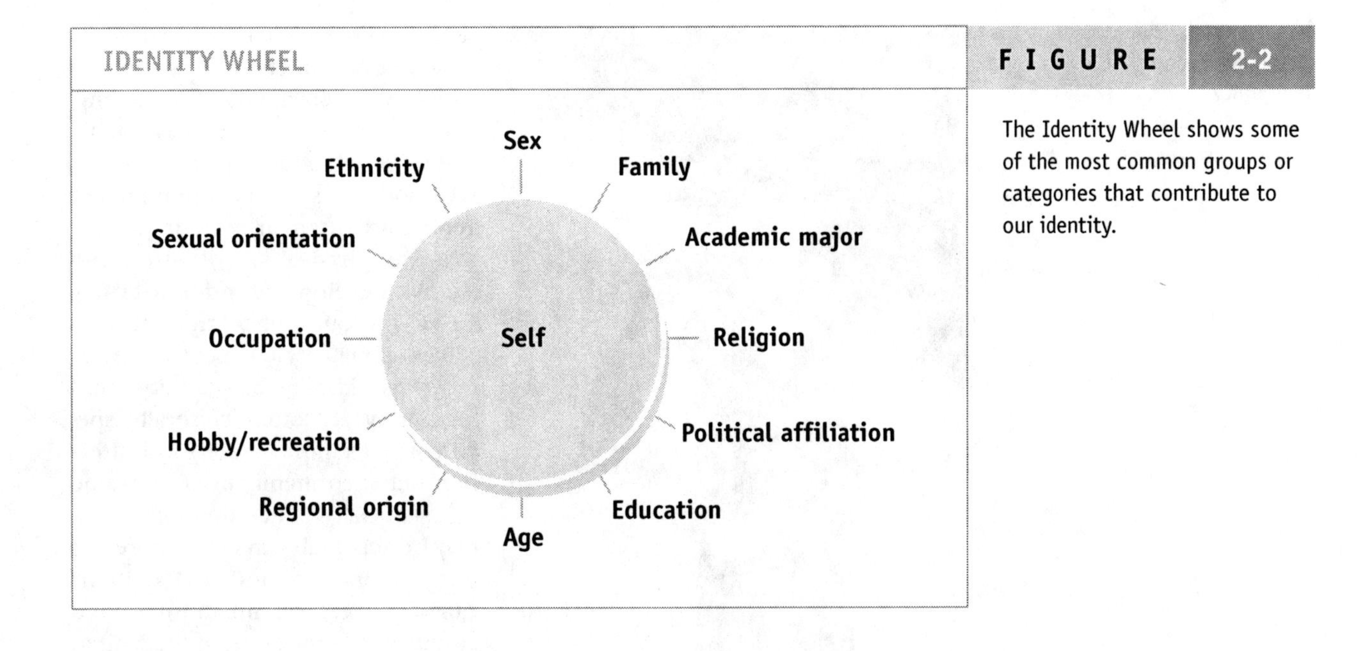

FIGURE 2-2

The Identity Wheel shows some of the most common groups or categories that contribute to our identity.

sex, or physical ability, or our association with other members of a group. For example, if a heterosexual male participates in a gay pride activity, some individuals might assume he is gay based on his association with gay men. Identity can even be constructed around a sense of place. Some residence halls place students together based on special interests, such as participation in outdoor sports or honors programs. Residents of public housing, by contrast, are often referred to as "living in the projects" and associated with violence and illicit drug activity owing to stereotypes of public housing perpetuated by the media (Vale 1995).

We draw from identity categories to guide our decisions about what to say and how to respond to others. Some of the most common categories are gender, social, and cultural identity.

Gender and Identity

Some people suggest that the most significant force in shaping identity and self-concept is an individual's sex and the corresponding gender identity associated with being female or male. Although many people use the terms "sex" and "gender" interchangeably, they do not mean the same thing.

Sex and Gender. Most people divide the human sexes into two categories, male or female. Everyone is placed into one of those categories based on genitalia and secondary sexual characteristics, such as the amount of facial hair or size of an individual's breasts. Think about the last time you filled out a survey or application. One of the first boxes on the form probably asked you to check "male" or "female." The public restrooms we use, the school athletic teams we join, and the prices we pay for haircuts and alterations are often determined by our physical sex.

These physical characteristics guide our assumptions about gender, which refers to the conception we have about what it means to be female or male, feminine or masculine, in our society. Perhaps you have noticed the difference between

Popular media images help shape our conceptions of femininity.

sex and gender in your everyday life, as when an athletic girl is called a "tomboy" or a man whistles at a long-haired passerby he assumes to be female. The communication behaviors we choose based on assumptions of gender are often far more important than the physical sex of an individual. We develop a **gender identity** based on our conception of ourselves as male or female. These conceptions about masculinity and femininity are often culturally specific. For example, displays of affection between members of the same sex, such as two men holding hands, may be acceptable in one culture but frowned upon in another. Definitions can also vary within cultures and countries; for instance, in the United States, one male might see his masculinity defined by how much money he can earn or how loudly he can shout down an opponent while another might base his self-concept on his degree of athletic skill or role as a father.

gender identity
The conception you have of yourself as a male or female, masculine or feminine.

Gender and Communication. From birth, people around us choose how to talk to us based on our gender. It doesn't matter if a baby is male: If he is dressed in pink, North Americans are likely to call him "pretty." A simple change of clothes to blue can make others perceive him as masculine and call him "handsome." For the rest of his life, others will talk to the boy based on assumptions about his masculinity, and as he grows up, his gender self-concept is likely to be one of the most important influences on his own communication style.

Deborah Tannen (1982), a scholar of language and communication, argued that men tend to perceive social relations as hierarchical and to use talk that is competitive and task oriented. In other words, their conversations establish "who's on top" and how things will get done. Through conversation, men negotiate their status, assert their competence, and preserve their independence because of their perceived identity as masculine males. Women who see themselves as feminine often perceive the social world as based on support and social connections and use conversation as a way to share feelings and achieve intimacy. According to Tannen, these different identities affect both the way women and men express themselves and how they perceive communication. Women are more likely to phrase preferences as questions, as in "Would you like to see a movie?" whereas men use statements such as "Let's see a movie." If someone offers a woman help with a task, the woman is likely to see the assistance as a gesture of support. The man, Tannen wrote, is more likely to see the offer as a possible insult to his competence.

"Of my two 'handicaps,' being female put more obstacles in my path than being black."
—Shirley Chisolm, first black woman elected to Congress

Tannen claimed that these differences are consistent between the sexes. Whether you agree with Tannen or not, gender is certainly an important part of a person's identity that contributes to one's self-concept and worldview, and that exerts considerable influence on how people communicate.

Social Identity

Some aspects of our identity are more "salient," or more important and meaningful to us at certain times than at others. The notion that we have many identities, some of which are more important to our self-concept than others, is addressed by **social identity theory** (Abrams and Hogg 1990). This theory states that our identification with social groups is important for our self-concept, and the relative *salience* of a given identity depends on the social context or setting we are in at a given time. We perceive different parts of our identity as more or less important based on the status (e.g., distinctiveness or prestige) that our identification with a particular group will bring us in a given social situation. For example, when there is only one woman in a group of men, her sex and gender become especially noticeable. If, on the other hand, there are many other women in the group, her gender is less likely to be important to her identity, and gender is less likely to have an influence on how others perceive her. Women in male-dominated workplaces who perceive themselves to be of a lower social status than men are likely to downplay their femininity (e.g., speak assertively and wear masculine clothes) and view themselves in terms of identities other than "female" (Swan and Wyer 1997). Or, consider the identity of a male construction worker who is also a wine connoisseur. When he goes to a party, he might choose to emphasize either his line of work or his passion for and knowledge of wine, depending on how he thinks others in the group will evaluate his social status.

social identity theory
Our identification with social groups is important for our self-concept, and the relative salience of a given identity depends on social context.

These examples illustrate social identity theory, which suggests that social contexts help to dictate which features of one's identity a person will choose to express. Think about the choices you make when talking to others about your age, family, career goals, or religion. You might be more inclined to mention your membership in an honor society to a potential employee than to a new friend. Your social identity, like your gender identity, makes up part of your self-concept that is both influenced by and helps to guide your interactions with others.

"My self . . . is a dramatic ensemble."
—Paul Klee, artist

Cultural Identity

In addition to our gender and social identities, our culture is another source of influence on our identity, self-concept, and communication patterns. It gives us a set of beliefs and assumptions that guide how we view the world. Culture includes everything that makes up our way of life, including shared values, knowledge, behaviors, and symbolic expression. We build cultures around both the social groups to which we choose to belong, such as religious organizations, and around physical characteristics, such as race. Consider the experience of Pam, an athletic, Chinese-American premed student. In college she is uncomfortable around some of her Asian friends, who she feels could perceive her as either "too Americanized" based on her direct manner and desire to be casual, independent, and creative, or "too traditional" due to her awe of college instructors and her acceptance of parental authority. Pam is not entirely comfortable with some of her Caucasian

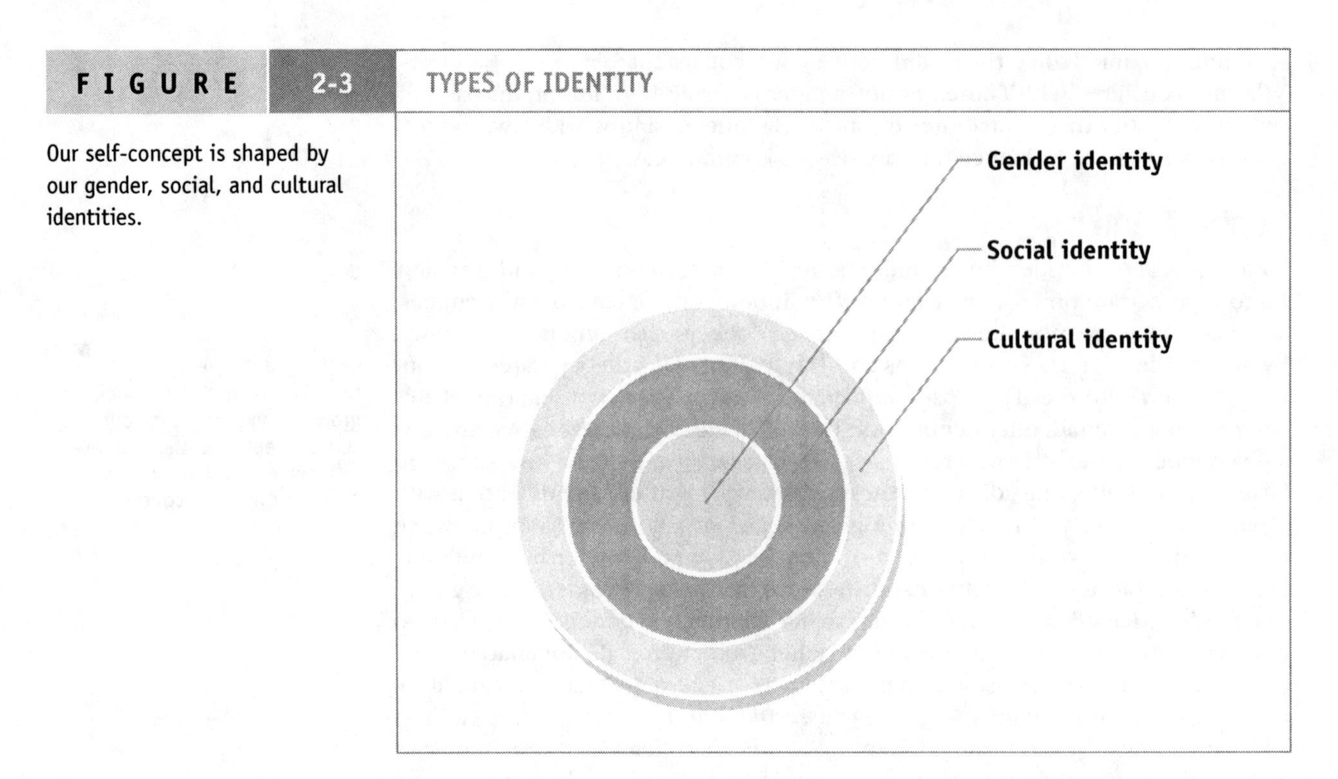

Our self-concept is shaped by our gender, social, and cultural identities.

peers, either. When she sees them skip class to watch soap operas and consume alcohol instead of studying, their behaviors reinforce her impressions that they lack discipline, self-control, and respect for authority. Pam will have to negotiate between two cultures and the conflicting identities that each fosters (Ly-Phin Pan 1998).

Our self-concept, identities, and cultural values all influence how we interact with others. We often see the world from the perspective of our cultures, and each culture has different expectations about communication behaviors. As Pam communicates with her friends and family, she is likely to use less eye contact and more formal, polite forms of talk with members of Asian communities than with her Caucasian peers. Pam's own sense of self will be guided by the culture with which she identifies the most. For example, in the United States, people tend to value personal independence and direct talk, while in many Asian countries, personal identity is based on relationships with families and communities, and the way people talk is guided by the expectations of others.

Our culture and identity enable us to see some things while not noticing others. When people talk to others who share their culture, they usually don't notice regional pronunciations or word choices (do you say "soda" or "pop"?) that would stand out to others. When watching television, young and middle-aged viewers rarely notice the under representation of elderly people (or women, most minorities, and disabled people) on the programs they watch (Norell 1999). Like gender and social identity, our cultural identity is apparent to us in some social contexts rather than others and influences both how we talk to others and how they respond to us. Figure 2-3 shows how gender, social, and cultural identities are interrelated.

Communicating Assumptions about Identity

Our assumptions about gender, social, and cultural identity guide our communication choices, which in turn can influence the ways others see themselves. Consider the identities that others have, in effect, created for you, from the first insult you might have heard on a playground to the label a friend might use when introducing you to someone new. For example, Sharika might introduce her friend Laura as a new mother or as the manager of a software company; the choice Sharika makes helps to define Laura and influence the impressions others have of her. The assumptions others make about Laura's identity will guide how they communicate with her.

Watch a video about the way culture influences self identity (CD Clip 2.1).

Allness. There are several ways that the words others use to describe us can influence our identity and self-concept. Sometimes, people resort to a practice called **allness,** which is the use of a single aspect of someone else's identity to describe that person without regard to her or his other qualities. Perhaps you have heard Linda Cohen, a talented and respected journalist, described as a female sportscaster. Although Cohen is certainly female, that particular feature of her identity probably has little bearing on her performance as a journalist. Allness is also an increasingly popular way to insult others, as in the banter of sports commentators who label each other based on how much hair the other has. Insults hurt, and the name-calling strategies we learn as children become refined in adulthood. Indeed, the most damaging names are those based on characteristics that we cannot easily change, such as race or physical peculiarities; such name-calling can do substantial damage to a person's sense of self (Farb 1994).

allness
The use of one aspect of our identity to describe our whole self.

Stereotypes. Like allness, the use of stereotypes limits our understanding of other people's identities. Whereas allness marks people based on a single feature of their identity, a **stereotype** is an unreliable generalization about a person based on a simplified image of a group to which the person belongs. Those who rely on stereotypes assume that individuals in a group are like everyone else in that group, be they blondes, lawyers, or Chicanos. Even so-called positive stereotypes have negative consequences. Sarriet, an Asian-American, provides an example: "nice, quiet, polite, subservient, traditional, good student, good girl—Asian women stereotypes. . . . I do fit some of the stereotypes. I have to distinguish which things are really inherent to my personal being and those I have because that's what people expect me to have." A racial *epithet,* often rooted in stereotypes, conveys images that can be internalized by those to whom it is directed and reinforces negative behavior among those who overhear the slur (Calvert 1997). Ultimately, when we treat people to doubt themselves based on one feature of their identity or label them in damaging ways, they can incorporate those perceptions into their self-concept and become less likely to succeed and reach their potential. Finally, stereotypes can be contagious. People who are surrounded by or exposed to denigrating stereotypes of others are likely to treat the victims of those stereotypes with less understanding and respect.

stereotypes
Specific kinds of labels that characterize people based on the assumed traits of others in their group.

Identity Tags. Another way that people are identified based on group membership is through identity tags, or labels used by advertisers who seek to target

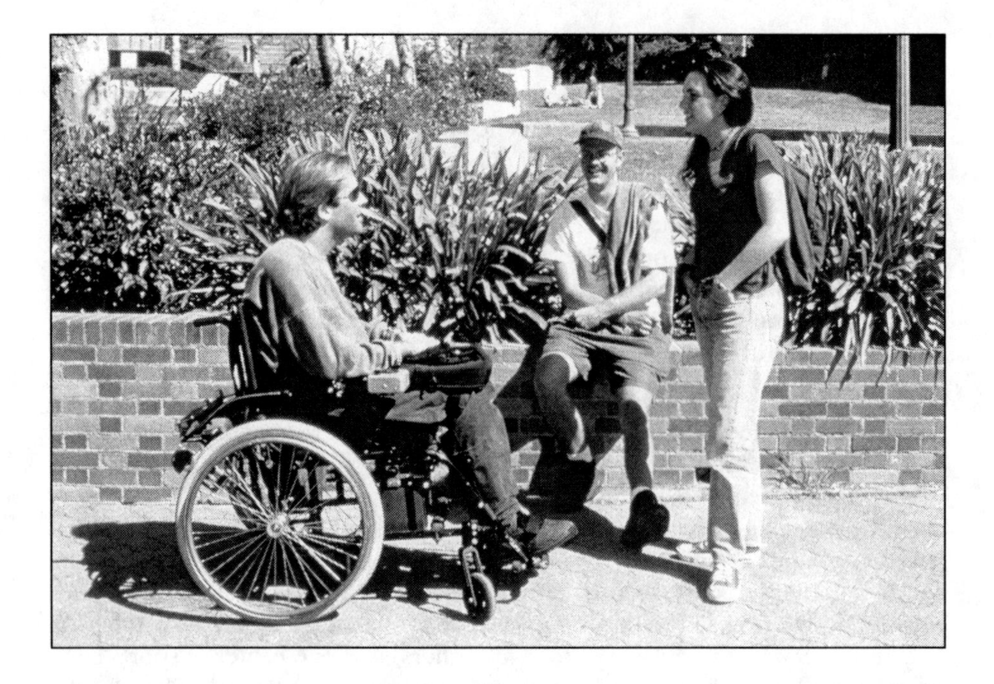

What are some of the assumptions these communicators might make about each other's identities?

a particular population or market for their product. You may be tagged instantaneously when you access websites on the Internet. When you visit many websites, you are automatically marked as a member of a group or class. As you shop on popular music websites, check scores on ESPN, or download software from *PC World,* advertisers are constructing an identity for you that may include your geographical location, browser type, Internet service provider, economic class, age, sex, and interests. From this kind of information, marketers develop lifestyle identities for you (which may be largely inaccurate) and may send you related e-mail promoting products or sites related to this profile.

The use of identity tags raises considerable questions about privacy and the ethics of acquiring and selling personal information. The identity tags that advertisers use are getting increasingly sophisticated. Consider technological advancements that have changed the ways ads are delivered. For instance, in one advertising campaign, women who visited the iVillage diet and fitness channel three times in a 45-day period saw a Snapple-a-Day (a meal replacement product) ad the next time they visited iVillage. Once the women were tagged as interested in diet and fitness, they were served Snapple-a-Day ads whether they read their horoscope or researched allergy medications (Oser 2004). Similarly, Google plans to scan confidential email to target users for specialized ads (Rupley 2004).

As with allness and other forms of stereotyping, identity tags tend to blend self-concept, identity, and culture into one feature or characteristic of a person. Although they may appear to be efficient ways to communicate, they can limit the knowledge and understanding that the best communication requires because they reduce people to simplified images or sets of characteristics. As you read the box, "Communicating with the Elderly in Health Care Settings," think about the assumptions many caregivers make about their elderly clients.

Applying Communication Concepts

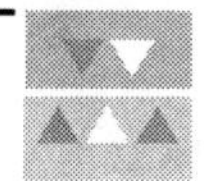

COMMUNICATING WITH THE ELDERLY IN HEALTH CARE SETTINGS

When people show signs of aging, such as having white hair, canes, and hearing aids, some speakers modify their speech by talking more slowly, using a demeaning emotional tone, referring to individuals with the inclusive term "we" (Are "we" ready to eat?), and calling elders "dear" and "sweetie." Not surprisingly, older people often feel disrespected, dependent, and less confident when addressed in this manner. The problem is particularly acute in health care settings such as nursing homes. According to one researcher, residents of nursing homes are being addressed in ways that are likely to reinforce dependency and that consequently have a negative impact on their physical and psychological well-being (Edwards 1995).

ASK YOURSELF:

1. How might this example illustrate allness or stereotyping?
2. How might caregivers address residents in ways that show respect and compassion?

Enhancing Self-Awareness through Interaction with Others

Throughout this chapter, we have emphasized how the things others say to us contribute to our self-concept and identity. There are also choices that we make in communicating with others that contribute to our own self-awareness and the development of our self-concept. Our self develops as we reveal ourselves to others, take on diverse communication roles, and interact with the many and varied forms of media. As the concept map in Figure 2-4 illustrates, there are many ways to enhance our self-awareness.

Revealing Yourself in Relationships

When Sergio first began seeing Chelsea, he thought of himself as a traditional, strong, and somewhat carefree guy. Although his friends saw Chelsea as too smart to be fun, Sergio enjoyed her company. They had gone to a few movies together and watched a basketball game when Chelsea suggested that they visit a local aquarium. The visit gave them the opportunity to spend several hours talking, and Sergio surprised himself by the things he revealed to Chelsea. By the time they parted that evening, Sergio imagined himself as slightly more introspective and willing to let Chelsea suggest the next outing together.

As Sergio talked with Chelsea, he began to discover new things about himself and reconsider which parts of himself he might want to reveal to her. Our self is a product of our past experiences, feelings and attitudes; it also includes an image of what you can become in the future, because you have the ability to reflect on your potential. As we communicate, we learn more about ourselves and make choices about what we will share with others. The **Johari Window** (Luft 1984), a model of self-awareness, diagrams this relationship between who we are and what we reveal to others (see Figure 2-5 on p. 51).

Johari Window
A model depicting an individual's degree of self-awareness.

FIGURE 2-4 SELF AWARENESS CONCEPT MAP

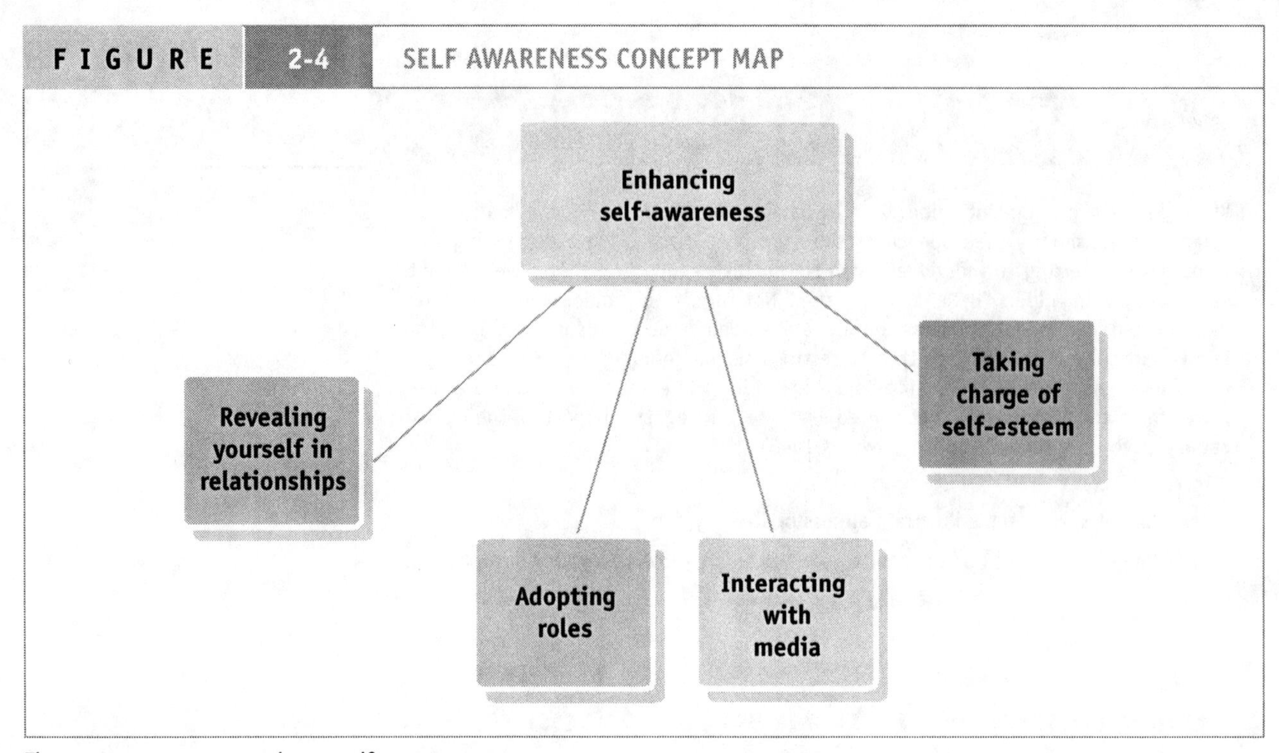

There are many ways to enhance self-awareness.

open quadrant
The part of yourself that is known both to you and to others.

The Open Quadrant. The model divides self-awareness into four areas, or quadrants. The **open quadrant** represents everything that you and others know about yourself. You present some characteristics, such as your physical appearance or general *demeanor,* in every interaction, but the more complex and meaningful parts of yourself usually require time and effort to understand and share with others. As you develop relationships with ***significant others,*** you also gain deeper awareness of yourself. The Johari Window diagrams the depth of awareness in a relationship by changing the size of the quadrants. If the open quadrant is relatively small, it represents a relationship that is new or "shallow," such as an acquaintance or classmate with whom you talk only once in a long while. If the quadrant is large, the model represents a long-term or intimate relationship between individuals who know themselves well.

hidden quadrant
Those things that you know about yourself but others do not.

The Hidden Quadrant. The **hidden quadrant** represents those things that you know about yourself but that others do not. These are attributes that you have managed to keep secret from others. Disclosing parts of yourself to others, often called "self-disclosure," helps increase your self-awareness as others either confirm or contradict these aspects of your self-concept. Self-disclosure can help build relationships as well as increase self-awareness, but it also carries some risks. In a newly developing relationship, self-disclosure is usually gradual and reciprocal. If you reveal too much of yourself too soon, the relationship might falter depending on the context of the relationship and the expectations

THE JOHARI WINDOW

FIGURE 2-5

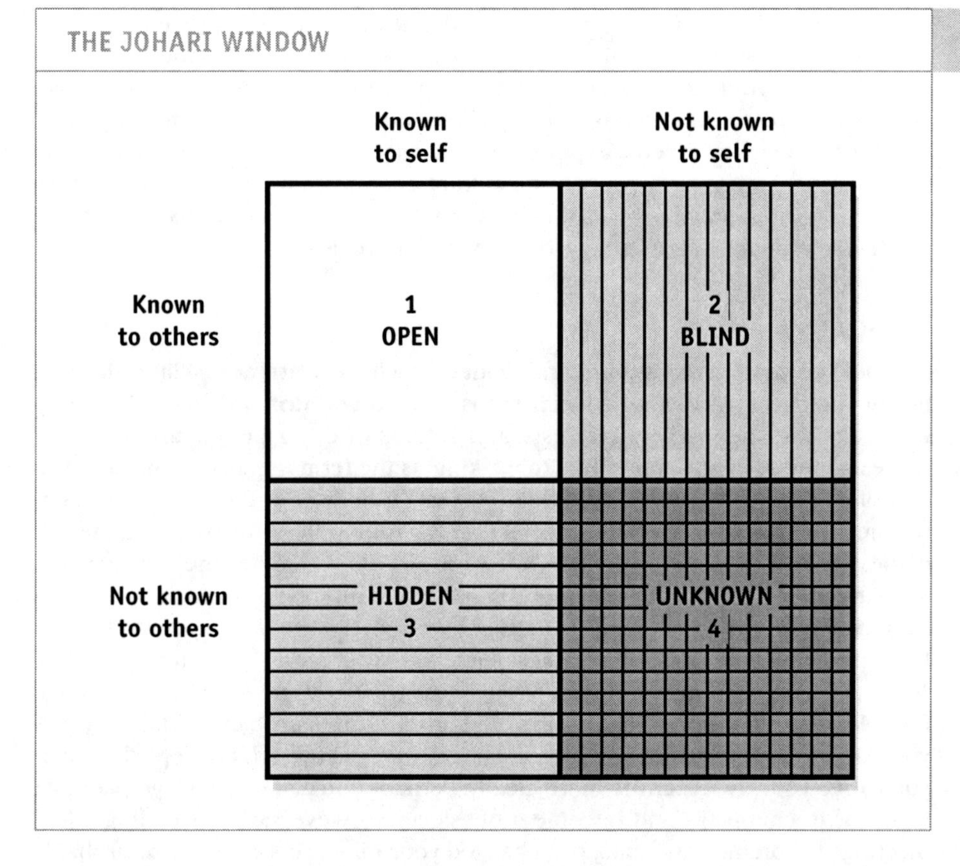

The Johari Window models the relationship between what we know about ourselves and what we share with others.

of the other person. Think about the starry-eyed individual who professes love early in a relationship. Saying "I love you" could thrill—or frighten—the other person! Significant disclosures should occur in a trusting relationship in which there is a history of mutual acceptance of each other's qualities. Again, the size of the hidden quadrant reflects the type of the relationship. A very large hidden area may represent either a new relationship or an ongoing one that is characterized by mistrust and caution. Conversely, a small hidden area represents a trusting relationship.

The Blind Quadrant. The **blind quadrant** represents those parts of yourself that others see but that you do not. Some of these characteristics might be unconscious behaviors that are noticeable to others, such as the way you fidget with a pencil or push sunglasses up the bridge of your nose. Other attributes in the blind area are more significant, such as self-interests that prevent you from clearly seeing your own weaknesses or strengths. Often others can see your own capabilities and liabilities before you do. For example, perhaps an elementary school teacher encouraged you to develop a skill, such as dancing, you did not realize you had. Some people are more introspective than others and have relatively small blind areas; others are much less self-aware. As others expose these attributes to you, your self-awareness increases and the blind area in the Johari Window decreases.

blind quadrant
The part of yourself that others know but you do not.

unknown quadrant
The category of things that neither you nor others know about yourself.

The Unknown Quadrant. Finally, the **unknown quadrant** represents qualities that neither you nor others know about yourself. Often these are attributes deep in your unconsciousness or are potential capabilities that you have not yet discovered. A large unknown quadrant often represents limited exposure to others or a lack of diverse experience. One way to reduce the unknown area is to experience new places, people, and cultures. As you communicate with diverse people in new situations, you gain chances to examine assumptions about yourself that you might not even have been aware of previously.

Adopting Roles

role taking
The act of understanding the motives, interests, and actions of other people and adopting those actions, at least temporarily.

Another way to explore assumptions about yourself and learn new skills is through taking different roles in your conversations with others. **Role taking** is the ability to understand the motives, interests, and actions of other people and to adopt those actions, at least temporarily. Role taking, as the term implies, is similar to the task of an actor who plays a particular part in a film or on the stage. Good actors become the character for the length of the show not only by memorizing the dialogue, but also by understanding what motivates the character they are playing. Similarly, in real life, humans attempt to understand motivations and adopt the behaviors of others to experiment with their own sense of self. When you started college, perhaps you tried new roles such as "neat freak," "studious scholar," "entrepreneur," or "nonconformist." Some of the roles you tried may have felt comfortable and ended up as lasting parts of yourself. Others probably did not. Even if you do not adopt the roles you play as a stable part of your self-concept, they help you to see your own identity more clearly. Perhaps you came to college planning to major in chemistry and become a physician. However, after attending a few meetings for premed students, you changed your mind. This experience probably helped you to assess your true interests and select a new major.

In any social situation, we take on roles based on the context, our perceived responsibility, and our degree of comfort. If Jorge's supervisor mentions his own marital difficulties at home, Jorge might be unsure about whether his supervisor expects him to take the role of comforter or problem solver. Role taking helps people understand both themselves and others more clearly. Communicators can construct mutual understanding if both parties can feel as the other feels. Although complete empathy is difficult, humans have a unique capacity to understand the perspectives of others and, over time, can bridge differences by playing the role of the other.

Interacting with Media

Communicating in relationships and practicing social roles are both ways that we learn more about ourselves. The growth and changes in our self-awareness are also influenced by the media, which permeate society. George Herbert Mead, writing about the development of the self in the early part of the 20th century, recognized the importance of media as windows into the motives of others, because media such as movies, radios, novels, and newspapers tell us stories that influence our attitudes and experiences (Mead 1934). Media now include advertisements, television, and computers, all of which provide portraits of others and show a variety of possible roles in society. By watching television, for instance, you can experience vicariously the plight of poor children in developing countries; the savagery of war; the senselessness of street crimes in cities; and the devastation of natural disasters such as earthquakes, hurricanes, and tornados. You can also view inspiring acts of heroism. For example, in 1989 the world watched as a solitary person stood in front of a column of Chinese tanks that were moving to suppress a student demonstration in Tiananmen Square. This act of defiance against overwhelming odds created one of the most memorable moments in broadcast history. Television depicts numerous moments of tenderness, empathy, honesty, and creativity each broadcast day. At its best, television can inspire our own self-growth by showing us the accomplishments and triumph of others.

But media can also have a destructive influence on the development of the self. As we mentioned in our discussion of channels, most mass media are commercial enterprises whose basic goal is to make money. Circulation and ratings are essential to profits and often influence the content of the media. The result is a mediated reality that distorts the picture of society and can also distort our own sense of self. One way that we understand our self is by comparing ourselves to others in a process called **social comparison** (Festinger 1954). For example, if you got a C on a term paper, you might ask others in the class what they received on the assignment. If everyone received C's or D's, then you would probably feel better and blame the professor for grading too harshly. Conversely, if everyone else received A's or B's, then you would probably experience disappointment and self-doubt.

social comparison
When we understand our self by comparing it to others.

The media provide an almost limitless number of images for social comparison. Often these images are distortions of reality and provide a false standard for measurement. For instance, if you compare your physical appearance to media images in magazines or on television, you may feel as if everyone is more attractive than you. Computers are frequently used to improve the images of models and actors you see in the media. This is especially true in fashion magazines where photographs of models are altered by computers to remove the smallest imperfections. The result is a false standard of beauty; even models are not as attractive as they appear to be in magazines. Sometimes people who compare themselves to media images feel inadequate about their appearance, and this leads to lower self-esteem. In one study, female students were surveyed after seeing pictures of models in fashion magazines. After viewing only 20 advertisements, the students voiced feelings of depression and hostility; think about the hundreds of photos in fashion and lifestyle magazines, billboards, televisions, and movies (Kay and Lindgren 1999). Another study demonstrated that after only 13 minutes of looking at fashion magazines, women became much more conscious and negative in their evaluations of their bodies (Turner, Hamilton, Jacobs, Angood, and Dwyer 1997).

Finding media images for social comparison is relatively easy for this group of students. How easy would it be for a group of disabled students? Elderly couples? Mexican-American families?

Beauty ideals are particularly oppressive for young women whose self-esteem is often based on their feelings about their bodies. Scholars have found that a significant percentage of white, middle-class, normal-weight girls misclassify themselves as overweight. These perceptions about body weight are more important to their self-image than their actual weight (Rierdan and Koff 1997). Even young women at or below normal body weight are influenced by mediated standards of beauty and may see themselves as inadequate or overweight. These negative and distorted perceptions of the body are the first step in a process that can lead to depression and eating disorders in young women.

The media similarly influence males. Most males on television are athletic, young, and tall. Men who are not athletic often feel inferior or different when they compare themselves to television stereotypes. Given the role of media and social comparison, what might be the responsibility of commercial media in providing images that promote positive self-growth? Is it ethical to use severely underweight women as models? What might be done to counteract the influence of media on the self-concept of young men and women?

Taking Charge of Self-Esteem

The keys to building a positive self-concept lie in managing the influences that shape the development of your self: interaction with others, role taking, and exposure to the media. Humans have a unique ability to critique their self-concept. It is hard to imagine a family pet that worries about being overweight or having bad breath. Our ability to think about and evaluate ourselves enables us to further develop and refine our self-concept. How we feel about ourselves is called **self-esteem** and is a critical part of who we are and how we communicate. Consider some common ways that people with low self-esteem are likely to interact with others. They may be less assertive and more easily persuaded to do something they don't want to do. People with low self-esteem are sometimes more lonely than those with high self-esteem and are less secure in their relationships with others (Brage and Meredith 1993, 1994). One study found that partners with low self-esteem were likely to engage in "clinging" or possessive behaviors in a relationship, such as spying on the other person, constantly checking up on or calling the other partner, and restricting access to potential rivals (Guerrero and Afifi 1998).

self-esteem
The value you attach to your self-concept.

Fortunately, just as the ways people communicate with themselves and others can contribute to low self-esteem, communication can also encourage personal growth. The following strategies can help you take charge of your self-esteem:

- Recognize that you are a complex person. At any one time, you display only a small portion of yourself to other communicators in a particular situation.
- Accept who you are as a starting point for change and set realistic personal goals. If your expectations are unrealistic, you are more likely to create negative self-fulfilling prophecies. Choose outcomes that are within reach; talk with others whom you trust to help evaluate those goals.
- Create supportive communication contexts. As you compare yourself to others, choose role models who are appropriate and make you feel good, rather than those who make you feel depressed. Similarly, invest your time talking to others who communicate positively about you and are willing to help, rather than those who highlight your weaknesses, prey on your self-doubts, or make you feel insecure.

- Be strategic about which parts of yourself to reveal to others. It can be comforting to have friends who know you well; remember to reveal yourself to others who share your respect, concern, and trust.

The people we talk to, the roles we take, and the images that provide us with social comparisons all influence how much we like ourselves. We do have the ability to improve our self-esteem: When we decide to change how we feel about ourselves and choose positive communication strategies, both our self-concept and our communication with others improves. In addition to raising our own self-esteem, we can also make active choices about the impressions we want to convey to others. The final section of this chapter presents some tips for how to best present yourself and manage the impressions others have of you.

Communicating Responsibly: Maintaining an Authentic Self

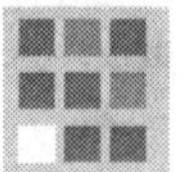

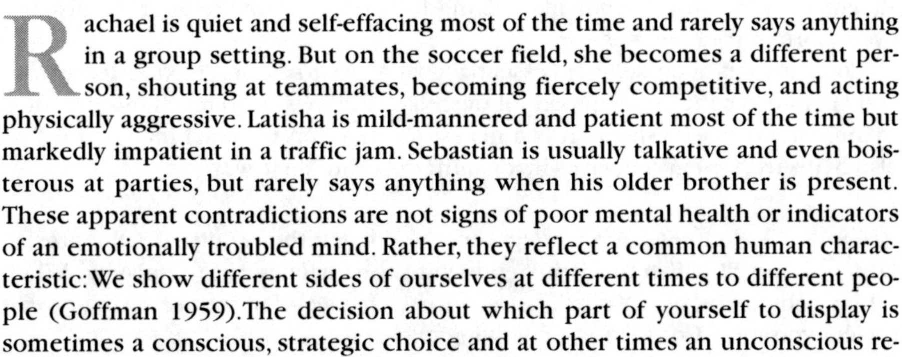

Rachael is quiet and self-effacing most of the time and rarely says anything in a group setting. But on the soccer field, she becomes a different person, shouting at teammates, becoming fiercely competitive, and acting physically aggressive. Latisha is mild-mannered and patient most of the time but markedly impatient in a traffic jam. Sebastian is usually talkative and even boisterous at parties, but rarely says anything when his older brother is present. These apparent contradictions are not signs of poor mental health or indicators of an emotionally troubled mind. Rather, they reflect a common human characteristic: We show different sides of ourselves at different times to different people (Goffman 1959). The decision about which part of yourself to display is sometimes a conscious, strategic choice and at other times an unconscious response to circumstances. Authentic communication involves presenting the image that is appropriate both for the situation and the outcome you desire, and is consistent with your self-concept. In general, there are three factors that influence whether we present an authentic self to others: those with whom we are communicating, the communication context, and the motivation or goal behind the interaction (Gergen 1971).

> "A multiple personality is, in a certain sense, normal."
>
> —George Herbert Mead, sociologist

Presenting Ourselves to Others

The other person (or persons) in an interaction is the single most influential factor determining which part of yourself to display. For example, think of the people you encountered after completing your first term of college. Everyone you met probably asked the same question, "How is school?" Did you give the same answer to everyone? If you are like most students, your answer varied depending on your audience. If you traveled far or left a family to attend college, you probably emphasized to your parents or partner how responsible you were by talking about your course work and the long hours you studied. With your best friends, however, you might have emphasized your independence and talked about your social activities. Finally, if you had a girlfriend or boyfriend back home, you probably stressed the absence of any romantic intention with others at school! Which of these responses was the "true" answer? In fact, all were true but incomplete. You chose to reveal particular parts of your college experience based on what you perceived the expectation of others to be.

facework
The act of presenting the self.

Sociologist Erving Goffman referred to the act of presenting the self as "maintaining face" or doing **"facework"** (Goffman 1967). Goffman, like many other social scientists, believed that facework is a collaborative effort with others in the communication situation. We not only present ourself to others, but we adjust our face based on their reactions to us. There are three possible reactions to the face we present others: confirmation, rejection, or disconfirmation (Watzlawick, Beavelas, and Jackson 1967).

confirmation
When others accept our presentation of self and act in harmony with the image we are displaying.

Confirmation. Other people confirm our "face" when they accept our presentation of self and act in harmony with the image we are displaying. This **confirmation** gives us confidence in the interaction and encourages us to display increasingly more of ourself to the other person or persons. For example, suppose you tell someone, "I really enjoy talking to you." If the other person confirms your statement by saying, "I really like talking to you, too," you are likely to disclose even more of your feelings.

Confirmation of ourself is an essential goal of day-to-day interaction. It nurtures and encourages the development of ourself and allows us to reach our potential by building our self-esteem. It is a necessary function of social interaction that also helps us present ourselves in an authentic, confident way.

rejection
When others contradict the presentation of ourself and act inconsistently with the image we are displaying.

Rejection. Other people reject our "face" when they contradict the presentation of ourself and act inconsistently with the image we are displaying. When others show **rejection** toward us, we either change what we are saying or end the conversation. Consider the following exchange:

Tyler: I'm beat. I can't believe how many hours I worked yesterday. I must've pulled a 12-hour shift.

Kellee: That's nothing. I work those shifts all the time, and I don't take hour-long lunch breaks like you do.

If you were Tyler, how would you react to Kellee's not-so-subtle rejection? Would you change the subject or stop talking to Kellee? Would you change your face by becoming angry and saying something spiteful? Perhaps you would accept Kellee's definition of the situation but feel hurt by her insensitivity.

Sometimes rejection, no matter how painful, is beneficial to the development of the self, because it helps us to see parts of ourself that we did not see before (the hidden area in the Johari Window) and enhances our understanding of how others see us. Perhaps Reyna thinks that she is being polite to her new assistants by coming in and out of the office without saying a word, until Tawana tells her that she and others in the office would prefer a "good-bye" to signal when she was leaving at the end of the day. Although Tawana might fear offending her new supervisor, the information she gave to Reyna was useful and important.

The fear of rejection is one of the reasons we reveal only a portion of ourselves to others. Our level of intimacy or degree of comfort with others determines much of our facework. Rejection often precludes intimacy and confines our presentation of self to a limited range of possibilities. Rejection can also limit our future encounters. Some people become "rejection-sensitive" and avoid all situations where they think rejection is possible. They also become defensive and tend to misinterpret the statements of others as personal attacks or rejection.

Disconfirmation. **Disconfirmation** occurs when others ignore our presentation of self and act with indifference to the image we are displaying. Disconfirmation is different than rejection. Whereas rejection communicates the message that "you are wrong," disconfirmation signals that "you do not exist" (Watzlawick, Beavelas, and Jackson 1967). Perhaps you have felt "disconfirmed" when someone ignored your comment in a group conversation, did not return your call or e-mail, or persistently called you by the wrong name. Disconfirmation can have very negative consequences; it can harm the victim's self-development and can lead him or her to feel alienated from others. Being disconfirmed robs people of any meaningful feedback and is rarely beneficial to either communicator.

disconfirmation
When others ignore our presentation of self and act indifferent to the image we are displaying.

Our efforts to preserve face and avoid disconfirmation can sometimes make our attempts to communicate seem ambiguous or misleading. Consider the "Exploring Communication Concepts" box, which explains how facework can affect intimacy.

Communicating the Self in Different Contexts

As we discussed at various points in this chapter, the way in which we communicate with others is influenced by the context in which an interaction takes place. At a very basic level, for instance, you probably would not talk to a friend in the university library the same way you would in the privacy of your home. Similarly, the setting influences how you present yourself. Goffman made a distinction

Exploring Communication Concepts

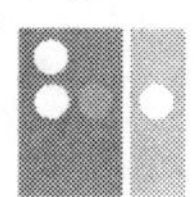

SAVING FACE AND COMMUNICATING RESISTANCE IN INTIMATE CONTEXTS

In heterosexual dating situations, men are usually expected to initiate and pursue physical intimacy while women are expected to set limits on it. There are various ways that a woman might try to communicate resistance besides saying "stop." For instance, she might say, "I'm seeing someone else" or "I don't think I know you well enough for this." These statements are called indirect resistance messages.

Research suggests that women use indirect resistance messages to stop or slow down sexual intimacy while preserving relationships. A man might feel rejected if she says, "I don't want to do this," and rejection can either end a relationship that the female wants to continue or result in retaliation by the male. So, women often communicate indirectly to avoid giving the impression that they are promiscuous, and thereby save face. They fear that if they agree to sexual intimacy too quickly, their partners will lose respect for them. Women also try to save face for their partners by avoiding outright rejection. Unfortunately, however, because the messages which women in these situations use are ambiguous, men sometimes hear them as confirming their own sense of self. Researchers found that the statement, "I don't think I know you well enough for this" was interpreted by only 26 percent of the male respondents to mean that the female wants to stop the escalation of sexual intimacy. Nearly half of the male respondents said that the statement means she wants to go further; she just wants to get to know the male better at the same time (Motley & Reeder 1995).

As this discussion suggests, it can be difficult to negotiate between confirming the self of someone else and presenting your own self authentically.

ASK YOURSELF:

1. What are the responsibilities of both communicators in these situations?
2. When are indirect messages appropriate, and how important is the preservation of face in deciding appropriateness?

between "front" and "back" communication contexts and used a theatrical metaphor to explain his concepts. As noted earlier, facework for Goffman is similar to what an actor does when playing a part on the stage. In front of the audience, the actor must be the character and play the part. But backstage, away from the audience, the actor can relax and be "out of character." In facework, a **front context** is a public setting where you actively manage the impression you project to others. A **back context** is a private environment that usually require a less conscious effort to manage the impression. Job interviews, first dates, and talking with your professor are examples of strong "front" contexts. Back contexts include being by yourself or with intimate friends and family members.

front context
A public setting where you actively manage the impression you project to others.

back context
A private environment that requires a less conscious effort to manage the impression you project to others.

The difference between front and back contexts influences your facework. There are faces that we will reveal in back contexts that we would never dare show in front contexts. Consider Paul Gilligan's cartoon, "Pooch Café."

In the comic strip, Gilligan captures both the embarrassment of being recorded acting foolishly and the increasing media fascination with *voyeurism*. The discomfort of presenting the self in front contexts is familiar to most people. For instance, have you ever walked in front of a very large group in an auditorium or amphitheater? If so, perhaps you experienced the awkward feeling of walking while everyone seems to be watching you. Suddenly you are conscious of every movement of your arms and legs and how you might appear to others. Similarly, in public contexts you become more conscious of every detail of your communication. The selection of your words, the way you say them, and how you stand or sit all become conscious decisions. In a job interview, for example, you are very careful to dress appropriately, say the right things, and present the best possible face to the potential employer. Conversely, when you are with your friends or by yourself, you are not as conscious of your communicative behavior.

Front and back contexts are interrelated and can never be completely separated. If you are at school, you actively manage your image as a student in front of your professors and other students. When you leave school for home, you are "backstage" and out of the "student" character. However, you present a different image, perhaps as a friend or roommate with your peers, and must take up that role. In that way, your presentation of self alternates between active and inactive, and private and public, and contributes to the variety of images and faces you present to others.

Source: Paul Gilligan, Copley News Service.

Social networking sites, like Facebook, further blur the lines between back and front stage. One study estimates that almost 90% of college students use Facebook each day and that most college students spend more time texting or online than they do watching television (Smith 2009). But young university students who are part of the "net-generation" may perceive the appropriateness of Facebook postings differently than their parents or prospective employers. One survey found that more than fifty percent of Facebook participants had pictures of themselves intoxicated or in romantic situations (Clark, Lee, and Boyer 2007). Most of these students saw the pictures as appropriate and said that they wouldn't mind if their parents accessed their Facebook pages. But employers and parents reported different definitions of the appropriateness of these photos which sometimes kept college graduates from getting hired (Palank 2006). Expectations about back and front nature of the Internet will continue to evolve as users reconcile opposing viewpoints.

Communicating the Self to Achieve Goals

In addition to choosing communication strategies that preserve face and are appropriate back- or frontstage presentations, authentic communication requires that you choose behaviors that are consistent with your motivation and goals. For example, if you are looking for a job, you should project a competent image that persuades others to hire you. You should dress appropriately, show up on time or even early for the appointment, provide a professional-looking résumé, and answer questions with specific details about your abilities. You should avoid revealing weaknesses and emphasize instead your strengths. Many people fail to be selected for jobs because they project the wrong image. The nature of the goal influences the presentation of self.

Not all situations require communication choices that are as strategic as those in a job interview. Your goal may be simply to maintain the image you have already established or to be anonymous by presenting as little face as possible. Or, you might be preoccupied with other thoughts and not even be aware of the image you are presenting. Some people are naturally better at image management than others and are highly aware of the image they project. As we discussed in Chapter 1, self-monitoring refers to an awareness of the image you are projecting. High self-monitors are acutely aware of how others see them. They make continual adjustments to the presentations of their self as the communication context changes. Awareness of how others evaluate you can be helpful in meeting their expectations and creating shared meaning. However, it can also lead you to become overly sensitive or cause you to change your communication in ways that contradict your self-concept or goals. Low self-monitors are insulated from disconfirming messages, but they can also be somewhat oblivious to the image they are presenting to others.

After our lengthy discussion of the presentation of self, you might think that facework is manipulative and phony, but it doesn't have to be. You can certainly lie and deceive others with carefully selected faces that are not connected to your true or authentic self. But most communicators want to be sincere or "genuine" in their interactions with others, and consistency between the face you present and the message you want to convey helps assure that you are communicating authentically. Be sincere while understanding the consequences of your messages and adapting your messages to the situation.

Finally, realize that interactions that challenge one's sense of self require careful, attentive, and conscientious efforts to communicate. When we feel a need to protect our identity or save face, we are most likely to become inflexible and destructive. If someone we care about tells us that our work on a project was sloppy, we are likely to defend our performance even if we know we completed it in haste. This impulse to shield ourself and preserve self-esteem applies to contexts as disparate as friends chatting with each other to corporate executives testifying in court. Knowing this, consider ways that you might improve your communication—by recognizing how others define their self-concept, creating positive expectations of them, valuing the many different facets of their identity, respecting aspects of their selves that they choose to reveal, and communicating as authentically as you can. The box that concludes this chapter, "Preserving Face in Communication," is designed to help you think about ways in which you can encourage others to present themselves in positive ways.

Applying Communication Concepts

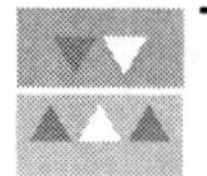

PRESERVING FACE IN COMMUNICATION

Communication scholars William Wilmot and Joyce Hocker (2001) offered the following guidelines for helping people protect their self-identity and reducing the need to save face:

Help increase self-esteem. Give people the benefit of the doubt; acknowledge that they have good intentions. Most people genuinely believe that they are doing what is best, and even if you disagree, it can be helpful to say, "I know you're trying to do the right thing" or "I appreciate the thought you've put into this."

Avoid giving directives. Direct threats are rarely productive, and even when we are certain we're right, it doesn't help to say, "If you don't do it, I won't ____ " (finish the job, speak to you, etc.). Give control to the other person, so that she or he can decide to take action without being coerced. Statements such as "I know I don't need to watch over your shoulder; you can get this done" are usually more productive and convey respect for the other person's sense of self.

Listen carefully to others and take their concerns into account. Sometimes we have the power to make decisions on our own without consulting others. However, when we show others that their concerns are respected, valued, and have been heard, it helps to preserve their self-concept and our relationship with them.

Ask questions that help the other person examine his or her goals. Although it can be easier to attack, asking questions often opens conversations and allows people to change rather than to respond defensively.

ASK YOURSELF:

1. Why might it be important to follow these guidelines?
2. What can saving face contribute to the quality of communication and the resolution of conflicts?

Resources for Review and Skill Building

Many of these resources are supported by the Connections CD-ROM and free Online Learning Center website.

SUMMARY

This summary is organized around the questions found at the beginning of the chapter. See if you can answer them before reading the summary paragraphs.

1. How does communication contribute to the development of the self?

   Our self-concept develops through interaction with others, making communication central in the development of the self. The self is also influenced by self-fulfilling prophecies and by self-evaluation. We evaluate ourselves based on how we see ourselves and how we think others see us.

2. How do identity and culture influence our self-concept?

   Our self-concept is defined partly by our gender, social, and cultural identities. Gender identity refers to the way we see ourselves as men or women, girls or boys. Social identity consists of the groups to which we belong. Our culture provides many of the beliefs and assumptions that guide how we communicate. Some identities are more important than others depending on the people with whom we are interacting at any given moment.

3. What are some of the challenges in communicating identity?

   When communicating identity, it can be tempting to define people based on one part of them. Sometimes we rely on allness or stereotypes, both of which limit communication effectiveness and can damage self-esteem.

4. How do we present ourself to others?

   The Johari Window is one model that depicts different parts of the self and the ways the self is revealed. At any given moment, we only present a small part of ourselves to others. The self also develops through role taking, when we try out roles and learn to empathize with others. In this way, we try out different identities and test parts of our self-concept. Our self is influenced further in our interaction with the media. We use images in the media as the basis of social comparison, whereby we judge ourselves in relation to the people we read about in newspapers and magazines and see on television and in movies. Media images can either harm self-esteem or help build a positive self-concept.

5. Why might communicating an authentic self be important, and what are the ways to do so?

   Communicating an authentic self requires consistency between your presentation of self and your self-concept. Our presentation of self depends on whom we are communicating with and is called facework. When our self is confirmed, we are likely to reveal more of ourselves to others. When we are disconfirmed or rejected, we also change our presentation of self in ways such as becoming angry or defensive. Our presentation of self also depends on whether the context is public or private, and how well we monitor the appropriateness of our communication. Although self-monitoring can sometimes feel manipulative, carefully managing the image you present to others can help you reflect parts of yourself that are both appropriate for the context and respectful of the needs of others.

KEY TERMS

Test your understanding of these key terms by visiting the Connections CD-ROM and Online Learning Center website at www.mhhe.com/dobkinpace.

allness 47
back context 58
blind quadrant 51
confirmation 56
disconfirmation 57
facework 56
front context 58
gender identity 44
generalized other 40
hidden quadrant 50
identity 42
Johari Window 49
open quadrant 50
rejection 56
role taking 52
self-awareness 39
self-concept 39
self-esteem 54
self-fulfilling prophecy 40
social identity theory 45
social comparison 53
stereotypes 47
unknown quadrant 52

FOR FURTHER REFLECTION

/dobkinpace
Join a conversation about chapter concepts by visiting the Online Learning Center website at www.mhhe.com/dobkinpace

One tool for bringing forth definitions of the self is the 20 statements test designed by Manford Kuhn (Kuhn and McPartland 1954). This test asks you to answer the question "Who am I?" 20 times, as if you were talking to yourself rather than somebody else. There are many ways to analyze your responses. Think about the roles you have chosen (daughter, father, friend), the groups with which you identify (communication student, Mexican-American, crew club), your interests and beliefs (Baptist, Libertarian, sports), and descriptions of your personality (intelligent, active, creative). Which categories are most central to your identity? How important are the words that capture your "self"?

BUILDING COMMUNICATION SKILLS

Identify an area of your self-concept that you would like to improve. You might want to be more outgoing, studious, productive, or confident. Next, make a list of the sources of influence on your self-concept: significant others, self-evaluation, role taking, and exposure to media. Choose one source and make an effort to actively change your self-concept. For instance, if you want to be more outgoing, pick an activity you enjoy and play the role of mentor or friend.

NET WORK

/dobkinpace

Note: While all the URLs listed were current as of the printing of this book, these sites often change. Please check our website (www.mhhe.com/dobkinpace) for updates and hyperlinks to these exercises.

1. Internet blogs are updated frequently and are often personal reflections about travel, work, or relationships. Popular blogs are listed at either http://www.bloglines.com/topblogs or http://weblogs.about.com/od/bestblogsindices/. Read two or three blogs that interest you. How do these journals communicate assumptions about identity? Do you see indications of allness, stereotypes, or identity tags? How do blogs blur the line between front and back contexts?

2. The Internet offers many opportunities for you to project an image of yourself by using the words of others. Sites such as www.bluemoutain.com or www.hallmark.com offer to send personal cards for any occasion in your name through the U.S. mail. Log on to one of these websites. Does it use identity tags to organize its messages? Are identity tags legitimate ways to present an authentic self to others?

MEDIA MOMENTS

The development of the self has provided the dramatic plot for many good movies. These films can effectively illustrate the many influences on self-concept, identity, and self-esteem. One example can be found in the 1996 movie *Shine,* which depicts the life of pianist David Helfgott (played by Geoffrey Rush). Consider viewing the film with the following questions in mind:

1. How do significant others contribute to David's self-concept?
2. What are the most important self-fulfilling prophecies in David's life?
3. How does David's generalized other change over time, and what is the effect on his ability to communicate?
4. In what ways do David's front and back communication strategies differ, and how do they help him communicate an authentic self?

Perceiving and Communicating with Others

3

CHAPTER

Stafford and Mike are hanging out at Mike's house, watching a reality TV show that features dramatic recreations of crimes. The program shows a black man breaking into a house at night, then being chased through a wooded neighborhood by police officers with dogs. The officers tackle the suspect, handcuff his wrists behind his back, and lie him face down on the pavement. Stafford says with irritation, "Why do we have to see this stuff all the time?"

Mike replies offhandedly, "Huh? What do you mean?"

"They always show black guys being chased," Stafford answers.

Mike dismisses Stafford's comment. "This looks believable to me."

Stafford's anger increases. "Yeah, well, that's because you see it all the time. Why don't they ever show a white guy being chased down and cuffed?"

Mike begins to get frustrated with Stafford. "It's just a stupid TV show. Why does everything have to be about race with you? I don't know what your problem is."

Stafford retorts, "I guess you just don't get it."

QUESTIONS TO FOCUS YOUR READING

1. Why is perception important to communication?
2. What are some factors that influence perception?
3. What are the main steps in forming perceptions?
4. What happens when we make attributions?
5. How can managing perceptions contribute to responsible communication?

Even though Stafford and Mike know each other well and are watching the same show, their perceptions of it vary considerably. As we discussed in Chapter 2, our identity and sense of self influence how we see the world and which communication behaviors we choose. Stafford sees himself as a critical viewer, attuned to the ways people of color are portrayed in the media, and he perceived the show to be racist. Although Mike has a different ethnic background, Stafford knows him well, and he probably assumed that Mike would share his view. Mike, however, saw Stafford's reaction as overly sensitive. Their different perceptions guided their conversation and, rather than exploring the basis of those perceptions, Mike and Stafford each clung to his own point of view and judgment of the other person.

Our perceptions of others guide the way we talk to and about them. Sometimes we're aware of the relationship between perceptions and behavior. We might acknowledge that our first impression of a fellow bus or airline passenger, for instance, has influenced our decision about whether to initiate a conversation. We are less likely, however, to think about how "who we are" dictates what we see. Indeed, relatively few people understand the process of perception in ways that lead to more accurate and responsible communication.

The power that perceptions have in guiding communication makes them particularly important to understand and manage. If you perceive a nonverbal gesture, such as someone waving her or his hand, as intentional, you are more likely to acknowledge the person who waved. The statement "Why don't you get some exercise?" can be perceived as a helpful suggestion or a negative comment about a person's weight or level of fitness. And the public figure who says "no comment" in times of crisis often leaves the door open for competing perceptions by observers, from holding the speaker responsible, to concluding that she or he lacks information. In every communication context, perceptions play a role in helping us to understand what others are saying and guiding our own efforts to communicate effectively.

perception
Process of assigning meaning to sensory information and experiences.

This chapter explores the relationship between communication and **perception,** the process of assigning meaning to sensory information and experiences. This process starts before you utter your first words and continues beyond any single interaction. By the end of the chapter, you should be able to:

- Understand factors that influence perception.
- Identify steps in the perceptual process.
- Recognize common attributional biases that impede communication.
- Begin managing perceptions in ways that foster productive and responsible communication.

Factors that Influence Perception

Our self-concept, past experiences, physical abilities, personality, and social environment combine to help make us who we are and to determine how we perceive other people and events in the world. How we perceive others influences the communication choices we make, from deciding whether to initiate a conversation to choosing whether to try to persuade someone who holds an opposing view on a particular issue. In Chapter 2 we explored how our identity, self-esteem, and degree of self-awareness influence how we perceive interactions and behave as communicators. In addition, perception is influenced by physical factors, personality, and culture.

Physical Factors

Some of the ways that one's physical features influence perception are easy to recognize. Physical characteristics such as age, height, and ability influence our attitudes and behaviors, and they play a role in how we perceive others and communicate with them. For instance, an elderly person might perceive being addressed by his or her first name as an insult, whereas a child would probably not think twice about it. The dark-skinned West Indian woman shopping in a Midwestern convenience store might perceive the "nude" label on beige-colored panty hose to be laughable (beige is only a "nude" skin tone for Caucasians). The person who is color-blind will see the world differently than one who is not. One color-blind woman wrote, "While there are days when I wish I could see all the colors in a sunset or appreciate the changing of the leaves, I usually just consider myself lucky that I see the world colored in a way that very few others do" (Rosenblatt 1998). Color-blindness affects both this individual's perceptions and how others might treat her. For instance, a carpet salesperson might misinterpret her lack of a reaction to different colors as indifference and move on to another customer.

Even *biorhythms* can determine what we see and how we interpret information. Studies of high school students show that morning classes are usually the least effective for them because the low point of alertness for adolescents is between six and eight o'clock in the morning. By the time they begin class at seven or eight o'clock, they are often sleep deprived from having to get up too early for class (Swet and Wisby 1998). So, although some students may not perceive their 7:00 A.M. teachers to be difficult or boring, their internal body clocks may make it difficult for them to master information or communicate effectively at that time in the morning, regardless of the skill, energy, or enthusiasm of the teacher.

Physical needs also influence our perceptions. The weary traveler sometimes sees the interior of an airport very differently when flights are delayed; bench seats and corners with carpeted floors become treasured spaces, and conversations with gate attendants can become tense. We can sometimes limit the extent to which physiological needs such as sleep and hunger influence us; nonetheless, they can be important factors in determining which stimuli we perceive and the way we communicate.

Finally, there are physical limits to the amount and type of information we can perceive. We cannot always see the gestures that a speaker makes, hear the dialogue of film characters when special effects are too loud, or listen carefully when we are very tired. Although we do not always think about the physical factors that may influence our perceptions, they do play a role in our ability to think about people and situations and to respond to them.

While the teacher of these students may perceive them as uninterested in the class, the reality may simply be that they are tired.

Personality

Just as self-concept, identity, and physical factors act as filters on our perceptions, our personality also affects how we perceive others. If you are generally an extrovert or an outgoing person who enjoys company, you might see a group of people talking at a party as a welcome opportunity for socializing. To a shy and introverted guest, that same group of people might appear intimidating and provoke anxiety. These initial perceptions will guide subsequent behaviors, so that the extrovert is likely to move toward the group and join in the conversation, while the introvert is likely to avoid interaction (Mudore 2002). Some researchers contend that inborn traits determine an individual's degree of comfort about communication; according to this view, anxiety about communication, or "communication apprehension," occurs independently of a person's social experiences (Beatty, McCroskey, and Heisel 1998). Certainly, the person who is predisposed to communication apprehension will perceive social situations differently than one who is not.

Culture

As individuals, we bring the composite of our self-concept and identity, physical characteristics, and personality into every communicative setting. In addition, we process perceptions through the filters of the cultures to which we belong. In Chapter 2 we noted how gender, social, and cultural identity all influence how we perceive others. A sexually charged joke might be appropriate in a Dutch workplace but be seen as harassment in the United States. A group of American workers might see their Indian peers as rude for talking in their own language when the Americans are present, whereas the Indians might be communicating in their native language solely because doing so makes it easier for them to explain problems to one another. An African-American male might not think twice about sharing his excellent test scores with his female Chinese-American classmate. Rather than seeing his comments as a legitimate expression of pride, however, she might perceive him to be arrogant and boastful.

Even same-sex groups form their own cultures. For instance, all-boy peer groups often perceive rules for games differently than all-girl groups. A group of boys playing a ball game is likely to see a borderline call as an opportunity for negotiation and constructive conflict, whereas an all-girl group is more likely to repeat the play or "do it over" to maintain good relationships with their friends (Pearson, West, and Turner 1995; Wood 1994). We even see others differently based on the sex of the company we're keeping at any given time. Consider the example of Jenny watching a horror film with a group of female friends. With her friends, Jenny might make fun of the predictable plot and act brave during the scarier parts of the movie. On a date with a potential boyfriend, however, she might feel scared, cringe at the violence, and possibly even lean on her date for support. This silent *accommodation* goes on all the time, as people adjust their perceptions and behavior on the basis of the cultural expectations of the people with whom they are talking, playing, or working (Tavris 1992).

Steps in the Process of Forming Perceptions

Our perceptions pass through physical, personal, and cultural filters so quickly that we rarely take notice of them. We perceive people and events before we begin listening or speaking, and we form new perceptions or refine existing ones as

STEPS IN THE PROCESS OF PERCEPTION

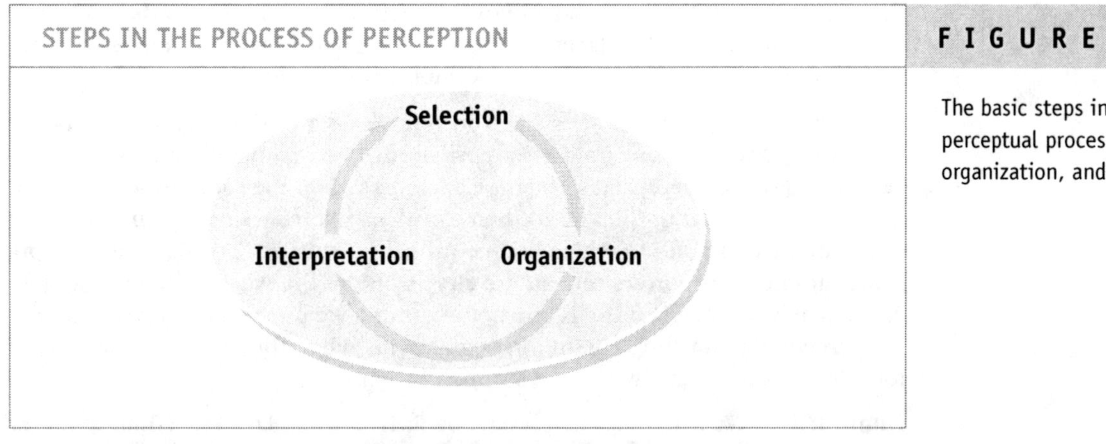

FIGURE 3-1

The basic steps in the perceptual process are selection, organization, and interpretation.

we communicate with others. The basic steps in the process of perception are selection, organization, and interpretation (Rao 2009). Although in reality it is somewhat difficult to break down the process into discrete stages, doing so helps us understand how perceptions are formed and made meaningful (see Figure 3-1).

Selecting

Without looking up, think about your surroundings. What is the color of the walls? If you have a pen in your hand, what is the color of the ink? How many windows are in the room? Who is sitting behind you? Perhaps you are more aware of the color of the words in your textbook than the details of your surroundings. You can probably answer some of the previous questions more easily than others based on which physical *sensations* you have perceived. **Selection** occurs when we focus on some sensory stimuli rather than others. This process has also been called the recognition of sensory information (Carterette and Friedman 1978), or selective perception. Because we are bombarded with so many stimuli throughout the day, it becomes necessary for us to consciously decide where to focus our energy. Most stimuli that we do perceive are filtered through our self-concept, past experiences, or expectations. The rest of the stimuli we simply miss (Toch and Smith 1968).

selection
Focusing on some sensory stimuli rather than others.

Selection includes not only what you decide to perceive, but also the moment you begin perceiving. For instance, the point at which you enter a conversation can determine your perception of it. If you start paying attention to an argument between your friends just as one of them leaves the room, you are likely to have a different perception of the person who left than if you had heard the argument as it erupted. Similarly, your perception of a central character in a movie will be different if you enter a film in progress rather than at the beginning. Although perception occurs continually, the point at which selection begins can influence considerably how you understand people and events.

There are two kinds of stimuli that we tend to select, salient and vivid. **Salience** refers to personal relevance or interest; **vividness** includes all of those sensations that seem to stand out from their surroundings. These two sets of cues are regularly exploited in the media by advertisers, radio announcers, and others in attempts to get audiences to focus on particular products or services. First we will examine salient cues that draw on novelty, familiarity, and repetition; then we will look at vivid cues such as intensity, size, figure and ground, and motion. Finally, we will address the role of social learning in selecting perceptions.

salience
Personal relevance or interest.

vividness
Includes all sensations that seem to stand out from their surroundings.

Salience. Our choices about what is worthy of attention are often based on how useful, interesting, or personally meaningful a specific stimulus might be. We tune in to *stimuli* based on our physical needs, the novelty of words or images, the familiarity of people, places, and things, the proximity or closeness of a sensation, or the frequency with which a stimulus is repeated.

Novelty You've probably seen signs on vehicles as a way to advertise a product or service. One Southern California pest-control company paints compact cars yellow and places large, black, rodent ears and a tail on the cars. These cars stand out in the stream of traffic due to their novelty. Advertisers realize that standing out from the competition with a unique product display is critical to gaining consumer attention; reporters rely on novelty as one of the ways to determine if an event is newsworthy. Novelty is one of the criteria we use in selecting stimuli that we perceive. Even young children recognize this when they try new ways to ask for things from parents who have stopped listening.

Familiarity We like things that are recognizable or similar to us. When we enter a room full of people at a reception or party, we are likely to be drawn toward and talk to those people we know or people we think might share similar backgrounds or interests. We might notice and talk to our neighbors if we run into them at a shopping center, and we are likely to develop friendships with people who work in the same office or take the same classes with us. Similarly, many of us can drive along a two-mile strip of fast-food franchises only to notice our favorite one. We also see the world through the experiences afforded by our occupations. An interior designer might see far more possibilities in color, furnishings, and window treatments for your bedroom, whereas an architect will talk to you about your rooflines and entry sequences. Familiarity helps us recognize particular features of our environment and find sources of information with which we are comfortable.

Repetition The first time you hear a song on the radio, you might not notice it. By the third or fourth time, the song may enter your *perceptual field.* And though most of us, particularly parents and teachers, rarely like to repeat instructions, repetition is a cue for the perceptual process to begin. Figure 3-2 illustrates how repetition might be used in advertising.

Vividness. Whereas salience refers to those perceptual cues that are personally relevant to you, vividness addresses the qualities of a word or image that make it stand out and become noticeable. The qualities of intensity, size, figure and ground, and motion all make some stimuli more vivid than others.

Intensity Bright colors, disturbing images, sounds of joyous laughter or deep distress all attract our attention because they are intense. Sometimes intensity makes people uncomfortable, leading them to block out stimuli. In the class of one of the authors, a Vietnam veteran became disturbed by a class discussion about military combat. He began reading a newspaper during class. The instructor first assumed that the student was communicating disrespect, but after talking with him, she discovered that the intensity of the discussion prompted the student to cope by blocking out stimuli. Morning newscasters recognize the risk involved in prompting selection through intensity, for although intense images will attract attention, they might also prove too unsettling for some viewers.

Size Although bigger isn't always better, we do notice things that are very large. North Americans tend to place considerable emphasis on size, highlighting features such as the tallest building, highest mountain, and biggest servings in restaurants. Size also affects how we perceive messages in electronic media. Substantial research suggests that people who watch larger television and film screens (70 inches or more) become aroused by the content and think what

REPETITION AND PERCEPTION

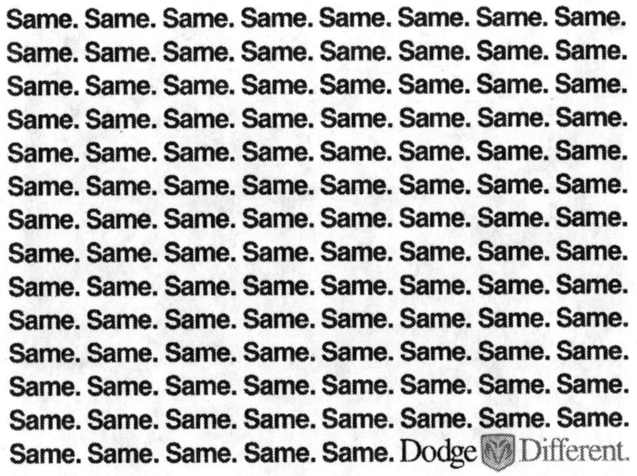

FIGURE 3-2

Same. Same. Same. Same. Same. Same. Same. Same.
Same. Same. Same. Same. Same. Same. Same. Same.
Same. Same. Same. Same. Same. Same. Same. Same.
Same. Same. Same. Same. Same. Same. Same. Same.
Same. Same. Same. Same. Same. Same. Same. Same.
Same. Same. Same. Same. Same. Same. Same. Same.
Same. Same. Same. Same. Same. Same. Same. Same.
Same. Same. Same. Same. Same. Same. Same. Same.
Same. Same. Same. Same. Same. Same. Same. Same.
Same. Same. Same. Same. Same. Same. Same. Same.
Same. Same. Same. Same. Same. Same. Same. Same.
Same. Same. Same. Same. Same. Same. Same. Same.
Same. Same. Same. Same. Same. Same. Same. Same.
Same. Same. Same. Same. Same. Dodge Different.

"Dodge is Different." How is repetition used to attract your attention? Does the ad use more than one perceptual cue?

Courtesy of BBDO for Daimler Chrysler. Used with permission.

they are watching is realistic partly because of the vividness of the images (Grabe et al. 1999). We also gravitate toward extremes in smallness, taking note of everything from short people, to miniature dog breeds, to the speaker whose voice drops to a whisper. The extremes of size are powerful perceptual cues.

Figure and Ground We see different things when we choose to focus on a single feature in a painting, print, or message rather than the image or meaning as a whole. Figure 3-3 shows three competing figures. The ones you focus on will dictate what you see in the image.

The part that you focus on is called "figure," and the surrounding images are often called "ground." You should be able to see a candlestick, a single face, or two profiles facing each other, depending on which image serves as a "figure" for you. If you're having trouble identifying the images, hold the picture at arm's length, then move it closer to you.

The principle of figure and ground has relevance for verbal as well as visual communication. During the first presidential debate between Vice President Al Gore and Texas Governor George W. Bush in 2000, Gore could be heard sighing heavily during Bush's statements. Some viewers came to perceive the sighing as "figure," so that their overriding impression of the debate was that Gore was rude. They selectively perceived his nonverbal communication as more important than the statements he made during the debate.

Motion Movement catches the human eye, making it an agent of vividness. If you walk into a room and a television is on, your senses will be drawn to it, even if you decide not to watch it. Perhaps you have had the experience of trying to study with the television on or attempting to have a conversation during a party in which the television sound is off, but there are still moving images on the screen. Similarly, if you are speaking to a room full of people, you are likely to notice the ones who check their watches or shift in their chairs. Although these movements might be disconcerting, your eye will be drawn toward them. You will then need to decide how to interpret the motion, a topic that will be addressed in a later section.

"Television has proved that people will look at anything rather than each other."

—Ann Landers, advice columnist

FIGURE 3-3 FIGURE AND GROUND

What do you see in the image?

Social Learning and Selection. Thus far, we have emphasized how cues from others, such as what people say, how they look, or the intensity of their emotions, influence the way we selectively perceive them. However, even perceptual cues such as size and intensity are affected by the way we learn to focus on some stimuli rather than others. **Social learning** is the general theory that we learn new behaviors, customs, and routines by watching others (Bandura 1977). Just as we learn about appropriate communication behaviors in our interactions with others, we also learn what to pay attention to in our environment. For instance, the person who has lived for years in a densely populated urban area is more likely to pick out obscure signs and traffic signals from a busy street scene than someone who comes from a more rural environment. The importance of social learning is demonstrated dramatically by people who acquire sensory abilities only as adults. The person who loses hearing as an infant and then regains it as an adult must learn a whole new process of sifting through stimuli, so that the barrage of sensory stimulation—new sights and sounds—does not become overwhelming.

social learning
The general theory that we learn new behaviors, customs, and routines by watching others.

Finally, because our decisions to select stimuli are based largely on past learning, we often put ourselves in familiar situations, see the same patterns, and focus on the same senses in ways that are predictable and comfortable. Perhaps you have a friend who has a habit such as saying, "You know." You are likely to notice that same pattern in an acquaintance, because it is one that you recognize. Past experiences are particularly resilient, because we often view them as our best form of evidence, and we don't like our image of the world to change. This resistance to change has been called **perceptual constancy,** or the tendency to maintain the same perception of people and events over time (Garrigan and Kellman 2009). Although our country has laws against double jeopardy, few of us recognize the principle in our personal relationships. If your roommate accidentally threw away an issue of your favorite magazine months earlier and now you can't find your most recent issue, you might be quick to accuse your roommate of misplacing it. Similarly, once you decide that a friend is absent-minded, a section of a nearby city is dangerous, or a talk-show host is trustworthy, you are likely to see each of these in ways that match your previous experience. First impressions are inevitable, but our tendency to cling to them can compromise subsequent perceptions and communication.

perceptual constancy
Tendency to maintain the same perception of people and events over time.

"We see what we expect to see, and we expect to see what we've already seen."

—Dr. James Tanner, sociologist

Organizing Perceptions

Perception occurs so quickly that we often are unaware of separate components in the process. We seem to process statements and images instantaneously. Think about the following scenario during which two young women, Jolene and Soleda, are on their lunch break. The two women are similar in age, height, and build. As they seat themselves, another woman from a nearby table waves to Jolene.

"Hey," she says, "I saw you at the gym this morning. You must go there fairly often."

Jolene replies, "I try to make it there five or six times a week."

The woman then turns to Soleda. "Do you work out, too?"

Soleda answers, "I used to, but I haven't had time lately."

Turning back to Jolene, the woman says, "Well, it certainly shows."

The *proximity,* or closeness of the woman's table, her movement toward Jolene and Soleda, and her familiarity with Jolene all contributed to their perceiving her presence. As this woman spoke, Jolene and Soleda quickly put her into one of several possible mental boxes. Perhaps she was perceived to be an intrusive stranger. Maybe she was seen as trying to establish a bond with Jolene. The mental category in which Jolene and Soleda placed her will influence how they interpret and respond to her.

Organization occurs when we place stimuli in a category or mental box to give them meaning and aid our retention. Several theorists have attempted to explain how the organization phase of perception occurs. For Gestalt theorists, selection and organization happen simultaneously in a sudden flash of recognition (Feldman 2009); it is a moment where things come together. Gestalt theory began as a critique of scientific methods that break things down into parts and led to seeing processes as wholes that are greater than the individual parts. Our instant recognition of a pattern or understanding of a perception sometimes feels like a Gestalt, and we don't think about the way we arrived at recognition or understanding. For communicators, however, understanding the process of organizing perceptions can unpack hidden assumptions and expectations about our interactions with others (see the "Applying Communication Concepts" box on categorizing inkblots).

organization
Placing stimuli in a knowledge structure or category to give them meaning and aid retention.

Applying Communication Concepts

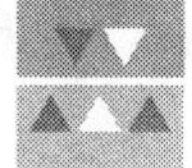

CATEGORIZING INKBLOTS

Once we perceive stimuli, we place them in categories that fit our image or worldview. Even the most ambiguous images are subjected to this process. Consider, for example, the Rorschach inkblot test, first proposed by Herman Rorschach in 1921. The inkblot test uses abstract designs to elicit associations that people make when viewing these designs. There are no "correct" answers to inkblot tests; rather, they are designed to evoke salient categories for organizing perceptions that are then interpreted by a therapist. The validity of the inkblot test for revealing personality traits is questionable. For our purposes, the inkblots are an excellent illustration of the way that people attempt to find meaning even for ambiguous perceptions. Study the inkblot in Figure 3-4A for a moment. The first one was posted on a web page and elicited the following responses on the site: (http://www.pigwig.demon.co.uk/inkblot/archive/98_11_responses.html):

FIGURE 3-4A. What do you see in the inkblot?

— It looks like someone making a leap on his skis.
— One very happy frog.
— A Russian folk dancer with pom-poms and clown shoes.
— A juggler standing on a bridge which is falling down.
— Some evil being with horns that is smiling, watching a tiny man with wings and really big feet dance on his lip.
— A pile of bones and flying geese. It makes me happy.

Now, look at the next inkblot (Figure 3-4B).

FIGURE 3-4B. What categories can you use to make sense of this image?

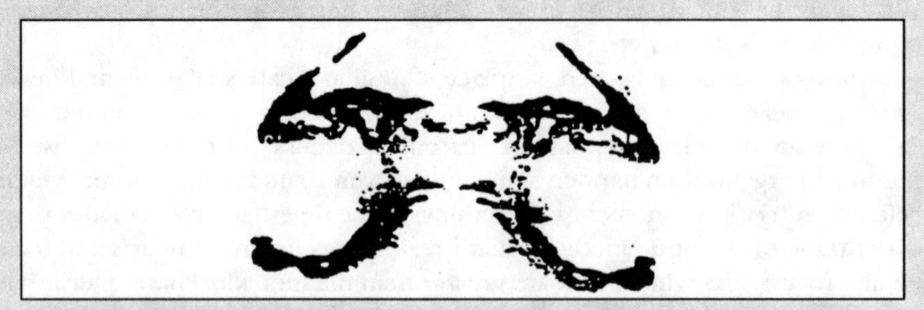

ASK YOURSELF:

1. How do you identify the image(s)?
2. What organization can you give them?
3. What might your responses tell you about yourself?

Gestalt theory and inkblot tests like the ones in the box may make the way we organize perceptions seem random and unknowable. In fact, there is much we do know about how perceptions are classified. The mental categories we use to organize perceptions are largely the product of our interactions with others. The relationship between the organization of perceptions and communication is addressed by the theory of **constructivism,** first proposed by George Kelly (1955). Constructivism suggests that people interpret and act on experience based on a mental system of organizing knowledge. This mental or cognitive blueprint is composed of personal constructs, prototypes, stereotypes, and scripts.

constructivism
Theory that people interpret and act on experience based on a mental system of organizing knowledge.

personal constructs
Categories by which people and events can be differentiated.

Personal Constructs. **Personal constructs** are categories by which people and events can be differentiated. We all have countless personal constructs, such as those that help us decide whether someone is sincere or insincere, generous or frugal, intelligent or unintelligent. We use these constructs to determine how closely our perception matches our previous experience and the qualities that the person or object might possess. Personal constructs provide an inventory of our beliefs. The more constructs we have, the more complex our understanding. For instance, North Americans see insects as pests rather than as a nutritional food source based on the definition of a construct called "food." Our personal experience will determine the complexity of constructs such as food, so the person who has sampled international foods and perhaps tried insect larvae will have a more multidimensional definition of things that are good to eat.

We rely on constructs all the time; they help us relate new words and images to those with which we are familiar, and they influence how we might respond to what we see and hear. Some communication theorists believe that we learn to categorize some of our perceptions based on what we see and hear in the media. The "Exploring Communication Concepts" box about media and perceptions of violence presents research that extends basic assumptions about using perceptual constructs.

prototype
A specific person, personality, or phenomenon that exemplifies a set of characteristics.

Prototypes. One of the most basic types of personal constructs that we use to organize perceptions is called a **prototype,** or a specific person, personality, or phenomenon that exemplifies a set of characteristics. Prototypes have been called ideal models of people or situations. For instance, you may have a prototype of the perfect teacher that you use as a basis of comparison for other teachers. You evaluate each subsequent instructor on the degree of similarity with your prototype. Many romantic comedies use the idea of prototypes as a plot device, as when the central character is with a partner who happens to fit her or his idea of the perfect mate. Although this mate seems prototypical, the protagonist discovers that another, seemingly inaccessible person is really closer to the prototype than he or she imagined. We have prototypes of star athletes, musicians, and news anchors as well. We might have one prototype for a marriage partner and a different one for a best friend. The individuals we use as prototypes help us classify our perceptions of people as we compare them with our ideal types.

Stereotypes. When our personal constructs are simplistic, we have difficulty recognizing and appreciating people's individual qualities. Stereotypes are among the most powerful and oversimplified constructs (Delia, O'Keefe, and O'Keefe 1982). As we discussed in Chapter 2, stereotypes are generalizations about people based on their group affiliation, rather than their individual characteristics.

Exploring Communication Concepts

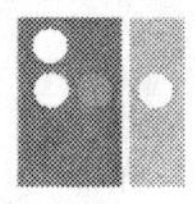

MEDIA AND PERCEPTIONS OF VIOLENCE

priming
Audience use of conceptual categories that have been emphasized in the media.

Television news anchors, talk-show hosts, and charismatic actors all rely on personal constructs to organize their perceptions, just like the rest of us. However, the constructs that influential communicators use to categorize people and events can have a significant influence on the perceptions of others. For instance, when television reporters present news stories, they rely on perceptual categories that are often adopted by viewing audiences. Once a person is identified as a criminal, for example, audiences are likely to use the construct of "criminal" each time they see another story about that person. This phenomenon has been called **priming,** or audience use of conceptual categories that have been emphasized in the media (Iyengar and Kinder 1988).

Research on media priming began with issues emphasized in the news, such as crime and poverty, and the influence of news on political campaigns. Contemporary research also considers the role of priming in the way film viewers perceive violence. For instance, we now know that watching violent videotapes leads to more aggressive thinking and increases the speed with which people react to aggressive, or "fighting," words (Bushman and Green 1990; Bushman 1998).

This research suggests that once we are presented with a conceptual category, we are likely to rely on it in organizing subsequent perceptions. If we repeatedly read in the local paper that a neighbor is a convicted sex offender, we are likely to see whatever that neighbor does as evidence of perversion. We might learn to react violently to some words and images or to associate a person with a category.

ASK YOURSELF:

1. Try to recall a news story or advertisement that was particularly appealing to you. How did it "prime" your perceptions?
2. What associations do you make with the person or product?

Familiar stereotypes might include the construct that poor people are lazy, overweight people have a good sense of humor, and homosexuals are promiscuous. A stereotype held by some police officers is that African Americans are likely to commit crimes. As one urban officer said, "I'm probably more suspicious of blacks, just based on my experience. There's more of a possibility of problems than with others"(Thornton, McKinnie, and Stetz 1999). This stereotype whether or not one thinks it is valid, leads some officers to behave more aggressively toward blacks whom they perceive to be suspicious and makes them more willing to detain and handcuff them than members of other racial groups. Remarks of the officers toward blacks are more likely to be condescending, accusatorial, and confrontational. Relying on stereotypes can have tragic consequences, as when a police officer shoots an unarmed African-American suspect or, as happened following the terrorist attacks of September 11, 2001, a deranged white man shot a turban-wearing Sikh thinking he must be an Islamic terrorist.

We often think that we can consciously avoid stereotyping, but we sometimes cling to them because they serve as a powerful shortcut in organizing perceptions; stereotypes are convenient mental boxes in which to place people. Some of the most convenient constructs are stereotypes about sex. From the time babies are born, we rely on our perceptions of their sex to help us understand them, and we create expectations about the way that they will communicate. In one study, for example, observers were shown videotape in which a child played with a jack-in-the-box. Half of the observers were told that the child was a boy; the other half that the child was a girl. When the child became agitated by the toy and cried, those who thought the child was a boy assumed he was angry, while those who perceived the child as a girl described her as afraid (Kimmel 2000).

We even stereotype inanimate objects. We often give ships and vehicles female names, and we refer to strong animals as males. At least one study reveals the strength of gender stereotypes in our perceptions of computers. In one experiment, all of the subjects denied having stereotypical perceptions of men and women. But when they sat in front of computers, they viewed male-voiced computers as being more knowledgeable about technology and female-voiced computers as being better teachers of love and relationships. Praise from a male-voiced computer was seen as more impressive than praise from the female counterpart. Finally, when the female voice of a computer was lowered to sound more masculine, people thought of that computer as more intelligent, with better reasoning skills and more persuasive abilities than the more feminine-sounding computer (Balint 1998). Such research demonstrates the pervasive reliance on stereotypes for understanding the world.

> "The first problem for all of us, men and women, is not to learn, but to unlearn."
>
> —Gloria Steinem, activist

Scripts. The mental patterns we use to organize perceptions include a final category of communication behavior called scripts. **Scripts** are guides to actions and expectations based on the way we have categorized our perceptions. When someone passes us on the sidewalk and asks "How's it going?" we might respond with, "Fine, thanks." The person who answers, "Well, pretty bad, really," or launches into a lengthy explanation of major life changes is likely to get a puzzled look from the greeter. Most of us categorize the event, "passing an acquaintance in the street," as an occasion that calls for a simple greeting. We have not scripted a conversation beyond two or three brief sentences. Similarly, if we hear a romantic partner say, "We need to talk," we might categorize the statement as a request for an intense examination of the relationship. The script that follows will be much more involved depending on our construct for the relationship.

> **scripts**
> Guides to actions and expectations based on the categorization of perceptions.

We develop scripts for all kinds of social situations; once we define a situation, a script will follow. As you read the "Think It Over" box about categorizing others and creating scripts, think about the earlier example of police officers who relied on stereotypes in their interactions with African Americans. Blacks in turn are likely to have their own scripts for interacting with local law enforcers.

Source: Cartoon by Kirkman & Scott, © Baby Blues Partnership. Reprinted by special permission of King Features Syndicate.

Think It Over

CATEGORIZING OTHERS AND CREATING SCRIPTS

Because some police officers rely on stereotypes of African Americans, some African-American parents try to reduce potential confrontations by teaching their children to use a script in the form of a checklist of do's and don'ts. For example: If stopped by an officer, "night or day, put both hands on the steering wheel. If it's night, turn your dome light on. Sit still until the officer gets to the car."

"Now he should ask you for identification, which is your driver's license. Wherever you have it on your person, you need to tell him, 'It's in my rear left pocket or rear right pocket.' And tell him, 'I'm not armed. You asked for my I.D. So I need to go into my pocket to get it.' " (Balint 1999).

Does your script for dealing with people change if you perceive them to be a threat? Are you more likely to be accommodating or confrontational?

How is your script influenced by your prototypes, personal constructs, or stereotypes?

Prototypes, personal constructs, stereotypes, and scripts all help us organize incoming perceptions in ways that make the world seem easier for us to understand. Organization is thus a critical step in creating meaning; placing a perception in one category rather than another will determine how we think about and respond to particular types of people and events. This whole system of mental categories, or templates, gives us a sense of security because it makes our world seem more predictable. This security can be deceptive, however, when it locks us into simplistic or rigid ways of thinking and communicating. When we experience something that either does not fit our categories or calls those categories into question, we may be forced to make a perception shift.

"Something which we think is impossible now is not impossible in another decade."

—Constance Baker Motley, first black woman in the United States to become a federal judge

Perception Shifts. **Perception shifts** are strategies for thinking creatively and managing different perspectives. They occur when people are willing to take risks and alter the way they perceive the world. The authors of the book *Fish!* discussed the power of choice that people have in the way they perceive their work (Lunden, Paul, and Christensen 2000). Although many people would consider the work at a fish market to be tedious, smelly, and boring, the fishmongers at Pike Place Fish decided that not only would they choose the kind of day to have at work, but they would also choose to be "world famous." Adopting the perception "we are world famous" meant that changes in behaviors had to follow. Making Pike Place Fish world famous required the workers to shift their perceptions of their jobs from being "merely a way to make money" to a setting where they had fun and were fully engaged with customers, such as making sure that they gave full attention to every customer with whom they spoke.

perception shifts
Strategies for thinking creatively and managing different perspectives.

New technologies often speed shifts in perception. Consider interactive health communication. At one end of the continuum are online physicians who dispense medical information in real time to Web consumers. At the other end is the more radical practice of treating urban patients in culturally specific neighborhoods through Internet connections and video-conferencing. Traditional health care has required people with limited mobility and English language skills to travel to a foreign environment, in which the language spoken and medicine practiced might seem strange and uncomfortable. With urban telemedicine, healthcare is delivered within the community of the participant. In a largely Latino environment, for instance, the website can be presented in Spanish and reflect Latino culture by providing information about both alternative and traditional treatments (Elegraby 1998). Some doctors argue that this form of health communication truly reflects a perception shift in the way that health care is understood and delivered (Murray et al. 2005).

You may have been asked to make a perception shift without even knowing it. Have you ever been told to view an unexpected event not as a "problem," but as an "opportunity?" If so, you were asked to make a perceptual shift by changing the way that you categorized the situation. The ability to make a perceptual shift is becoming increasingly valued in the workplace. Employers regularly state that they desire employees who can think "outside of the box," which means being able to adopt a new way of thinking about issues and organizing perceptions. Such thinking is difficult because it requires looking beyond the categories that we typically use to organize our perceptions.

When someone makes a request, issues an order, gives us information, or expresses emotion, the way we perceive and organize this information determines our responses to them. The boxes we use to organize information—the prototypes, personal constructs, stereotypes, and scripts—help us manage perceptions and decide how to interact with others. When we change the boxes by shifting our perceptions, we change our behaviors and our interpretations. We now turn to the last stage in the perceptual process: interpretation.

> "Some people are always grumbling because roses have thorns. I am thankful that thorns have roses."
>
> —Alphonse Karr, French writer and editor

Interpreting Perceptions

Interpretation is the stage in the perception process in which we determine the meaning of an event or interaction. It is the process by which we explain our perceptions. Interpretation sometimes seems to happen at the same time as organization, because as we have seen, the way we organize perceptions can also help us understand them. Both organization and interpretation give meaning to perceptions, so the distinction sometimes seems artificial. At times, though, we process our perceptions in distinct steps. We use context, closure, and attributions to help us interpret our perceptions. Each of these concepts will be described in the following sections.

interpretation
Stage of perception in which we determine the meaning of an event or interaction.

Context. The first way we make sense of our perceptions is by placing them in the context of an interaction. We don't need complete information to draw conclusions; indeed, we understand a lot by thinking about the nature of the situation or our relationship to the person to whom we are talking. Context can often help us to interpret the meaning of someone's statements or actions. Consider the relationship partner who snaps at you as soon as he or she comes home from work. If you know that your partner has had a particularly stressful day, that might make it easier for you to be sympathetic, rather than reacting with anger.

Closure. Another strategy that we use to interpret perceptions is closure, or filling in the gaps between stimuli. Closure helps us read the words at the edge of margins when we receive a document with the final letters missing at the end of each line:

> The Board of Trustees, in accordance wi
> the recommendation of the President and t
> Faculty of the Graduate School at the Uni"

We know that the missing letters complete the words "with," "the" and "University." Similarly, we can read the pages from printers that need new print cartridges; the bottom half of each line can be missing, and we'll still be able to read the print. We interpret vanity automobile plates using closure and can probably fill in the letters of the following examples:

BLK DMND   SXY WMN   GN FSHN

The same process happens when people who know each other well finish each other's sentences. In all of these situations, closure allows us to draw conclusions based on unfinished, incomplete, or limited information.

attribution
The assignment of meaning to the actions of ourselves and others.

Assigning Attributions. Drawing conclusions on the basis of our perceptions of words and images may seem relatively easy. Interpretation becomes much more difficult when we try to explain the behaviors of others. When we make an **attribution** we assign meaning to the actions of ourselves and others (Aronson 1984). For example, an adult friend might enjoy looking at the sky and finding animal shapes in the clouds. You could call your friend's behavior either childish or childlike, depending on what you thought about your friend and how you interpreted the activity. Suppose that you are talking to a woman who frequently checks her watch or looks to see who else is in the room. If you have just met her, you might categorize her behaviors as those of an impatient person. If you know her, you are likely to decide what her behaviors mean in the context of your relationship. Does she have to be somewhere else that is more important, or is she bored with what you are saying? Is there some immediate physical need that she has to address, or is there someone else she'd rather talk to? The attributions you make regarding her behaviors signal the move from organizing your perceptions to interpreting them.

External and Internal Attributions At a general level, we interpret the actions of others as being caused either by external forces, such as the social situation or physical environment, or internal causes, such as personality characteristics and individual beliefs. When we perceive people to be acting consistently, we attribute their behavior to internal causes. When a specific situation seems to be causing their behavior, we see external forces as responsible for their actions. Parents struggle with this as they try to figure out whether their children's behavior is part of a passing phase or an indicator of a more enduring *predisposition.* The parents who perceive their three-year-old son's hysterical sobbing to be part of a passing phase are more likely to respond gently to him than those who conclude that such an emotional display is likely to be repeated throughout his childhood. If a driver cuts you off on a freeway, you might see that person as someone rushing due to an emergency or as an angry, aggressive individual. Your nonverbal gestures—from pulling out of the way to waving in anger—will reflect your attribution. In the first instance, behavior has been attributed to a specific, external occurrence; in the second, the behavior is perceived to be the result of an internal, stable condition. Each attribution leads to different communication strategies in response.

We make judgments about external and internal attributions based partly on our conceptual categories for people. For instance, considerable research has demonstrated that our gender schemas, or conceptual categories about what it means to be male and female, determine how we rate the success of men and women. When a man performs well, both men and women are likely to attribute his success to internal factors, such as his individual abilities and talents. When a woman succeeds, some people are more likely to attribute it to external forces, such as luck (Valian 1998). These gendered attributions negatively affect women in a range of occupations, from professors to mathematicians and computer scientists (Bachen and McLoughlin 1999; Doyle 2000).

Our decision to interpret behaviors based on external or internal factors often depends on how much responsibility we think others have for their situations. Those decisions then influence how we treat and communicate with others. For instance, throughout history we have used disease classifications to explain the degree of responsibility that people have for their actions. As Joseph Gusfield (1981) demonstrated, people driving under the influence of alcohol can be seen as social drinkers who are sometimes involved in accidents, as criminal "killer drunks," or as people struggling with the disease of alcoholism. How we define people who drink and drive will determine our responses to them. We will treat them differently if we view them as people with an illness rather than as criminals.

The way we organize perceptions is directly connected to our interpretations of internal and external causes. If we like people, we tend to see their misfortunes as caused by forces outside their control; if we dislike them, we are more likely to hold them responsible for the things that happen to them. Consider the following example of press coverage of two athletes, former Olympic diver Greg Louganis and NBA star Magic Johnson, both of whom contracted the AIDS virus. In an analysis of press coverage of Louganis and Johnson, Wachs and Dworkin (1997) showed how Louganis, a self-identified gay man, is presented as a victim or carrier of the disease, and Johnson, a heterosexual, is presented as a hero. Louganis is seen as responsible for contracting the disease, while Johnson, who admittedly engaged in promiscuous and high-risk behavior, is not seen as acting in ways that might have contributed to contracting the disease. Because of these different attributions, Louganis was held to higher standards of morality, while Johnson was forgiven for his behavior.

Think about the last time you were angry with someone. Perhaps another driver made an unsafe lane change, a customer didn't leave a tip, or a friend did not return a phone call. Did you assume that the behavior was intentional—for example, the driver was a rude person or the customer was being cheap? Or did you attribute the behavior to external cause—for example, your friend who owed you a call was unusually busy? How did your attribution of the other person's actions influence the way you responded to that person? How would your script change if you changed your attribution?

Watch a video about potential mistakes people can make in their attributions (CD Clip 3.1).

Biases in Attribution. Our attributions are vulnerable to biases in interpretation that can hamper our communication effectiveness, because they lock us into narrow ways of understanding and responding to others. Attribution biases can take the form of fundamental attribution error, self-serving bias, attractiveness bias, and similarity bias.

fundamental attribution error
The overestimation of the degree to which other people's behaviors are due to internal factors and underestimation of the significance of external forces.

Fundamental attribution error Perhaps the most basic kind of perceptual bias is the **fundamental attribution error,** which occurs when we overestimate the degree to which other people's behaviors are due to internal factors and underestimate the significance of external forces. For example, a student who arrives late to a class may have been involved in a traumatic incident such as a traffic accident. However, some professors will automatically assume that the tardiness is due to rudeness or poor planning by the student. In this case, the fundamental attribution error may lead the professor to criticize the student or to ignore the student's attempts to participate in class.

self-serving bias
The tendency to attribute external causes to our own misfortunes, but not to those of others.

Self-Serving Bias The **self-serving bias** also addresses common tendencies in the way we interpret external and internal causes of behavior. The self-serving bias refers to the tendency to attribute external causes to our own misfortunes, not to those of others. Self-serving bias is the idea behind the phrase "the devil made me do it." Suppose that you just completed an important job interview. During the interview, you gave a seemingly bizarre answer to a question, such as a 200-mile drive would be a reasonable commute. You could explain your answer as a fluke caused by too much caffeine or by the inattentiveness of the interviewer. Or you could attribute the statement to your own inexperience with interviewing. The self-serving bias suggests that you are more likely to attribute the statement to caffeine or the demeanor of the interviewer. We are much better at finding internal reasons for our own behavior when we want praise, whereas we often attribute our own behavior to factors beyond our control when we have done something that might be criticized.

"It's not my fault."
—Han Solo, *Star Wars*

attractiveness bias
The tendency to think better of attractive people than unattractive people and to make positive attributions about their behavior.

Attractiveness Bias A third common attributional bias is based on our positive evaluation of people who are physically attractive. The **attractiveness bias** suggests that we tend to think better of attractive than unattractive people, and we tend to make positive attributions about their behavior. Additionally, as long as beautiful people don't abuse the power of their looks, we will hold them less accountable for bad behavior than their less attractive counterparts (Aronson 1984). Interestingly, this bias doesn't always work in favor of attractive people; research on sexual harassment found that attractive people are more likely to be perceived as flirtatious, whether they intend to flirt or not (Solomon and Williams 1998).

similarity bias
The attribution of our own motivations to someone else's behaviors.

Similarity Bias A fourth attributional bias is the tendency to think that the people we like are similar to us. The **similarity bias** occurs when we attribute our own motivations to someone else's behaviors. After all, part of liking someone is the feeling that your perspective is shared. For instance, suppose that Drew and Kane are co-workers who frequently take lunch breaks together. Kane might like Drew and assume that he would find the same joke to be funny. But Drew might consider the joke to be offensive. Or perhaps you have become friends with another member of a club to which you belong. You mention that you would like to get something to eat after the club meeting, thinking that the new friend would like to continue discussing an upcoming activity. The new friend, however, assumes that you are asking for a date.

Attribution theory prompts us to consider the ways that we account for our own behaviors and those of others, and to recognize the potential biases in doing so. In the final section of this chapter, we explore some strategies to manage our perceptions and the way we communicate more effectively and responsibly.

Perception and Responsible Communication

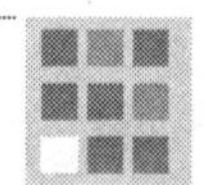

As we have seen, understanding the process of perception is critical to effective communication, because perceptions provide the basis for our assumptions about ourselves and others. These interpretations inform our decisions about how and what to communicate. And although all perceptions are important, not all perceptions are equally valid. Here we will look at ways to evaluate perceptions and act in ways that take responsibility for doing so by owning perceptions, overcoming attributional bias, using perception checks, and practicing perspective taking.

Own Your Perceptions

When people argue that perceptions are less important than reality, they fail to note that we often treat our own perceptions *as* reality, and we hesitate to acknowledge the importance of perceptions that are different from our own. For instance, if Naomi believes that Kyle has lied to her, Naomi might interpret everything that Kyle says as an attempt to cover up the lie, regardless of whether Kyle lied in the first place. You might perceive a popular instructor as someone who gives high grades without hesitation, when in fact she has high expectations, evaluates students with rigor, and is popular because she motivates students to learn. Your perceptions about her as "easy" might guide your interactions with her until you are faced with the reality of her grading standards. The first step in owning your perceptions is recognizing why your perceptions might be different than those of the person you are talking to.

Owning your perceptions also means realizing that others might not share your perceptions. Often, we try to argue with people who don't share our perceptions, rather than acknowledging that, for them, their perceptions are just as valid as ours. Suppose that you work for a company that surveys employees about its process of giving salary increases based on merit or perceived excellence at work. The survey reveals that over 60 percent of the employees feel that the merit pay process is unfair. Company supervisors might push this perception aside by saying "that's just the opinion of some disgruntled employees; it's not reality. Of course the way we give raises is fair." Nonetheless, the perceptions of employees about whether standards are fair, or how well they are meeting the standards, can be just as important as the existence of the standards themselves. In this case, company supervisors will need to own their perceptions and acknowledge the perceived reality of their employees before they can address issues of low employee trust and morale.

> "What difference does it make if the thing you are scared of is real or not?"
>
> —Toni Morrison, *Song of Solomon*

Overcome Attributional Bias

The move from selection to interpretation in the process of perception happens quickly, and the speed with which this occurs can be our biggest obstacle to effective communication. Overcoming attributional bias can be as simple as slowing down and examining your assumptions about yourself and others. Consider the following tips:

- *Avoid mind reading.* Just because someone appears to be wealthy, or elderly, or happy, doesn't mean that you can predict how he or she will feel, think, or act. Many salespeople have missed out on closing a sale because they didn't think a customer looked affluent enough to make a purchase.
- *Be charitable in accounting for the actions of others, just as you would be toward yourself.* If a close friend or relative doesn't send a card on a special occasion, don't assume that a slight was intended. If you've ever been late or forgetful, you know that a little understanding can go a long way. Postpone judgment.
- *Finally, acknowledge your mental shortcuts and how they influence your evaluations of other people.* We have all formed a few convenient mental constructs, or stereotypes based on our past experiences. The responsible communicator is aware of his or her biases and works to minimize their influence in every interaction.

"I always prefer to believe the best of everybody—it saves so much trouble."

—Rudyard Kipling, author

Use Perception Checks

A **perception check** is a tool that gauges the accuracy of your perceptions by engaging in conversations with others. You have probably used perception checks without realizing it. For instance, you might perceive a classmate to be unapproachable and then ask a fellow student if he or she shares your perception. A perception check, such as a conversation with the classmate, might challenge your initial perception. People who seem unapproachable are often labeled as arrogant or cold, when they may be merely shy or reserved. Sometimes a single conversation can serve as a perception check. Perception checks can help us decide if someone's behavior is due to stable qualities, such as personality traits, or based on external circumstances. We should seek verification for that first impression we form based on an initial encounter.

perception check
Tool that gauges the accuracy of your perceptions by engaging in conversations with others.

What might be the script between these communicators? What perceptual biases might influence the communication between these people?

To verify an impression, take the following steps:

- Describe the behavior you've observed ("You didn't eat much of your lunch").
- Acknowledge that there is more than one way to interpret the behavior ("I'm not sure if you didn't like the food, or you aren't hungry").
- Ask for clarification ("Can I get you something else?").

Without using this process, your perception could be inaccurate. You could think that your friend is being rude or is depressed rather than finished with a meal.

In general, perception checks show others that you are genuinely interested in understanding them and what they think. Although you can always revert to statements like "I can't believe you did that!", doing so is not likely to initiate a mutually satisfying dialogue. Perception checks are vital to good communication.

Practice Perspective Taking

Although you can never see the world exactly as another person sees it, you can practice **empathy,** the ability to accurately perceive the experience and behavior of another person, and to communicate the insights gained from those perceptions. Taking the perspective of others is particularly important when conflict exists. When you disagree with people, do you try to see their point of view? Do you ask questions about their experience? Think about the scenario at the beginning of the chapter. Stafford and Mike clearly had different perceptions about the television show they watched. Rather than try to take the perspective of the other person, each stubbornly clung to his own opinion and communication broke down. What could Mike have done to empathize with Stafford? What was the probable effect of Stafford saying, "You just don't get it?"

empathy
The ability to accurately perceive the experience and behavior of another person.

Perspective taking can also mean seeing something from a new angle. Think back to the definition and examples of perception shifts. If someone you respect says you are a bit aggressive and have an "edge," you can take the comment as an insult or you can try to communicate in ways that make the other person feel more comfortable. As you get to know how others see the world, you become more aware of the possible reasons for their behavior. Finally, when you demonstrate that you can voice the perspective of another, you have shown that person invaluable respect, even if you disagree with the perspective.

The study of perception sometimes feels abstract, as if perceptions are merely ideas in our heads. However, ideas have consequences. The way that we choose to perceive, categorize those perceptions, and assign meaning to them all determine how effectively and responsibly we will be able to communicate. Perceptions only become a liability when we close our minds and take them for granted. Know who you are, and why you perceive the world the way you do. Be willing to explore the connections between your identity, the roles you play, your culture, and the attributions you make about yourself and others. Take risks; once you know "the box," thinking outside of it might help you to change the world around you.

Resources for Review and Skill Building

Many of these resources are supported by the Connection CD-ROM and free Online Learning Center website.

SUMMARY

This summary is organized around the questions found at the beginning of the chapter. See if you can answer them before reading the summary paragraphs.

1. **Why is perception important to communication?**

   Our perceptions form the basis of interpretations about ourselves and others, and we communicate based on those interpretations.

2. **What are some factors that influence perception?**

   Specific factors that influence perception include physical characteristics, such as ability, age, and height, and personality traits. Perception is also affected by the cultural context of interaction.

3. **What are the main steps in forming perceptions?**

   There are three steps in the process of forming perceptions: selecting, organizing, and interpreting. We often do all three simultaneously, and it can be particularly difficult to separate organizing, the placing of stimuli into categories, and interpreting, the process of explaining our perceptions. Environmental cues of salience and vividness help us select some stimuli rather than others. Salience includes novelty, familiarity, and repetition. Vividness consists of intensity, size, figure and ground, and motion. We also select perceptions based on our past experiences, and we tend to maintain perceptions of people and events over time.

   We use personal constructs, prototypes, stereotypes, and scripts as ways to define what we see and hear and to organize our perceptions in manageable ways. Some of the most creative thinking occurs when we shift our perceptions, develop new constructs, and adopt new ways to perceive people and events. When we attempt to understand and explain how we have categorized our perceptions, we are engaged in interpretation.

4. **What happens when we make attributions?**

   We rely on attributions to assign meaning to the behavior of others. Attributions are commonly based on how much responsibility we think people have for what they say and do. When explaining our own behaviors, we tend to take credit for actions we're proud of and blame external factors for things we don't like. We often evaluate others based on the degree of control we think they have, and their degrees of physical attractiveness and similarity to us. The attributions we make influence the way we communicate about ourselves and with others.

5. **How can managing perceptions contribute to responsible communication?**

   Perceptions are the basis for decisions about how to communicate appropriately and effectively, because how we perceive people or events will influence our responses to them. The perceptions we have are always important, even if they seem to differ from the perceptions of those around us. Overcoming attributional bias helps us evaluate our perceptions and limit the quick judgments of others that can lead to communication based on unfair stereotypes. Perception checks help us determine the accuracy of perceptions and can communicate respect to others. Finally, perspective taking helps us empathize with others and see things in new ways.

KEY TERMS

Test your understanding of these key terms by visiting the Connections CD-ROM and Online Learning Center website at www.mhhe.com/dobkinpace.

attractiveness bias 82
attribution 80
constructivism 75
empathy 85
fundamental attribution error 82
interpretation 79
organization 73
perception 66
perception checks 84
perception shifts 78
perceptual constancy 73
personal constructs 75
priming 76
prototypes 75
salience 69
scripts 77
selection 69
self-serving bias 82
similarity bias 82
social learning 72
vividness 69

FOR FURTHER REFLECTION

Join a conversation about chapter concepts by visiting the Online Learning Center website at www.mhhe.com/dobkinpace

Read the following essay by Danzy Senna (1998):

I have never had a comfort zone of a given racial identity. My mother is a Bostonian woman of WASP heritage. My father is a Louisiana black man of mixed African and Mexican heritage. Unlike people who are automatically classified as black or white, my race has always been up for debate. I am forever having to explain to people why it is that I look so white for a black girl. . . . It's not something that I should have to explain, but in America, at least, people are obsessed with this dissonance between my face and my race. Particularly white Americans have a difficult time understanding why someone of my background would choose blackness. With Tiger Woods proclaiming himself a Cablinasian, multiracial activists demanding new categories, and *Newsweek* declaring it hip to be mixed, it strikes most people as odd that I would call myself a black girl. . . .

In those situations where I was silent in the face of racism, where I "passed," I felt a part of me die. I was a witness to things that white people say when they think they're alone. My school friends were forever talking about "niggers" and "spics," then chummily patting me on the back and saying, "Don't worry, Danzy. We're not talking about you." For me not to assert myself as black in these situations was an act of betrayal against those people whom I loved the most. It was also a betrayal of myself. . . .

These days, when people ask me what I identify with, instead of answering them with a simple word, I often turn the tables and ask them why they want to know . . . I want people to think more about what they are asking me. We have all become so lazy about race, just eating up the folklore that is shoveled our way: black equals athletic, poor, brown-skinned, left-wing, rap-music; white equals intellectual, wealthy, pale-skinned, right-wing, rock music, etc. We hold onto these archaic definitions despite a world that is increasingly blurred. I want to make people define the terms they so often use without thinking. . . . Are we all simply what we appear?

How have prototypes, personal constructs, and stereotypes contributed to the author's identity? What are your perceptions of her? What kinds of perception checks might be appropriate when talking to her?

BUILDING COMMUNICATION SKILLS

As you leave class, begin to take notes on all of the things that you observe. Continue doing so until you reach your next destination; include observations about people as well as the physical environment. On what basis do you seem to select stimuli? Can you apply the categories of salience and vividness? What interpretations did you make about the people you encountered, and did you consistently notice the same things (e.g., style of dress, height, weight, eyes, social groupings)? What do your perceptions tell you about how you see yourself?

NET WORK

Note: While all the URLs listed were current as of the printing of this book, these sites often change. Please check our website www.mhhe.com/dobkinpace for updates and hyperlinks to these exercises.

1. Look at the listings of chat rooms through a local Internet service provider. Choose one based on a category of identity that is important to you and participate in a few exchanges. What perceptions do you have of the other participants? Do you think that those who agree with you share characteristics such as age, race, and gender? Who do they think you are and are their perceptions accurate? Have you engaged in perception checks and are they useful?
2. Take a look at a website devoted to optical illusions, such as http://www.encyclozine.com/Illusion or http://www.colorcube.com/illusions/illusion.htm. See if you can identify the use of figure and ground, size, or intensity. Do you see different images depending on your perspective? How easy is it for you to shift perspective?

MEDIA MOMENTS

Many popular films play with the idea of challenging perceptions, as considerable suspense can be built around the violation of audience expectations. Particular playwrights, such as David Mamet, are known for their use of perceptual twists. One good example of the differences in perceptions and their consequences can be found in Mamet's film *Oleana* (1995). This film addresses a possible case of sexual harassment between a university student and professor. Consider viewing the film with the following questions in mind:

- How is the same behavior viewed differently by both Carol and John? Does either one commit attributional biases?
- How might John and Carol have used perception checks and perspective taking in more constructive ways?
- How do you explain the outcome of the conflict?
- Can you separate reality from perceptions?

Listening and Responding to Others

CHAPTER 4

The documentary film, The Listening Project *(2008) asks the question, "What does the world think of America?" The film follows four Americans as they ask this question of people around the world in countries like Afghanistan, Tanzania, Russia, South Africa, and China. The responses to the question include numerous compliments and favorable opinions of America. But it also includes many unsettling observations and disparagements. One Afghani woman, who lost her family to an errant American bomb, says as she cries, "They [the Americans] could have helped. But they never even came to see." American audiences of the film find it easy to listen to the praise of their country but difficult to listen to the criticism. They often become defensive and stop listening. But those who persist in listening find hope in the words of others. While America is certainly not perfect, there is still a tremendous opportunity to help the world community. Americans can only help others if they understand their needs and can only understand their needs if they listen carefully.*

QUESTIONS TO FOCUS YOUR READING

1. Why is listening essential for effective communication?
2. What are the stages of the listening process?
3. What are the differences between active and passive listeners?
4. What are some important obstacles to effective listening?
5. What are the four types of listening goals?
6. How can you be an effective and responsible listener?

Listening is a major part of communication that many of us take for granted. As Figure 4-1 illustrates, we spend as much as 53 percent of our total communication time listening (Barker et al. 1981). Despite this, most of us are poor listeners. As communicators, we are preoccupied, distracted, or forgetful as much as 75 percent of listening time, and we typically remember less than 20 to 25 percent of what we hear (Listening Factoids 2000). We also assume that listening is easy and natural when it actually requires skill, energy, and concentration.

Good listening skills are important in both our professional and personal lives. Many business executives identify listening as one of the most important work related skills they look for in their employees (Staiano 2006). According to one expert, business executives spend as much as 80 percent of their time listening (Wycoff 1994). Listening is also an important part of interpersonal relationships. The time we spend listening in a relationship helps us to grow personally and to convey to others that we respect them and want to understand them. Listening is basic to overcoming feelings of loneliness and isolation; we all want to feel that others are willing to listen to us (Nichols 1969). Improving your listening skills will make you a better communicator, assist you in your professional life, and enrich your interpersonal relationships. After reading this chapter, you should be better able to:

- Distinguish between hearing and listening.
- Identify parts of the listening process.
- Establish listening goals.
- Identify and manage obstacles to effective listening.
- Practice ways to be a responsible and effective listener.

"The most called-upon prerequisite of a friend is an accessible ear."
—Maya Angelou, poet

Hearing and Listening

hearing
The act of perceiving sounds or other related stimuli.

Many of us confuse the concepts of hearing and listening. **Hearing** refers to the process by which sound waves are converted into electrochemical impulses that travel to the brain and are deciphered into recognizable sounds. The physical ability to receive and decipher sounds varies considerably among individuals and can be affected by inherited properties of the ear, illness, aging, or environmental damage. Many of us take this ability for granted, even though increasingly fewer of us hear well. For instance, recent advances in audio electronics, such as headsets and surround sound, have contributed to the acceleration of hearing loss among adolescents and young adults (Levine 1999). Although most of our discussion focuses on listening rather than the physiological process of hearing, it is worth noting the real, physical limitations that some of us face in trying to hear.

listening
The process of perceiving, constructing meaning from, and responding to spoken or nonverbal messages.

The International Listening Association (2000) defines **listening** as "the process of receiving, constructing meaning from, and responding to spoken and/or nonverbal messages." When we listen, we move from the physiological process of hearing to the process of communicating. Suppose, for instance, that you turn on the television while you study. If the television is simply background noise and you are not paying any attention to what is being broadcast, then you

FIGURE 4-1 COMMUNICATION TIME SPENT LISTENING

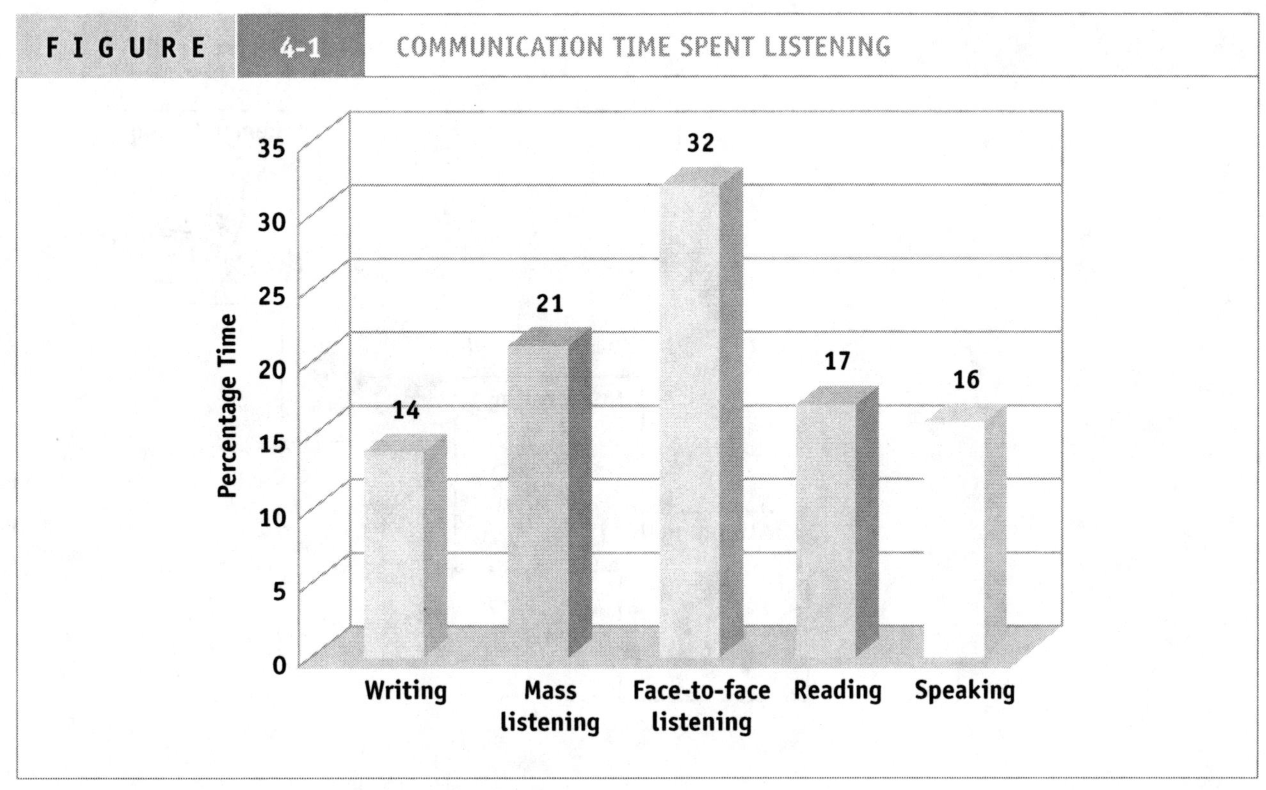

Over half of our time spent communicating is devoted to listening.

are only hearing the noise. But if a program or newscast catches your attention and you set aside your schoolwork to watch more closely, then you are listening. Sadly, many of us hear other people like we hear the television; too often, we expend little effort to listen to and communicate with others. Gaining a basic understanding of the process by which we figure out what others are saying is the first step toward improving our listening skills.

The Listening Process

The listening process is similar to the perception process we described in Chapter 3 and can be divided into four stages: attending, interpreting, responding, and remembering.

Attending

Listening begins as soon as we perceive that a message is being sent and decide to pay attention to that message. **Attending** involves making the conscious choice to listen. Earlier, we noted that the process of perception begins when we select or focus on stimuli. Listening works the same way. We may begin to listen when someone says our name or when we hear our favorite restaurant mentioned in conversation. Attending also means that we must often make choices

attending
The first stage in the listening process involves making the conscious choice to listen.

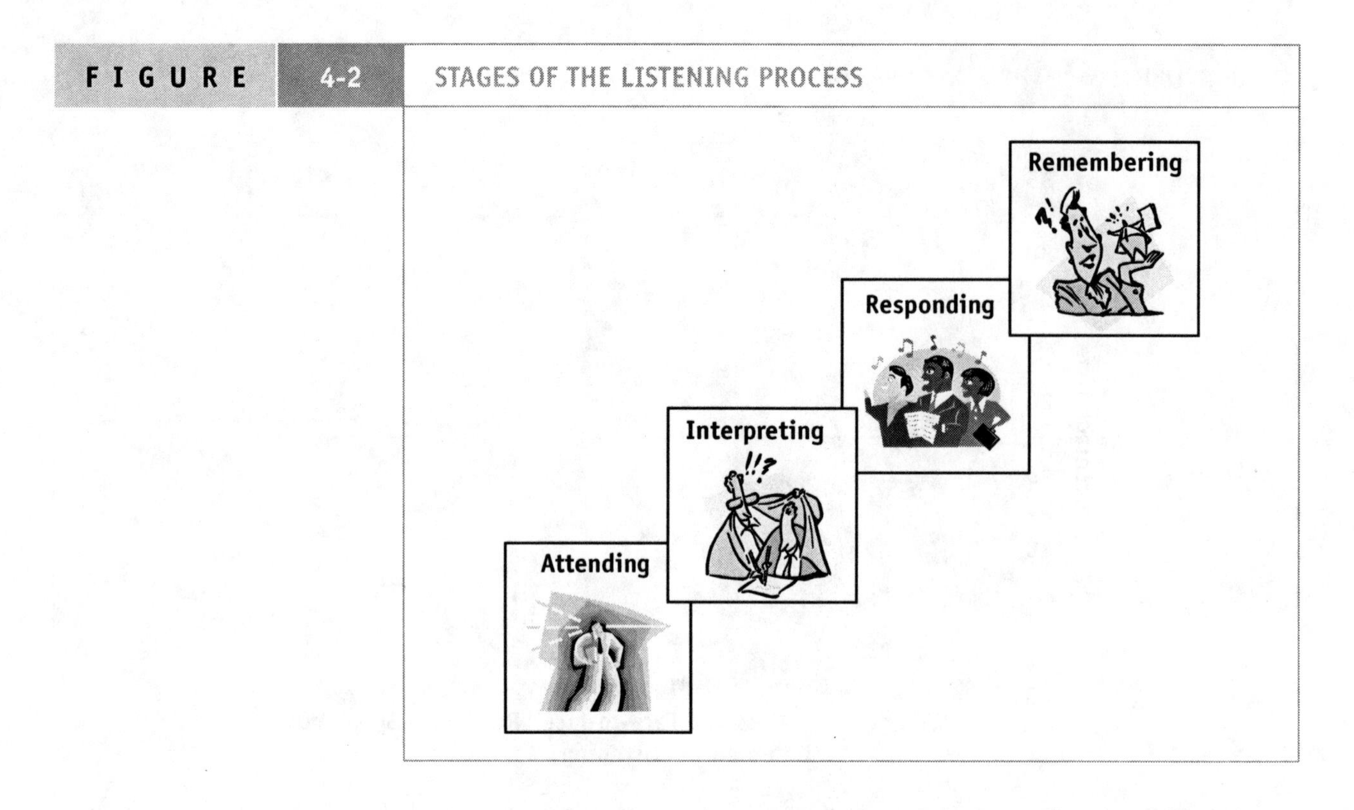

FIGURE 4-2 STAGES OF THE LISTENING PROCESS

about competing messages in our environment by "tuning out" certain stimuli while focusing on others. Think about the busy parent who tries to talk on the phone while a toddler nearby clamors for attention. The parent might be used to tuning out a demanding toddler while the caller may be distracted by the commotion in the background. Both the caller and the parent must decide which interaction warrants attention. Once we choose to listen, we are committing both mental and physical energy to the communication process, and we are making choices about what we will listen to. As you read the "Think It Over" box on listening and deaf people, consider the different ways that a hearing-impaired person might listen.

Interpreting

interpreting
The second stage in the listening process involves giving meaning to sounds or related stimuli.

As the box on deaf people illustrates, we can "listen" to many nonverbal behaviors and use visual, olfactory, and tactile sensations to guide the listening process. Once we decide to listen and pay attention, we begin **interpreting** what we hear. We might start to wonder why someone mentioned our name in a conversation we overheard, or we might focus on someone who gives a rave review of our favorite restaurant. As we converse, we watch facial expressions and gestures to help us decipher the meaning behind words; for instance, a touch on the shoulder or pat on the back can affect how we interpret a statement. Sometimes we use all of our senses to interpret what is being said. Movie producers have long recognized that the emotional and physical reaction of fright is elicited primarily from the sounds in a film. The kinds of music that foreshadow danger in a film are familiar to most moviegoers, as is the snarl of an alien creature that helps us interpret its sinister intentions.

Think It Over

DO DEAF PEOPLE LISTEN?

Although most people think of listening as based on the reception of sound, listening is a process that involves more than the ears. The blending of visual and auditory cues is particularly relevant to hearing-impaired and deaf people. People who can hear tend to use metaphors of sight, such as lipreading, to explain the communication process of deaf people. However, the least effective communication between hearing and deaf people is speech and lipreading (Burgher 1995). Lipreading reduces the listening process of merely seeing one visual cue rather than moving through all of the stages of listening. Deaf people listen to every body movement, gesture, and facial expression being made by the person with whom they are communicating. Some communication scholars argue that deaf people are more attentive listeners than people who rely on spoken words, because deaf people must be more aware of the movements that accompany speech when they listen (Stein 1995).

Do we listen for messages that go beyond sound?
Can we listen with our eyes?

Although these communicators cannot hear, are they listening to one another?
© Bob Daemmrich

Responding

When listening to others, verbal and nonverbal cues help us interpret what they say and guide our reactions to them. We might decide to join in the conversation about that favorite restaurant of ours or make a joke about being the subject of someone else's conversation ("OK, be sure you only say the good things now that I'm here!"). **Responding** to a message includes any discernable reaction,

responding
The third stage in the listening process involves any discernable reaction including both verbal and nonverbal feedback.

including both verbal and nonverbal feedback. When we listen, we usually offer feedback. It may be verbal, such as asking questions or making statements, or it may be nonverbal, such as a head nod, eye contact, and leaning forward. Although we are not always aware of the responses we make while we listen, all feedback communicates important information. Checking our watches, looking around the room, or changing the subject of conversation are also ways of responding as we listen, but they communicate our lack of involvement in the interaction.

Even when we do respond intentionally, our style of responding can have unintended effects. Since there is so much variety in what individuals, groups, and cultures consider to be appropriate responses, even the most sincere and well-intentioned responses can be misinterpreted. The misunderstanding that can occur between members of different cultures is exemplified in the following example about a German and a North American attempting to converse (Tannen 1998). For Germans, aggressive and forceful responses to the arguments of others are signs of intelligence and knowledge, while Americans see such behavior as self-aggrandizing, defensive, and humiliating. The refusal of Americans to use this response style often makes it appear to Germans that Americans either don't know or don't care much about what they are saying. Even when we think we are responding in ways that communicate respect and understanding, our behaviors can be easily misunderstood.

Our satisfaction with our interactions with others depends largely on the quality of our responses as listeners. Sometimes the quality of our responses suffers because our attention is pulled in many directions. Think about how the influence of everyday technologies affects your ability to listen and respond. Wireless telephones have made it possible to do many other activities while talking with others. It is now common to work on a computer, drive a car, wash dishes, or fold laundry while using the phone. How do you feel when you hear other activities in the background at the same time you're having a conversation? Can you hear the clicking of a computer keyboard or running water when you are talking to a friend? Are you distracted when you hear someone eating on the other end of the phone? Which sounds command your attention, and how do you know if you're being listened to?

> "The greatest compliment that was ever paid me was when one asked what I thought and attended to my answer."
>
> —Henry David Thoreau, author and philosopher

Remembering

remembering
The final stage in the listening process involves the retention and recall of the messages.

The final stage in the listening process, **remembering,** is the retention of messages. As noted earlier in the chapter, communication research suggests that we remember less than half of a message immediately after we listen to it, and that just eight hours later our retention decreases to as little as 20 percent of what we heard (Nichols 1995). Many factors affect retention. Interestingly, the way we respond to a message often determines how well we remember it. As our involvement increases, so does our memory. For instance, when people actually participate in conversations, they tend to remember more information than they do if they only observe others in conversation (Benoit and Benoit 1995). Participation can take a variety of forms, including talking, taking notes, and asking questions, all of which enhance memory. These forms of participation are also strategies for practicing active listening.

We often try to listen while engaged in other tasks.
© Bob Daemmrich

Active and Passive Listening

We listen best when we take the role of **active listeners.** Active listeners choose to focus on the moment, are aware of interactions as they unfold, respond appropriately, and resist physiological and psychological distractions. Active listening is a fundamental skill in establishing and maintaining relationships, managing information, responding to crises, and speaking in public. Despite its importance, we don't often listen carefully or with the needs of the speaker in mind. Instead, we tend to be **passive listeners** who expend little or no energy in the listening process. The difference between active and passive listeners is often attitudinal; active listeners are willing to invest mental and emotional energy in the listening process. Passive listeners assume that they are listening accurately and that any misunderstandings that arise are the fault of the speaker. Suppose Karyn knows that Lea isn't working on the weekend and says wistfully, "I really wish someone could cover my shift on Saturday." Lea responds, "Simone can't do it. She's already working that shift," and changes the subject. If Karyn and Lea listen to each other passively, each is likely to leave the conversation with an inaccurate picture of the other. Karyn might think Lea is avoiding her request ("Why can't you do it?"); and Lea might assume that Karyn only wants Simone to cover the shift. Each might blame the other for not being a good listener. Active listening would require Karyn and Lea to listen carefully for the needs of the other.

active listeners
People who focus on the moment, are aware of interactions as they unfold, respond appropriately, and are aware of distractions.

passive listeners
People who expend little or no energy in the listening process.

Active listeners want to be involved in the interaction while passive listeners do not. The differences between passive and active listeners lie in (1) the responsibility each takes for communication, (2) the energy each puts into becoming interested in a message, (3) the importance each places on both verbal and nonverbal messages, (4) the value each places on interaction, (5) the willingness each has to listen to an entire message, and (6) the effort each invests in taking notes (Floyd 1985). These differences are summarized in Table 4-1.

TABLE 4-1 Passive versus Active Listeners

CHARACTERISTIC	PASSIVE LISTENER	ACTIVE LISTENER
Does the listener accept responsibility for communication?	Believes that speakers are solely responsible for the quality of communication and blames them for communication failure. Often evaluates a speaker's delivery instead of the content of the message. "My professor was so boring that I fell asleep during the lecture."	Understands that speakers and listeners share responsibility for the success or failure of communication. Evaluates the content of a message and looks past monotone or ineffectual delivery. "If you listen carefully, Professor Leon has some really interesting things to say."
Does the listener make an effort to develop an interest in the message?	Easily bored and unreceptive to new areas of interest. Stops listening to new, complex, or unusual messages. "Physics is so dry and useless."	Works to discover areas of interest and exhibits a willingness to tackle new, complex, and unusual messages. "How can an understanding of physics help me?"
Does the listener understand the importance of both verbal and nonverbal messages?	Believes that verbal communication is straightforward and ignores or is distracted by nonverbal messages. "The speaker's hands were shaking so hard I thought they were going to fall off."	Listens to both verbal and nonverbal messages and understands the importance of the entire message. "Why is the speaker so anxious?"
Does the listener understand that listening is an interactive process?	Sits back, shows no signs of understanding, and talks very little during the interaction. "When is the speaker going to stop talking?"	Leans forward; displays nonverbal feedback such as head nods or vocal reassurances. Often asks questions, makes comments, or seeks clarification. "I didn't understand the last part. Could you repeat the explanation?"
Does the listener listen to the entire message?	Listens off and on or only at the beginning. "This speaker keeps saying the same thing over and over."	Works to understand the entire message. "How is that related to what the speaker said a few minutes ago?"
Does the listener take notes?	Does not take notes. "I can remember this information. I don't need to write anything down."	Looks for opportunities to take notes. "Let me write down this information so I can review it later."

Source: J. F. Floyd, *Listening: A Practical Approach* (Glenview, Il: Scott, Foresman, 1985), p. 24.

As Table 4-1 illustrates, active listening requires a commitment to participate fully in an interaction, knowledge of effective listening strategies, and willingness to respect the different interpretations that people may have when they listen to others.

Obstacles to Effective Listening

So far we have discussed the importance of listening, the stages of the listening process, and the important distinction between simply hearing a message and actively listening to one. In this section we will discuss common obstacles to effective listening. In any communication situation, there is ample time for obstacles to intrude in the listening process. This is especially true in everyday speaking situations, because most people can listen much faster than they can talk. On average, people speak at a rate of 120 to 150 words a minute, whereas most listeners can process language four to seven times faster, at 400 to 800 words a minute (Wolff and Marsnick 1992). That's one reason why people's minds wander while listening, and why reading a book is so much faster than listening to it. Many different kinds of listening barriers can slip into the time gap between speaker and listener. Some of these barriers are external, whereas others are created by the listener's attitude toward the speaker.

Overcoming External Distractions

When we listen, several aspects of the communication context sometimes seem as though they are beyond our control and distract us from listening. The communication context, such as the physical environment, messages that compete for our attention, and the medium used to communicate can all create barriers to effective listening.

Physical Environment. The physical environment can pose immediate and substantial obstacles. Some locations simply make it difficult to listen. At your college or university, for example, you have probably noticed substantial differences in classrooms. Some rooms might echo and seem hollow while others might absorb sound and seem hushed or overly quiet. In both instances, listeners and speakers struggle with the acoustics of the physical environment that make it difficult to communicate. Other settings contain extraneous sounds that overwhelm any attempt at communication. Trying to converse in a noisy restaurant or at a crowded party makes hearing, never mind listening, difficult. Many experts worry that our modern environment is becoming too loud. John Wheeler, president of the Deafness Research Foundation, coined the term *"toxic noise"* to describe the high decibel levels of concerts, personal stereos, and contemporary movies that are affecting the hearing of an increasing number of Americans (Tolson 1999). Finally, there can be many distractions in the environment that compete for the attention of listeners. Distracting or annoying sounds may divert attention, for instance. Have you ever sat in front of a student with a persistent cough or one who drummed his or her fingers mindlessly on the desk? Such sounds may not overwhelm communicators, but they certainly make it difficult to pay attention.

Sometimes physical conditions seem to be outside our control. However, there are simple steps we can take to minimize the distractions created by environmental noise. If transportation vehicles such as airplanes or ambulances create a distraction, ask the speaker to pause or repeat a statement. Students often like to sit near the back of classrooms, when sitting closer to the speaker is an easy way to minimize distractions. Finally, turn down the volume on electronic devices. Doing so could save your ears for years to come.

Message Context. Just as the physical environment creates a particular context for listening, so does the message context, or placement of a particular message within a system of messages. Sometimes the first words or phrases said distract us from hearing what follows them or influence our interpretation of what has been said, sometimes to the extent of forgetting what we have heard. For example, we often pay more attention to criticism than compliments. No matter how many times your best friend tells you that you are attractive, you are still likely to focus on and remember the one comment he or she made about your bad hair cut. Similarly, a professor can read dozens of positive course evaluations but is nevertheless likely to focus on and remember the negative comments, even if they are infrequent. Sometimes we need to be reminded about positive evaluations of ourselves, because in our attentiveness to criticism, we don't hear praise.

The influence of message context on listening can be illustrated in many ways. One study found that television viewers who were shown advertisements during violent programming such as kick boxing were far less likely to remember the advertised products than viewers who watched nonviolent programming (Yam 1999). Conversely, message context can sometimes prompt us to listen more carefully. In an effort to reach African-American women, the University of California at San Diego Cancer Center trained salon cosmetologists to talk about breast cancer, mammograms, self-examinations, weight loss, and smoking. Placing the messages in the context of the salon was so successful that the Cancer Center expanded its program to include information about diabetes (Mind/Body Flash 1998). When we understand and pay attention to the context in which we listen to messages, we become more careful and effective listeners.

Media Noise. In many contemporary listening situations, the medium used to communicate can affect listening. Some communication theorists suggest that messages transmitted over radio are received more actively than those presented on television, because we focus primarily on stimuli received through our ears when we listen to the radio. Perhaps you have heard a movie review over the radio and seen a trailer for the movie on television. If you listen to the movie clip without the visuals, you will probably focus on the dialogue between characters and the *ambient sounds.* You are more likely to be involved in the interaction between characters, and you are in a better position to think about what they are saying to each other. If you watch the trailer, you are more likely to miss pieces of dialogue and form more general impressions

Active listening requires people to disregard social and physical distractions.

about the movie based on its visual appeal. Subtle differences in the way we listen to different media can also pose obstacles; think about the difference between talking to someone on a grounded telephone versus a cellular or speakerphone. Although we regularly think of transmission difficulties or noise as obstacles to effective communication, we are less likely to consider the influence of the mode of transmission itself, or the medium chosen, as an obstacle to effective listening. If you are about to have an important conversation, such as asking someone for a substantial favor, requesting money or time from an employer, or discussing the future of a relationship, think about the influence that the medium will have on the listener's ability to understand you. Some conversations are best held in person!

Overcoming Attitudinal Obstacles

Our attitudes pose the single biggest challenge to effective listening. Attitudinal obstacles to listening are often harder to recognize than physical ones, because we don't stop to scrutinize our own listening behaviors. Indeed, we sometimes blame the physical environment ("The classroom was just too hot for me to concentrate") for the shortcomings in our attitude. Most attitudinal barriers stem from preoccupation with the self, preconceived attitudes and beliefs, personal investment, and indifference, or lack of interest due to message overload, boredom, or impatience.

Preoccupation with the Self. When we are unsure of ourselves, our ability to listen effectively is diminished, particularly if we have poor self-esteem. New situations that test our competence can make us feel anxious about what others are saying. Clinical psychologist Mary Pipher, author of *Reviving Ophelia* (1994), offers a dramatic example in discussing the *imaginary audience syndrome,* the tendency of teenage girls to think that other people are obsessed with evaluating their appearance and behaviors. As teenagers grow more self-aware, many become increasingly concerned about what others think of them. For girls, becoming a young woman can mean meeting fairly rigid expectations about proper appearance, achievement, and behavior. As a result, they have a tendency to see themselves as constantly being scrutinized by an imaginary audience. An insecure teenage girl might listen to her basketball coach say, "Good try" in praise of her effort and think, "Yeah, right; the coach is calling attention to my horrible ball handling." To some extent, the imaginary audience syndrome affects most of us. Think about the first time you joined a new group, whether an employee organization, student club, or even meeting the parents of a new relationship partner. You may have been so preoccupied with the impression you were creating that you didn't hear what was said to you. ("Hello; it's so nice to meet you." "Hi, I'm fine, thanks.").

Similarly, the person with low self-esteem is likely to hear even *mundane* comments ("Wow, I didn't expect you to get here so quickly!") as attacks, and to respond accordingly ("Are you sure you wanted me to come over?"). This form of self-absorption affects listening considerably, as it becomes hard for the listener to accurately assess the meaning of messages and the motives of speakers. Conversely, people with an inflated sense of self barely listen to the speaker at all, and focus instead on turning topics of conversation toward themselves. This usually leads to a desire to talk instead of listen. Communicators who are consistently thinking about what they are going to say instead of listening to others miss much of the meaning in messages.

Preconceived Attitudes and Beliefs. Sometimes our preoccupation is tied to a particular attitude or belief about a topic or person that we bring to the listening situation. Preconceived attitudes and beliefs often interfere with our listening effectiveness by leading us to categorize messages before fully understanding them (see Chapter 3). We often come to listening situations with prejudices that cause us to jump to conclusions or block out what others are saying. Our prejudices may be based on our views about race, class, sexual orientation, education, religion, or any other category of people. For instance, we might think that high-achieving students have nothing worthwhile to say about relaxing on the weekends, and thus tune out when someone we think of as a "brain" tries to give us good tips about little-known bike trails.

Preconceived beliefs even interfere with our ability to solve basic riddles or make sound inferences. See if you can explain the following situation: "A blind beggar had a brother. The blind beggar's brother died, but the brother who died had no brother." How might you account for this seemingly contradictory situation? Most people have trouble, because they assume that the beggar is a male. The riddle only makes sense, though, if the beggar is a female; the brother who died had no brother but had a sister instead. Often our assumptions about categories can limit our ability to understand simple relationships.

Other kinds of preconceived attitudes and beliefs operate more subtly than prejudices. Our sense of our own previous experience or knowledge can give us a false sense of security so we might not listen because we assume that a speaker has nothing new to tell us. We might judge the speaker's appearance or credibility and decide not to listen. Or the information being conveyed might be complex or challenge our beliefs. In either case, we may opt to listen passively, if at all.

Listening to beliefs that contradict your own values can be an especially difficult listening experience. The "Exploring Communication Concepts" box on cognitive dissonance explains some of the challenges we may face in such situations.

Personal Investment. Preconceived attitudes and beliefs have the strongest influence on our listening ability when we also have a personal investment in the speaker or topic. For example, if you feel strongly that women should not compete in contact sports, such as football or boxing, then you are not likely to listen actively to a female boxer talk about her experiences or to a speaker who argues in favor of co-ed football teams on campus. If the person were speaking about women's advancements in professional golf or tennis, you might listen more carefully.

Personal investment can lead to three listening barriers: selective attention, ambushing, and avoidance of threatening information. Each of these barriers can serve us well at times. For instance, when faced with competing messages, we will selectively attend to the message that seems to be more important. However, selective attention can become problematic when it prevents us from hearing important information. When we care deeply about a person or subject, we are more likely to listen to the parts of a message that support our beliefs. Personal investment can also make us more likely to engage in *ambushing* the speaker, or listening for ways to respond or attack. We might listen only until we hear something that sparks a thought of our own. One author compared this process to throwing a stick for a dog; as soon as the speaker throws the stick, you are off—you don't need to know the reason for throwing it in the first place (Browning 1999).

Exploring Communication Concepts

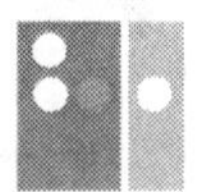

COGNITIVE DISSONANCE

One of the widely held psychological theories that has influenced communication research is Leon Festinger's (1957) theory of **cognitive dissonance.** According to Festinger, when two things that we think, believe, or do are related but also conflict with each other, we experience uncomfortable tension. For instance, the proud new owner of a sport utility vehicle (SUV) is less likely to pay attention to messages about increasing gasoline prices and the need to conserve fuel, even though he or she believes that wasting resources is wrong.

Cognitive dissonance helps explain why we avoid listening to information that challenges our existing beliefs. According to Festinger, we seek consistency between attitudes, and between attitudes and behaviors, and we try to find ways to resolve contradictions. The SUV owner, for example, can do this by changing her or his opinion of the vehicle or the value of conserving gas. Or, if changing one of these beliefs is uncomfortable, the SUV owner might avoid the contradiction altogether by ignoring information about fuel consumption or discounting its credibility. Cognitive dissonance can prompt us to tune out information that makes us uncomfortable. Unfortunately, by not listening to someone whose views challenge our own, we are losing an opportunity to learn and to grow, for dissonance can stimulate new and powerful ways of understanding (Salibrici 1999).

ASK YOURSELF:

1. Under which conditions are you most likely to experience dissonance? For example, think about personal habits that you consider distasteful or unhealthy, or an uncomfortable point of view held by someone you care about.
2. What might you do to eliminate your discomfort?

cognitive dissonance
The uncomfortable tension listeners experience when two ideas, concepts, or things that they believe, value, or do are related but contradictory.

Finally, personal investment can lead us to avoid speakers or topics altogether. One of the authors can recall a time when she gave a student an extension on a paper, only to discover that the student had not been listening. The student had been avoiding the professor because he felt bad about not having started the assignment; rather than truly listening and absorbing the news about the extension, he assumed that no late papers would be accepted. In that case, avoidance cost the student a substantial grade reduction in the course. Our emotional involvement can limit our ability to hear others at times when active listening is called for, and it can make us feel more easily threatened and less likely to take the risk of actively listening and learning new information.

Sometimes emotional involvement in a topic is triggered by a particular word or phrase used by a speaker. This form of distraction is called **semantic noise.** For instance, if a health practitioner tells you, "We need to have a glucose test," you might latch onto the word "we" because *you* are the one who requires the test, not the practitioner! In this case, the use of a specific word can distract us from focusing on the primary message of the speaker.

semantic noise
A barrier to listening triggered by a particular word or phrase used by a speaker.

indifference
A lack of interest in listening.

Indifference. Although preoccupation with the self and personal biases often prevent us from listening carefully, sometimes we exhibit **indifference.** We

FIGURE 4-3 ACTIVE LISTENING REQUIRES ENERGY

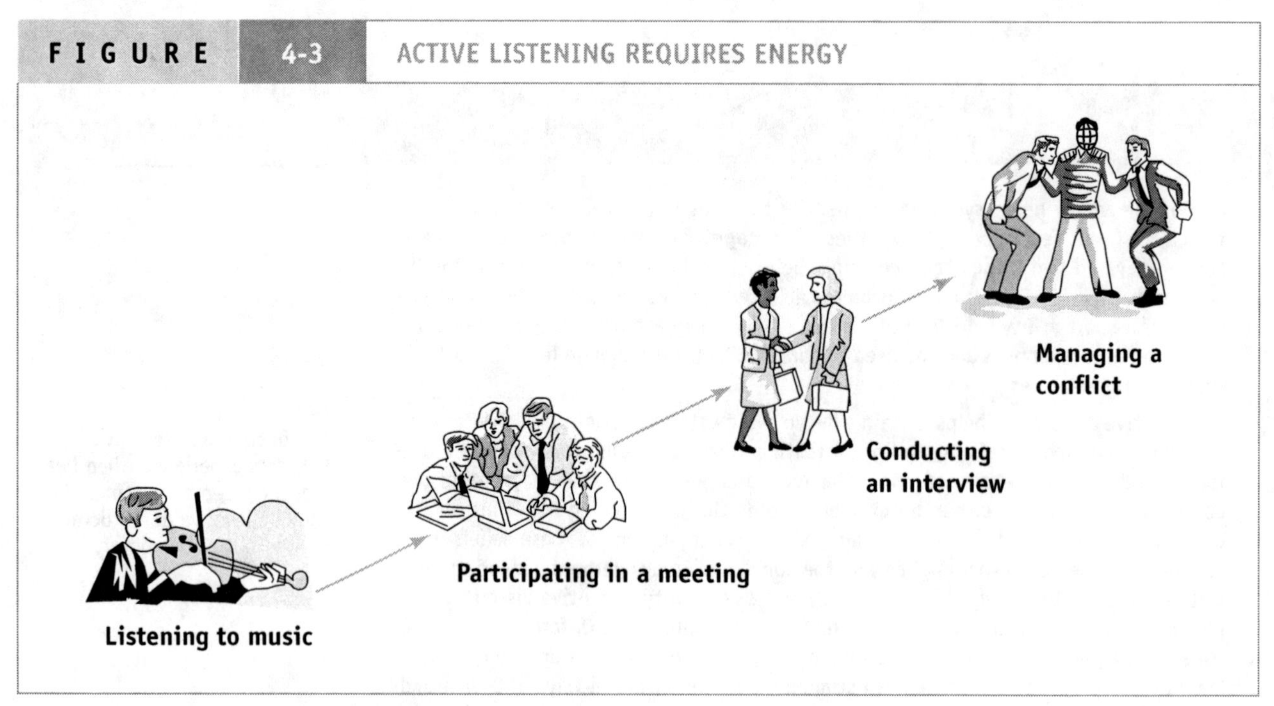

Some contexts require more energy to listen than others.

are simply not willing to invest time and energy into a listening situation. Consider Figure 4-3. Whereas some contexts require relatively little energy, other listening situations can be quite demanding for the listener who chooses to be active.

Many factors can prompt our indifference and lead to passive listening and poor responses to speakers. Due to the constant barrage of messages we receive from television and radio to the conversations in which we participate or overhear, it's not surprising that at times we experience *message overload.* Usually we focus selectively on some messages rather than others, but sometimes we just become overwhelmed and tune out everything. Or boredom may strike, and rather than searching for ways to listen actively, we amuse ourselves with distractions such as assessing the speaker's appearance. We may also become impatient or frustrated with complex material. The difficulty in understanding a different speech style or accent can lead to impatience with the listening process as well. Though we don't like to admit it, these forms of indifference amount to laziness, and they are among the most troublesome listening obstacles. The indifferent listener has chosen to avoid a relationship with the speaker, making constructive communication hard to achieve.

pseudolistening
Pretending to listen.

Indifference often results in **pseudolistening,** or pretending to listen. Most people have some sense of how the active listener behaves. The pseudolistener adopts some of those behaviors, such as nodding, giving eye contact, and even providing minimal vocal encouragement. However, behind the behaviors lies indifference, because the listener is not really paying attention to the speaker.

Pseudolistening can be a form of politeness intended to spare the feelings of a speaker we find boring. As with all forms of indifference, however, pseudolistening can limit our ability to interact constructively with others. Sometimes pseudolistening might feel like a survival tactic, but does it really show respect for the other person? The next section in this chapter offers some strategies to help you become a more effective and responsible listener.

> "Let us draw closer to the fire, so that we might better be able to see what we're saying . . . ."
> —Chinese Proverb

Becoming a Responsible and Effective Listener

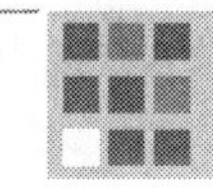

After reading about the many obstacles to effective listening, you may have concluded that being a good listener is more difficult than you thought. Perhaps you can recall a time when you listened actively at a concert by a favorite musician, at a political presentation for a cause you endorse, or during an emotional conversation with a close friend. Regardless of the circumstances, listening responsibly and effectively is more likely to occur if you take the following steps:

- Identify your listening goal.
- Prepare to listen.
- Listen with an open mind.
- Choose your response carefully.
- Make the interaction memorable.

Identifying Listening Goals

We choose to listen for many reasons. We often listen to television or film for relaxation or recreation. We go to concerts to be energized, entertained, or inspired by the music. We listen to presidential debates or class lectures to become better informed about relevant issues or topics. We listen to the worries of friends about finding a job because we care about them. In each of these situations, we have made a decision about why we want to listen. As our goals for listening vary, so do listening strategies. The following section identifies four different listening goals: appreciation, comprehension, empathy, and evaluation. As you read, keep in mind that the most satisfying interactions occur when speakers and listeners share the same goals.

appreciation
The goal of listening for pleasure or enjoyment.

Appreciation. Sometimes, we listen because doing so brings us joy. **Appreciation** is the goal of listening for pleasure or enjoyment. We watch movies, listen to music, and go to comedy performances because we find them entertaining and appreciate the experience. Listening for appreciation has benefits beyond immediate pleasure; at least one study demonstrated that surgeons who listen to the music of their choice while operating improve their performance (Choo 1994). Sometimes we listen to speakers because we like their use of language or sense of humor. Listening for appreciation isn't always easy; as with all types of listening, the most memorable interactions are those in which we make a personal investment through active listening. One way of making a personal investment is by providing feedback; responses that show appreciation include applause, rhythmic body movement, and verbally responding to the speaker. In some cultures, appreciation can even take the form of "talking back," or commenting on and arguing with speakers, performers, and mediated presentations.

"Knowledge speaks, but wisdom listens."

—Jimi Hendrix, rock musician

comprehension The goal of listening for understanding.

Comprehension. When our goal is **comprehension,** we listen to gain information or understanding. While enjoying a new song on the radio, you might struggle to understand the artist's meaning behind a particular phrase or lyric. When this happens, you have moved from appreciative to comprehensive listening. We seek comprehension in many contexts. In everyday conversation, we want both to understand our friends and be understood by them. In school and on the job, we need to follow the comments and instructions of teachers and employers. Even the best listeners can never know with absolute certainty that what they have heard is what the speaker meant; however, we can take steps to improve our comprehension when we listen to others. By questioning speakers or making comments, we often discover errors in our understanding of what has been said. Consider the following exchange and listening errors that are discovered through simple feedback.

Oz: How was your summer?

Eli: [Speaks softly] Not much fun.

Oz: Excuse me. Did you say fun or not much fun?

Eli: [Louder] Not much fun. I took a full load of courses over the summer so that I can graduate early.

Oz: Are you graduating this semester?

Eli: No, no. I still have three more semesters but that's early for me. I'm only a sophomore right now. How was your summer?

Oz: Great. I just returned from Panama City.

Eli: Oh, I have always wanted to go to Central America. I was in Argentina once, but I have never been to Central America.

Oz: I said, Panama City, in Florida.

Eli: Sorry. My mistake. How was Florida?

Our conversations are full of such instances in which we misunderstand what we hear. Too many times, however, we let these errors slip passively by us without clarifying our perceptions. Being attentive and active improves our chances of comprehending what others say.

Listening for comprehension also includes understanding the point of view of others and listening objectively. Doing so can be difficult, particularly if the information is complex or the topic is controversial. As the box on cognitive dissonance implied, we aren't always willing to listen to someone with whom we disagree, even for the sake of learning. One study of college students found that fewer than 3 percent sought to discuss controversial topics, such as race, as a way to acquire new information and perspectives (Trosset 1998). Suppose your housemate has a poster of Cesar Chavez, a well-known organizer of migrant Hispanic farm workers, prominently displayed in his or her bedroom. Would you see the poster as an opportunity to learn more about your housemate's knowledge of labor issues? Many of us avoid conversations about which we are indifferent or that we fear might lead to conflict, and few of us are willing or able to recognize our own biases and set them aside. Yet doing so improves our ability to comprehend messages and establishes a foundation for the next listening goal, empathy.

Empathy. We listen to enjoy and to learn, and we also listen to establish connections with others. This aspect of listening is the basis of personal relationships. When we listen with empathy, we seek to understand and support the feelings or emotional state of others. As we discussed in Chapter 3, empathy is the ability to accurately perceive the experience and behaviors of another person. Empathy is easily confused with *sympathy,* which means feeling sorrow and having compassion for another person's point of view. Empathy goes beyond sympathy and involves identifying with another person. In popular language, empathy is to walk in other people's shoes, to see what they see, to feel as they feel. When we listen to establish empathy, we listen for more than understanding the content of a message; we listen to share the emotional experience of the speaker. **Empathetic listening** establishes common ground between people by acknowledging the legitimacy of feelings and giving support to others.

empathetic listening
Establishes common ground between people by acknowledging the legitimacy of feelings and giving support to others.

expressive communication
Verbally acknowledging how others feel and sharing experiences.

instrumental communication
Listening or responding to help others solve problems or accomplish goals.

As with other types of listening, there is considerable variation in the way people show that they are empathetic listeners. Some people show empathy nonverbally, with a gentle touch or a nod. Other people are more comfortable responding verbally. For some people, emotional support is best conveyed through **expressive communication,** such as verbally acknowledging how the other feels and sharing experiences ("How terrible! You must have been so upset."). We often expect expressive communication to be used by females, and thereby associate it with femininity. Other empathetic listeners are more comfortable responding with **instrumental communication** (Tannen 1990; Wood 1997), or talking to help solve problems and accomplish goals ("You know, you really should report that to her supervisor"). Our culture stresses problem solving as a virtue and classifies it as a masculine trait, which means that we are more likely to expect men to use instrumental communication. These gendered expectations guide our responses when listening to a friend or partner in distress. For example, women often talk about dilemmas they face as a way to establish connections with others and express their feelings about daily

Expressive communication is an important part of empathetic listening.

© Monika Graff/The Image Works

struggles. On the other hand, men are taught to respond to problems with solutions. As a display of care and competence, a man might try to "fix" a woman's problem. He might say, "If you're so worried about that exam, why don't you just find a tutor?" For the person who wants emotional support, this response might be perceived as critical and disconfirming. Likewise, the female listener who does not respond to a speaker's distress with emotion is often labeled as cold and uncaring. Empathetic listening requires responding to the speaker based on his or her needs. Sometimes being an empathetic listener means moving beyond stereotypical expectations and trying to find out what kind of response the other person is seeking.

Expectations for empathetic listening frequently extend beyond personal relationships to business contexts. For instance, many companies and government agencies require their supervisors to monitor the calls made by their employees. Call monitoring is not new; companies routinely announce, "Your call may be monitored for quality of service." Recently, however, some companies have been evaluating their phone representatives on their level of empathy. Rodney Ho reported in *The Wall Street Journal* that companies such as Nextel have been appraising their employees based on their support for customer feelings and expressions of care and concern. Representatives are advised to use phrases such as "I understand your frustration"; "Don't worry. I'm sure I can straighten that out"; and "If I were in your shoes, I'd feel the same way" (Ho 1999). As customer expectations rise, so do the pressures on phone representatives to add empathetic listening to their repertoire of skills.

Empathetic listening is important in both everyday and professional situations. The doctor who listens only for medical data misses vital information about the emotional and mental states of patients. Perhaps you have had a conversation similar to this one:

Patient: My throat has been hurting for days, and I can't even get any sleep. I'm a wreck; I can't function very well.

Doctor: How long has it been sore?

Patient: For three, maybe four, days, and I haven't slept since.

Doctor: Well, you need to clear up that drainage for your sinuses, so I'm going to prescribe a decongestant. It will probably make you wired.

In the patient-doctor interaction, the patient has said twice that sleeplessness is a problem, but the doctor has missed this information and prescribed a drug that will probably make the patient feel worse. Lack of empathetic listening between doctors and patients can create far greater problems. For instance, one doctor recalled discussing a patient's sinus condition but failed to listen to the patient's hints of suicidal thinking (Swirsky 1999). Parents who listen to their children describe their day's activities sometimes miss the emotional significance of what the children are trying to convey, and spouses who sense that their feelings are not being taken seriously are rarely satisfied with their marriages. Empathetic listening involves listening "between the lines." It helps communicators form new bonds and affirm existing ones, making it an essential listening goal.

evaluation
The goal of listening to render an opinion or judgment.

Evaluation. Most of us like to think that we can listen critically and make sound judgments based on what we hear. Listening with the goal of **evaluation**

means we are listening to render a judgment about what we have heard. As a listening skill, evaluation goes beyond expressing an opinion to making a thoughtful assessment based on an understanding of a message. Although evaluative listening occurs most often when we encounter a persuasive message (e.g., an advertisement, request for a favor, or attempt to influence our beliefs), we take evaluative stances toward many kinds of messages. Evaluative listening means we assess arguments and claims made by others. It also helps us test and modify our own beliefs, attitudes, and values.

Building on comprehensive listening, listening for evaluation begins with a careful analysis of the message. Doing this requires that we delay or suspend judgment until we understand the content of the message and the speaker's intentions, rather than forming an opinion even before the speaker finishes conveying a message. Such premature evaluation rarely results in an accurate or sound appraisal. As we listen to a message, we should concentrate on understanding its content, observing important nonverbal actions made by the speaker, and generally seeking clarity and comprehension.

Evaluative listening, when done well, requires that we consider both the information or evidence that is presented and the reasoning the speaker has used to draw her or his conclusions. Standards of evidence are discussed in more detail in Chapter 15, which focuses on persuasive speaking. In general, though, when a claim is made, there must be adequate, recent, and trustworthy information offered to support it. For example, a speech about televised violence might include research performed by prominent communication researchers about the effects of violence in the media. A speech on the same topic could revolve around a graphic description of a scene from a dramatic television series. The speech that makes a strong connection between the information presented and the conclusion drawn about the effects of media violence is more likely to be judged as credible. If the speaker wanted you to support restrictions on televised violence, which would you find to be more compelling: research on the effects of violence or the example of a violent scene? Your judgments of the speaker's credibility, your personal experience, and your ability to use sound reasoning will influence your ability to evaluate what you hear.

At its core, evaluative listening requires thinking critically about messages. Evaluation is a process of judging messages, such as deciding whether a rumor about a friend is true or whether a film is suitable for a younger sibling. Critical thinking goes a step further; it is the ability to explain why some messages are effective, ethical, or truthful whereas others are not (Cohen 1998). So, how do you know whether the rumor about your friend is true? By what standard are you measuring a film's suitability for children?

When listening for evaluation, we often make assumptions or fill in the gaps in what we hear to form a conclusion; we draw inferences. An **inference** is a projection or interpretation based on facts. If a friend shows up late for a lunch date and we know that there is considerable highway construction occurring nearby, we might infer that our friend was caught in a traffic jam. Although we didn't observe our friend trapped in traffic, we make an inference based on what we do know.

inference
A conclusion, projection, or interpretation based on facts.

We draw inferences from information all the time but rarely call attention to them. The salesperson who tells you that a particular brand is the most popular wants you to infer that since other people found the brand appealing, you should, too. Suppose you are about to enter a restaurant when you see a driver standing next to a limousine parked in front of the restaurant. When you ask the driver whom he is waiting for, he says, "The governor." You might infer that the governor is dining at the same restaurant as you, when in fact you have not seen the governor. Conclusions based on inferences must always be evaluated because they are only as solid as the accuracy of the inference. We will revisit the role of inferences in more detail when we examine persuasive communication (Chapter 15).

In some communication contexts, the "soundness" of our judgment has little to do with proper inferences from facts. Rather, we judge some messages based on our own experience or the way in which the message was constructed. The "Exploring Communication Concepts" box on evaluative listening and narratives explores one such context and presents an alternative way of evaluating messages.

Thus far, we have focused on the listening process, goals, and obstacles to effective listening. We have emphasized the importance of being a good listener and the effort that this requires. By reviewing each of the stages in the listening process, we can now identify key strategies that you can use to help you become a more responsible and effective listener. These skills will determine the quality of your interactions and can help deepen your relationships with those around you.

Preparing to Listen

Once you make the choice to listen actively, take the following steps to help you focus on what you hear.

1. *Clear your mind.* Do your best to remove those preoccupations that may distract you, such as wondering about what you will eat next, who your best friend is dating, and what you think the speaker might say.
2. *Eliminate distractions.* This can be as simple as turning off the ringer on a phone or closing a door.
3. *Set goals.* Decide why you want to listen, rather than what you think the speaker might say. Anticipation can clutter your mind. Once your mind is clear and focused, you are ready to begin listening.
4. *Take notes when listening to presentations.* We usually think of note taking as a way to keep a physical record. This is certainly important, but taking notes will also help you stay focused and remember what has been said. There are many ways to take effective notes: You might divide your paper in two columns, using one column for content and the other to jot down personal impressions; you might outline the speaker's comments or you might note the most significant impressions that the speaker is making.

The simple act of paying attention is rarely taken as seriously as it should be. It sets the stage for the listening experience. The "Applying Communication Concepts" box on listening effectively to electronic media suggests one way of taking notes on the films and videos you see in class.

With so much information coming to you through electronic sources, critical listening and viewing skills are essential. Active listening will help you appreciate, retain, and evaluate mediated messages.

Exploring Communication Concepts

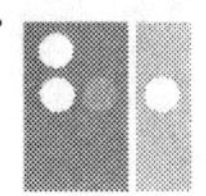

EVALUATIVE LISTENING AND NARRATIVES

We often think of listening to stories as pleasurable, as good opportunities to learn from the experiences of others, or as ways to offer support to speakers by showing an interest in their personal lives. We are less likely to recognize that stories can also serve as arguments, and that listening for evaluation can and should extend to stories.

The idea that storytelling, or narration, might be instrumental to how we form beliefs and opinions is central to the work of Walter Fisher, a scholar at the Annenberg School of Communication. Fisher (1989) suggested that many people look at arguments as statements about evidence, inferences, and conclusions ("First I saw her enter the store, then I noticed the book was gone, and she was, too. She must have stolen the book"). While we certainly might assess the strength of the witness's inferences, there are other standards that we often use to evaluate stories or everyday accounts of events.

Fisher proposed two alternative standards as ways to evaluate narratives, or stories. First, **coherence** asks whether a story makes sense based on the details, order of events, credibility of the storyteller, behaviors of the characters, and comparisons with other similar accounts. Many *urban legends* stay alive because they are dramatic, but since their details are often outlandish and they seem to be isolated events, they lack coherence. Even if we find that a story makes sense, it might not fit what we already believe to be true. **Fidelity** refers to the truthfulness of a story based on the facts and relevance to personal experience or values. Suppose you heard a rumor that a friend you trusted and respected had cheated on an exam. If you had studied and taken the exam with your friend, you probably wouldn't believe the rumor; the story would lack fidelity.

coherence
The standard of evaluating narratives that asks whether a story makes sense based on the details, order of events, credibility of the storyteller, behaviors of the characters, and comparisons with similar accounts.

fidelity
The standard of evaluating narratives that refers to the truthfulness of a story based on the facts and relevance to personal experience or values.

Fisher's work has prompted substantial interest and inquiry into the ways stories function as arguments. For instance, lawyers use stories to persuade juries. Read the following story by attorney Gerry Spence as he attempted to persuade an audience. Think about how you would evaluate it:

> I was driving down Beach Creek Road today. I had my four-year-old daughter, Sarah, with me. I strapped her as tightly into the seat as I could, because I knew the road could be very dangerous, and I strapped myself in as well. Although this was a dangerous road, it was the only one Sarah and I could take to town.
>
> As usual I drove very slowly, hugging the shoulder all the way. As I was coming to that first blind curve, I thought, What would happen to us if a drunk comes around that corner on the wrong side of the road? What if a speeding driver barreled around that curve and slid slightly over the centerline? There would be no escape for us. The shoulder is narrow. There is a deep drop-off. I looked at my little daughter and I thought, she is innocent. Why should she be subjected to this danger?
>
> And then when I was well into the curve I saw the approaching vehicle. A lot of thoughts flashed through my mind . . . there had been four deaths on this road in the past ten years, and I don't know how many wrecks that resulted in serious injury. . . .
>
> As you can see, this time Sarah and I made it. This time the driver wasn't drunk or inattentive. This time the driver was in control . . . . But there was not much room to spare. I could have reached out and touched his car. The question is, when will Sarah and I become just another statistic on this road? Will you remember me standing here, imploring you to do something about this? Especially for her? Please. (Spence 1995).

ASK YOURSELF:

1. What is your reaction to this story?
2. With stories such as this one, how would you listen for evaluation?
3. Is the story coherent? How would you test its fidelity?

Applying Communication Concepts

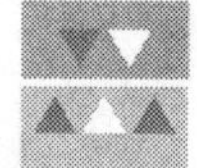

LISTENING EFFECTIVELY TO ELECTRONIC MEDIA

Much of the information we receive comes from electronic sources such as film, video, and television. Usually we approach these media as sources of entertainment, for "mindless" viewing, or as a time to passively absorb information. However, multimedia, film, and video are increasingly part of classroom and business settings. Part of your success as a student, employee, and consumer will depend on your ability to listen actively to information in a variety of mediated presentations. The following steps can help you become an active listener/viewer of electronic media:

1. *Prepare yourself for the experience.* Review material that may be relevant, such as course materials or film reviews. Determine the intent of the message source if you can; is there a message behind this movie, or is the main purpose to make money? Finally, assign a purpose, such as appreciation or comprehension, for viewing.
2. *Take notes in columns.* Use the left side for observations and the right side for your interpretations and/or responses to the presentation. Suppose you are required to watch the psychological thriller, *Swimming Pool* (2002). Your notes for the opening sequences might look like this:

Dark water, gentle waves; not a Swimming Pool-(title shown). Pans up; oh, Big Ben, it's London—to people on subway. Older woman reading book looks up, seems to notice someone. "You're Sarah Morton." Other woman says no; "I'm not the person you think I am." Cut to her in bar ordering whiskey.	Music is eerie, quiet, unsettling. Focus shifts to that woman who's probably an author. She's eccentric and introverted, maybe hiding something? Seems really uptight. Can't handle something because she's going straight to the bar. Something about her isn't right.

Taking notes like these, particularly when watching films you consider to be primarily intended for entertainment, requires substantial attention and energy. However, the records that you keep will help you recall both the words and images that impressed you and the reactions and questions that you had while viewing.

3. *Share your impressions with your peers following the presentation.* Check the accuracy of story and factual details, and discuss your interpretations with others who have seen the presentation.
4. *Synthesize and generalize information from the presentation.* Draw main points together and relate them to your own knowledge and experience. What did you learn? How would you evaluate the presentation? What are you left wondering about?

These steps help turn passive viewing into active listening. Listening actively to visual media may seem difficult, but it is similar to the steps fans take when watching a sporting event or favorite TV program. They prepare for the event with background information and predictions, note details of the event and their interpretation of what happened, discuss and argue about the event with other fans and talk back to performers, and draw conclusions for future reference. The next time you view a media presentation, try to be an active listener.

ASK YOURSELF:

1. Are you prepared to view the presentation?
2. Can you separate stimuli from your interpretations?
3. Did you participate in a discussion about the presentation?
4. What were the central ideas?

Improving Comprehension

As soon as we focus our attention, we begin assigning meaning to what we have heard. Interpreting messages accurately and effectively means not only being able to match the speaker's intent with your understanding, but knowing how to place those messages in a context that makes them significant for you. Effectiveness here revolves around two key skills: maintaining an open mind and using perception checks.

Maintaining an Open Mind. We know that perceptual biases exist but to overcome them, we need to acknowledge the effect that they can have on our ability to interpret messages. Try the following steps:

1. *Recognize your own interests and biases.* If you are preoccupied with yourself or rush to judgment, you will short-circuit your ability to understand others.
2. *Separate the message from its source.* Whether you like a speaker or dread hearing him or her talk, try to listen with respect.
3. *Identify key points in the message.* One test of how actively you have been listening is whether you can pick out the most important parts of a message.
4. *Listen for unanticipated information.* If you listen only for a particular kind of message, such as the direct answer to a question that you have asked, you might miss important information.

Open-mindedness requires the willing suspension of one's biases and the urge to evaluate. For example, a younger student in one of our classes was assigned to work with a middle-aged student on a course project. The younger student was fearful that the older student would be distracted by family and job responsibilities. The older student was worried that the younger student would not take the project seriously. We encouraged both students to be open-minded and to move past their preconceived notions about different age groups. By the end of the project, both students had learned to appreciate what the other contributed to the assignment. Their willingness to remain open-minded not only produced an excellent project, but also established a mutually respectful relationship.

Using Perception Checks. Perception checks are ways to assess whether you have heard what the speaker intends. For instance, you could paraphrase in your own words what the speaker said. *Paraphrasing* the message aids recall and comprehension by forcing you to reconstruct the speaker's ideas and feelings. Another perception check is the use of additional sources to compare what you have heard. You could discuss the message with other listeners, contrast the message with other messages from the same speaker, or compare it with similar messages from different speakers. If you have heard that a local community college has the best painting classes in your area, you might try to find out if other people have gotten the same recommendation, visit the college website to see how their program is described, or talk to people who have taken one of the classes.

Perception checking includes asking questions and identifying areas of agreement with the speaker. For instance, a speaker might facilitate a group discussion by saying, "Marcella's arguments about increasing parking fees for faculty are really convincing to me, because I agree that we really need to keep costs down for students. What do you think?" By giving credit for an idea to another group member and paraphrasing that idea, the speaker increases goodwill in the group and then invites others to participate. All of these perception checks—paraphrasing, asking questions, and identifying areas of agreement—serve as safeguards against misinterpretation and establish a foundation for shared meaning.

Choosing Your Response

One important aspect of listening effectively is responding appropriately. Imagine what happens if in response to another shopper's request to get by ("Excuse me, could you move your cart, please?"), the person to whom the request is made snaps back ("What's your problem? I'll be done in a minute"). Although communication has certainly occurred, neither person is likely to be pleased with the outcome. Appropriate responses when listening let the speaker know that he or she has been understood. Responses facilitate the flow of conversation by providing energy and direction. As a respondent, you are acknowledging your role in the interaction by both your verbal and nonverbal behaviors. The response you make will influence what happens next in the interaction, so whatever your listening goal, consider the following guidelines for providing useful feedback.

1. *Make active choices about your feedback.* Ambiguous responses, such as a shrug of the shoulders or saying, "Whatever" are rarely helpful to the speaker and they mask your thoughts and feelings as a listener. Try to determine your goal in responding and choose both verbal and nonverbal feedback that matches your goal and the needs of the speaker. There are many ways for you to indicate involvement in a conversation. Sometimes a simple nod or smile is enough to demonstrate your interest; at other times, speakers will pause in anticipation of a question or comment. Individual and cultural differences can dictate very different kinds of feedback. For instance, some speakers will end several sentences with questions such as "Right?" or "Do you know what I mean?" These speakers are searching for confirmation that they have been heard; they are looking for a nod, or a verbal "uh-huh" from the listener.

2. *Be careful about using negative feedback.* Sometimes we don't even realize we are giving feedback that offends others. One student summed up several poor listening behaviors: "He interrupted me, told me what I should have done, and always topped me," all of which made her feel "very unimportant" (Roefs 1998). When people feel unimportant, interaction begins to deteriorate and the opportunity for further communication can be lost. If you think an evaluation of a speaker's message is necessary, giving constructive criticism ("You might try using more contrast in the background colors on your PowerPoint presentation") that is specific, offered in the spirit of helping, and wel-

Luann by Greg Evans

Source: LUANN reprinted by permission of United Features Syndicate, Inc.

comed by the speaker is generally preferable to making harsh judgments about people and their ideas ("Looks like you couldn't figure out how to make your presentation attractive").

3. *Validate the speaker.* Think about the last time you felt as though you had been understood, accepted, and supported. Someone around you probably responded to you in a way that showed understanding not just of what you meant, but how you felt. Responding in ways that validate the speaker go beyond simple confirmation of what was said. It often calls for using the same emotional intensity and involvement as the speaker. The woman who announces, "I'm pregnant," probably wants to hear more than "Are you sure?" from her partner, and the friend who says, "I got switched off my favorite account at work," probably wants some follow-up questions rather than a nod and a smile. Offer clear verbal responses, encouragement, and follow-up questions that invite the speaker to convey what is most important. Show your involvement in the conversation and your willingness to understand more than the surface meaning of a statement. The good listener creates a bond of trust and respect with the speaker by acknowledging both the importance of the speaker as a person and the value of what she or he is saying.

   Validation can even be given to people with whom you disagree; the main goal is to disagree without being disrespectful of others. To do this, practice using an **empathetic echo** (Browning 1999), or restating what you have heard in your own words. The empathetic echo can function like a perception check, but the point here is less to check the accuracy of your perception than to show the speaker that you have paid attention. For instance, validation can come through self-disclosure or the sharing of stories rather than giving advice before it is requested. ("I can't believe that mechanic charged me $200 to replace the battery." "That's horrible. I dread getting my car fixed; one time, they charged me an extra $50 just to 'clean' my engine.")

empathetic echo
A listening or response technique that paraphrases or repeats a message.

Making Communication Memorable

Just as attending, interpreting, and responding can all be improved with a little work, so can your ability to remember what you have heard. We often hold the speaker responsible for keeping our attention and helping us remember, rather than taking responsibility ourselves for all phases of the listening process. As a college student, many of the tips you hear will probably be related to remembering information for tests and examinations. However, some of these same skills can be useful in interactions with family and friends as well as in public life. Some of us seem to be born with better memories than others, and all of us seem to lose some of our capacity to remember as we age. Regardless of our relative abilities, we can benefit by staying involved while listening and organizing information to aid our memory.

Staying Involved While Listening. As we mentioned previously, the best way to remember an interaction is to make an investment in it. Participation can take many forms: We can take notes, ask questions, or offer comments that make a connection to what has been said. Sometimes it also helps to associate what the speaker is saying with your own personal experience or impressions. Of all the memory difficulties that people have, one of the most common seems to be remembering people's names. We commonly hear people say that they can remember faces, but not names. Given the significance that we attach to our names, this oversight is considerable. Remembering someone's name is the first step in

Applying Communication Concepts

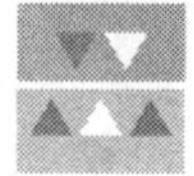

LISTENING AND RESPONDING DURING INTERVIEWS

Interview situations are a good example of settings in which we often are highly motivated to respond appropriately. In any interview, it is especially important to listen carefully to questions, make sure that you understand them, and think before you respond. The response you choose depends on the purpose of the interview.

Employment questions are best answered in ways that show you at your best. Be sincere, succinct, direct, and honest. Try to highlight your qualifications without exaggerating or claiming expertise that you don't have. Practice helps, both in listening to questions and rehearsing your answers. You can expect to hear questions such as, "What particular skills do you bring to the position?" You can also expect the question, "Why do you want to work for us?"

Basic interview skills can also be used in less formal contexts. When you ask people for information, initiate a network with a new group of co-workers, or talk to prospective roommates, you are using skills similar to those used in an interview. Whether you are the interviewer or interviewee, you need to be a good listener. When you're the one conducting the interview, encourage the speaker by demonstrating your interest; lean forward, use direct eye contact, and vary your verbal responses. Use questions that the speaker might anticipate to create trust and build confidence ("What do you like best about your current job?").

ASK YOURSELF:

1. Are your questions clear and direct?
2. How might you rephrase your questions if the respondent has difficulty understanding you?
3. Have you thought of follow-up questions that will allow the speaker to stress points more clearly?

Additional tips and strategies for improving interviewing skills are presented in the Appendix.

making a connection with them. Often we don't remember names because we never learn them in the first place; we are too busy thinking about ourselves rather than listening to the other person. The next time you are introduced to someone new, try to (1) remember what they are interested in, (2) make a mental note of the person's appearance, (3) note a distinguishing feature, and (4) repeat the person's name at least once, make sure you get it right, and write down the name if necessary. Most people are very appreciative of the effort taken to remember a name, and it creates an important context of respect for future interaction.

Organizing Information. It is often easiest to remember information that comes in stories or neatly organized packages. Stories help people process facts, explain principles, and apply ideas. Outlines and lists also aid retention, but few speakers are obvious in their use of them. To be effective, the listener must often identify key points and regroup material.

Everyone wants to feel valued and respected. The good listener stays active in the process and responds in ways that acknowledge the worth of the speaker and strengthen the bonds that make good communication happen.

Resources for Review and Skill Building

Many of these resources are supported by the Connections CD-ROM and free Online Learning Center website.

SUMMARY

This summary is organized around the questions found at the beginning of the chapter. See if you can answer them before reading the summary paragraphs.

1. **Why is listening essential for effective communication?**

   We spend as much as 53 percent of our total communication time listening, yet most of us are poor listeners. We are preoccupied, distracted, or forgetful as much as 73 percent of the time we are listening and we remember less than 25 percent of what we hear. By improving our listening skills, we strengthen the foundation for shared meaning in communication and increase satisfaction with our interpersonal relationships.

2. **What are the stages of the listening process?**

   The four stages of the listening process are (1) attending, (2) interpreting, (3) responding, and (4) remembering. The listening process begins when we actively select, or attend to, stimuli in our environment. We assign meaning to the selected stimuli in the interpretation stage of listening. Responding to a message involves any discernable reaction to a message. We respond to messages verbally and nonverbally. Finally, the remembering stage involves the retention and recall of messages.

3. **What are the differences between active and passive listeners?**

   Active listeners frequently remember more information than passive listeners. Active listeners focus on the moment, are aware of interactions as they occur, and resist distraction in the communication situation. Passive listeners, by contrast, expend little effort in the communication process, lack focus and awareness of the interaction, and are easily distracted.

4. **What are some important obstacles to effective listening?**

   There are many obstacles to effective listening in every communication situation. Sometimes we encounter external obstacles such as poor acoustics or distracting environmental noises. Events that occur prior to or after the interaction can also present challenges. In addition, our attitude toward the communication situation can also influence our ability to listen. Low self-esteem, preconceived attitudes, personal or emotional investment in a speaker or topic, and indifference can all diminish our ability to listen effectively.

5. **What are the four types of listening goals?**

   The four listening goals are (1) appreciation, (2) comprehension, (3) empathy, and (4) evaluation. When our goal is appreciation, we listen for pleasure and enjoyment; when we listen for comprehension, our goal is to understand the message. Empathetic listening involves not only understanding the message, but also recognizing and supporting the feelings and emotional states of others. Finally, evaluative listening helps us render an opinion or judgment about the message.

6. **What can you do to become a more effective and responsible listener?**

   Listening is a skill that can be improved. Some of the ways to listen responsibly and effectively that were discussed in this chapter include preparing physically and mentally to listen, talking notes, being open-minded, using perception checks, actively providing feedback, demonstrating comprehension, staying involved throughout the interaction, and organizing material and information.

KEY TERMS

Test your understanding of these key terms by visiting the Connections CD-ROM and Online Learning Center website at www.mhhe.com/dobkinpace.

active listeners 97
appreciation 105
attending 93
cognitive dissonance 103
coherence 111
comprehension 106
empathetic echo 115
empathetic listening 107
evaluation 108
expressive communication 107
fidelity 111
hearing 92
indifference 103
inference 109
instrumental communication 107
interpreting 94
listening 93
passive listeners 97
pseudolistening 104
remembering 96
responding 95
semantic noise 103

FOR FURTHER REFLECTION

/dobkinpace

Join a conversation about chapter concepts by visiting the Online Learning Center website at www.mhhe.com/dobkinpace

1. We often use the expression, "I hear you," to indicate that we have listened to what someone else has to say. Our language is filled with examples of "hearing"; we have congressional "hearings," and the concept of a "day in court" is based on a judge or jury "hearing" a case. If a case has been presented but no one has listened, has communication occurred? If we say we have heard someone but we have not listened to him or her, how does this affect the quality of our conversation?
2. The goal of empathetic listening is to understand and support the feelings and emotional state of the speaker. Part of feeling supported and valued comes from the sense that others understand us. How do perception checks let us know if we are understood? How might they help create a bond between speaker and listener?

BUILDING COMMUNICATION SKILLS

1. When we discussed listening for evaluation, we mentioned that many misconceptions occur when we make faulty assumptions or inferences from facts. Indeed, sometimes it's difficult to distinguish facts from opinions. Analyze each of the statements below and determine if the conclusion is based on reasonable inferences or if the inference is questionable.
   - Robert was calling to see which auto parts store has replacement sunroofs, so his must be broken.
   - Brand X is the best sport nutrition bar because it has the most vitamins and minerals in it.
   - Dr. Sampson gives the lowest grades in the department because no one received an A in any of his courses last semester.
   - My sister says that candidate G is most likely to win the upcoming election because he won last year.
   - The driver next to me was shaking his fist at the driver of the car in front of him, who must have cut him off.

(Answers: 1-inference; 2-opinion; 3-if true, fact; 4-inference; 5-inference)

2. Often many listening obstacles exist simultaneously. For instance, one student described his first week as an intern at a television station this way: "There was a lot of noise caused by the producers looking over my shoulders every five minutes. This caused information not to be received with 100 percent clarity . . . in the editing room there are ten televisions on at once; sometimes six or seven of them will have the volume up full blast. This makes it extremely difficult to differentiate which broadcast you're actually listening to. Fortunately I'm getting better at singling out the one broadcaster's voice by volume, rate, and pitch" (Skinner 1999). Analyze this situation. What kinds of listening is this intern trying to do, and what kinds of listening obstacles does he face?

NET WORK

Note: While all the URLs listed were current as of the printing of this book, these sites often change. Please check our website www.mhhe.com/dobkinpace for updates and hyperlinks to these exercises.

1. The home page for the International Listening Association, http://listen.org/, contains much information on the process of listening. Visit the page and look at the section on listening exercises for skill-building activities to improve your listening ability. Also, explore the listening resource section for interesting facts about listening; links to books, journal articles, and tapes about listening; and an online assessment of your listening ability.
2. National Public Radio has an archive of audio stories (http://www.npr.org/programs/morning/100years.html) that profile people who have lived to be at least 100 years old. Each profile contains first-person audio clips describing the challenges and opportunities of living so long. Listen to four different stories with four different goals in mind. Listen to one for enjoyment or entertainment and to another for comprehension. Listen to one critically to form an opinion about the quality of life of the elderly and listen to a final one for empathy. What obstacles hinder your ability to empathize with these centenarians? What attitudinal obstacles did you encounter as you listened to the stories? What factors hindered your ability to listen empathetically?

MEDIA MOMENTS

The television show *The Office* (NBC 2008) is a comedy that depicts a self-centered boss named Michael Scott (Steve Carell). Many of the shows funniest scenes involve Michael's poor listening skills as he projects his needs and insecurities onto his employees. Watch an episode of *The Office* and answer the following questions:

- How does Michael's preoccupation with the self hinder his ability to understand others?
- What preconceived attitudes and beliefs keep Michael from listening accurately?
- What are some examples of Michael misinterpreting communication with others?
- Why is listening such an important skill in the work place?

Understanding and Shaping the World through Verbal Communication

5

CHAPTER

Shauna and Elise ran into each other while waiting for the campus tram. "Hey," said Elise, "I was ego surfing and saw the picture of me you posted last week."

"Finally. Did you like it?" asked Shauna.

"Yeah, it looked better than the real thing. Did you Photoshop it?"

"I gave you green eyes and put the guy in the background" replied Shauna.

"Bob liked it. He was over last night" confided Elise.

"Bob! Is he still coming over? He is such a milker."

"He didn't stay long and he really liked your photos."

"Really, well maybe he is alright then. Got to go to my cloud computing class. Catch you later."

"You are such a technophile."

QUESTIONS TO FOCUS YOUR READING

1. What are the fundamental properties of words?
2. How do words imply actions and attitudes?
3. How do words influence thoughts?
4. Why is it important to understand different levels of meaning in words?
5. What roles do codes play in verbal communication?
6. How can language be used responsibly?

Regardless of whether you belong to "Generation Net" (those born after 1982), you probably recognize most of the words used by Shauna and Elise. You might even be able to think of words that you and your friends or co-workers have adopted from a favorite television show, movie, or song lyric, or you might share words or phrases that have special significance based on your relationship. At its most basic level, verbal communication occurs when people use words in an attempt to create meaning. We encounter new words throughout our lives, from our parents, friends, teachers, and popular media. When we communicate with others, we give those words meaning. Our words and those of the people around us shape our understanding of ourselves, as when someone pays us a compliment or uses a label to describe us. From the time a toddler discovers that "move," "stop," and "eat" can be used to direct the behavior of others, he or she learns that words carry power to shape the world. Words can also bring about change when they influence others, deception when they are used to lie or confuse, and empowerment when they create possibilities for self-growth.

verbal language
The systematic use of words and symbols to create and convey meaning.

This chapter explores the power and possibilities of **verbal language,** the systematic use of words and symbols to create and convey meaning. We will first look at the smallest unit of verbal communication, words, and their place in larger systems of meaning. Language changes depending on the context in which it is used, so we will also examine verbal communication and culture. Finally, because being an effective communicator requires the use of appropriate, responsible, and ethical language, this chapter will offer strategies for using language responsibly. After completing this chapter, you should be able to:

- Understand the process by which verbal communication becomes meaningful.
- Identify the units of language.
- Appreciate the place of language in culture.
- Know how to use verbal communication responsibly.

Verbal Communication and Meaning

From the time we learn to understand words and to speak, verbal communication is central to how we think about ourselves and others and act in the world around us. We might not often think about choosing our words very carefully, because they often seem to come naturally to us. However, the better we are able to understand the process by which words become meaningful, the better able we are to communicate effectively. This section of the chapter provides an overview of the fundamental properties of words as symbolic, arbitrary, ambiguous, and changeable. Then, it explores the idea that language is never neutral and that it influences the way we think. These properties of language underlie all verbal communication.

Words are Symbolic, Arbitrary, Ambiguous, and Changeable

Words are central to the way we create and share meaning. As we discussed in Chapter 1, verbal communication can be either written or oral. Although many characteristics of written language apply to spoken words as well, oral communication is usually less formal and more personal, interactive, and transient than written communication. In Chapter 2 we noted that the words we use to define our self, identity, and culture all influence the way we communicate about ourselves and to others. In Chapters 3 and 4 we saw how the words we use and listen to influence our perceptions and either help or hinder understanding. Our words allow us to shape and name our experiences, create shared meaning with others, express ourselves in varied and sometimes ambiguous ways, and create new words to describe our changing world.

symbolic
The property of words that allows us to talk about things without being the things themselves.

Words are Symbolic. Words are **symbolic** in that they represent ideas or objects and allow us to talk about them. In addition to describing our everyday world, symbols allow us to talk about things that do not exist, such as events in the past or fictional characters. When we see an object, like a book on our desk, a tree outside, or a friend walking in the room, we attach a word to that thing so that we can think and talk about it with others. We learn to connect words to objects and ideas through communication. As we write and talk to other people, we share understanding about what the words mean. One of the simplest ways to show how we attach meanings to words is through a "triangle of meaning" originally credited to C. K. Ogden and I. A. Richards (1923). (See Figure 5-1).

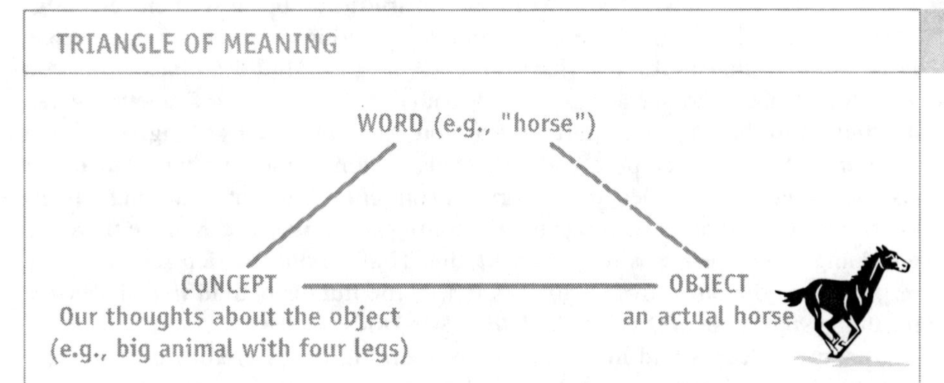

FIGURE 5-1

The triangle of meaning shows the relationships between words and the things they represent.

Since the original presentation of the "triangle of meaning," scholars have offered variations on the model. However, they all illustrate the relationship between words and the things they represent. The line connecting the word and concept shows that each person will have her or his own meaning for a word. The person who lacks experience with either an actual horse or the word "horse," would have difficulty making sense of the word. The line from object to concept shows that once a person encounters an object or, in the example above, a horse, the person forms a mental image of that object. The word "horse" at the top of the triangle represents the combination of an object or idea and a person's mental image of that object or idea.

This process of attaching meaning to words makes words symbolic because they stand apart from the things they represent. Words refer to objects, ideas, and actions, and they help us communicate with others. Our verbal language lets us share knowledge; through language, we can remember the past and imagine the future. We can invent new behaviors, such as "line dancing" and "spamming" (sending unwanted mail through the Internet), and we can recognize these activities as new and meaningful once we agree upon a word for them.

arbitrary
Words that have no direct connection to the objects they represent.

Words Are Arbitrary. Our words are **arbitrary** in that they have no direct connection to the objects they represent. A "chicken" can be "la poulet" in French without changing a thing about the bird. The word, then, is not the thing it represents. Some words seem to have a natural relationship to physical objects; for instance, we might think that a barking dog sounds like "woof" and the Chinese character for house ("房") resembles the actual building. But even these words make sense primarily because the people using them have a shared understanding of what these words mean.

The idea that words are arbitrary is significant because we often act as though there is a necessary relationship between a thing and the word we use to talk about it. Think about a difficult conversation between two friends. One might call the conversation a "disagreement," whereas the other might call it a "fight." Both people would be right, because the connection between the conversation and how each chooses to label it is based on his or her perceptions. There isn't one correct word that necessarily defines the conversation. Because words are arbitrary, we have to negotiate their meaning when we communicate with others.

ambiguous
Words that do not have a clear meaning.

Words Are Ambiguous. Words are **ambiguous** because their meanings are not always clear, and a wide variety of interpretations are sometimes possible. Professor Bartello can tell you that your essay is "good," but that doesn't tell you what "good" means to her. For example, "good" could correspond to a letter grade, it could mean that Professor Bartello was entertained by your writing, or it could be your professor's attempt to end further discussion about your work. She might also be trying to acknowledge the worth of your effort without criticizing aspects of your writing or embarrassing you. The ambiguity of words can make them entertaining and inspiring as well as frustrating. Think about the rich and varied interpretations that arise from a good poem, or the humor behind the advertising for the 1998 release of the film *Godzilla:* "Size Does Matter."

In some cultures and in some contexts, ambiguity is vital to communication, because being clear and direct might be inappropriate or embarrassing. For example, someone who has participated in a job interview but was not offered a position might not want to know exactly why an offer wasn't extended. Often employers will send ambiguous messages, such as, "We regret that we cannot offer you a position at this time," rather than being direct. A letter that says, "We were disappointed that you showed lack of confidence and creativity in your interview" might be less ambiguous, but it might also be hurtful to the job candidate.

Although the meanings of words are arbitrary, our conventions for using them are not. Think about the person who has been woken up by a phone call and says to the caller, "Sorry, I have a frog in my throat." The word "frog" isn't meant to be taken literally—that an amphibious creature is jumping on the speaker's vocal chords. However, our rules about language use determine where the word "frog" will be placed in the sentence, regardless of its meaning. These conventions, or our shared agreement about how to use language, make communication possible.

changeable
Words based on social, political, and cultural contexts, and the historical time in which they are located.

Words Are Changeable. Finally, words are **changeable** in our meaning for and use of them. Words change based on social, political, and cultural contexts, and the historical time in which they are used. The meanings of many words in the English language have changed over time. For example, the phrase "colored people" has undergone a transformation to become "minorities" and, more recently, "people of color," which now not only refers to African Americans, but to people from a wide range of ethnicities. At least one urban government, the San Diego City Council, has adopted a policy of avoiding the words "majority" and "minority" when referring to racial and ethnic groups, because "minority" can be considered disparaging (Huard 2001). For years, people with disabilities were called "cripples," which unfairly labeled them as incompetent, social outcasts. By changing our use of language, we can show respect, increase the accuracy of our communication, and sometimes enhance self-esteem.

Additional examples of words whose meanings have changed or use has expanded over time include:

- *bimbo*—from a generic term for a man, to a sexually promiscuous or stupid woman.
- *gig*—from a fish spear, to a performance event, to a measure of computer space.
- *juke*—from being disorderly, to a part of a jukebox, to outmaneuvering by feint or deception.
- *lift*—from raise, pick up, or move (or an elevator in Britain), to steal.
- *steep*—from sharp rise in a slope, to excessive or expensive.

The symbolic, arbitrary, ambiguous, and changeable properties of words bring richness to communication and provide countless opportunities for creativity. The English language has expanded not only by changing the meanings of existing words, but also by appropriating words from other languages. Consider how the words from other languages have become part of the traditional American breakfast: After beginning with juice or fruit, such as "melon" (Greek origin through French), we might have some "bacon" (French) and "eggs" (Old Norse) with "toast" (French). Perhaps we will put "butter" (Latin) or "marmalade" (Portuguese) on our toast. We might also drink "coffee" (Arabic), "tea" (Chinese), or "cocoa" (Mexican Spanish). Whereas other cultures might import foods and devise new names for them, English language speakers have historically appropriated both the products of other peoples and the words they have for them (*The Word Tree* 1998). Many words in the English language have been *appropriated* from other languages. Table 5-1 provides a few examples.

Unfortunately, the qualities that make language so interesting can also make it difficult to learn. Some people find the English language particularly hard to acquire and use correctly. Although English requires few inflections or changes in tone, the way words are spelled does not always correspond to their pronunciation. Consider the four pronunciations of "cough," "rough," "through," "though." Furthermore, the same word can have many different meanings and the rules for combining words are riddled with exceptions. Understanding these features of verbal communication is the first step in gaining control over language and influencing the processes by which people construct meaning.

> "It was not so very long ago that people thought that semiconductors were part-time orchestra leaders and microchips were very small snack foods."
>
> —Geraldine Ferraro, D-New York, former U.S. House of Representatives

TABLE 5-1

APPROPRIATED WORD	LANGUAGE OF ORIGIN
alcohol	Arabic
barbecue	Arawak
boss	Dutch
yen ("craving")	Chinese
robot	Czech
kayak	Eskimo
emotion	French
alphabet	Greek
rocket	Italian
tycoon	Japanese
lilac	Persian
cafeteria	Spanish
taboo	Tongan
yogurt	Turkish

Source: P. Farb, *Word Play: What Happens When People Talk* (New York: Bantam, 1973), p. 340–341.

Words Imply Actions and Attitudes

The symbolic, arbitrary, ambiguous, and changeable properties of words can make them seem incredibly elastic, open to the broadest interpretations, and ready to be used at will. However, because words gain their meaning when people use them, one person alone rarely has the power to create new words or meanings for them. Think about what happens when a musician such as Marshall Mathers, also known as Eminem, decides to use offensive language in his lyrics. Supporters of Eminem have argued that although he uses language that endorses violence against women and gay people, he is free to use *repugnant* words without being held responsible for the ways in which his lyrics are interpreted (Sanneh 2001). This does not mean that Eminem's listeners will not be offended. The language we are taught has existed before us and, most likely, will continue to be used after us. When someone like Mathers says he is acting out a role and doesn't endorse the actions in his lyrics, as in "went to gym in eighth grade, raped the women swim team" (Mathers, Bass, & Bass 1999), his words, nonetheless, are likely to be interpreted literally by his listeners. Words carry with them conventional meanings that are inescapable, and conventions only change when groups with enough clout adopt new meaning so that shared understanding can occur.

Words have a powerful capacity to influence our thoughts and actions. The understandings we have for words often determine the actions we take toward the objects they represent. Theorist Kenneth Burke (1966) has written extensively about the ability of language to influence both *what* we see and *how* we see. For instance, if Kendra shows you a large pane of glass in a building and calls it a "door," you might look for a handle and try to exit the room that way. Your actions are likely to be different if she tells you it is a "window." Or, if she tells you she is "arthritic," you might try to help her open the door. In this sense, language is never neutral; all words imply actions or attitudes. The degree to which members of a group share understandings about these actions or attitudes determines the power that words can have.

Even the basic descriptions of events suggest an evaluation of the thing being discussed. The front-page newspaper headline, "Mexico's Violent Powder Kegs—Festering Rebellions Erupt in Deadly Clashes" (*San Diego Union-Tribune* 1998) combines the words for an inert, apolitical substance ("powder kegs") with those for a foul wound ("festering" and "erupt"). The story is about attacks by army troops on rebel groups in rural Mexico, and it implies that the rebel groups are diseased, violent, and without legitimate political purpose. An alternative headline, "Mexican Army Continues Attacks on Rebel Peasants," would create a far different impression. Although we may expect news headlines to be as objective as possible, they often illustrate the principle that words carry meaning beyond mere description.

Finally, words tell us how to think and act in the world around us. If a woman introduces herself as *Mrs.* Williams, she is letting people around her know that she identifies herself as a married person. She is likely to create a different impression if she uses a hyphenated name, such as Mrs. Arias-Williams, and still another if she goes by Ms. Arias. More than one survey suggests that a substantial portion of the American public believes that women who keep their names or hyphenate them after marriage are less apt to be attractive, like to cook, or be a good wife or mother than those who take their husband's names (Murray 1999). Undoubtedly, most married women do not make a decision about changing or keeping their name based on how they want their cooking to be perceived. But because language is never neutral, we cannot always escape the attitudes that are embedded in words. The "Think It Over" box on whether words really matter offers another example of how our choice of words can have profound implications.

Words Influence the Way We Think

The community that agrees to use words in similar ways often shares beliefs, attitudes, and values, in part because sharing a language leads to related patterns of thinking. Think about the way high school seniors change their language if they go directly to college after graduation. Words such as "homerooms," "teachers," and "lunchrooms" are replaced by "professors" and "dining commons." According to the **linguistic relativity hypothesis,** our thoughts are influenced by the words

linguistic relativity hypothesis The idea that our thoughts are influenced by the words we know and the patterns of language that dominate our culture.

Think It Over

DO WORDS REALLY MATTER?

Members of the scientific community recognize how powerful words can be in influencing attitudes and actions. Consider the difference between using the phrase "fetal tissue" and "unborn baby." The difference between these phrases is at the heart of one of the most hotly debated issues in the United States: Should human fetal tissue be used in scientific research? (Maggio 1997). The notion of conducting medical research on "babies" is offensive to most people, whereas the idea of using "fetal tissue" is less controversial. Although the human tissue used for research is the same regardless of the phrase—stem cell research is conducted on tissue from fetuses that have been miscarried or aborted—the way we describe the research influences the degree of public support for it.

Under which circumstances would you use the word "baby," particularly when discussing medical or reproductive issues?

How might your choice reflect the policies you are likely to support?

that we know and the patterns of language that are dominant in our culture. The linguistic relativity hypothesis was formulated by Edward Sapir (1921) and later extended by his protégé, Benjamin Whorf (1956). Sapir argued that our words act as a lens shaping how we see the world.

The linguistic relativity hypothesis suggests that two people speaking different languages will necessarily have different perceptions of reality. A person whose native language is Mandarin will probably perceive extended family members differently than a native English speaker, because the Mandarin language has a far more complex set of words to describe families. For example, if you are a native English speaker, you lack a specific word for your "sister-in-law's mother." Cultures that place more emphasis on extended families also have the vocabulary to easily discuss these relationships. In addition to emphasizing vocabulary, Whorf studied the structure of language. In his study of Hopi Indians, Whorf found that the Hopi had no words for "time," so the concepts of "early" and "late" had no meaning for them. Whereas European languages measure time by fixed points on a continuum (morning, noon, night) or as an object to be manipulated (buy or save time), Hopi language describes the passage of time through a sequence of events (preparing for and participating in an activity). Similarly, Hopi prophecies are less concerned with *when* a catastrophe might happen than with *living a life that is prepared* for that moment, whenever it might be (Macy, Gomes, and Kremer 2000).

The linguistic relativity hypothesis suggests that language can expand the range of our thinking because, if we have a wider vocabulary, we have more words at our disposal to help us think about or describe a situation. Technical language is a good example. If you are not a mechanic, you might have trouble describing the problem with your brakes: If you can say "the caliper sliding surfaces are binding," not only will you impress your mechanic, but you will be able to give a clearer picture and demonstrate your knowledge (and you are likely to save some money as well). In addition to expanding possibilities, language can also constrain our thoughts, because without words to convey our ideas, those ideas might never become part of our reality. A simple exercise in visualization illustrates this. Think about your grandfather's face. Now, see if you can describe the area below his nose and above his upper lip. Unless he has a mustache, you might have a hard time "seeing" this part of his face. Since there is no common English word for that space, few people have as clear an image of it as they do of the eyes, nose, and mouth.

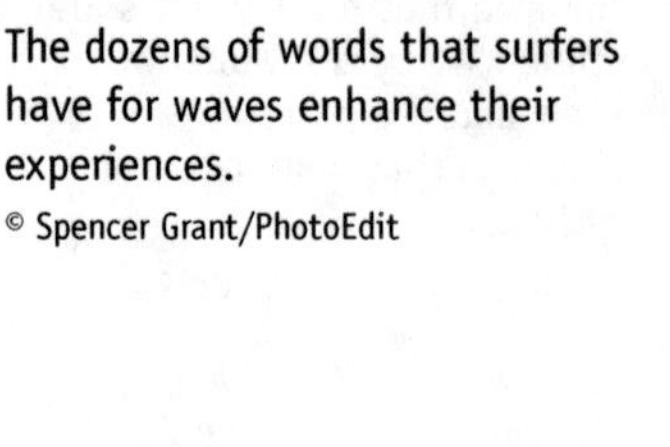

The dozens of words that surfers have for waves enhance their experiences.

Our words and language patterns are powerful, then, in their capacity to shape our perception of reality. We see the world differently based on the words we have to think about it. The dozens of words surfers have for "wave" makes their experience of them richer than the non-surfer, for they are likely to see breaks, soups, lips, and sledgehammers. Travelers who know the languages of the countries they visit come closer to appreciating the perspectives of other peoples, for they are one step closer to seeing their culture as they do.

> "The choice of what words we may use determines what dreams we are able to express."
> —Gloria Steinem, author and activist

Understanding the Meanings of Words

Thus far, we have been exploring the properties of words as they function in verbal communication. We have said that words become meaningful in interaction, when people use them and share understandings of them. Words are largely symbolic because they stand for something else—an object or idea. At a deeper level, each language uses particular kinds of words that have denotative and connotative meanings, and that are organized in systems and operate based on codes. In the following section, we will explore the levels of meanings for words and the ways they work within a system of rules or codes.

Denotation

As we have seen, words have many possible meanings, which is why verbal communication can be so ambiguous. The most concrete meaning for a word is often referred to as its denotative meaning. You may have heard **denotation** defined as the dictionary definition of a word. This is a useful start that needs to be refined. The dictionary includes many kinds of definitions, beginning with *referential meanings* (as in indicating a loose spot in a piece of rope and calling it "slack"), and adding the values ("slack" as lazy) and contexts ("my supervisor is slack") in which a word might be found. So, think of denotative meaning as the most tangible, specific, and objective meaning of a word. This often happens to be the most widely shared meaning of a word as well.

denotation
The most concrete, specific, and objective meaning of a word.

Words with readily available, denotative meanings are often called **concrete** words because they come as close as possible to an objective description of reality. Particular kinds of words denote objects or things and have simple, referential meanings. Most of the words used to describe everyday objects, such as lamp, chair, desk, shoes, or window, are concrete words with referential meanings. Words of this kind do not convey feelings or emotions (Richards 1976). Think about the earlier discussion in this chapter about words as symbolic. We used the example of "horse" to illustrate the relationships between a person, the word, and an actual object (see Figure 5-1). At the level of denotation, the word "horse" functions at a concrete, descriptive level. The "horse" is little more than a particular kind of mammal that is recognizable by people who understand the English language. At this simple, referential level of understanding, the word has denotative meaning. However, a horse can also elicit many highly personal thoughts based on our experience (or lack thereof) with the animal. For one person, the horse might call forth the romantic imagery of the American West; for another, it might represent a European culinary delicacy. Some of those associations may be evoked for a person any time the word is used. Those personal associations move beyond denotation into the next level of meaning: connotation.

concrete
Words that come as close as possible to an objective description of reality.

Connotation

connotation
The meaning of words based on individual or cultural experiences or values.

In addition to denotation, our words also have connotative meanings. **Connotation** refers to the meanings of words based on specific individual or cultural experiences or values; often these meanings are invested with emotion. Think about the rectangular piece of cloth we call a "flag." Once it consists of red and white stripes and white stars on a blue background, we call it an "American flag," and it comes to mean much more than a piece of cloth. Through our verbal communication about the meaning of the flag, we might automatically think of duty to country, freedom, and democracy. The flag becomes symbolic of the values espoused by citizens of the United States of America. If we fought in a foreign war, were born after the Vietnam War, or flew a flag following the September 11, 2001 attacks, the flag might take on additional meanings. Or think of a dinner date during which a woman presents a man with a diamond ring. In many cultures, the diamond stands for love and commitment; for the woman, it might also be an attempt to initiate a new stage in the relationship. At the denotative level, the ring is only a piece of jewelry with a carbon crystal in it. How does the type of stone (the diamond) affect the meaning of the ring as a symbol? How might the man respond if the ring's stone were black onyx? Many people expect men to present symbolic gifts as part of courtship; so, does the presentation of a diamond ring by a woman have its own meaning?

abstract
Words that refer to thoughts, ideas, or theories.

One way to illustrate the way that concrete words take on connotative meaning is through an abstraction ladder (Hayakawa 1964). **Abstract** words have no physical referent; they refer to thoughts or theories. When read from the bottom up, the ladder begins with pure physical matter and progresses to more abstract, symbolic levels (see Figure 5-2).

As the abstraction ladder suggests, even everyday items can take on abstract levels of meaning. Few words are completely concrete or purely abstract. Their level of abstraction is relative to other words in our vocabulary and to the context in which they are used. A word like "lipstick" can refer to an object when on a shelf in a beauty supply store; when worn by a young girl, it can be interpreted as evidence of her desire to be older.

Connotative meanings for words vary based on the relationship of participants and the cultural context in which they are communicating. Nonetheless, the diamond ring and the flag usually have connotative meanings rather than merely denotative ones. Some meanings of words become so ingrained in members of a culture that the values and feelings they invoke seem inevitable and inseparable from the objects they represent. Most U.S. citizens would experience extreme discomfort if asked to step on their country's flag; for them, the cloth has become equivalent to the country's core values. The flag no longer functions at the level of denotation. The same process occurs when people violate our expectations of them based on our understanding of them as "mother" or "Olympic athlete." Think about the disbelief that often accompanies charges of illegal activity by Olympic athletes. When an Olympic medalist or star athlete is charged with drug use, it can be difficult for fans to take the charge seriously. The phrase "Olympic athlete" has denotative meaning, but we often treat the people to whom it refers as a set of values rather than as individuals. As a word or image takes on connotative meanings, we are likely to respond to the cultural ideas, emotions, and values associated with it.

Sometimes separating connotative and denotative meanings can remind us that words are arbitrary representations of reality. A key strategy of critical think-

FIGURE 5-2 THE ABSTRACTION LADDER

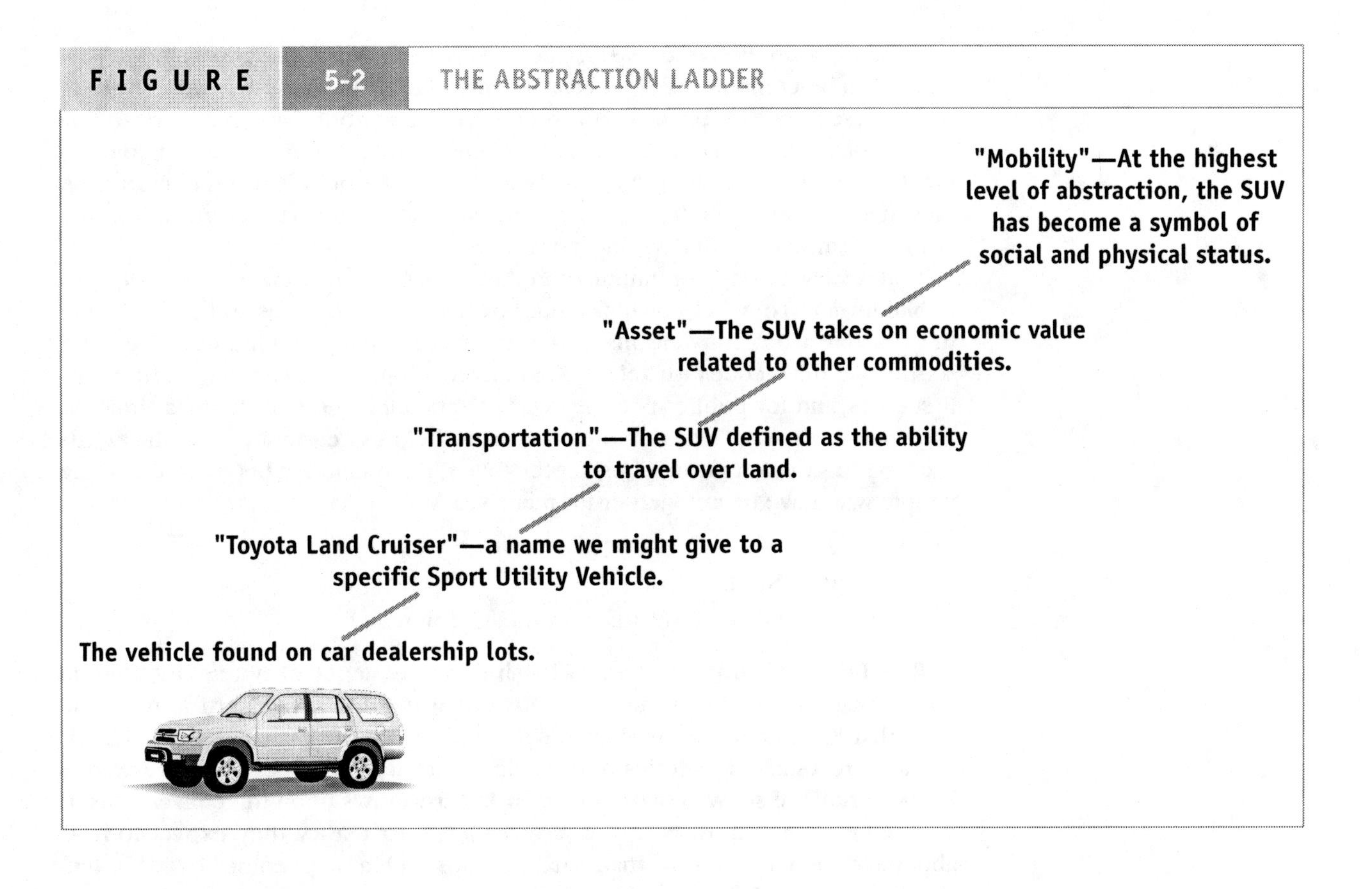
"Mobility"—At the highest level of abstraction, the SUV has become a symbol of social and physical status.
"Asset"—The SUV takes on economic value related to other commodities.
"Transportation"—The SUV defined as the ability to travel over land.
"Toyota Land Cruiser"—a name we might give to a specific Sport Utility Vehicle.
The vehicle found on car dealership lots.

ing involves untangling the denotative and connotative levels of meaning, from exploring the decision to call someone "girlfriend" to assessing the implications of calling a conflict "war." Perhaps you have been in a situation in which someone referred to you as "girlfriend" or "boyfriend," and you were uncomfortable with the label because it suggested a degree of exclusivity that you were not prepared to claim. Or, once a partner started to use this word to describe you, his or her expectations about the amount of time you should spend together suddenly changed. In both cases, a discussion about the meaning of "boyfriend" or "girlfriend" would be a good idea! This kind of critical thinking can help us uncover assumptions and underlying values, and help us evaluate the basis on which we are asked to make sacrifices, as when patriotism is invoked to inspire us to pay taxes or wage war. Analyzing the common understandings of such words is also the first step in changing their meaning and gaining access to the potential power of language.

"A word is not a crystal, transparent and unchanged; it is the skin of a living thought, and may vary greatly in color and content according to the circumstances and the time in which it is used."

—Oliver Wendell Holmes, physician, poet, and humorist

Codes

All verbal communication is governed by codes, which help us make sense of words and the contexts in which they are uttered. A **code** is a set of conventions or rules that is shared by members of a culture and which governs the use of

code
A set of conventions or rules shared by members of a culture and which governs the use of words and symbols.

words and symbols (Fiske 1987). Codes provide us with guidelines about how words can be combined and what words mean in relationship to other words in a phrase, sentence, or passage. For instance, it takes more than an understanding of the English language to know that a diamond ring signifies love and commitment when presented by a man to a woman. Both participants in the interaction must understand the code, or the cultural expectations and rules surrounding the symbol "diamond," to understand its meaning.

Codes vary among communication contexts, from personal conversations to public forums. They help us figure out how to interpret words and symbols, and they establish the conventions by which we habitually communicate. As with scripts, we have codes for telephone conversations, for classroom lectures, for first dates, and for public speeches. Our scripts tell us how to define a situation and what to expect. Codes, on the other hand, help us determine what the words used in the situation mean. Consider the following interaction between a working couple who have been together for many years:

Raj: What is your day like today?

Bettina: Not too bad.

Raj: I'll be in the area around lunchtime.

Based on the history of the relationship and sequence of statements, Bettina knows that Raj will call around 11:30 A.M. that day and invite her to lunch. The code that Raj and Bettina share helps them interpret the words as an invitation. Children recognize the codes of television at a very early age: When the credits begin to run, the show is over. Television, in turn, draws upon the conventions of storytelling. When most North Americans listen to a story, they expect to hear about a sequence of events that usually begins with a "happening," builds in tension, and ends with a temporary or permanent resolution to the change caused by the initial happening.

Personal ads in newspapers provide interesting and often humorous examples of messages that are coded in very specific ways. Consider the following advertisements. You might have trouble understanding all of the statements without knowing the conventions for language use on which they rely:

> Older woman, you know about love! 28-year-old SNAG seeking you. Me: 6′2″, 200 lbs, Gemini, accomplished professional. You: 30–40, petite, nonmaterialistic, uninhibited, and ready for us.
>
> DSWF, blond/green, 30s, 5′4″, 125 lbs, no baggage, commitment-oriented. Seeking financially secure, active, devoted gentleman for walks, talks, sunsets.

It might be difficult to discover that "SNAG" means "sensitive, New Age guy" or that "DSWF" means "divorced, single white female." Think about other features of the code for personals. What is the primary interest of the first author? What do "blond/green," "no baggage," and "financially secure" mean in the context of the second ad? The "Exploring Communication Concepts" box on communication codes and talk shows gives another example of a way that codes operate in mediated contexts. As with personal advertisements, the way people use language on talk shows is governed by rules based both on the context of the communication and the shared culture of participants.

Exploring Communication Concepts

COMMUNICATION CODES AND TALK SHOWS

Communication researchers such as Donal Carbaugh (1991) have looked extensively at the way culture affects how we interpret codes. In his analysis of *Donahue,* a popular television talk show in the 1980s, Carbaugh emphasized the importance of individualism as part of a code that views personal struggles rather than social factors as being responsible for problems such as racism, poverty, and unemployment. Based on this code of individualism, if you heard that someone was denied a loan because he or she was Hispanic, you would assume that the denial was based on some personal shortcoming of the individual, rather than potential discrimination in the banking industry. Of course, either (or both) could be true.

Carbaugh gives the example of a discussion about race and unemployment on *Donahue,* when a "guest expert" tried to demonstrate empathy with poor people by saying, "We are on the side of individuals who are trying to make it." The idea that both black and white individuals try to make a living was "heard to be a common cultural denominator," a point that was presented as more important than any differences in opportunities people may experience based on race. In other words, speakers on the show used a code of conversation that placed unemployment in the context of individual struggles and avoided discussion of more divisive social problems such as racism (Carbaugh 1991).

Subsequent studies of communication on television talk shows have extended this research. One scholar, Patricia Priest, argued that the code of conversation, which emphasizes the individuality of the guests, has encouraged people who are socially deviant to appear on these shows (Priest 1995). In other words, even though people realize they might be ridiculed on daytime talk shows, they want to appear on them because they think it will be a place to tell their personal stories, gain support, and sometimes even receive free therapy or counseling (Grindstaff 1997).

ASK YOURSELF:

1. Do you think that television viewers are interested in seeing talk show guests as social outcasts? As individuals responsible for their own circumstances?
2. Does the talk show format, or code, promote connections or divisiveness among people?

Communication codes regulate our private conversations as well as our public ones. We have rules for everything from greeting a stranger on the street to choosing appropriate language during a public presentation. In the United States, a typical conversation with a new acquaintance might begin with a question such as, "So, where are you from?" An Australian aborigine might be more likely to ask, "Who does your father belong to?" Public presentations have codes of communication as well; speakers are usually expected to use formal language, speak fluently, and structure what they say with a clear beginning, middle, and end.

Codes provide frameworks for structuring our verbal communication. They help us determine how to interpret words and regulate the ways we use them. We rely on communication codes to help us predict what people will say to us and expect from us. Breaking communication codes can be risky. For instance, some families have a hard time discussing emotions openly. For those families, saying "I love you" might violate a code about appropriate disclosure of emotion and make other members of the family uncomfortable. Codes also tell us which words are appropriate. In most college classrooms, for example, students are expected to address their instructors with the title of "professor" or "doctor." On one occasion, a student approached one of the authors and said he couldn't call her "doctor" because she "just didn't look like a doctor." The student might not have been aware of his own code violation, which could have easily been interpreted by the author as evidence of sexism.

Although codes can be intentionally broken to shift our perceptions or to grab our attention and shock us, breaking codes is risky. When expectations are violated, communicators can become confused or offended, leading to barriers in communication. Once we understand the codes that govern our use of language, we can decide whether violating them is necessary or ethical. We have said that codes are based on context, culture, and the relationships between people. Codes also establish group membership, because knowledge of them can determine who is included and who is excluded in a group. For example, some organizations have unstated rules about where business transactions can be discussed. The employee who doesn't share a gym membership with supervisors might be left out of important business decisions, and the person who repeatedly disrupts meetings might not be asked to participate in future meetings. These special codes based on our membership in groups help to define our identity and will be discussed further as we continue to explore the connection between verbal communication and culture.

Communicating Culture through Language

Our collected and repeated use of signs and symbols form the basis of our culture. As we stated in Chapter 2, culture includes everything that makes up our way of life, including shared values, knowledge, behaviors, and symbolic expression. How we talk and what we talk about are central to our cultures. The following section explores these connections more deeply by looking at communication and the development of co-cultures, language and gender, and the function of taboos.

Communication and Co-Cultures

reference groups
Groups with which we most strongly identify.

The language we use to describe our personal identities necessarily includes names and labels for the groups to which we belong. The groups with which we most strongly identify function as **reference groups.** Although American society is divided into many groups, the most prominent divisions among people occur along the lines of gender, ethnicity, socioeconomic status, age, and sexual orientation. Particular reference groups, such as those whose members are female, nonwhite, working or lower class, or nonheterosexual, often develop co-cultures, or cultures that reflect both their connection to and distinction from dominant culture (Samovar and Porter 1994). Every society has a dominant culture that communicates acceptable behaviors, common beliefs, shared values, and social hierarchy to its members. Some features of dominant culture in the United States include individualism as a core value, capitalism as the preferred economic system, heterosexuality as the legitimate form of sexual orientation, and the nuclear family as the most appropriate familial unit. Co-cultures share features of the dominant culture but establish distinct boundaries based on the shared identities of group members. For example, bodybuilding has become a significant part of many gay co-cultures. Gay men who engage in body-building are sometimes trying to establish a strong connection to traditional masculinity, even though many heterosexual men do not see gay men, under any circumstances, as masculine. This gay co-culture is connected to, but also distinct from, dominant culture.

Sports fans often form co-cultures with their own codes of expression.
© Mike Blake/Timepix

People of color often experience pressure from members of the dominant culture to declare allegiance with a particular reference group. As one Asian-American explains, "When I was in college I had an identity crisis. It was the first time I was away from my family. I learned the meaning of 'banana': yellow on the outside, white on the inside" ("If the Shoe Doesn't Fit" 1995). Metaphors such as "banana" imply that one has internalized the beliefs, values, and norms of the dominant white culture while maintaining a superficial relationship to an ethnic co-culture. Co-cultures can provide support networks through which people affirm their identities and receive encouragement.

The language used by members of co-cultures when talking with one another can also help to create and maintain boundaries, provide a means of identification, and ensure privacy. For example, boundaries between groups are often created and reinforced through unique codes of expression. Members of co-cultures might use slang, technical language, new words, or street language to demonstrate unity. Aida, an African-American woman, says: "I can talk the street language in East Palo Alto. If someone says, 'Wassup?' I answer, 'Wassupwitchu?' I know I'm more accepted by people I can communicate with. Acknowledgment of people is important" ("If the Shoe Doesn't Fit" 1995). The specialized language of co-cultures, also called **argot,** becomes a way for people to acknowledge their membership in a group, and it can provide a sense of solidarity between group members. Think about how the editors of *YM (Young and Modern)* tried to adopt the language of a teenage girl in their response to the following letter to the editor. The letter posed the question: "I'm 16, and I've never had a boyfriend. I have a great personality, so it's 'cause I'm fat, right?" The magazine responded, "Wrong! Enough with the bod-bashing! Our readers . . . are way more critical of their looks than the rest of the world is. So stop harshing on yourself. When you mirror-gaze focus on what you dig . . . ." (Letters 1998).

argot
The specialized language of a co-culture.

Some groups identify themselves based on music. Their "soundtrack" provides a connection with friends, and paraphernalia such as T-shirts makes the connections visible (Roefs 1998). Proud fans of Alicia Keyes might wear a new concert T-shirt, whereas Deadheads (fans of the Grateful Dead) are likely to get together based on shared MP3 files and bootlegged tapes. Although these special codes are sometimes misunderstood by those outside the co-culture, they can help create affinity among group members.

Like the words borrowed from other languages, the special codes of co-cultures are sometimes appropriated by the dominant culture. For instance, entire industries have emerged based on the look and language of hip-hop music. But with the exception of communication that has become commercialized, the verbal communication used by co-cultural groups is rarely accepted as legitimate within the dominant culture. Because of this discrepancy, members of co-cultures often learn **code-switching,** or the ability to adopt a preferred code based on the group with which one is interacting.

code-switching
The ability to adopt a preferred code based on the group with which you are interacting.

In general, groups with lower social status must become more adept at code-switching. Aida, the African-American woman from East Palo Alto, must drop her use of street language in formal business settings, whereas her male counterpart is less likely to be judged harshly for using words common to his co-culture. Girls learn early in life that code-switching will ease their movement into different social groups, which explains why girls often use language that is more sophisticated and grammatically correct than that of boys. Girls also learn a code of appeasement—polite expressions ("If you don't mind . . ."), questions ("Am I making sense?"), tentative wording ("It's just my opinion . . .")—that can reflect or communicate a subordinate position. With their peers, girls will often switch to the less formal language of their co-culture (Tavris 1992). The relative powerlessness of some co-cultural groups makes code-switching necessary for their survival. Recognizing the codes of co-cultures promotes learning about the expression and identity of others, and it brings us one step closer to bridging communication gaps.

Taboos

taboos
Prohibited words or the behaviors that those words describe.

In every culture there are words which, by convention, are deemed inappropriate or unacceptable to speak (Farb 1973). **Taboos** are prohibited words or the behaviors that those words describe. Although every culture has them, the behaviors and words considered as taboo vary both across cultures and within time spans of individual cultures.

DILBERT reprinted by permission of United Feature Syndicate, Inc.

Taboo words are interesting because they reveal the values and privileges of a culture. Consider that many taboo words in the English language refer to sex or natural bodily functions. "Talking dirty" can be a way to mock or challenge social conventions, to attract attention in public forums such as talk radio and television, and to provoke confrontation. When used by individuals of lower social status, taboo words can be a source of social stigma or shame. Finally, taboo words provide clues to the social anxieties of a culture.

One topic that has been treated as taboo in English language is female menstruation. At the end of World War II, nearly 100 expressions for menstruation were in use, including "wearing the rag," "flying the red flag," and "entertaining the general" (Farb 1973). Although the contemporary expression, "having a period," might seem to be an improvement, its use is still considered to be taboo in some contexts. In talking about her work for CBS on a situation comedy dealing with menopause, actress Cybill Shepherd (Coping 1998) said, "We were told that we couldn't say the words 'menstruation,' 'vagina,' or 'cervix'. . . . I had to fight CBS in order to say the word 'period' " (p. 74). Our discomfort with using some words reveals unresolved tensions in contemporary society and has real consequences.

For instance, girls who begin menstruation without talking about it first may think they are dying, and some older women have great difficulty discussing menopause with their physicians. In fact, the discussion of the normal bodily functions of women is still so scandalous to some people that the examples you just read might be considered offensive (see the Dilbert cartoon).

Given the discomfort that taboo language causes some people, think about situations in which it might be appropriate to raise taboo topics or use taboo language. Is it acceptable to mention taboo topics for the purpose of educating others? Is it ethical to use taboo language on television and radio for entertainment purposes? Do you ever use it to achieve a desired effect, such as shocking someone? Knowing the beliefs and values of your audience can help you decide whether using taboo language might be an appropriate and effective means of communication.

Ethical Challenges in Verbal Communication

At the beginning of this chapter, we suggested that words carry power to shape the world. Our language choices convey attitudes, influence others, shape the way we think, help define our individual and group identities, and signal areas of social tension. Words can transform people's sense of self and move them to action. Indeed, many of our social institutions are based on this belief in the power of language. Our legal system includes libel and slander laws to protect people from the potential harm done by words. Law enforcement officers must orally read

Some of our most important personal transformations are conveyed and legitimated through verbal communication.
© Michael Newman/PhotoEdit

people's rights. Courtroom procedures lead to a pronouncement of "guilty" or "not guilty" to determine people's fates. Our rituals, such as the exchange of wedding vows and the reading of names at commencement ceremonies, indicate changes of personal status and identity through declarations of our accomplishments and commitments to others. And we often value oral testimony, such as eyewitness accounts, above all other forms of evidence precisely because of our faith in the ability of verbal communication to reveal truth.

Watch a video about the way words influence self-identity (CD Clip 5.1).

The power of language makes understanding its ethical use particularly important. This final section of the chapter begins with a discussion of deception and gossip. It then offers several strategies for using effective and responsible forms of verbal communication.

Deception

At its most fundamental level, verbal communication involves building relationships. We tend to engage in more frequent and deeper communication with people we know, and few people will hold conversations with people they consider to be insincere or deceptive. Effective verbal communication requires trust among participants. Deception has the potential to destroy trust, so it deserves consideration here. In this section we will focus on euphemisms, doublespeak, and gossip.

Euphemisms. The features of language that make it ambiguous and changeable also make it susceptible to manipulation. As we noted, words such as "good" may be vague in their specific meaning, and other words change across time and contexts. Some people exploit these qualities and use words in purposefully ambiguous ways. One fairly benign use of ambiguity is the **euphemism,** a socially accepted word or phrase substituted for an uncomfortable or unacceptable one. Euphemisms, such as saying someone "passed away" when he or she died, serve to avoid directness and maintain social conventions of politeness. Our unwillingness to speak of death is reflected in many euphemisms. Consider, for example, that "life insurance" really insures against death and should be called "death insurance." Similarly, the use of "women's sizes" or "full-figured" to mean clothing for large women are euphemisms that attempt to avoid calling attention to physical size. Unfortunately, they also equate "women" with being large. With 40 percent of American women wearing sizes 14 to 24 (Henderson 1997), this means that the "average" American woman is sent to shop in separate clothing sections or stores that imply she is too heavy. Compare our references to female body size to the ones we use for males. We don't use euphemisms for "big and tall" men's clothing, because there is less need to be sensitive about men who are large; size is a positive sign of stature for men. Men's clothing departments are far less likely to have many items in a size "small" than those in "XXL."

euphemism
A socially accepted word or phrase substituted for an uncomfortable or unacceptable one.

Like other forms of ambiguous verbal communication, we use euphemisms to make others comfortable. Euphemisms can be misleading and have unintended consequences, but they are rarely intended to deceive. They are similar to "white lies," everyday forms of verbal deception designed to make potentially awkward social situations more comfortable. White lies, as in making up an excuse for being late to an engagement or insincerely complimenting someone's appearance, may temporarily ward off tension. However, like any form of deception, they can damage trust between communicators if discovered.

Doublespeak. **Doublespeak** occurs when we use language to intentionally obscure, confuse, *equivocate,* or deceive. Government and corporate communication provide countless examples of doublespeak. For instance, in attempts to obscure his support for new taxes, former President George Bush called the taxes "revenue enhancement" and "receipt strengthening." Other politicians have referred to ordinary sewage as "regulated organic nutrients" that "exceed the odor threshold" (Lutz, in Simon 1997). And in an ironic acknowledgment of his own deception, Lieutenant Colonel Oliver North, accused of selling arms to terrorists, described some of his testimony before Congress during the Iran-Contra scandal of the 1980s as "at variance with the truth." Doublespeak can be found in explanations as well as words or phrases. Scott Kominkieqicz (1996) noted the following statement made by a former special assistant to the president of a major U.S. trade union:

doublespeak
The use of language to intentionally obscure, confuse, equivocate, or deceive.

> It's just not accurate to believe that blacks were confined somehow to the lowest-paying jobs; rather, there was some tendency for blacks to be congregated in certain units which had a variety of characteristics including, in some instances, a somewhat lower average pay than some units where there might be a heavy concentration of white employees. (p. 24)

In the example above, the speaker uses language to obscure racial discrimination practiced by the trade union.

Doublespeak, unlike euphemisms, goes beyond politeness to mislead and confuse. Euphemisms are usually employed in an attempt to be sensitive to the listener's feelings, whereas doublespeak attempts to protect the speaker's interests. By using this form of deceptive communication, speakers can lead others to support beliefs and actions to which they might otherwise object. Detecting doublespeak can be difficult. See if you can match the everyday words for their doublespeak equivalents by taking the "Doublespeak Quiz."

Applying Communication Concepts

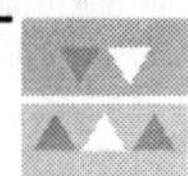

A DOUBLESPEAK QUIZ

Take the following doublespeak quiz by matching the words and phrases with their more common meanings.

1. ______ resources control package	A. greeting cards
2. ______ friendly fire	B. malpractice
3. ______ social expression products	C. failure
4. ______ safety-related occurrence	D. pencil
5. ______ ethnic cleansing	E. defoliation of forests
6. ______ incomplete success	F. accident
7. ______ downsizing personnel	G. chicken coop
8. ______ portable handheld communications inscriber	H. killing own troops
9. ______ therapeutic misadventure	I. genocide
10. ______ single-purpose agricultural structure	J. firing employees

Answers: 1-E, 2-H, 3-A, 4-F, 5-I, 6-C, 7-J, 8-D, 9-B, 10-G.

As the examples found in the box on doublespeak illustrate, deceiving others through language can happen in contexts ranging from the workplace in which an employer notifies employees of impending layoffs ("downsizing personnel") to the armed forces in which the troops commit genocide ("ethnic cleansing"). Language is also used to deceive in more personal contexts, from people betraying those who are close to them ("It wasn't really an 'affair.' We just hung out together and kissed a few times") to individuals who try to impress others by fabricating information or credentials ("Yes, I graduated summa cum laude in astrophysics"). In all of these cases, deception damages relationships and makes further communication with those who deceive difficult, if not impossible.

Gossip

gossip
Talk about an absent third party.

Like the euphemism, gossip is never wholly good or bad. Despite its negative connotations, **gossip** is merely talk about an absent third party, and can range from imparting information about other people, such as births and promotions, to the dissemination of rumors or false information. Gossip serves many important social functions. It can promote understanding of the social environment, bonding among group members, and the establishment of a group's moral codes. Sometimes people use gossip to check their perceptions about the behaviors of others with a friend or confidant. Two male friends might discuss a romantic interest in a third individual, and one of them might mention that the individual already has a partner. Or two students might talk about the grading policies of an instructor. One could have "inside" information, and tell the other that the instructor is particularly strict about grammar and editing for written assignments. In yet another example, two co-workers might share the difficulties they have working with another employee and discuss options for working together effectively. Gossip can help people acquire important information, build relationships, and evaluate the appropriateness of their actions.

One of the most significant misunderstandings about gossip is that only women and girls engage in it. Both males and females participate in gossip with similar frequency and with comparable levels of negativity (Westen 1996). Males and females do differ, however, in the subjects about which they gossip. Females are more likely to discuss relationships, whereas men's gossip often focuses on individuals at work or in the public eye. For example, talk about recent contracts for professional athletes or who is maneuvering for a raise at work, and rumors about the sexual conduct of politicians exemplify the kind of topics about which men are more likely to gossip. News of marriages and discussions of neighbors and their parenting styles are more often found in women's gossip. Although we often think of women as the sex that gossips, it is an important form of verbal communication for both sexes.

"Show me someone who never gossips, and I'll show you someone who isn't interested in people."
—Barbara Walters, newscaster

Problems from gossip arise when it is misunderstood, spreads false and malicious information, or is used to exclude people from membership in a group. Having privileged information about a third party is a form of power that can enhance status in a group. If you are the first in a circle of friends to know that an old high school classmate is engaged, your friends will probably make you the center of attention as they ask for details. Unfortunately, insecure people who want to elevate their importance are the ones most susceptible to and likely to transmit false or misleading information, partly because of their insecurity and their awareness of the power of gossip. The result is that gossip is often disseminated by those most likely to exaggerate or betray trust (Westen 1996). Gossipers who lie, spread rumors, or reveal private information about others usually do so for personal gain. It might help them forge a bond with the person to whom they are gossiping, enhance their self-esteem, or result in a personal reward. Even if the intentions of the gossiper are harmless, as in a person talking about a third party to gain advice, once gossip has been started, it can take on a life of its own through the *proverbial* grapevine.

Although gossip is a common verbal communication strategy, the potential harm it causes makes it a risky practice. Some topics of gossip, such as the intimate relationships of celebrities and public figures, the intentions of influential stockholders, and the private stories disclosed to talk show therapists are not only socially acceptable to many people, but they make up a substantial part of our entertainment industry. Even these forms of gossip carry risks. Once a statement is made, it cannot be retracted; the person sharing gossip, even with a close confidant, cannot control the life of the information once it has been shared.

Using Language Responsibly

Thus far, we have focused attention on verbal communication practices that carry with them considerable potential for harm. Although all language use has this potential, there are practical steps that can be taken to communicate verbally in effective and appropriate ways. This section asks you to consider ways to use language clearly, precisely, creatively, and with the needs of others in mind.

Qualifying Inferences

As we discussed in Chapter 4, inferences are the interpretations or conclusions we draw based on specific statements or facts. All generalizations and stereotypes are based on inferences. Two verbal communication skills, indexing and dating, help to counter the potential confusion and damage caused by some inferences.

Indexing ties evaluations to a specific circumstance to make them unique. We often need to index our statements to explain our judgments. For instance, if we say that our partner is lazy, he or she will want us to provide specific information to understand the basis on which we have made that judgment. Similarly, if we hear someone say that "kids today have no manners," we might want the speaker to index this statement by noting a particular circumstance in which this seemed to be true.

indexing
A process that ties evaluations to a specific circumstance to make them unique.

Another method of qualifying inferences is **dating,** which places observations in a specific time frame to suggest that change is possible. Although it may feel correct and appropriate to say, "Math scares me," it might be more useful and convey more information to say, "When I took math in high school, it really scared me." We often make judgments about others that we treat as *impervious* to change; dating inferences can acknowledge that people grow and change ("When I first met her, she seemed really worried about keeping her scholarship"). Both indexing and dating make verbal communication clearer, more sophisticated, and less likely to perpetuate misleading generalizations and stereotypes.

dating
A process that places observations in a specific time frame to suggest that change is possible.

Finally, inferences can be qualified by separating fact and opinion. One way of acknowledging your point of view can be to simply preface your comment with,

"In my opinion . . . ." This kind of qualifier lets listeners know that you are aware that others might disagree with you. Another way to separate fact and opinion is to be clear about the basis on which your opinions have been formed. If a friend says, "That's a really good restaurant," you might want your friend to explain why the restaurant is good. Has he eaten there or just seen the ads for it? Are the prices reasonable? Is the atmosphere exciting? Are the portions large or is the food prepared in a special way? This kind of information moves the conversation from a single opinion to a discussion and can contribute to mutual understanding between communicators.

Including Others

inclusive language
Verbal communication that demonstrates respect for others by using language that values them as individuals.

Verbal communication often establishes boundaries of identity and acceptance, implying who is acceptable and who is not. **Inclusive language** addresses this imbalance and enhances the quality of communication by demonstrating respect for others by using language that values them as individuals. Considerable research has been done on the effects of exclusive language on women; the use of generic "man" and "he" for humans or both sexes, and the suffix "-man" on the end of occupations such as fireman contribute to perceptions among girls and young women that they are not being addressed (Bate and Bowker 1997). Although substantial attention has been focused on gender, inclusive language is relevant to any person, group, or class that is seen as less than or outside the mainstream of society. Think about the following words and phrases. Can you think of ways to make them more inclusive, as has been done in two of the examples?

Oriental (Asian)	Handicapped (Disabled)
Old woman	Retarded
Man and Wife	Male nurse

There are many ways that the words listed above can be changed to be more inclusive. Most people do not wish to be called "old"; "elderly" is a more appropriate word. "Retarded" is a powerful word that disparages people and can damage self-esteem. Using "learning" or "mentally" disabled, depending on which term is more accurate, shows respect. Although the phrase "man and wife" is still common, it suggests that the man is more important in the relationship, and his spouse is defined primarily in relationship to him. The phrase "husband and wife" defines both people by their relationship to each other. Finally, "male nurse" singles out the man as someone who is performing women's work, when nursing can be done equally well by people of either sex. Referring to him as a "nurse" avoids perpetuating this stereotype.

Some people resist using inclusive language and argue that such changes are really a form of doublespeak or a waste of time. One popular argument is that people who urge the use of inclusive language are really "whiners" who are interested in promoting a political agenda. However, regardless of your politics, using inclusive language is a good idea. You probably learned at a very early age that some words were best avoided in some contexts. You probably spoke differently with your friends than you did with your parents. Similarly, you learned the appropriate way to address people depending on the context, and you probably made careful decisions about when to refer to someone by his or her first name rather than the last name. Using inclusive language merely requires this same level of awareness and effort.

People often feel left out of verbal communication not just because language is exclusive, but also because the words people use can be a way to exert power and make others feel subordinate. Effective and inclusive language can require speaking to others as more than members of groups and without recourse to specialized codes such as jargon. **Jargon** is a technical language often associated with a particular profession. Mechanics and computer technicians can use the words of the trade to mystify a vulnerable customer ("Your USB port is shot and you need a new motherboard"). Lawyers can use legal phrases to intimidate clients and witnesses in a court case.These strategies reinforce real power imbalances between communicators and threaten to undermine the trust necessary for good verbal communication. As with the use of abstractions, jargon should be used only when communicators share a common base of knowledge that makes participation equal.

jargon
A technical language often associated with a particular profession.

Practicing Civility

Speaking appropriately and effectively requires thought and effort, particularly when you have something difficult to say, or you are with others who violate your sense of appropriate behavior.We will talk more about conflict and difficult conversations in Chapter 9; even here, though, in our discussion of language, the importance of practicing civility deserves mention. As we stated at the beginning of the text, civility includes being an active participant in society and acknowledging the validity of other points of view. Practicing civility also means using language that empowers rather than disparages, builds trust rather than deceives, and helps others rather than hurts them. Civility applies in all communication contexts. Suppose a rude driver cuts in front of you. Do you hurl insults at the driver or do you let it go? If a friend disagrees with you, do you say something like,"No one with half a brain would agree with you," or are you willing to learn more about her or his position? If someone you respect uses language to degrade another person, do you remain silent or do you politely ask that some forms of language be avoided? And if a member of your company or organization doesn't want to contribute to a new program, do you label that person as uncooperative or do you look for other ways for that member to be productive?

Practicing civility also means keeping teases and taunts in check.We learn very early in life that verbal abuse gets attention; as we grow older, we see plenty of examples of teasing, bullying, and other forms of verbal attacks that seem to be rewarded. One researcher observed teenage boys playing basketball and recorded how much time they spent shooting the ball as opposed to "trash-talking"; in 20 minutes, one boy took one shot."The rest of the time, the players threw insults and epithets instead of balls as they dribbled around the court" (Taylor 1998). Hurling insults can be a form of play, but often participants ignore statements or expressions that indicate a boundary between fun and ridicule has been crossed. Deep down, most of us realize the power of words to hurt. Consider the following exchange between two students in class:

Professor: What question would you like a member of the opposite sex to answer?

Female Student: I want to know if guys are more threatened by beauty or brains.

Male Student: Oh, that's easy. If a woman's smart, it's pretty hard to make her feel stupid. She can argue with you. But it's easy to make her feel ugly. Just ask her if she's put on weight or something.

> "When we take the time to be courteous to one another, we find that we are happier and less likely to engage in nuclear war."
> —Dave Barry, humorist

We often know how to use words to hurt, even if we don't acknowledge our choice to use words that way. If you like to tease, ask yourself why you are doing it. Is it because you gain a sense of power over the other person? How does it make you feel about yourself? If you are the target of put-downs, ask yourself why you allow yourself to be spoken to in such a manner, and object to the comments.

Speaking with Cultural Sensitivity

cultural sensitivity Possessing the knowledge, awareness, and skills to communicate effectively and appropriately with diverse people.

The suggestions given here can at times feel overwhelming. In a time of changing meanings of words and a culture that thrives on charged language and exaggeration, sifting through the strategies of verbal communication to find the most effective and appropriate word choices can be a staggering task. Much of this difficulty can be surmounted, however, by demonstrating **cultural sensitivity,** which requires possessing the knowledge, awareness, and skills to communicate effectively and appropriately with diverse people. Sometimes cultural sensitivity can be demonstrated simply through the willingness to engage others in conversation. You might not know whether to refer to someone as an Asian-American or an Asian-Pacific Islander; often the best approach is to ask the other person how she or he prefers to be identified. Doing so demonstrates sensitivity and respect for others and can reduce unnecessary anxiety.

Beyond the ethical reasons for practicing cultural sensitivity are sound economic ones. Think about the skills necessary for succeeding in the workplace. If you do not take the views and values of those from other cultures into account, not only might you offend someone with whom you do business, but you might also damage working relationships. Consider this interaction: During the noon lunch hour, a receptionist at a public relations firm receives a call from the cousin of a new intern with the company. When she pages the intern, she tells him, "I'm really tired of interns getting personal calls at work. It's really a disruption from my work." The intern is likely to think that the woman is rude, it's not his problem, and maybe he should rethink his willingness to volunteer for the company. For the receptionist, cultural sensitivity might include indexing. Rather than classifying this intern as being "just like all the others," she could acknowledge that he is new and could be responding to an urgent situation. Then, a polite reminder of company policy about personal phone calls would be less condescending. For the intern, cultural sensitivity might include "dating" or recognizing the receptionist's concerns as legitimate based on her past experience with interns from cultures other than her own.

Cultural sensitivity goes beyond indexing, dating, and inclusive language to include the willingness and desire to accommodate and respect the needs and perspectives of others. Sometimes this can appear to be a form of *moral relativism,* in which all perspectives and needs have equal merit. Being culturally sensitive, however, does not mean that you must abandon all of your core beliefs and values. Rather, it requires you to suspend judgment of others and use communication strategies that enable you to build trust and understanding. The skills presented here are a start in building this common ground.

Verbal communication can sometimes seem like a minefield, ready to destroy relationships when used in naive, careless, or malicious ways. However, verbal communication also has the potential to build common bonds, redefine identities, and shape the world. Appreciation for the way words shape our lives and the power and possibilities of language is the first step in becoming a capable, discerning, and responsible communicator.

Resources for Review and Skill Building

Many of these resources are supported by the Connections CD-ROM and free Online Learning Center website.

SUMMARY

This summary is organized around the questions found at the beginning of the chapter. See if you can answer them before reading the summary paragraphs.

1. What are the fundamental properties of words?

   Words are symbolic because they allow us to talk about things without being the things themselves. This symbolic quality allows us to use language to create new meaning, share knowledge, remember the past, and imagine the future. Words are also arbitrary in that they have no direct connection to the things they represent, and they are ambiguous because they are open to interpretation. The meanings of words also change over time and place.

2. How do words imply actions and attitudes?

   Language is never neutral; words have the ability to influence our thoughts and actions. Although the conventional meanings of words can be changed, words carry with them the weight of the culture, so we cannot always escape the attitudes that are embedded in our words.

3. How do words influence thoughts?

   According to the linguistic relativity hypothesis, our thoughts are influenced by the words that we know and the patterns of language that are dominant in our culture. The wider our vocabulary, the broader and deeper our range of thinking, because we see the world based on the words we have to think about it.

4. Why is it important to understand different levels of meaning in words?

   Words have both denotative and connotative levels of meaning. Although many words have relatively simple denotative meanings, some words can also be abstract and complex. The more connotative a word becomes, the more important it is to understand the values associated with the word, because we often forget that the meaning of the word might not be shared.

5. What roles do codes play in verbal communication?

   Codes establish rules or norms that guide our use of language, depending on the context in which verbal communication takes place and the culture of the communicators. Codes regulate private conversations and public performances, and they help us interpret the meaning of words. They also help create and reinforce boundaries among groups. Codes can be intentionally broken, but it is usually risky to do so.

6. How can language be used responsibly?

   Effective communication depends on trust. Some forms of deception, such as euphemisms, are intended to help rather than harm others, but most forms, such as lying and using doublespeak, violate the trust necessary for building relationships. Other means of building trust and credibility through verbal communication include qualifying inferences, using inclusive language, practicing civility, and speaking with cultural sensitivity.

KEY TERMS

Test your understanding of these key terms by visiting the Connections CD-ROM and the Online Learning Center website at www.mhhe.com/dobkinpace.

abstract 130
ambiguous 124
arbitrary 124
argot 135
changeable 124
code 131
code-switching 136
concrete 129
connotation 130
cultural sensitivity 144
dating 141
denotation 129
doublespeak 139
euphemism 138
gossip 140
inclusive language 142
indexing 141
jargon 143
linguistic relativity hypothesis 127
reference groups 134
symbolic 123
taboos 136
verbal language 122

FOR FURTHER REFLECTION

Join a conversation about chapter concepts by visiting the Online Learning Center website at www.mhhe.com/dobkinpace

1. Popular media such as television, film, and advertisements sometimes break codes for creative or commercial effects. Consider the following case:

   In August 1995, Calvin Klein, Inc. halted an advertising campaign that critics claimed imitated "kiddie porn." Voice-overs, camera angles, and suggestive language met outrage from media analysts and the American Family Association, which charged the ads approached child pornography. . . .

   One television ad showed a young man standing before the camera with a male voice-over, "You got a real nice look. How old are you? Are you strong? You think you could rip that shirt off of you? That's a nice body. You work out? I can tell."

   In response to the outrage of critics, Calvin Klein officials said the ads were designed to convey a "positive message" that "young people today . . . have a real strength of character and independence" and that the company was "taken aback" by the association with child pornography. Spokesmen also denied that the ads were designed to generate the kind of controversy that would quickly bring vast publicity—free media exposure—to Calvin Klein and the company's products (Folkerts 1996).

   - Was it a good idea for Calvin Klein to break a code?
   - Think about advertisements, movies, or books that break conventions and force you to think about words, symbols, and stories in different ways. Does breaking codes usually constitute a violation of ethics?

2. Think about a co-culture to which you belong.
   - Can you identify the argot and code for that co-culture?
   - Do you switch the code when a new person enters the group?

3. Think about words like "blackmail" and "black magic," and contrast them with words such as "white magic" and "white lie." Our language tends to associate negative images with blackness, and positive ones with whiteness. How does our language sometimes help perpetuate racism, sexism, and other forms of intolerance?

BUILDING COMMUNICATION SKILLS

1. Examine the headlines of your local newspaper. What attitudes are reflected in the headlines? Who is given responsibility for problems and crises?
2. Listen to a close friend, family member, or roommate who answers the phone. Can you tell who the person is talking to by the code he or she uses? In what ways does your verbal communication change when speaking with someone to whom you are attracted?

NET WORK

Note: While all of the URLs listed were current as of the printing of this book, the sites often change. Please check out our website www.mhhe.com/dobkinpace for updates and hyperlinks to these exercises.

1. For a further look at language and verbal communication, see the website, "Happy Fun Communication Land": http://www.rdillman.com/HFCL/TUTOR/tutor0.html. Under the tutorial, "Signs and Language," there is an excellent explanation of the relationship between words and meaning.
2. The website for Random House Webster's College Dictionary outlines a system for determining the "offensiveness quotient" for words (http://www.randomhouse.com/words/language). Terms are ranked based on the initiator (does the person who uses the word intend to be hurtful?) and the interpreter (is the person being described offended?). For instance, using "guy" to refer to a woman is rarely taken as offensive, whereas using "baby" is likely to offend her. Check the list to see if you might be using terms that offend others, even if that is not your intent.

MEDIA MOMENTS

Many popular films explore the struggles of individuals trying to negotiate between their co-cultures and the dominant culture. Others explore the power of language, particularly in the classroom, the courtroom, and in the political arena. One film that captures both the power of language and the ethical challenges of breaking codes and code switching is Spike Lee's *Malcolm X* (1992, starring Denzel Washington, Angela Bassett, Albert Hall, S. Albert Freeman, Sr.). Consider watching this film and think about how it addresses the following questions:

- How was the young Malcolm Little labeled based on his race? What language was used to describe him and how did it shape his identity?
- How did Malcolm X's preaching reflect the codes of a co-culture? How were his words interpreted by the dominant culture?
- What word choices did Malcolm X make to convey his message? Was he effective? Did he use language responsibly?

Appreciating and Using Nonverbal Communication

CHAPTER 6

QUESTIONS TO FOCUS YOUR READING

1. What basic characteristics distinguish nonverbal from verbal communication?
2. What are the functions of nonverbal communication?
3. What are some ways we use our eyes and face to communicate?
4. How do we use gestures to communicate with others?
5. How do we use personal space to communicate nonverbally?
6. What messages do we communicate through touch?
7. How do we use our voice to communicate nonverbally?
8. What are some ways we communicate through the use of smell, time, and objects?

Roberto, a young American Peace Corps volunteer, approached a Kikuyu farmer in the coffee-growing region of Kenya. The farmer smiled broadly and embraced him in a friendly greeting. The Peace Corps worker smiled and returned the greeting. He wanted to talk to the farmer about a water purification project that the Peace Corps was working on, but he noticed that the farmer was dressed in clean clothes and walking in the general direction of the town. He assumed that the farmer was on an important errand, since the hard-working Kikuyu rarely ventured from their fields. Roberto concluded that this would not be a good time to talk. A look of frustration showed momentarily on the American's face, and the farmer sensed his disappointment. "Is anything wrong?" the farmer inquired. Roberto replied haltingly in the Kikuyu language, "I wanted to talk about our project, but I see you are busy." The farmer laughed. "Coffee farmers are always busy. Tomorrow I will gladly talk with you." As the farmer said the word "gladly," his eyes looked directly into the face of the American, he smiled once more, and opened his arms in an inviting gesture. "What time should we meet tomorrow?" asked Roberto as he pointed at his watch. Again the farmer laughed as he displayed his arm to remind the American that he wore no watch. "We will meet when the sun is there," said the farmer. As he spoke the word for "there," he pointed to the sky about three quarters of the way up the horizon, and off he went to town. This time Roberto laughed. Pointing at the sky was too imprecise for his own "to the second" American view of time, and he knew that tomorrow he would be standing in the field for over an hour waiting for the sun to be "there," unsure exactly when the farmer would arrive. But arrive he would—smiling, friendly, and eager to listen.

Perhaps, like the American Peace Corps worker, you have found yourself in a different culture with only limited ability to communicate verbally. If so, you may remember relying on nonverbal gestures, facial expressions, and body movements to communicate. Most of the communication between the Kikuyu coffee farmer and Roberto occurred without words. Smiles, a friendly embrace, the manner of dress, looks of disappointment and reassurance, pointing at a watch, and tone of voice all helped the young Peace Corps worker and the Kikuyu farmer overcome a language barrier.

You do not need to be in a different culture to appreciate the importance of nonverbal communication. Much of the meaning in our daily communication comes from nonverbal behaviors, or cues, such as hand gestures, eye contact, styles of dress, and voice inflections. Many communication scholars are convinced that nonverbal messages account for much, if not most, of the meaning in our daily interaction with others (Knapp and Hall 1997). Whatever the context, familiar or new, understanding nonverbal cues can help you become a more effective communicator. After reading this chapter, you should be able to:

- Understand the basic characteristics of nonverbal communication.
- Distinguish several functions of nonverbal communication.
- Identify communicative effects of specific nonverbal cues.
- Use nonverbal cues responsibly.

Basic Characteristics of Nonverbal Communication

It seems like something of a *paradox* to describe nonverbal communication using words when the very essence of the subject is outside the realm of words. The study of nonverbal communication is full of such contradictions. For instance, we use some nonverbal gestures spontaneously and without much thought, such as yawning to indicate we are tired. Others are carefully planned and carried out, such as a first kiss on a date or a firm handshake in a job interview. Some nonverbal gestures are instantly recognizable to many people, like the wave of a hand goodbye or tears of sadness. On the other hand, some gestures are very individualistic or specific to a particular culture or relationship, such as the Kikuyu gesture for time. Some nonverbal gestures clearly reveal our feelings, such as laughter when we are happy or shaky hands when we are nervous. Other gestures, however, conceal our feelings to protect us from the scrutiny of others, such as a "stoic face" when we are hurt or a "straight face" when we are lying. In short, nonverbal communication can be spontaneous or carefully crafted, universal or context specific, and truthful or deceptive. Many of these apparent contradictions stem from the broad range of nonverbal behaviors available to us. Nonverbal communication includes such diverse ways of communicating as gestures, eye contact, tone of voice, touch, and smell. Although each of these cues is distinctly different, they share some common characteristics that generally distinguish nonverbal communication from verbal interactions (Anderson 2008).

"We will try to persuade with our words, but if our words fail, we will try to persuade with our acts."

—Martin Luther King, Jr.

Nonverbal Communication Is Not Language

The academic study of nonverbal communication first flourished in the late 1960s and early 1970s. Experts from fields such as psychology, sociology, and anthropology, as well as communication, realized that this important and powerful aspect of human interaction was largely unstudied. Since that time, a tremendous amount of research has been conducted about many different aspects of nonverbal communication. Much of this research is sophisticated, important, and useful. Unfortunately, one persistent holdover from those early days is the popular term "body language." Before you enrolled in your communication course, you may have thought "nonverbal communication" and "body language" were interchangeable terms.

Most communication experts view body language as a *misnomer* for two reasons. First, the word "body" is too narrow to describe accurately the wide variety of nonverbal cues available to us. For example, the term "body language" would exclude the use of objects, like the car you drive or the clothes you wear, to communicate. Second, nonverbal communication is not a language (Dunn 1998). You may remember that in Chapter 1 we defined **nonverbal communication** as messages expressed through symbols other than words or as **nonlinguistic** or outside of language. Simply put, verbal communication is composed of words; nonverbal communication consists of nonwords. Verbal messages have different structures than nonverbal messages. For instance, they have a prescribed word order, called *syntax,* whereas nonverbal messages do not. Suppose you are surprised by a good grade on a test. Surprise is often communicated through facial expressions such as raised eyebrows, eyes opened wide, jaw dropped, and lips parted (Ekman and Friesen 1975). The order in which these facial gestures occur does not matter; all three will probably occur simultaneously. On the other hand, word order is essential to verbal messages. Consider the difference in meaning between these two statements when the word order is changed: "I am surprised." "Am I surprised?" Languages also use word forms to distinguish tense, number (singular/plural), and masculine/feminine. Nonverbal messages do not change by tense or number—there is no past tense of a smile or plural version of eye contact. These structural differences help distinguish verbal from nonverbal messages.

nonverbal communication
Messages expressed through symbols other than words.

nonlinguistic
A characteristic of nonverbal communication indicating that nonverbal messages are outside languages.

The nonlinguistic nature of nonverbal communication makes nonverbal messages more general and often less precise than verbal symbols. For example, think back to your look of surprise at the unexpectedly high test score. People who saw your facial expressions would know that you were surprised, but they might not know what preceded the emotion (This is the first good thing to happen to me today), why you were surprised (This is my highest grade in this class), or what you plan to do next (celebrate!). Most likely you would provide much of that information in words accompanying your facial expressions. Still, nonverbal messages are a powerful means of communication that often have more impact on communicators than words.

"Emotion constantly finds expression in bodily position."
—Mabel Elsworth Todd, dancer, educator, author

Nonverbal Communication Is Often Linked to Our Emotions

intrinsic
A characteristic of nonverbal communication indicating that nonverbal messages are inherently connected to our emotions and mental states.

When you feel angry or confused, your face reflects your emotional state. Much nonverbal communication is **intrinsic**, or inherently connected to our inner feelings or emotions (Tracy and Matsumoto 2008). Facial expressions, hand movements, and actions often spring naturally and spontaneously from thoughts and feelings. If friends are feeling sad or distressed, you might hug them spontaneously or put a hand on their shoulders in an attempt to provide comfort. When you are nervous, you might squirm in your seat, absent-mindedly scratch your face, or tug at your hair. If you are late for an appointment, you are likely to look at your watch and walk or drive quickly to your destination. Or, if you are speaking to a friend about your golf game, you might *pantomime* a golf swing as you describe a memorable shot.

The intrinsic nature of nonverbal cues leads us to perceive them as more truthful or genuine than verbal communication. When a nonverbal message contradicts a verbal message, we almost always believe the nonverbal one. For example, suppose your mother looks worried and downcast—she is frowning with her head bowed and shoulders hunched. Concerned, you ask her if she is feeling OK and she responds, "Yes, I am fine." It is unlikely that you would believe your mother's verbal response. Instead you would probably conclude that she is troubled by something and doesn't want to burden you with her problems.

The intrinsic nature of nonverbal messages also makes some of them more universal than verbal messages (Castellano et al. 2007). Languages vary from culture to culture, but certain nonverbal expressions appear to transcend cultures. In pioneering research, Paul Ekman and Wallace Friesen (1975) discovered that certain facial expressions were virtually universal across cultures. Most of these expressions were associated with basic human emotions. The researchers discovered that in countries as diverse as Japan, Papua New Guinea, Brazil, Chile, and the United States, facial expressions of surprise, fear, disgust, anger, happiness, and sadness were remarkably identical. Some hand gestures, such as waving hello or goodbye, and some gestures of insult also have the same meaning in many different cultures. In almost all cultures, material possessions communicate wealth and privilege, and hugs and kisses are viewed as gestures of affection. At the same time, however, many nonverbal cues differ from culture to culture. In our opening example, the young American had a very different concept of time than did the Kenyan. These differences result because many nonverbal messages are specific to the culture or the particular situation in which they occur.

Nonverbal Communication Is Highly Contextual

Nonverbal messages often get their precise meaning from the communication context. Suppose you fold your arms across your chest. The meaning of this gesture depends on the situation. If you are listening to a sermon, your gesture might be a sign of reverence. If you are outside on a chilly evening, your gesture might reflect your feeling cold. Or, if you are at a social gathering, your gesture might be an attempt to close yourself off from the approaches of others. To understand the meaning of your gesture, someone observing you would need to understand the context.

Nonverbal expressions of grief transcend cultures.

© Jeff Greenberg/PhotoEdit

One important contextual cue for nonverbal communicators is the nature of their relationship. Nonverbal cues are especially effective for communicating *affective* or emotional messages. Often, when we cannot accurately describe our emotions with words, our nonverbal behavior conveys our mood and feelings. For instance, at a funeral we might not know what to say to the family of the deceased. We want to comfort the bereaved, but words seem inadequate. Instead, we rely on nonverbal actions. We may hug them, pat them gently on the back, put an arm around their shoulders, wipe away their tears, or use other gestures that show support and caring (Angell 1998). Most important relational messages, such as those intended to convey intimacy, support, love, and inclusion, are communicated primarily through nonverbal behavior. Similarly, messages that indicate that a relationship is in trouble or about to end are communicated nonverbally. Most people in long-term relationships know when their partner is angry not so much by what is said but through facial expressions, tone of voice, body posture, and gestures.

Some relationships are also characterized by the use of nonverbal communication to exert power or control over others. Research has shown that people communicate dominance over others in one of several ways:

- Touching them more than they are allowed to touch back.
- Initiating and ending conversations.
- Borrowing possessions without permission.
- Smiling less and frowning or scowling more than the other person.
- Interrupting others as they speak but ignoring their attempts to interrupt you.
- Using less frequent but more direct eye contact.
- Talking more in conversations than the other person.
- Initiating and ending periods of silence.
- Using a louder voice and more angry tones and inflections than the other person (Edesu and Burgoon 1996).

Think about a situation in which you have used one or more of these nonverbal cues. What effect did you intend to have? How did your behavior influence further communication with the other person? The use of nonverbal cues to exert power and control stifles both verbal and nonverbal communication and inhibits the development of healthy relationships.

Nonverbal Communication Is Influenced by Culture and Gender

The way we use and understand nonverbal messages is also dependent on our cultural knowledge and values (Marsh et al. 2010). Various cultures and co-cultures use different repertoires of nonverbal cues, just as different languages use different sounds. For instance, some cultures use eyebrow movement for specific meanings such as hello (many Asian cultures) or no (Turkish) while other cultures use eyebrow movement more generally to emphasize an emotion (European American). In Thailand there is a rather precise code of nonverbal appropriateness that would seem unusual to Americans. Thai students, for instance, sit with their feet flat on the floor because it would be insulting to show the soles of their shoes to another person. It would also be disrespectful for Thai students to place textbooks on the floor or pass anything over the head of another student. American students, by contrast, often cross their legs or prop up their feet in class, displaying the soles of their shoes for everyone to see. They also place books on the floor and pass handouts over the heads of other students. Gestures deemed insensitive in Thailand go unnoticed in the United States.

We often turn to cultural expectations to interpret nonverbal messages, but because expectations vary among cultures and co-cultures, we sometimes misunderstand the message. Below are a few examples of communication problems arising from different cultural interpretations of nonverbal cues.

- European Americans tend to make direct eye contact when listening in a conversation. African and Asian Americans (who often prefer indirect eye contact as a sign of deference and respect) sometimes find such direct eye contact invasive and confrontational. Conversely, European Americans interpret indirect eye contact as a sign of inattention (LaFrance and Mayo 1976).
- Latin Americans tend to touch more in social conversation than European Americans who find such touch invasive and overly friendly. Latinos, on the other hand, find European Americans somewhat "cold" when they step back to avoid social touch (Lustig and Koester 1999).
- Hawaiian students tend to look down to the floor in a classroom setting as a sign of respect for the authority of the teacher. When these students study in the mainland United States, their professors sometimes interpret such behavior as being unprepared or reluctant to participate (Mercer 1994).
- Vietnamese Americans are traditionally reserved about the expression of emotion. They see the external expression of emotion as undignified. A Vietnamese boss who is pleased with a co-worker will not usually smile or express satisfaction. Western European workers might mistake this stoic expression for arrogance or displeasure.

The potential for misunderstanding nonverbal messages makes knowing about the expectations of other cultures particularly important.

Like people from different cultures or co-cultures, men and women sometimes use different nonverbal cues. For instance, men are more likely to display anger in response to jealousy or infidelity, whereas women often respond with expres-

Exploring Communication Concepts

GENDER DIFFERENCES IN NONVERBAL COMMUNICATION

In his review of research, Anderson (2008) discovered that there are more similarities than differences between men and women in their use of nonverbal cues. However, he also discovered that research over many years does point to consistent differences in the way men and women communicate nonverbally. Below is a sample of these differences:

Attentiveness. Women tend to notice nonverbal cues more than men. Research indicates that women are often more sensitive and accurate interpreters of nonverbal behavior. Women also tend to use nonverbal gestures more frequently than men, especially to convey positive messages of support and caring.

Interpersonal Distance. Women usually stand closer together in conversation. Women also stand more closely to each other than men do when they are talking with other men. When men and women talk together, the men adopt the closer distance of women. Men tend to use more space when they work, relax, sit, or stand, whether by themselves or with others.

Voice. Men usually speak more loudly than women. They also use more vocal pauses, such as "um" and "ah," than women. Women are more likely to vary their voices and end sentences in a raised pitch.

Facial Expressions and Gestures. Women tend to be more expressive than men, revealing their emotions more accurately and often. Happiness is more likely to produce smiles in women than men, but women are less likely than men to display anger when mad. Women are more likely to notice and remember specific facial characteristics than men, whereas men are more likely to fidget with their hands and feet. Women gesture more often than men, but men use larger gestures.

Eye Contact. Women usually make and sustain eye contact more than men. Women in conversation have the most eye contact, and men talking together typically have the least.

Touch. Men are more likely to initiate touching behaviors in casual dating relationships, but women initiate touching behaviors more often in marital or other intimate relationships. In long-term heterosexual relationships, partners appear to initiate touch about the same number of times.

ASK YOURSELF:

1. How do you differ from the general tendencies listed above?
2. How are you similar?
3. Why do you think men generally make less eye contact than women?
4. What are some possible reasons that men use more space than women?

sions of sadness (Bank and Hupka 1996; Pines and Friedman 1998). Many communication problems between men and women come from different uses and interpretations of nonverbal cues. The "Exploring Communication Concepts" box on gender differences in nonverbal communication further explores this cultural influence on nonverbal messages.

Nonverbal Communication Is Continuous

Nonverbal messages flow in **continuous,** or steady, streams of cues rather than individual, distinct bits of information. Verbal communication is somewhat less

continuous
A characteristic of nonverbal communication that indicates that nonverbal messages are streams of cues.

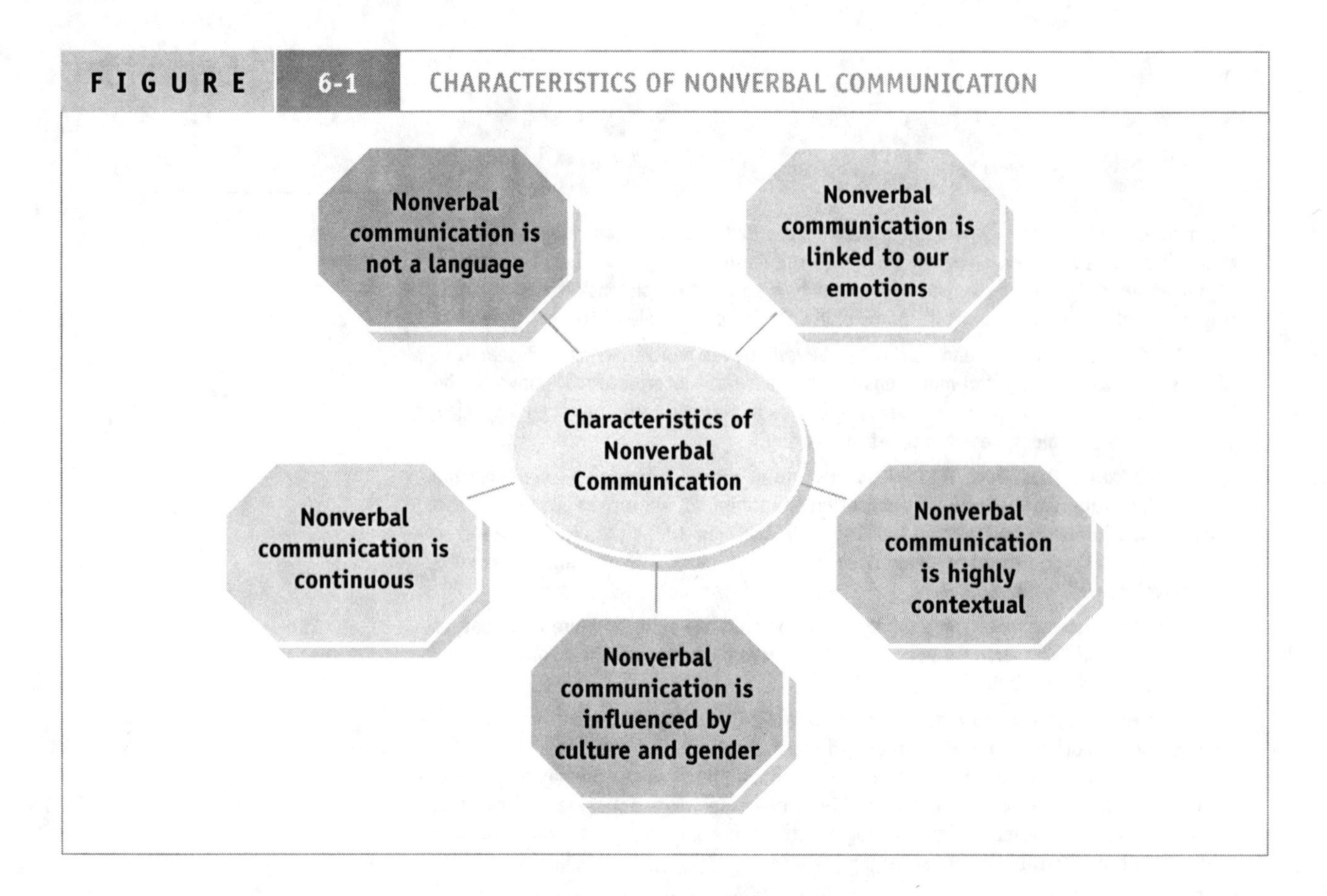

continuous and can be divided into discrete parts such as individual words, syllables, and sounds. Instead of being divided into words or sentences, nonverbal messages are often combinations of several cues displayed *simultaneously*. Consider the following example: Suppose your supervisor is interviewing you for a possible promotion. During the interview, you can use many different nonverbal cues simultaneously to impress your employer. A firm handshake, direct eye contact, professional appearance, promptness, and a confident smile all communicate competence at the same time. This ability to use many nonverbal cues in a continuous stream of messages is one reason that nonverbal communication is so powerful.

Functions of Nonverbal Communication

Nonverbal communication functions in a variety of ways that are closely related to the verbal communication that is taking place at the same time. Researchers have identified six ways that verbal and nonverbal communication are interrelated (Knapp and Hall 1997). Nonverbal communication can accent, complement, contradict, regulate, repeat, or substitute for verbal communication.

accent
A nonverbal function that highlights, accentuates, or emphasizes verbal messages.

Accenting Verbal Communication

Nonverbal cues **accent** verbal communication when they highlight, accentuate, emphasize, or draw attention to phrases or words. Your voice accents much of your communication. If you want to emphasize a particular word, you might increase the volume and inflection to make it stand out in the sentence. For example, you might say of a friend, "She is *SO* funny." Your emphasis on "so" indicates that your friend is beyond "average" funny, and is "extraordinarily" funny. Similarly, other nonverbal cues heighten our verbal interactions. Suppose that you want to tell someone a secret. Verbally, you might say, "I have a secret to tell you." At the same time, you emphasize the confidential nature of the message by lowering your voice, glancing over your shoulder to see if anyone else is listening, standing closely, or maybe even touching a finger to your lips in a gesture of silence.

Complementing Verbal Communication

Nonverbal cues **complement** verbal communication when they augment or add meaning to the interaction. Suppose that you are talking to someone about a recent accident and say, "I got a bruise right here," while pointing at a mark on your bicep. Without the accompanying nonverbal gestures, the listener would not know the exact location of your injury. By complementing verbal communication, nonverbal gestures reduce much ambiguity in our language. Pointing, as did the person with the bruise, is often a complementary gesture that clarifies meaning. A professor might point at a student while saying, "Will you help me?" You might tell a delivery person, "Put the package there," while pointing at a table, or you might say to your roommate, "Pass me that," while pointing to a coffee mug.

complement
A nonverbal function that adds meaning to verbal messages.

Other nonverbal gestures are complementary as well. Your tone of voice can augment meaning. The meaning of sarcastic comments, for example, is conveyed almost entirely in the nonverbal cues that accompany the statement. The statement, "That was really smart," might be a genuine compliment or an insult about somebody's intelligence depending on your tone of voice. Similarly, your tone of voice tells others if you are kidding around or are serious. Suppose a friend asks to borrow your car and you respond, "Sure, if you have twenty dollars." If you say the line with little intonation, your friend may not understand your intent and may even ask, "Are you kidding?" But you can send a clearer message by saying the line in jest, with great exasperation accompanied by a smile. In hundreds of ways each day, we clarify our words with such nonverbal complements.

Contradicting Verbal Communication

Nonverbal messages **contradict** when they oppose, deny, or disagree with verbal messages. Contradictions can be confusing for communicators. For instance, if a male friend tells you that he is "carefree" or "laid-back" but always wears a starched and pressed dress shirt to class, you might begin to wonder which message is accurate. Although these contradictory messages can be confusing, we often believe the nonverbal message over the verbal one. For instance, in the previous example, you would likely believe that your well-dressed friend was not as carefree as he claims.

contradict
A nonverbal function that opposes, denies, or disagrees with a verbal message.

Even when we attempt to mask or hide emotions, our nonverbal behavior often gives us away. Nonverbal experts call this contradiction **"leakage"** (Talwar and Lee 2002). Leakage often "gives us away" when we are lying. Usually at least one of our nonverbal cues will signal anxiety or nervousness when we try to deceive someone. But not all contradictions are calculated lies. Sometimes, the contradiction accurately communicates our confused emotions. Public speakers might say they are not nervous, but their shaky hands and cracking voices reveal apprehension. Accident victims in shock say that they are feeling fine without realizing that the trauma they have experienced is revealed in their facial expressions.

leakage
A nonverbal cue that reveals emotions we are trying to conceal.

Regulating Verbal Communication

regulate
A function of nonverbal communication that controls, adjusts, or alters the flow of verbal messages.

We use nonverbal cues to **regulate** verbal messages by controlling, adjusting, or altering the flow of interaction. Nonverbal gestures can open or close channels of communication, signal whose turn it is to talk, encourage someone to talk more, or discourage someone from talking as much. For example, one researcher observed students at a university library approaching the reference desk for help. The researcher wanted to find out if the nonverbal actions of the librarian discouraged students from asking a question. Her observations confirmed the importance of nonverbal communication in regulating verbal interactions. If the librarian made eye contact or smiled, the student usually approached the desk and asked a question. On the other hand, if the librarian was on the phone, using the computer, or conversing with someone else, the student usually did not approach the desk (Radford 1998). In this way, nonverbal cues serve as traffic signs during verbal interactions, telling us when to stop, go, yield, and merge.

Repeating Verbal Communication

repeat
A function of nonverbal communication that reiterates verbal messages.

When we replicate or reiterate verbal messages with nonverbal gestures, we **repeat** our communication. For example, when you give directions, you probably repeat your verbal instructions with hand gestures. You might say, "Go north two blocks and turn right," at the same time you point north and mimic a right turn with your hand. This act of repetition has communicative value. Researchers have long understood the importance of redundancy in oral communication because repeating a message helps listeners better comprehend the information. Reading teachers use this principle when instructing young children. As they say a vowel sound, they exaggerate the sound with their mouth and use a hand gesture to reinforce the meaning. For instance, they might teach the long "o" sound by saying, "Boooooat," forming their mouth in an exaggerated O, and tracing the outline of their mouth with the index finger. Students learn to associate a particular sound with the mouth formation and hand gesture. Such techniques accelerate the learning process.

Redundancy can also add intensity to a message. For example, some counselors mirror messages as they listen to patients. If the patient leans forward, the counselor leans forward; if the patient looks distressed, the counselor subtly mirrors the same facial and hand gestures. While such behavior may seem contrived, research shows that these messages of reinforcement actually increase feelings of empathy and trust in a therapeutic relationship (Sandhu and Reeves 1993). Similarly, intimacy in relationships is often communicated through mirroring, such as using similar hand gestures and facial expressions as people converse. Although communicators may not be aware of these behaviors, nonverbal reinforcement of verbal messages increases feelings of intimacy (Ebesu and Burgoon 1996).

Substituting for Verbal Communication

substitute
A function of nonverbal communication that takes the place of verbal messages.

Nonverbal gestures **substitute** for verbal messages when they take the place of or replace verbal words or phrases. Sending roses to say "I love you" or waving goodbye are just two gestures that most people would recognize without verbal confirmation. Strong emotions are often difficult to talk about; instead, we allow our nonverbal messages to tell others how we feel. For instance, we rarely need to tell others that we are embarrassed. We might blush, laugh or giggle nervously, blink excessively, swallow rapidly, and touch our face more than normal (Cuvelier 2002).

Objects or pictures can also substitute for verbal communication. Some office workers use a series of colored blocks, called Protoblocs, to indicate their avail-

FIGURE 6-2 INTERNATIONAL ROAD SIGNS

Because nonverbal signs are more universal than verbal languages, countries often substitute pictures for words on traffic signs. Can you understand the following international road signs? Which ones are more difficult or unclear? Why? Do you need some context (where and when the sign is posted) to understand the pictures?

Answers: side wind, trucks with trailers prohibited, traffic jam, painting in progress, vehicles transporting explosives prohibited, quay or river bank, unsteady materials on the road, children near roadway, and tramway crossing.

ability. They place these blocks on a cubicle wall or desk where co-workers can see them. Each block has a specific meaning. A red cube means "Do not interrupt me under any circumstance"; a green pyramid means "I am available to talk with you"; and the yellow sphere means "Caution, talk to me if it is important" (Koudsi 1999). Like these office symbols, we use signs to regulate behavior such as the flow of traffic. Some of these signs are verbal, like the word "STOP." Other signs rely on pictures or symbols to convey their meaning (see Figure 6-2). Communicators chatting online, emailing, or texting have developed their own nonverbal cues that substitute for verbal expressions. Like road signs, these symbols and

Applying Communication Concepts

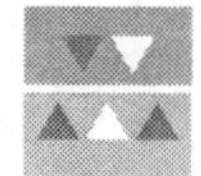

TEXTING SYMBOLS AND ABBREVIATIONS

Communicators often use symbols or abbreviations as a shortcut to full words when emailing or texting.

As we mentioned in Chapter 1, texting and emailing are somewhat lean media that eliminate many of the nonverbal cues found in face-to-face conversations. Symbols and abbreviations can compensate for the absence of such cues by simulating voice inflection or facial expressions. These symbols and abbreviations can enhance the conversational quality of texting and add nonverbal meanings to an otherwise verbal media. Specific symbols come in and out of vogue and new forms are constantly emerging. Also, different groups use variations on basic symbols. Use the symbols carefully and understand your audience. While your friends may appreciate your abbreviations in a text message, your professor is likely to disapprove of them in a term paper.

Here are a few symbols and their meanings that you have probably used in your own communication.

:)	User is happy	:-(	User is frowning (sad)
cm	Call me	cul	Call you later
g2g	Got to Go	jw	Just wondering
:-O	User is surprised	;-)	User is winking
wu	Whats up	:-(O)	User is yelling
btw	By the way	QSPA?	Que Pasa?

ASK YOURSELF:

1. How can using symbols and abbreviations in texting prevent miscommunication?
2. How might they create misunderstandings?
3. Why do some people dislike symbols and abbreviations?
4. Are texting abbreviations nonverbal or verbal symbols? Are they both?

abbreviations are widely understood by users. The "Applying Communication Concepts" box on texting symbols and abbreviations describes some of these communicating conventions.

Types of Nonverbal Communication

kinesics
The use of body motion to communicate nonverbally.

Nonverbal communication takes many forms. Whether it is giving a look to our partner when he or she makes a rude comment or spreading our arms in a spontaneous welcome when our partner walks into the room, many of our nonverbal behaviors employ **kinesics,** the use of body motion to communicate nonverbally. There are other means of nonverbal communication as well. The smell of a hayloft, the swiftness of your response to a question, the tone of a voice, and the kind of posters that cover the walls of your room all convey a message. This section looks at the various ways nonverbal communication occurs. It begins with one of the most powerful forms of nonverbal communication: facial expressions.

"Your expression is the most important thing you can wear."
—Sid Ascher, author

Facial Expressions

Most nonverbal experts believe that your face is the richest source of nonverbal cues. Ekman and Friesen (1975) divided the face into three parts that are capable of independent movement: (1) the top region including the brow and forehead; (2) the middle region including eyes, eyelids, and nasal passage; and (3) the lower face including the mouth, rest of the nose, cheeks, and chin. Each of these areas can act alone or in concert with the other two regions, providing great variety and subtlety to facial expression. For example, Ekman and Friesen described disgust as follows: "The upper lip is raised, while the lower lip may be raised or lowered; the nose is wrinkled; the lower eyelids are pushed up, and the eyebrow is lowered" (p. 68). Your face, however, can communicate subtle differences in the standard "disgust" gesture including the intensity of the emotion. If you were only mildly disgusted, for example, you would wrinkle your nose less and raise the upper lip only slightly. You often display two or more emotions on the face simultaneously. For example, if you felt contempt as well as disgust, you would likely press your lips together instead of apart. Expressions of disgust, contempt, and anger often blend together to reflect a remarkable range of emotion.

We often try to control or mask our facial reactions to strong emotions by conforming to social norms called display rules. **Display rules** are cultural expectations about the public display of emotions (Ekman 1997). We cannot help feeling the way we feel, but we can sometimes control our reactions to those feelings. Anderson (2008) identified five general display rules that help us manage and control our facial communication:

display rules
Cultural expectations about the public display of emotions.

1. *Simulation* is displaying an emotion that you do not feel. For example, you might look interested in a film or a play that your date is enjoying even though you are really feeling ambivalent about the story.
2. *Intensification* is displaying more emotion than you feel. You might act more interested in your mother's profession than you really are because you know it is important to her—your display matches her expectation.
3. *Neutralization* is often called a "poker face" and is used to conceal something or protect privacy. In business negotiations, neutralization is often employed to protect your interests and to keep others from taking advantage of you.
4. *Miniaturization* refers to the display of less emotion than you are experiencing. For instance, you might appear less excited about your big raise at work when talking with a co-worker who received a smaller increase.
5. Finally, *masking* is displaying the emotion opposite to the one you are feeling. For example, you might act nonchalant during a job interview even though you are very nervous or you might act interested in your professor's lecture even though you are very bored.

Eye Contact

Your eyes communicate a variety of emotions. You roll your eyes to indicate disgust or disapproval, bat your eyes flirtatiously to signal your attraction to someone, close your eyes as a sign of reverence, or wink at someone to indicate that

Think It Over

TELEVISION AND DISPLAY RULES

You have probably noticed that people act differently when they are on television than they do offscreen. For instance, at sporting events fans sometimes become more animated, shout more loudly, and gesture more wildly when the camera is pointed at them than they do when the camera is not. Why?

Do we have norms about the display of emotion on television?
How should news reporters react on camera to dangerous or tragic situations?
How do celebrities, talk show guests, demonstrators, athletes, eyewitnesses to a crime, or people in the background of news reports act when a camera is pointed at them?
How do we learn these display rules?

you are talking in jest or kidding around. Eye contact, or how long you gaze or look at someone, is an especially powerful communication tool. Researchers estimate that in the United States, the average listener in a conversation looks at the person talking about 60 to 75 percent of the time while the speaker looks at the listener about 40 percent of the interaction. Mutual gaze can last from one to seven seconds; on average, communicators look into each other's eyes for three or four seconds before one or both break off eye contact (Bavelas, Coates and Johnson 2002). However, the duration of eye contact increases as the distance between communicators increases. We seem to use prolonged eye contact to compensate for lack of physical proximity.

Eye contact acts as a nonverbal regulator. For instance, establishing mutual gaze in a conversation is usually an invitation to talk, and prolonged eye contact is virtually a demand to interact. Eye contact also helps regulate taking turns in a conversation. As we mentioned, the listener usually watches the speaker, but the speaker does not always look directly at the listener. As the speaker's turn ends, he or she will look at the listener and establish mutual eye contact. As the listener begins to speak, he or she will look away until the turn ends, at which point the whole process will be repeated. Alternating eye contact in this way facilitates a smooth transition from speaker to listener.

Eye contact communicates involvement and interest, whereas the lack of eye contact signals indifference and disinterest. Public speakers, for instance, communicate their interest in the audience by looking at them. Speakers who look at their notes instead of the audience are usually less effective than those who make a conscious effort to establish and maintain eye contact. Eye contact also communicates interest and connection in interpersonal relationships and often indicates acceptance, warmth, and closeness (Anderson 2008). Prolonged mutual gaze has long been associated with flirtation and sexual interest. Eye contact can communicate acceptance and involvement in nonromantic relationships as well. People being interviewed for employment who make prolonged eye contact are usually perceived as more competent than those who avoid looking at the interviewer.

> "The soul, fortunately, has an interpreter—often an unconscious, but still a truthful interpreter—in the eye."
>
> —Charlotte Brontë, English novelist

Gestures

Communication scholars have long understood the power of gestures. Speech teachers from the ancient Greeks and Romans (e.g., Aristotle, Quintillian, and Cicero) to modern professors have talked about the importance of animating delivery with hand and arm movements (Graf 1991). **Gestures** are defined as a significant movement of the body that expresses a message to a receiver (Thomas 1991). **Emblems** are gestures with clear and specific meanings. They are widely recognized within a specific culture and often substitute for words. Can you think of hand gestures for the following phrases? Quiet! Come here. Speak more loudly. Stop. Go away. Look. I'm full of food. Absolutely no! Most of us would understand the specific emblem associated with these phrases. Such emblems permeate our society and are used in many different contexts.

gestures
Significant body movements that convey a message.

emblems
Nonverbal gestures with specific and definitive meanings, often substituting for explicit verbal words.

Emblems can be used to signal membership in religious, civic, social, or even criminal groups. Sororities and fraternities have secret handshakes, military personnel salute each other, and gangs use hand signs as gestures of identification. As with all nonverbal cues, emblems vary from culture to culture. Table 6-1 illustrates various emblems of greeting in different cultures.

Using Gestures to Regulate Interactions. We use gestures to initiate, coordinate, and terminate communication. For example, indicating whose turn it is to speak is largely a matter of nonverbal cues such as regulating gestures. In class, you raise your hand to speak and the professor calls on you when it is your turn. In conversation, the gestures are less obvious but just as important. When you want the other person to keep talking, you nod your head, lean back in a receiving posture, and maintain direct eye contact. When you want to speak, you will nod your head rapidly as a signal that the other person's turn is finished, lean forward or straighten your posture in preparation to speak, raise your index finger slightly, and make an audible noise such as drawing in your breath loudly enough to be heard. Similarly, when you want to end the interaction, you might break eye contact, turn your shoulders perpendicular to the other person's body, take a step backward, glance at an exit, or look at your watch. In this way, we use gestures to synchronize our communication.

Using Gestures to Adjust or Adapt. We also use gestures called **adaptors** to adjust or adapt to our environment. These include gestures such as fanning ourselves when it is hot or absent-mindedly twisting a ring on our finger when we are bored. Adaptors are often unconscious habits that occur without much intended meaning. Nevertheless, adaptors often communicate an inner feeling of boredom or anxiety that is obvious to observers. We use adaptors to make ourselves comfortable, such as wiping perspiration off our brows, covering our mouths when we yawn, blowing on our hands when it is cold, or stretching when we are tired. Adaptors also include grooming gestures such as brushing teeth, combing hair, or adjusting clothing.

adaptors
Nonverbal gestures that we use to adapt to our environment, such as fanning ourselves when we are hot.

Using Gestures to Illustrate. Speaker's gestures, or **illustrators,** are important communicative tools that emphasize, accent, or clarify our verbal communication. Several studies have documented that illustrators contribute

illustrators
Nonverbal gestures that accent or clarify verbal messages.

TABLE 6-1 EMBLEMATIC GREETINGS

The handshake is the most common greeting in the United States. But other countries have different emblems for friendly greetings. The following is a sampling of different emblems used as greetings in different cultures around the world.

EMBLEM	CULTURE
Raising handshake. After the traditional handshake, communicators clasp right hands and raise them high in the air where they are disengaged.	Bantu
Touching noses. The nosetip is brought into contact with the nosetip of another person or with another part of his or her head. (See the photo at the beginning of the chapter.)	Finnish, New Zealander, Bedouin, Polynesian, Melanesian, and Inuit
Deep bow. Communicators bow with hands at their waist. The depth of the bow is a sign of social status, gender, or age.	Japanese
Slight bow. Communicators make a slight bow at the waist while placing their hands, palms together, under the chin.	Thai, Laotian, Khmer
Wiggling thumb and little finger. Communicators raise their arms and wiggle the hand gently. The thumb and little finger are extended with the other fingers curled.	Hawaiian
Blowing a kiss with the fingertips. One communicator touches fingertips to the lips and moves the hand away from the mouth, in the direction of the other communicator, while spreading the fingers.	Maltese, Sicilian, Sardinian, Portuguese, Swedish
Hands together. Two communicators join palms in the front of the chest and point fingers upward.	Much of Asia
Index fingers together. Two communicators place their index fingers side by side.	North African

Source: UNESCO, "Body Language," *UNESCO Courier* 50 (1997), p. 35.

important information to communication interaction (Beattie and Shovelton 1999). For instance, illustrators can be used to indicate size and shape. You might say, "My professor assigned a book to read that is this thick," while holding your thumb and forefinger three or four inches apart. Illustrators can point at or request objects. You might stretch forth your hand in a receiving motion while requesting, "Please pass the pepper," or point at a parking lot while telling a friend, "I am parked over there."

Proxemics

Popular phrases like "You stood by me," "You were there for me," and "We are very close," indicate the importance we place on space in nonverbal communication. The study of space is called **proxemics** and is divided into two types: personal space and territoriality.

proxemics
The use of space to communicate nonverbally.

Personal Space. Edward Hall (1966) was one of the first investigators to recognize the importance of personal space in the communication process. He noticed that people regulate the space around their bodies according to the degree of intimacy in a relationship. Hall theorized that there are four levels, or zones, of space that act like invisible barriers and control the distance between an individual and others.

1. The *intimate zone* is the closest space and extends approximately 18 inches from your body. Standing in this zone is a sign of familiarity and closeness. When two communicators are standing within 18 inches of each other, they are likely to touch in some manner. Caresses, hugs, pats, and other forms of touching characterize the intimate zone.
2. The *personal zone* extends from 18 inches to four feet from your body. People in this zone are usually familiar and friendly with each other, but not intimate enough to engage in touching behavior. Two people in this zone can communicate without others hearing the conversation.
3. The *social zone* extends four to eight feet from your body. Strangers and formal acquaintances usually stay in the social zone. Groups of friends also stand in this zone so that everyone can hear the conversation.
4. The *public zone* extends beyond eight feet from your body. There is little privacy in this zone, and anyone can hear the conversation between two people talking eight feet apart. For example, most of your college classes are conducted in the public zone, and other students passing by in the hall or outside the window might very well hear the lecture.

There is a great deal of variation among cultures about what is considered to be an appropriate use of personal space. Hall's research applies primarily to North Americans and is less applicable to people in other parts of the world. In some Asian countries, for instance, public intimacy is still discouraged, and even romantic partners will not stand within 18 inches of each other in public spaces. Conversely, in some Middle Eastern cultures, almost everyone stands within two feet when conversing whether they are intimate or not. These differences can sometimes cause misunderstandings when two people with different expectations attempt to communicate. Consider this example from a professor teaching in the United States.

> I advised a student from the Middle East. He would stand very close to me when asking a question. Uncomfortable at his closeness, I would take a step backwards to give myself more room. He would immediately take a step forward. Whenever we talked it would turn into a dance of sorts, with me stepping backwards trying to get away and the student stepping forward to get closer. We sometimes moved across the entire room during a single conversation.

After thinking about this conversational dance, the professor realized that his student felt like he was running away just as the professor felt the student was invading his space.

territoriality
The tendency of humans to mark and defend a particular space.

haptics
The use of touch to communicate nonverbally.

Territoriality. **Territoriality** is the human need to mark and defend space. The numerous signs indicating city, county, state, and national borders are examples of our strong need to communicate the boundaries of our territory. In our personal lives, we communicate boundaries by building fences around homes or putting names on office doors. Objects or signs used to communicate ownership or control of a space are called territorial markers. Territorial markers often communicate possession of a space. National and state parks always post signs indicating their boundaries. Landscaping not only beautifies one's yard but also communicates, "This is my land." Gangs "tag" territory with graffiti or other recognizable symbols. Even universities construct elaborate entrances to identify the boundaries of campus and to restrict access from unwanted visitors. Territorial markers also extend personal space. For example, you might place your coat or books on the chair or seat next to you at the library or on a bus. Finally, territorial markers personalize and distinguish space. For instance, many office workers mark their computer monitors with pictures, stickers, or drawings. Similarly, many university students mark their apartment or dorm room with pictures, posters, or other personal items.

Students often personalize their living spaces based on their interests and identity.

Touch

Haptics is the use of touch to communicate nonverbally. Touching is perhaps the most powerful and personal of the nonverbal cues. Touch often communicates messages of intimacy including love, acceptance, encouragement, and sexual desire. Many researchers believe that positive touch, or affection, is necessary for healthy development of humans and that the lack of touch can cause serious developmental problems. Unfortunately, touch can also send hurtful messages of hate, discrimination, and harassment. Effective use of touch can enhance a communicative interaction and relationship, but the misuse of touch can harm not only relationships but the people in them as well.

There are many types of positive touch, including functional-professional, social-polite, friendship-warmth, and love-intimacy (Knapp 1978). *Functional-professional* touches are the least personal type of touch and are associated with occupational functions. Doctors, dentists, nurses, and many other professionals touch clients, customers, or patients as part of their work-related responsibilities. *Social-polite* touches are associated with interaction rituals and formal situations. This type of touch is usually governed by explicit social norms and is used in greetings, religious ceremonies, and festive rituals. Social rituals, such as getting pinched on St. Patrick's Day, involve social-polite touches. *Friendship-warmth* touches communicate immediacy and acceptance. Friendship gestures are intimate but platonic touches that include hugs, pats, and embraces. Playful slaps or wrestling are bonding gestures in some cultures, as are nonromantic kisses. *Love-intimacy* touches are personal gestures that convey deep commitment. These gestures are usually limited to a few family members, special friends, and romantic partners. Love-intimacy touches are longer and more intense than friendship touches. In romantic relationships, love-intimacy touches include gestures to arouse sexual desire and pleasure.

Vocalics

Vocalics is the use of the voice to communicate nonverbally. It is not the study of the actual words or language spoken, but of how those words are said and other sounds the voice makes. Vocalics include a wide range of nonverbal behaviors such as sounds that are not words, laughter, pauses and silence, breathing patterns, and voice qualities. When you are excited or surprised, you often emit short bursts of sound that accompany other nonverbal gestures. Laughter is an almost universal sign of happiness and good feelings. Pauses during a conversation can convey a variety of meanings, including confusion, concentration, thoughtful reflection, anger, or suspense. The way you breathe often reflects your emotional state. Patsy Rodenburg (2000), the long-time voice coach for the Royal Shakespeare Company, recognized the communicative value of breathing. She insisted that actors incorporate breathing patterns into characterizations and performances. She believed that each character should have a specific breathing pattern and that as a character's emotional state changes, so should the actor's breathing patterns. As with actors on stage, one's breathing is often an indicator of his or her emotional state. Breathing quickly and loudly might signal arousal, physical exertion, or anxiety, whereas breathing slowly might communicate that one is relaxed or tired. Vocalics also includes vocal pauses such as "um," "aaa," and "and a" and other unintelligible sounds. Vocal pauses are called *disfluencies* and are often unconscious behaviors. These disfluencies are sometimes a sign of a nervous, unprepared, or distracted communicator.

vocalics
The use of your voice to communicate nonverbally.

Probably the most important aspect of vocalics is voice quality. The quality of your voice accompanies your words every time you speak and can add considerable meaning to what you are saying. This is especially true in public speaking

"This is Daddy, honey. That was Daddy's office voice."

when you use your voice to capture the audience's attention, enhance the meaning of words, and convey commitment to your topic. The cartoon above captures how we sometimes use different voice qualities with different people.

We add meaning to our words using three main voice qualities: rate, volume, and inflection.

1. *Rate* is how fast you talk. When you are anxious, impatient, or excited, you talk very quickly; when you are discouraged, depressed, contemplative, or melancholy, you speak very slowly.
2. *Volume* is the loudness of your voice. When you want to get someone's attention, you raise your voice; when you are confiding a secret, you speak very quietly.
3. *Inflection* is the vocal emphasis you place on words. By changing the inflection of your voice, you can transform a statement into a question, highlight specific words, or add meaning to sentences.

Odor

Although odors are sometimes forgotten nonverbal cues, our sensory environment is full of pleasant and unpleasant smells that communicate a variety of messages. While many of the messages conveyed by smells are unintentional, we also use smell to communicate overt messages. Consider the following example from a student in one of our classes.

> I was mad at my roommate who seemed inconsiderate and borrowed things without permission. My roommate was a vegetarian, so to get even, I woke up early and fried bacon each morning for a week. The smell filled the apartment and sent a clear message that "this apartment is mine too!"

Experts believe that our sense of smell developed early in the evolutionary process as an important survival skill. Early humans used smell to detect food, find mates, and warn against predators. Modern humans still have a tremendous *olfactory* capacity with over 1,000 genes that detect and encode smells (Givens 2004). Recent research indicates that our olfactory capacity is so sensitive that each nostril is capable of detecting a different smell simultaneously and that we can distinguish approximately 10,000 different scents (Milius 1999).

> "Smells coat us, swirl around us, enter our bodies, emanate from us. We live in a constant wash of them. Still, when we try to describe a smell, words fail us like the fabrications they are. Words are small shapes in the gorgeous chaos of the world."
>
> —Diane Ackerman, poet and journalist

Smells are often associated with or "trigger" strong emotions and memories (Givens 2004). The smell of coffee brewing in the morning might be a strong reminder of your childhood. The smell of a new car might be associated with the excitement of owning your first new automobile. You can even buy an aerosol spray that duplicates the smell of new car leather, rubber, plastic, and vinyl. Presumably, marketers will use the scent to persuade customers to buy products. Similarly, the scent of perfume or cologne might trigger romantic feelings or sexual desire. Smells can be used to communicate approach or avoidance in many situations. You are drawn to pleasant smells that you associate with positive emotions and memories and stay away from unpleasant odors. For example, mall-based cookie franchises attempt to lure you into the store with the inviting smell of freshly baked, chocolate-chip cookies. On the other hand, you may avoid walking past a trash dumpster on campus!

Culture plays a big role in what smells communicate. Other people or cultures might consider smells pleasant that you find repugnant. For example, the intense aroma of spicy curry or barbeque may strike you differently if you are European American than if you are Arab American. Your first impressions of a new culture are often the unusual smells in the environment. Different plants, foods and spices, animals, or people themselves might smell differently. At first you may find these new odors unpleasant. But as you get to know the culture and the people, you become accustomed to the new smells and may even find them inviting. People in the United States, are especially concerned with body smells, spending a great deal of money to prevent bad breath and natural body odors. We equate such smells with the lack of personal hygiene. Most other cultures, however, find bodily smell natural and are bewildered by our attempt to disguise such odors with deodorant, mouthwash, and toothpaste. An essential aspect of intercultural communication is the ability to suspend judgment and to accept new sensations, including unusual smells.

Time

Chronemics is the use of time to communicate. We communicate many different messages, such as power or status, by the way we spend and manage our time. Americans are especially time conscious. We coordinate work, school, and meals

chronemics
The use of time to communicate nonverbally.

with precise measures of time. We even time our leisure activities. The National Basketball Association decided that a single "second" was not a precise enough measure of time and now times the last minute of a game in "tenths of a second." Clocks and time displays are *ubiquitous* fixtures in our lives. Almost everyone who can tell time wears a wristwatch. You probably have a clock in the living room, on the kitchen wall, and one or two alarm clocks in the bedroom. Time is also displayed on your television, VCR or DVD player, oven, microwave oven, radio, car stereo or CD player, cell phone, electronic games, and maybe even on your pen.

Time as an Indicator of Money and Status. The popular saying "time is money" equates time with a monetary reward. Like money, Americans think of time as a valuable and scarce resource and, accordingly, the way we use the resource communicates many different things. Time is a strong indicator of power and status in our society. For example, work supervisors can tell subordinates how to spend their time, but the reverse is usually not true. Supervisors schedule, conduct, and close meetings. They assign work hours, tasks, and other professional uses of time. Supervisors can drop in on a subordinate without an appointment, but subordinates must make an appointment to see the boss.

In the larger social context, time indicates privilege and status as well. The "idle rich" can travel, golf, and engage in other leisure activities without the burden of work. Patients or clients must wait for doctors, dentists, or counselors. If you fail to show up for a dentist appointment you will probably be billed for the appointment anyway. But that same dentist can cancel or reschedule your appointment without financial liability. The truly disadvantaged and poor in our society often must wait prolonged amounts of time for even basic services such as health care or transportation. These long waits reinforce the social position and lack of power of the underprivileged. Similarly, the control of another person's time communicates power or lack of power in our everyday conversations. A person with more power usually takes more turns, speaks longer on each turn, and interrupts others more than those with less power.

Time as an Indicator of Competence. We also use time as a nonverbal indicator of competence. For example, people who are "on time" for appointments are thought of as responsible and organized. People who are continually late, on the other hand, are often seen as lazy or unorganized. Our vocabulary is sprinkled with such evaluations. Competent people might be referred to as punctual or prompt and their actions seen as efficient, prompt, timely, and economical. Incompetent people are referred to as lazy, sluggish, or slow-witted. Finally, time can indicate relational involvement. Spending time with someone is a clear signal of interest and commitment. Conversely, not spending time with someone you know is often seen as apathy toward the relationship.

Cultural Views of Time. Albert Einstein is famous for his theory that time is relative. Einstein was talking about the physics of time, but his notion could also refer to a cultural conception of time. Many cultures are not as obsessed with time as people in the United States. Think back to the example at the beginning of the chapter. The Kenyan farmer's notion of time was centered on the work he did in the field. He would meet his American friend when the work was done, not at some predetermined hour or minute. Cultural differences such as these can lead to misunderstanding. For instance, the amount of time one is expected to wait for a scheduled appointment or meeting varies considerably around the world. Waiting times in Latin American countries are often much greater than in the United States. This difference can cause considerable anxiety for some U.S. business executives and can create a difficult communication barrier for them (Givens 2004).

Many cultures view time as circular, in which events happen concurrently. This view of time is called **polychronic.** Most people in the United States have a monochronic view, in which time is perceived as a linear sequence of events. In a restaurant, for instance, Americans would expect that customers would be served in the order they were seated—first come, first served. In a polychronic culture, no such expectation would exist. Several appointments might be scheduled at the same time or several shoppers in a market might call out their orders all at once (Burgoon 2000). While many Americans view time as **monochronic,** they may find themselves in situations that are more polychronic in nature. Doctors often schedule several appointments at the same time, and traders on the Wall Street and Chicago markets shout orders at the same time. As with most nonverbal cues, the context or situation has much to do with the precise meaning of time.

polychronic
Cultures that view time as circular rather than linear.

monochronic
Cultures that view time as linear rather than circular.

Artifactics

Artifactics is the use of objects to communicate nonverbally. Our clothes, jewelry, cars, and houses all say something about us and are sometimes important expressions of our personalities, values, and interests. The authors of this text ask students each semester to describe a "meaningful object they own." One student selected a pearl necklace and wrote of its significance:

artifactics
The use of objects to communicate nonverbally.

> It was a gift from my parents on my 16th birthday and also happens to be my birthstone. I wear very little jewelry, but when I do it tends to be simple and elegant. I think this represents my own simplicity, my appreciation for natural beauty, and my ties to family. Some women wear lots of jewelry. I am content with the plain and gentle accent of my necklace (Walker 2002).

What do your artifacts communicate about you? Table 6-2 is a brief sample from other students. Do any of them sound familiar?

Artifacts also communicate status. Objects that convey power and control are present in almost every aspect of our lives. A large house, expensive car, and designer clothes all convey the nonverbal message of privilege and wealth. Military uniforms communicate very precise ranks and status. Similarly, high school letter jackets communicate specific ranks or awards such as captain, all-league, or champion with a series of bars, letters, or patches. At commencement, students graduating with honors sometimes wear robes or cords and those with PhDs wear special hoods. Basketball referees can stop action on the court by blowing the whistle they carry, and police officers can stop cars by turning on their flashing patrol car lights. Finally, artifacts can communicate inclusion in or identification with a group. Students often wear caps or sports jerseys from the their favorite team or school. License plates can communicate a person's home state while bumper stickers reveal a person's favorite musical group, political party, religious preference, or a social cause.

TABLE 6-2 ARTIFACTS COMMUNICATE MESSAGES ABOUT OUR PERSONALITIES AND VALUES

Artifact	Message
A daily planner	I am a very punctual person and have a need to be organized.
An autographed photo of Steven Spielberg	I am interested in film and want to be a director.
A keyboard	I have played the piano since the third grade and am a music major.
A cell phone	I love to talk with my friends and family. I also like to be "connected."
House plants	I try to "water" and nourish people as well as plants in my life.
A photo album	I like to share pictures of family and friends from back home. Even though I am a sophomore, I still miss them.
A karaoke machine	I am a total "ham." I love to be the center of attention, to be on stage, and to sing silly songs to a crowd of people.
A suitcase	My father was a marine until he retired last year. I have packed that suitcase more times than I want to remember and have lived all over the world. Now Indiana finally seems like home.
Athletic shoes	Working out and appearing fit are important to me.

Communicating Responsibly: Managing Nonverbal Cues Effectively

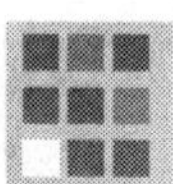

Using nonverbal cues effectively and responsibly often poses a challenge for communicators. The intrinsic nature of nonverbal cues makes them difficult to manage, especially if one is experiencing strong emotions. Additionally, the contextual nature of nonverbal communication makes it easy to misuse a cue, and the powerful nature of nonverbal communication makes is easy to offend others. Despite these difficulties, people can learn to manage their use of nonverbal cues more effectively and responsibly. This section suggests some strategies for doing so.

Monitor Your Nonverbal Messages

The first step toward using nonverbal communication effectively is being conscious of the messages you are sending. Understanding the material in this chapter should help you grasp the various ways that you can communicate nonverbally. But understanding the various types and functions of nonverbal behavior when reading about them is different than recognizing them in action. You need to go one step further by monitoring your own actions and trying to understand how others are interpreting them. Use the feedback process to monitor your messages and align your intentions with your nonverbal cues. For instance, if someone seems offended by a touch or a gesture, ask this person, "Did I do something inappropriate?" Opening yourself up for this kind of feedback takes something of a "thick skin," but the payoff is generally worth the risk because it allows you to find out if you have been understood as you intended. Consider the following example:

> Early in Professor Stark's teaching career, a student commented that he seemed uninterested in his student speeches. The comment surprised the professor because it absolutely was not true—student speeches were one of his favorite parts of the course. So he asked, "Why do you think I am uninterested?" The student responded, "Because you are always looking down at your desk while I speak." Suddenly Professor Stark understood what the problem was. While his students were speaking, he was looking down at their outlines to follow their speeches. Even though Professor Stark was listening carefully, he was sending an inadvertent nonverbal message of apathy. Now he makes it a point to make eye contact with student speakers and to follow their outlines more discreetly.

Similarly, by probing others about your nonverbal behavior, you can gain a deeper understanding of nonverbal cues and how others interpret your actions.

Avoid Intrusive Nonverbal Cues

Nonverbal communication is powerful, and it can easily be misused in ways that violate the privacy of or threaten others. So, you need to ensure that others are comfortable with your nonverbal messages. Eye contact, for example, can communicate negative emotions, such as disdain, or exert dominance over another person. Sometimes combatants, like boxers or two people who are arguing, stare intensely at each other in a struggle to establish dominance and to see who will blink first. Eye contact that is unwanted is almost always threatening. Uninvited watching is such a basic form of intimidation that it can rarely be done innocently. Examples range from openly ogling a stranger to even more insidious forms of sexual harassment, such as surveillance and stalking. The difference between establishing positive immediacy and communicating harassment, hate, or domination is usually a matter of context and other nonverbal cues. If you are looking at someone to communicate love and respect, your words, voice tone, facial gestures, and posture should indicate the compassion and interest that you want to establish.

Is this supervisor using touch appropriately with his employee?

© Bob Daemmrich/The Image Works

Similarly, touch should be used in a responsible fashion. Touch is a very individualistic nonverbal cue. Some people enjoy touch and look for many opportunities to engage others in touching behaviors. Others, however, avoid physical contact with most people; they are comfortable touching only a small number of close friends or a romantic partner. Social touch is governed by many norms and expectations. Remembering social expectations can help you use touch in responsible and respectful ways. Some of these expectations are:

- Don't use touch to communicate physical dominance. Don't move people, even small children, out of the way with touch. Don't shove or push, even in a large crowd.
- Don't interrupt someone with touch. Even in very intimate relationships, you shouldn't try to kiss someone while they are talking or hug someone in the middle of a chore or professional responsibility.
- Don't be "critical" through touch. Don't scold a young child while thumping his or her chest.
- Don't touch someone who does not want to be touched.
- Don't hurt someone with touch, even when wrestling playfully (Anderson 2008).

Remember the Cultural Context of Nonverbal Cues

Being sensitive to and tolerating the difference between cultures is one of the most important communication skills you can develop. This is especially true of nonverbal cues that are often linked directly to cultural practices and values. Gestures, for instance, often have different meanings in different cultures. Consider the differences in these nonverbal cues and how easily miscommunication could occur.

- *Waving.* Waving means good-bye to most Americans, but it means "no" to many Europeans who wave good-bye by bobbing the hand up and down.
- *Beckoning.* Most Americans would beckon someone to come by turning over their hand, palm up, and moving the hand towards them. However, in some European countries and most of Asia this is how people beckon dogs and other animals. Such a gesture would be insulting when used with humans. Instead, they place the palm down and make an itching action with their fingers.
- *The OK gesture.* In France, the OK gesture means zero; in Japan it means money; and in Brazil or Germany it is an obscene gesture. Similarly, the "got your nose" gesture that many Americans use in jest with small children is a vulgar gesture in many parts of Europe and Asia.
- *Thumbs-Up.* Most people in the United States think of thumbs-up as either "good going" or an indication that one is hitchhiking. In Nigeria, however, it is a rude gesture; in Japan or Germany it is often the signal for the number one, and in Australia it is an obscene gesture, especially if the hand is pumped up and down.
- *You're crazy.* In Argentina, this very familiar American gesture of twirling a finger by your ear means you have a telephone call (Imai 2001).

Responsible communicators need to be cautious in interpreting nonverbal cues. Try to understand the complete context, including the cultural values and practices of the communicators. Again, tolerance goes a long way toward preventing miscommunication and misunderstanding.

Resources for Review and Skill Building

Many of these resources are supported by the Connections CD-ROM and free Online Learning Center website.

SUMMARY

This summary is organized around the questions found at the beginning of the chapter. See if you can answer them before reading the summary paragraphs.

1. What basic characteristics distinguish nonverbal from verbal communication?

   Nonverbal communication is nonlinguistic. It is often intrinsically connected to the emotions we feel. Much nonverbal communication is contextual. The precise meaning of messages is influenced by the situation, particularly one's culture and the relationship between communicators. Nonverbal communication flows in a continuous stream of cues and actions.

2. What are the functions of nonverbal communication?

   Nonverbal communication can augment, repeat, or highlight words or phrases. It complements language by adding additional meaning to a message, and it can contradict it when the nonverbal cue seems to contradict spoken words. Nonverbal communication can also regulate verbal language by controlling or altering the flow of interaction. Finally, nonverbal communication may substitute for language by replacing words entirely.

3. What are some ways we use our eyes and face to communicate nonverbally?

   Eye movements such as blinking, winking, rolling your eyes, or shutting your eyes are all forms of nonverbal communication. Eye contact, or how long to gaze or look at someone, is a powerful nonverbal cue. We use eye contact to compensate for lack of physical proximity, to regulate verbal interaction, to establish immediacy or closeness with others, and to exert control or dominance.

4. How do we use gestures to communicate with others?

   Kinesics is the use of body movement to communicate nonverbally. One form of kinesics is the use of gestures or any significant or communicative movement of the body. Some gestures, called emblems, substitute for verbal words, while others regulate verbal interaction. We use other gestures to adjust to our environment, such as fanning ourselves when we are hot, or to illustrate verbal language.

5. How do we use personal space to communicate nonverbally?

   Proxemics is the use of space to communicate nonverbally. One aspect of proxemics is use of personal space. We communicate the nature of a relationship by regulating the distance between communicators; we allow intimate friends or family to stand closer to us than mere acquaintances or strangers. Also, we mark and defend our space to communicate territoriality.

6. What messages do we communicate through touch?

   Touch conveys a variety of messages depending upon the relationship of the people touching. There is the functional-professional touch of a doctor examining a patient, the social-polite touch of acquaintances greetings, the friendship-warmth touch we use when we embrace close friends or relatives, and the love-intimacy touch that communicates the deep commitment of lovers.

7. How do we use our voice to communicate nonverbally?

   We use our voice to communicate messages other than words. We use vocalics such as laughter, pauses, silence, and breathing patterns to communicate nonverbally. Also, varying voice qualities such as rate, volume, and inflection add meaning to the words we speak.

8. **What are some ways we communicate through the use of smell, time, and objects?**

   Smells often trigger strong emotions or associations, but they are also culturally specific—that is, what smells bad in one culture may be a very desirable smell in a different culture. Time can be used to communicate power or control (How long do we expect others to wait for us?). We also communicate relational involvement by the amount of time we spend with others. Finally, the objects we own, display, or wear often communicate our personality, status, and membership in a specific group.

KEY TERMS

Test your understanding of these key terms by visiting the Connections CD-ROM and Online Learning Center website at www.mhhe.com/dobkinpace.

accent 156
adaptors 163
artifactics 171
chronemics 169
complement 157
continuous 155
contradict 157
display rules 161
emblems 163
gestures 163
haptics 166
illustrators 163
intrinsic 152
kinesics 160
leakage 157
monochronic 171
nonlinguistic 151
nonverbal communication 151
polychronic cultures 171
proxemics 165
regulate 158
repeat 158
substitute 158
territoriality 166
vocalics 167

FOR FURTHER REFLECTION

/dobkinpace

Join a conversation about chapter concepts by visiting the Online Learning Center website at www.mhhe.com/dobkinpace

1. Think about objects that you own.
   - Which objects are expressions of your personality, values, or interests?
   - What do you believe these objects symbolize about you?
   - Where do you keep these objects—in public or private? Why?
   - What artifacts would indicate your status or membership in a specific group?
2. Think about the proxemics of your university or college.
   - How does your school mark its territory (gates, fences, or streets)?
   - How is space allocation a symbol of power?
   - Who has the most desirable parking spaces?
   - Who inhabits the nicest building and what does that say about the values of the college?
   - What messages does your school try to convey through the architecture, landscaping, and design?

BUILDING COMMUNICATION SKILLS

Go to a public place such as a food court at a shopping center or a common area on campus. Watch two or three people converse from a distance where you cannot hear what is being said and analyze their nonverbal communication.

- What can you tell about the people by the way they are dressed or the objects they are carrying?
- What can you tell about their relationship based on the use of personal space?
- What can you tell about their mood by their use of facial expressions or hand gestures?

NET WORK

Note: While all the URLs listed were current as of the printing of this book, the sites often change. Please check our website www.mhhe.com/dobkinpace for updates and hyperlinks to these exercises.

1. The Center for Nonverbal Research has an online collection of descriptions, explanations, and illustrations of many nonverbal terms and behaviors. The website is located at http://members.aol.com/nonverbal2/index.htm. Most of the entries in the collection are fascinating, but the following ones are especially interesting: body adornment, deception cues, eye-blink, love signals, lips, swagger walk, and tongue-show. When and where might you use these nonverbal messages? How might these definitions be influenced by culture?
2. For an extensive list of cultural differences in gestures and other body kinesics, check out the website http://www.csupomona.edu/~tassi/gestures.htm. What are some differences in typical Western and Asian gestures? How do other parts of the world interpret American gestures?
3. There are several good sites with extensive lists of unique and interesting texting symbols and abbreviations, including: http://mobiles.maxabout.com/kb/sms_dict.aspx. Which symbols on this list would you use? Why?
4. Go to YouTube and search for videos with the phrase, "personal space." How is personal space established, maintained, or invaded in these video clips?

MEDIA MOMENTS

The film, *How to Lose a Guy in 10 Days* (2003) tells the story of two people with hidden agendas who meet and form a relationship. Ben (Matthew McConaughey) is trying to win a bet by making a woman fall in love with him. Andie (Kate Hudson) is writing a story for a magazine on how to lose a guy in ten days. Each of the main characters uses distinctive nonverbal cues to establish his or her personality. Analyze each character and note how they differ in voice quality (rate, volume, inflection), hand gestures, facial expressions, use of space, touch, and use of time.

- How are Ben's actions consistent with the gender differences discussed in text? How are they different?
- How are Andie's actions consistent with expectations? How are they different?
- View a scene without the sound. Can you tell what is happening based solely on nonverbal cues?
- Play the scene again with the dialogue. What aspects of nonverbal communication accent, complement, illustrate, or contradict the verbal messages?

Communicating in Interpersonal Relationships

CHAPTER 7

HOLLY: *Hello.*

MAYA: *Hey, Holly. How is everything?*

HOLLY: *Wow. The long lost Maya. I thought you had forgotten my number. Are you sure you have time to talk with me?*

MAYA: *Why the hostility? I always have time to talk with you, Holly.*

HOLLY: (Sarcastically) *Right, you talked to me a grand total of twice all last year.*

MAYA: *That's an exaggeration. I left you a couple of messages just last month and you didn't return a single one.*

HOLLY: *Every time I called, you were out with your college friends. I can't help it if your roommates can't take a message. Besides, all you ever talk about is your sorority sisters or how much fun college is.*

MAYA: *It's not my fault that you have no ambition to go to college. I came home at Christmas break and you would hardly talk to me. You went skiing with Laura and the Pattersons. What's up with that—you barely talked to them in high school.*

HOLLY: *I have fun with them. They are interested in me.*

MAYA: *And I'm not?*

HOLLY: *Not anymore. You don't even know that I've been in college since January.*

QUESTIONS TO FOCUS YOUR READING

1. **What is interpersonal communication?**
2. **How is intimacy communicated in interpersonal relationships?**
3. **What role does attraction play in relationship formation?**
4. **What role does communication play in the development of a relationship?**
5. **How can appropriate self-disclosure help maintain intimacy in an interpersonal relationship?**

MAYA: (Astonished) *College? Really. You never told me. Where did you go?*

Holly: *Just over at State.*

MAYA: *That's great, Holly. I knew you would do it. You don't need to apologize. State is a really good university.*

HOLLY: *It's not as good as your "hoity-toity" private school.*

MAYA: *That's not fair. You know this is a good opportunity for me.* (After a long pause) *But sometimes I do feel so out of place—seems like everyone else has more money than I do.*

HOLLY: *I just can't believe that you joined a sorority. You are like the "anti-sorority sister."* (Laughing) *I wear more makeup than you do and I don't even own any lipstick.*

MAYA: (Also laughing) *My sorority sisters are all really nice. You would like them if you gave them a chance.* (After another pause) *Holly, it's good to hear your voice. I missed you.*

HOLLY: *Oh, don't get gooey on me. That sorority thing is starting to affect you. Why don't you come over and I will tell you about my classes.* (Pause) *Maya?*

MAYA: *Yeah.*

HOLLY: *It's good to hear your voice too.*

Maya and Holly are two friends struggling to understand each other and their changing relationship. For Maya and Holly, the things that were said, the way they were said, and, importantly, the things that were not said during the year after high school created tension in their friendship. Maya felt *estranged* from her friend as the frequency and quality of their interaction decreased. She recognized that their conversations were less personal and more distant than before. Similarly, Holly felt left behind, neglected and perhaps inferior to Maya because she didn't go directly to college after graduating from high school. She resented Maya's preoccupation with her new life and avoided talking with her at winter break by going on a skiing vacation. Their friendship, however, also provided a solid foundation that enabled them to move past these relatively new tensions. Drawing on previous experience and trust, Maya and Holly begin to confide in each other—expressing fears, admitting insecurities, and exchanging compliments. Their relational foundation allowed them to reconnect and eventually to express a renewed commitment to their friendship. Communication shaped their relationship and the relationship, in turn, shaped their communication.

Few of us think about the fundamental importance of communication within a relationship. Relationships are created, expressed, altered, strengthened, weakened, postponed, reaffirmed, or terminated through communication. The way that we communicate with each other reflects the essence and substance of our relationships. In this chapter, we will discuss communication in interpersonal relationships. By the end of the chapter, you should be able to:

- Define the characteristics of interpersonal communication.
- Understand the role of attraction in the formation of interpersonal relationships.
- Comprehend and illustrate various communication stages of relational development.
- Understand the role of self-disclosure in fostering and maintaining intimate relationships.

"The easiest kind of relationship for me is with 10,000 people. The hardest is with one."
—Joan Baez, singer

Basic Characteristics of Interpersonal Communication

interpersonal communication Occurs when individuals treat each other as unique and interact in an individual or customized way.

Interpersonal communication is interaction among a small number of people and is characterized by more personal and individualized communication than that which takes place in larger groups. This definition can be understood by looking at the basic characteristics of interpersonal communication. It is personalized, it occurs in a relationship, and it is influenced by culture and gender.

Interpersonal Communication Is Personalized

People communicating in interpersonal relationships speak and relate to each other as unique individuals. They do so by communicating in ways that are distinctive to the relationship. These distinctive ways of communicating put the "personal" in interpersonal communication. If a personalized approach is absent, the communication that takes place is not considered interpersonal in nature. For example, fast-food attendants speak to many people while doing their job. If an attendant simply says the same kinds of things to each customer ("Do you want fries with that burger?"), then the communication is not personalized. On the other hand, if the clerk remembers a repeat customer and inquires about family members or some other personal matter ("Hey, how did the job interview go last week?"), then the communication is decidedly more personalized.

Personalization makes interpersonal communication different from mediated or public communication. In those settings, communicators, like the customers in the fast-food restaurant, are generally treated as though they were interchangeable (Stewart and Logan 1998). For example, television programming is usually aimed at a "target group"; media executives assume that younger adults will like "Grey's Anatomy" and that older people will watch "60 Minutes." Similarly, public speakers often address the audience as one entity or unit rather than as a collection of individuals. A college professor delivers the same lecture to all students in the class. Most of the time it is simply impractical to teach each student the same material in different ways. There might be individual moments of interpersonal communication within a televised message or a public speech (a football player might say "Hi, mom" into a camera, or the professor might ask a specific student to share a relevant personal experience), but the overall interaction is qualitatively different and usually not interpersonal.

Interpersonal communication can occur in many different situations. Over time, family members, friends, romantic partners and even co-workers establish distinct and personalized ways of interacting with each other. Interpersonal communication may take place in small groups of four or five people or even in larger groups, such as an athletic team or campus club, where individuals come to know each other particularly well. But generally, interpersonal communication flourishes in smaller contexts, especially when two people engage in dyadic communication. One college senior, speaking to first-year students about making the most of their education, suggested that they seek out one-on-one conversations with their professors.

> I like to talk with my professors during their office hours at the beginning of the semester. In the classroom, you get to know your professors in a general way. But talking one-on-one, you get to know them as individuals while developing a better feel for what is expected in the course. The professors also get to know something about me—my educational goals, likes and dislikes, and career plans. Even a brief conversation can make the professor and the course so much more interesting for me.

The personalized nature of interpersonal communication reflects the responsiveness of the communicators to each other. This responsiveness manifests itself in many different ways. Interpersonal communicators often cocreate a message by anticipating each other's intentions, completing unfinished statements, or speaking at the same time. Feedback is continuous and immediate in interpersonal communication. Messages reflect the unique circumstances and nature of the relationship and are tailored to the particular individuals; you say things to those close to you that you would not say to others. People in close relationships often develop specialized meanings for words and phrases that take the form of verbal shortcuts (Knapp and Vangelisti 1996). For example, consider this dialogue from longtime partners planning a routine dinner date.

Eva: What time should I pick you up?

Daniel: How about the usual? Will that give you enough time to solve the Buster problem?

Eva: Oh yeah. The Buster problem isn't nearly as involved as last time. If I take the shortcut, I should have plenty of time.

Daniel: [*Laughing*] The shortcut isn't always short. Where should we go?

Eva: How about the place where that guy wore the wild hat last time?

Daniel: You mean the place on Market Street?

Eva: Yeah.

Daniel: Sounds great.

Phrases like "the usual," "the Buster problem," "the shortcut," and "the place where that guy wore the wild hat" are instantly recognizable to Daniel and Eva but not necessarily to anyone overhearing their conversation. Interpersonal conversation is full of specialized vocabulary and nicknames. Communicators in close relationships also become keenly aware of subtle nonverbal cues. Nonverbal gestures such as the shrug of a shoulder, the tilt of a head, a certain smile, or a particular stance convey clear and concise messages. Most of you can probably tell when your mother is angry simply by the set of her mouth.

Interpersonal Communication Occurs in a Relationship

Interpersonal messages are heavily influenced by the nature of the relationship between communicators. You talk differently with your professor than you do with your parents, and your conversation is more intimate with a best friend than it is with an acquaintance. In Chapter 2 we discussed the presentation of *self* and noted that people disclose different aspects of themselves to different people. Similarly, different types of relationships influence how to communicate with others. For instance, in an intimate relationship you might be willing to discuss sensitive topics like your fears, embarrassing moments, weaknesses, hopes, desires, or aspirations. You would be unlikely to discuss those same topics with someone you didn't feel as close to or trust as much. Even in your own family, you might talk differently with your mother than with your father. At work you are likely to have different kinds of relationships with different co-workers and bosses, as the student in the following example did.

> At work I have three bosses and I have a different relationship with each of them. One of them is very serious all of the time and intimidates me. I try not to talk to her, and when I do it is always about work. Another boss is very friendly but a little older. She owns a boat and I always talk to her about water skiing, which I enjoy, and other boat stuff. The third boss is a good friend and I can talk to her about anything. We always talk about dates and personal things.

We mentioned in Chapter 1 that all messages contain a content and a relationship dimension. The content dimension is the substance of the communication or the overt purpose for the interaction. The relationship dimension establishes the nature of the connection between the sender and receiver. Almost all messages conveyed in an interpersonal interaction express the nature of the relationship, though the relationship dimension of a message is often implicit or unstated. The implied nature of relational messages can lead to misunderstandings. For example, consider the following interaction between Blaine and his boss, Megan:

Blaine: It's kind of slow tonight, and I have a big test at school tomorrow. Would you mind if I take off early to study?

Megan: Well, I . . . I suppose that would be all right. Go ahead and take off.

Blaine requests both permission to leave (Can I leave early?) and reassurance that the relationship is still on good terms (Do you mind?). He gets a clear response to the content request (Go ahead and take off) but the relational dimension of the message is much less clear and full of ambiguity. What was the meaning of Megan's hesitation ("I . . . I suppose")? Was she angry, disappointed, distracted by something else, or just thinking through the request? Just as important, do both Blaine and Megan interpret the hesitation in the same way? Does one think of it as disappointment while the other thinks it is simply careful consideration of the request?

Scholars and counselors suggest that interpersonal communicators should openly discuss the relational dimension of messages. The relationship between communicators in interpersonal interactions is so important that periodic discussion of the exact nature of that relationship is essential to prevent misunderstandings. For example, consider this account from a college graduate student.

> One of the other graduate students in our program was a huge New York Mets fan. One year the Mets had a terrible season and I would tease him about the team's poor performance. I would cut the standings out of the paper and place it on his desk and rib him about the success of the Yankees. I thought all of this was in good fun and something of a bonding experience. I expected him to tease me back about my favorite team, which was also near the bottom of the standings. But he never did. He started to avoid me and when we did talk, our conversations were very short. He rarely looked me in the eye. When I finally realized what was happening, I raised the subject with him ("Does my teasing bother you?"). We had an honest exchange of feelings about our communication. I told him that I saw my teasing as a sign of true friendship. To my surprise, what I saw as "affirming our relationship," he saw as hostility. I should have recognized the need to talk about our friendship earlier.

Both friends in this example understood the content of the message but misunderstood the relational implications until they explicitly discussed their friendship. Such discussion is important because relationships are an essential part of our lives, and the success of those relationships often depends on the effectiveness of our communication. Relationships can help us realize our full potential. In trusting relationships, we can conquer insecurities, discover and overcome faults, learn new skills, and solve problems.

Interpersonal Communication Is Influenced by Culture and Gender

Think about the last time you talked with someone and the conversation did not go smoothly. Perhaps a friend tried to tease you, and you thought your friend was being inconsiderate. Perhaps a supervisor or professor asked a question, and the room got very quiet as the tension built. Perhaps you got frustrated with another person's point of view and insulted or snapped at that person. Perhaps you said something that seemed to offend the other person, and you had no idea why. Or perhaps you withdrew from the conversation because you thought there was no way the other person could understand you. When situations such as these occur, you are often left wondering what happened. You and your friend might have very different ideas about what boundaries can be crossed in teasing, your professor or supervisor might be violating a taboo in your group, or you might grow impatient when people don't provide the feedback you expect. These conflicts could be based in part on cultural differences in communicating. Understanding

Think It Over

LEARNING FROM RELATIONSHIPS

We said that "good" relationships help us to realize our potential.
Can bad relationships also help us to become better people?
What can you learn from the breakup of a relationship?
How can a bad relationship hinder self-esteem?

How might expectations about gender and culture affect this relationship?
© Michael Newman/PhotoEdit

the role of culture in influencing interpersonal communication is an important part of the communication process.

Patterns of communication that are influenced by culture can be difficult to recognize, because we do not notice them until they cause friction. Once friction occurs and others react in ways we do not anticipate, we often blame them for not understanding us or following our rules. We mentioned earlier that different cultures have different expectations about forming lines in public places, such as bus stops. Cultural expectations vary at all levels of interpersonal communication. In some languages, such as French, people use different words depending on the closeness of the communicators ("vous" is formal, "tu" is more casual or familiar). A Japanese couple is less likely than a North American one to be comfortable displaying their affection in public. Co-cultures also influence patterns of communication in relationships. For example, while many gay couples feel comfortable discussing their relationship status with other gay people, they are also likely to realize that many heterosexual people would be uncomfortable discussing relationship issues with them.

Just as people have preferences about interpersonal communication styles based on their cultural backgrounds, they also come to expect certain communicative behaviors based on gender. In general, most people expect men to interact in ways that are stereotypically masculine (direct, unemotional, aggressive, competitive, task-oriented) and women to use communication in ways that are stereotypically feminine (indirect, emotional, passive, cooperative, and relationship-oriented).

We expect males and females to interact in these gendered ways because we have been taught to recognize and adopt them since birth (Wood 1994). As early as preschool, boys and girls in the U.S. exhibit gendered ways of negotiating hierarchy in their peer groups (Kyratzis 2000). Boys are encouraged to play together in team sports that have clear rules, are highly competitive, require aggression, and often involve physical risk. Girls are more likely to play indoors and in smaller groups, and they are encouraged to be less competitive. Girls gain status through performing well academically and cultivating relationships with a close-knit peer group, while boys gain status through physical performance, public displays of humor, and attracting the attention of authority figures. These gendered experiences give boys more opportunities to practice direct, assertive, task-based, and public forms of communication, and they give girls experience in using talk to establish and maintain relationships, express emotion, and respond to a range of needs.

As a result, women are expected to show interest in others, self-disclose in relationships, and be cooperative, whereas men are expected to use talk to achieve goals. Substantial communication research suggests that women and men do tend to communicate in these ways (e.g., Wersfeld and Stack 2002). Women are more likely to talk about private feelings and thoughts, especially to their female friends, and men are more likely to talk about external topics, such as work and politics (MacGeorge, Gillihan, Samter and Clark 2003; Palomares 2008). Imagine the potential conflicts between a man and a woman who wish to begin a friendship with one another. She might value him as a person who will not ask too many personal questions, and he might be looking for someone with whom he can share emotions and confidence.

Men and women are also likely to talk about their concerns differently. Wood (1994) identified four common misunderstandings that may arise when women and men communicate.

- Women often share stories to build relationships. ("I can't believe how long Steve kept me on the phone. I really wanted to get off work in time to help Leila move into her new apartment.") Men are likely to offer advice ("So why didn't you just get Steve off the phone?") rather than communicate support ("That's the pits. Do you think Leila's doing OK?").
- Men and women often talk differently about physical and personal problems (Granito 2002). Men are more likely to resist being probed about their worries, whereas women are more likely to expect questioning if they seem troubled.
- Women and men often have different ways of relating their experiences. Women's stories are more likely to be detailed and involve more characters, whereas men's stories are more likely to focus on specific actions that lead to a conclusion.
- Men and women have different ways of talking about relationships. Because women see communication as a process in creating and maintaining relationships, they are more likely to initiate discussion about feelings and boundaries in the relationship. Men often see such discussions as threatening, assuming that if the woman thinks the relationship needs to be discussed, then she must have a problem that he will need to fix.

We tend to label the behaviors associated with men as "masculine" and those associated with women as "feminine." However, men often adopt feminine interaction styles and women adopt masculine ones, depending on the sex and status of the person(s) with whom they are communicating and the context of the conversation. You can probably tell the sex of the other person on the line when a close friend or roommate is talking on the telephone based on her or his style of interaction. For example, a male is more likely to sound feminine when talking with a potential romantic partner, and a woman is more likely to sound masculine when talking to business associates. Although interaction styles vary across contexts, we often fall back on rigid gender expectations. Recognizing both the gendered expectations that we place on others and the ways that individuals vary in their interaction styles can help us meet our communication goals and accommodate the needs of others.

Intimacy, Interpersonal Relationships, and Communication

In a single day you might talk with your dentist, chat with a family member, ask a professor a question, help a co-worker solve a problem, and study with another student for an exam. The nature of the communication with each of these people would vary greatly in mood, formality, and purpose depending on the closeness or level of intimacy in the relationship. **Intimate interpersonal relationships** are characterized by high levels of trust, warmth, and affection, while nonintimate relationships are more impersonal, distant, and formal. The degree of intimacy in a relationship can often be measured by its breadth and depth. **Breadth** refers to the width of the relationship, or how many different contexts communicators experience with each other. For example, suppose that you have a teammate in an intramural sports league at your school. If the only time you talk with this teammate is at practice or during a game, you would have a "narrow" interpersonal relationship. But if you interact with this teammate in other contexts—in a class, at a party, or even as a housemate—then you have a broader relationship. Quite naturally, broader relationships are more intimate than narrower ones.

intimate interpersonal relationships
Characterized by high levels of trust, warmth, and affection; nonintimate relationships are more impersonal, distant, and formal.

breadth
The number of contexts in which communicators interact in a relationship.

depth
The amount of time communicators interact and the personal level of information they exchange in a relationship.

The **depth** of a relationship refers to the amount and type of interaction you have with another person. Often depth is a factor of time—the more you interact with a person, the more intimate and personal the communication. Not surprising, long-term relationships usually have more depth than newer ones, although some new relationships can achieve substantial depth through intensive interaction. Still, the depth of a relationship reflects much more than time; it involves the amount of trust that develops between communicators. Trust in a relationship increases intimacy. For instance, you may interact with particular co-workers every day but still not feel comfortable discussing sensitive issues like your love life or religious values with them. On the other hand, exploring such topics with your closest friends is much more likely.

One theory that explains the depth of a relationship based on the type of topics discussed is called **social penetration theory** (Altman and Taylor 1973). Social penetration theory states that we disclose and discuss more personal information as our relationships become more intimate. The theory likens the development of a relationship to the peeling of an onion. To get to the core of an onion, you must first peel away the outer layers. Similarly, to reach the intimate core of a relationship, you must first "peel away" the outer layers. Relationships develop intimacy as communicators move through the outer impersonal layers and eventually understand each other's beliefs and values. Figure 7-1 illustrates this metaphor.

social penetration theory
We disclose increasingly personal information about ourselves as the relationship develops, and we reserve discussion about our most private thoughts for our most intimate relationships.

At the first level of depth, we discuss topics like the foods we eat, the films we see, and the music we prefer. Interpersonal discussions at the middle layer include the sharing of political views and social attitudes, such as revealing what groups we belong to or whom we voted for in the last election. The next level, the inner layer of intimacy, is much more personal than the previous ones and includes topics that require a substantial amount of trust to discuss. For example, in this level we might discuss our spiritual values, hopes, goals, fantasies, secrets, and deep fears. In the final, most personal level—the core shown in the figure—we reveal

FIGURE 7-1 SOCIAL PENETRATION THEORY

To reach the intimate core of a relationship, you must first "peel away" the outer layers.

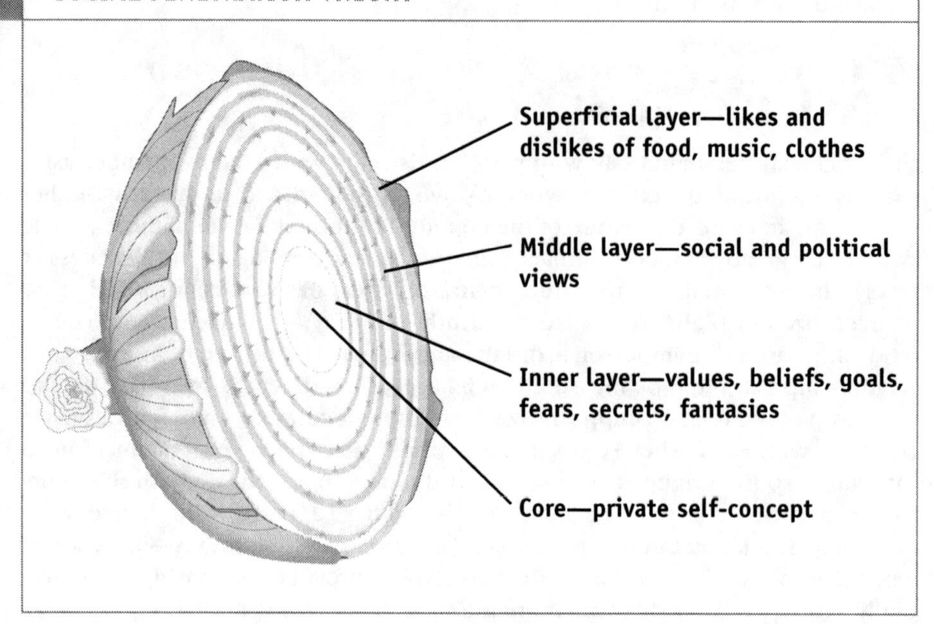

our most basic and private self-concept with someone else. This requires a great deal of trust so that other people will not reject or make fun of how we view ourselves. Such a discussion is usually reserved for our most intimate relationships, those that have developed areas of mutual trust as they progressed through the layers of the "onion."

Your most intimate relationships, then, would be those in which you interact with the other person frequently and in many different contexts, and discuss personal topics that you would not discuss with others. However, relationships are also dynamic and the level of intimacy *fluctuates* as the relationship changes. Some impersonal relationships grow in intimacy, whereas other relationships decline in intimacy as spouses, lovers, or close friends break up or drift apart. Some communication experts also worry that relatively new communication technologies inhibit the growth of intimacy in relationships. The "Exploring Communication Concepts" box introduces the idea that our modern dependency on such technologies reduces human contact in social interactions and decreases intimacy.

Interpersonal Attraction

Some of our relationships occur by circumstance, and we have little or no choice in the selection of the other person. These relationships might include most family members, some co-workers, teammates, or assigned partners in a class project. In other circumstances, however, we make a conscious choice to form a relationship. In these situations, attraction plays a major role. Interpersonal attraction is both simple and complex. It is simple and mostly accurate to say that we form relationships with people to whom we are attracted. But it is much more complicated to figure out why we are attracted to some people but not to others. Attraction is more than a simple list of physical or personal characteristics. Rather,

Exploring Communication Concepts

COMMUNICATION TECHNOLOGIES AND ONLINE RELATIONSHIPS

Communication technologies such as cell phones, discussion groups, computer chat, instant messaging, and e-mail often expand communication opportunities and lead to the formation of new online relationships. Initially, experts worried that excessive use of the Internet was psychologically harmful to communicators because it led to loneliness and a sense of detachment (Paterson and Kraut 1998). Although preoccupation with online relationships might lead some people to withdraw from other forms of social interaction, recent research has established the viability of online relationships. Here is a sampling of research findings regarding online relationships:

- The use of the Internet to establish and maintain interpersonal relationships is very popular. For instance, in a national survey as many as 54% of adolescents between the ages of 10 and 17 reported communicating online with someone they did not know, and 39% reported establishing either a casual or close online friendship within the last year (Wolak, Mitchell, and Finkelhor 2002). Although online communication is most popular with young people, users of all ages are increasingly relying on the Internet to meet people and establish relationships. These communicators are not necessarily the stereotypical computer enthusiasts portrayed in popular books and films. Rather, communicators of all ages, personality types, and socio-economic levels are using the Internet and other communication technologies to meet people and establish relationships (Bonebrake 2002).
- Romantic online relationships often develop in a predictable pattern. Communicators usually meet each other in a public discussion group where they notice or are attracted to the other person's postings and ideas. This interest usually leads to a more personalized form of communication, such as e-mail or instant messaging followed by phone conversations. As the relationship becomes more intimate, communicators exchange pictures and finally arrange to meet face-to-face (Baker 2000).
- Communication technologies provide new opportunities to establish and maintain relationships. These new opportunities often arise out of the convenience of being online. Communicators separated by great distances can meet and get to know each other, and new relationships can happen at unusual times such as while doing homework, at work, or during the middle of the night. Additionally, the Internet provides new ways to maintain "offline" relationships, whether it is parents staying in closer touch with their college-age children, grandparents communicating on a regular basis with their grandchildren, gay teens finding out that they are not alone, or co-workers exchanging ideas after they leave the office (Baker 2000).

Communication technologies help shy or introverted communicators overcome their inhibitions and extend their social network. The anonymity of the Internet, the lack of the need to reveal their physical appearance, and the ability to carefully construct messages provide a safe place for introverts to confront their fears and meet new people (Amichai-Hamburger, Wainapel, and Fox 2002). The Internet is especially attractive to adolescent communicators who are socially awkward but eager to connect with others (Wolak, Mitchell, and Finkelhor 2002). The Internet also helps even the most extroverted of communicators through uncomfortable and anxious situations, whether it is finding a lost love, reuniting with high school acquaintances, or contacting the never-forgotten ex (Lee 2000).

ASK YOURSELF:

1. How might online relationships facilitate the development of interpersonal similarity?
2. How is the pattern of online relationship development different from or similar to the stages of relationship development discussed in the text?

attraction is a combination of many factors. Among them are interpersonal similarity, proximity, and physical attributes.

Liking Those Who Are Similar

interpersonal similarity
Occurs when we share common attitudes, values, habits, and communication styles with other members of a relationship.

Probably the strongest factor in interpersonal attraction is **interpersonal similarity.** We are attracted to people with similar attitudes, interests, values, habits, and communication styles (Khohnen and Shanhong 2003). Again, think about a good friend. You probably share many common interests with this person. You might like the same music, enjoy the same films, and eat similar foods. Indeed, these similarities were probably one of the reasons you became friends in the first place. Common preferences draw us into relationships of all kinds. For example, employees are often most comfortable with co-workers who share similar attitudes, and patients tend to select or stay with doctors or counselors who share common perspectives (Glaman and Jones 1996; Speight and Vera 1997). Our perceptions of similarities change as a relationship develops. At the beginning of a relationship, demographic similarities (e.g., age, appearance, or ethnicity) might be very important. But as a relationship develops, similar attitudes and values typically become more meaningful.

Similarity is attractive for many reasons. For one thing, it reduces the amount of uncertainty in a relationship. Most of us have at times experienced a degree of anxiety at the beginning of a relationship. Usually such anxiety decreases as we get to know the other person better and as the relationship becomes more predictable. In a new relationship, the more we have in common with the other person, the less uncertainty there is. We know, for example, what we would do in a specific situation and have some degree of confidence that a person with similar interests and values would act in the same way. Also, we are less likely to have initial disagreements with someone whose interests are similar to ours. Conflict frequently produces anxiety, so it is not surprising that we are attracted to relationships we believe will produce fewer disagreements.

Similarity to others also validates our view of the world. We have an inherent need to organize and understand our environment. When we form a relationship with someone who sees the world as we do, our perceptions are validated by this person. We also expect that the other person will enjoy doing what we like to do, so the relationship will be more rewarding. Furthermore, common experiences and perspectives establish a basis for effective communication. For example, suppose that you enjoy growing a garden. You probably find it easier to discuss your hobby with other gardeners who have experienced the same challenges and rewards of horticulture than with someone who thinks that gardening is boring or a waste of time. This mutual interest provides a common vocabulary, topics, and insights for effective communication; the lack of common perspective might prevent shared meaning and satisfying communication.

Even though similarity is a strong factor of attraction, we can form meaningful relationships with those very different from us. The saying that opposites attract is at least partially true. In certain cases, similarity can be stifling and limit personal growth. Someone who is different from you in particular ways may fill a need. For example, suppose you are extremely shy. You might be attracted to someone who is social and outgoing because this person draws you out and helps you feel more comfortable with others. Also, your perceptions of similarity might change as the breadth and depth of the relationship increases. Someone you initially perceive as similar may turn out to be quite different in the long run. For example, someone who shares your love of mountain climbing or music might turn out to have a very different attitude toward honesty. Or someone with whom you originally had little in common might turn out to share important values. Finally, two people with many differences can develop, over time, common perspectives and experiences. Similarities forged out of differences are frequently powerful bonds and can provide the basis for a strong relationship between two seemingly different people.

"It's only through our relations with others that we . . . come to believe in our own capabilities and inner goodness."

—Joan Borysenko, psychotherapist and biologist

Liking Those Who Are Familiar

Earlier in the text we discussed proximity as a factor of nonverbal communication and defined it in terms of physical space, such as how close you stand next to someone. When talking about interpersonal attraction, however, **social proximity** refers to common places where we meet and interact with people. Distance in social proximity is measured by the frequency with which we visit these places. Areas of close social proximity include your neighborhood or apartment building, workplace, and the clubs you frequent. At school, areas of close social proximity would be the classrooms you go to, the places you eat, and where you study. Not surprisingly, we are attracted to and form relationships with people we meet in these places. Think about your closest friendship. Chances are the two of you were either in the same school classroom, worked at the same job, or lived near one another when you began your friendship, even if this is no longer the case. While encounters with strangers are much talked about in novels or popular magazines, in reality the vast majority of our relationships are formed with people who are already familiar to us and in fairly close social proximity.

social proximity
Refers to "social closeness"; we are often attracted to people who live near us, belong to the same groups or organizations, or attend the same school.

Close proximity does not necessarily enhance our attraction to others as much as it provides the opportunity to interact in a setting that is convenient and safe. Talking with someone we see everyday is often less intimidating than initiating a conversation with a stranger. Think about your communication classroom. Somehow it is easier to strike up a casual conversation with the student sitting next to you than it is with someone across the room. Similarly, we tend to talk with those whom we see often and who are close by. As we do so, we begin to form relationships. As we form relationships, we tend to interact more frequently. This cycle of talk, deepening relationship, and more talk starts with the notion of proximity.

At least two studies have verified that our relationships often emerge from those in close proximity. One study looked at childhood friendships; the researchers discovered that the majority of junior high school students made friends with students they met in their classes. The researchers also found that these students were likely to befriend other students who lived close to them. This was especially true for people of color attending predominantly Caucasian schools (Clark and Ayers 1992). What is true of junior high students is also true for older people. Another study tracked subjects in their sixties and seventies to discover how their closest friendships changed over time. The researchers discovered that many older people formed new friendships late in life as longtime friends moved away, became ill, or died. The common thread in almost all of these new friendships was close proximity; older people formed relationships with

Applying Communication Concepts

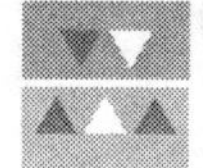

NEW RELATIONSHIPS

One implication of research on proximity is that those who want to meet new people should extend their social and professional circles. In addition to more traditional ways of meeting others, such as joining a club or gym, trying intramural sports, or taking a new assignment at work, people are increasingly turning to Internet dating. In fact, half of all single adults in the U.S. visit online dating services each month (Mulrine and Hsu 2003).

ASK YOURSELF:

1. Why might broadening social and professional circles be a good way to meet others and form new relationships?
2. How do interpersonal similarity and social proximity work together when forming new relationships?
3. What might make some dating services more successful than others?

those who lived close by or attended the same church or clubs (Wenger and Jerome 1999).

These studies confirm the importance of proximity in forming relationships. Many universities have adopted an approach to promoting tolerance on campus that takes this principle into account. They integrate students from very different backgrounds into residence halls, courses, clubs, intramural teams, and other types of university activities in the hope that students will overcome prejudices and form relationships with those who live in close proximity or who participate in the same activities. This approach has been successful in promoting friendships that might not otherwise develop, and demonstrates the power of proximity on attitudes as well as relationship development (Light 2001).

Liking Those We Find Attractive

physical attraction
Occurs when we are attracted to someone's appearance through such attributes as facial features, height, body type, and hair color.

attractiveness
What we visualize as the "perfect look" or idealized physical attributes.

You probably associate **physical attraction** with romantic interest, but it is also an important aspect of most other kinds of relationships. Physical attributes such as facial features, height, and hair color are some of the first things we notice about another person, and they play a part in our decision to either pursue or avoid a relationship with that individual. We tend to develop relationships of all kinds with people who attract us physically. Defining physical attributes that are attractive is difficult because our perception of "good looking" is quite personal. There are, of course, some common cultural stereotypes of physical beauty, such as being slender or having large eyes. But physical attraction is different than physical attractiveness. **Attractiveness** is the idealized appearance of physical attributes, what we visualize as the "perfect look." In forming relationships, we seem to separate the ideal from the attainable and do not necessarily form relationships with people who have the perfect look. Instead, we form relationships with those whom we find attractive to us even though their appearance may diverge from common stereotypes.

Have you ever noticed that two friends, or two people dating, often look like each other? We are frequently attracted to those who look like us. Also, as a relationship develops, our physical attraction to the other person may increase or decrease. Someone you originally thought of as physically attractive might not seem as good looking when you get to know this person better. Similarly, a person's physical appeal may increase as you interact with him or her. Even a simple relational connection, like knowing the other person's name, can increase attraction. As we get to know other people's attitudes, beliefs, sense of humor, likes and dislikes, and other aspects of who they are, we often find them more attractive.

Communication and Relationship Development

Like plants, animals, and people, relationships grow and progress through somewhat predictable life cycles. Scholars have identified several developmental phases that most relationships experience as they progress from beginning to end. **Stages of relationship development** are patterns or life cycles that relationships pass through as they develop or deteriorate. Relationships have a beginning, middle, and eventually an end. Each relationship, however, progresses through developmental stages differently. Some speed through the beginning while others linger. Some end quickly while others last a lifetime.

stages of relationship development
Patterns or life cycles that relationships pass through as they develop or deteriorate. Relationships have a beginning (or birth), middle (coming of age), and an end (death).

Communication scholar Mark Knapp offered a descriptive model that identifies stages in relationship development and focuses on the type of "talk" that occurs within each stage (Knapp and Vangelisti 1996). The model applies to most types of relationships, but it is a more accurate description of close friendships and romantic relationships than of family or professional relationships. Few relationships follow all the stages. Rather, the model describes, in general terms, 10 possible stages of development (see Figure 7-2). Knapp called the first five stages "coming together"; these stages describe a relationship as it becomes increasingly intimate. The second five stages represent the stages a relationship goes through as it disintegrates or declines and are called "coming apart." We will briefly describe each stage of Knapp's model and then discuss how particular relationships develop unique communication patterns.

Coming Together

Initiating. The first stage of interaction in a relationship involves meeting another person and initiating communication. In this stage of relational development, we try to gain the attention of the other person and establish open lines of communication. The actual interaction includes conversations that are familiar and comfortable to both communicators, such as: "Hi, how are you?" "Where are you from?" or "What is your major?" These questions are safe for communicators in the beginning of a relationship because social and cultural conventions provide commonly accepted scripts. If we say, "Hi, how are you?" others automatically know to respond, "Fine, how are you?" Of course, we are not really asking about the other person's health. Instead, we are saying, in essence, "We recognize and want to talk with you." At the same time we are asking, "Do you recognize and want to talk with us?"

Experimenting. The experimenting stage is characterized by the exploration of mutual interests and circumstances. The exploration phase still occurs at a relatively safe social level. Communicators continue to rely on common scripts,

FIGURE 7-2 STAGES OF RELATIONSHIP DEVELOPMENT

Relationships go through stages of "coming together" and "coming apart."

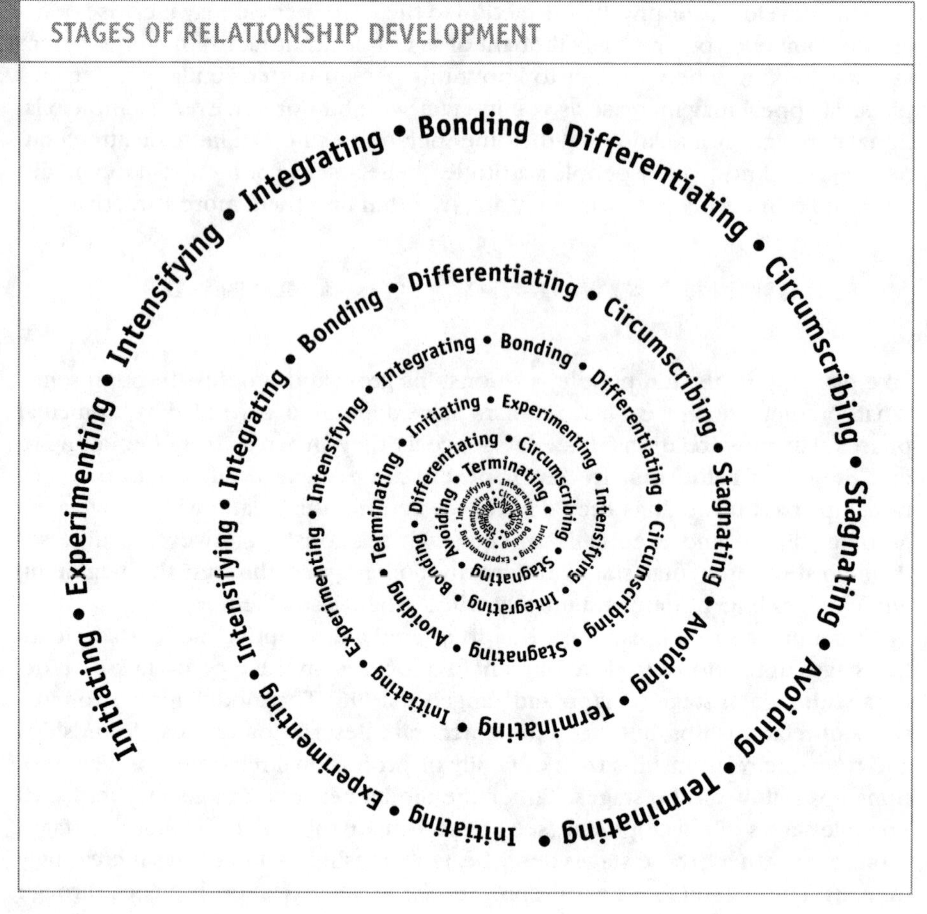

integrating topics
Areas of common interest that members of a relationship enjoy discussing.

but they also engage in "small talk." For instance, they might discuss the weather, people they both know, or movies they have seen recently. Much of the experimenting stage involves the discovery of **integrating topics,** areas of common interest that both parties enjoy discussing. These topics serve as the focal point for interaction during the experimenting stage and provide convenient opportunities to renew the relationship each time the parties meet. Suppose, for instance, that you formed an acquaintance with a fellow student in your cultural anthropology class. Chances are that every time you encounter this person on campus, you begin your conversation by discussing some aspect of the course, such as the professor, other students, or the difficulty (or ease) of the course material. In the experimenting stage, there is little commitment to each other besides the willingness to discuss integrating topics. Small talk gradually begins to reveal both personalities in the relationship and gives each person a glimpse of a "deeper" or more intimate aspect of the other person's self. If those glimpses are intriguing or attractive, the relationship probably moves on to the next stage of interaction, the intensifying stage.

Intensifying. In the intensifying stage, we experience an increase in the breadth and depth of the relationship, seeing each other more often and in a greater number of contexts. We still exercise caution when it comes to expressing

Exploring Communication Concepts

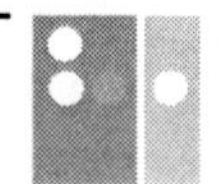

WHO SAYS, "I LOVE YOU" FIRST?

Some of our common stereotypes about heterosexual relationships include the ideas that females are more likely than males to express their emotions, and males are more likely to avoid commitment in relationships. So, you might think that women usually say "I love you" first in intimate relationships. However, communication researchers have found that men are more likely to make this declaration first (Pearson, West, and Turner 1995). There are several reasons that men may take this leap: As in other phases of courtship, women often wait for men to initiate this stage in the relationship. Additionally, men might say "I love you" to persuade their partners to commit more fully to the relationship or to pursue sexual advances (Brantley, Knox and Zusman 2002).

Because women often wait for men to initiate each new phase of a relationship, women can be left wondering about their partner's level of commitment. One strategy that researchers have noted is the "secret test," in which a woman tries to get information about the status of the relationship without asking her partner directly (Baxter and Wilmot 1984). Perhaps you have used or been subjected to a secret test. Have you ever tried to make your partner jealous just to see what the response will be? Have you used situations such as meeting relatives or babysitting to see how your partner interacts with family members or children? Secret tests are common, particularly when one person in the relationship is uncomfortable talking directly about love or levels of commitment.

ASK YOURSELF:

1. Besides saying "I love you," how can you tell if someone is committed to a relationship?
2. Have you used secret tests to determine your partner's commitment in a relationship? Did they work?
3. Why might such indirect or secret tests be necessary?

affection, and our desire for more intimacy creates a certain amount of uncertainty and fear of rejection. So we actively seek confirmation of our intentions through *reciprocity.* If we give a gift, we expect a gift in return; if we offer affection; we expect affection from the other person.

Interaction in this stage is also characterized by self-disclosure of increasingly intimate aspects of our self. As we open ourselves to wider scrutiny through the disclosure process, the communication becomes less safe and we become more vulnerable. When we disclose something personal, we expect the other person to reciprocate by disclosing something of a personal nature. In romantic relationships, explicit expression of affection and attraction intensify the relationship, and we expect such expression to also be reciprocated. If we say "I love you,"we expect the other person to respond "I love you, too."The utterance of these words inevitably changes the relationship. The "Exploring Communication Concepts" box looks at the implications of the "I love you "statement and which member of the relationship is likely to initiate the exchange.

During the intensifying stage, communication becomes more *idiosyncratic* to the relationship. We develop nicknames, unique patterns of interaction, and verbal shortcuts that emerge out of common experiences. In the opening to this chapter,

Maya and Holly had developed personalized forms of interaction such as referring to personal information about each other ("I wear more makeup than you do and I don't even own any lipstick"). Such unique communication patterns often start in the intensifying phase and continue throughout the life of the relationship.

Integrating. As relationships develop, the people in them may begin to integrate numerous activities, coordinate daily schedules, and develop common interests, attitudes, and values. They may also merge their social circles: The friends of one become friends of the other and vice versa. Communication at this stage of the relationship is characterized by heightened empathy ("You don't want to go out, do you? You look exhausted") and the growing ability to predict the other person's behavior. Increasingly, the other person's attitudes and values become part of our inner dialogue—we can hear the other person's perspective in our thoughts ("Max would love this book"). As we acknowledge and accommodate this new stream of talk in our thoughts, integration occurs at new levels of intimacy. Together we develop unique ways of perceiving the environment and forge a common vision about the relationship. In this stage we also use inclusive pronouns—"we" and "us"—frequently in public conversations (Wood 1997). We also explicitly discuss the nature of our communication and engage in more **metacommunication.** Metacommunication is communication about communication or analyzing the content and style of our interaction ("I feel left out when you say 'my' place instead of 'our' place"). Metacommunication occurs in all stages of the relationship but increases as we try to integrate the relationship and establish a foundation for the next stage of development, bonding.

metacommunication
Communication about communication; discussing the relationship dimension of messages is one type of metacommunication.

Bonding and Ongoing Intimacy. The bonding stage occurs as we make long-term commitments to the relationship. Bonding in a relationship is often institutionalized through some kind of ritual or ceremony. Marriage is the most obvious form of such a ritual; others include initiation into a fraternity or sorority, commitment ceremonies, cohabiting, exchanging rings, or making other public pronouncements of relational devotion. With or without a public ritual, bonding implies an interpersonal contract of mutual obligations and responsibilities. These obligations and responsibilities are unique to each relationship and often include pledges of loyalty, support, and exclusivity. The contract is usually implicit but may be explicitly stated or even written. Wedding vows, prenuptial agreements, or fraternity/sorority pledges are examples of written contracts. Often the obligations and responsibilities of a relationship are discussed through metacommunication, as people talk about what it means to be a best friend, spouse, or partner within a specific relationship. Ongoing intimacy at this level also includes the successful management of conflict. Conflict and disagreement emerge at all phases of a relationship, but the bonding stage is a pivotal point between coming together and coming apart. The successful management of disagreement at this stage of the relationship becomes especially important. We will discuss effective communication in intimate, ongoing relationships later in the chapter. But first, we consider the stages of relationship disintegration and what happens when a relationship begins to "come apart."

"Kindness and intelligence don't always deliver us from the pitfalls and traps; there are always failures of love, of will, of imagination. There is no way to take the danger out of human relationships."
—Barbara Harrison, writer

Heightened empathy and shared perspectives can lead to bonding and ongoing intimacy.

Coming Apart

Differentiation. At a certain point in a relationship, we begin to take note of the differences that exist between our partner and ourselves. This may undo some of the integration of the two previous stages. We might reestablish separate social circles with new or old friends, have less contact with our partner, and discover basic personality differences that are difficult to reconcile. Differentiation is characterized by talk about differences, expressions of dissatisfaction, and the assertion of individual wants and needs. Not surprisingly, there is considerable arguing or fighting in this stage. Differentiation can lead the relationship in either direction. Often, differentiation can make the relationship stronger as individual needs are recognized and accommodated. We might also learn from our disagreements and build relational norms about how to successfully manage conflict ("We should never go to sleep mad at each other" or "I now know to stay clear of you when you are cleaning the garage"). As a result, differentiation can lead us back to ongoing intimacy as we alternately discover and reconcile differences. Conversely, differentiation can also lead to further disintegration in the relationship. Unresolved conflict usually escalates and leads to even more separation of activities and daily routines. This divergence in the relationship leads to the next phase, circumscribing.

Watch a video about ways of managing differences (CD Clip 7.1).

Circumscribing. If a relationship continues to deteriorate, we may begin to circumscribe it by reducing the breadth and depth of the relationship significantly. We establish clearly defined boundaries of interaction and confine our discourse to relatively safe topics. Progressively, however, even safe topics may become sources of new disagreements as unresolved conflicts accumulate. Discussing simple topics like where to eat, how to drive, or what to wear can create significant tension and disagreement. This often leads to decreases in interaction and a spiraling sense of isolation. Dissatisfaction with the relationship greatly increases in this stage and leads to what the prominent interpersonal scholar, Steve Duck (1984), called "intrapsychic brooding." Intrapsychic brooding is *ruminating* over and over in our minds about the inadequacies of the relationship. Communication during this stage is often characterized by superficial pleasantries and the absence of personal discussions of feelings. Frequently we put off any discussion of relational troubles by saying, "Lets talk about this later" or "What's the use—talking never solves anything." In public, we still play the role of intimate partners, but in private, silence is often the dominant form of interaction.

Stagnating. In this stage, interaction flattens out and stops growing in either direction. We may feel a sense of hopelessness and stop trying to repair the relationship. But we may also be reluctant to end the union, believing that doing so will be more painful than staying in a counterproductive relationship. Interaction in this stage resembles talk between strangers and is carefully planned to be neutral; conversation often becomes rigid, formal, and awkward. The list of safe topics becomes very small and talk about the relationship is almost nonexistent. Both parties believe there is nothing new to say. Intrapsychic brooding increases and we may carry on imagined conversations with the other person in which we rehearse what to say about the inadequacies of our relationship in our own mind instead of discussing these with the other person. The stagnating nature of the relationship increasingly displays itself in public as we stop pretending that intimacy exists.

Avoiding. There is some degree of avoidance in any stage of relational decay, leading both partners to experience a great deal of emotional separation in the differentiation and the circumscription phase. In the avoidance stage, the separation becomes physical as partners actively avoid any face-to-face contact. Interac-

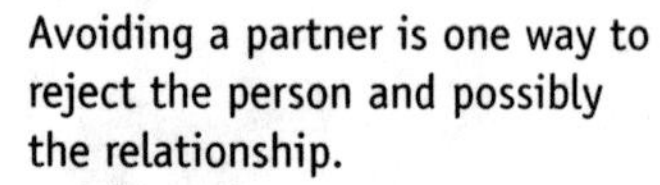

Avoiding a partner is one way to reject the person and possibly the relationship.

tion in this stage is characterized by the lack of conversation or even contact. The lack of contact communicates a strong message about the increasingly permanent nature of the separation. If interaction does occur, it is usually blunt and to the point. Sometimes, interaction is laced with hostility and unpleasantness, but almost always the interaction serves to close channels of communication. Extreme forms of avoidance may include ignoring the other person even when that person is in close physical proximity. This "disconfirmation" of the other person inevitably signals the rejection of the person as well as the relationship.

Terminating. In the terminating stage we negotiate the end of the relationship. We try to make sense of our new circumstances, cope with the situation, and understand what benefits we gained from the relationship. Often the end of a relationship is the beginning of something new, including a new definition of the old relationship. For example, a partner or spouse might become an "ex" with new expectations and even obligations. A symbolic gesture of dissolution such as returning personal property, defacing or burning pictures, or obtaining a final decree of divorce often accompanies termination. Interaction is often pragmatic and businesslike as we establish formal procedures of exit. Table 7-1 summarizes the purpose and types of interaction in each stage.

Unique Development Patterns

Although the stages we have discussed generally apply to many close relationships, every relationship develops in unique ways and follows different paths through the stages. Particular relationships may skip a stage, move through a stage in an abbreviated or short period of time, revisit earlier stages, and, in general, develop a unique sequence of events. Consider the following scenarios:

- Two people meet and experience an instant and strong attraction. They either skip or abbreviate the experimenting stage and move directly into intensification.
- One member of a long-term relationship betrays the trust of the other person. The betrayal causes the relationship to fall apart very quickly and the relationship moves almost directly from ongoing intimacy to circumscription.
- Two longtime friends become romantically involved. Although they were close as friends, the new relationship goes back to the experimenting and intensifying stages as the "friends" discover different types of intimacy.
- Finally, a marriage comes apart in a predictable way, going through each of the stages of disintegration. But after a separation, the couple reunites, establishes intimacy, and returns to the bonding stage.

The path of a relationship is forged through the interaction between participants as they discover and define the stages of the union. Often a particular event, feeling, or interaction changes the direction or intensity of the relationship. These **turning points** help explain the uniqueness of a relationship as different experiences create different responses (Baxter and Bullis 1984; Wood 1997). Saying "I really like you as a friend" can be one of these turning points in a relationship. For some, uttering these words creates a barrier that ultimately ends the relationship. Each relationship develops in different ways as the participants act and react to each other, to events, and to patterns of communication.

turning points
Particular events, feelings, or interactions that change the direction or intensity of a relationship.

TABLE 7-1 Stages of Relationships and Interaction Characteristics

STAGE	PURPOSE	INTERACTION CHARACTERISTIC
Initiating	To gain the attention of the other person and open lines of communication.	Socially safe talk governed by social convention.
Experimenting	To gain information about the other person and begin an initial exploration of the costs and rewards of a relationship.	Extension of socially safe "small talk" including the discovery of integrating topics of common interests.
Intensifying	To increase the breadth and depth of a relationship and to secure reciprocity of our intentions for a more intimate relationship.	Increasingly personal self-disclosure.
Integrating	To integrate activities, schedules, interests, attitudes, and social circles. To develop common expectations concerning the relationship.	Heightened empathy and the ability to predict the behavior of the other person. Integration is expressed in the use of plural pronouns "us" and "we." Engagement in more metacommunication.
Bonding and ongoing intimacy	To establish long-term commitments to the relationship and develop mutual obligations and responsibilities.	Ongoing metacommunication about the nature of relational obligations/responsibilities and effective management of disagreement.
Differentiating	To establish individual differences, needs, and wants. To provide increased opportunities for discussion of conflict management. Differentiation can strengthen a relationship through the successful management of conflict or it can lead to further disintegration.	Expressions of dissatisfaction, assertions of individuality, and talk about differences. Increased arguing and fighting.
Circumscribing	To significantly reduce the breadth and depth of the relationship and to establish clear boundaries of interaction.	Communication increasingly consisting of superficial pleasantries around safe topics. Lack of discussion about the relationship and a reluctance to solve disagreements.
Stagnating	To avoid either a return to intimacy or complete dissolution of the relationship.	Interaction becomes formal and awkward, resembling communication with a stranger. Participants carry on "imagined dialogues" about the inadequacies of the relationship. Participants avoid discussion of the relationship.
Avoiding	To close channels of communication and establish entirely independent routines.	Avoidance of contact. If interaction occurs, it is often blunt and impersonal.
Terminating	To end the relationship.	Symbolic gestures of dissolution and the end of most interaction. Communication often concerns making sense of the relationship and redefining perceptions of each other.

Maintaining Ongoing Intimacy through Appropriate Self-Disclosure

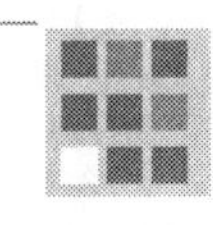

Effective communication is at the center of most long-term, successful relationships, and one key element to effective interpersonal communication is self-disclosure. **Self-disclosure** is the act of revealing one's personal thoughts, preferences, feelings, and experiences to another person within the context of an interpersonal relationship (Jourard 1964; Dindia and Fitzpatrick 1997; Knight 2009). Self-disclosure does not usually apply to the public presentation of self, such as a professor telling a class that he or she loves jazz music or the accidental discovery of personal information about another person. Suppose you observe a friend cheating in class. Such behavior would certainly affect your view of that friend, but it does not represent intentional disclosure. It is very different from your friend admitting to you what he or she did and to become subject to your reaction to the confession.

self-disclosure
The intentional revelation of personal aspects of your self, including thoughts, preferences, feelings, and experiences, to another person within the context of an interpersonal relationship.

The Advantages of Self-Disclosure

Self-disclosure is important in maintaining an intimate relationship for two reasons. First, it builds trust. By confiding in your friend something, such as a family problem, that you would not normally share with other people, you are communicating your faith in the friendship. Similarly, your friend's acceptance of your disclosure without revealing the information to others further justifies your trust and increases the likelihood of additional disclosure. Second, self-disclosure builds a foundation for meaningful communication within the relationship. Repeated self-disclosure enables you to know and understand the other person more intimately than any other form of communication would allow and provides you with the basis for understanding verbal and nonverbal nuances of interpersonal interaction ("I know why she doesn't want to go to River Park—that's where she used to take her dog before it died").

The Risks Inherent in Self-Disclosure

There are also personal and relationship risks associated with self-disclosure. Any disclosure of personal information makes you more vulnerable and raises the possibility of hurt feelings or even rejection. For instance, in the heat of an argument, a friend may be tempted to use self-disclosed information against you. Suppose, for example, you confide in a friend that you are struggling in school. Initially, he may reassure you and try to boost your confidence in your academic ability. But later, during a fight, he might retaliate for something you said by making fun of your poor grades. Those closest to you often know how to hurt you the most.

> "I think it is almost self-evident that you cannot love another person . . . unless you know what (s)he needs. And you cannot know what (s)he needs unless (s)he tells you."
>
> —Sidney M. Jourard, clinical psychologist

When Is Self-Disclosure Appropriate?

Appropriate self-disclosure helps a relationship grow and progress, whereas inappropriate disclosure hurts the relationship and places a burden on one or both of the people in the relationship. Separating effective from ineffective disclosure is not easy. Confessing betrayals of

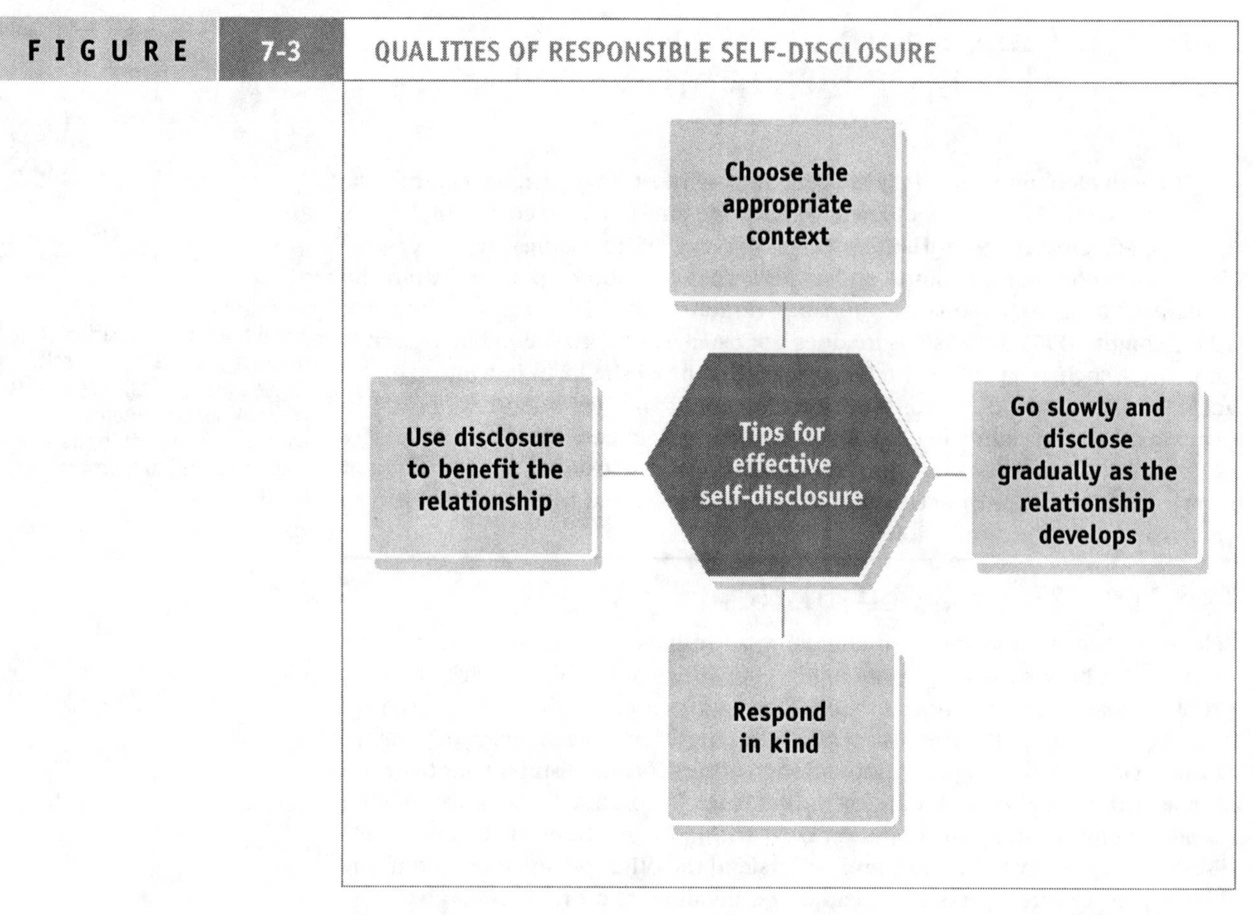

FIGURE 7-3 QUALITIES OF RESPONSIBLE SELF-DISCLOSURE

trust within the relationship, for instance, may very well harm or even end the relationship ("I had lunch with my old girlfriend yesterday"). Perhaps, though, such a confession was necessary to the relationship, even if it created much anguish. The painful confrontation of relational problems might eventually lead to new levels of commitment and ongoing intimacy. The possibility of rejection, however, means that you should think carefully about any act of self-disclosure. Although disclosure varies according to the specific situation, some general guidelines may help you decide what and when you should reveal yourself to another person (see Figure 7-3).

Choose the Appropriate Context for Disclosure. The amount and type of self-disclosure should match the communication situation and cultural context. Perhaps you have had an experience similar to the one described by a high school teacher.

> I was chatting with fellow teachers in the faculty lounge during lunch break. We were discussing the usual topics of student performance, bad cafeteria food, and the ineptitude of district administrators. Several teachers excused themselves from the conversation and left to prepare for the next period. The only other person remaining in the lounge was a history teacher I hardly knew. I looked at him and said, "How's your lunch?" He paused and said, "I have a horrible indigestion

problem; everything I eat wants to come back up." That was certainly more information than I wanted to know!

Before disclosing personal information, consider the time, place, mood, and your relationship to the other person or persons. In the preceding example, the history teacher picked the wrong time (there were only a few minutes left before class started), place (people usually avoid discussing health problems while eating), mood (the conversation had been about general school topics, not individual problems) and relationship (the two hardly knew each other) to share his health troubles. Disclosures that do not match the situation are often rejected or ignored, leaving the person making the disclosure feeling hurt and vulnerable. Make sure that the other person has the time and willingness to explore your disclosure. Broaching a serious topic when there is little time to discuss it will only frustrate efforts to exchange personal feelings. Similarly, you should not drastically alter the prevailing mood of the situation. If the situation is casual, friendly, or lighthearted, any disclosure should not be very serious. If the situation is more private and solemn, a disclosure of a more serious nature is appropriate. Most important, the disclosure should fit the relationship. Save very private details for your most trusting relationships and disclose only semiprivate details to less intimate ones. For example, stepparents often try too hard too early to bond with their new family. They sometimes disclose very personal information to stepchildren in the hope of accelerating the bonding process. Stepchildren, however, may resent this "instant" intimacy and prefer less personal conversation until the relationship develops more fully (Martin, Anderson, and Mottet 1997).

Go Slowly and Disclose Gradually as the Relationship Develops. In most cases, relational intimacy develops through the gradual sharing of personal information. The gradual progress of disclosure allows time for two people to develop mutual expectations about the nature and extent of disclosure. Too much disclosure too early can place an excessive burden on both parties and prevent the growth of intimacy. Both the amount and intensity of disclosure should increase gradually. In newer relationships, disclosure occurs infrequently. When it does occur, it is usually brief and limited to a single topic ("My father died when I was 14"). But as the relationship develops, disclosure becomes more frequent and extends to multiple topics, often increasingly personal in nature. For example, in a new relationship you may disclose impersonal details such as biographical data. As the relationship progresses you may begin to disclose increasingly personal information, moving from biographical data to preferences in music, food, and forms of entertainment, to personal aspirations, and finally to deeply held fears, and insecurities. Someone who tries to force a degree of intimacy by disclosing too much too soon risks overwhelming the other person and forcing a premature acceptance or rejection of the relationship.

Respond in Kind. One of the strongest expectations in a developing relationship is reciprocal disclosure. If we disclose something personal about ourselves, we expect the other person to do likewise. Reciprocity refers to both the frequency and level of intimacy of our disclosures. Relationships in which one person does all of the disclosing are often one-sided and not as intimate as those in which both parties participate equally. Similarly, the level of intimacy should match the other person's disclosure. If one person discloses that he or she likes chocolate-chip cookies, this would not be a signal to discuss religious preferences. Reciprocal disclosure has many benefits for the relationship; reciprocity is a good index of the mutual involvement in the relationship (Vanlear 1991). By exchanging disclosures both parties are saying, in essence, that they are committed to the relationship. Symmetrical disclosure patterns also establish an expectation of shared power—how you feel and how the other person feels are both equally important to the relationship. Finally, reciprocity builds mutual empathy in a relationship and establishes a common understanding for ongoing intimacy and growth of the relationship (Karlsberg and Karlsberg 1994).

Use Disclosure to Benefit the Relationship. Self-disclosure should be constructive for the relationship and beneficial to both parties. Selfish reasons for disclosure are rarely constructive or beneficial. Disclosures that aim to make the other person jealous ("At work today, I found myself thinking of my ex, Jason"), establish power or superiority ("I hate it when you talk about Jason. Besides, I heard the loser lost his job"), or create feelings of guilt ("I never think about my ex. Why do you always think about Jason?") ultimately do not help ongoing intimacy. Whenever you are disclosing, you should consider the burden you are placing on the other person.

If you are intentionally, or even unintentionally, placing an unreasonable burden on the other person, you should consider carefully what you are saying. Such burdens often thwart attempts to continue the relationship. You should have a reasonable expectation that the other person has an interest in listening to your disclosure. For example, suppose you have a problem with your parents that you need to discuss with someone. Before disclosing your problem to a friend, you should have a reasonable expectation that he or she will want to help you and that your disclosure will not be an unwanted burden. Perhaps a friend has discussed a similar situation with you in the past or another friend has made a sincere offer to discuss anything that troubles you. On the other hand, you probably will not find much comfort from friends who are preoccupied with serious problems of their own or who might see your problem as trivial or burdensome.

Cartoon © Hilary B. Price. Reprinted with special permission of King Features Syndicate.

Resources for Review and Skill Building

Many of these resources are supported by the Connections CD-ROM and free Online Learning Center website.

SUMMARY

This summary is organized around the questions found at the beginning of the chapter. See if you can answer them before reading the summary paragraphs.

1. What is interpersonal communication?

Interpersonal communication is interaction among a small number of people and is characterized by more personal and individualized communication than that which takes place in larger groups. Interpersonal communication occurs when people speak and relate to each other as unique individuals. Interpersonal communication is shaped by the nature of the relationship between the communicators and, in turn, the nature of the communication shapes the relationship. We communicate differently in different relationships. The nature of relationship is often communicated in the "relationship" component of a message.

Interpersonal communication is also influenced by culture and gender. Different cultures have different expectations about relationships and how people should interact within those relationships. Some men and women also have differing expectations about interpersonal communication. Women are expected to show interest in others, self-disclose in relationships, and be cooperative, whereas men are expected to use talk to achieve goals. Women are more likely to talk about private feelings and thoughts, especially to their female friends, and men are more likely to talk about external topics such as work and politics.

2. How is intimacy communicated in interpersonal relationships?

High levels of trust, warmth, and affection characterize an intimate relationship. Relationships vary by breadth and depth. Breadth is the variety of contexts and types of topics discussed in a relationship. A narrow relationship is one in which you talk about the same thing in the same context. A broader relationship is one in which you encounter the same person in different contexts and talk about a wide range of topics. Depth refers to the amount of interaction you have with another person. Often depth is a factor of time—the more you interact with a person, the more intimate and personal the communication. Our most intimate relationships have both great breadth and depth.

3. What role does attraction play in relationship formation?

Interpersonal similarity, proximity, and physical attributes all affect the degree to which we are attracted to someone. We are often attracted to people with similar attitudes, interests, values, habits, and communication styles. We are attracted to people who live near us, belong to the same groups or organizations, or attend the same school. We are also attracted to those we find physically appealing, but our idea of "good looking" is very personal and varies greatly. Our physical attraction often increases as the relationship develops.

4. What role does communication play in the development of a relationship?

Communication is the substance of relationships. Through communication we establish, maintain, and end relationships. Although relationships are as unique as the individuals in them, there are general stages of development that many relationships experience as they mature. These stages are often characterized by particular communication patterns. Two general patterns of relationship development are relationship formation and relationship breakup.

Relationship formation is characterized by increasing intimacy and commitment. In the initiating stage of a relationship, we open lines of communication. We gain more information about the other person in the experimenting stage. In the intensifying stage, we increase both the depth and breadth of the relationship. We assimilate activities, schedules, and interests in the integrating stage. The bonding stage establishes mutual obligations and responsibilities and creates a foundation for long-term relationships.

Relationships that disintegrate usually start to do so in the differentiation stage, when we become dissatisfied with the relationship and focus on individual needs and preferences. We may significantly reduce the breadth and depth of the relationship in the circumscribing stage, actively avoid either a return to intimacy or further deterioration in the stagnating stage, and close channels of communication in the avoiding stage. Finally, in the terminating stage we end the relationship and try to make sense of the experience. Each relationship develops in its own way. Some may abbreviate or skip particular stages while others may move back and forth between just one or two phases.

5. **How can appropriate self-disclosure help maintain intimacy in an interpersonal relationship?**

   Effective communication is essential to manage ongoing intimacy in a long-term relationship. Self-disclosure can build trust and commitment in a relationship and is necessary, in some degree, to maintain ongoing intimacy. Self-disclosure should be suitable to the context, gradual, reciprocal, and have an appropriate purpose.

KEY TERMS

Test your understanding of these key terms by visiting the Connections CD-ROM and the Online Learning Center website at www.mhhe.com/dobkinpace.

attractiveness 192
breadth 187
depth 187
integrating topics 194
interpersonal communication 181
interpersonal similarity 190
intimate interpersonal relationships 187
metacommunication 196
physical attraction 192
self-disclosure 201
social penetration theory 187
social proximity 191
stages of relationship development 193
turning points 199

FOR FURTHER REFLECTION

Join a conversation about chapter concepts by visiting the Online Learning Center website at www.mhhe.com/dobkinpace

1. In the opening example, we said that Maya and Holly's friendship had changed when Maya went away to college.
   - Why is it difficult to maintain intimacy in a long-distance relationship?
   - What can communicators do to maintain intimacy in a long-distance relationship?
2. Examples of gendered communication styles are often easy to identify in popular media. Movies, television shows, and music videos all provide us with models of expected communication behaviors between men and women.
   - Can you tell whether a film is designed primarily for a male or female audience?
   - What are the different types of story lines?
   - How might the dialogue differ between men's and women's movies (e.g., who does most of the talking)?
   - What is different about the plots and character development in the two types of movies?
   - How do the differences in film types reflect stereotypes about male and female communication?

BUILDING COMMUNICATION SKILLS

1. Interpersonal communication is very responsive because communicators rapidly adapt to the uniqueness of the individuals and the relationship. To experience an extreme form of this responsiveness, do the following activity. Hold a conversation with a friend, partner, or family member. Instead of the normal format of taking turns, alternate *every* word—the first person says the first word, the second the second word, the first the third word, and so on. After you are finished, answer these questions:

   How was the conversation unique? Responsive?

   How did your relationship with the other person help you anticipate what was going to be said?
2. People communicate differently in different relationships. Suppose that you loan your car to a roommate to go shopping. While the roommate is at the mall, your car is stolen. Tell each of the following people about your problem.

- A police officer (reporting the crime).
- Your parents (they bought you the car).
- Your chemistry professor (your backpack with all your class notes and texts was in the trunk).
- An insurance agent (filing a claim).
- Your best friend (whom you were supposed to drive home for the weekend).

  How would the conversation with each person vary?

  To whom would you disclose the most information? Least? Why?

NET WORK

Note: While all the URLs listed were current as of the printing of this book, the sites often change. Please check our website (www.mhhe.com/dobkinpace) for updates and hyperlinks to these exercises.

1. There are many different self-assessment tests on the Web that deal with interpersonal communication. The site at http://www.queendom.com has several relationship assessments including those for self-disclosure, communication skills, conflict management, commitment readiness, and relationship satisfaction. The site at http://www.drphil.com/ articles/article/339 is a webpage for the television psychologist, Dr. Phil. On this site, he has tests for relationship chemistry and partner awareness. Finally, the site http://www.wellnessnet.com has a test of stress and its effect on interpersonal relationships. Take any of these tests and analyze the results. Do they seem accurate, informative, helpful, or not? Why?
2. The website http://www.ivillage.com has many interesting articles concerning online dating. Read two or three of these articles. How does the advice in these articles agree with or contradict the information presented in this chapter? How are online relationships different from other forms of relationships?

MEDIA MOMENTS

The film *Juno* (2007) tells the story of an unconventional high school relationship. Juno (Ellen Page) is a 16-year-old high school teen who discovers that she is expecting a child with another high school student named Paulie (Michael Cera). Juno doesn't consider Paulie to be her boyfriend and as she decides what to do with the baby, their relationship connects and disconnects several times. Watch the film and answer these questions:

- How was the relationship development similar to the sequence of stages presented in this chapter? How was the development different?
- What turning points occurred to move the relationship from one stage to the next?
- How did disclosures help the relationship grow or deteriorate?

Building Common Ground in Interpersonal Relationships

8

C H A P T E R

Adele and Paul were enjoying a quiet evening at the beach. They had been dating for some time, and Adele was struck by the beauty and peacefulness of the moment. Her silence was unnerving to Paul, who insisted that she tell him what she was thinking. Adele tried to put her feelings into words. "I just feel lucky to be alive and here with you. Relationships can take over your lives; you give everything to them, and they can be gone at any moment. That's why this moment, here with you, is so precious."

Paul wasn't sure how to interpret Adele's words. They were a bit scary to him. He knew that her family was putting pressure on her to get married and have a family, because Adele, at 25, was considered "old" to be single, particularly by her Cuban father. And Paul's mother didn't approve of Adele because she was Catholic. On the other hand, although he really liked being with Adele, Paul wasn't sure if he wanted to make a commitment to her anyway. Is that what she was asking?

Paul sat stiffly and silently, looking away from Adele. She grew tearful. What could he be thinking? She continued, "Anyway, I can't explain it, but I'm just thankful to be here, with you, now."

QUESTIONS TO FOCUS YOUR READING

1. How can conflict be valuable?
2. What are some common sources of conflict?
3. What are the different ways of handling conflict?
4. How can dialectical tensions be managed in relationships?
5. How can communication help build common ground among people who are different?
6. What are some important steps to remember in trying to resolve conflicts?

This was hard for Paul to hear. He said, "Sometimes I don't get you. You take everything so seriously, and you just get too emotional. Sometimes I think you're too intense."

At this point, Adele grew quiet and sad. She didn't think she was overly emotional, and she feared that Paul might never be able to understand her.

Differences between people can arise in any communication context, from the most intimate to the most unfamiliar. Indeed, the closer we get to someone else, the more likely we are to see the differences between that person and ourselves. For Adele and Paul, a quiet, romantic evening became strained as a result of different communication styles, expectations about their relationship, and understandings of cultural and religious backgrounds. To build common ground between them, they need to resolve the tensions and potential conflicts that grow out of their different expectations, feelings for, and understanding about each other.

Differences between people can be a source of conflict or personal growth. You probably like some friends because they seem to be just like you; they share the same values, like the same movies, or enjoy the same food. However, you might have other friends who are quite different from you, and these differences might be part of the reason you enjoy spending time with them. Perhaps they wear clothes that you wouldn't dare to try on, engage in activities you consider strange, or are several years younger or older than you. Differences can range from individual characteristics, such as the way someone talks, to cultural differences, such as what people consider to be proper rules for courtship, cooking, living arrangements, and employment. Conflicts occur when people who are in relationships—whether at home, in the workplace, or in shared social and political contexts—see their differences as incompatible or unmanageable.

conflict
A condition of disharmony and disagreement that exists when people who depend on one another see their needs, beliefs and values, or goals as incompatible.

Conflict is a condition of disharmony and disagreement that exists when people who depend on one another see their needs, beliefs and values, or goals as incompatible (Wilmot and Hocker 2001). By themselves, conflicts are neither good nor bad; depending on how we respond to them, however, conflicts can become either constructive or destructive. Disputes can arise between people from widely varied backgrounds or from those who seem to be quite similar. Some of the most frequent and intense conflicts erupt between siblings who have shared the same family, friends, and culture.

This chapter will explore ways that personal and cultural differences influence communication and the conflicts that these differences can produce. To the extent that no two individuals are identical, all communication involves issues of difference. This chapter focuses on communication patterns that such differences create and the ways to build common ground with others. This chapter will help you to:

- Identify the types and sources of conflict.
- Understand different conflict management styles.
- Distinguish between destructive and constructive responses to conflict.
- Respond to conflict in ways that build common ground.

The Value of Conflict

Most of us see conflict as uncomfortable at best, and destructive at worst. Conflicts can range from arguments about trivial preferences (e.g., whether toothpaste should be squeezed from the middle or the end of the tube) to more serious disagreements about beliefs, values, and the distribution of resources (e.g., whether scholarships should be based on need or merit). Large or small, these disagreements affect the quality of our communication and our ability to relate to others. The way we engage in conflict affects our romantic relationships, our mental health, the physical and mental health of our families, and our success at work and school (Wilmot and Hocker 2001).

From our earliest interactions with our families, we learned about ways to handle conflict. For example, your family talked about disagreements or perhaps they avoided them. In some families, loud voices and emotional outbursts are common signs that people are passionate. In other families, these ways of responding to conflict are frowned upon. You might have been taught to dismiss arguments rather than "holding on" to them, or you may have come to expect verbal or physical abuse as part of conflict. The ways you communicate when you disagree can be helpful to others and productive in your relationships, or they can be harmful and destroy the climate of trust on which good communication is built.

> "It is within families themselves where peace can begin. If families can learn to respect their members, and deal with conflict resolution, that would be the first step to keeping peace on a global level."
>
> —Susan Partnow, management consultant and peace activist

Conflict can provide opportunities for growth and change, and it can be a sign of a healthy relationship. When conflict is handled well, there can be several potential benefits (Brinkert, 2010).

Establishing Boundaries and Norms. One potential outcome of conflict is the establishment of relationship boundaries, working patterns, and norms. For instance, suppose you and your roommate have an argument because she borrowed a CD without permission. One positive result of this conflict might be a clearer definition of what property can and cannot be shared. Presumably, your roommate would also think twice in the future about borrowing your things without permission. Similarly, perhaps a new employee at your store does not see stocking shelves as part of his duties, but your supervisor expects everyone to assume that responsibility. The conflict that results from different expectations can lead to clearer understanding and shared expectations between employees and their supervisors.

Expressing Feelings. Conflict can also be a vehicle for expressing feelings. Suppressed feelings often build in intensity; conflicts provide an outlet for such feelings. Think about how you feel when someone close to you says something hurtful. If you can't talk about how you feel, you are more likely to withdraw from the relationship. Similarly, businesses and organizations need to know when customers and members are dissatisfied. Conflict is one way by which organizations become aware of problems and can assess their performance.

Identifying Individual Needs. Another potential benefit of conflict is that it can help identify individual needs within relationships. The expression of individual needs will inevitably produce tension between people whose preferences and needs are different. The resulting conflict can be the means through which individuals can express their preferences and grow within a relationship. For example, if you never tell your parents that you don't like the clothes or food they usually send for your birthday, they will continue to send them to you each year.

Balancing Power. Conflict can also be a way to balance power within relationships. If one member of the relationship is always submissive and rarely expresses personal preferences or needs, the power inequity in the relationship will increase. One reason that groups come together in organizations such as trade unions is to give workers the opportunity to voice their concerns about unequal relationships between employees and managers. The conflict that often results can remind members that power should be equitable and continually negotiated.

Building a History of Survival. Finally, having and resolving a disagreement can demonstrate to both members that the relationship can withstand conflict. For instance, when romantic partners successfully survive their "first big fight," they begin to build a history of handling conflict that helps them prosper in the future (Siegert and Stamp 1994). They may even establish a set of ground rules for fighting, such as distinguishing topics or strategies that will be tolerated from those that cross a line. Understanding the positive functions of conflict is the first step in managing and resolving disagreements constructively, both for people in close relationships and for people who don't know each other very well. The box, "Applying Communication Concepts: Building a History of Shared Expectations," asks you to consider how potential conflict might be the impetus for creating harmonious living arrangements with others.

Sources of Conflict

At the beginning of the chapter, we defined conflict as a condition of disharmony and disagreement between people who depend on each other and see their needs, beliefs and values, or goals as incompatible. When people depend on one another, what one person does makes a difference to the other person. You might disagree strongly with your friend about when to arrive at a social event, but as long as the two of you do not plan to share a ride, the difference is unlikely to cause conflict. Once people become interdependent, whether in sharing a ride or raising a family, the potential sources for conflict accumulate. We will look at three sources of conflict: competing relationship needs, different beliefs and values, and incompatible goals.

Competing Relationship Needs

Every relationship, healthy or unhealthy, can evoke contradictory feelings and tensions among the people involved. For example, parents may both love to be around their children and also cherish some privacy. Communication scholars call these contradictory feelings **dialectical tensions** (Baxter 1990; Vanlear 1991). In interpersonal relationships, dialectical tensions are dynamic; they change and evolve with the relationship. Although they vary with particular circumstances, three dialectics occur in most relationships: autonomy/connection; stability/change; and expression/privacy (Baxter and Montgomery 1996).

dialectical tensions
Ongoing, changing needs that are often opposite or contradictory.

Applying Communication Concepts

BUILDING A HISTORY OF SHARED EXPECTATIONS

Sharing living space with others in a residence hall, apartment, or house creates many opportunities for disagreement and conflict. Starting college can be a particularly difficult time for those students who face shared living arrangements, as 90 percent of first-year students now arrive on campus having never even shared a bedroom (Beddingfield 2002). Conflicts can occur over differing expectations about everything from neatness to noise levels and smoking habits.

One of the keys to avoiding problems is to establish and communicate clear norms about various aspects of sharing a living space. Discussing explicit norms in the areas listed here can help prevent conflict. When disagreements do occur, they present opportunities for establishing shared expectations and boundaries.

- *Personal Belongings.* What belongings can others use? Do they need permission? What belongings are off limits? Which food items will you buy together? Which will you buy individually?
- *Noise Levels.* How loudly can you play a stereo or television? At what hours? Will you set aside quiet time for study?
- *Telephone Use.* Should you limit the length of each call? Should modem time be limited based on time spent (two hours each) or hours of the day (2 P.M. to 4 P.M.)? Who is in charge of paying the bill? Where should messages be left? What is the policy on answering call waiting?
- *Cleanliness.* What is your definition of cleanliness? How often do you clean your area? What chores should be shared and how often should they be rotated?
- *Guests.* Are guests allowed? How long should they stay? Are parties or social events allowed? If so, who will clean up?
- *Security.* When will the door be locked and when will it be open? How will parking spaces be shared or assigned?

These are just a few potential areas of conflict when living spaces are shared.

ASK YOURSELF:

1. Are there other areas of conflict that you have experienced when living with others?
2. Has discussion of expectations and norms led to a positive outcome?
3. What are some unresolved sources of tension that need to be addressed?

Autonomy/Connection. The opposing needs for **autonomy,** the need to retain independence, and **connection,** the need to be included in a relationship, can create tension in a relationship. You might feel this tension early in a relationship when integrating activities with someone else alters your established, personal routine. You want to explore the relationship and be with the other person, but you might also feel that you are losing some of your freedom. Another example of this tension might have occurred when you went to college. While you were excited to be "on your own," you probably missed your family and friends. You will also feel this tension in relation to other social connections at college. For example, maybe you wanted to go to a new friend's home during a vacation but also worried that you would disappoint your parents if you did not see them. Levels of comfort with autonomy and connection can vary based on an

autonomy
The desire to retain independence.

connection
The need to be included in a relationship.

Expectations about autonomy and connection often need to be discussed when a family member leaves home.
© David Young-Wolff/PhotoEdit

individual's personality, culture of origin, or life stage. Perhaps your father was somewhat distant when you were young, but suddenly became very interested in your daily activities and called you frequently as he reached and passed middle age. Like all dialectical tensions, the contradiction between connection and autonomy is a strong one and a source of much friction throughout all stages of a relationship.

stability
The need to control our environment through safe and conventional routines.

change
The need for novelty and new experiences.

Stability/Change. The stability and change dialectic is the tension between the predictable and the novel. We have a strong need for **stability,** to feel in control of our environment and establish routines that are safe and conventional. But we also desire **change,** or novelty and new experiences; we like surprises. In relationships, we are comforted by the status quo, yet become bored by redundancy. Too much predictability is dull, but too much spontaneity is overwhelming. This tension might be especially pronounced in long-term relationships that have set daily routines. Many of these routines are mundane but necessary. Perhaps one person feeds the dog each day while the other waters the plants. The routine is safe, because each person knows his or her role and carries out the responsibility. But repeated routines can also become rigid and confining. Eventually each partner may wonder, Why don't you ever feed the dog? or Why don't you water the plants for a change? It is not uncommon to hear one member of a long-term relationship complain: "We do the same thing every weekend. Let's try something new." The stability/change dialectic also exists in workplace relationships. Although performing the same tasks repeatedly is comforting to some people, others thrive on the challenges posed by new knowledge and activities.

We also experience the tension between stability and change within our larger social circles. We may feel pressure to have our relationship conform to cultural or co-cultural expectations. At times, though, we may desire to have a new or unconventional relationship. This desire is particularly strong in cultures that tolerate uncertainty. For instance, some observers argue that the media's emphasis on youth, spontaneity, and change in the United States prompt people to become easily dissatisfied with long-term relationships. Conversely, people in cultures that set strict boundaries for the behaviors of relational partners often have more long-lasting relationships. For example, in India, where many marriages are arranged, divorce is far less common than in the United States.

Expression/Privacy. People in relationships often wrestle with opposing needs to express themselves and maintain privacy. At times, the need for personal **expression** is strong; individuals want to be open, candid, and confiding and desire others to be as well. At other times, people want **privacy;** they are restrained, circumspect, and distant (Vanlear 1991). As we have discussed, disclosing oneself to another person builds trust in relationships and promotes intimacy. But people also have a strong need to protect themselves from embarrassment and to establish and maintain a separate identity. Excessive openness can lead a person to feel a loss of control and a need for privacy. This need for privacy occurs at all stages of a relationship, even our most intimate ones. For example, spouses may be keenly aware of and discuss each other's daily activities, goals, and feelings, yet still keep correspondence and financial information private. Students do not often tell their parents everything they are doing at college, and parents typically withhold some information from their children. This tension between expression and privacy, like the other dialectics, also occurs in the broader social context of the relationship. For instance, if you become friends with a supervisor at work, you may feel free to discuss your friendship with some co-workers but conceal it from others. You want to be both public and private about your circumstance at the same time. Like the other dialectics, both impulses are legitimate and need attention. Learning to manage these contradictory needs is one key to cultivating intimacy in a relationship.

expression
The need to be or have others be open, candid, and confiding.

privacy
The need to be or have others be restrained, circumspect, and distant.

Dialectical Tensions across Communication Contexts. As we have seen, dialectical tensions can affect all kinds of relationships, from those with friends to those with parents, spouses, and co-workers. Workplaces have increasingly become places where people make friends and find life partners. Over the past 50 years, the amount of time at work spent interacting with others has increased rapidly, so much so that one-fifth of us meet our spouses or life-partners through work, and 7 out of every 10 men and 9 out of 10 women make lasting friendships at work (Reeves 2001). Conflicts can arise when people create social relationships in professional situations and attempt to manage their need for autonomy/connection and expression/privacy. Norms about phone conversations, nonverbal behaviors, and appropriate use of e-mail should be discussed with one's colleagues, because communicators may not share expectations about behavior.

The need to balance expression and privacy has also become increasingly challenging because of the wide array of communication technologies. Cell phones, pagers, e-mail, and "instant messaging" all raise the expectation that people should be accessible to others regardless of time and place. Tensions arise in situations ranging from maintaining a networked calendar at a worksite, where fellow employees have access to a down-to-the-minute schedule of co-workers, to relational partners in conflict who can interrupt each other on the computer through instant messaging to extend a heated discussion. Consider the following situation exchange between Paul and Adele, the couple introduced at the beginning of the chapter. Adele wants to end the relationship and will not answer phone calls from Paul, who breaks in on one of her Internet chats.

Paul: I know you're there.

Adele: Busted.

Paul: I'm sorry about last night. I just wanted to talk to you. When you get back from Mexico, will you have dinner with me?

Adele: No. I'm sorry if I sound harsh, but you are extremely self-centered if you think you can just slip back into my life.

Paul: All I wanted was a little space.

Adele: That's fine. Space. Breeeathe. You have lots of it.

Paul: I did nothing wrong. I was honest with you, completely honest! All I wanted was for you to understand and now, when I want to share my feelings with you, you're telling me I'm a phony. What do you need, attention twenty-four/seven?

Adele: No, I don't need that at all. I'd probably flip out. But your asking me that makes me laugh. What's the point of me telling you what I want? The minute you tell someone what you want, it's not the same. It's either there or it's not.

Watch part of an interview with Dr. Barbara Montgomery on competing tensions in relationships (CD Clip 8.1).

Was it appropriate for Paul to interrupt Adele? Consider the dialectical tensions in this relationship. Paul has violated Adele's privacy because of his own need to express his feelings. Clear tensions exist between Adele's desire for autonomy and Paul's need for connection. Adele wants spontaneity while also having some consistent (if unidentified) relational needs met. Managing dialectical tensions that emerge in a variety of communication contexts will be critical if this couple plans to stay together.

Differences in Beliefs and Values

Intelligent people with good intentions sometimes come into conflict, not because only one of them is "right," but because they have different sources of knowledge, different perceptions of events, or different values, or because they have different ways of communicating about conflict. Conflicts also arise when people have different assumptions due to unequal access to information. Suppose that a father is traveling several hundred miles to visit his two adult sons, both of whom live in different households in the same city. Several days before his trip, the father tells one son that he is coming but does not tell the second son until he arrives at the home of the first. As a result, conflict is likely to erupt between the father and his second son, and perhaps between the two sons as well. Simple misunderstandings about what happened, if not addressed, can also grow into major conflicts. One person's harmless joke can be perceived as harassment by someone else, one person's dinner invitation to a friend might be interpreted by the friend as a romantic proposition, and one person's belief that he or she does most of the household chores might be disputed by another member of the household.

What Is Worth Fighting About? The more long-standing and difficult conflicts occur when people have different values about what constitutes conflict and how conflicts should be managed. These differences are often easiest to identify when people violate the expectations of others about appropriate ways to disagree (Gundykunst and Kim 1997). Suppose, for example, that Lars, a student, disagrees with Professor Ali about the way an assignment was graded, and he tries hard to communicate this belief constructively. He gives Professor Ali his best persuasive reasons for rejecting the grade and thinks he is listening actively and responding respectfully to his professor. Professor Ali, however, seems to be insulted. Rather than acknowledge anything Lars says, Professor Ali points to the diplomas hanging in her office and reminds Lars of how many years she has been teaching at universities. Lars and Professor Ali probably will not get the chance to discuss Lars's grade until they manage their cultural differences about appropriate ways to communicate with each other.

Lars and Professor Ali seem to be communicating past one another because they are operating from different cultural assumptions about how students and professors should relate to each other. Lars considers himself relatively equal to the professor and expects her to value his opinion. Professor Ali, on the other hand, sees Lars's comments as challenges to her authority about matters that he should not question. Cultural differences do not always cause conflict, and conflict can occur just as easily between people who share the same culture. One middle-aged African-American woman from Georgia might work in a family planning clinic while another woman from the same background stands outside, protesting the existence of the clinic. But whenever people come from varied backgrounds and see others as having different values, the likelihood and complexity of conflict increases because of different expectations about how conflict should be managed.

> "Every belief we hold, every behavior we cherish as normal, every social or economic arrangement we perceive as fixed and unalterable can be and is regarded by other people as bizarre, inexplicable, and wholly irrational."
>
> —Stephen Brookfield, philosopher and educator

High/Low Context. In Chapter 1 we discussed specific features of messages and noted that some statements seem to have direct, clear meaning while others made sense based on the relationship between the people interacting or the context in which the communication took place. When communication is **high context,** people expect others to figure out implicit meanings based on the situation or the relationship between communicators. For instance, there might be enough shared history between Ed and Liliana so that they change their topic of conversation when Charlize enters the room. Or, one of them might say to the other, "I had lunch with the devil yesterday," and both know who the "devil" is without having to use a name. **Low context** communicators, in contrast, expect information to be direct and explicit. For example, two cardiologists are likely to use exact and descriptive language when talking to each other about a patient.

high context
An interaction style in which people expect others to figure out implicit meanings based on the situation or the relationship between communicators.

low context
An interaction style in which communicators expect information to be direct and explicit.

Problems can arise when high- and low-context styles come together. The cardiologist who uses low-context communication when talking to a patient who is terminally ill might deeply offend the patient, who expects the cardiologist to adopt more empathetic language. In some Asian cultures, moreover, medical professionals are not supposed to give patients the details of their illness, because talking in such a direct way would violate the privacy of the patient's body.

Differences in low- and high-context styles of interaction show up in more subtle ways as well. Suppose Stan offers to give his friend Brian a relatively new futon bed. Brian offers to pay Stan, but Stan refuses the money. Later in the conversation, Stan says that he really needs a dining room table. Although he hasn't suggested directly to Brian that he expects anything, a few weeks later Stan says, "So, are we still trading the futon for a table?" Stan could think that Brian is being manipulative, or he might understand that Brian's high-context style of communication meant that he would rather maintain a friendly, casual atmosphere than turn the exchange into a business transaction.

People from different cultures often prefer and use different levels of context when they communicate. In cultures that emphasize group identity and prioritize community needs, high-context communication is more common. Since people place high value on the quality of relationships, they are more likely to talk to each other in ways that preserve those relationships. People in cultures that emphasize individual needs, rights, and identity tend to use and prefer the more exact and explicit style of low-context communication. When the two styles meet, impatience and frustration can result. The low-context communicator wants ideas and intentions stated up front, to "cut to the chase." The high-context communicator is likely to see such communication as rude and abrasive, particularly if speaking with someone he or she perceives to have lower social status.

As always, knowing the expectations and preferences of others is an important first step in creating shared understanding among communicators. In Chapter 2 we discussed the importance of preserving face in communication. Low-context communicators need to address high-context communicators in ways that acknowledge the importance of their relationship and reinforce their self-esteem. High-context communicators might consider the needs of others for specific information and remove ambiguity when possible. The box, "Communicating Across Cultures in Business," asks you to think about the different values and expectations of communicators from China and Western Europe.

Incompatible Goals

Just as conflict can occur over different needs, beliefs, and values, it can also arise from incompatible goals. Sometimes goals are easy to identify, such as the desires to occupy land, obtain resources, or earn prestige. At other times, personal goals may be hidden. Suppose that Grant wants his supervisor, Ursella, to be fired so that he can apply for her position. He might avoid her, challenge her in group meetings, or delay completion of her projects without her awareness of his underlying goal. Conflicts occur when people see the goals of others they depend upon as either unimportant or standing in the way of progress toward their own goal. Such conflicts range from those due to relational partners with competing goals in conflict over which television program to watch, to countries in conflict over which ethnic or religious group should be allowed to live within their borders.

Conflicts over goals often occur because the people involved are focusing on points of disagreement rather than trying to build a common ground. Once they focus on their own position on an issue, they are less likely to see how their goals might be compatible. Consider the conflict between Mia and Arlie, who share responsibility for the care of their younger brother, Thomas. Mia wants to attend a weekend seminar that will help her earn credit toward her certificate in dental hygiene. While Arlie supports Mia's career goals, she believes that she

Exploring Communication Concepts

COMMUNICATING ACROSS CULTURES IN BUSINESS

As joint ventures between businesses from different cultures become more common, so do the instances of cultural conflict. Several recent studies have explored the nature of and strategies for dealing with these conflicts. In her analysis of communication between Chinese and Western European business people involved in joint ventures, Linda Beamer (1998) found several sources of misunderstanding. Because the Chinese emphasized relationships, foreign managers had difficulty getting information from Chinese government officials, whereas their Chinese partners obtained information through their personal relationships with those officials. In the United States, cultivating friendships with officials to gain favors has often been seen as unethical, but cultivating such ties was the only way to get work done in China.

The Chinese managers also tended to rely on past models of problem solving, whereas Westerners tended to prefer experimentation and creativity. Chinese managers preferred to repeat past approaches to problem solving because projects that were unsuccessful could then be blamed on the model used rather than the people making decisions. Westerners were also more direct in their communication than their Chinese counterparts. For instance, they expected employees to ask for and provide reasons to justify a raise. Chinese managers said that such a request would prompt them to ask the employee to resign because raises should only be awarded to groups, not individuals.

Because of differences such as these, Beamer (1998) argued that the recognition of cultural differences in communication between businesspeople is "critical to prevent small misunderstandings from developing into large problems" (p. 58). She suggested that companies employ "culture interpreters" to explain misunderstandings and mediate conflicts.

ASK YOURSELF:

1. If you were a "culture interpreter," what advice would you give the Western managers? The Chinese managers?
2. Would you use a high- or low-context style in asking for a raise? What would such a request sound like?

already takes care of Thomas most weekends and wants some time to begin a new exercise program. Mia is likely to see Arlie's goal as less important and Arlie's request as impeding her own goals. Arlie is likely to resent Mia, become angry, and insist that her goal of starting a solid exercise routine is just as important as Mia's goal.

Arlie and Mia are locked into their positions, rather than thinking about their common interests. Both could benefit from focusing on their shared responsibility for their brother, so that the issue becomes one of dividing that responsibility rather than arguing over whose goals are more important. Perhaps Mia can commit to watching Thomas every other weekend, or Mia and Arlie can negotiate regular times for Arlie to establish her exercise routine. The ability of Mia and Arlie to move beyond their positions and build common ground will depend on the effectiveness of their conflict management skills.

Ways of Handling Conflict

As we have noted throughout the chapter, people handle conflict in a variety of ways. We develop expectations about conflict based on what we learn from our families, peer groups, and co-cultures; our styles of responding to conflict depend on both our personal background and our experience with different conflict management strategies. In this section, we will identify common styles of conflict management, destructive responses to conflict, and ways of handling conflict constructively.

> "Some couples have gotten into a habit of yelling at each other whenever they disagree . . . one partner turns up the volume and the other switches off."
>
> —Lisa Parkinson, family therapist

Identifying Your Conflict Management Style

There are several common approaches to conflict. The one you rely on most often depends on your personality, experience, values, and culture. If you find conflict to be particularly unpleasant, if you have suffered physical or emotional trauma, if you place a high value on relationships, or if you come from a culture or co-culture that steers clear of confrontation, you are likely to adopt a style of accommodating others or avoiding conflict. If, on the other hand, you come from a co-culture that emphasizes direct expression of ideas, competition, and the importance of accomplishing tasks, you are more likely to be drawn to a style of persuading others to accept your viewpoint. Figure 8-1 identifies six possible styles of managing conflict: coercion, persuasion, collaboration, compromise, accommodation, and avoidance.

coercion
Psychologically or physically forcing the other person to accept your point of view.

Coercion is forcing the other person, psychologically or physically, to accept your point of view. The list of coercive techniques includes an unpleasant assortment of threats, blame, punishment, blackmail, abuse, and ridicule. Coercion can be as simple as telling others that they either do things your way or they find someone else to be with or work with. Sometimes coercion can happen through manipulation, as when one person forces another to agree through the exploitation of circumstances. Coercion through manipulation includes leaving the room during an argument, intentionally crying to stop discussion, purposefully withholding information, and other indirect methods of forcing one's point of view on the other person. People sometimes resort to such tactics out of desperation, ignorance, or deep-seated psychological troubles. In a very small number of situations, such as a parent forcing a child to stop engaging in dangerous behavior,

FIGURE 8-1 CONFLICT MANAGEMENT STYLES

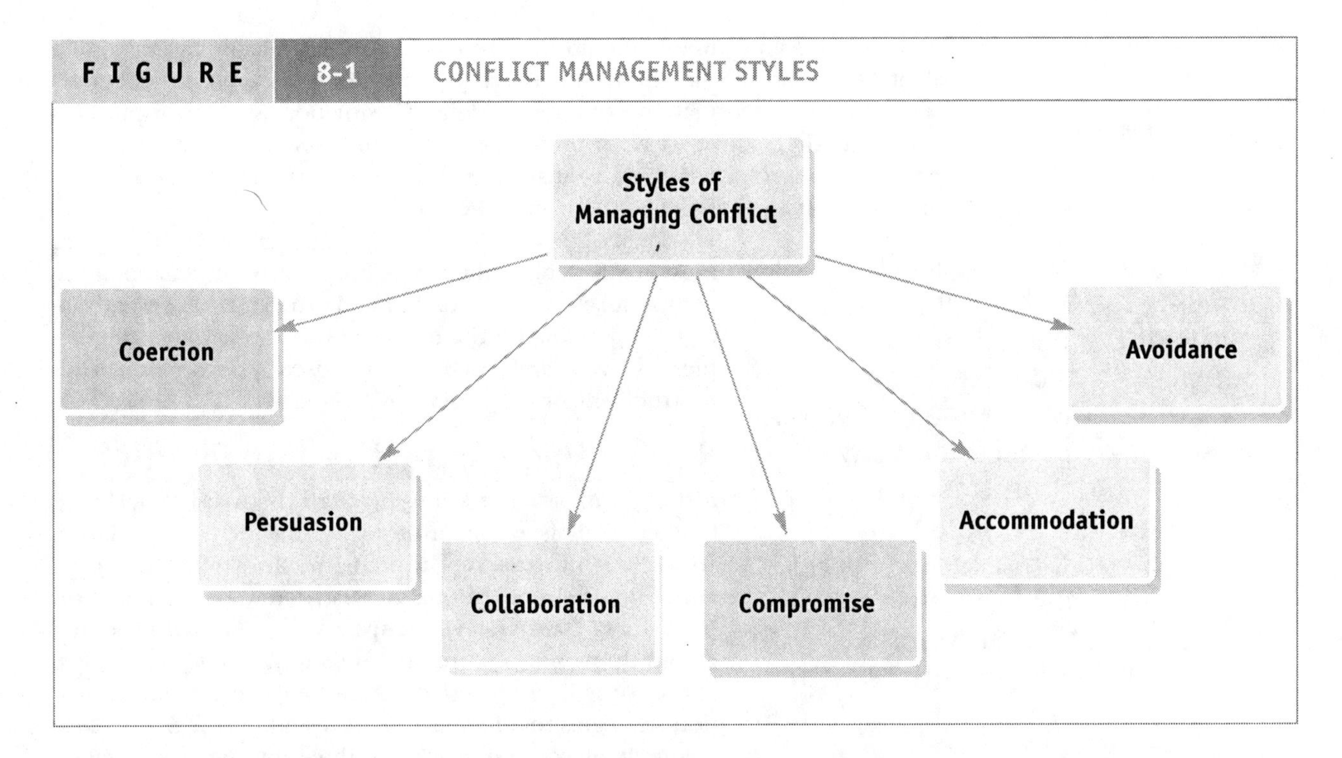

coercion is arguably acceptable. However, employing these methods for conflict management, even in small doses, can be harmful to relationships. Any selfish benefit gained from these tactics comes at the expense of the other person.

Persuasion is the attempt to get others to change their point of view. Persuaders usually believe that they have the best grasp of the issues and know how to get things done. Many people who have grown up in the United States know about and are comfortable with this style of managing conflict, as public debate, written argument, and confrontation are common in many co-cultures. Among other co-cultures and for some individuals, persuasion can seem overbearing and inflexible. Sometimes persuaders can become competitive and see the conflict as a "win–lose" proposition.

Collaboration requires working together to reach consensus. This approach is often called a "win–win" strategy, because it synthesizes the best parts of each perspective. Collaborators believe that people can work together to resolve issues and are usually open to new ideas. People from cultures that place a high priority on relationships tend to favor collaboration, whereas people who want quick resolutions often get frustrated by the time that collaboration can take. Like collaboration, compromise is a conflict management style that tries to level the playing field of participants and promote equal representation of different interests. **Compromise** occurs when members in a relationship give up something in order to achieve an acceptable resolution to the conflict. Compromisers see conflict management as requiring negotiation, or give and take, for everyone to benefit from resolution of the conflict.

The two remaining styles of conflict management move further away from self-interest and closer to satisfying others as a primary goal. **Accommodation** means sacrificing, in whole or in part, one's own preferences and points of view. Accommodators usually let other people have their way and downplay the importance of issues. They will concede to others for the sake of resolution. Sometimes accommodators support others by listening and helping them sort through

persuasion
Attempting to get others to change their point of view.

collaboration
Working together to reach consensus.

compromise
Giving up something in order to find an acceptable solution to the problem.

accommodation
Sacrificing, in whole or in part, your own preferences and points of view.

avoidance
Attempting to evade conflict.

information. **Avoidance** is the attempt to evade conflict, usually by remaining silent or leaving the situation. Sometimes people choose to avoid conflicts because they lack information or understanding of a situation. Avoidance can be a way to let others move ahead or protect oneself from coercion, or it can be an attempt to show resentment or dissatisfaction with others. At other times, avoiders might use humor to distract others and relieve tension.

"I once believed, as most do, that arguments are to be won, the opponent pummeled into submission and silenced. You can imagine how that idea played at home. If, in accordance with such a definition, I won an argument, I began to lose the relationship. Winning an argument merely meant that I had won the right to live in silence with the woman and children I loved."

—Gerry Spence, *lawyer and author*

Each of us has a conflict management style that we are most comfortable using. Coercion, persuasion, collaboration, compromise, accommodation, and avoidance all have advantages depending on the nature of the conflict and the people involved, and each can be used to respond either destructively or constructively to conflict.

Responding Destructively to Conflict

Although most of us know through firsthand experience that conflict is often unpleasant, not all conflict is destructive. Unfortunately, though, much of what we learn about conflict contributes to destructive communication behaviors. **Destructive responses to conflict** entail competition, self-centeredness, hostility, and *defensiveness.* Participants in destructive conflict engage in communication strategies that increase anxiety and hurt feelings, close channels of communication, reduce intimacy, or escalate conflicts, sometimes to the point of violence. Rather than trying to achieve solutions that benefit more than one person or group, participants take a "win-lose" approach assuming that one person's gain is another's loss. Some of our more popular communication technologies make it particularly easy to lapse into destructive communication. Think about the speed and potential anonymity of e-mail, telephone calls, and Internet discussion groups. The hostile communication of Internet *flaming* happens partly because people who attack others on the Internet do not have to face their victims. People who cannot be identified or can respond instantly are likely to communicate destructively in the heat of anger, because they can use these technologies to shield themselves from their relationships with others.

destructive responses to conflict
Communication characterized by competition, self-centeredness, hostility, and defensiveness.

Gottman (1999) called the following four behaviors the "four horsemen of the apocalypse" because they are so destructive that they can indicate the end of a relationship is near.

1. *Setting a critical tone.* Gottman suggested that the first minute of conflict between spouses can indicate whether 96 percent of them will stay together or divorce. Disagreements that start with attacks and accusations ("you never," "you always," "you are so . . .") set a negative tone that is hard to overcome. Suppose Kim is angry that her partner is late. As soon as her partner walks in the door, Kim says, "I can't believe you're so inconsiderate!" Instead of blaming her partner, Kim might say, "I really get frustrated when I have to wait for you."

   Another, more subtle way of setting a critical tone happens when communicators use **passive aggression.** Rather than retaliating with directly aggressive messages, communicators who use passive aggression express hostility through sarcasm ("Can't you take a joke?"), guilt ("If you really think you've

passive aggression
Indirect expression of hostility, often through the use of humor, guilt, or inconsiderate behavior.

spent enough time with the kids this week, I guess I can watch them for you tonight"), or inconsiderate behavior ("I didn't tell you he called? I suppose I could start writing down your phone messages"). If you find yourself using passive aggression, think about the behaviors that make you feel hostile and try to identify those for the other person. If someone uses these tactics in conflicts with you, avoid responding with a counterattack (this can be difficult!); instead, try to start an honest exchange about what behaviors are triggering the other person's hostility ("Sometimes I can't tell that you're joking. I need to know if that's really how you feel").

2. *Acting out of defensiveness.* When people feel threatened or attacked, they often respond by retaliating, whining, or reneging (going back) on what they said. You might have acted defensively when someone broke a promise to you or criticized you. Or you might have felt attacked by a simple statement based on the history of your relationship with someone else. Consider the following exchange:

   Chris: We should clean the yard this weekend.

   Lee: I always clean up around here, and you just watch TV all weekend. I shouldn't have to be in charge of keeping everything nice for you.

   Chris: What's your problem? I said *we* should clean the yard. I didn't say *you* should do it yourself.

   Lee's defensive response suggests that there is a deeper issue about equal participation in chores that needs to be discussed. Lee and Chris would both benefit from a discussion about shared responsibilities.

Watch a video that contrasts defensive and supportive communication (Clip 8.2).

3. *Stonewalling.* When people refuse to talk about conflicts or problems, ignore them, or try to keep others from raising them, they are *stonewalling.* In the example at the beginning of the chapter, Paul was stonewalling when he avoided looking at Adele and didn't respond verbally to her. Similarly, stonewalling occurs when a member of a group refuses to participate in resolving disagreements. Although stonewalling may seem to be a way to prevent conflicts from escalating, it prevents everyone involved from dealing constructively with them. As a result, feelings of dissatisfaction *fester* and become more intense with time.
4. *Communicating contempt.* The person who communicates *contempt* discredits others by attempting to establish his or her superiority through insults, mockery, or sarcasm. Contempt is a form of hostility. Telling someone "You must be nuts to let this bother you so much" communicates superiority, because it suggests that the other person is weak or overly emotional. Sneers, heavy sighs that convey the attitude, "yeah, right," are also ways to communicate contempt. Once conflicts are reduced to this level, it becomes increasingly difficult to address them in ways that respect the beliefs and integrity of everyone involved.

Ultimately, conflict that is managed poorly or avoided altogether can destroy individual relationships, communities, and nations. Criticism, defensiveness, stonewalling, and contempt occur across all communication contexts. Once participants become accustomed to using them, they can be hard habits to break. On the other hand, being able to recognize these tactics and choose different responses to conflict is a first step in managing tensions constructively.

Remaining rational, understanding others, and maintaining open communication are keys to handling conflict constructively.
© Bob Daemmrich/The Image Works

Handling Conflict Constructively

Conflict is an inevitable part of human relationships. The ways we handle conflict are what make it either constructive or destructive. As the previous section illustrates, some degree of conflict can be beneficial to relationships and in certain cases, it can increase intimacy. Cooperation, shared interests, flexibility, open discussion, and support of differences characterize **constructive responses to conflict.** Conflicts become constructive when people focus on shared interests and try to achieve "win-win" solutions. Even the most difficult dilemmas can be approached constructively through communication behaviors that improve the relationships among people.

constructive responses to conflict
Communication characterized by cooperation, shared interests, flexibility, open discussion, and support of differences.

A good relationship is one that can deal successfully with the differences between people (Fisher and Brown 1988). The following guidelines can help you manage differences and handle conflicts constructively:

1. *Remain rational.* Do your best to balance emotion with reason, even when passions run high. Sometimes this means taking a mental "time out," so that you can separate how you feel from your decision about how to treat or communicate with others.
2. *Try to understand others.* Often when you disagree with others, you feel as if they don't understand you. Although you might want to make sure that you are understood, sometimes it is more important to try to see things from the other person's point of view.
3. *Maintain open communication.* It can be hard to listen when you want to be heard. However, to handle conflict constructively you need to listen carefully and consult others when you make decisions, particularly when your decisions affect them.
4. *Be reliable.* There might be times when others try to deceive or manipulate you. Try to suspend judgment of them and disagree without resorting to your own deception or manipulation; be straightforward and honest.

5. *Avoid coercion.* Be open to persuasion and try to persuade others without resorting to force.
6. *Separate the person from the issue.* Try to focus on ideas rather than personalities; allow others to retreat gracefully from their positions.
7. *Remain open to others.* Even if others reject you and your concerns, try to remain open to their ideas. Show that you care about them, even when you disagree with them.

These guidelines are ambitious, and keeping all of them in mind when you are in the heat of an argument can be difficult. However, if you practice at least a few of them, you will foster the constructive management of conflict.

"Honest disagreement is often a good sign of progress."
—Mahatma Gandhi

Building Common Ground with Responsible Communication

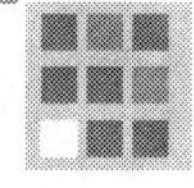

Thus far, we have identified many differences in attitudes and behaviors toward conflict, cultural knowledge, and styles of communicating, all of which influence the way we perceive and respond to others. Sometimes those differences produce tensions that can be either threatening or liberating. They are threatening when we fear them or lack the ability to respond to them appropriately and effectively. They are liberating when we learn how to identify the basis of differences, challenge our own assumptions, and communicate in ways that build bridges with others. This final section offers specific strategies for managing conflicts and building common ground in ways that maintain personal integrity, show respect for others, and build lasting and productive relationships.

Managing Dialectical Tensions

Although dialectical tensions are in some ways irreconcilable, they can be managed. Effective management of dialectical tensions through selection, separation, neutralization, or reframing can help relationships grow while acknowledging the different needs of relational partners.

Selection. The strategy of selection requires focusing on one need while suppressing or ignoring the other. For example, as we noted earlier, most parents feel the need to be with their children but also desire some private time together. Many parents, however, suppress their desire for autonomy as a couple for the sake of their children. Selection is an effective technique in situations where one of the desires is clearly dominant for both members of the relationship. It is less effective in situations where both urges are strong or when the two parties in a relationship experience the dialectic differently. In such cases, suppressing the neglected feeling will produce frustrations and resentment. Suppressed feelings often surface with even more intensity until they are managed in a different way.

Separation. Another alternative is to manage dialectics by meeting both needs separately in different situations through a process called separation. For example, you might tell your parents that you are going to your friend's home for winter break but that you will return home for spring break. Or a newlywed couple might ask their parents not to come to their apartment unannounced, but they might also create a routine of spending one Sunday a month with them. A couple might establish expectations within their relationship that they will be open about most things but reserve the right to withhold some information with the understanding that some amount of mystery can strengthen the relationship. Some cultures are particularly *adept* at using separation to manage tensions. For instance, some Asian cultures avoid religious conflict by separating public and private prayer. A Japanese person who is raised Catholic is free to participate in a Buddhist ceremony and then return home to say a Catholic prayer, because the Japanese see public participation in a religious ceremony as separate from, and thus not necessarily in conflict with, private religious beliefs.

Separation works well in situations where clear boundaries can be established between the tensions. It is less effective when the tensions coexist in many areas of the relationship, where drawing boundaries reduces relational intimacy, or where separation promotes the needs of only one member of the relationship.

Neutralization. You can also neutralize dialectics through a process of compromise and accommodation. Neutralization is rarely an ideal solution to problems, but it can be effective in limited use. Sometimes neutralization means acknowledging the other person's unique needs and tolerating the difference, which can show a commitment to the relationship. Although compromise is not the ideal solution since neither person is completely satisfied with the outcome, it often produces a workable way of managing hard-to-solve conflicts. For example, suppose you prefer to study with music playing, but that music bothers your roommate. One compromise would be to play music on even numbered days and not on odd numbered days. Neither you nor your roommate is entirely happy with this arrangement, but it does provide a solution that you both may be able to accept.

Long-term relationships involve many such compromises and sacrifices. However, if one member of the relationship continually gives in to the other, compromise can become a form of avoidance or manipulation that serves the purposes of only one person in the relationship. This power imbalance almost inevitably leads to feelings of dissatisfaction and distrust. Neutralization does not work in areas of strong preference where compromise is seen as "halfhearted" and only frustrates everyone involved.

Reframing. Finally, you can try to redefine or reframe dialectic tensions. Reframing takes much effort and time but can be successful in creating new ways of "seeing" tensions. For instance, a couple can learn to see time apart as a bonding activity. Although it is difficult, many couples conduct long-distance relationships by redefining what being "together" means, so that phone calls, e-mail, and seeing each other on weekends begin to meet that definition of togetherness. Reframing is the most difficult strategy in dealing with dialectic tension but one that can open channels of communication and significantly increase the quality of relationships.

> "Human beings draw close to one another by their common nature, but habits and customs keep them apart."
>
> —Confucius

FIGURE 8-2 STEPS IN VALUING DIFFERENCE

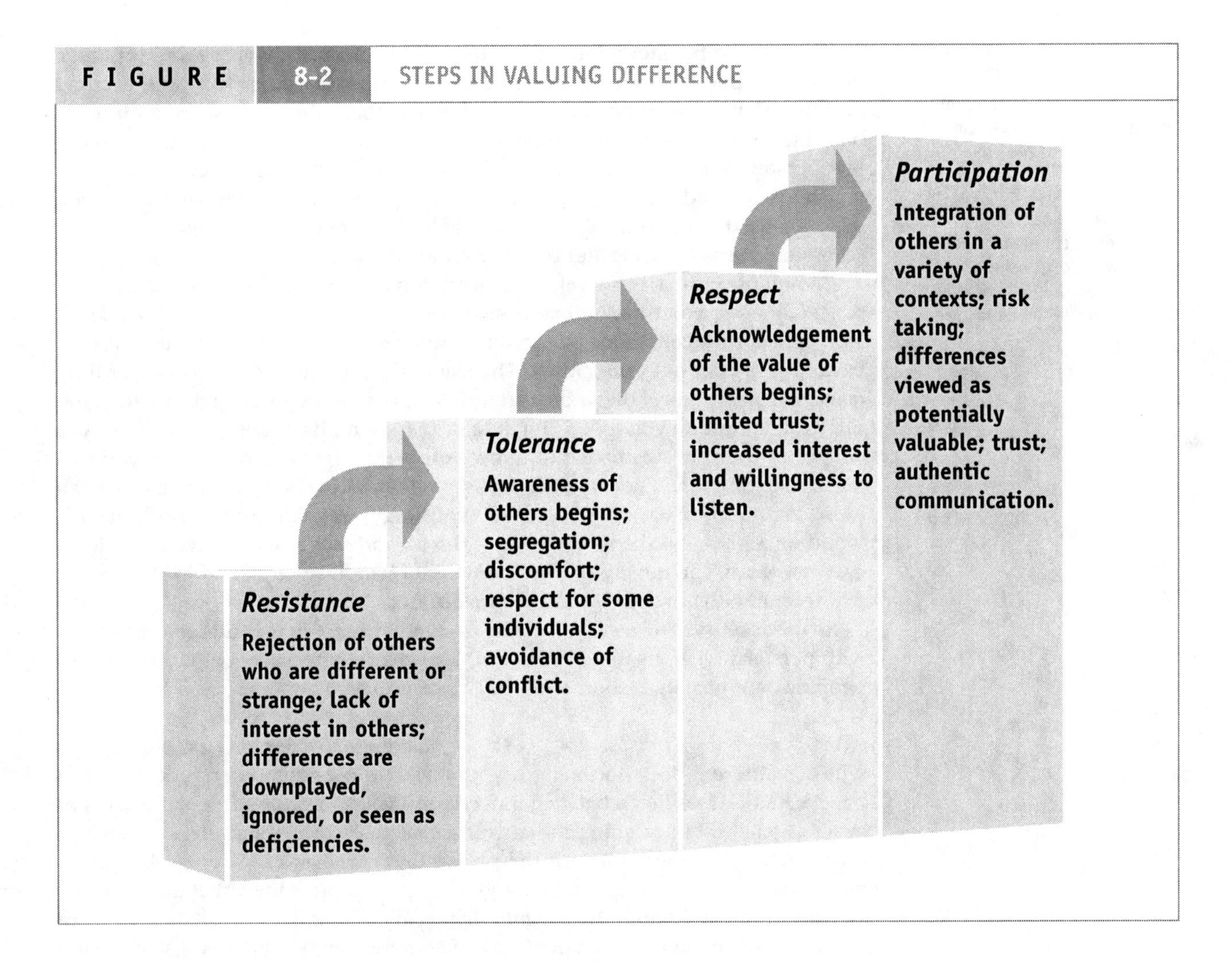

Resistance
Rejection of others who are different or strange; lack of interest in others; differences are downplayed, ignored, or seen as deficiencies.
Tolerance
Awareness of others begins; segregation; discomfort; respect for some individuals; avoidance of conflict.
Respect
Acknowledgement of the value of others begins; limited trust; increased interest and willingness to listen.
Participation
Integration of others in a variety of contexts; risk taking; differences viewed as potentially valuable; trust; authentic communication.

Communicating across Differences

Our relationship needs, beliefs and values, goals, and ways of handling conflict influence what we consider to be a conflict and how we communicate when we encounter others who are different. Our first response to others who are different might be to ignore, avoid, or judge them. However, as we come to understand and appreciate those differences and to build relationships with people who are different, we increase the potential for building common ground and move further up the model of inclusion to full participation with others. Figure 8-2 illustrates the steps in creating common understandings among people from different groups.

At the first level, **resistance,** we judge others who are different and avoid or reject them. We might decide not to invite members of that group to social events or working groups, we might live in communities or go to schools where we don't have to encounter them, or we might choose to ignore the fact that they are different. At the next level, **tolerance,** we are willing to acknowledge that differences exist and are likely to adopt a "live and let live" attitude. We prefer not to talk too much about our differences, because doing so might lead to disagreements,

resistance
The level of communication where we judge others who are different and avoid or reject them.

tolerance
The level of communication where we are willing to acknowledge that differences exist.

respect
The level of communication where we begin to see value in the ways that others are different.

participation
The level of communication where we accept others who are different as unique, valuable, and integrated into our lives.

and that would be uncomfortable. At the level of **respect,** we begin to see value in the ways that others are different; life becomes more interesting and exciting because of the unique perspectives and beliefs that others can share with us. At this stage, we might begin to trust a member of a different group and consider that person to be a good friend. Finally, when we reach the **participation** stage, we have accepted others as unique and valuable, and have integrated them into our lives. We do not avoid conflict with them, and when we do disagree, we try to communicate as honestly and respectfully as we can.

Communication at the level of participation can be difficult. Suppose that you are the first woman to attend an all-male institution, such as a military academy. Members of these organizations are likely to reject you at the outset; after all, they have been, by definition, exclusive. The leaders of the organization, however, have mandated that you be allowed to attend. So, a few of the men might be tolerant. They do not talk to you much, but at least they don't harass or sneer at you. As a couple of your classmates get to know you better, they begin to invite you to a few social functions. They might even ask you what it's like to be the first woman there. Finally, if you're very fortunate, you might develop a friendship, having found someone who shares activities with you, and sees you both as an individual *and* a woman. The quality of your conversations with that friend is likely to be better than with anyone else in the organization.

As this example suggests, the ability to communicate across differences begins with personal relationships. Relationships span differences most effectively when people communicate resourcefully and respectfully.

Communicating Resourcefully. Building common ground with others who are different does not mean adapting to others at the expense of what you believe, but it does mean balancing needs and learning from the perspectives of others. Sometimes searching for consensus silences voices and turns into "coercive harmony" (Nader 2001), or the pressure to conform to beliefs or behaviors with which you disagree. Instead of giving up the core values that are most important to you, hold onto them while also trying to identify with people who are different, understand their unique ways of communicating, and establish common goals and values. For example, suppose that you view yourself to be a religious person, and you consider sitting in a church pew before an altar the appropriate way to pray. Your roommate, Abubakar, prays by kneeling and putting his head to the floor. Although his behavior initially may seem strange to you, consider asking him about his faith and understanding of prayer. You are likely to find new connections between yourself and Abubakar without necessarily questioning your own convictions. Communicating resourcefully means both understanding others *and* taking your own points of view seriously (Arnet 1986; Hones 1999). Use your cultural knowledge to interpret and adapt to other cultures, change your own understandings when necessary, and build common ground with other members of the wider communities to which you belong.

> "I have found it of enormous value when I can permit myself to understand another person. . . . If I let myself really understand another person, I might be changed by that understanding."
>
> —Carl Rogers, psychologist

Communicating Respectfully. Earlier in this chapter, we suggested that showing respect was one stage in the process of creating inclusive communication practices. Remember that there is a cultural basis to respect. For example,

Think It Over

COMMUNICATION, COMMUNITY, AND RESPONSES TO RACIAL CONFLICT

On April 10, 2001, the city of Cincinnati erupted in four days of violent protest over the fatal police shooting of Timothy Thomas, a young, unarmed, African-American man. Thomas was the 15th African American to die in Cincinnati police custody since 1995. The shooting came within a month of a lawsuit filed against the city based on accusations of racial profiling. Following Thomas's death, the U.S. Department of Justice launched a federal investigation of the Cincinnati Police Division's "patterns and practices."

One outcome of the lawsuit and investigation was an agreement among the police, city officials, and community to embark on an elaborate, six-month mediation process that would include thousands of community members. The process would begin with people sitting down and talking, first within their own identity groups, and then with people from different groups. The encounters would be structured to address issues of dignity, respect, and opportunity, so that relations between police and the community could be based on shared understanding and goals (LeBlanc 2001).

Why might it be important to have these discussions? Who should be included in them? Can you generate a list of ground rules for how communication should take place?

giving praise ("Your speed in completing that project was outstanding!") to someone from Japan might be considered boasting and therefore insulting, even if given to someone you know well, because praise is reserved for group performance. Indeed, some Japanese use *lavish* praise as the ultimate form of insult, because they expect it to be interpreted sarcastically. Communicating respectfully means that you maintain a careful balance between your own needs and values and those of the wider groups to which you belong. Developing community requires engaging in dialogue with those who are different while embracing higher values of civility and tolerance of diversity and plurality (Gundykunst and Kim 1997). Gundykunst (1994) called this "graceful fighting."

As we noted in our discussion about the value of conflict, one way of determining how a couple, group, or community might talk respectfully about conflict is by generating ground rules for discussion. Communicators might agree to take responsibility for making themselves understood, keep comments confidential, avoid interruption, use considerate language, and check the accuracy of their assumptions about what others mean (Pearce and Littlejohn 1997). The "Think It Over" box illustrates one community's attempts to establish common ground by building relationships among members of the community.

Creating Common Ground from Conflict

All communication begins with a relationship between people. The quality of this relationship and the climate in which it unfolds will determine how well conflicts are addressed. **Communication climate** refers to the way people feel about their interactions with others, either in relationships or in groups. You have probably been in relationships or groups where the climate was noticeably "chilly."

communication climate
The way people feel about their interactions with others, either in relationships or in groups.

Perhaps some group members dealt with conflicts destructively, ignored one another, and exchanged insults, or one individual dominated all discussion. "Warmer" communication climates occur when people trust one another, contribute freely, and use responsible strategies for intervening in conflicts.

Conflicts can be handled responsibly through careful timing of responses, a focus on the present, tentative and descriptive statements, discovery of how others feel, persuasive arguments, a focus on strengths, and the search for a mutually satisfying resolution.

- *Be sure the timing is right.* If your partner has just gotten home after a particularly stressful day, it might be best to wait until later in the evening to discuss the visit to your parents that she is dreading. Choose a place and time where participants can listen attentively and comfortably.
- *Try to focus on current behavior.* You may be particularly adept at remembering what someone said days or weeks ago, and though the statement may have been painful, try to focus on what is being said now. For example, a classmate may have made an insensitive remark about one of your speeches, and now you disagree over how to approach a group project. Talk about issues connected with the group project rather than bringing up the previous comment.
- *Be tentative in your statements and be willing to modify one or both points of view.* Accommodate the objections of the other person. Suppose you participate in a committee that is selecting finalists for a job with your organization. Although you were not impressed with one of the candidates for the position, other committee members want to schedule a follow-up interview. By being flexible, you might find that the candidate exceeds your expectations.
- *Find out how others feel.* Be sure to ask why the other people in the group are impressed with the job candidate, and make sure that you have compatible goals for the new employee.
- *Use descriptive communication.* Define problems as clearly as you can and identify specific behaviors that create tension. Perhaps you have decided that you no longer want to carpool with a friend to school. Let your friend know why you want to stop sharing rides. Concentrate on using "I" language. Instead of saying, "You just can't handle being in the car with me," identify the source of tension and how it makes you feel. "When you keep making comments about my driving, I feel like you don't trust me."
- *Focus on strengths as well as weaknesses.* Identify positive behaviors and shared values or interests, and incorporate them with your own by combining ideas. Often both points of view in an argument are compatible, but we become emotionally invested in our point of view and the disagreement becomes competitive. A rational discussion of ideas often reveals that you can combine both points of view into one solution.
- *Offer your most persuasive arguments with support and development.* If your ideas are good and your evidence convincing, then the other person may not only accept your point of view but also embrace it. For example, suppose you and a friend are planning a vacation to California. Your friend wants to fly and you want to drive. You could try to persuade your friend on the merits of driving to California by showing your friend a map of the drive with interesting spots highlighted along the way. Discover what would interest your friend and plan a route to accommodate those interests.

- ***Search for a solution that satisfies the needs of everyone involved.*** Look for common needs and interests, and generate new ideas that go beyond the original disagreement. Sometimes creativity is the best solution to old problems. It satisfies our need for spontaneity, moves past the original objections, and finds "win-win" solutions that both parties like.

Although real arguments can be hard to manage, if both parties make a sincere effort to discuss problems, different points of view can often be integrated into a single solution. Even when everyone's needs cannot be accommodated, the outcome is more likely to be accepted if all involved have participated in a careful and considerate process of deliberation.

Building common ground among people requires both strong voices and a process of communication by which individuals and groups can build relationships and make sound decisions. Whether between people in close relationships, strangers brought together by circumstance, working groups at school or business, or within entire communities and cultures, conflicts can either destroy people or bring them together. Careful, considerate, and effective communication is perhaps the most important means of bringing people together in mutually satisfying and productive ways.

> "If communication is about anything, it's about building common ground between groups."
>
> —Jim Applegate, former president, National Communication Association

What are some advantages and disadvantages of town hall meetings as places for communication about conflict?

Resources for Review and Skill Building

Many of these resources are supported by the Connections CD-ROM and the free Online Learning Center website.

SUMMARY

This summary is organized around the questions found at the beginning of the chapter. See if you can answer them before reading the summary paragraphs.

1. How can conflict be valuable?

   Conflict can be a way to establish relationship boundaries and norms, express feelings, identify individual needs, balance power, and build a history of survival within relationships.

2. What are some common sources of conflict?

   Conflict is a condition of disharmony and disagreement that exists whenever people who depend on one another see their needs, beliefs and values, or goals as incompatible. Competing relationship needs can cause dialectical tensions, which are contradictory feelings in relationships. Some of the most common dialectics are autonomy/connection, stability/change, and expression/privacy. Different beliefs and values about what happened, what constitutes conflict, and how to communicate about conflict can become complicated by the high- or low-context preferences of communicators. People also come in conflict when they see their goals as incompatible or perceive others to be standing in the way of achieving their goals.

3. What are the different ways of handling conflict?

   Individual conflict styles can be characterized as coercion, persuasion, collaboration, compromise, accommodation, or avoidance. Conflicts become destructive when communicators criticize, act out of defensiveness, stonewall, and convey contempt. Constructive responses to conflict include remaining rational, trying to understand others, maintaining open communication, being reliable, avoiding coercion, separating people from issues, and remaining open to others.

4. How can dialectical tensions be managed in relationships?

   Dialectical tensions can be managed by fulfilling one need while suppressing the other (selection), managing competing needs in different situations (separation), compromising by giving up a need (neutralization), and creating new meanings and definitions for tensions (reframing).

5. How can communication help build common ground among people?

   Often people resist talking to, working with, or living alongside people they perceive to be different. When people tolerate difference, they acknowledge that everyone is not alike but still prefer to be with others who are similar to them. When people of different cultures respect each other, they start to see differences as valuable and may form new friendships. Participation occurs when people are willing to include others in a range of activities and can see them as both unique and full participants or members of a shared community.

   Building common ground requires communicating resourcefully and respectfully. Resourceful communicators know their own core beliefs and values but are also willing to identify with people who are different, understand their ways of communicating, and establish common goals and values. Respectful communicators practice civility and tolerance by observing ground rules such as preserving confidentiality, avoiding interruptions, using considerate language, and checking the accuracy of their assumptions.

6. What are some important steps to remember in trying to resolve conflicts?

Most conflict situations improve when communicators carefully choose the timing of discussion, focus on current behavior, are willing to modify beliefs and find out how others feel, use descriptive statements, focus on strengths as well as weaknesses, use persuasive arguments, and generate creative solutions that satisfy the needs of everyone involved.

KEY TERMS

Test your understanding of these key terms by visiting the Connections CD-ROM and Online Learning Center website at www.mhhe.com/dobkinpace.

accommodation 221
autonomy 213
avoidance 222
change 214
coercion 220
collaboration 221
communication climate 229
compromise 221
conflict 210
connection 213
constructive responses to conflict 224
destructive responses to conflict 222
dialectical tensions 212
expression 215
high context 217
low context 217
participation 228
passive aggression 222
persuasion 221
privacy 215
resistance 227
respect 228
stability 214
tolerance 227

FOR FURTHER REFLECTION

1. Identify your own preferred style of conflict management.
   - What are its advantages? Disadvantages?
   - How would you communicate with someone who is two styles removed from you (see Figure 8-1)?
   - Can you think of situations in which it might be best to use one style rather than the other?
2. Suppose you are at the grocery store and in a hurry. You are standing in the express line with a few items in a basket. The express line next to you is moving along quickly, but the man in front of you has 15 to 20 items in his cart.
   - How do you feel?
   - Do you say anything to the man? Why or why not?
   - Would it make a difference if the person were a woman?

Join a conversation about chapter concepts by visiting the Online Learning Center website at www.mhhe.com/dobkinpace

BUILDING COMMUNICATION SKILLS

1. Compose a "Family Fighting Inventory" by making note of the amount of fighting in your family, the topics most often fought about, and topics that should never have been argued about in the first place.
   - What communication patterns have you come to expect?
   - In what ways are they constructive? Destructive?
   - How might you change your approach to conflict?
2. Attend a meeting or event at which you are a stranger. Engage in a conversation with someone at that event.
   - How did he or she respond to you?
   - Were there sources of discomfort, and if so, how did you deal with them?

NET WORK

Note: While all the URLs listed were current as of the printing of this book, these sites often change. Please check our website (www.mhhe.com/dobkinpace) for updates and hyperlinks to these exercises.

1. Several websites offer helpful guidelines for communicating across cultures. See, for example, www.casagordita.com/diverse.htm for a discussion of "How to Make Meetings Work in a Culturally Diverse Group." What are some of the behaviors you might value and expect of others? What are some ways to be an effective leader even when those expectations are not met?
2. Visit the website, www.silkrc.com and explore the link to foreign nationals who discuss their feelings about "the American workplace." What are sources of tension for them? How often are their difficulties based on misunderstandings in communication? How might these misunderstandings be overcome?
3. The Public Conversations Project, (PCP), www.publicconversations.org offers resources designed to promote constructive dialogue about potentially divisive public issues. Enter one of the PCP dialogue forums. How might the groundrules for contributions encourage constructive rather than destructive conflict?

MEDIA MOMENTS

The film *American Beauty* (1999) tells the story of a suburban family whose routine becomes thrown out of balance. Lester and Carolyn, a married couple, struggle with tensions in their relationship, and Lester attempts to deal with his feelings about employment, his daughter, and his sexual desires.

Consider watching the film and answering the following questions:

- What are some of the dialectical tensions in this family? How are they managed (or mismanaged)?
- Can you identify destructive conflict strategies? What might make some of the conflicts more constructive?
- What effect do the communication strategies of Lester and Carolyn have on their daughter Jane?
- What cultural dimensions does Lester demonstrate? How do his internal conflicts reflect tensions about cultural and gender expectations?
- Do Lester's behaviors conform to the expectations of those around him? How do others respond when their expectations of Lester are violated?

Communicating in Groups

CHAPTER 9

Charlotte Bustamante had a choice to make. She was a terrific high school basketball player. During her junior year, she led the league in scoring and received much attention as one of the best players in the city. Charlotte was very competitive by nature and, going into her senior year, wanted to win the MVP trophy given annually to the best basketball player in the league. She also wanted to win the league championship.

During the summer, Charlotte's coach asked her to switch positions from the team's shooting guard to its new point guard. As a point guard, Charlotte would be the team leader but not the team's leading scorer. Charlotte accepted the coach's challenge, and the team worked together to reevaluate each person's position and contributions to the team. Her teammates elected her captain, a responsibility she took seriously, actively trying to build team unity. She talked often with the newer players about their abilities and how they could fit in with the returning players. During practice she would compliment teammates on good plays but also quietly correct any player who made a selfish play. Charlotte also met regularly with the coach to pass along team concerns and to solve any problems that were occurring. During games Charlotte shouted instructions and encouragement to teammates.

QUESTIONS TO FOCUS YOUR READING

1. What are some of the different types of small groups in society?
2. What are some of the advantages and disadvantages of group decision making?
3. How do norms and roles influence group communication and decision making?
4. How can groups organize a discussion effectively when making a decision?
5. What is the role of a responsible leader?

Charlotte was no longer the highest scorer on her own team, but her team was winning. During the final game, Charlotte's strong defense, smart decision making, and accurate passing helped the team win the coveted championship. She was not voted the league MVP, but she felt good about the leadership skills she developed, the progress of the other players, and the sense of accomplishment of winning a team championship.

Charlotte's experience with her team is typical of many successful small groups. Individuals often sacrifice their individual goals for the achievement of the group. Members have clearly defined roles within the group, including a good leader like Charlotte. Like the basketball team, groups must coordinate and *synchronize* the actions of individual members. Successful groups usually feel a sense of togetherness, or cohesion, in the pursuit of a common goal and members work hard to resolve conflicts. Importantly, effective communication is essential for the success of a group. Through communication, groups coordinate their actions, provide leadership, define and accept roles within the group, solve problems, and build cohesion. In short, one characteristic that separates successful groups from less successful ones is the effectiveness of communication.

All of us belong to groups. Humans are inherently social creatures, and we seek opportunities to be with others (Ebstein et al. 2010). We work in groups, study in groups, join clubs or associations, live in groups, and play sports in teams. Being a part of a group has many rewards, including the feeling that we belong to something and are needed. Group membership, however, can also cause frustrations due to disagreements or interpersonal problems with other group members. Regardless of whether groups are a source of frustration or comfort, they are a part of our lives. Positive group experiences can be enhanced and negative ones improved by understanding some basic characteristics of group communication. This chapter will help you to:

- Understand the importance of groups in society.
- Identify the advantages and disadvantages of group participation.
- Identify various group communication norms and roles.
- Use a structured approach to decision making in groups.
- Understand what it takes to lead a group in an effective and responsible manner.

"Never doubt that a small group of thoughtful, committed citizens can change the world; indeed, it's the only thing that ever does."

—Margaret Mead, anthropologist

Small Groups Are Essential in Our Society

In the quote above, Margaret Mead expresses the sentiments of many experts: Small groups have more power than individuals to change society. Societies are organized around individuals, small groups, and complex organizations that are made up of several small groups. For example, individuals belong to a family, several families make up a neighborhood, and several neighborhoods make up a city. The bridge between the individual and the larger, more complex society is the small group. To understand how groups influence society, one needs to know what a small group is and what types of groups exist in our society.

Small Groups Exist through Communication

People gather in large and small crowds all the time. You might be standing in line with several people to use the campus ATM machine. Or, you might be sitting in the bleachers with hundreds of other fans watching a soccer game. Perhaps you are studying at a table in the library with several other students whom you do not know. Do you think of yourself as a member of any of these "groups"? Do any of these gatherings even constitute a group? According to most small group theorists, they don't. People who happen to be in the same place at the same time are not a group. If this is true, then, what is a small group? A **small group** is composed of a limited number of individuals who communicate interdependently to achieve a common goal. Let's look at the various parts of this definition.

small group
A limited number of individuals who communicate interdependently to achieve a common goal.

Groups Consist of a Small Number of Members. The actual number of people is not as important as the opportunity to interact. That opportunity is what separates a large group, such as all members of the Audubon Society or Atlanta Falcons fan club, from a small group. Small groups usually consist of three to seven people. Communication researchers often differentiate between two people and three or more because the dynamics of communication between two people are considerably different than the dynamics between three or more. The number of communication channels, the possibility of distortion and noise, the opportunity to share diverse resources, the number of individual preferences to be accommodated, and the likelihood of conflict all increase in a group. In a group of three people, for example, two of the members could form a majority to "outvote" the other member. These communication dynamics become more complex as the group becomes larger. For instance, business managers have long recognized that supervising a group of 15 people is far more challenging than managing 3 people (Span of Control 2004).

According to our definition, small groups are made up of "individuals" who bring their own personalities, biases, and goals to the group. This diversity of perspective, experience, and resources can help a group to be successful, but accommodating individual differences is also one of the real frustrations of the group experience. For example, you may have been in a study group that included a few members who didn't want to study. Instead, they wanted to talk about current movies, relationship problems, and the weather—anything but the course material! By leading the study group off on tangents, individual members can waste the time of the other members and diminish the ability of a group to accomplish its goal. Ideally, at least one member of the group will realize what is happening and bring everyone back to the topic at hand. One of the challenges facing a group is to find ways to harness the individual talents of each member and contribute to a common goal while preventing idiosyncratic behavior from distracting the group from its purpose.

Group Members Interact with Each Other. The people standing in line to use the campus ATM machine, for instance, are not really a group because they are not interacting with each other. Through communication, the group establishes its own identity apart from simply a collection of individuals.

Communication also enables the group to accomplish goals and maintain member relationships. The definition of groups implies an expectation that communication among members will be ongoing and somewhat constant. Members who rarely talk to other members are really not a part of the group. Similarly, individuals in the group are interdependent. If you are a member of a group, there is an expectation that you will participate and contribute to the group. If you choose not to participate, then the group is altered. In this way, each member affects the group as a whole.

Small Groups Have a Common Goal or Purpose. There are many different purposes of groups, ranging from problem solving to simple socializing. But whatever the common goal is, it defines the group and gives it purpose. Without this purpose, the group stops existing. A jury, for example, is a group charged with the purpose of deciding the innocence or guilt of a defendant. When the decision is made, the group disbands. The word "common" also implies that members have a mutual interest in the outcome. They may disagree over how to achieve it, but a common goal is necessary to link members together. If a group disagrees about the fundamental nature of the goal, it rarely continues to exist.

Types of Groups

There are many different types of groups that enrich our society. You may belong to a few or to many of these and are no doubt aware that different groups meet different needs. As you review the following descriptions of various types of groups, think about the impact they may have on your life.

Primary Groups: Satisfying Basic Needs. Primary groups exist to fulfill the basic human needs of survival, safety, and inclusion. Primary groups include nuclear families, extended families, friendship groups, and other intimate groups of people. Primary groups are called "primary" because they are one of the earliest and most important influences on our socialization. Socialization is the process of teaching individual members about society's expectations, customs, values, and rules. Primary groups are an important part of our lives, and the feelings of love and support that they provide shape our sense of worth and value. The lack of such support can have a lasting effect on our identity and our overall quality of life. Research on older people, for instance, indicates that those who participate in social groups and have close friendships are healthier and live longer than those who do not ("Socializing Elderly Live Longer" 1999; "Living to Age 100" 1999).

Social Groups: Having Fun with Friends. Social groups provide members with opportunities for recreation, relaxation, and entertainment. These groups include sororities, fraternities, clubs, and hobby groups. In such social groups, getting together with others is sometimes more important to group members than the stated purpose of the group. Social groups frequently provide members with an opportunity to meet and form relationships that evolve into primary groups or other significant associations. They also may offer significant fringe benefits as discussed in the box on "Exploring Communications Concepts," which explores some of the benefits and liabilities of group memberships for college students.

Exploring Communication Concepts

GROUP INVOLVEMENT AND COLLEGE SUCCESS

Alexander Astin, professor of education at the University of California at Los Angeles, conducted a far-reaching survey of college student behaviors and discovered significant benefits of joining student groups. Astin's study, published in the book *What Matters in College?* (1993), surveyed 25,000 students at approximately 200 colleges and universities in the United States. Astin was interested in discovering what aspects of the college environment and student behavior contributed most to the personal development of students and their academic performance. He discovered that while there were many differences between students who succeed at college and those who do not, one of the strongest factors correlating with success was joining a student peer group.

Students who joined campus government groups, clubs, sororities and fraternities, sports teams, or even class discussion groups were more likely to perform well in college than those who did not. In particular, those who joined peer groups reported greater increases in leadership abilities, interpersonal skills, and public speaking proficiencies than students who didn't join peer groups. Joining a group was also positively related to overall academic development including higher grade point averages, stronger analytical and problem-solving skills, greater cultural awareness, and a broader knowledge base. Membership was also correlated with social activism, satisfaction with the faculty, and intellectual self-esteem. Finally, students who joined peer groups reported feeling less depressed than students who did not. Positive correlation does not mean that group membership caused these positive outcomes; that is, joining a group will not necessarily improve your grades. Still, many college counselors believe that participation in one or more groups, together with a strong network of friends and groups, helps students adjust to college life and is often an enriching experience (Light 2001).

ASK YOURSELF:

1. How might joining a group help students improve their analytic problem-solving skills? Interpersonal skills?
2. How might joining too many groups hinder a student's overall academic performance?

Help Groups: Self-Improvement through the Support of Others. Help groups are unique because their goal is the improvement of individual members rather than group success. Help groups include counseling and therapy groups, consciousness-raising groups, and skill-building groups. Counseling and therapy groups usually have a trained facilitator who helps members confront and solve problems. These trained professionals know that group support can be an important part of overcoming challenges and encouraging individual betterment. Support groups are composed of members who share a common problem, want to exchange information, discuss issues, share insights and resources, and provide empathic understanding. For instance, there are support groups for parents of children who are hearing impaired, victims of domestic abuse, and people who feel lonely. Members of support groups often find a renewed strength to handle their challenges after joining such groups.

Civic Groups: The Power of Participation. Civic groups are local government and education groups that operate within the official structure of public institutions. Some of these groups are composed of members who are elected by local citizens. These groups include oversight boards for hospitals, regulatory commissions for public utilities, school boards, and city councils. Some smaller municipalities still make decisions in town meetings where any citizen can attend, discuss, and vote on policies. Other civic groups are composed of members who are appointed or volunteer to serve on various city and education committees. They include parent, student, and teacher associations (PSTAs), school site counsels, local historic preservation groups, museum boards, and juries and grand juries. Through participation in these civic groups, individual citizens engage in the democratic process and influence local politics.

Grassroots Groups: The Power of Common People. Grassroots groups are local groups organized outside the official government structure. Grassroots groups are often called Non-governmental Organizations (NGO) or Community Based Organizations (CBO). Some of these groups work in collaboration with government officials. For example, neighborhood watch groups work closely with local law enforcement agencies to help reduce crime in many communities, and local better business bureaus work with authorities to ensure fair business practices. At other times, Grassroots groups help supplement services that the local governments do not offer or which are insufficient to meet community needs. Many such groups help feed and clothe the homeless, visit older citizens in their homes, and provide care for Alzheimer's patients. Finally, some grassroots groups, such as animal rights groups, offer an alternative voice to official government positions. This alternative position is important in local governance. Groups such as the Southern Poverty Legal Center or antidefamation organizations help to protect the rights of minorities and other marginalized groups. The alternative voice that these groups offer ensures diversity of opinion in our local communities. Special interest groups monitor and advocate policy on specific issues such as the environment or land use. The strength of grassroots groups lies in the commitment group members feel toward a common goal and their willingness to work together to advance their cause.

Virtual Groups: Networking through Computers. Virtual groups transcend time and distance; that is, group members are not at the same location or even communicating at the same time. There are many different types of virtual groups. There are social networking groups such as those found on Facebook. There are virtual help groups, civic groups, and problem-solving groups. Many grassroots groups are virtual groups as well.

Some virtual groups, like social networking groups, are very informal and lack the official structure of leaders and deadlines. The common purpose in many of these groups is social connection and the opportunity to converse with others online (Perry and Schneider 1999).

A more focused type of virtual group is a discussion group (Perry and Schneider 1999). Usually these groups discuss a specific, common interest. These groups function as information outlets and decision-making groups. For example, the Online Learning Center that accompanies this text provides an opportunity to form a discussion group about course concepts. Discussion groups tend to be more topical and less anonymous than chat rooms. While there may be more than one topic of discussion, there usually is a limited series of related topics that group members refer to as threads. Discussion groups are often sponsored by specific organizations. For instance, many professors create discussion groups for college courses where students can exchange and discuss course concepts. While these conversations are more topical than those in chat rooms, they do wander considerably more than face-to-face conversation. Also, because communication in discussion groups, as well as chat rooms, is more anonymous than face-to-face communication, the conversation can become aggressive at times with some members resorting to insults and other forms of offensive communication. Some groups include a discussion monitor who edits postings and, when necessary, reminds participants of discussion rules.

The ability to solve problems and make decisions in groups is a fundamental communication skill that everyone should develop.
© Cindy Charles/PhotoEdit

Problem-Solving Groups: Focused on the Task at Hand. Most professional organizations, including businesses, civic groups, and NGOs, use small groups to solve problems or make decisions. Because solving problems and making decisions are so fundamental to a wide variety of careers and situations, the National Communication Association (NCA) identifies the ability to work in a group as one basic communication skill everybody should develop (National Communication Association 1998). Many employers rank the ability to work in a group as a qualification they are seeking in an employee because numerous contemporary businesses are organized around work teams (Kolb 1999). Some of these work teams, called **ad hoc groups,** are temporary in nature and are created for the purpose of making a specific decision or solving a unique problem. Once the problem is solved or the decision made, the ad hoc groups are disbanded. Another type of group, called a **standing group,** has a broad mandate and works continuously on a variety of related problems. For example, many businesses have quality control teams that evaluate the quality of customer service or products. Your professional life will be filled with work teams and your ability to work effectively within these groups will be important to you.

ad hoc groups
Temporary groups created for the purpose of making a specific decision or solving a unique problem.

standing group
A group that has a broad mandate and works continuously on a variety of related problems.

> "A committee is a group that keeps minutes and loses hours."
> —Milton Berle, comedian

The Rewards and Costs of Group Decision Making

Perhaps you think of committee and group work as a waste of time—too much talking and too few decisions. If so, you are not alone. Some professional managers become frustrated when working with groups and prefer simply to make decisions themselves. However, there are some important benefits to group decision making. Consider the situation of Lorraine, a manager in a medium-sized business seeking to expand. She is assigned the task of deciding which products and services to increase and which to curtail. She can research the problem and make the decision herself, or she can form a group and involve her co-workers in the decision-making process from the beginning, explaining the problem to the group, giving co-workers some basic guidelines such as deadlines and budget, and ultimately letting the group make the decision. Which method of decision making would you select? An increasing number of managers are using groups to make decisions. They believe that the rewards of group decision making, especially if the group discussion is efficient, outweigh the costs. Group problem solving has several benefits over individual decision making, but there are also problems associated with it. In the next sections we will look at the comparative advantages and disadvantages of group decision making.

Advantages of Group Decision Making

Groups often make better decisions than individuals for a variety of reasons.

1. *Group members bring with them different abilities, resources, and knowledge.* This diversity enables a group to develop a broader perspective on a problem than any one individual can, allows the group to see a wide range of possible solutions to the problem, and ultimately leads the group to select a better alternative (Hirokawa 1982, 1983; and Hirokawa and Pace 1983). By integrating diverse perspectives, the group often performs at a level beyond the capabilities of any one member. This phenomenon is called group synergy. **Group synergy** occurs when group members combine their abilities to produce an outcome greater than the sum of their individual abilities (Engleberg and Wynn 1997). For example, a sports team of less talented players will often win a game against a more talented team because they play together so well that they transcend their individual limitations. Working as a team enhances each player's ability. Similarly, in a decision-making group or a management team, the process often produces a better outcome than would be expected from individuals comprising the group (Ranganathan 2001).

group synergy
Group members combine their abilities to produce an outcome greater than the sum of their individual abilities.

2. *A group decision allows for a division of labor.* In a group, you can divide a task into *discrete* parts and have each member assume responsibility for a different element. By dividing the labor among the group, no one person is burdened with all of the work, which typically means that a group can accomplish more than an individual acting alone. For instance, consider a communication club that is sponsoring a faculty-student reception. Instead of handling all of the arrangements by herself, the club president assigned each student and faculty member a specific task. Some members brought items of food or drink. Others worked on the invitations and still others arranged a program of guest speakers. The reception was a great success and no one in the group felt overwhelmed by the effort.
3. *Finally, group members will be more committed to a decision that they make collectively than one that is made by only one or a few members.* Shared decision making empowers group members to shape their own goals and future. The feelings of autonomy and self-determination that develop when one participates in a group often produce an attachment to the group and the group's decision. This sense of attachment, solidarity, and camaraderie that binds a group together is called **cohesion**. Cohesion motivates members to

cohesion
A sense of attachment, solidarity, and camaraderie that binds a group together.

continue to participate in the group. Members feel as if they have a stake in the success of the group and are more supportive of and enthusiastic about implementing the decisions they make.

Disadvantages of Group Decision Making

While there are many benefits to group decision making, there are also liabilities. Usually the advantages of group decision making outweigh the liabilities, but it is important to understand the disadvantages so that you can mitigate the negative effects of a group experience and make the best decision possible.

1. *Group members must often sacrifice their individual preferences for the will of the group.* Integrating diverse opinions into a collective group decision is one of the real strengths of group decision making. But a frustrating by-product of this integration is the loss of individual choice. You have probably had this experience. Several of your friends want to go a movie together, but they cannot agree on which one to see. After several suggestions, they finally settle on a movie that you have already seen. Being a good sport, you go to the movie anyway. The group's preference may be different than any one member's choice, and it is sometimes difficult for a particular individual to modify his or her preference to accommodate the collective will of the group.
2. *Group decision making can lead to conflict.* Since groups are composed of unique individuals with different perspectives, conflict often occurs. Not all conflict is bad. Conflict can force a group to see new perspectives and actually make a better decision. Indeed, groups that have no conflict often make bad decisions because they do not test their ideas through disagreement. Conflict can become counterproductive, however, when it escalates into personal attacks and selfishness. Some conflicts create factions or coalitions within the group as members choose sides and square off against each other. Such coalitions hurt group cohesion and adversely affect the discussion.

   Although conflict is inevitable and even necessary in group decision making, it still makes the experience difficult for members, who may experience anxiety as a result. With experience, however, participants can learn to minimize such anxiety and maximize the benefits of conflict.
3. *Group decision making takes more time than individual decision making.* Integrating the opinions and preferences of members into an acceptable solution is a complex and sometimes slow process. The logistics alone of assembling all of the members together can be time consuming. Also, a frequent complaint about working in committees or groups is the amount of time participants spend talking about *tangential* subjects. A certain amount of socializing is healthy for a group and helps to build cohesion, but some groups engage in excessive socialization to postpone or forestall working on the group project, a phenomenon called **task-avoidance.**
4. *Finally, group decision making can mean working with members who do not do their share of the work.* Groups frequently contain members who are, for one reason or another, undependable. Most often, other group members must work even harder to compensate for these slothful members. This

task-avoidance
Engaging in excessive socialization to postpone or forestall working on the group project.

causes considerable resentment and prevents groups from achieving their optimal performance. To avoid such a scenario, groups should establish clear work expectations for each member who is accountable for a particular share of the workload. Clear and accurate communication is the key to effective performance evaluation. Vague hints that some group members are "not fulfilling their responsibility" rarely produce a change of behavior. But even with clear expectations, some members will not fulfill their obligations and others must make up for this lack of effort.

Although the disadvantages of group decision making often lead to frustration, the advantages provide real benefits such as better decisions and more committed group members. Group decision making does not need to be tedious and unduly time consuming. Skilled groups can use time efficiently and still produce a sound decision. Also, a decision that takes some time to reach is sometimes a better decision than one that is made quickly. Group decision making inherently restrains individuals from rushing into hasty and ill-conceived courses of action.

Norms and Roles Are Established through Group Communication

Leaders and supervisors can often maximize the advantages and minimize the disadvantages of group decision making by creating clear expectations for success. These expectations are communicated through the norms and roles that groups establish. In this section we will examine group norms and roles and how they are established through communication (see Figure 9-1).

Group Norms Establish Communication Guidelines for Members

group norms
Expectations, established through interaction, about how members should behave.

Group norms are expectations, established through interaction, about how members should behave. Generally, norms are prescriptions for action. They become the guidelines that members use to evaluate acceptable and unacceptable behavior. The group establishes these expectations as they communicate with each other. Norms change and develop over the course of group life. What is unacceptable at the beginning of a group's existence may become acceptable later. In families, for instance, younger children often have more freedom than their older siblings; as their children grow, parents change their expectations about what constitutes acceptable behavior.

Explicit Norms. Some norms are explicit rules. Explicit rules are usually communicated in a direct fashion and often written to emphasize their importance. Frequently, these norms have specific sanctions for a member who violates them and another member who is in charge of enforcing the rule. At your place of employment, for instance, there might be an explicit expectation that you will wear a uniform with the company name on it when you go to work. This company norm would probably be written in the employee handbook and supervisors would be charged with enforcing the rule. If you did not wear the uniform, your supervisor might issue you a written reprimand.

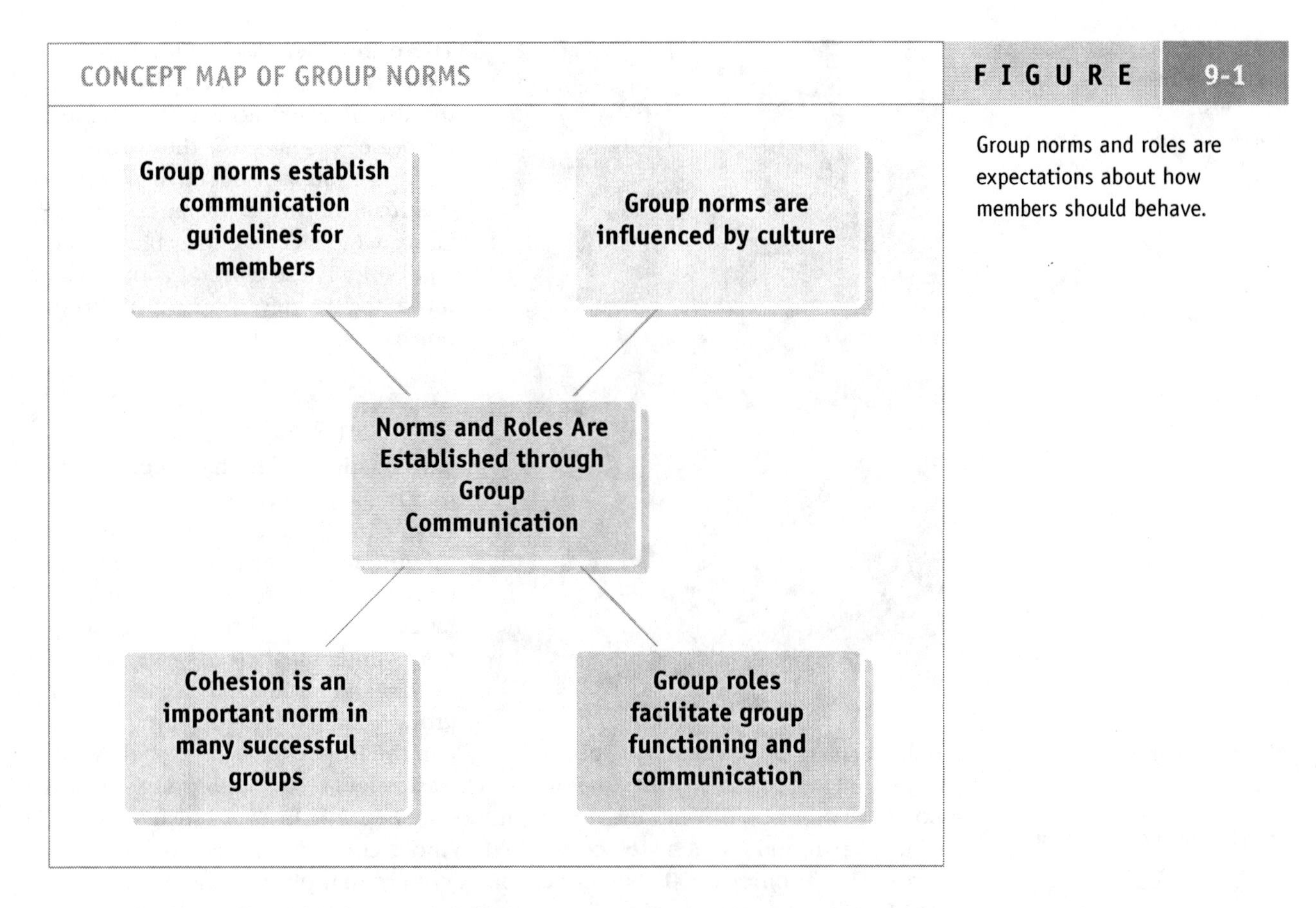

FIGURE 9-1

Group norms and roles are expectations about how members should behave.

Implicit Norms. Norms are implicit when they are assumed to exist but are rarely discussed openly. Through interaction, members gradually learn the expectations of the group. Classroom norms, for instance, vary from course to course. In some classrooms, professors encourage class participation and welcome comments from the students. In other courses, the professors expect students to listen and not to talk. These expectations become clear to students through classroom interaction, even though the expectations are not written anywhere. If a professor ignores raised hands, does not listen to student comments, or becomes impatient when a student asks a question, students quickly learn to sit quietly in class. By contrast, a professor who calls on students by name for comments, listens to those comments carefully, and welcomes questions invites students to contribute to the discussion. Groups of all kinds establish implicit norms about most aspects of group work. Miscommunication sometimes occurs when implicit norms are vague and confusing. Often, making these implicit norms more overt helps clear up misunderstandings.

Group Norms Are Influenced by Culture

Group norms and expectations about communication often differ from culture to culture or from co-culture to co-culture. For instance, we previously discussed the differences between high- and low-context cultures and noted that members of high-context cultures prefer implicit norms, whereas members of low-context cultures would be much more explicit in discussing communication expectations.

Group norms can vary based on the cultural identities of group members.

© Fujifotos/K. Kai/The Image Works

There are other basic cultural characteristics or dimensions that shape the use of group norms. This section introduces some of the broadest cultural contexts: collectivism and individualism, power distance, uncertainty avoidance, and masculinity and femininity. These cultural contexts all influence the development of group norms (Hofstede 1997).

Collectivism and Individualism. The first dimension, individualism-collectivism, has been called the primary dimension on which cultures vary (Triadis 1995). **Individualism** refers to the tendency of some cultures to emphasize the importance of individual rights over group rights, individual needs over group needs, and individual identity over group identity (Ting-Toomey 2000). Individualism is the dominant value of people in the United States and many Western European cultures. **Collectivism,** in contrast, refers to an emphasis on the importance of group obligations, needs, and identity. People from countries such as China, Japan, and Mexico are accustomed to more collectivistic, group-based cultures (Ting-Toomey 2000). Someone from a culture that places great value on individuals acting alone is likely to be more self-focused and expressive, whereas people from collectivistic cultures are more likely to be aware of and adjust what they say based on the expectations of others.

individualism
Emphasis on the importance of individual rights over group rights, individual needs over group needs, and individual identity over group identity.

collectivism
Emphasis on the importance of group obligations, needs, and identity.

As with all of the countries mentioned in this section, each country contains co-cultures with varying expectations; within cultures and co-cultures, individuals may interpret the expectations of others differently. However, understanding dimensions such as individualism and collectivism provides a starting point for appreciating some of the most widely held expectations in a culture. If you are from an individualistic culture such as the United States, you might have difficulty appreciating why your Mexican-American roommate sees going home on weekends to be with family members as more important than studying with other students for a final exam. Collectivist cultures are often more comfortable with groups than individualistic cultures and will view group cohesion as more important than individual achievement.

Power Distance. **Power distance** refers to the relative value that cultures place on status and power in relationships. When people at the bottom of a hierarchy accept the idea that there is a great deal of power or status between themselves and those at the top, they exemplify a high power distance culture (Hofstede and Bond 1984). Members of low power distance cultures believe that power should be distributed as equally as possible; there are very specific instances where people can legitimately claim power over others. For instance, an Egyptian worker, coming from a high power distance culture, might think that she is performing perfectly for her supervisor because she does exactly what she is told and doesn't ask questions. Her Swedish supervisor, however, coming from a

power distance
The relative value that cultures place on status and power in relationships.

low power distance culture, might see the Egyptian as lacking initiative and assertiveness.

When people from different power distance cultures interact, misunderstanding is likely. Think about the way most students in the United States expect to be treated by their teachers. At the end of the semester, they are likely to evaluate their teacher's ability to make course material interesting, promote discussion, and provide thorough explanations that they can understand. Students from China are more likely to be interested in whether the teacher is competent and maintains authority in the classroom. You can probably imagine the potential conflicts that happen when an American student attends a Chinese school or a Chinese teacher joins an American faculty.

Uncertainty Avoidance. **Uncertainty avoidance** refers to the degree of uncertainty tolerated by members of a culture or group. In cultures where uncertainty is accepted, members are more likely to accept change, speak against ideas, and push the boundaries of social norms. In cultures where uncertainty is to be avoided, members are less tolerant of people with deviant ideas or behavior and desire more formal rules about how to communicate. People who expect certainty are likely to interact in very structured, ritualistic ways, and those who tolerate uncertainty can be frustrating to those who don't. For example, some professors may prefer to give writing assignments with very general directions, whereas many students like specific instructions about the topic, length, and style of the paper.

uncertainty avoidance
The degree of uncertainty tolerated by members of a culture or group.

Masculinity and Femininity. Cultures that place a high value on **masculinity** emphasize power, assertiveness, independence, materialism, and rigid distinctions between expectations of males and females. Cultures that are high in **femininity** emphasize interdependence, quality of life, and variability in the roles that females and males are expected to perform. In cultures where the status of women is relatively low in terms of rights, opportunities, and wealth, masculine characteristics are more likely to be celebrated (Kimmel 2000).

As with all of the cultural dimensions we have been exploring, the valuing of attributes stereotypically labeled "masculine" and "feminine" varies within cultures, groups, situations, and individuals. Nonetheless, understanding differences based on masculinity and femininity can be useful. Think about the reaction of male group members to a feminine leader who frequently uses emotional language and pronounced gestures. In more feminine cultures, feminine leaders would seem normal in a group, whereas in masculine cultures, women in general are more likely to be treated with suspicion.

masculinity
Emphasis on power, assertiveness, independence, materialism, and rigid distinctions between expectations of males and females.

femininity
Emphasis on interdependence, quality of life, and variability in the roles that females and males are expected to perform.

Collectivism and individualism, power distance, uncertainty avoidance, and masculinity and femininity are dimensions of culture that can influence any level of communication. Table 9-1 illustrates some of the implications of these cultural differences for communication in groups.

Cohesion Is an Important Norm in Many Successful Groups

An important norm that develops in most groups concerns the amount of cohesion between members. Cohesion is the feeling of unity and togetherness among group members. The amount of cohesion that develops in a group greatly influences group communication. Members in a highly cohesive group will be enthusiastic about participating, concerned about the group outcome, and generally committed to the group. From sports teams to business work teams, experts have

TABLE 9-1 Dimensions of Culture that Influence the Development of Group Norms

COLLECTIVIST	INDIVIDUALIST
(China, Japan, Mexico, Philippines, Venezuela)	(Australia, Canada, France, Germany, United States)
Members often think in terms of "we."	Members often think in terms of "I."
Harmony is desired; direct confrontation is avoided.	Honesty is desired and demonstrated by speaking your mind.
Relationships are often more important than tasks.	Tasks are often more important than relationships.
HIGH POWER DISTANCE	**LOW POWER DISTANCE**
(India, Iran, France, Korea, Nigeria, South Africa)	(Israel, Canada, Germany, New Zealand, Sweden, United States)
Inequalities among people are expected and desired.	Inequalities among people should be minimized.
Group members expect to be told what to do.	Group members expect to be consulted.
Privileges, status symbols for leaders are expected and popular.	Privileges and status symbols are frowned upon.
HIGH UNCERTAINTY AVOIDANCE	**LOW UNCERTAINTY AVOIDANCE**
(Austria, Greece, Ecuador, Korea, Spain)	(Canada, India, Jamaica, Hong Kong, United States)
Uncertainty is threatening and must be fought.	Uncertainty is normal and accepted.
Aggression and emotion may be displayed at the proper time and place.	Aggression and emotion should be hidden.
Difference is dangerous.	Difference leads to curiosity.
Members desire structured discussions.	Members are comfortable with open-ended discussions.
Innovation is resisted.	Innovative ideas and behavior are tolerated.
FEMININE	**MASCULINE**
(Costa Rica, Denmark, France, Portugal, Thailand)	(Brazil, Ireland, Switzerland, Venezuela, United States)
Dominant values in society are caring for others and preservation.	Dominant values in society are material success and progress.
All members are supposed to be modest.	Men are supposed to be assertive, ambitious, tough.
Both men and women members take care of relationships.	Women are expected to take care of the relationships.
Leaders use intuition and value consensus.	Leaders are expected to be decisive and assertive.

discovered that highly cohesive groups are more productive than less cohesive groups (Galanes, Adams, and Brilhart 2000; McGrath 1984). There are some basic ways that group members can establish norms to develop cohesion.

1. Create a strong sense of teamwork in the group. Try following the lead of collectivist cultures and use the word "we" instead of "I." This simple change of pronoun encourages inclusivity and establishes a sense of group identity.
2. Develop group traditions that foster a climate of togetherness. These traditions might include starting the meeting the same way each time, celebrating group successes together, or even making "inside" references or jokes pertaining to past group experiences.
3. Develop shared goals. Cohesion is strongest in groups when all members are committed to the group goals. Similarly, members are most committed when they are empowered to help establish those goals. Goals are better established by the group as a whole than they are when created by an individual member. Cohesion develops as members feel a sense of satisfaction when group goals are accomplished. Conversely, group members become dissatisfied if the group never accomplishes anything. In the process of achieving the overall goal of the group, look for and celebrate smaller accomplishments.
4. Respect and accept all group members. Togetherness increases when members feel needed and appreciated by the group.
5. Recognize individual efforts and accomplishments of group members.
6. Respect differences between members and find ways to use individual differences to accomplish group goals.
7. Finally, develop a sense of cooperation in the group. The essence of cohesion is the willingness of members to help each other. Members need to feel like they are connected and working together to accomplish the group goal. When group members realize that they can accomplish more working together than they could by themselves, the group begins to reach the extent of its full potential (Engleberg and Wynn 1997; Rothwell 1988).

While cohesion is generally a positive quality in groups, excessive cohesion can cause problems. When cohesion increases, groups tend to enforce norms more rigidly. This strong enforcement of group values can stifle communication and creativity. Members may be reluctant to voice disagreement or express individuality out of fear of group *recrimination.* Strong cohesion inevitably leads to a pressure to conform to what the group expects. Groups can protect against the pressures of conformity by developing a supportive climate where group members can voice disagreement without feeling attacked or defensive. The "Exploring Communication Concepts" box examines groupthink and the dangers of creating climates in which disagreement is stifled.

Watch a video clip about the power of conformity in groups (CD Clip 9.1).

Roles Facilitate Group Functioning and Communication

Group roles are a collection of common expectations that define a specific purpose, need, or capacity within the group. Role expectations are narrower than general group norms, which apply to all members in the group, because they set expectations for specific individuals. Some roles are very formal in nature and are explicitly assigned to a particular member. Someone in the group, for instance, might be in charge of physical facilities and arranging meeting times. Other roles

Exploring Communication Concepts

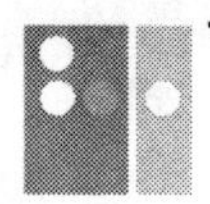

IRVING JANIS AND GROUPTHINK

Perhaps the most influential theory about the negative effects of group cohesion is Irving Janis's theory of groupthink (1983). Janis theorized that groups with strong cohesion develop a type of tunnel vision that prevents them from seeing flaws in their decisions. This narrow perspective develops because members of the group feel the need to agree with the collective point-of-view rather than critically challenge ideas. Janis developed his model of groupthink by analyzing government decisions that did not turn out as expected. After analyzing these historical cases, Janis hypothesized that there are three general causes of groupthink.

- *Groups overestimate their power.* Excessively cohesive groups create an illusion of invulnerability where members believe they can do no wrong. This sense of false power often comes from *dogmatic* members who believe in their inherent morality; they are right and everyone else is wrong. This false sense of power lures the group into making quick decisions and avoiding critical thinking and reflection.
- *Groups become closed-minded and narrowly focused in their discussion.* Consequently, such groups develop "collective rationalizations" which they employ to discredit warnings or danger signals that indicate that they are on the wrong track. Often these rationalizations are rooted in their false sense of power. Group members might argue, for instance, that the danger signals come from uninformed sources that do not know as much about the problem as the group. Groups create negative stereotypes of competing groups or dissidents outside the group. They label those who disagree as stupid, extreme, harmful, or evil.
- *Groups pressure members to conform to rigid norms.* Members are afraid to voice disagreement. They engage in self-censorship or withdraw into silence. The group creates an illusion of unanimity even though some members may privately disagree with the policies of the group. In some extreme forms of groupthink, members of the group actively pressure dissenters by threatening or alienating them.

Groupthink prevents effective decision making. Groups that engage in groupthink rely on incomplete information, do not critically evaluate the information they collect, fail to examine a full range of possibilities before selecting a solution to a problem, and do not create contingency plans in case their preferred solution fails. In addition, they fail to examine the potential risks associated with their decision. Not all cohesive groups develop groupthink, and there are a few relatively simple things group members can do to prevent it.

1. Encourage members to voice disagreement.
2. Encourage the critical assessment of ideas. If no one disagrees with a decision, maybe the group should reexamine the policy in more detail.
3. Assign someone to play "devil's advocate," a person who argues against the group just to test an idea.
4. Take warning signals seriously and refrain from negative stereotypes of those who disagree.
5. Consult outside experts frequently and regularly invite nonmembers to meetings.

By establishing a supportive climate in which members can disagree without feeling threatened or pressured, a group can be cohesive and still make good decisions.

ASK YOURSELF:

1. What are some recent group decisions, either based on news accounts or from your personal experience, that illustrate the theory of groupthink?
2. How would using perception checks also help to prevent groupthink?
3. Besides groupthink, what are some other disadvantages of overly cohesive groups?

are not assigned but emerge as the discussion progresses. One or two members, for example, might worry that the group is beginning to argue too much and act as mediators to resolve conflict. There are three types of group roles: task, group maintenance, and individual (Benne and Sheats 1948).

Task roles facilitate the group goal or purpose. In a decision-making group, these would include roles such as gathering information, evaluating information, contributing to the group discussion, recording group decisions, and coordinating group activities. **Maintenance roles** serve to build relationships within the group and to create a sense of teamwork. Someone who helps solve conflict, makes sure everyone participates, supports others, or relieves tension with appropriate humor is taking on a group maintenance role. Finally, **disruptive roles** satisfy member's needs at the expense of the group. These roles are often self-serving and are generally considered dysfunctional and counterproductive to the group goal. They include members who seek recognition, dominate the discussion, block group efforts, and refuse to participate. Table 9-2 lists several examples for each type of group role.

task roles
Facilitate the group goal or purpose.

maintenance roles
Serve to build relationships within the group and to create a sense of teamwork.

disruptive roles
Satisfy member's needs at the expense of the group.

Difficulties associated with group roles can create communication problems for a group. In general, there are three types of role problems: role conflict, role ambiguity, and role load (McGrath 1984). Role conflict occurs when members have competing expectations. For example, some members may want a group leader who is decisive while others may want a more democratic leader who consults them about all group decisions. These competing expectations can create role conflict for a leader. Role ambiguity occurs when expectations are not clear to members. Sometimes role expectations change during the course of discussion and the new expectations are not clearly communicated to everyone. Members may also have difficulty translating ambiguous role expectations into behaviors. For example, suppose a member assumes the role of evaluator without explicitly acknowledging his or her intentions. Some members in the group might be confused and think of that person as a disruptive cynic rather than a constructive evaluator. The evaluator can clarify the role explicitly by saying things like, "Although the ideas sounds good, let me play devil's advocate," or "Please don't take this personally, but I would like to take a closer look at this idea." Finally, role load problems occur when group expectations are unevenly distributed. If one member has too many roles to perform effectively or a single member is assigned two competing roles, problems are likely to occur.

"The essential feature of common thought is not that it is held in common but that is has been produced in common. . . . The core of the social process is not likeness, but the harmonizing of differences."

—Mary Parker Follett, management expert, sociologist

CULTURAL INFLUENCES AND GROUP ROLES

Look at Table 9-2 and ask yourself the following questions:

How might the different dimensions of a culture influence your choice of role to play in the group?

Which roles might someone from a collectivist or individualistic culture select? Someone with low or high power distance? High or low uncertainty avoidance? Masculine or feminine?

TABLE 9-2 **Group Roles**

Roles define a specific purpose, need, or capacity within the group

TASK ROLES	DESCRIPTION	EXAMPLE
Initiator	Suggests directions and proposes solutions.	"I think we should start by reviewing the architect's plans for the skate park."
Information and opinion seeker	Researches discussion topics, asks for facts and suggestions, and invites members to share personal experiences and viewpoints.	"Charlene, how much money did the Associated Students budget for the skate park?"
Information and opinion giver	Provides relevant facts and evidence, draws conclusions from the data, and shares opinions.	"We already have six intramural fields. I think students would prefer a skate park to another softball diamond."
Clarifier	Clears up misunderstandings, clarifies ambiguous statements, and simplifies complex ideas.	"I said that the insurance company would cover our liability in the park. However, I'm also sure that it will cost us more money."
Elaborator	Explains, expands, and develops ideas and suggestions.	"It is not just a skate park. There is a place to ride bikes and an area for roller hockey."
Coordinator	Organizes the activities of the group and assigns task responsibilities.	"Charlene, will you call our insurance company by next meeting and get an estimate on the increased costs?"
Evaluator	Tests ideas and makes judgments about the value of information and suggestions.	"I have looked over these plans and I still don't believe that there is room to put a skate park between the basketball arena and the tennis courts. It would be much better down by the swimming pool."
Tracker	Keeps the group on task, clarifies the agenda, and reminds members of the group goal.	"I don't think we should discuss the menu for the snack bar before we decide where to put the park."
Recorder	Keeps the group record, prepares reports and agendas, and maintains the minutes.	"Does anyone have an item for next week's agenda?"

MAINTENANCE ROLES	DESCRIPTION	EXAMPLE
Gatekeeper	Promotes open discussion, encourages reluctant members to join the discussion, controls channels of communication, and ensures even participation.	"Pauline, you haven't said much. What's your opinion?"
Norm setter	Establishes group expectations and standards.	"We shouldn't talk all at once. When someone else is speaking, everyone in the group should listen."
Harmonizer	Resolves conflict, manages disagreement, and promotes compromise.	"Andrea, would you support Bill's proposal if we could reduce the costs by 10 percent?"
Tension reliever	Relieves tension through humor, welcomes new members, and reduces status distinctions.	"Everyone, this is Michelle. She will be joining our group. Introduce yourselves and make her feel welcome."
Supporter	Expresses positive feelings for others, builds group cohesion, and counsels/consoles other members.	"Dana, your report was well written. I certainly learned much by reading it."

DISRUPTIVE ROLES	DESCRIPTION	EXAMPLE
Blocker	Prevents group progress, constantly raises objections, argues trivial points, and frequently reintroduces controversial topics.	"Harriet, let me interrupt you. Before we move on, I would like to reconsider the decision we made last meeting."
Recognition seeker	Seeks individual achievement, attention, opportunities, or pleasure at the expense of the group.	"If we adjourn early, I could get home before the traffic gets too heavy."
Isolate	Withdraws and refuses to participate.	"It doesn't matter to me. I'm only here because Professor Jobs said I had to come."
Aggressor	Puts down others, engages in conflict for the sake of conflict, and tries to "one up" others.	"Lynn, you never make any sense. Your next good idea will also be your first good idea."
Cynic	Doubts all ideas, needlessly discourages others, and encourages failure.	"We're never going to solve this problem, so why try?"

Using the Problem-Solving Agenda to Make Effective Decisions

One common complaint from members in decision-making groups is the inefficiency of the process. Some people feel that groups waste everybody's time and take too long to reach decisions. Group members might also struggle with uncertainty when they are asked to make an important decision without any prior notion of what would be the best course of action. Nonetheless, scholars of small groups have discovered that well-organized groups can be both efficient and effective in making decisions.

agenda
A written guide that lists the order of tasks to be accomplished and topics to be discussed by the group.

problem-solving agenda (PSA)
A standard approach to group problem solving that maximizes critical thinking while minimizing rash or impulsive decisions.

Knowing *how* to make group decisions often helps reduce uncertainty and facilitates effective decision making. One key to running effective group meetings is using a good **agenda,** a written guide that lists the order of tasks to be accomplished and topics to be discussed. An agenda provides a visible structure to the group process. Using an agenda in meetings helps groups focus their attention, cover more business, and reduce the tendency to wander into unrelated and counterproductive topics. The **problem-solving agenda (PSA)** is a standard approach to group problem solving that maximizes critical thinking while minimizing rash or impulsive decisions. Research shows that groups that consider only one solution to a problem often make poor decisions (Hirokawa and Pace 1983). The PSA ensures that groups do not rush to adopt the first solution that they consider but instead generate and analyze many different solutions before selecting the best one. The general steps in the PSA are (1) define and understand the problem, (2) establish explicit criteria for an effective solution, (3) generate possible solutions to the problem, (4) select the best possible solution to the problem, and (5) implement the solution and reevaluate the decision (see Figure 9-2).

Define and Understand the Problem

The first step of the problem-solving agenda is to obtain a thorough understanding of the group's responsibility for solving the problem, define the specific nature of the problem, comprehend the causes of the problem, and discover the harm or damage caused by the problem.

group charge
The overall or main objective of the group.

What Is the Group Supposed to Do?

The **group charge** is the overall or main objective of the group. The term "charge" implies that someone has expectations for the group and has given the group a responsibility. While this may sound simple, understanding the charge is essential to the success of the group. Many groups fail at this most basic step. For instance, they may not understand their task: Should they be a fact-finding group, a group that makes recommendations, or a group that takes some action? A group charged with exploring ways of increasing campus recycling will have a very different goal than a group charged with actually increasing campus recycling by 15 percent. The first charge is largely a fact-finding responsibility, while the second group would need a specific plan of action. If the charge is unclear, the group should actively seek clarification from the person who determined the group's objective. The group should know what power and responsibilities they have, the rationale for forming the group, the nature of group performance, who will receive the output, and what will be

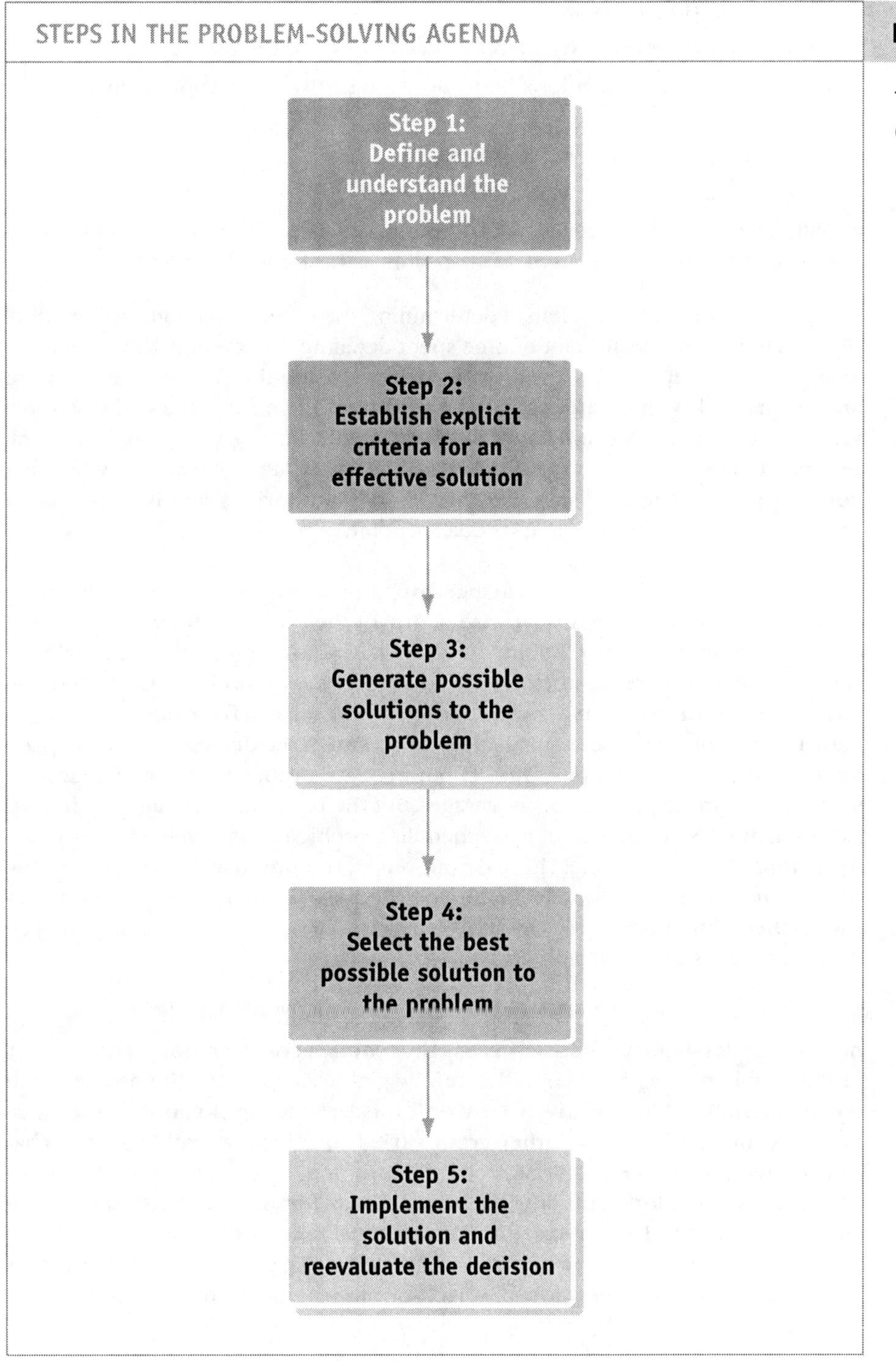
STEPS IN THE PROBLEM-SOLVING AGENDA
Step 1: Define and understand the problem
Step 2: Establish explicit criteria for an effective solution
Step 3: Generate possible solutions to the problem
Step 4: Select the best possible solution to the problem
Step 5: Implement the solution and reevaluate the decision

FIGURE 9-2

The Problem-Solving Agenda (PSA) has five steps.

done with the output. For example, suppose your university has a parking problem (most do), and you have been asked by the student association to participate in a problem-solving group to suggest possible solutions. To find out what is expected, you might ask the following questions:

- What power do you have?
- Is there money or other resources available to solve the problem?
- What should your report look like—how long, how many copies, what style of writing?
- When should the report be completed?
- Who will see the report when it is done?
- Will your group be charged with implementing the solution or will your responsibilities be over as soon as the report is finished?

Part of defining the problem is determining the extent of the group's responsibilities toward it. The amount of time spent detailing the solution will depend on whether the group has the authority to develop a solution, or whether they are mainly charged with creating a picture of the problem for others who will develop a solution. If the group has been charged with issuing a report, group members need to know who will read the report, and why. These issues, too, will affect how the group frames its task. A report to city authorities will be different in scope from a report to the campus quality of life committee.

What Is the Problem? The next step in the process is defining the problem. Groups should define the precise nature of the problem and understand the context in which it occurs. Careful consideration of the problem will usually reveal unexpected dimensions to the situation, and how a problem is defined will ultimately determine the type of solution a group selects. For example, in examining the lack of adequate parking, the problem might be defined as too few parking spaces on or near campus. This definition of the problem will naturally lead to solutions like more parking lots or garages. But the problem might also be defined as too many cars on campus or as a scheduling problem that brings too many cars to campus at the same time. These definitions of the problem might lead to solutions such as incentives for car pooling, restrictions on the number of permits issued, scheduling more classes early in the morning or at night, and maybe even decreasing the size of the student body.

What Causes the Problem? Having defined the problem, the group needs to understand its causes. This usually requires consideration of the history of the problem. The group should carefully gather facts about the problem and try to determine if it is relatively new or if it is a recurring situation. If the situation is recurring, how have other groups tried to solve the problem, and what can you learn from their experience? If the problem is relatively new, the group should generate a list of possible causes and look for any relationship between and among causes. The parking problem, for instance, is probably the result of several factors, such as too many cars, a shortage of parking spots, lack of mass transit, lack of land to develop, and lack of money and resources to solve the problem.

What Harms or Damages Result from the Problem? Finally, the group should make a list of the negative consequences created by the problem. Specifically, who is being harmed and in what ways? Negative consequences usually include the loss of money, opportunity, or health. Trying to quantify the loss in this way will also yield an understanding of the magnitude of the problem. The lack of adequate parking results in lost time for students as they hunt for parking spots and miss educational opportunities when they are late for class. It also costs them money as they pay for a service they cannot always use. And too many cars produce air pollution that causes environmental degradation, illness, and increased medical bills.

Establish Explicit Criteria for an Effective Solution

Before proposing a solution the group should carefully consider the characteristics of an effective solution. Three general or universal criteria should be applied to all problems: feasibility, workability, and acceptability. First, an effective solution should be feasible. Feasibility means that there are resources available to carry out the solution. A feasible solution is affordable (in terms of money and resources), uses available technology, and allows adequate time for implementation. Workable means that the solution will solve the problem. Many proposed solutions to a problem are feasible but will not solve the problem. For instance, building another parking lot is not likely to ease the traffic congestion and may even encourage more people to bring cars to campus rather than car pooling. Increasing parking spaces might need to be combined with incentives for car pooling and restrictions on driving. Finally, a good solution should be acceptable to those who implement it. A feasible and workable solution will not solve the problem if those who must implement it are reluctant to do so. One possibility to solve parking problems is simply to cement or asphalt every square inch of campus, including playing fields, gardens, and walkways. But most students and faculty value the aesthetic nature of their campus and would reject a solution that would turn their environment into one large parking lot. If a solution is not acceptable, workable, and feasible, it should not be adopted and other solutions should be sought.

Generate Possible Solutions to the Problem

Once criteria are established, a group should generate possible solutions to the problem. Members should do careful research to see how others have solved the problem. Very few problems are unique and a group can benefit greatly from someone else's experience. The group should also generate new and unique ideas. The object of this step in the PSA is to think of as many potential solutions as possible. Routine and often tired ideas are the easiest to think of and usually come first in the discussion, so group members should not settle for the first one or two suggestions that are generated. The more ideas a group considers, the better their chances of finding good solutions. During this idea-generating stage, it is important not to criticize possible solutions. Criticism often stifles creativity and reduces the number of possible solutions that are proposed. Even wildly impractical suggestions sometimes lead to ideas that are feasible, workable, and acceptable.

Select the Best Possible Solution to the Problem

Once a group has generated a number of potential solutions, the next step in the process is to select the best alternative to solve the problem. To accomplish this goal your group should systematically apply the criteria you have established (phase two) to each of the solutions your group generated (phase three). Sometimes a clear choice will emerge from the possibilities and the decision will be obvious. More often, however, two or more choices will look attractive and deciding on one of these will be difficult. There are essentially three ways to make any decision in a group.

Majority Rules. The first way to make a decision is by a vote in which the majority wins. "Majority rules" is a quick and efficient method of decision making. It satisfies most of the members of the group, gives everyone a chance to participate in the process, and is an easy method of conflict resolution. But majority rule also divides members of the group into "winners" and "losers" and therefore tends to be less satisfactory to the members who did not vote for the selected choice. This dissatisfaction can lead to opposition to the decision and possibly even *alienation* from the group. Voting should occur after the group has had a chance to discuss each alternative thoroughly and each member has had an opportunity to express an opinion.

Authority Decision Making. A second method of decision making is decision by authority. "Authority decision making" charges one person or one subgroup with making the decision for the whole group. The group's responsibility is to provide the authority with carefully constructed arguments for and against each alternative. The authority may be the leader of the group, a judge or arbitrator, or an established expert. Decision by authority forces the group to evenly consider the pros and cons of each decision and often to carefully write justifications for each position. But decision by authority also takes the decision out of the hands of group members and is the least participative of the decision-making methods.

Decision Making by Consensus. Finally, consensus decision making is reaching unanimous agreement through group interaction. Consensus decision making is the most difficult and time-consuming method, but it is potentially the most beneficial. Reaching consensus forces a group to evaluate and reevaluate ideas, alter proposals to meet objections, critically evaluate all possibilities, combine good ideas, and reject bad ones. Also, once a group reaches consensus all members of the group are committed to the outcome.

Implement the Solution

The last step of the PSA involves determining how the group will implement the decision. A good decision with poor implementation rarely works. The key elements of implementation are what, who, and when. The group should divide the implementation into the key activities and actions that must be taken. This list should be comprehensive, but each action item should be discrete. Duplications of action waste time and resources. Assignments should be based on expertise and abilities. For instance, the task of editing the final group report should be assigned to a member who is particularly good at writing. The work should be equally divided among the group members so that no one person is burdened with too many responsibilities. Finally, the group should establish a timeline for completion of the project. Generally it is better to have a series of *interim* due dates rather than one final deadline, since this approach allows the group to assess problems as they occur. Clear communication among group members is essential for effective implementation of a solution. Members should know their exact responsibilities and have a firm deadline for completion. Too often, implementation fails because no one is sure who should be doing what.

Becoming an Effective and Responsible Leader

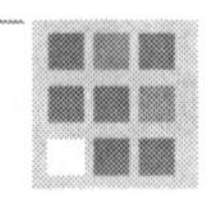

Probably the single most important factor in any small group is the type of leadership it enjoys. Group leaders set the style and tone of group communication. **Leadership** is the process of exerting positive influence over other group members. A leader can exert influence in many ways. In this section, we discuss styles and principles of leadership.

leadership
The process of exerting positive influence over other group members.

Styles of Leadership

There are many different methods of influencing group members. A stereotypical image of a leader is someone who directs the group by giving commands or orders. In truth, this is only one style of leadership, and it is perhaps the least effective. There are actually three basic styles of leadership. Each has its place in influencing groups, but each also has its limits. The three styles are authoritarian, laissez-faire, and democratic.

Authoritarian Leadership. **Authoritarian leadership** is predominantly autocratic. The leader makes all decisions for the group. Some authoritarian leaders ignore group input entirely and make decisions with little regard for group members. Other authoritarian leaders are more concerned about the welfare of group members and actively seek their advice. But both types of authoritarian leaders do not trust members to make decisions. Authoritarian leadership is often quick and decisive, and there are some situations, such as a military group in combat, where this strong leadership style is effective. In many more cases, authoritarian leadership is *despotic* and repressive. Group members eventually feel alienated from the decision-making process and resent the leader.

authoritarian leadership
The leader of the group makes all decisions for the group.

Laissez-faire Leadership. **Laissez-faire leadership** is a nondirective style of leadership in which the leader exercises a hands-off approach to influence. A laissez-faire leader gives minimal guidance to the group and allows group members to work with little or no structure. In many ways, laissez-faire leadership is the opposite of authoritarian leadership—it is leadership by no leadership. Groups with many experienced members, or creative and artistic groups where any structure inhibits the imaginative process, often benefit from laissez-faire leadership. However, the lack of structure and guidance often creates a lack of direction and frustrates members who want to accomplish the group task efficiently.

laissez-faire leadership
The leader of the group gives minimal guidance and allows group members to work with little or no structure.

Democratic Leadership. **Democratic leadership** allows members to participate fully in the decision-making process. A democratic leader facilitates group discussion and allows members to make important decisions. Decision making under democratic leadership takes more time than under authoritarian leadership but usually produces more satisfied and committed group members. Most of the discussion in this chapter has assumed the democratic leadership style.

democratic leadership
The leader of the group allows all members to participate fully in the decision-making process.

Developing Group Leadership Skills

Being a group leader is an important responsibility. The leader is the most visible member of the group, and other members look to the leader to set the climate for the group. At some point in your life, you will probably be a group leader. Here are a few basic suggestions to help you be more effective as a leader.

Be Organized, But Flexible. Distribute a clear notice of the meeting, including the time and place, to each member prior to the meeting date. Also, prepare and distribute an agenda before the meeting. Carefully plan time limits and the sequence of topics, but be flexible. Use the agenda as a guide to discussion and be willing to deviate from the agenda if the group so desires. Recognize that some group members from high uncertainty avoidance cultures might welcome a detailed agenda, whereas others will appreciate an opportunity to help shape the agenda. Also, leaders can influence the behavior of other members by modeling behaviors of acceptance and tolerance. Be accepting of diverse ideas that are expressed responsibly in the discussion.

Facilitate and Manage the Discussion. The leader is responsible for ensuring a productive discussion by encouraging participation and guiding the discussion. Thomas Scheidel and Laura Crowell (1979) list five aspects that leaders should consider when managing the discussion.

1. The leader should "locate" the discussion by providing a clear understanding of the status of the discussion. ("OK, we have agreed that there is a need to reduce the time we spend on paperwork, but we haven't yet figured out the best way to do this. Next, we should decide which forms we could eliminate.")
2. The leader should "summarize" the discussion at important points of the process to ensure clear and accurate recall of past activity. If the discussion takes place over the course of several meetings, the leader should provide a summary of each meeting in the form of minutes or other written records.
3. The leader can "open" new topics of discussion by providing transitions from one aspect of the discussion to the next. When possible, limit the discussion to just one topic and resist the urge to revisit a topic unnecessarily.
4. The leader can also "track" the discussion by connecting related points and discussing the relationship of ideas. It is also the leader's responsibility to bring the group back to the topic if group members wander off into irrelevant discussions.
5. Finally, the leader should "pace" the discussion by allocating time to each topic. The pace of the discussion should be appropriate for the complexity of the issue. You want to be thorough but not waste time. Group members will become impatient with a discussion that moves too slowly or discusses the same issues at every meeting.

Be an Active Participant. Leaders often play the important role of group participant. As a leader, you have an obligation to do research, take and fill regular assignments, suggest solutions to problems, and critique ideas in addition to your leadership responsibilities. But be careful. Because you are the leader, you are also the most visible member of the discussion; use this power responsibly. Work hard to be fair and open minded. Let others participate in discussion, and minimize favoritism. Most leaders can augment their status by being involved in the action of the group rather than staying at a safe distance. If you have a good suggestion for the group, offer it to them as a participant, not as the leader. One of the symptoms of groupthink is that members may accept suggestions from the leader without thinking about them, so be sure that the group tests your ideas with the same critical nature that they apply to all ideas.

In Most Circumstances, Be a Democratic Leader. Trust members to make important decisions. In some situations, the group might prefer the leader to make unimportant decisions autocratically. For example, a long discussion about where to meet as a group might be a waste of time. Be sure that there is clear agreement in the group about which decisions the leader should make autocratically and which can be the province of the entire group. Help members establish procedures for decision making and accept the decision they make even if it is not your preferred alternative. Your first instinct when you become a leader might be to give orders and direct people. Remember, democratic leaders facilitate more than they command. Help members to make decisions by identifying and securing key resources and by organizing the discussions, but allow members to make democratic decisions.

Do Not Overreact. One of the main responsibilities of the leader is to provide stability to the fluctuating group process. When exercising your power as leader, look for trends rather than isolated instances. Do not let the group be excessively satisfied by small accomplishments and, conversely, do not let them become overly depressed at setbacks. Establish a group climate that values hard work, responsibility, and achievement. Recognize individual achievement while stressing group accountability and success. Insist that members treat each other with civility by encouraging tolerance of people and perspectives. Be critical of ideas and accepting of people (Fisher and Ury 1981). The "Applying Communication Concepts" box looks at some of the challenges in applying effective and responsible leadership skills to civic groups.

Applying Communication Concepts

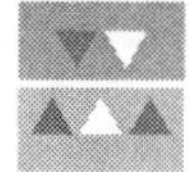

LEADING A COMMUNITY-BASED GROUP

Leading a community-based organization (CBO) poses many unique challenges and opportunities. CBOs are grassroots groups that operate outside the official government structure. They are usually organized around a single problem or task, such as advocates for the homeless or neighborhood watch groups. Leading a CBO can be a lonely affair. Leaders must arrange the structure and support for the group and often end up doing a variety of tasks, ranging from fund-raising to custodial chores. Nonetheless, leading CBOs also offers many opportunities. One strength is the commitment group members feel toward a cause or goal. This strong sense of commitment often makes leading a CBO a rewarding experience.

Perhaps the most daunting challenge in leading a community group is achieving the best possible results with limited resources. Generally, there are four phases to consider when organizing and leading a CBO: engagement, prioritization, activation, and assessment (Ouellette, Lazear, and Chambers 1999; Bobo, Kendall, and Max 1996).

Engagement. In the engagement phase, the leader identifies and defines the problem and enlists volunteers to participate in the group. The leader's first task is to make people aware of the problem and to recruit members who can help the group and begin to arrange resources. The core group of volunteers should stay relatively small at the beginning of the process as it is better to train a few people well than many people poorly. In this phase, leaders should also identify those with the power to solve the problem. These people may be elected officials, business leaders, or the media. The group should determine why these people have not solved the problem in the past and what is necessary to move them to action now.

Prioritization. The second phase in leading a CBO is to set priorities. There are usually more needs than resources. A leader will need to figure out what is most important to accomplish first and focus on that. A successful CBO often must win real improvements in people's lives or improve situations. Member enthusiasm will wane quickly if nothing changes (Bobo, Kendall, and Max 1996). The group should divide the main objective into smaller tasks and establish achievable and noticeable goals with a specific plan of action including "what will be done," "when it will be done," and "who will do it."

Activation. Having set priorities, the leader's next task is to implement the plan of action. The group can enlist the help of other groups with similar problems to increase support for the project and encourage sympathetic government officials to speak out on the group's behalf. Someone in the group should plan and carry out a public relations campaign that includes contacts with the media. Also, the leader can encourage a grassroots movement by having group members solicit the support of their neighbors and friends. Resources and participants will increase as the group accomplishes noticeable changes.

Assessment. Finally, the leader assesses the accomplishments of the group by continually revaluating plans and objectives. Many efforts require some readjustment of the group's original tactics. Accurate information is essential in this phase. Members sometimes become discouraged by the lack of success. The key to many difficult problems is determination and perseverance.

ASK YOURSELF:

1. What are some CBO groups on your campus that operate outside the official structure of the administration or student government?
2. How is the advice for leading a CBO similar to or different from the problem-solving agenda discussed earlier in the chapter?

Resources for Review and Skill Building

Many of these resources are supported by the Connections CD-ROM and free Online Learning Center website.

SUMMARY

This summary is organized around the questions found at the beginning of the chapter. See if you can answer them before reading the summary paragraphs.

1. What are some of the different types of small groups in society?

   A small group is composed of a limited number of individuals who communicate with each other to achieve a common goal. There are many different types of groups in society. Primary groups fulfill our basic human needs of survival, safety, and inclusion. They include families and relationships. Other types of groups include social groups, help groups, civic groups, community-based groups, virtual groups, and problem-solving groups.

2. What are some of the advantages and disadvantages of making a decision in a group?

   There are several advantages to group decision making. Groups often make better decisions than individuals because they bring a variety of viewpoints, resources, and talents to the problem. Through division of labor, groups can also divide a task into parts and ask each member to take responsibility for a different element. This often allows groups to achieve more than a single individual could possibly accomplish. Finally, group members will be more committed to a decision that they help make. This commitment helps implement the decision and builds group cohesion.

   Disadvantages of group decision making include the following: Members may have to sacrifice their individual preferences for the will of the group, which can be frustrating for particular members. Group decision making inevitably creates a certain amount of conflict that may also cause anxiety and frustration for some members. Finally, group decisions sometimes take more time than those made by individuals, and members often must "cover" or compensate for other members who do not do their share of the work.

3. How do norms and roles influence group communication and decision making?

   Group norms are expectations about how members should behave and are established through interaction. Some norms are implicit and unstated while others are more overt or explicit. One norm is the level of cohesion or attachment members feel toward the group. Groups that develop cohesion often are more productive than groups that do not, although groupthink is a risk. Group norms are influenced by a culture's view of collectivism versus individualism, power distance, uncertainty avoidance, and masculinity versus femininity.

   Group roles are common expectations that define a specific purpose, need, or capacity with the group. Some roles facilitate the group task and include gathering and distributing information, evaluating ideas and suggestions, and coordinating group activities. Maintenance roles serve to build relationships within the group and include members who solve conflicts, arrange compromises, and support other members. Finally, some roles are counterproductive. Individual roles that satisfy a member's needs at the expense of the group include seeking individual recognition, blocking group efforts, or withdrawing from the discussion.

4. **How can groups organize a discussion effectively when making a decision?**

   One way to structure a discussion in which a decision needs to be made is to use the problem-solving agenda (PSA). A PSA is a written guide to a group meeting that helps structure the decision. The problem-solving agenda has five steps: (1) define and understand the problem, (2) establish explicit criteria for an effective solution, (3) generate possible solutions to the problem, (4) select the best possible solution to the problem, and (5) implement the solution and reevaluate the decision.

5. **What is the role of a responsible leader?**

   Leadership is the process of exerting positive influence over other group members. There are three styles of leadership. Authoritarian leadership is autocratic in nature with the leader making all of the decisions for the group. Laissez-faire leadership is nondirective leadership with the leader providing only minimal, if any, guidance. Finally, democratic leadership is participative in nature with the leader allowing members to make important decisions.

   A responsible leader should be organized but flexible. Leaders have the responsibility to facilitate and manage group communication as well as actively participate in the discussion. A good leader is usually democratic and does not overreact.

KEY TERMS

Test your understanding of these key terms by visiting the Connections CD-ROM and Online Learning Center website at www.mhhe.com/dobkinpace.

ad hoc groups 243
agenda 256
authoritarian leadership 261
cohesion 244
collectivism 248
democratic leadership 261
disruptive roles 253
femininity 249
group charge 256
group norms 246
group synergy 244
individualism 248
laissez-faire leadership 261
leadership 261
maintenance roles 253
masculinity 249
power distance 248
problem-solving agenda (PSA) 256
small group 239
standing group 243
task roles 253
task-avoidance 245
uncertainty avoidance 249

FOR FURTHER REFLECTION

/dobkinpace

Join a conversation about chapter concepts by visiting the Online Learning Center website at www.mhhe.com/dobkinpace

1. Make a list of the groups to which you belong. What types of groups are they? What are some explicit norms that occur in these groups? What are some implicit norms? Which ones are cohesive and which ones are not? Why? What roles do you play in each group? What type of leadership occurs in each?
2. We said that task-avoidance often distracts a group and wastes valuable decision-making time. However, sometimes a divergence can help group morale. When and how might task avoidance help a group?

BUILDING COMMUNICATION SKILLS

1. Try the problem-solving agenda (PSA) on a current problem at your college or university. If you have difficulty thinking of a problem, read the campus newspaper for ideas. Define the problem and make an extended list of difficulties the problem is creating. Generate a list of specific criteria for an effective solution. Decide which of the criteria are the most important, and generate possible solutions to the problem. Finally select the best alternative using the criteria. Did using the PSA help you select a good solution? Why or why not?
2. Join a campus club or group. Affiliation with a club or social group in college, as we mentioned in the "Exploring Communication Concepts" box on student involvement, can have unexpected benefits. Sometimes the relationships you form in these groups can turn into professional opportunities. Finding a job after graduation is often a matter of networking—talking to people who know people who have job opportunities. Sororities, fraternities, or other clubs can provide those networking opportunities. Communication clubs on campuses are a great place to meet others who have the same professional interests as you. The National Communication Association sponsors a student honors society called Lambda Pi Eta. This group provides networking opportunities for communication majors from around the country. If your campus does not have a chapter of Lambda Pi Eta, contact the National Communication Association about starting one.

NET WORK

Note: While all the URLs listed were current as of the printing of this book, these sites often change. Please check our website (www.mhhe.com/dobkinpace) for updates and hyperlinks to these exercises.

1. Brainstorming is an activity that helps you generate possible solutions to a problem. There are many good brainstorming activities on the Internet. One site is located at: www.mcli.dist.maricopa.edu/authoring/studio/guidebook/brain.html. This site has a step-by-step approach to brainstorming. How does brainstorming help groups generate solutions to a problem? Why is withholding criticism during brainstorming so important?
2. The Internet contains many exercises to help groups build cohesion. Two such sites are located at: http://www.teambuildingproductions.com and http://wilderdom.com/games/InitiativeGames.html. Analyze two or three of these activities. Will they help groups build cohesion? Why or why not?

MEDIA MOMENTS

The film *Breaking Away* (1979) illustrates many of the group concepts discussed in this chapter. The film depicts teenagers in a typical college town "coming of age" as they decide what to do with their lives after graduating from high school. Although the film is more than 20 years old, the issues it discusses are still relevant as the young men in the film try to establish an identity apart from and yet connected to the university. There are three main groups in the film: Dave Stoller's family, a group of high school friends, and a fraternity at the university. All three groups come together in annual bike race at the university in the film's finale. After viewing *Breaking Away,* answer these questions:

- How do group norms differ between each of the groups in the film?
- What roles do each of the four friends assume in the group? How do these roles change as the story progresses?
- How cohesive are the friends? Does the competition between the friends and the fraternity increase the cohesion?
- How are group norms influenced by the culture of the three different groups?

Exploring Mediated Communication

CHAPTER 10

In April 1999, two teenaged boys opened fire on students at Columbine High School near Littleton, Colorado. Before they took their own lives, Eric Harris and Dylan Klebold killed 12 other students and one teacher. Their actions marked the peak in a string of school shootings across the country that left 30 people dead over the previous 18 months. Shortly after the deaths at Littleton, experts and opinion leaders began offering explanations for the boys' killing spree. Some people began taking a harder look at the role of media in creating images of violence and possibly inspiring violent behavior. Critics blamed the string of fatal assaults on the influence of performers like Marilyn Manson, movies such as The Matrix, *websites aimed at recruiting alienated teenagers, and video games that teach players how to use firearms. Parents of shooting victims filed lawsuits against several media companies, including Time Warner, Nintendo, Sony, Atari, New Line Cinema, and Polygram Film Entertainment.*

QUESTIONS TO FOCUS YOUR READING

1. What is the distinction between mediated and mass communication, and why might this distinction be important?
2. What are the stages in the coevolution of communication technologies and audiences?
3. Why is there so much concern about the effects of media?
4. What are the functions of mass media?
5. Why is media literacy important, and how can consumers and users of media communicate responsibly?

The public discussions about the relationship between media and violence prompted by the Littleton school massacre followed decades of research and speculation about the role of contemporary media in society. Like many technologies, those associated with mass media have been credited with an array of effects on individuals and society. Mass media have been held responsible for everything from ushering in the Renaissance and prompting revolutions in Eastern Europe to creating a population of alienated, overweight, and out-of-shape youth.

Certainly, mediated communication has a profound influence on our lives. The books, magazines, newspapers, computers, radio, movies, television, and popular music that make up mass media all contribute to our understanding of the world and our place within it. Because of the mass media, we know what the inside of an operating room looks like, though few of us have been in one; we have a mental image of the polar ice caps, though few of us have visited them; we are familiar with the language of lawyers and law enforcement officers, though few of us have worked in these fields; and we recognize the clothing of 19th century British royalty, though none of us were alive then. Modern media influence our knowledge, perceptions, attitudes, and behavior. Increasingly, we may also find ways to make our own voices heard through media, whether by composing music, publishing websites, becoming activists, or producing our own videos and films.

Much communication today takes place through media, transmitted electronically by unseen producers making decisions that affect millions of viewers whom they will never know. Communication through the media affects all of us, but the scope and nature of those effects are not entirely clear. This chapter looks at the types of mediated communication that have evolved over the years. It pays particular attention to technological developments in electronic communication, including their positive and not-so-positive effects. Finally, it offers some guidelines to help readers become more critical consumers of media, who are aware of what is being communicated, by whom, and for what purposes. After completing this chapter, you should be able to:

- Distinguish between mediated and "mass" communication.
- Understand audiences and how the media they use have evolved.
- Recognize the effects and functions of media.
- Be a critical and literate consumer of media.

Defining Media and Mass Communication

At the beginning of this text, we defined communication as a process of creating shared meaning, and we noted that various kinds of channels carry messages between communicators. We engage in mediated communication when we use technology as the channel to carry our messages. When messages are produced by large industries and designed to produce a profit, people often use the phrases "the media" or "mass media" interchangeably to talk about those industries. Although your text will certainly discuss the significance of mass media industries, it focuses on the process of creating and sharing meaning with messages that have been mediated. Distinguishing between "mass communication" and "media" should sharpen this focus.

Mass Communication

mass communication
The creation of meaning through messages sent to a large, unseen, and anonymous audience.

Mass communication refers to the creation of meaning through messages sent to a large, unseen, and anonymous audience. The word "large" is somewhat ambiguous, but most people consider a mass audience to be a larger number of people than can congregate in the same place at the same time. Thus, the mass audience can number in the thousands or millions. For instance, in 2010 over 19 million viewers watched the final episode of *Dancing with the Stars,* 10 million viewers watched *Wheel of Fortune* nightly, and the Superbowl between the New Orleans Saints and Indianapolis Colts drew an astonishing 106 million viewers, making it the most watched program in television history (Nielsen 2010).

Producers of mass communication, such as a prime time television series, rely on large audiences to generate advertising revenues that will cover production costs. Those costs are substantial. For example, in 1998, a single episode of "ER" or "The Sopranos" cost more than $13 million to produce (Mandese 1998). The more resources, such as money, time, and advanced technology, used to produce a message, the larger the audience needs to be for the communication effort to be cost effective. That's why test audiences screen big-budget movies before they are released. Based on initial audience responses, the movie's ending or other features might be changed to draw as large an audience as possible and maximize investor profits. The same is true for much television programming. The phrase "Least Objectionable Programming" was coined to emphasize the goal of drawing as large an audience as possible by not offending any particular segment of viewers. Expensive, mass entertainment doesn't need to be *excellent;* it just needs to be good enough to appeal to a large group of people and thus be profitable.

As audience size increases, the personalization of messages decreases. Mass communicators are separated visually and emotionally in time and space from their audiences, so the quality of the mass communication process differs from the other communication contexts you've studied. Because the audience is anonymous, the personal connection in mass communication is limited. Audience members aren't known as individuals either to the source of the messages or to each other. Although members of particular audiences, such as fan clubs, may feel they share a special bond, they probably have not met a substantial number of other people in that audience. Clever solicitors sometimes try to circumvent the anonymous quality of mass communication. For example, you have probably received mass mailings that are addressed to you personally, sometimes in what appear to be handwritten envelopes. Even supposed prize notifications from national organizations such as Publishers Clearinghouse may be addressed this way. Advertisers want you to feel as though they know you personally and are in some way "present" when you receive your mail.

Because of its reach, mass communication has been a cornerstone of social organization for centuries. Some anthropologists claim that mass communication was first practiced in ancient Egypt as a strategy for the pharaohs to rule over their conquered subjects (Henderson 1994). The pharaohs spread tales of terror through word of mouth and pictographs so that people they had never met knew of their power and potential for destruction. Through the mass communication of fear, the pharaohs controlled large, unseen, and somewhat anonymous groups of people.

Mass communication is even more fundamental today in the governance of modern and technologically advanced societies. As participants in a democracy, we rely on mass communication to facilitate decision making by providing us with sound information and a forum for exchanging knowledge and ideas with others. Through radio and television, we can hear and see political candidates debate; through newspapers, magazines, and television, we can learn about public problems; and through call-in shows, Internet discussion lists, and letters to editors, we can participate directly in public conversations. Although ideally we would all participate directly in the decisions that affect us, if each citizen in the United States were to speak for only two minutes about one political issue, it would take over 950 years to hear everyone speak (Page 1996). Instead of many people sharing information about public affairs, we rely on specialized, professional communicators such as journalists to interpret events and bring us timely information.

Media

media
The vehicles that carry messages.

Today mass communication is aided by technologies such as television, radio, computers, and print processing that influence how we send and receive messages. These technologies are called **media,** the vehicles that carry messages. Not all communication that travels through electronic devices is generated for a "mass" audience; in fact, as media become increasingly specialized and interactive, audiences become smaller, are sometimes present at an event, and are known to the sender of the messages. Your campus may have a closed-circuit television system that shows campus events, a small weekly newspaper, newsletters for academic departments, or courses that support online discussion groups, all of which exemplify mediated communication.

The Coevolution of Mass Media and Audiences

The origins of media can be traced back as far as the first uses of pictures and symbols to convey meaning. Communication first became mediated when language moved from spoken to written form. As media and their audiences evolved, the dominant forms of communication changed as well. Oral cultures became literate ones as people learned to read and write. Ultimately, technological developments led to the creation of the electronic society that we have today.

Oral Culture

oral cultures
Cultures in which speaking and hearing are the dominant forms of communication.

Before the advent of writing and continuing through the early days of printing, all cultures were based on oral communication. In **oral cultures,** speaking and hearing are the dominant forms of communication. Information is passed from person to person, the history of the community is shared through story and verse, and all communication occurs among those who are present with the speaker, with only the memories of those present to carry on traditions and beliefs. Authority and power is conferred on those who master storytelling and oral teaching.

Even centuries after the development of the alphabet, oral cultures remained dominant because only an elite group of individuals, usually members of a business, intellectual, or religious class, could read and write. This division of oral and literate people persisted into the Middle Ages, when manuscripts were read aloud both to listening audiences and in private, as a way to better understand a text.

In the thousands of years since they were dominant, some oral cultures have persisted. Some cultures, such as the Hmong in Southeast Asia and many Native

American tribes in the United States, still emphasize face-to-face communication, the perpetuation of culture and tradition through the stories of elders, interdependence of community members, and the status of storytellers. Think about the connections between the features of oral culture and rap music or poetry "slams," where the spoken word is particularly important. In both types of cases, people use oral communication to build community, tell stories, and convey historical traditions.

"Introduce the Alphabet to a culture, and you change its cognitive habits, its social relations, its notions of community, history, and religion."

—Neil Postman, author

Literate Culture

With the development of written communication came **literacy,** the ability to comprehend and use written symbols. Reading and writing allowed people to separate themselves from others in their immediate community. Speakers and listeners no longer needed to be together for communication to occur, and people could read information privately. Written documents allowed people to travel to new and remote places with the aid of maps and to record information about social, economic, and religious life. Social status and power began to shift too from those who were accomplished storytellers or possessed special skills to those who could read and write. Written communication enabled those who mastered it to control the history of a culture; records of property, taxes, and inheritance; and rules of governance.

literacy
Ability to comprehend and use written symbols.

The changes brought about by writing took centuries to fully emerge. As late as the 12th century in England, written financial accounts were still checked by having them read aloud. People understood and trusted their ears more than their eyes, so an "audit" literally meant "hearing" rather than reading a written document (Ong 1991). As with many changes in how we communicate, the most substantial cultural shifts came about as a result of technological advances that made new forms of communication accessible to great numbers of people, such as the advent of the printing press (McLuhan 1964; Ong 1998).

Although Johannes Gutenberg has been credited with the development of the movable printing press in 1455, the Chinese had been using wooden block presses for centuries, and Koreans had been using metal type presses since the 13th century. Gutenberg, however, used lead molds that could be rearranged infinitely to produce virtually identical copies of books in mass quantities. With this technological advance in printing, Gutenberg began the mass production of the Bible in 1456. The social and economic changes that followed were tremendous. The development of print prepared the ground for the Protestant Reformation, because copies of the Bible could be read and interpreted by *lay people.* Print allowed people to publish maps and records, facilitating the European exploration of the globe. The development of print also gave rise to the modern sciences, changed sex role expectations, and altered the way people understood and participated in political life (Eisenstein 1979).

This first true form of mass communication, print, had a profound effect on society because it made reading and access to written materials available to a wider range of people from different socioeconomic classes. With literacy came changes in the way people received and understood information. Reading requires linear thinking, in which knowledge is acquired bit by bit, one piece at a time. Words are interpreted in a progression, from the start of a sentence to the end. Rather than relying primarily on hearing to understand language, seeing and visual perception become dominant. The changes in thought and perception that come with written communication are described in the "Think It Over" box.

Think It Over

LOGIC AND LITERACY

Studies of *preliterate* cultures illustrate the effect that the ability to read may have on the way we think. For instance, members of a mostly preliterate tribe in a remote area of Russia listened to the following statements: "In the far North, where there is snow, all bears are white. Novaya Zembla is in the far north, and there is always snow there." The listeners were then asked, what color are the bears in Novaya Zembla?

The statements above resemble a syllogism, the classic form of deductive reasoning (All places with snow have white bears. Novaya Zembla is a place with snow. Therefore, Novaya Zembla has white bears). For the literate thinker, the connections follow logically, in a progression. For the tribal members, however, the typical response was: "I don't know. I've seen a black bear. I've never seen any others. Each locality has its own animals." Preliterate peoples are more likely to think situationally, based on their own experiences, customs, and local knowledge (Stephens 1991).

Understanding written language may rob us of some things, such as the ease of acquiring foreign languages, which becomes increasingly difficult as we become entrenched in the writing of our native language. This might be one reason why learning a second or third language is easier when we are very young. However, literacy seems to enable us to think more easily in abstractions and to explore connections and contradictions among statements (Stephens 1991).

Some experts argue that without the ability to read and write, people lose much of the mental skill necessary for critical thinking, such as the ability to follow complicated arguments, uncover falsehoods, and recognize contradictions. Other experts counter that some preliterate cultures have elaborate decision-making processes, and intelligent people who have not learned to read are still capable of thinking critically.

Is literacy necessary for critical thinking?

Should literacy be required for voting or obtaining a driver's license? Why or why not?

As literacy spread, Western European cultures placed increasing importance on the ability to think in a linear, logical fashion. Formal education became more of a necessity, new ideas were disseminated more quickly and easily, and audiences began to demand both printed information and entertainment in the form of books and magazines. Literacy also became a cornerstone of democracy. U.S. citizens were expected to acquire knowledge, learn customs, and vote using written materials. For example, the 19th century black press promoted the ideals of democracy and helped keep alive dreams of American citizenship and equal rights (Hutton 1993, 34). Foreign-language newspapers provided immigrant populations with a connection to their homeland while extending to them knowledge about the United States. By the 20th century, the printing press had led to the creation of mass-produced books, newspapers, and magazines. Throughout the 20th century, each medium would struggle with the conflicting demands of appealing to a broad enough range of people, or "mass," to be profitable while retaining some degree of specialization or distinctive identity to be competitive. The Calvin and Hobbes cartoon provides a commentary on the effect that rapid editing of TV images might have on critical thinking.

Communication in an Electronic Society

By the early 20th century, print society in this country was flourishing with the mass production of books and newspapers. At the same time, the first elec-

Television images come so quickly that viewers may not be able to think critically about them.

tronic communication—radio, film, and television—began to emerge. As these newer media technologies evolved, they forced changes in the form, content, and function of print media. Table 10-1 provides a timeline of key dates in the development of modern media dating back to the Roman Empire and illustrates the substantial innovations that took place between the late 1800s and 1900s.

Electronic media have influenced all forms of communication, either directly or indirectly, leading to an **electronic society.** We continue to hold intimate conversations with friends, pass on family traditions through stories, and write personal notes with pen and paper, but electronic media have affected even these forms of communication. We share secrets, rumors, and stories on the telephone and by e-mail. We learn much about what to expect from others and how to behave based on television shows and movies. Our family stories are recorded in photographs, on videotapes, and on Web pages. Finally, many of our personal greetings are written on computer-generated cards and extended with telephones, voice mail, and e-mail conversations.

electronic society
The stage at which all forms of communication have been influenced, either directly or indirectly, by electronic media.

As these new modes of communication become more prevalent, older forms of communication persist but are altered. Electronic society has brought back some of the traditional features of oral cultures, such as placing emphasis on how people look or their social standing in a community to determine whether they should be believed (McLuhan 1964). History is shared though the new electronic storyteller, television. Electronic media shape how we talk to each other, when we work and play, and how we structure our society. For example, popular words and phrases are borrowed from the media, social gatherings are organized around televised sporting events, dates are often structured around "dinner and a movie," and public spaces like conference centers and courthouses are designed with the needs of the news media in mind. One result of our television viewing is to make us more social in our activities. Reading a book is a private, solitary experience, whereas watching television with someone else can be seen as a social event—even if we never speak to the other person! When we view a television program, we do so at the same time as countless others in a mass audience, thus sharing a similar experience despite separations in distance and environment.

TABLE 10-1 Selected Innovations in the Evolution of Modern Mass Media

59 B.C. —	Romans post daily news sheets, called *acta diurnal.*
100 A.D. —	Chinese use paper for written communication.
1300 —	Koreans use metal type presses.
1455 —	Johannes Gutenberg develops the movable type printing press in Germany. Five years later he prints the Bible, which is credited with spawning the Protestant Reformation.
1534 —	Henry VIII of England imposes strict measures to control printing. British control of English-language printing and newspapers in the colonies continues until the American Revolution.
1783 —	The first American daily newspaper, *Pennsylvania Evening Post and Daily Advertiser*, was started in Philadelphia.
1827 —	The first black newspaper, *Freedom's Journal*, is published.
1828 —	The first American Indian newspaper, the *Cherokee Phoenix*, is published.
1833 —	The *"penny press"* is inaugurated with the *New York Sun.*
1877 —	Thomas Edison and John Kruesi build the first phonograph.
1883 —	Beginning of the *Ladies Home Journal.*
1897 —	Guglielmo Marconi receives a patent for the wireless telegraph.
1889 —	Edison develops a motion-picture projection system.
1903 —	Edwin Porter develops narrative film in *The Great Train Robbery.*
1905 —	The first permanent motion-picture theater, the nickelodeon, appears.
1910 —	There are 2,600 U.S. daily newspapers, more than at any time before or since.
1920 —	The first commercial radio station, KDKA in Pittsburgh, begins operation.
1927 —	The first talking movie, *The Jazz Singer*, opens.
1939 —	Television debuts at the New York World's Fair.
1941 —	First commercial telecasting begins in the United States.
1950s —	Television growth increases dramatically; radio and magazine formats begin to specialize (e.g., *Mad Magazine*, *Playboy*).
1966 —	All networks run complete color prime-time schedules.
1975 —	First consumer marketing of VCRs (videocassette recorders).
1981 —	Warner-Amex introduces MTV; first music video is by The Buggles, "Video Killed the Radio Star."
1985 —	Compact disks (CDs) enter the market; by 1987 CD sales double LP album sales.
1994 —	A live Rolling Stones concert footage of 20 minutes is made accessible to the world through video streaming on the Internet.
1995 —	The Lucky Goldstar group, a South Korean conglomerate, acquires Zenith, the last American-owned manufacturer of television sets.
1997 —	Movie titles are released on DVD (digital videodisk).
1998 —	America Online (AOL) and Netscape join to provide the largest and easiest access to the World Wide Web.
1999 —	Nearly half of all homes in the United States have personal computers; about 35% use modems (Campbell 2000).
2002 —	An estimated 561 million people worldwide are online (www.glreach.com/global-reach.biz/globstats)
2004 —	HDTV programming is broadcast to 99% of U.S. households (White 2004)

Television has become a primary storyteller in American culture.
© Tannen Maury/The Image Works

As people in countries around the world see some of the same movies and television shows, they begin to share some of the same interests, tastes, and values. Although each individual viewer might interpret a movie or TV show differently. U.S. media producers play a substantial role in defining the range of images available to viewers around the world. For instance, mass media products are the second-largest U.S. exporter after aircraft, and American movies, television shows, music, and software have penetrated all global markets (Garten 1998). English-language films command 80 percent of worldwide box office receipts (Frank 1999). While the United States is a worldwide exporter of mediated messages, it also draws from cultural dreams, fears, and folklores around the world, transforming and repackaging them for worldwide audiences (Pells 2002). The possibility of a new sense of shared identity and community across national boundaries and cultures led one of the first popularized scholars of contemporary media, Marshall McLuhan, to coin the phrase "global village" to express the sense of connection that electronic media make possible on a global scale.

Technological Convergence in the 21st Century

For those who value the individualism, privacy, and critical thinking of print culture, McLuhan's vision of electronic society was perhaps too optimistic. McLuhan died in 1980, long before many of the technological advances that we now take for granted had become part of mainstream society. As media and audiences have evolved together, the lines between personal and public, or individualized and mass media have become increasingly blurred. We have grown accustomed to hearing about the intimate relations of celebrities and politicians, to seeing televised confessions of talk show guests, and to watching the mundane, domestic activities of ordinary people on the Internet. The ways we use media have also changed, so that we can combine pager, e-mail, and telephone communication; access Internet data from our televisions; view concerts, movies, and sporting events from digital satellites; and buy toys, games, and movies from the same entertainment distributor.

The result of recent advances in electronic communication has been **technological convergence,** or the union of different, specialized media to meet the individual needs of users. Because our society is increasingly driven by and dependent on the transfer of data and the production of messages, some scholars

technological convergence
The union of different, specialized media to meet the individual needs of users.

have suggested that we are a *network society* (Van Dijk 2000) that reflects the integration of several communication technologies into a new social system. The combination of technologies offers countless new ways to create, store, and access mediated messages and has had numerous effects on the ways we communicate. We expect people to be more accessible for conversations, and we conduct business at all hours and locations. Whereas people have days or weeks to respond to traditional mail, many of them become impatient if their e-mail recipients do not respond within 24 hours. The places where we used to gather and talk to new people with shared interests, such as sporting events, concerts, and movies, are often replaced by cable and satellite TV.

Media Functions and Effects

Each cultural shift from the oral, to the print, and finally to the electronic era has brought with it new thinking about media and new patterns of communication. For example, Adolf Hitler's use of radio and film to spread Nazi propaganda in the 1930s led some scholars to study the significance of media in aiding his goals. In the 1960s television was increasingly recognized as an important social force. When John F. Kennedy and Richard Nixon appeared in the first televised presidential debates, commentators and market researchers blamed Nixon's apparent loss to his sweating and poor complexion that were vividly captured by the camera (Schudson 1991; Wilson-Smith 2000). As technologies such as film, radio, and television became widespread, researchers began to look for direct and measurable effects of media.

Predicting Media Effects

Whenever new technologies emerge in a culture, they are met with both optimism and fear. In the late 1920s, when movies became a widespread form of family entertainment, social scientists warned of the damaging effects movies might have on children. By the late 1930s, radio had a dominant role in mass communication and entertainment, leading researchers to question the effects of this medium as well. We have censored books, banned films, instituted rating codes for popular music, and restricted access to magazines based on concerns about the effects of media on the attitudes and behaviors of individuals. These efforts to regulate media have been fueled partly by research suggesting that media have direct effects on thought and behavior.

The SMCR (Source-Message-Channel-Receiver) model captures the original logic behind the direct view of media influence (Berlo 1960). Figure 10-1 illustrates the transmission of a message, "beef can be bad for you," to a particular viewing audience.

hypodermic needle model Explains direct media effects by suggesting that a specific message can be "shot" into an unsuspecting audience.

The idea that powerful media have a direct effect on audiences has been called the **hypodermic needle model,** which is also referred to as the "magic bullet theory" or "direct effects model" (Campbell 2000). This model suggests that a specific message can be "shot" into an unsuspecting audience. Based on this model of communication, a researcher might conduct a telephone survey to see if viewers of the "Oprah" segment now believe that beef is not healthy. The researcher could also track consumer behavior to see if beef sales decreased after people watched the show. In fact, following the 1996 "Oprah" show, Texas cattle ranchers alleged that Oprah's comments had caused beef prices to fall to a 10-year low. The crash in market prices was large and swift enough for ranchers to bring a libel suit

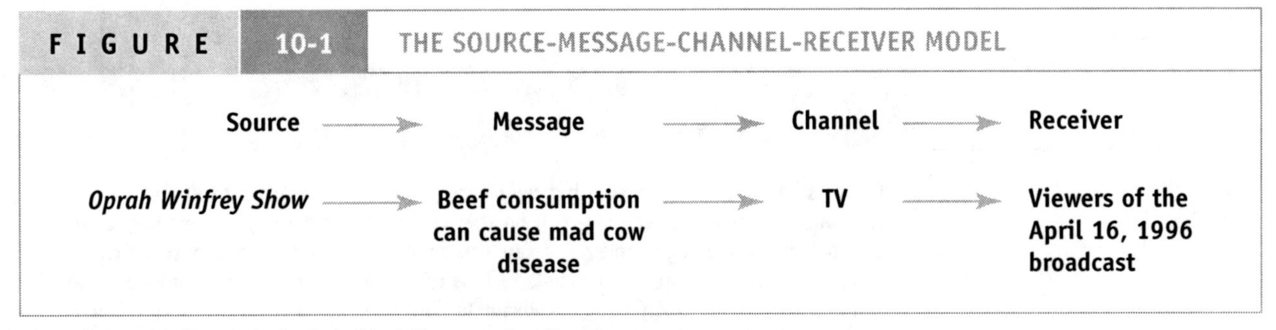

The SMCR model shows the logic behind direct media effects.

against Oprah Winfrey. As with most allegations of direct media effects, however, the degree of responsibility assigned to Oprah Winfrey for falling beef prices was difficult to prove, and her acquittal was upheld in February 2000.

Direct effects of media exposure on individual beliefs, attitudes, and behavior are difficult to prove because so many competing factors can explain the way people think and act. Just as people choose when to listen to someone in a conversation, they engage in **selective exposure** and **selective retention** when consuming media. It is difficult to say that a person voted for a candidate because of his or her performance in an on-camera interview, when it is quite likely that viewers chose to watch a particular candidate because they have already decided that they like the candidate. Similarly, viewers might have remembered the "Oprah" segment on beef because they are vegetarians or value Oprah's opinion on healthy lifestyles. As with other forms of communication, people pay attention to and remember messages that are familiar and that confirm what they already believe. So, in most cases, media may reinforce existing beliefs and behaviors rather than cause significant changes in what people think and do (Wicks 1996; Klapper 1960).

selective exposure
People choose to watch or listen to media messages that confirm existing beliefs.

selective retention
People choose to remember media messages that confirm existing beliefs.

Although proving that there are direct, measurable effects of media exposure is difficult, they certainly exist. They include isolated incidents ranging from the gang rape of two little girls by boys who had seen the made-for-television movie, *Born Innocent,* to the young men who died after imitating a scene in a football movie in which the actors played "chicken" by lying in the middle of a highway at night. Although few people respond to direct media messages in such disastrous ways, decades of research have demonstrated that media do influence attitudes and behaviors. We know that children are particularly vulnerable to media influence. For instance, children are both more likely to become aggressive and fearful after watching frightening and violent movies and television shows, and they are more open to learning successful coping skills for stress (Hoffner 1997; Bandura 1983). Consumers of pornography are more likely to be violent and accept rape myths (e.g., women ask to be raped based on what they are wearing) than nonconsumers (Allen, D'Alessio, and Brezel 1995).

"Violence is an inspiration to the unstable."

—Peggy Noonan, former presidential speechwriter

Concerns about the effects of electronic media have motivated both the general public and political leaders to argue for restrictions on media content. For example, the end of the 1990s saw passage of the Telecommunications Act, which mandates that all new television sets contain V-chips so that parents can block

Exploring Communication Concepts

USING TELEVISION TO PROMOTE POSITIVE SOCIAL CHANGE

From its beginnings, television has been recognized as a potentially valuable teaching tool. Although much of the research on the impact of television programs has focused on troublesome messages, television can also be used to promote positive social change. Advocacy campaigns are one example of how television can be used to convey socially responsible messages. In 1988, for example, Jay Winsten, a professor at the Harvard School of Public Health, introduced the idea of the "designated driver" to television writers, producers, and executives. By 1994 the designated driver "message" had been the main topic of 25 programs of 30 minutes or 60 minutes and had aired on 160 prime-time shows in four seasons.

Adult viewers both noted its appearance on television and appear to have been influenced in their behavior. The percentage of adults who refrained from drinking to serve as designated drivers went up, and within a year of the campaign, drunk-driving fatalities dropped significantly. Of course, these messages occurred as part of a broader campaign that included public service messages and stricter drunk-driving laws. For new information to be retained and have an impact, it needs to appear in a variety of contexts over an extended period of time (Rosenweig 1999).

ASK YOURSELF:

1. What are some other ways that television might be used to promote positive social change?
2. What lessons have you learned from television?

programming they believe is unsuitable for children. Measures such as these reflect widespread concern about the potentially negative influence of media. However, the influence of media doesn't have to be harmful. The "Exploring Communication Concepts" box looks at the potential of television to help reduce drunk-driving fatalities.

Another way to understand the role of media in shaping culture and influencing individuals is by looking at the functions of media in society. The next section introduces three general functions of mass media: gratifying audiences, defining public agendas, and cultivating worldviews (Wood 1998).

Gratifying Audiences

Most of us like to think that we actively choose what to watch, listen to, or read. We also assume that there is a good reason behind our choices. We might pick up a newspaper to find out about the latest financial news, sports statistics, or community events. We probably have some criteria in mind for choosing one movie over another. The **gratification function** of media refers to our active use of media to fulfill these needs and desires. Our motivations for consuming media include the fulfillment of four basic needs: surveillance, information, entertainment, and social utility (see Figure 10-2).

> **gratification function**
> The active use of media to fulfill needs and desires.

Surveillance. Most theories of the press in the United States begin with the "watchdog" function of journalism, or the responsibility of journalists to monitor

FIGURE 10-2 CONCEPT MAP OF MEDIA GRATIFICATIONS

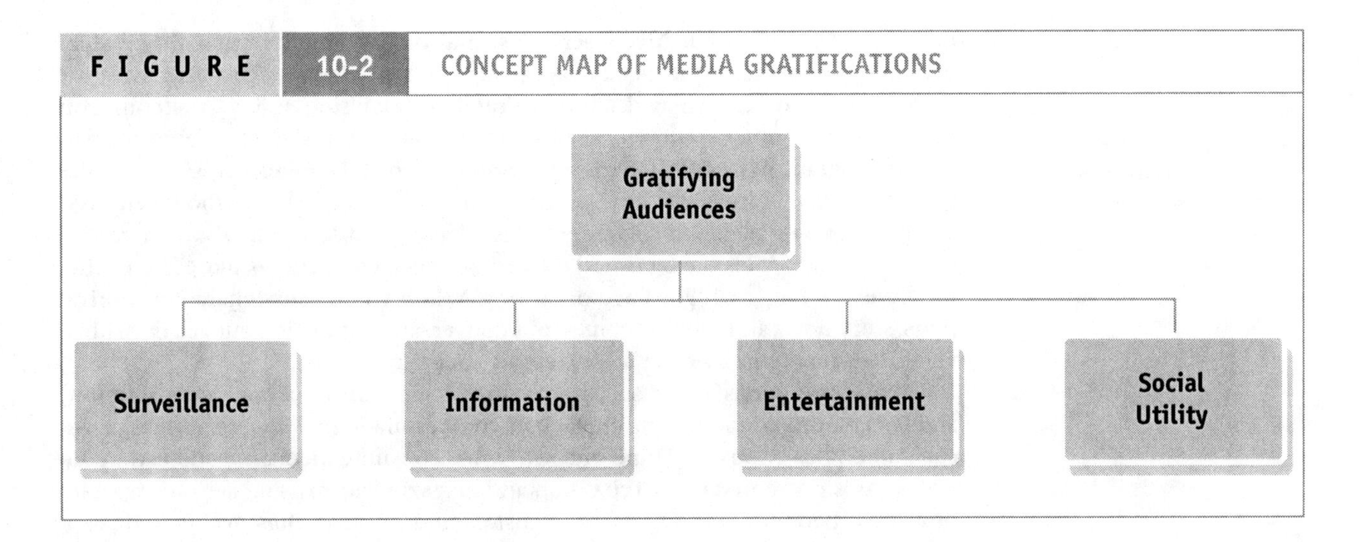

the activities of those in positions of power and expose wrongdoing and corruption. In doing so, good journalists fulfill an important audience need—that of **surveillance,** or keeping watch on important social and political events. When a natural disaster strikes, a scandal brews in Washington, or corrupt leaders threaten a community, many people turn to the mass media to alert them to danger and help them respond. The surveillance function addresses this need to know about events and their potential consequences for individuals and their communities. Our desire to know about the activities of others is satisfied by several media outlets in addition to traditional journalism. Television newsmagazines, trade journals, and special interest publications such as *Ebony, Details,* and the *Advocate* also perform the surveillance function, as do online sites such as Netflix.com, Salon.com, and Sportingnews.com.

surveillance
The function of media to keep the public informed about social and political events.

Information. Whereas media serve a surveillance function when they alert us to newsworthy events, they gratify our need for **information** when we are seeking knowledge, when we are curious, or when we have a personal investment in a topic. Specialty television programming, such as that found on Home and Garden Network, the Discovery Channel, and the History Channel; reference books; and documentary films all address this need.

information
When discussing media gratification, the desire for knowledge based on curiosity, personal investment, or need.

entertainment
The form of gratification we get when media function as a form of wish fulfillment, providing satisfying images and stimulating emotions.

Entertainment. Perhaps the most common motivation for consuming mass media is the desire to be entertained. As **entertainment,** media can serve as a form of wish fulfillment, providing satisfying images and stimulating our emotions. We also turn to media to divert our attention from everyday pressures or to provide a form of companionship. The entertainment function is one of the most commonly cited motivations for consuming media, as well as the one most often misunderstood. As media entertain, they also inform, enlighten, and persuade in ways that are obscured when we consider media to be "mindless." Think about your favorite prime-time drama. You may have learned much of what you know about the medical or legal profession based on this show.

Social Utility. After every televised award show, morning talk show hosts spend considerable time commenting on who was wearing what and on upcoming fashion trends. Media serve a **social utility** function in that they identify common topics about social relationships and provide models of behavior for discussion. If you are an avid fan of a dramatic television series or sitcom, you probably know others who share your enthusiasm for the show. Sometimes a particular program will spark controversy; when Ellen DeGeneres revealed that she was gay on the "Ellen" show, even people who had never seen the show ventured an opinion about Ellen's sexual orientation. Countless discussions about marriage, money, and sex roles have ensued following episodes of shows like "The Bachelor," "Average Joe," and "For Love or Money." When you discuss character motivations, story lines, and plot outcomes as a conversation topic in your relationships, you are using media to serve a social utility need.

social utility
The function media serve when they provide common topics about social relationships and models for behavior.

Each of the needs addressed here—surveillance, information, entertainment, and social utility—focuses on the active choices made by viewers. Although we can sometimes choose to "tune out" when we consume media, we still can't control what is presented to us. Television and magazine advertising are inescapable, unwanted banners that pop up on websites, and popular films may include representations that we do not appreciate or find offensive. Even if we could filter out all unwanted communication, the messages we choose to consume can still influence our personal beliefs, behaviors, and the cultural environment around us in ways that may not be entirely positive. Although the gratifications offered by media are certainly an important part of media consumption, there are other, more powerful and sometimes less obvious ways that media affect our lives.

"Television in the main is being used to distract, delude, amuse and insulate us."
—Edward R. Murrow, journalist

Defining Public Agendas

When media professionals turn their attention to an event, they may do so relentlessly. Think about the never-ending stories generated about Congressman Gary Condit following the disappearance of Chandra Levy, the year-long scrutiny of President Bill Clinton and Monica Lewinsky, the focus on perceived "front-runners" in political campaigns, or the considerable attention given to celebrity misfortune or drug addiction. When news editors choose to place an item on the front page of a newspaper or as a lead story on the evening news, they are performing a gatekeeping function. **Gatekeepers** are the editors, producers, webmasters, and other media managers who decide which messages will get produced. We often trust and grant them power by relying on them to filter out information for us that we might not consider important. Once a gatekeeper decides that a topic is worthy of attention, the media production process crafts that topic into a story that is informative, profitable, and often entertaining.

gatekeepers
Editors, producers, webmasters, and other media managers who decide which messages will get produced.

The ability of media to capture the public imagination was identified as early as 1921 by Walter Lippman, a widely read journalist and essayist, who suggested that because of the process by which events are transformed into news stories, we respond to "the pictures in our heads" rather than actual events. For example, most of us will remember September 11, 2001, through vivid images of planes crashing into the World Trade Center in New York City and subsequent pictures of destruction. Of course, mass media provide us with those pictures.

Understanding the construction and influence of the pictures in our heads is critical because we base so many of our decisions on them. In the United States,

What kinds of emotions are these images likely to evoke?
© AFP/Corbis

we rely on media to provide us with information that is both clear, accurate, and relevant, and also diverse enough to encourage multiple perspectives on public problems. The quality of our decisions about our own lives and the freedoms and rights we are willing to grant others depends on the nature of some of those same pictures referred to by Lippman in 1921. Following the September 11 attacks, we saw images of New York City firefighters and police officers, grieving families of victims, portraits of Osama bin Laden and the Taliban in Afghanistan, and portrayals of the Afghan countryside that guided our opinions about how the United States should respond to the attacks.

When media turn human events into stories for public consumption, they are setting a public agenda. **Agenda-setting,** a term coined by communication theorists Maxwell McCombs and Donald Shaw (1977), refers to the idea that media identify and structure salient issues for audiences. At its core, agenda-setting rests on the beliefs that news media "may not be successful in telling us what to think, but [they are] stunningly successful in telling us what to think about" (Cohen 1963, 13). Media can help put some issues in the forefront of public consciousness. So, when a U. S. president declares a "war on drugs," which is then amplified in news accounts, audiences are likely to identify drugs as a major social problem.

agenda-setting
The process by which media identify and structure important and meaningful issues for audiences.

Media do not act alone in building public agendas. Powerful political leaders and interest groups, natural or human-triggered catastrophes, and organizations of concerned citizens can all contribute to the building of public awareness. Even entertainment media, such as popular movies, can play a role. Think about trends in "message" movies, such as *The Green Mile* and *Dead Man Walking* (the death penalty), or *Armageddon* and *The Day After Tomorrow* (disaster movies). News media play an independent role, however, in conferring legitimacy on some people and events rather than others and in setting the boundaries of public debate. The conferral of status is easiest to see when a particular group or individual is

TABLE 10-2 Terms Used to Report on the Persian Gulf War, 1991

They	We
Destroy	Take out, suppress
Kill	Eliminate, neutralize
Cower in foxholes	Dig in
They launch	**We launch**
Sneak missile attacks	First strikes
Without provocation	Preemptively
Their troops are	**Our troops are**
Brainwashed	Professional
Cowardly	Cautious
Cannon fodder	Daredevils
Blindly obedient	Loyal
Fanatical	Brave
Their planes are	**Our planes**
Shot out of the sky	Suffer a high rate of attrition
Zapped	Fail to return from missions
Saddam Hussein is	**George H. W. Bush is**
A crackpot monster	Assured
Demented	At peace with himself
Defiant	Resolute

labeled as outcast or deviant. For instance, when former sports celebrity O. J. Simpson was charged with the murders of Nicole Brown Simpson and Ronald Goldman, *Time* magazine alluded to his presumed deviant nature by adding shadows to his portrait on its cover. Media shape public debate on broader scales as well. Consider Table 10-2, which illustrates the choices made by journalists in describing armed conflict in the Persian Gulf (Allen 1999). How might these word choices have contributed to public support of U. S. war efforts against Iraq?

Ultimately, the choices made by journalists reflect the routines and standards of their professions as dictated, to some extent, by the interests of the publishers who employ them. Journalists cover stories that are timely and unusual; contain conflict, human interest, or consequences for their readers and viewers; and involve prominent and/or deviant people. They capture events that occur in predictable places, such as the courthouse and city hall, because these are the places that journalists routinely expect newsworthy events to occur. They cover the activities of Republican and Democratic leaders who can make quotable statements ("sound bites") and look good on camera. Finally, journalists are most likely to interview people who are like themselves in terms of gender and race. Regardless of whether individual readers or viewers agree with the choices of stories or people presented in the news, these journalistic choices help determine which stories are important and who has the authority to speak publicly about them.

Cultivating Worldviews

As you might imagine, media do more than fulfill individual needs and contribute to public discussion and decision making. Mass media also play a part in shaping the way we see the world by providing resources and ideas, and by reinforcing particular attitudes and behaviors. Among the vast array of possible images and stories to present, our contemporary media producers retell some stories more than others and show many of the same people, places, and events. Think about the standard plot of an action-adventure movie. You can probably predict the story: A hero with a checkered past is faced with an event that brings him (almost every action hero is male) back to a lifestyle long since abandoned. Duty calls; he will endure grave physical stress, kill without apparent remorse, and overcome evil in a spectacular battle.

Cultivation Theory. Each of these stories tells us about what is important, who is allowed to use violence, and what counts as evil. Some media critics place media at the center of society and argue that the cultural heritage once passed down in stories told by parents and grandparents, churches, and schools is now conveyed largely through media. This view of media and society is called **cultivation theory,** and suggests that media consumption has a cumulative influence in promoting a shared worldview that cuts across most individual and cultural differences (Gerbner et al. 1994).

cultivation theory
An approach to media research which argues that media consumption has a cumulative influence in promoting a shared worldview.

George Gerbner, who formulated cultivation theory, was concerned with ritual viewing which, he argued, is the most common kind of television consumption. Ritual viewing means turning the TV set on at the same time every day or to pass time, rather than choosing a particular program and watching only for that defined amount of time. Rather than seeking media to fulfill a specific need, some of us might, out of habit, turn on the television at a specific time of day. Think about your own viewing habits. You probably turn on the television most often to fit in with other activities. Perhaps you like to have the television on when you have breakfast in the morning, or maybe television keeps you awake for late nights of studying. Researchers of cultivation theory believe that over time, this ritual viewing amounts to quite a bit of time spent watching television.

> "For the first time in human history, children are hearing most of the stories, most of the time, not from their parents or school or churches or neighbors, but from a handful of global conglomerates that have something to sell."
>
> —George Gerbner, media researcher and founder, Cultural Environment Movement

Most people do view television in large quantities; Americans spend a third of their free time in front of the television (Stossel 1997), and a TV is on for nearly seven hours a day in the average U. S. home (Nielsen 2004). Over a 65-year life, the average person will have spent nine years glued to the TV. During that time, each viewer will see repeated character types, situations, and actions that cut across differences in individual programs (Morgan, Shanahan, and Harris 1990). Researchers interested in the cultivation of beliefs and behaviors began by looking at one of the more troubling patterns in television programming: the proliferating portrayals of overt physical violence. Someone sitting down to watch primetime television is likely to see five violent scenes an hour, including five murders, before the evening has ended. By age 18 the typical American child has witnessed 40,000 murders and 200,000 other acts of violence on television (Stossel 1997).

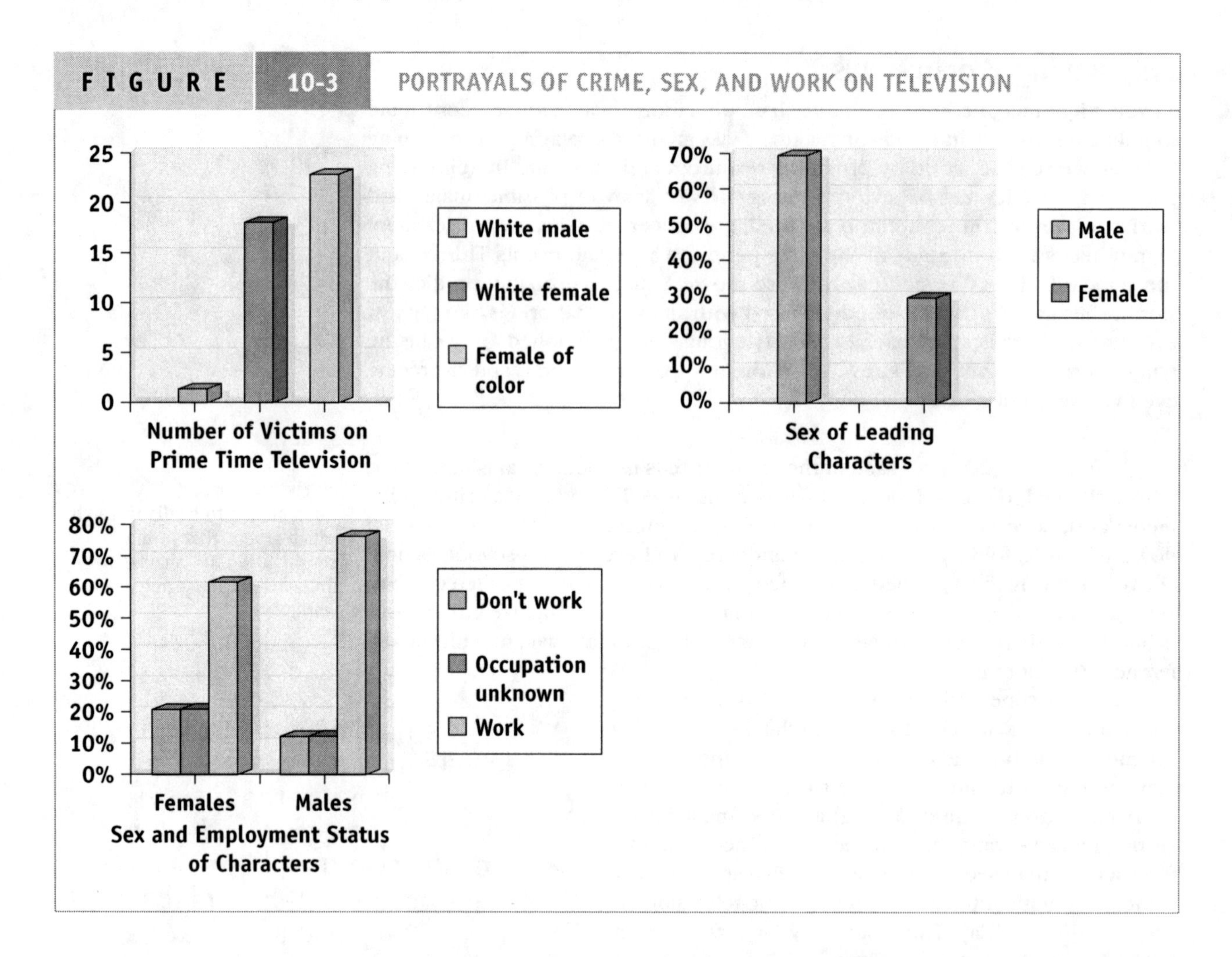

Although portrayals of violence gained the initial attention of researchers, other patterns in programming have also emerged. For example, two-thirds to three-quarters of all leading characters are males; members of the lower classes are almost invisible on television, making up only 1.3 percent of prime-time characters; villains are disproportionately male, lower-class, and Latino or foreign; and for every white male victim there are 17 white female and 22 minority female victims (Stossel 1997; Weiman 2000). Figure 10-3 provides percentages on three patterns of TV characters.

The Influence of Repeated Images. Some researchers argue that the recurring themes and images in media have measurable influences. For instance, prime-time viewers see a world in which crime rates are a hundred times higher than in real life. These viewers are more likely to become desensitized to victims of violence, to feel more vulnerable to crime, to invest in personal security systems, and to favor strict anticrime policies (Signorelli and Morgan 1990). Gerbner and his associates call this the "Mean World Syndrome," a point of view about the world that makes people more suspicious, distrustful of strangers, and willing to impose strict penalties on all kinds of social outcasts. Some research suggests that television viewing can create even more fear of crime than being a victim (Van Den Buick 2004).

Beyond the specific examples of crime and violence, electronic media, above all, reinforce the commonsense assumptions that we make about our world and the people within it. Children who watch a lot of television tend to stereotype occupational roles for each sex and say that men are born with more ambition than women (Signorelli 2001). As we saw in Chapter 2, women who see repeated images of models in fashion magazines are more likely to feel depressed and hostile, and they are more likely to show symptoms of eating disorders (Cantor 1997). Adults who consume sexually explicit materials are more likely to show greater acceptance of male dominance and female submission and greater acceptance of premarital and extramarital sex. When that sexual content is combined with violence, consumers are more likely to say they would be willing to force a women to have sex (Weimann 2000).

> "If you came and you found a strange man . . . teaching your kids to punch each other, or trying to sell them all kinds of products, you'd kick him right out of the house, but here you are; you come in and the TV is on, and you don't think twice about it."
>
> —Jerome Singer, psychology professor

Although these research findings may seem shocking, they do not suggest an independent, direct effect of media images. Rather, they illustrate the potential of our most pervasive form of communication, mass media, to influence our tastes, values, and beliefs. The images we see are drawn from our broad culture, but they are done so selectively, so that some values and perspectives are kept alive while others are neglected. The "Exploring Communication Concepts" box offers a practical way to identify the images that recur in popular media programming.

The Media as an Industry. The recurrent images of people and stories on television can be explained by looking at mass media as an industry. Above all, programming is designed to make a profit. Shows like "Buffy the Vampire Slayer," "Felicity," and "Lois & Clark" stayed on the air not because they attracted a large share of the viewing audience, but because the people who watched them were relatively young, affluent, and willing to change their buying habits, thereby attracting sufficient advertising dollars to pay for production costs and make a profit for the network (Campbell 2000).

Exploring Communication Concepts

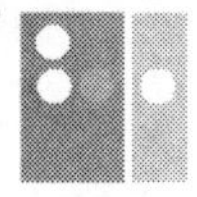

UNCOVERING THE PATTERNS IN TELEVISION'S REALITY

Take an evening to sit down with your television, your remote control, and a DVR. During a prime-time hour, record 60 seconds of each channel. Your examples might range from a news program, to an advertisement, to a feature film, to a sitcom, to professional wrestling. Do not edit your choices; simply record a minute of every channel that you can. Then, once you have compiled your videotape, go back and watch your selections. Count the number of times you see lead characters in categories based on sex, class, race (e.g., Caucasian, African American, Hispanic, Asian, Native American), age (e.g., under 12, 13–19, 20–30, 30–55, 55 and over), and occupation (e.g., professional, service, athlete, law enforcement). You might even count acts of aggression or violence.

ASK YOURSELF:

1. Who is the perpetrator? Who is the victim?
2. What is the sex, class, race, and profession of the lead characters?
3. Whose interests do these representations serve? What stereotypes might they help to perpetuate?

TABLE 10-3 Consolidation in Media Industries: AOL/Time Warner

America Online, Columbia House, Time Inc., Time Warner Entertainment, Turner Broadcasting System, and Warner Music

America OnLine, Compuserve, Netscape: MusicNet, Digital City, moviefone, mapquest, Spinner.com, Winamp, and Shoutcast

Time, Inc: *Entertainment Weekly, People, Southern Living, Sports Illustrated, Time, People en Español, Teen People, Field & Stream, Golf, Yachting,* IPC Media (UK)—*Marie Claire, Loaded, Horses & Hounds*

Time Warner Entertainment: Warner Brothers TV, video, DVD; HBO; one-half owners of Comedy Central and Court TV

Turner Broadcasting System: CNN, Cartoon Network, Turner Classic Movies, TNT, Atlanta Braves/Hawks/Thrashers, Goodwill Games, WB Network

Warner Bros: film studios (Warner Bros., New Line, and Fine Line Features), Warner Home Video (with AT&T), UCI (with Viacom)

Warner Music: Atlantic, Elektra, London, Reprise, Warner Bros. Records; Artists: Green Day, Madonna, Faith Hill, Red Hot Chili Peppers; rights to more than one million songs

Source: M.C. Miller, "What's Wrong with This Picture?" *The Nation*, January 7, 2002.

media synergy
The use by media conglomerates of as many channels of delivery as possible for similar content.

The images presented on television fall into stable patterns because they are produced by a relatively small group of people. The number of people who make decisions about media content is ever-shrinking due to the consolidation of media industries. The move toward **media synergy,** or the use by media conglomerates of as many channels of delivery as possible for similar content (Baran 1999), contributes to the repetition of themes and images reflected in contemporary media.

Media mergers in the 1990s have contributed to synergy. Consider the Walt Disney Company, which has movies, studios, a regular television network (ABC), major newspapers, radio stations, books, stores, character licensing, and stakes in online ventures such as NFL.com and Movies.com (Miller 2002). This conglomerate can control every stage in the production process, from creating content to controlling distribution, to presenting programming and advertisements in the home. Disney can produce an animated feature for theatrical and home release, spin off a cartoon for an ABC Saturday morning slot, publish a book version of the movie, air "the making of" shows on their cable channel, place characters from the movie at their theme parks, put toy characters in McDonald's Happy Meals, and license products ranging from CD-ROM games to lamp shades (Campbell 2000). Even magazine publishers expand their influence beyond their articles by coordinating magazine content with advertisements. Examples of "complimentary copy" include articles on beauty tips that feature the products in corresponding ads or special reports on high-performance automobiles that are advertised in the magazine. Like the larger media conglomerates, print media publishers such as Condé Nast and Simon & Schuster have partnered with electronic media so that they can cash in on magazine and book ideas that turn into TV programs, videos, and films. Table 10-3 looks at another example of media conglomeration in AOL/Time Warner.

Some experts worry that media consolidation limits the diversity of views and quality of news and entertainment we receive. When Dixie Chick Natalie Maines criticized President Bush at a concert, Cumulus and Cox Radio banned their music. Clear Channel radio dropped Howard Stern due to his controversial comments, Wal-Mart refused to sell *Maxim* and shielded the covers of *Glamour* and *Redbook* based on "racy" content, Walt Disney ordered Miramax to drop distribution of Michael Moore's documentary *Fahrenheit 911,* and Sinclair Broadcasting (ABC) pulled a *Nightline* tribute to fallen soldiers, charging that it was an anti-war statement (Billboard 2004, Granatsein 2004). Events such as these raise questions about the influence of media consolidation on political and artistic censorship.

Using Media Responsibly

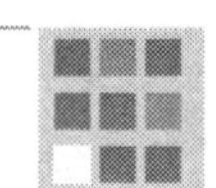

The effects and functions of media, from framing public debate to inspiring violence-prone individuals, might make media seem threatening and all-powerful. However, an audience of critical readers, viewers, and creators can minimize the potentially negative influence of media. Becoming an effective and responsible media consumer or communicator requires the ability to understand media from the perspective of a producer. Just as written literacy requires the comprehension and use of verbal symbols, **media literacy** requires an understanding of the language of media and an ability to critically assess the contribution of media to society. There are three general steps involved in developing media literacy: identifying whose interests are served, identifying the techniques used to create images, and assessing the beliefs and values that are conveyed. Becoming media literate will also help you create your own mediated communication effectively and ethically.

media literacy
Ability to understand the language of media and critically assess the contribution of media to society.

Identifying Underlying Interests

As we noted above, media industries are increasingly consolidated. A good start in developing media literacy, then, is to recognize the profit motive of media conglomerates and the groups most likely to benefit from the media you consume. For example, you might expect *Entertainment Weekly* to promote a new HBO movie, or NBC news to avoid negative stories about its parent company, General Electric.

Because media need to make money, they are also likely to air programs that support values such as buying the newest products, acting on impulse, and instantly gratifying needs. Ask the following questions of the media you consume:

- Whose point of view is reflected?
- Whose point of view is left out?
- Who benefits from this portrayal?

With the hundreds of information media available to the average citizen, including daily and weekly newspapers, local newsletters and newsmagazines, AM and FM radio, commercial and educational television, Internet news providers and websites, the average American can choose from a vast array of media with differing points of view. However, most of us return to the same media outlets, many of which reflect the interests of a few major conglomerates. Stretch your consumption habits to explore different points of view. If you read *Time,* try reading *The New Yorker* or *U. S News & World Report.* Pick up a magazine that seems to be targeted to someone from a different group. See a movie made in a foreign country. Read a section of the local newspaper that you usually ignore. Watch the cable access station or late-night public television. Take advantage of diverse types of entertainment and points of view to increase your media literacy and help support unique media sources.

Identifying Production Techniques

Any mediated message uses its own language of representation. You are probably familiar with many techniques of film and video: When camera work appears shaky, the images are given a documentary or amateur feel. Close-up shots make people seem more intimate, and when a film cuts from one scene to another, we usually assume a relationship between two events, as when a person leaves a house and in the next image is seated behind the wheel of a car. We assume that the person walked from the house to the car, even though we do not see this happen. Think about why some images are chosen rather than others, how they are framed and lit, and where conversations are cut or edited. For example, does a character appear in shadows to convey a sinister impression? Do words seem to be edited out? These decisions affect the impression you will form of mediated communication. Ask the following questions:

- How does the sound track ask me to experience these images? Do the words being spoken match the pictures?
- Does it look like words or points of view were left out? Where might I find a more complete version of this story?
- How does the camera lighting and angle make me feel about this person?
- How do I know that I can trust what I see?

Increasingly, media use dramatic re-creations and digital alteration of images to make a point or achieve an effect. During the CBS coverage of the New Year's celebrations on December 31, 1999, images of Times Square were altered so that a competing network's logo, part of the physical environment of Times Square, was erased. How much airbrushing or image manipulation is acceptable? When historical film footage is mixed with entertainment film, does this change our sense of history? Media literacy means, in part, understanding the way that images are produced and being able to check your perceptions.

Assessing Beliefs and Values

Finally, your consumption of media should always involve a questioning of your own beliefs and values. Some images probably make you feel uncomfortable; others may be damaging to yourself and others. Think about and support programming that looks at the world in ways that are different from yours, and that voices alternative perspectives. For instance, does an exciting sporting event always involve the spectacular star performance that is highlighted and replayed, or

Commercial media messages are carefully crafted to produce a desired effect.
© Bob Daemmrich/The Image Works

does it showcase talented, cohesive teamwork? Can you find images of beautiful people who are of a different ethnicity than your own, or who are over 60 years old? Does a story about violence always have to include violent images? Ask the following questions:

- Are the images and stories disrespectful of an individual or group of people?
- What are the underlying values reflected?
- Does the material presented arouse my emotions so much that I can't think clearly?
- How might this story be told differently?

Media literacy includes the analysis of messages, an awareness of why images are presented the way they are, whose interests are reflected, and what some alternative images and perspectives might be. For example, what standards of beauty are promoted in music television shows like "Grey's Anatomy" and "America's Next Top Model"? How are your emotions manipulated in revenge sequences such as those in films like *The Patriot?* We may think of ourselves as fairly critical viewers, but most of us have a ways to go to achieve true media literacy. This is due in part to a tendency to embrace the **third person effect,** the belief that media influence others more than ourselves. Most of us want to believe that we are immune to harmful effects of media (Salwen and Dupagne 1999). Acknowledging the potential influence of media on ourselves makes us more aware consumers, more responsible citizens, and more creative members of our society.

third person effect
The belief that media influence others more than ourselves.

Creating Responsible Media

Few of us are likely to become prominent producers of commercial media, but most of us have the opportunity to create or promote responsible, mediated communication. We might engage in Instant Messaging conversations with friends or acquaintances, produce amateur videos or photo presentations, design our own website, record an answering machine message, or publish an organizational newsletter. As you become more media literate and create your own forms of communication, ask yourself the following questions:

- Am I presenting myself authentically, without compromising the values I consider to be important?
- Am I presenting my message authentically, so that any manipulation of words or images is easy to identify? For example, do the statements people make appear in proper context? Are dramatizations and re-creations clearly labeled?
- Am I giving the consumers of my messages the ability to respond to me?
- Is anyone likely to be hurt by my communication; if so, am I prepared to take responsibility for my behavior?

Throughout your personal and professional life, you will use media in a variety of ways to communicate with a broad range of people. Sometimes, you might be asked to promote ideas or products that you find objectionable. For example, some of the biggest companies in Hollywood routinely design and market R-rated movies for children as young as nine (Carvajal 2000). Think about Serafin, a student intern who was told to give away toys, T-shirts, and posters for the R-rated movies *South Park* and *The World Is Not Enough* as part of a publicity event for a local radio station. When eight- and nine-year-olds approached the booth, he was told to give them the free items. Should Serafin have objected to this request?

There are many ways to respond to those media messages that you do find objectionable. In addition to creating your own images and stories, you can call radio and television stations, e-mail webmasters, and write letters to newspapers and magazines. Some organizations, such as the Institute for Global Communications (http://www.igc.org), Center for Media Literacy (http://www.medialit.org), and Adbusters (http://www.adbusters.org) are devoted exclusively to the creation and promotion of diversity in media. In addition to improving your own critical awareness and creative ability, responding to media producers leads to more diverse and high quality media content and improved discussion about media. The box, "Applying Communication Concepts," gives specific tips for answering questions in front of a camera.

Applying Communication Concepts

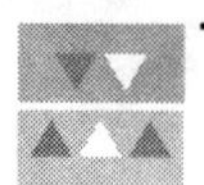

SPEAKING TO THE MEDIA

At some point in your professional or student life, you will probably be asked to appear in an on-camera interview. If you choose a career working in a public institution or within the communication industry (e.g., public relations, marketing, or journalism), you are even more likely to interact with media professionals.

The following hints will help you work successfully with the media:

- **Prepare** your message. You will probably know why you are being contacted, so think about possible questions and the message you would like to deliver.
- **Listen** carefully to each question. Maintain eye contact with the interviewer rather than worrying about the camera.
- **Answer** each question briefly.
- **Bridge** your answer to your message. Use a phrase such as, "Let me add that . . ." for a transition to your message. Be honest; if you can't answer a question, don't be afraid to say so.

ASK YOURSELF:

1. Which part of the process might be the most difficult for you?
2. How might you practice before you get in front of a camera?

Resources for Review and Skill Building

Many of these resources are supported by the Connections CD-ROM and free Online Learning Center Website.

SUMMARY

This summary is organized around the questions found at the beginning of the chapter. See if you can answer them before reading the summary paragraphs.

1. What is the distinction between mediated and mass communication, and why might this distinction be important?

   Mass communication refers to the creation of meaning through messages sent to a large, unseen, and anonymous audience. The more resources used to produce a message, the larger the audience needed to make a profit. Although many of us consume mass communication, we also participate in mediated communication, which includes any communication that is sent or received using technology.

2. What are the stages in the coevolution of communication technologies and audiences?

   Over the centuries we have moved from an oral to a literate and finally to an electronic society. With each new era of media have come fears about their effects and hopes for a better society. Before the advent of writing and printing, communication was based on speaking and listening. Oral communication became mediated when language first moved from spoken to written form. In some parts of the world oral culture is still dominant, but in most parts of the world, literacy became dominant with the development of the printing press. The reproduction of the Bible has been called the first form of mass media.

   Literacy brought with it changes in thinking, social structure, and commerce. Some of these changes still exist in the electronic society of the 21st century. Electronic society has brought back some features of oral culture, such as focusing on listening, using personal appearance to evaluate believability, and sharing public events with large audiences. Several communication technologies, such as telephone lines, digital satellite services, and personal computers have been combined to bring us new ways to communicate with mediated messages.

3. Why is there so much concern about the effects of media?

   With every new mass medium has come a concern about media effects. Direct effects of media are difficult to prove, because competing factors such as selective exposure can often explain behavioral change. However, some research does suggest that mass media can have a direct effect on audience beliefs and behaviors, particularly among children and consumers of sexual and violent media content.

4. What are the functions of mass media?

   Through media we can learn what remote parts of the world look like; how we expect others to behave in work, education, and leisure; who appears fit to run our country; what behaviors we will tolerate; and even how we should look on a date. Mass media fulfill audience desires for surveillance, information, entertainment, and social utility. Media managers function as gatekeepers who decide which messages will be produced, and when media turn human events into stories, they can build public agendas.

   Media also cultivate worldviews by providing audiences with a steady stream of recurring stories, themes, and images. For instance, the patterns of portrayals on prime-time television reinforce stereotypes about sex roles, contribute to fear of crime, and encourage acceptance of violence. The most profitable and common images are repeated, and the potential diversity of images and voices can be lost.

5. **Why is media literacy important, and how can consumers and users of media communicate responsibly?**

   Media literacy requires becoming knowledgeable about media production, acquiring the skill to evaluate media messages, and encouraging the creation of ethical communication. It requires the ability to identify underlying interests behind messages, understand production techniques in mediated communication, assess beliefs and values that are reinforced by media, and create responsible communication through authentic portrayals of self and others, providing opportunities for feedback, and responding to objectionable media content. Only by becoming careful, responsible, and critical media consumers can we ensure that the creative and liberating potential of media be achieved.

KEY TERMS

Test your understanding of these key terms by visiting the Connections CD-ROM and the Online Learning Center website at www.mhhe.com/dobkinpace.

agenda-setting 283
cultivation theory 285
electronic society 275
entertainment 281
gatekeepers 282
gratification function 280
hypodermic needle model 278
information 281
literacy 273
mass communication 271
media 272
media literacy 289
media synergy 288
oral cultures 272
selective exposure 279
selective retention 279
social utility 282
surveillance 281
technological convergence 277
third person effect 291

FOR FURTHER REFLECTION

Join a conversation about chapter concepts by visiting the Online Learning Center website at www.mhhe.com/dobkinpace

1. As noted at the beginning of the chapter, the more resources that are devoted to film or television programming, the larger an audience needs to be for a studio to make a profit. Look at the list of top-grossing films worldwide. Are there any common themes in these films? What themes are missing and why?

Worldwide Box Office Receipts
(in millions of U.S. dollars)

1.	*Titanic* (1997)	$1,835,300,000
2.	*The Lord of the Rings: The Return of the King* (2003)	$1,129,219,252
3.	*Pirates of the Caribbean: Dead Man's Chest* (2006)	$1,060,332,628
4.	*Harry Potter and the Sorcerer's Stone* (2001)	$968,657,891
5.	*Pirates of the Caribbean: At World's End* (2007)	$958,404,152
6.	*Harry Potter and the Order of the Phoenix* (2007)	$937,000,866
7.	*Star Wars: Episode I—The Phantom Menace* (1999)	$922,379,000
8.	*The Lord of the Rings: The Two Towers* (2002)	$921,600,000
9.	*Jurassic Park* (1993)	$919,700,000
10.	*Harry Potter and the Goblet of Fire* (2005)	$892,194,397

Source: http://www.imdb.com/boxoffice. Retrieved May 16, 2008

2. Keep a log of all the media you consume for two days. Include, for example, the radio or CD that serves as a morning alarm, the music or television program that starts your day, and the billboards you pass as you drive. Then, try to go "cold turkey" for a day and eliminate all media consumption. How much media do you consume? What needs are met by your media consumption? How difficult was it to avoid all media?

BUILDING COMMUNICATION SKILLS

Broadcast commercials and print advertising can be some of the most entertaining forms of mass communication. Advertisements do more than promote products; they also sell attitudes, values, and lifestyles. For example, a commercial for a luxury sport utility vehicle (SUV) shows several adults, dressed in the latest designer weekend clothes, running through a forest, laughing, with flashbacks to when they were young children. They might be playing tag or some other game. They gleefully run to the edge of a cliff and jump off, into a pristine swimming hole below. The ad then cuts to the SUV, swerving among trees in a blur, and asks you to capture the experience of youth by driving the SUV. Think about the implications of this lifestyle for personal safety, responsibility, and environmental preservation.

The same critical analysis can be brought to any product advertisement. Flip through the pages of a popular magazine and consider the following questions:

- How quickly and easily are problems solved?
- Does the ad appeal to basic human needs?
- What age, race, class, and gender is targeted by the ad? Does one group appear to have power or control over another? How can you tell?
- How is success measured? How is beauty measured?
- What kind of lifestyle is promoted, and what are the implications?

NET WORK

Note: While all the URLs listed were current as of the printing of this book, the sites often change. Please check our website (www.mhhe.com/dobkinpace) for updates and hyperlinks to these exercises.

1. Several websites offer perspectives on public affairs that differ considerably from those presented by more well-known news organizations. One site maintained by "Project Censored" illustrates the power of news media as gatekeepers. Each year Project Censored publishes a list of stories that the organization feels have not received adequate coverage in mainstream publications. Visit its website: http://www.projectcensored.org. Are you familiar with any of the stories Project Censored lists as important? Why do you think these stories didn't get more widespread coverage?
2. Many internet sites promote media literacy and diversity. Compare two or more of these websites: www.poppolitics.com; www.mediawatch.com; www.mediaawareness.com; www.prwatch.org/cmd/; www.changingchannels.org. What objectives do these sites share? How do they address issues of media responsibility?

MEDIA MOMENTS

View a segment of reality-based television, such as "America's Most Wanted," "The Bachelor," or even a daytime talk show. Reality programming is among the least expensive to produce.

- Whose interests are served?
- Do such shows perform a social utility function?
- Why might people participate in them?

Planning Public Presentations

CHAPTER 11

It was just a few minutes before Grant Hayes was to speak to a gathering of college students, and he was hurriedly trying to prepare his presentation. The president of Associated Students, Jackie Nguyen, had asked Grant to speak at an orientation program for first year students. Other students had been asked to speak on behalf of a number of campus organizations. Grant was to discuss the benefits of service learning opportunities. He was the student coordinator for a program that placed students in service opportunities ranging from tutoring underprivileged elementary school students to outreach programs for the homeless. But Grant had been so busy setting up this semester's programs that he had run out of time to prepare his presentation properly. He hurriedly grabbed a few sign-up forms for the program, an old folder with a few overhead transparencies from a previous presentation to faculty members, and a couple of pages of quotations that he had pulled off the Internet about a similar program at another university.

When Grant arrived at the orientation, he was nervous. The crowd was larger than he had expected, and there was no overhead projector. Jackie introduced Grant: "Now, Grant Hayes will talk about the benefits of our Service Learning Opportunities program."

QUESTIONS TO FOCUS YOUR READING

1. How do I choose a topic for my speech?
2. What is the difference between a general speech purpose and a specific speech purpose, and how do they affect my speech?
3. How can analyzing the situation improve my speech?
4. What kind of research should I do for my speech?
5. How can I plan a responsible presentation?

Grant began, "Thank you, Jackie. But I really didn't prepare a speech on the benefits of SLOs. I thought I would just talk about how to sign up for the program. I have some forms here, but I really don't have enough for everyone. I will pass out the few I have but if you don't get one, come by our office in the Student Center. There are two kinds of SLOs. There are SLOs for credit and SLOs for noncredit."

Jackie interrupted, "Maybe you should tell them what a SLO is, Grant."

Grant continued, "Right. SLO stands for "service learning opportunities" and there are two kinds of SLOs—SLOs for credit, called SLO-Cs and SLOs for no credit, called SLO-NCs. You use the green form for SLO-Cs and the blue form for SLO-NCs. I have some overhead transparencies that show how many students signed up for SLO-Cs and SLO-NCs last semester but there is no projector, so I'll just read them to you. I also have a quote I want to read about SLOs. It's about a program that builds houses in Boston for disadvantaged people. We don't have such a program here, but we have others that are really great." After several anxious moments, he said, "I can't seem to find the quote right now, but if you are interested, come up after the program and I will tell you all about the programs you can sign up for."

Grant sat down feeling disappointed. He knew that his presentation had gone poorly.

Benjamin Franklin's oft-quoted statement, "by failing to prepare, you are preparing to fail," applies to Grant's presentation. Grant had good intentions but missed an opportunity to tell first-year students about his program. Where did he go wrong? First, he misjudged the purpose of the speech. The audience expected Grant to give a persuasive speech on the benefits of service learning, but Grant simply explained how students could sign up for his program before they knew much about it or had any desire to do so. He also misjudged how much the audience knew about his topic, using, for example, abbreviations that the audience did not understand (SLO-Cs and SLO-NCs). In addition, Grant did not carefully analyze the speaking situation. Not only did he overestimate the audience's knowledge about his topic, but also he underestimated the size of the audience and did not have enough forms for everyone. In addition, he assumed an overhead projector would be at his disposal rather than checking the room in advance to make sure one was available. Finally, Grant did a poor job of gathering materials that would be relevant to his audience. The materials about the program that he did use were a series of numbers on last semester's participants that had little meaning for the audience, and he referred to a program in Boston that was not relevant to his audience. As a result of his lack of preparation, Grant's speech was largely ineffective.

The skills needed to compose and deliver a speech in front of an audience are valuable ones. Surveys of Pace and Harvard University Business School graduates and prospective employers have all rated oral communication and presentation skills as one of the most important factors for career success (Ulinski and O'Callaghan 2002; Sears 1994). In a survey of chief executive officers of large U.S. companies, 84 percent of the respondents said that the ability to speak to groups of colleagues and to make public presentations was "very important," yet many of the respondents also said that the communication skills of their staff were "seriously deficient" (Moss 1995). College graduates who complete a public speaking course are seen as significantly better at giving business briefings and presentations than those who have not (Harris 1994).

Public speaking is also an important skill outside one's work and career. A growing number of college students and graduates become involved in **civic engagement,** actively participating to create change, organizing others who share a common vision, and working to improve communities and organizations (Halstead and Lind 2002; Van Benschoten 2000). Civic engagement includes volunteering to work with others on community problems such as health, discrimination, and the environment. It also requires dialogue with other interested and concerned citizens through public speaking (Penn State Center for Public Speaking 2002). Standing up and expressing oneself is not only a basic freedom in a democracy, but also an important skill in improving communities.

civic engagement
Participating to create change, organizing others who share a common vision, and working to improve communities and organizations.

In this course, your immediate concern is probably an assignment to prepare and deliver a speech to your class. The process you will use to prepare and deliver a classroom speech is the same as that needed in professional and civic contexts. Careful preparation is the foundation of an effective speech. In this chapter we will consider the steps involved in planning and preparing a speech. After completing this chapter, you should be able to:

- Select a topic for your speech.
- Identify a general and specific speech purpose.
- Analyze the speaking situation.
- Gather appropriate materials and information on your topic.
- Plan a responsible presentation.

"Spectacular achievements are always preceded by unspectacular preparation."
—Roger Staubach, football star

Selecting a Topic

Choosing a topic presents a challenge to many students. In many speaking contexts outside the classroom, such as speaking in a business meeting to colleagues or clients or to members of a civic organization, the topic of your speech will be dictated by the agenda. For example, your boss might ask you to speak to another work team about a project you are working on, or the PTA president might ask you to speak to parents about the next fund-raiser. In both instances, your topic is predetermined. In those cases, your task as a speaker is to address that topic in an appropriate way through a careful analysis of the situation, a process we will discuss later in this chapter.

In many college courses, however, instructors ask students to choose their own topic for speaking assignments. Some students know right away what they want to speak about, while others are bewildered by the range of choices available. Students sometimes spend considerable time trying to select the best possible topic, reasoning that the "perfect" topic will mean a good speech and ultimately a good grade. As a result, students sometimes do not spend enough time preparing their speech and end up with below-average grades. The authors of this text have a combined total of more than 40 years of experience teaching public speaking. We have listened to thousands of student speeches, and our experience has taught us that there is no such thing as the perfect topic. Some topics that might appear to be *intrinsically* interesting often turn out otherwise, whereas other topics that might appear to be fairly dull are often presented in interesting ways. In general, the following guidelines have proven useful to students selecting a topic for classroom speech.

Pick a Topic of Interest to You

If the topic interests you, you are likely to be motivated to prepare thoroughly and to deliver an animated speech. Your natural enthusiasm for the topic will also enhance your credibility with the audience. If the topic interests you, it is likely to engage interest your classmates as well. Conversely, audiences can usually detect a lack of enthusiasm in a speaker who is not especially concerned about the topic of his or her speech.

Look for a Topic by Analyzing Your Interests

Make a list of possible topics by making an inventory of things that appeal to you. Ask yourself what college courses you enjoy, what activities you participate in outside of class, what current events interest you, or what kinds of books you read for enjoyment. Sometimes, students overlook an obvious topic because it is so commonplace in their lives that they forget that others might be interested in it. For example, a student in one of our classes was struggling to find a topic. Finally, we suggested that she speak about her hometown, Las Vegas, Nevada. She replied that everyone already knew everything about Las Vegas and wouldn't be interested in a speech about it. Nevertheless, she began to ask classmates about her hometown and soon discovered that many of them knew very little about the city and were eager to know more. She eventually prepared an effective speech about "little-known places" to visit in Las Vegas. Often the topics you know the most about are those about which you can prepare the most absorbing and effective speeches. The box "Applying Communication Concepts" will help you make an inventory of possible topics for a speech.

Get Feedback on Your Topic Ideas

Almost any subject can be the topic of a successful speech. Ultimately, it is not the topic that makes a speech successful but how effectively you adapt the topic to your audience. Like the student from Las Vegas, talk to your classmates, friends, or instructors about possible ideas for a speech. Through this conversation you will begin to narrow your possible topics. For instance, Raoul figured he loved soccer so much he would do his speech on this sport. He knew that soccer wasn't a big sport at his school, so his audience would probably not know much about it. He decided to focus on something that he knew people thought of when it comes to soccer—heading the ball (or hitting the ball with your head). He asked his roommates what they were most interested in learning if they heard about heading a soccer ball, and they replied: "Does it hurt? How far can you send it?" Who's the best?" Raoul was beginning to get some ideas for his speech. Talking with others as Raoul did will not only help you select a topic but will also help you focus your ideas.

Applying Communication Concepts

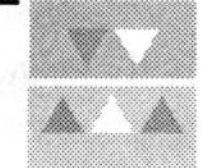

SELECTING A TOPIC

To help inventory your interests, take a few minutes to complete the following exercise on paper. This structured experience should help you to generate some possible ideas for speeches. When it comes to developing a topic for your speech, remember to consult your instructor and course materials for the specifics of your assignment. Not all topics are appropriate for all assignments, and your professor may have specific restrictions or recommendations on the selection of a topic.

Answer each of the following questions in as much detail as possible.

School

1. What is your major? Minor?
2. What class or classes have you enjoyed the most?
3. What lectures have interested you this semester (or quarter)?
4. What topics or lectures have you discussed with friends or roommates?

Job/Careers

1. What jobs have you had?
2. What do your parents do?
3. What do you see as your ideal job after you graduate?
4. What unusual jobs have your friends, relatives, or acquaintances had?

Interests

1. What do you do when you are not in the classroom?
2. What hobbies or special interests do you have?
3. What are the last three books you read outside the classroom?
4. What are your favorite magazines?
5. Where have you traveled?
6. What is interesting about your hometown?
7. What sports do you enjoy participating in or watching?
8. What type of music do you listen to?
9. Do you enjoy plays, opera, or other forms of performance?
10. Do you play a musical instrument?
11. What were the last three events you paid to attend?

Beliefs

1. What are three strong values you believe in?
2. What political movements do you participate in?
3. What was the last long discussion you had with your roommate, best friend, or spouse?
4. Look at a newspaper—what stories interest you?
5. What current events worry you?
6. Which sections of the newspaper do you read first? Why?
7. How have your participated in your community? What service activities or charities have you participated in?

ASK YOURSELF:

Some students would prefer to be assigned a speech topic and avoid the trouble of selecting their own topic.

1. Why do you think many professors have students select their own topics?
2. What would you like others to know about you?

Still having trouble picking a topic? Try the topic helper.

Set a Deadline for Selecting a Topic

It is best to select a topic promptly so that you have ample time to prepare your speech. A deadline will help you avoid procrastinating. One of the secrets to success in public speaking is preparation and practice. Too many students delay their preparation by failing to select a topic in a reasonable amount of time. Pursuit of the perfect topic usually leads to procrastination, which gives way to panic as the date of the speech approaches. With these pitfalls in mind, select a topic that interests you and start doing the research for your speech as early as possible.

Focusing Your Speech Topic

Once you have selected a topic, develop a clear sense of your goals for the speech. What is it that you want to accomplish? Beginning speeches often lack focus because speakers haven't sufficiently considered the goals of their speech. For instance, suppose your speech is meant to alert people to the dangers of pesticides on the fruit they buy in the supermarket. What aspects of the topic would you need to cover? Should you talk about the actual chemicals that might be present, or focus on how to avoid them by purchasing organic produce? Every topic presents such questions.

The best way to ensure a focused presentation is to clearly identify the purpose of your speech at the outset. When planning your speech, consider your audience and what you think you can reasonably expect to accomplish. There are two types of purposes in public speaking: general and specific (Gregory 2002). The **general speech purpose,** as the name implies, is the broad objective of your speech. The **specific speech purpose** is the precise goal that you want to achieve. Both are important to your speech, and we will discuss each in the following sections.

general speech purpose
The overall objective of the speech, such as to inform, to persuade, or to entertain.

specific speech purpose
The precise goal the speaker wants to achieve with the audience.

Determine Your General Purpose

There are three general purposes of a speech: to inform, to persuade, and to entertain. Although these goals sometimes overlap, speakers need to identify the general purpose that is most appropriate for their speech.

Speeches to Inform.

In a **speech to inform,** the speaker explains a concept, idea, or process to the audience. For example, a professor's lectures on Renaissance sculpture or a lab demonstration of photosynthesis are speeches to inform. The goal of a speech to inform is to have the audience understand something about a topic. Speakers delivering an informative speech must assess what the audience already knows about the topic and then build upon that knowledge. In business, a human resource officer might sponsor a training workshop on time management while managers often conduct business briefings on sales projections. A baseball coach could demonstrate how to bunt, and a ballet teacher could teach students to pirouette. Televised cooking shows, home improvement demonstrations, and documentaries all aim to inform the audience about particular subjects.

speech to inform
A speech whose overall objective is to explain a concept, idea, or process to an audience.

speech to persuade
A speech whose overall objective is to influence an audience to accept a belief, agree with a value, or take an action.

Speeches to Persuade.

In a **speech to persuade,** the speaker tries to influence the audience to accept a belief, agree with a value, or take an action. For example, political candidates give speeches to persuade voters to choose them; lawyers speak to jury members to convince them of the innocence or guilt of defendants. Some persuasive speeches aim to instill a belief or attitude; others aim to persuade the audience to act, such as signing a petition, buying a product, or refraining from driving while intoxicated; and finally, some aim to reinforce or strengthen a belief already held by the audience, as in a speech about helping the poor or protecting the environment.

Speeches to Entertain. Sometimes the general goal of a speech is to entertain by amusing, enthralling, cheering, charming, or otherwise pleasing the audience. The goal of a **speech to entertain** is for the audience to enjoy the speech. Messages intended to entertain audiences abound in our culture. Most television programming is aimed at audience pleasure and enjoyment. Stand-up comics deliver a specialized form of speeches to entertain. Speeches to entertain are given at many special occasions, such as after-dinner speeches for professional organizations or toasts at a wedding.

speech to entertain
A speech whose overall objective is to amuse, enthrall, cheer, charm, or otherwise please an audience.

Most speeches will include elements of all three general speech purposes. A speech to inform might very well be entertaining, and a speech to entertain might persuade some audience members to change their beliefs about a particular topic. For example, an entertaining speech about the rigors and rewards of snow camping might prompt some audience members to consider trying it. Although speeches can address more than one purpose, focus on the primary goal of your speech when trying to narrow your topic. While your speech to inform might have a secondary goal of entertainment, your primary objective is to have the audience understand your information. Having too many goals for a speech may confuse the audience and spread the resources of a speaker too thin. Select an achievable general purpose for your speech that will help you focus your resources and efforts.

> "You grow up the day you have your first real laugh at yourself."
> —Ethel Barrymore, silent film star

Develop Your Specific Purpose

The specific purpose states your objective for the speech in precise detail, much like a thesis statement in a well-written paper states the purpose of the writer. The specific purpose provides focus for the speech. In almost all speaking situations, the topic chosen will be too broad to cover in the available time. A specific purpose narrows the general subject of your speech by focusing it on a specific aspect of the topic. For example, if you want to give a 10-minute informative speech about chocolate, you might focus on the process of making chocolate, the history of chocolate, or even the health benefits of chocolate—but not on all three topics. A specific purpose should be stated in the form of a goal. What do you want the audience to know or do once the speech is finished? In writing a specific purpose, you should be able to complete the following sentence: I want my audience to (understand, believe, or do): ____________________. For example, consider one of the following specific purposes for a speech on chocolate:

- I want my audience to understand the steps in making chocolate.
- I want my audience to understand the history of chocolate in Europe.
- I want my audience to believe that chocolate is an excellent health food.

Refine and Focus Your Specific Purpose. As you gather materials and organize your speech, you are likely to refine and provide further focus to your specific purpose. The most common mistake is to set specific purposes that are too broad. Specific purposes like, "I want my audience to understand the history of the Vietnam War," are too wide ranging for a single speech. A more suitable specific purpose might be, "I want my audience to understand how the Tet Offensive led to the escalation of the Vietnam War in 1968." Similarly, specific purposes like "I want my audience to understand the history and technique of bicycle racing" separate rather than unite a topic because they suggest two speeches instead of one. Here are some ways that the specific purposes for a speech about chocolate might be refined and be made more precise:

- I want my audience to understand three steps in making chocolate: (1) nibbing—preparing and shelling the cocoa bean, (2) crumbing—roasting and pressing the cocoa bean into a paste, and (3) conching—mixing in other ingredients and churning the paste to make it smooth.
- I want my audience to understand three important periods in the early history of European chocolate: (1) 1519, when Cortez brought back chocolate to Spain from the Aztecs in Mexico; (2) the 1650s, when the European nobility began to enjoy sipping hot chocolate drinks; and (3) the 1690s, when Belgian and Swiss chefs popularized chocolate by adding it to cakes and other desserts.
- I want my audience to believe chocolate makes an excellent and tasty health food, because chocolate contains antioxidants, flavonoids, and fatty acids that are good for you.

An old speech adage says, "Bite less and chew more." It is better to cover less material in depth than to cover too many main points superficially. The more precise your specific purpose, the better your speech will be.

Develop Your Specific Purpose with Your Audience in Mind. Sometimes speakers develop a specific purpose that is too narrow. Although this happens rarely, it usually occurs when speakers incorrectly assess the audience's level of knowledge and come up with a specific purpose beyond the audience's

Speakers need to consider both their audience and the occasion as they develop their presentations.

ability to comprehend. Consider a student who gave a speech about the rail, a type of bird that cannot fly. The student's specific purpose was: "I want my audience to understand the metabolic rate of land-based rails." The topic was too specialized for a nonscientific audience. A more appropriate specific purpose might have been, "I want my audience to understand that rails are flightless birds."

Analyzing the Situation

As the experience of Grant Hayes at the beginning of the chapter shows, it is also important to analyze your speaking situation. The situation includes everything from the size of the room to the makeup of the audience and is one of the first things to think about when planning your speech. By analyzing the situation, speakers can discover many opportunities to enhance their presentations. Consider the opening example again. Can you think of opportunities or challenges that Grant missed? He was addressing a large crowd of first-year students who were interested in learning about his program, he had a chance to persuade the audience about the value of his program, and his introduction by the student body president added credibility to his presentation. Grant was also faced with several challenges, including an audience that knew little about his program, a purpose regarding service that might not grab the audience's attention as easily as one about intramural athletics or campus concerts, and a restless audience that had already heard many presentations. Had Grant responded to these opportunities and challenges, his speech would have been much more effective.

All speaking situations are a dynamic and changing mix of several characteristics including speaker, audience, and occasion. By analyzing each of these three areas, you will discover opportunities to enhance your speech and challenges to overcome. The "Applying Communication Concepts" box identifies questions to help you develop your speech by analyzing the speaking situation.

Evaluate Your Strengths and Weaknesses as a Speaker

All speakers have strengths and weaknesses. Some speakers might have a knack for using jokes to engage the audience but have trouble explaining concepts clearly. Others might have tremendous knowledge to offer the audience but tend to be dry and long-winded. Knowing your own strengths and weaknesses as a speaker will help you to work on areas that may be difficult for you and to develop strategies for taking advantage of your abilities. For example, perhaps you are speaking on a subject about which you have limited knowledge. Once you recognize and accept that you are not an expert on the topic, you can make a concentrated effort to learn more about it by doing the necessary research. Similarly, if you know that people generally think you are humorous, you can make plans to integrate humor into your speech.

To accurately assess the situation, you need to understand your biases toward a topic. Your perspective on the topic can limit your ability to understand the audience's view of the subject. For example, students in colleges and universities that are close to the U.S.-Mexico border often give speeches on traveling in Mexico. Some of these students speak Spanish, have lived in Mexico before, or are even Mexican citizens. They have extensive experience with the country and a clear understanding of the culture. Occasionally, however, a student's only experience with Mexico is a vacation to a beach resort or a day trip across the border. These students sometimes do not realize the limits of their understanding, and

Applying Communication Concepts

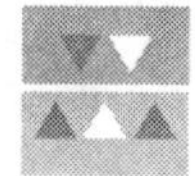

ANALYZING THE SPEAKING SITUATION

Speakers can discover opportunities and challenges by doing a careful analysis of the situation. The following questions should help you prepare your speech with the audience's knowledge and interests in mind.

Speaker

How much do I know about the topic?
What are my biases toward the topic?
What are my strengths as a speaker?
What are my limitations as a speaker?

Audience

What is the age range of my audience?
Is my audience composed of men only? Women only? Both sexes?
What is the socioeconomic status of my audience?
What is the ethnicity or nationality of my audience?
What is the level of education of my audience?
What are the professional interests of my audience?
How much does the audience know about my topic?
How does the audience feel about my topic?
What does the audience expect to happen in the speech?

Occasion

What is the purpose of the gathering?
What is the mood of the occasion?
How much time do I have to speak?
What is the time of day, month, and year of the speech?
What is the physical setting of the speech?
Who speaks before me?
Who speaks after me?

ASK YOURSELF:

Earlier in the chapter we mentioned a few unique characteristics of the speech situation in a college classroom.

1. What are some additional challenges and opportunities present in your classroom assignment(s)?
2. How might these opportunities and challenges differ from those you may face in speaking situations outside the classroom?

they present a stereotypical image of Mexico that is almost always inaccurate and occasionally offensive. For instance, students might talk about the many nightclubs just across the border that cater to Americans and assert that the locals don't mind serving alcohol to underage customers. The message of irresponsible drinking can be offensive, particularly to residents of Mexico who are likely to be insulted by characterizations of their country as a place for Americans to get intoxicated and by claims that the locals do not care.

To be a successful speaker you need to understand your biases and work to expand your viewpoint. Even if you do not explicitly present alternative perspectives in your speech, an awareness of them will help you effectively adapt your topic to the audience.

Evaluate Your Audience

The most effective speeches are "audience centered." **Audience centered** means that a speaker adapts the speech to the audience's needs, level of knowledge, background, and interests. We have already emphasized the need to assess the expectations an audience is likely to bring to a speaking situation. In addition, the speaker should analyze the audience's demographic characteristics, attitudes, and expectations.

audience centered
Speakers adapt the speech to the audience's needs, level of knowledge, background, and interests.

Determine the Demographic Profile of Your Audience.

In preparing your speech, consider the **demographic characteristics** of your audience, including their age, sex, socioeconomic status, ethnicity, nationality, level of education, and professional interests. The generalizations drawn from such observations should be a starting point but not the only method used to understand your audience, because the information generated from such analyses is often very general and can be dangerously biased. If audience members think you are stereotyping them in your speech, they will feel resentful. For example, although many people in their 40s and 50s have shared experiences that are particular to post–World War II America, they often grow tired of being referred to as the "baby boom" generation. Similarly, a younger audience is generally more computer sophisticated than an older audience, but many young people distrust computers, and one of the fastest-growing segments of Internet users are retired people. Use the information gathered from demographic analysis carefully to provide general insights into your audience. In your classroom speaking assignments, for example, it would be helpful to know what academic majors are represented in the audience, what level of exposure to other cultures your classmates have, and what kind of life experiences they are likely to have encountered. In this way, demographic analysis becomes a starting point for finding out more useful information about your audience, rather than becoming a justification for perpetuating stereotypes. The "Exploring Communication Concepts" box employs the example of commercial television to illustrate some of the uses and limitations of demographics to understand audiences.

demographic characteristics
The age, sex, socioeconomic status, ethnicity or nationality, level of education, and professional interests of the audience.

Find Out about Your Audience's Attitudes.

The simplest way to find out about your audience's attitudes is to interview members of the actual audience. Many times, however, this is impractical or even impossible. Instead, you might interview the person who asked you to speak or other people who have spoken to the audience before. For example, suppose that Dr. Newhorst was invited to speak to her university's alumni association about the *curriculum* of the Communication Studies Department. To learn about the audience, she asked the director of the meeting about those who were likely to attend. She also called other professors who had spoken to this group on previous occasions. Finally, she was able to talk with a couple of actual audience members. From these sources, she learned that the group of recent graduates was most concerned about employment opportunities. This information was helpful in preparing her presentation.

Exploring Communication Concepts

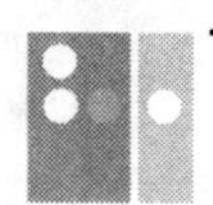

DIFFICULTIES WITH DEMOGRAPHICS

As identity groups such as Asian Americans, Catholics, or working mothers have achieved higher disposable incomes, commercial television producers have sought to appeal to them as distinct audiences. This trend is called "niche marketing" and is evident in specific programs, such as "SpongeBob SquarePants" on Nickelodeon (aimed at middle-class, 12–24 year olds), and entire cable channels, like Black Entertainment Television (for African Americans).

To some media critics, however, niche marketing plays on some of our worst cultural stereotypes. Demographic analysis produces very broad generalizations of audiences, and then television executives decide what it means to be part of that demographic group. The Lifetime Channel presents women as interested in diets, affairs, weddings, and fashion. PrideVision, a Canadian cable channel, attempts to appeal to gay people by featuring programs that emphasize exhibitionism and promiscuity (Whitaker 2002).

Consider watching a few programs on a cable station that targets a particular type of audience.

ASK YOURSELF:

1. What does the channel assume about the interests and values of its audience?
2. What are some limitations in relying on audience demographics to design messages?

She decided to talk about her department's internship program and emphasize that the program prepared college graduates for career opportunities. The speech was successful in part because she adapted her topic to her audience. Similarly, suppose you are giving a speech about the interpretation of dreams. You need to know if the audience believes that dreams have meaning or if they are hostile to the idea.

audience expectations
What the audience believes is going to happen during the speech.

Determine Your Audience's Expectations. Another important aspect of audience analysis is **audience expectations,** or what they believe is going to happen during the speech. If you miscalculate their expectations, you may mistakenly offend or bore your audience. Many commencement speakers at college graduations fail to analyze audience expectations correctly. Students and their parents come to a commencement ceremony wanting to celebrate the completion of a college degree, receive a diploma, or applaud and cheer the graduate. They anticipate certain formalities such as an address by the valedictorian and another by an honored guest. They usually expect the speaker to address the graduates with some words of advice concerning their transition from college into the "real world." Above all, they expect that the speaker will be brief and to the point. Both parents and students are uneasy with speakers who violate these expectations, such as local or national politicians who use the opportunity to deliver election-style orations. Once the audience senses that the speaker is ignoring their expectations, they quickly lose interest. They begin to fidget in their seats and chat with each other as they become anxious for the speech to end and the diplomas to be handed out.

Audiences will also have specific expectations about the length, formality, and outcome of the speech. The expected length of the speech is always a concern to audiences. Instructors learn this lesson quickly in a college classroom. No matter how interesting the lecture, students will stop taking notes when the instructor goes past the time to dismiss the class. Some situations are more formal than others, and again the speaker should be aware of the situation. Speakers who dress informally, use *colloquial* language, or sit down to deliver their speech in a formal situation such as an awards program might appear disrespectful. Similarly, speakers who dress up, use more formal language, and deliver a monologue with little audience interaction in an informal situation will appear stiff and unresponsive. Finally, the audience comes to the presentation expecting a certain outcome. An audience that is invited to an informative presentation will probably resent a "hard core" sales pitch, and an audience that expects to be entertained will probably not listen to a lengthy informative demonstration. Few things please audiences more than having their expectations met, so timing the length of your speech, choosing an appropriate style, and adapting to the audience's anticipated outcomes will help you craft a successful presentation.

Audiences have clear expectations for commencement speakers.

Consider the Occasion

Just as audience members have expectations based on the topic of a speech, the occasion for speaking also creates anticipation for both the speaker and audience. An **occasion** is defined by the purpose of the gathering, and the mood, time, and physical setting of the speech. A person's retirement dinner is a very different sort of occasion than the same person's surprise birthday party. Lighthearted and frivolous occasions, such as bachelor parties, make it difficult for a serious-minded speaker to deliver a somber message successfully.

occasion
The time, mood, and setting of the speech.

Think It Over

EXPECTATIONS ABOUT CLASSROOM TOPICS

When you listen to speeches for a class, you are likely to hear a variety of topics. What are your expectations for speeches by classmates? Are there particular topics you wish they would avoid? Why? How might they make such topics more appealing to you?

Consider the Purpose of the Gathering. In any situation the speaker must know the reason for the gathering. For some occasions, speeches will revolve around a similar theme or central topic, but in others, as in your classroom assignments, the occasion allows you to change the subject or even contradict other speakers on the program. Speakers should be aware how their speech might influence others on the program. If applicable, look at the agenda for the meeting and notice who speaks just before and after you. The speech just before you may influence the audience's receptiveness to your speech. The previous speaker's ability and choice of topic may motivate the audience to listen attentively to you or may predispose the audience to respond to your speech with hostility or apathy. Similarly, you need to consider the potential impact of your speech on the receptiveness of the audience to the speaker who comes after you.

Consider the Mood of the Occasion. There are as many moods as there are speaking opportunities. Most occasions, however, will have a prevailing mood that might be cheerful, urgent, playful, or serious. In the classroom, with a series of speakers, the mood is usually fairly serious yet supportive because of the sense that everyone is learning together; each audience member must also speak when it is his or her turn to do so. Classroom speeches sometimes vary in mood and tone; one student may give a lighthearted speech about dating while another will deliver a very serious speech about people with AIDS. In speaking situations outside the classroom, there will be a more pervasive mood within which the speaker must work. Suppose you are at a business meeting with your work team. The purpose of the meeting is to develop strategies for finishing a project on time to meet an urgent deadline, and you are expected to summarize your recommendations. In this urgent, "time-tight" mood, you probably should not engage in long personal anecdotes or jokes, but rather be brief and to the point. Yet if you are with that same work team at a dinner celebrating the completion of the project, it may be perfectly appropriate to relate personal anecdotes. In this way the mood can directly shape the content of the speech.

Consider the Timing of the Speech. The time includes both the expected length of the speech and the time of day, month, or year the speech is being given. The time available to speak is usually prescribed by the occasion. For example, in the famous Lincoln-Douglas debates of 1858, the first speaker, usually Stephen A. Douglas, would speak for one hour; then Abraham Lincoln would respond for one and one-half hours; and finally, Douglas would finish the debate with a 30-minute rebuttal. They engaged in these debates seven times over 26 days (Postman 1985). At the Fifth Communist Party Congress of Cuba in 1997, President Fidel Castro spoke to the delegates for seven hours without a break (Castro Opens Party Congress 1997). Certainly, most student speakers will not have that much time and should be sensitive to the expectations of the audience and the time requirements of the assignment. Careful preparation can help speakers make the most of the time they are given.

The time of day can also be important. Suppose that you have a class which begins at noon. Speaking during this time period is always problematic. Some students will come to class distracted because they are hungry and anticipating lunch, while others who have eaten will be lethargic and sleepy. Speakers in this situation find that they must work especially hard to motivate their fellow students to pay attention. Sometimes speakers can use the timing of an occasion to their advantage. Holidays, seasons, or other yearly events can be rich sources of topics for student speakers, such as patriotic speeches on the Fourth of July or speeches about effective study habits at the end of the semester as final examinations approach.

Consider the Physical Setting. Martin Luther King, Jr., delivered his now famous, "I Have a Dream," speech in the vast plaza before the Lincoln Memorial in Washington D.C. With more than 200,000 audience members stretched out in front of him, King realized that the opening of the speech would have to produce an impact to capture their attention. King also knew in advance that he would be standing directly in front of the Lincoln Memorial. Everyone in the audience, even those at the farthest end of the reflecting pond, would see the statue of Lincoln looming over him. He decided to use this powerful symbol not only as his backdrop to the podium but in his introduction by echoing Lincoln's Gettysburg Address. King began by saying, "Five score years ago . . ." King was so effective, in part, because he understood the physical setting of the speech and used it to his advantage.

If you are unfamiliar with the physical setting where you will deliver your speech, try to undertake some *reconnaissance* before the actual event by checking it out at least a few days before you will give your speech. Notice how big the room is and how its size will influence your speech. In a very large room, you may need a microphone or some other aid to help project your voice. Assess the audiovisual and computer resources available and decide which ones, if any, will be useful in your presentation. Also, consider the shape of the room. In a long and narrow room, you need to pay particular attention to the audience members sitting in the back and project your message to those farthest away. In a shallow but wide room, it is important to make a conscious effort to establish eye contact with those on either side of you. Observe what is behind you (e.g., a pull cord for a pull-down map, strange piece of artwork) that might distract the audience. Sometimes you can adjust the physical setup in advance to head off potential distraction on the day of your speech.

Gathering Materials for Your Speech

As with any research project, gather more material than you will need to use in your actual speech. Even if your personal knowledge of the topic is extensive, you should supplement what you know with other sources of information; doing so will enhance the credibility of your presentation. There are many possible sources of information. Sources that might be helpful to you in preparing your speech are traditional printed materials, electronic resources, interviews with knowledgeable people, and your own personal experiences with the topic.

Printed Materials Can Enhance Knowledge of Your Topic

Books, journals, newspapers, and other printed materials provide a rich source of information on almost any topic. Most of these sources can be found in your campus library, which also offers many services to help you research your topic. Libraries organize their materials in catalogs or indexes by title, author, or subject. Most of these catalogs consist of electronic listings of every item the library owns and identify each item with a unique call number indicating where the item is stored. If you have trouble locating items, many libraries have a reference librarian available to answer questions about your search and help you locate books and other materials. If your library does not have a particular item, many college libraries also offer an interlibrary loan service that allows you to borrow items from other libraries. Consult your campus library for details about its catalog, reference librarians, and interlibrary loan program. Table 11-1 lists some of the printed materials you might find useful in researching your speech topic.

Electronic Resources Can Help You Gather Speech Material

The computer's ability to store, retrieve, sort, and deliver information has radically changed the way many speakers find material for their speeches. There is a wealth of resource material on the Internet, but searching for it can be time consuming and frustrating. Knowing something about the electronic resources you are using will facilitate your search. For those of you who are familiar with these basic forms of election information, the discussion that follows will serve as a review. If you are a beginner, here is a quick guide to information on the Internet.

Searching the Internet for Information.

The Internet is a convenient but unreliable source of information. The Internet has much useful, accurate, and credible knowledge. But it also contains many outdated facts, mistakes, and deliberate falsehoods. Check with your instructor about using the Internet to research a speech because many professors now limit the use of information from the Internet. If your instructor does allow Internet research, critically assess the information you are gathering before using it.

Once you have obtained information you think you can use to prepare your speech, evaluate it carefully. Answering a few simple questions can help you analyze information from the Internet (Hanson 2000; Cornell Library 2001).

1. What is the source? The source often helps you decide if the information is likely to be accurate or if you should be cautious or skeptical about its validity. Make sure that the source and its qualifications are clearly stated on the Web page. Generally, unattributed content is less reliable than information with a stated source. The website address, called a URL (uniform resource locator), should be clearly identified and can also help you identify the source. Each address ends in a suffix that identifies the type of organization that sponsors the pages (.edu = educational institutions, .gov = government organizations, .com = commercial websites, and .org = nonprofit organizations).
2. Is the source a primary or secondary one? A **primary source** is firsthand knowledge, testimony, or direct evidence about the topic you are researching (Yale University Library 1996). The authors of primary sources create content. A **secondary source** is based on the observation or research of other people. Authors of secondary sources simply compile secondhand information. Keep in mind that primary sources are generally better than secondary ones.

primary source
Firsthand knowledge, testimony, or direct evidence from authors who created the information.

secondary source
Information based on other people's observation or research.

TABLE 11-1

ITEM	DESCRIPTION	EXAMPLES	COMMENT
Books	"Book" is a general category that refers to any printed work with pages bound along one side. Some books are about a single subject while others are collections, called anthologies, of shorter pieces bound together.	*The Oxford Guide to Library Research* by Thomas Mann; *Malcolm X Speaks: Selected Speeches and Statements,* edited by George Breitman.	Books are one of the oldest and still one of the best sources of information. Like all types of information, books vary greatly in quality. Try to locate books that are objective and have up-to-date information about your topic.
Scholarly journals	Contain articles on research and experiments within a specific discipline written for experts and other specialists	*The Quarterly Journal of Speech; Human Communication Research*	Most scholarly journals are *peer reviewed,* meaning that experts in the discipline select only the best articles to publish. Some articles can be very technical and hard to understand.
Magazines	Magazines contain articles of general interest on a variety of subjects for non-expert readers. Magazines are usually published weekly or monthly.	*Time, Newsweek, The Economist, Travel and Leisure*	While some magazines publish articles about a wide range of topics, most publish articles around a single theme such as business, politics, fashion, hobbies, or special interests.
Newspapers	Daily news with local, national, and world coverage	*The New York Times, The Wall Street Journal, Washington Post*	Back issues of newspapers are frequently stored on microfilm or microfiche.
Encyclopedias	A collection of detailed articles written by experts for nonexpert audiences. Some encyclopedias cover many different subjects and others are specific to a discipline.	*Encyclopedia Britannica, McGraw-Hill Encyclopedia of Science and Technology, Encyclopedia of Islam*	Many general encyclopedias are now CD-ROMs, but many discipline-specific encyclopedias are still in book form on library shelves.
Almanacs	Collections of facts and statistics	*World Almanac and Book of Facts, Baseball Almanac, Computer Industry Almanac*	Almanacs are a good source of up-to-date statistics for your speech.
Dictionaries	A collection of definitions for words and terms	*Oxford English Dictionary, Black's Law Dictionary, Saunders Comprehensive Veterinary Dictionary*	Specialized dictionaries often have more detailed definitions than those found in general dictionaries.

Printed materials in your college library are an excellent source of information for your speech.

Source: Duke University Libraries, "Finding Background Information," retrieved June 3, 2002 from www.lib.duke.edu/libruide/background.htm

3. How current is the information? Much of the information on the Web is out of date. Beware of a website that has no date or seems obsolete. It takes much time and effort to maintain a good website and, sadly, some websites are rarely updated. As a result, the material becomes dated. Higher quality websites are updated frequently and clearly display copyright and revision dates.
4. What is the intended purpose and audience? There are many reasons for posting information on websites; some reflect a narrow or biased perspective. Some websites want to sell you a product and are unlikely to be objective about the weakness of that product, while others may be scholarly in nature and more objective. Many websites are personal postings in which the information reflects just one person's perspective on the topic. There are also websites that simply want to attract attention and users to support advertising revenue.
5. How thoughtful does the site appear to be? The format and design of the site often yields clues about the accuracy of the information it provides. Websites that are disorganized and hard to navigate are often less authoritative than those whose creators take the time to present their information carefully. An authoritative site exhibits some of the following design characteristics that help visitors find information:
   a. The website's Internet address is clearly listed in a prominent place on the Web page.
   b. The site is logically organized and information is easy to find. Popular and frequently requested information is clearly linked to the homepage. A search engine on the homepage allows visitors to search the contents of all pages linked to the site.
   c. The writing is clear, understandable, and free of grammatical mistakes and misspellings.
   d. Sources of information are provided and ideas are correctly attributed to their originator.

Figure 11-1 illustrates these principles on a website from the National Geographic Society.

Use Interviews to Gather Information from Experts and Other Authorities

Another method of gathering materials for your speech is to interview someone who is an authority on your topic. Interviews often yield information that is unattainable in other ways. For instance, in preparing a speech on the Vietnam War, one student supplemented books and articles on the subject with an interview of a neighbor who was a former prisoner of war in the infamous "Hanoi Hilton." The veteran had a wealth of firsthand knowledge that the speaker was able to incorporate into the speech, which added an element of human interest that was well received by the audience. Most experts, if approached in the right way, are often flattered and quite willing to help college students with their assignments.

Interviewees appreciate interviewers who already know something about them and their field, so before the interview, do some research to find out as

FIGURE 11-1 EVALUATING WEBSITES AS SOURCES

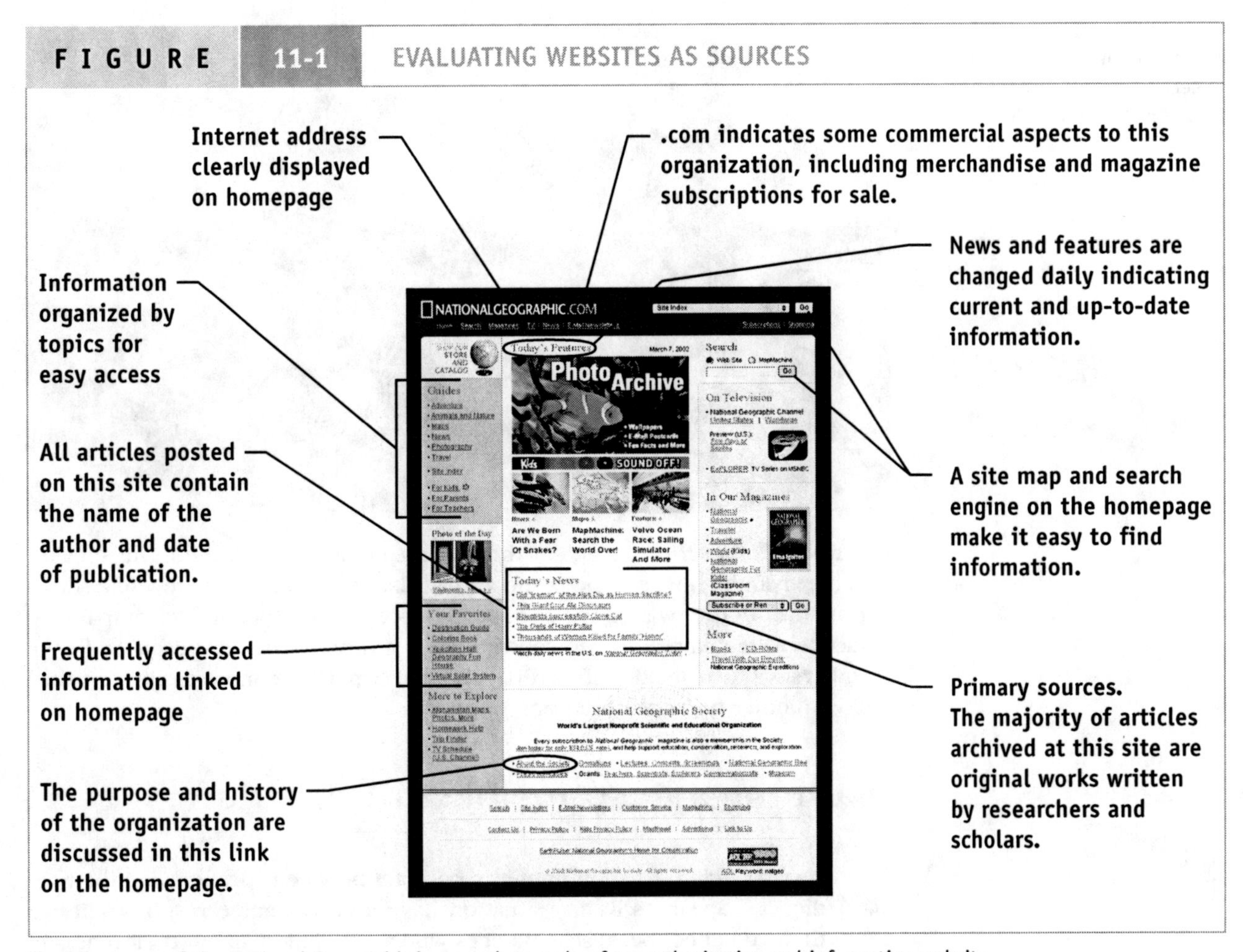
Internet address clearly displayed on homepage
.com indicates some commercial aspects to this organization, including merchandise and magazine subscriptions for sale.
News and features are changed daily indicating current and up-to-date information.
Information organized by topics for easy access
All articles posted on this site contain the name of the author and date of publication.
A site map and search engine on the homepage make it easy to find information.
Frequently accessed information linked on homepage
Primary sources. The majority of articles archived at this site are original works written by researchers and scholars.
The purpose and history of the organization are discussed in this link on the homepage.
NATIONALGEOGRAPHIC.COM
Photo Archive
SOUND OFF!

The homepage of the *National Geographic* is a good example of an authoritative and informative website.

much as possible about the person. For example, a champion stock car racer will appreciate that you already have learned what a stock car is and know the major races he has won. Background research will also help you formulate effective questions in advance. When setting up a meeting place, schedule a time that is convenient to both the interviewee and yourself, and be sure to arrive at the interview promptly. Be respectful of the interviewee's needs by staying only as long as the agreed-upon time, whether that is 10 minutes or an hour. For additional help in conducting interviews, see Appendix A, "A Brief Guide to Interviewing."

CONNECTIONS

Watch a video clip of a student speaker who uses personal experience to develop her speech (Clip 11.1).

Use Your Own Experiences in the Speech

Drawing upon your personal experience in a speech can enhance your credibility and make your speech unique and memorable. Consider a student who talked about the effectiveness of automobile air bags in saving lives. Most of the supporting material came from outside sources. But the final example was a graphic

Interviews can be an excellent way to obtain information for a speech.
© Mary Kate Denny/PhotoEdit

description of a serious accident the student herself experienced. The speaker calmly explained how seat belts and air bags had saved her own life while showing pictures of the twisted car and accident scene. The story and accompanying evidence were compelling and contributed to a very successful speech. Audience members will usually identify with a personal experience more easily than they will with other types of stories and statistics.

Planning a Responsible Presentation

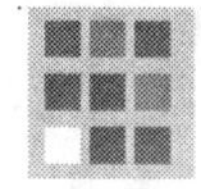

Every speaking situation implies a contract between speakers and their audiences. Speakers in any situation have a considerable responsibility to their audiences because audiences who are willing to invest their time and energy in listening expect speakers to honor their expectations and interests. Speakers can plan a responsible presentation by selecting an appropriate topic for the audience and occasion, presenting a balanced perspective, and identifying the sources of their information.

"The ultimate sin of any performer is contempt for the audience."
—Lester Bangs, journalist, critic

Select an Appropriate Topic for the Audience and Occasion

READ ALL

Speaking to an audience is both an opportunity and a responsibility. The audience provides an opportunity for speakers by listening to them, and the speaker is responsible for speaking about something that is worthwhile and beneficial to the audience. One way that speakers can show respect for an audience is by selecting an appropriate topic. Being "audience centered" means that the speaker should think about the audience and select a topic that helps them develop their abilities and improve their lives. Not all topics need to be serious, but they should not be offensive. Topics that perpetuate negative stereotypes of race, gender, and sexual orientation should not be used. Avoid topics that are likely to make the audience feel unnecessarily uncomfortable or awkward; audiences do not want to be insulted or embarrassed. Also, topics that advocate illegal actions or demonstrate illegal activities are often irresponsible, as is the promotion of excessive and illegal alcohol consumption and irresponsible sexual behaviors. In general, speak with *deference* to the audience, treating the members with respect and consideration.

Present a Balanced Perspective

A good speech balances outside sources with the speaker's own perspective and analysis. Some students fall short of balance by using one source exclusively. In a written paper, this kind of misuse is easy to spot because the reader can look at the references or footnotes and see the lack of other sources. It is sometimes more difficult to detect this problem during a speech in which references are not stated. Students who misappropriate their time and rush to complete their speech before the speaking deadline often have this problem. The use of a single source of information is often a symptom of procrastination and contributes to many other problems. For example, your information may be unreliable, and you will not have the knowledge to detect these inaccuracies.

Use a range of sources to win credibility with your audience and make your speech interesting. Devoting the proper time and resources to your speech will help you draw from a range of materials and reduce the influence of bias on your presentation. Speeches that are based on a single source are usually less interesting and more likely to sound *banal* and *trite,* whereas those with accurate, diverse, and credible information are interesting and compelling for the audience.

Identify the Sources of Your Information

The Internet provides students with many opportunities to use someone else's work in its entirety without proper attribution. While plagiarism is often viewed as a problem in written works, it has become an increasing problem in speeches as well. The American Association of University Professors defines **plagiarism** as "taking over the ideas, methods, or written words of another, without acknowledgement and with the intention that they be taken as the work of the deceiver. . . . It is theft of a special kind, for . . . a fraud is committed upon the audience that believes those ideas and words originated with the deceiver. . . . It is the antithesis of the honest labor that characterizes true scholarship" (AAUP 1990).

To avoid plagiarism, speakers should clearly identify, or make **attribution** of, all sources they use, in a bibliography to the speech and in the actual speech itself. Attribution means crediting or referencing the source of the information, much like a footnote in a paper ("Oprah Winfrey's website, Oprah.com, has an excellent recipe for Chilean seafood stew that I would like to share with you"). The wording of your speech should be your own and not the work of others. Obviously, if you take a document from the Internet and read it as your own speech, you are guilty of plagiarism. But it is also plagiarism if you pirate the structure of a document for your speech, rearranging material only slightly, or use any original idea or concept without proper attribution.

plagiarism
Using other people's ideas, methods, or words without proper acknowledgment.

attribution
Crediting or referencing the sources of information.

Think It Over

PLAGIARISM AND HONOR CODES

Research by the Center for Academic Integrity (McCabe 2002) seems to indicate that cheating varies greatly from one university to another depending on how seriously the students embrace the school honor code.

Does your school have a strong honor code?

Do you think cheating at your college is less or more common than at other schools?

Plagiarism is not limited to sources from the Internet. Any attempt to deceive your audience, such as using a speech you prepared for a different class, using a speech from another student, or listing sources that you do not consult, constitutes academic dishonesty.

Careful preparation can turn a good speech into an excellent one.

© Marc Grimberg/Getty Images/ The Image Bank

Resources for Review and Skill Building

Many of these resources are supported by the Connections CD-ROM and free Online Learning Center website.

SUMMARY

This summary is organized around the questions found at the beginning of the chapter. See if you can answer them before reading the summary paragraphs.

1. How do I choose a topic for my speech?

   Pick a topic that interests you. Your enthusiasm for a topic will be contagious to the audience and help you deliver a lively presentation. Almost any topic can be a successful speech. Select a topic early and spend most of your preparation time gathering material for your speech and adapting your topic to the audience.

2. What is the difference between a general and a specific speech purpose and how do they affect my speech?

   The general speech purpose is the overall goal of your speech, such as to inform, persuade, or entertain your audience. A speech to inform explains a concept, idea, or process to the audience. A speech to persuade motivates the audience to believe or act in a certain way. A speech to entertain amuses, enthralls, cheers, charms, or pleases the audience. The specific speech purpose states your objective for the speech in precise detail. An effective specific purpose should narrow the topic and focus the speech. It should clearly indicate what you expect of the audience once the speech is over. One way of formulating an effective specific purpose is to complete the following sentence: I want my audience to (understand, believe, or do) ____________________ .

3. How can analyzing the situation help my speech to succeed?

   A careful analysis of the situation includes an examination of your strengths and weaknesses as a speaker, the audience, and the occasion. When analyzing yourself, determine how much you know about the topic and identify any biases you might have toward the topic. When examining the audience, consider the age, sex, socioeconomic status, ethnicity, and levels of education of the members. You should also consider your audience's familiarity with and attitudes toward your topic. In analyzing the occasion, consider the time, mood, purpose of the gathering, and physical setting of the speech. It is also a good idea to take into account any speakers who talk immediately before and after you. Consider how those speeches might influence the audience's reception of your topic.

4. What kind of research should I do for my speech?

   You will want to gather more information than you can use in the presentation. An abundance of research allows you to select the most interesting or persuasive material for use in your speech. Thorough research will also make you a more credible and trusted speaker. The computer's ability to store, retrieve, sort, and deliver information has radically changed the way many speakers find material for their presentations. Electronic indexes catalog types of speech materials, including newspapers, magazines, journals, books, audio files, video collections, and photographs. The World Wide Web can also enable you to access an enormous amount of material directly through homepages on the Internet. Much of this information is valuable, but much of it is also dubious. Critical researchers evaluate the reliability of the information by examining the source and currency of the information they find, the consistency of the material contained on the Web page, the intended purpose of the computer site, and even the actual design of the homepage.

5. How can I plan a responsible presentation?

   You can prepare a responsible presentation by selecting an appropriate topic for the audience and occasion, and presenting a balanced perspective by using information from a variety of sources. A responsible speaker also makes proper attribution of all sources used in the speech, either in the bibliography or in the actual speech itself. You should not plagiarize the work of others. Take the time to carefully prepare your speech, using your own ideas and words.

KEY TERMS

Test your understanding of these key terms by visiting the Connections CD-ROM and Online Learning Center website at www.mhhe.com/dobkinpace.

attribution 317
audience centered 307
audience expectations 308
civic engagement 299
demographic characteristics 307
general speech purpose 302
homepage 312
occasion 309
plagiarism 317
primary source 312
secondary source 312
specific speech purpose 302
speech to entertain 303
speech to inform 302
speech to persuade 302

FOR FURTHER REFLECTION

/dobkinpace

Join a conversation about chapter concepts by visiting the Online Learning Center website at www.mhhe.com/dobkinpace

1. The stages of planning described in this chapter are: (*a*) selecting a topic, (*b*) focusing the topic, (*c*) analyzing the situation, and (*d*) gathering materials.
   - Is the order of these steps significant?
   - In what ways does selecting a purpose help you analyze the situation?
   - How does an analysis of the situation help you focus your research?
2. President Theodore Roosevelt is credited with saying, "My father gave me these hints on speech-making: "Be sincere . . . be brief . . . be seated."
   - Do you think most audiences share this same expectation of speeches? Why or why not?
   - How do you know when a speech is long enough? Too long?

BUILDING COMMUNICATION SKILLS

1. Write three different specific purpose speeches (one to inform, one to persuade, and one to entertain) for each of the following topics: laundry, income taxes, car tires, phobias, civil rights, game shows, personal safety, laughter, collectibles, bubble gum, and proper diet. How do the different general purposes influence the formation of specific purposes?
2. Perform an audience analysis by discussing your speech topic with members of the class. Some of the following questions might help your analysis:

- What do you know about my topic?
- What experience do you have with my topic?
- Have you, your family, or friends recently discussed my topic?
- What have you read recently about my topic?
- Have you ever seen a film or television show that discussed my topic?
- What aspect of my topic interests you most? Least?
- How do you feel about my topic?

NET WORK

Note: While all the URLs listed were current as of the printing of this book, these sites often change. Please check our website (www.mhhe.com/dobkinpace) for updates and hyperlinks to these exercises.

1. Several websites offer advice about evaluating information found on the Internet. Two excellent sites are http://campusgw.library.cornell.edu/olinuris/ref/research//webeval.html at the Cornell University Library, and http://www.library.ucla.edu/libraries/college/help/critical/index.htm at the University of California, Los Angeles (UCLA) Library. Compare the two sites. How is their advice for evaluating information from the Web different or similar? Select one of your Web sources and evaluate it based on the advice from one of these sites. Does your source seem authoritative? Why or why not?
2. The website for the History Channel has a large archive of speeches from politicians, entertainers, sports figures, and activists. Look up the website, http://www.historychannel.com/speeches/index.html, and choose a speech for analysis. Try to identify the types of information the speaker used, including any examples of testimony, literal analogies, figurative analogies, brief illustrations, extended illustrations, or statistics.

MEDIA MOMENTS

Many films about legal battles contain dramatic speeches to a jury. One such older film is *The Verdict* (Brown 1982), starring Paul Newman. Written by David Mamet and directed by Sidney Lumet, the film tells the story of a lawyer of questionable ethics, personal problems, and a dwindling practice who stumbles across the case of a lifetime. The verdict in the case remains in doubt until the final climactic scene in which Paul Newman delivers a speech summing up his client's case. Watch the film and analyze the speaking situation based on the following questions:

- What are the speaker's strengths and weaknesses?
- Who is the audience? What do we know about the audience's values? How does the speaker use this information in the speech?
- What is the occasion of the speech? How do the time, mood, and location influence the speech?
- What are the opportunities and challenges in the speaking situation?

Organizing and Outlining Public Presentations

CHAPTER 12

Esperanza Valdez had less than 10 minutes to prepare the most important presentation to date of her career. Her marketing company was trying to land a lucrative account, and today they were "pitching" their proposal to the clients. But William, who was to give the first presentation, was not yet there. Corrine Kush, the company president, entered the room and headed for Esperanza, who had helped with research for the marketing plan but had not anticipated speaking about it. "William is stuck in traffic and can't make it. Can you prepare some remarks in the next few minutes?"

"Of course," replied Esperanza, sounding more confident than she was. "Remember," said Corrine, "speak no longer than 10 minutes and then turn the time over to me." Esperanza knew the information, but how was she going to organize all the thoughts she was having? She remembered her speech class in college and wrote on her notepad: introduction, body, *and* conclusion. *She started with the body. She wanted to talk about how the proposal could meet the needs of the clients. She thought for a moment and then under the word* body, *she wrote,* problem *and* solution. *Under each of those points she noted a couple of examples. Next she wrote a concise introduction that she hoped would get the clients' attention.*

QUESTIONS TO FOCUS YOUR READING

1. How do I organize the main points of my speech?
2. How do I support and develop the main ideas of my speech?
3. What is an effective introduction to my speech?
4. What is an effective conclusion to my speech?
5. How do I outline my speech?

Finally, she wrote a conclusion that summarized the material and provided a transition to Corrine.

Esperanza's brief preparation and notes gave her some comfort. When Corrine introduced her to the clients, she summoned up her courage. "My name is Esperanza, which means 'hope' in English, and today I hope to convince you that our proposal can meet your business needs." The clients chuckled at the word play on her name. "I will show you," Esperanza continued, "the problem with your current marketing approach and how our plan can solve that problem. The problem, as we see it . . . ." Esperanza defined the problem and illustrated it with specific examples. She then said, "Our solution to this problem is . . . ." She explained how the proposal would solve the problem and illustrated her points with examples. Then she finished, "In summary, we believe that your advertising dollars have not been spent wisely. We can solve those problems by buying more cost-effective media opportunities. Now our company president, Corrine Kush, will compare our marketing approach to that of our competitors." Esperanza sat down. Corrine gave her an approving look and then launched into her presentation.

Esperanza faced the same dilemma as students in preparing for a speech. How should information be organized? Esperanza had plenty of information, but she needed to organize the material in a meaningful and memorable manner. Her introduction quickly caught the audience's attention and previewed the main points of her speech. She used a simple and effective structure for the body of the speech, choosing "problem" and "solution" as her two main points. Next, she selected meaningful examples to illustrate her main points. Finally, she summarized her information for the audience and provided a transition to the next speaker. This simple structure built her confidence and contributed to a successful presentation.

Chapter 11 emphasized the importance of analyzing the audience and gathering material to prepare for a speech. Once these steps are completed, information must be organized so that it is meaningful to the audience. Like all oral communication, speeches are transient, and the audience is not likely to have a printed copy to refer back to after the speech is finished. A well-organized presentation helps the audience remember what was said long after the speech is finished. A tightly organized, coherent presentation also helps speakers remember the main points of their speeches. Beginning speakers often comment after a speech, that they forgot to mention a major point or "mixed up" information as they spoke. A strong structure will help prevent this problem. In this chapter, we will discuss ways to organize a speech. After completing this chapter, you should be able to:

- Select a logical structure for the main points of your speech.
- Effectively support and develop the main points of your speech.

- Construct an effective introduction to your speech.
- Construct an effective conclusion to your speech.
- Produce an outline of your speech.

"We are all aware that speech, like chemistry, has a structure."
—Roger Brown, writer

The Overall Structure of Your Speech

Traditionally, speeches are organized around a three-part structure—introduction, body, and conclusion. An old speech axiom goes something like this: "A speech should tell your audience what you are going to tell them (introduction), tell the audience what you are telling them (body), and finally tell the audience what you just told them (conclusion)." Each of these parts to a speech is necessary, and each has a distinct function. The introduction is the speaker's opportunity to capture the audience's attention and provide them with a strong reason to listen carefully. The body is the substance of the presentation and is used to accomplish the goals of the speech. Because the body is the longest and most detailed portion of the speech, it needs to be carefully organized so the audience can follow and understand the material. Finally, the conclusion is the speaker's last chance to impress the audience and make the speech memorable. In general, the introduction and conclusion of the speech should be approximately 10 to 15 percent of the presentation, and the body should be 85 to 90 percent. Most speakers find it helpful to develop the body of the speech first and then work on the introduction and conclusion afterward.

Ways of Organizing the Body of the Speech

The main points of the speech should flow smoothly in a logical way that allows the audience to understand at all times during the speech where the speaker has been, where the speaker is now, and where the speaker is going. There are seven traditional ways of organizing the body of the speech: chronological, narrative, spatial, topical, comparison, cause and effect, and problem/solution. The choice of organizational strategy will depend to some degree on the topic of your speech. A discussion of the merits of electric cars, for instance, would not lend itself to a chronological organization as much as to a comparison organization. But many topics will lend themselves to one, two, or more structures. To acquaint you with these different types of structures, we will describe each type.

Chronological Speech Structure

A **chronological speech structure** organizes a speech around segments or sequences of time. Many different uses of time are possible, such as speeches about the history of a person, place, or event. A speech about the history of your university, the discovery of electricity, the development of the computer, or a reenactment of the Battle of Gettysburg might all be organized around the chronology of key events. For instance, a speech about Alcatraz Island in San Francisco Bay might be organized around four important time periods.

chronological speech structure Organizes a speech around segments or sequences of time.

Specific Purpose: I want my audience to understand the four main time periods in the history of Alcatraz Island.

I. 1775: Spanish explorer Juan Manuel de Ayala discovers the island.

II. 1850–1933: The United States Army uses the island for a military base that houses prisoners.

III. 1933–1963: The Federal Bureau of Prisons uses the island as a maximum-security, minimum-privilege penitentiary.

IV. 1972–Present: Congress designates the island as part of the Golden Gate National Recreation Area.

Speeches that explain a process or sequence can also be organized around chronology. A *process speech* describes how to make or do something by listing the essential steps of the process in time order, from the earliest to the latest. For example, a speech instructing the audience how to snowboard, write a résumé, make a dream catcher, or create a Web page could all use a time format to organize the main points of the speech. A speech on developing black-and-white film could be organized around the following basic steps:

> *Specific Purpose:* I want my audience to understand the four basic steps in developing black-and-white film.

I. Load film onto the developing reel.

II. Place film into the developer.

III. Place film into the stop bath.

IV. Place film into the fixer.

narrative speech structure
Organizes a speech around one or more stories.

Narrative Speech Structure

A **narrative speech structure** organizes a speech around one or more stories. A typical narrative structure tells a story in chronological order with a beginning, middle, and end. Narratives often contain some form of dilemma or conflict that is resolved in the end. Fiction writers use narrative structures in novels and short stories. Similarly, a speech can achieve a specific purpose by the detailed retelling of a single incident or a series of stories. Sometimes speakers use personal stories as the body of their speech. Speakers addressing the topic of an eating disorder, for example, could organize a speech around their own experiences with discovery, struggle, and treatment of the problem. A speech about learning to skydive in a single day could be organized around the following key events in the experience.

> *Specific Purpose:* I want the audience to understand my first day of skydiving.

I. 8:30 A.M. to noon: Learning the basics

II. Noon to 2:00 P.M.: Practicing the basics

III. 2:30 P.M.: Jummmmmmmmmmping!

spatial speech structure
Organizes a speech around familiar relationships in the environment, such as near and far, up and down, right and left, or east and west.

Spatial Speech Structure

A **spatial speech structure** organizes the speech around familiar relationships in the environment, such as near and far, up and down, right and left, or east and

Spatial structure works well for presentations about locations and buildings.

west. Often, a familiar building such as a library, school, or museum can make a good speech as can a familiar map. A speech about Hawaii, for example, could be organized around the five major islands in that state.

> *Specific Purpose:* I want my audience to understand the unique character of each Hawaiian island.

I. Kauai is the "Garden Isle."
II. Oahu is the "Gathering Place."
III. Lanai is the "Pineapple Island."
IV. Maui is the "Valley Isle."
V. Hawaii is the "Big Island."

Often a visual aid depicting the spatial relationships helps the audience follow the structure of the speech. The human heart, for example, has two halves (right and left), and each half has two chambers, one that pumps (the ventricle) and one that receives (the atrium). A speech on this topic could be organized around the four spatially related parts while using a visual aid to help the audience follow the organization (see Figure 12-1).

> *Specific Purpose:* I want my audience to understand the function of each of the four main parts of the heart:

I. The right atrium receives blood from the body.
II. The right ventricle pumps blood to the lungs.
III. The left atrium receives blood from the lungs.
IV. The left ventricle pumps blood to the rest of the body.

FIGURE 12-1 MODEL OF THE HUMAN HEART

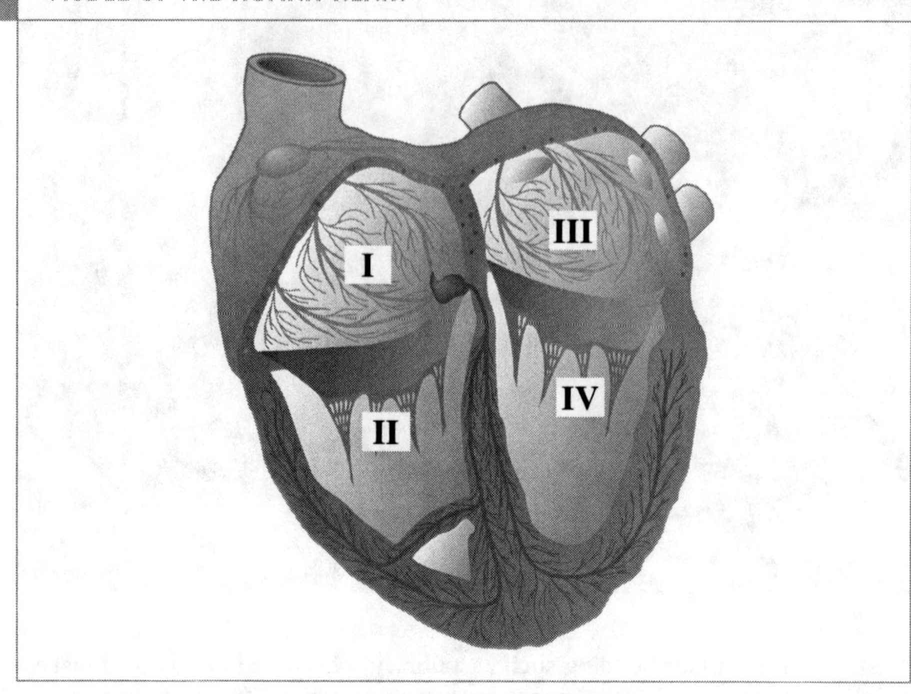

A good visual aid helps the audience follow the structure of speech.

Topical Speech Structure

topical speech structure
Organizes a speech around types or categories.

A **topical speech structure** organizes a speech around types or categories. Topics that do not lend themselves easily to other forms of organization can often benefit from a topical structure. Most topics will suggest a natural classification that divides the topic logically. A speech on dance, for instance, might be organized around three distinctive styles (jazz, ballet, and modern). A speech on clouds could be organized around the three types of clouds (cirrus, stratus, and cumulus). A speech on the basic rituals in practicing Islam could be organized like this:

> *Specific Purpose:* I want my audience to understand the basic rituals, called the Five Pillars of Islam, that all faithful Muslims perform.

I. *Shahda* is saying the confession of faith.
II. *Salat* is praying five times daily.
III. *Saum* is fasting during the month of Ramadan.
IV. *Zakat* is giving alms.
V. *Hajj* is making a pilgrimage to Mecca.

Comparison Speech Structure

comparison speech structure
Organizes information around distinct points of similarity or difference.

Another way to organize a speech is to compare or contrast different aspects of the topic. A **comparison speech structure** organizes information around distinct points of similarity or difference. A speaker might compare and contrast two computers such as Macintoshes and PCs, the experience of living off campus to living in a residence hall, or seeing a play on stage or a film based on the same script. In comparing the various items, the speaker should select two or three distinct points of comparison or characteristics that highlight the similarities or differences. For example, suppose a speaker wants to compare the two types of diabetes (Type I and II) across three points of comparison (characteristics, symptoms, and treatment.) The speech might look something like this:

Specific Purpose: I want my audience to understand that the characteristics, symptoms, and treatment vary between Type I and Type II diabetes.

I. Characteristics

A. Type I diabetes begins in childhood.

B. Type II diabetes begins in adulthood.

II. Symptoms

A. A symptom of Type I diabetes is excessive thirst.

B. A symptom of Type II diabetes is blurred vision.

III. Treatment

A. Type I diabetes is treated with insulin injections.

B. Type II diabetes is treated with diet, exercise, and medication.

"When we recognize a pattern, we expect its completion. This expectation of the future allows us to listen with intelligence . . . . We can anticipate what will come next, be alert for evidence and reasoning necessary to make a case, listen with increased critical sensitivity, and evaluate how the thought, argument, or theme fits with the overall pattern of the whole speech."

—Gerard A. Hauser, communication scholar

Cause and Effect Speech Structure

A **cause and effect speech structure** divides the speech into the causes of some phenomenon and the effects that result from it. A speaker informing the audience about a disease, for example, could talk about the causes and symptoms of the ailment. A speaker addressing the social problems of urban areas could talk about the causes of poverty and the effects of such problems. A speech on the global warming or the "greenhouse effect" might have the following main and subpoints:

cause and effect speech structure
Divides the speech into the causes of some phenomenon and the effects that result from it

Specific Purpose: I want my audience to understand the causes of global warming and the effects of increased temperatures on our atmosphere.

I. Global warming is caused by increases in carbon dioxide in the atmosphere.

A. The burning of gas, oil, and wood increases carbon dioxide.

B. Deforestation of the rain forests increases carbon dioxide.

II. Increased temperatures change the ecosystem and climate of the earth.

A. Polar ice caps are melting.

B. Ocean levels are rising.

C. Precipitation patterns are changing.

Problem and Solution Speech Structure

problem/solution speech structure
Organizes information in a speech around one or more problems and one or more solutions to those problems.

In the chapter opening, Esperanza organized her business presentation by mentioning the problems her clients were having with their marketing approach and the solutions her company was proposing. Esperanza's presentation was based on the **problem/solution speech structure,** which organizes information around one or more problems and one or more solutions to those problems. A speaker might speak about the problem of domestic violence and possible solutions, or the problem of voter apathy and solutions. A speech on the problem of air pollution also could be organized around the problem/solution structure.

> *Specific Purpose:* I want my audience to understand the health problems of air pollution and three possible solutions they can use as individuals.

I. Problem. Air pollution causes health problems.
   A. Air pollution has been linked to breathing and respiratory problems.
   B. Air pollution has been linked to cancer.

II. Solutions. Individuals can help reduce air pollution.
   A. Individuals can reduce air pollution by using solar energy to heat their homes and water.
   B. Individuals can reduce air pollution by using mass transit.
   C. Individuals can reduce air pollution by using electric lawn mowers.

Choosing a speech structure that is clear and easy to identify doesn't have to be difficult. The "Applying Communication Concepts" box helps you practice recognizing types of speech structures.

Applying Communication Concepts

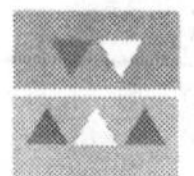

IDENTIFYING SPEECH STRUCTURES

Identify the speech structure (chronological, narrative, spatial, topical, comparison, cause/effect, or problem/solution) suggested by each of the following topics:

a. Exercising regularly reduces the risk of heart attack.
b. The music department is located in three different buildings on campus.
c. A sport utility vehicle (SUV) differs from a truck in three significant ways.
d. There are three simple steps in ironing a shirt.
e. There are four types of blood.
f. Causes of anemia can often be treated with an iron-rich diet.
g. We can all learn to be better businessmen and businesswomen from the life of Sam Walton.

(Answers: *a.* cause/effect, *b.* spatial, *c.* comparison, *d.* chronological, *e.* topical, *f.* problem/solution, *g.* narrative).

ASK YOURSELF:

1. How could each of these topics be organized with a different structure?
2. How might two or more structures be combined into a logical organization?

Developing and Supporting the Main Ideas of Your Speech

Once speakers have arranged their main points in a logical order, they should develop each idea with supporting material that extends ideas and adds detail to central concepts. The basic structure of the speech is like the skeleton of the human body; it is the framework that holds the speech together. Supporting materials act as muscle tissue that provides detail, texture, and strength to the body. Without a skeleton, the muscle of a body would be useless; without muscle, the skeleton could not move. Similarly, without a coherent speech structure, the supporting ideas would make no sense; without proper development of each of the main points, the structure would be empty and meaningless. An effective speech provides enough support to be credible and interesting without overloading listeners with redundant and unfamiliar material. There are many different forms of support available to speakers. This section discusses six types of supporting material: testimony, examples, analogies, statistics, explanations, and definitions.

Using Testimony

testimony
Stated opinion in support of an idea.

Testimony is a stated opinion in support of an idea. Testimony from someone who is believable ("The American Dental Association recommends changing your toothbrush every three months") can provide powerful support of an idea. Testimony from unrecognizable or self-interested people ("Buy this car from my dealership") is often questionable. The benefit of testimony is its ability to add another voice to your argument or description in support of your ideas. If the testimony is particularly articulate, it may add memorable details to your speech. Like courtroom witnesses, the best testimony is based on firsthand knowledge, eyewitness accounts, or substantial expertise in the subject. Less effective testimony comes from witnesses who gained their knowledge secondhand or who are biased in their observations. For example, celebrity spokespeople may be famous, but they rarely know much about the products they are paid to sell ("I'm not a doctor, but I play one on TV"). In using testimony, follow these simple guidelines:

- Look for objective testimony from sources that have nothing to gain by their opinion. Suppose for example, that you are giving a speech about camcorders. A salesclerk at the local electronics store is sure to recommend a model that the store carries. On the other hand, you could consult ratings of camcorders by *Consumer Reports* for a more objective opinion.
- Look for expert testimony. Find people with educational or practical experience related to your topic.
- When possible, use testimony from sources your audience recognizes. For instance, if you are giving a speech on health, you could find testimony from the Surgeon General, the American Medical Association, the Mayo Clinic, the *American Medical Journal,* or some other credible, well-known source.
- Look for testimony that is articulate and well stated. If a quote is difficult to understand, you might as well attribute the information to the source and paraphrase the idea in your own words.

"[Although] stories are considered not quite as satisfying as statements and statements not quite as satisfying as statistics . . . in the long run, a people is known, not by its statements or its statistics, but by the stories it tells."

—Flannery O'Connor, writer

- Keep the testimony short and to the point. Don't read long passages of complicated, obscure, or insignificant prose to your audience. Instead, select testimony that is concise, easy to understand, and relevant.

Using Examples

examples
Illustrations or stories that explicate a particular point.

In a speech, **examples** are illustrations or stories that explicate a particular point. There are three types of examples: brief, extended, and hypothetical. A *brief example* is an illustration familiar to the audience which therefore requires very little detail. Brief examples are often used in a series to heighten their effect. For example, you might illustrate the sentence, "The South has produced many popular writers," with several examples, such as William Faulkner, Anne Rice, Eudora Welty, and Walker Percy. An *extended example* is a single illustration retold with greater detail and context. In the following extended example, Colonel Eileen Collins (2001), tells of her observations of earth from outer space while piloting the space shuttle:

> I had grown up to think of the world in terms of the Northern Hemisphere . . . and the Southern Hemisphere . . . in terms of the United States . . . Europe, Asia, and Africa. But this is not the world I saw from space. From space, there was no geography class in neatly etched states . . . no continents with the rigid national boundaries. From space, I saw, instead, the serene beauty of flowing landscapes . . . the brilliant radiance of sun-glinted lakes . . .
>
> The world I saw from space had no divisions of people . . . no artificial separations of human interests and human needs. All I saw was one fragile blue planet . . . From space, this is the way the world appeared to me. A world of shared dreams. A world of shared destinies.

A *hypothetical example* is an illustration that is not real, but imaginary. Many of the chapter opening vignettes in this textbook are hypothetical examples. Hypothetical examples are often concise and easy for audiences to understand. For instance, in a speech about the difficulty of a physically challenged student attending college, a speaker could lead the audience through a typical day of a fictional student. This hypothetical example could condense all of the challenges faced by physically challenged students into a single day.

Examples add texture and interest to the speech. The audience will remember a well-told illustration more than they will other forms of support because they often become involved with the speech through their identification with the situation and the circumstance of the story. However, examples can be time consuming, and sometimes speakers use illustrations that are irrelevant, boring, or both. Examples can also become more memorable than the point they are trying to illustrate. When using examples, keep the following suggestions in mind:

- Provide enough detail and texture to involve the audience in the story.
- Be sure that the illustration supports the main point and is relevant to the situation.
- Carefully choose the number of examples to use. Too many personal stories narrows the focus of the speech unnecessarily and limits audience interest. Balance the effects of personal examples with other forms of support, such as

statistics or explanations. You might balance a personal story about the joys of scuba diving with statistics that show the number of people who participate in the pastime.

- Be sure to identify hypothetical examples as imaginary or unreal.

Using Analogies

An **analogy** compares or contrasts two things. In general, one unfamiliar concept or object is compared to something that the audience already knows or understands. There are two types of analogies: literal or figurative. A *literal analogy* compares two concepts, objects, people, or places that are inherently similar to each other—that is, the two items being compared come from the same class or broad category. For instance, you might compare the size of two objects that are similar. A speaker might say, "Ireland is half the size of Florida" (both land masses). To explain what a kumquat tastes like, a speaker might say it is "sour like a lemon" (both citrus fruits). One speaker described the summer climate in Washington, D.C., using this comparison: "Daily life in a Washington summer is sort of like living in Bangkok or Manila, but having to dress like you're in London" (Evans 1999).

analogy
Compares or contrasts one unfamiliar concept or object with something that the audience already knows or understands.

A *figurative analogy* compares two concepts, objects, people, or places from different classes or categories. Because the things being compared are inherently different, a figurative analogy is a type of *metaphor.* For example, the American writer Langston Hughes (1951) uses a series of figurative analogies to compare the despair many Americans feel about their future with other objects or feelings. "What happens to a dream deferred? Does it dry up like a raisin in the sun, or fester like a sore and then run? Does it stink like rotten meat or crust and sugar over like a syrupy sweet? Maybe is just sags, like a heavy load. Or, does it explode?" A more lighthearted example comes from a college student explaining how to change the oil in a car. The last step in the process was changing the oil filter. To stress the importance of this step, the student used the following figurative analogy: To change the oil but not change the filter would be like taking a bath and putting your dirty underwear back on. While the class groaned its revulsion of this image, it was an effective reminder about the importance of this last step.

The benefit of an analogy is the powerful connection between something familiar and something unfamiliar. By comparing something new with something the audience already understands, their knowledge is extended and the material becomes memorable. When using analogies, you should:

- Keep the analogy simple. Complex analogies usually raise as many differences as similarities.
- Explain the similarities. Do not expect the audience to understand the comparison, especially in figurative analogies, without some explanation.
- Make sure the audience recognizes the familiar part of the analogy. Saying that Ireland is half the size of Florida means nothing to an audience that doesn't know the size of Florida.

Using Statistics

Statistics are numerical representations used to quantify ideas or concepts. Statistics are popular with speakers because they can briefly summarize and clarify concepts. For example, John Lawson (1998), senior vice president of Deere and Company, said when speaking about the increased production of U.S. farms: "Fifty

statistics
Numerical representations used to quantify ideas or concepts.

years ago, one farmer could feed roughly 20 people. Today, a single farmer can put bread in the mouths of . . . 130-some people—better than a sixfold increase since the 1940s." Similarly, in a speech about the increasing diversity of America and its impact on U.S. businesses, Richard Notebaert (1998), chairman of Ameritech, used the following statistics:

> And let me tell you about . . . customer base. According to the Department of Commerce, the buying power of Americans of African, Asian, and Hispanic descent is already $1 trillion. That's trillion with a 'T.' By 2050 . . . the African-American population will double and the Hispanic population will triple. Those groups that we now refer to as minorities will make up nearly half of the American population. What company can afford to ignore these evolving customer demographics and perspectives? Certainly none that intend to prosper into the new millennium.

Statistics have inherent credibility, and audiences often believe that "numbers" are unbiased evidence. This is not always the case, because statistics can be manipulated and used to mislead an audience just as easily as other forms of information. Nonetheless, statistics that are calculated correctly can be authoritative and useful in your speech. The following few tips can help you in using statistics.

- Use statistics sparingly. Too many statistics will bore your audience and lead to confusion.
- Round off statistics whenever the "rounding off" does not distort the intent of the statistic. Instead of "10.34 percent" you could say, "10 and a third percent" or simply "a little over 10 percent."
- Provide context for statistics, including who collected the data and calculated the statistics ("According to the Center for Disease Control [CDC], almost 1 million children have some form of lead poisoning"), when and where the statistics were reported ("As revealed in a CDC report released last October for National Lead Poisoning Prevention Week"), and any other information that will help the audience understand the numbers ("Although 1 million children is a large number, the CDC believes that lead poisoning is the most preventable environmental disease of young children").
- Interpret the statistics for the audience. Audiences frequently need explanation and clarification of the numbers a speaker is reporting ("These survey results confirm that teachers are generally as committed to their profession as are lawyers and doctors even though they make substantially less money").
- Whenever possible, make the statistics visual with graphs or diagrams. Visual aids help the audience easily comprehend the numbers. We will discuss the use of visuals aids in more detail in Chapter 13 on delivering your speech.

Using Explanations and Definitions

explanation
Clarifies some concept or idea by further identifying its source, explaining how it works, or relating it to other concepts.

Explanations and definitions are used to describe and define the main points of a speech. An **explanation** clarifies some concept or idea by further identifying its source, explaining how it works, or relating it to other concepts. Explanations are especially useful in informative speeches, such as explaining how milk is pasteurized, where Mardi Gras originated, or how interest rates are related to inflation.

Statistics can be presented with visual aids such as bar graphs.
© Walter Hodges/Getty Images/Stone

Explanations are also frequently used in persuasive speeches, where they often lay the foundation for the audience to accept a speaker's point of view or argument. For example, in speaking to the U.S. Congress, Mexican president Vicente Fox (2001) began his speech with an explanation of the mistrust that has characterized relations between the two countries.

> I am aware that for many Americans and for many Mexicans the idea of trusting their neighbor may seem risky and perhaps even unwise . . . . This perception has deep roots in history. In Mexico, they derive from a long-held sense of suspicion and apprehension about its powerful neighbor. And in the United States, they stem from previous experience with a political regime governing Mexico which for the most part was regarded as undemocratic and untrustworthy.

After laying this foundation, Fox then went on to explain how the situation had changed with his election, and he proposed several joint programs in migration and trade.

Speakers use a **definition** to establish the meaning of words or concepts. In this textbook, we have defined many key terms in each chapter to help you understand our explanations and clarify concepts. Similarly, speakers should define

definition
Establishes the meanings of words or concepts.

important terms, technical jargon, and other words that the audience may not know. A good definition clarifies meaning by distinguishing between related concepts or words. For example, you could distinguish between large and small businesses by defining "small businesses" as businesses with fewer than 100 employees. You could define a "hurricane" as an ocean storm whose winds reach 75 miles per hour, "acupuncture" as a traditional form of Chinese healing using thin metal needles, the "Middle Ages" as a 1,000-year period in European history which began with the fall of the Roman Empire in the fifth century and ended with the Renaissance, or "Venus" as the second planet from the sun. Each of these definitions not only identifies what the concepts are but also what they are not (Venus is not the third planet from the sun.)

Explanations and definitions help the audience to understand the concepts and words you are discussing. When using explanations and definitions, keep the following suggestions in mind:

- Explain or define any concepts that are unfamiliar to your audience. A careful audience analysis can help you identify important points that need clarification.
- Keep explanations and definitions simple. Explain and define concepts with words that the audience knows and understands (defining words in a definition becomes too complex for audiences).
- Illustrate explanations and definitions with examples or other forms of support to reinforce the meaning of the concept.

Using Transitions in the Body of the Speech

transitions
Verbal bridges that move the speech from one point or idea to the next.

The body of the speech also needs transitions to connect the various points of the speech. **Transitions** are verbal bridges that move the speech from one point or idea to the next. Transitions can be as brief as one or two words ("First, I will talk about . . .") or as long as several sentences. Good transitions help the audience see a relationship between different parts of the speech ("Even more important is my next point . . ."), follow the organization of the speech ("The second step in the process is . . ."), remember what was said ("As I mentioned . . ."), or anticipate what will be said ("Next, I will explain how you can help").

Two useful types of transitions are signposts and internal summaries. Just as road signs guide drivers down the highway, *signposts* tell an audience where they are and where they are going in a speech. A speech on making bread, for instance, might use this signpost between steps of the process: "Now that we have mixed the ingredients together, I will show you how to knead the dough." An *internal summary* reviews concepts or ideas to help remind the audience of key points and to move the speech to the next important point. For instance, one student gave a speech about New York's Metropolitan Museum of Art using various exhibit areas of the museum as a spatial organization. The student used this internal summary to move the speech from one main point to the next: "So far in the speech, we have seen modern European sculptures on the first floor and ancient Asian art on the second floor. Next, we will visit the art of medieval Europe in the part of the museum called the Cloisters." An internal summary could finish this section of the chapter and provide a transition to the next: "In summary, then, we have discussed how to structure the body of your speech using one of the standard forms of organization, how to develop the main points of the speech with various forms of support, and how to add transitions to connect various parts of the speech together. In the next section of the chapter, we will discuss how to construct an effective introduction to a speech."

Starting Your Speech with an Effective Introduction

An introduction to a speech is like an appetizer to a fine meal; it should be interesting, leave the audience wanting more, and set up the main course. An effective introduction has four goals:

1. Gain and maintain audience attention.
2. State the purpose of the speech and preview the main points.
3. Establish the speaker's credibility.
4. Give the audience a reason for listening to the speech.

These goals are not mutually exclusive and can sometimes be accomplished with a statement or two. For example, a speaker might successfully gain the attention of the audience by providing a strong reason for listening. Other times, however, a speaker will need to use several statements to ensure that each of these goals is accomplished.

Gain and Maintain Audience Attention

An introduction should gain and maintain **appropriate audience attention.** This means focusing the audience's thoughts on the topic of the speech. Inappropriate attention distracts the audience and diverts their attention from the topic. For instance, banging a loud drum, screaming loudly, and insulting the audience would unquestionably gain the audience's attention but would also distract their focus from the topic of the speech. The "Think it Over" box asks you to consider effective and ethical ways to gain the attention of an audience.

appropriate audience attention
Focuses the audience's thoughts on the topic and purpose of the speech.

The audience's attention should be gained as early as possible in the speech with an effective attention step. An **attention step** is an explicit attempt by the speaker to gain the audience's interest and should be the very first statement or series of statements in the introduction. There are several different types of attention steps.

attention step
An explicit attempt by the speaker to gain the audience's interest.

Think It Over

INAPPROPRIATE ATTENTION

Consider the following attention step. A student speaking about insects started the speech by eating several live worms, beetles, and even a cockroach. The speaker certainly gained the audience's attention. Was this "appropriate attention"? What would be the advantages and disadvantages of starting a speech like this? Would the speaker be able to maintain the audience's attention throughout the speech? What would the audience be thinking? What will the audience remember about the speech—the topic, the attention step, or both? What are some other ways the speaker could have introduced the topic?

Anecdotes. An *anecdote* is a brief story that illustrates some aspect of the topic. A good story should include characters, plot, and some conclusion or resolution. First-person stories are especially effective and often establish your credibility as well as gain the audience's attention. One student started a speech on the addictive qualities of methamphetamine with a firsthand account of drug rehabilitation. The anecdote was so full of vivid detail about the cost and pain of overcoming drug addiction that the audience was anxious to hear more about the topic.

Quotations. A quotation repeats another person's words with attribution. To gain the audience's attention, the quote should be "catchy" or clever and make the audience think about the topic of the speech. A speech on conquering phobias could begin with Marie Curie's quote, "Nothing in life is to be feared. It is only to be understood." The audience is more likely to respond favorably to the quote if they recognize the source and the source is given before the quote. For a speech comparing the process of cremation with traditional burial methods, a student used this Woody Allen quote, "It's not that I'm afraid to die. I just don't want to be there when it happens." More than one student has started a speech with the familiar Jack Nicholson line from *A Few Good Men* (1992), "You can't handle the truth."

Provocative Statements. A provocative statement is a *pithy* declaration that makes the audience think about the topic. Provocative statements should be concise and intriguing. Consider this interesting opening: "Thomas Jefferson and John Adams, political rivals throughout their lives, died on the exact same day—July 4th, 1826. Today I would like to tell you about another Fourth of July, in 1776, when these two men and other revolutionaries signed the Declaration of Independence and gave birth to our country."

Interesting Statistics. Interesting statistics can capture the audience's attention and focus their thoughts on the speech. A statistic used in the introduction should be simple enough for the audience to comprehend easily, and its connection to the topic should be obvious. For example, in a speech to the Executive Club of Chicago, the CEO of the Coca-Cola Company used the following statistics to emphasize the magnitude of his company: "A billion hours ago, human life appeared on Earth. A billion minutes ago, Christianity emerged. A billion seconds ago, the Beatles performed on "The Ed Sullivan Show." A billion Coca-Colas ago was yesterday morning" (Goizueta 1996).

Humor. Finally, a speaker can use humor to start a speech. Audiences usually appreciate a sense of humor in a speaker and often listen carefully to a well-told joke, pun, or humorous story. Comedian Bob Newhart (1997) started a commencement speech to Catholic University of America with this introduction: "My son graduated from here in 1989 with a degree in English literature, specializing in the poetry of Yeats. As you all know, when you pick up the classified pages you just see page after page of jobs for Yeats scholars." A student speaking on the decreasing value of the American dollar started a speech with this humorous observation: "When my great-grandmother read the back of a dollar bill it said, 'redeemable for silver.' When my grandmother read the back of a dollar bill, it said 'backed by gold.' Today, however, when I read the back of a dollar bill it says, 'In God We Trust.' "

State the Purpose of the Speech and Preview the Main Points

The purpose of the speech should be clear to the audience from the beginning. Sometimes novice speakers organize a speech like a suspense novel and hide their purpose until the very end. Such a strategy rarely works; rather, it often frustrates and confuses the audience. An explicit and clearly stated purpose in the introduction helps the audience anticipate and remember the speech material. Speakers should reword the specific purpose they developed while preparing the speech for use in the introduction. For example, the specific purpose, "I want my audience to understand the basic rituals that all faithful Muslims perform, called the Five Pillars of Islam," might be stated in the introduction like this: "My speech will introduce you to the basic ritual that Muslims perform, called the Five Pillars of Islam."

The speaker should also state the main points of the speech in the introduction. For example, an introduction to a speech on a possible destination for "spring break" might contain this statement of purpose and preview of main points: "Today I want to convince you that South Padre Island in Texas is one of the best spring break destinations in the country because South Padre Island has (1) plentiful sun and beautiful beaches, (2) an abundance of inexpensive hotels and restaurants, and (3) many college students from around the country who come to enjoy their vacation." In this manner, a speaker tells the audience what to expect from the main points of the speech. Table 12-1 reworks three specific purposes presented earlier in the chapter for use in a speech introduction.

Establish the Speaker's Credibility

An effective introduction should establish the speaker's credibility. **Credibility** is the audience's perception of the expertise, character, and goodwill of the speaker. Expertise refers to the competence and skill the speaker has with the speech topic. Character is usually defined as the speaker's trustworthiness, and goodwill is the extent to which the speaker is concerned with the audience. If the audience perceives the speaker as credible, they will be motivated to listen to the speech. Credibility, like attention, should be established and maintained throughout the speech. We will discuss credibility in more detail in Chapter 14, but for now, here are a few simple tips for establishing credibility during the introduction.

credibility
The audience's perception of the speaker's expertise, character, and goodwill.

Mention know-how and experiences with the topic. Audiences appreciate first-hand knowledge of a topic, so speakers should briefly establish their expertise with the topic ("I have spent the last two spring breaks in Texas at South Padre Island, and I believe that it is one of the best places in the country to vacation").

Establish the credibility of the sources. If speakers have no direct experience with the topic, they should establish the credibility of their research material ("The travel service, Student Express, lists South Padre Island as one of the very best destinations for spring break vacations").

Avoid being apologetic. Speakers often make the mistake of saying something like: "I am not very good at speaking, so I hope you won't be too bored." Such an admission, even if the speaker is feeling anxious, does not help establish credibility. In their introduction, speakers should refrain from discussing nervousness, inexperience, or fears.

TABLE 12-1 Introducing Your Speech

SPECIFIC PURPOSE	STATEMENT OF PURPOSE AND MAIN POINTS IN THE INTRODUCTION
I want my audience to understand the four basic steps in developing black-and-white film.	"In my speech, I will discuss the four basic steps in developing black-and-white film, which are: first, loading film onto the developing reel; second, placing film into the developer solution; third, inserting the film into the stop bath; and fourth, putting the film into the fixer."
I want my audience to understand the unique character of each Hawaiian island.	"Today I will speak about the unique character of each Hawaiian island and introduce you to: Kauai the 'Garden Isle,' Oahu the 'Gathering Place,' Lanai the 'Pineapple Island,' Maui the 'Valley Isle,' and Hawaii the 'Big Island.'"
I want my audience to understand the health problems caused by air pollution and three possible solutions they can use as individuals to reduce it.	"By the end of my speech, I hope you will understand that air pollution has been linked to breathing and respiratory problems and to lung cancer. I will also tell you what you can do personally to reduce air pollution by heating your homes and water with solar energy, riding mass transit, and using an electric lawn mower."

A good introduction should state the purpose and preview the main points of the speech.

Keep the introduction short and relevant. An introduction that is too long, antagonizes the audience in some way, or is clearly irrelevant hurts the speaker's credibility.

Give the Audience a Reason for Listening to the Speech

The introduction should give the audience a reason or motivation to listen. Most audiences come to a speech with a strong, unstated question: Why should I listen to this speech? Speakers should answer this question as soon as possible. Speakers might demonstrate how a speech will save the audience money, help them with a common problem, or make them better people. A statement such as, "I know that most of you, like myself, are on a college budget, and one great thing about South Padre Island is the low cost," is likely to motivate audiences to listen. If the topic does not apply immediately to the audience, the speaker should indicate some future relevance. For example, a student might use this motive for listening to a speech about buying life insurance: "I know most college students don't think about life insurance and the possibility that they will die. But life insurance is a wise investment for the future, and buying it now is much cheaper than buying it when you are 50, 40, or even 30. Buy now, save later."

Finishing Your Speech with an Effective Conclusion

The conclusion to the speech is the last chance for speakers to have an impact on the audience and should bring the speech to a noteworthy and effective end. The conclusion to the speech should be like a dessert after a fine meal; it should complement the entire meal and leave the diners with pleasant memories. Similarly, the conclusion to a speech should (1) summarize key points and (2) reinforce the purpose of the speech with a clincher (Gregory 2002).

Summarize Key Points

At the beginning of the chapter, we said an introduction should "tell the audience what you are going to tell them," the body should "tell them," and the conclusion should "tell them what you told them." Although it may seem redundant to novice speakers, telling them what you told them is an important function of a conclusion. Reminding an audience of the key points of the speech helps them remember the information after the speech is over. The summary should be brief. There is no need to repeat all the information from the body of a speech. The most effective summaries simply remind the audience of the main points from the body of the speech. The following conclusion from a speech about responsible pet ownership illustrates a brief but effective conclusion: "As you can see, responsible owners need to provide their pets with a healthy and varied diet, plenty of exercise, and proper vaccinations and licenses."

Reinforce the Purpose of the Speech with a Clincher

The most important function of a conclusion is to reinforce the purpose of the speech in a memorable way. A clincher is a vivid ending to the speech that "seals the deal." It should motivate the audience to embrace the purpose of the speech. There are many ways of clinching the purpose of the speech. Many of them are similar to the types of attention steps discussed earlier in the chapter. For instance, the speech could end with a provocative statement, anecdote, quote, or statistic that strongly reinforces the purpose of the speech. The conclusion to the speech about pet ownership might end with this statement: "Remember, the golden rule applies to pets as well. Treat your pets as you would want them to treat you if they were your owner." Speakers can also challenge the audience to take some action or make some commitment as a way of clinching the purpose of the speech. For instance, the following challenge might work with the pet speech: "I have a copy of the Responsible Pet Owners Pledge from our local humane society for each of you. Today, I challenge each of you to sign the pledge as a promise to your pet that you will be a responsible and loving owner." Whatever clincher the speaker selects, it should be compelling. Speech teachers often say that the speech should end with a bang, not a whimper.

Making the Most of Your Conclusion

Here are a few additional tips and reminders to help you develop an effective conclusion to your speech.

- The conclusion should promote a mood in keeping with the rest of the speech. If the speech has been very serious, a lighthearted conclusion will trivialize the central idea. Similarly, if the speech has been somewhat lighter, the audience will resist a drastic change of mood to something grave or serious.
- The conclusion should clearly signal the end of the speech. You can use some traditional ending phrases such as, "In conclusion . . .," "In summary . . .," or "Finally, . . ." as a transition to the conclusion, but do not end the speech more than once! Audiences do not like to be told "in conclusion" three or four times.
- Be brief and concise, but not too abrupt. Like the cartoon character Porky Pig, too many speakers simply end their speeches by saying, in essence, "That's all, folks." These speakers miss an opportunity—remember, the conclusion is your last chance to influence your audience.
- Avoid being apologetic or making excuses for your speech ("I'm happy to tell you that this is the end of my speech"). Such apologies reduce your credibility.
- Do not open new areas of discussion. Introducing new topics in the conclusion leaves the audience with doubts and questions rather than the central ideas you have tried to convey.
- Finally, be relevant. Much as an irrelevant joke in the introduction distracts the audience, a comment off the subject in the conclusion will confuse listeners about the speech purpose.

Watch a video clip of a student speaker using some of these tips to conclude her speech (CD Clip 12.1).

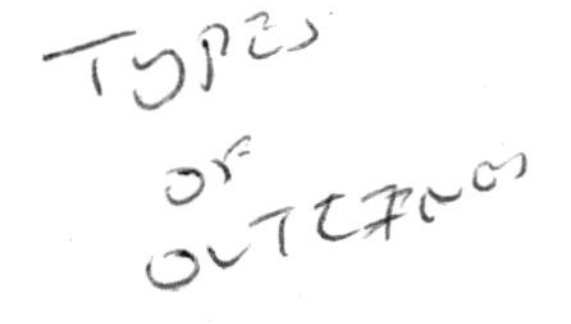

Communicating Responsibly: Developing a Sound Structure

Now that you have organized your information, you are ready to outline your speech. Just as good audience members listen attentively, good speakers develop ideas clearly, in a systematic way, with the audience's understanding in mind. An **outline** is a concise synopsis that displays the structure and relationship of speech ideas and concepts. Outlining helps you learn and remember your speech material. In addition, creating an outline is the first step in an effective delivery because your outline will eventually be used, in some form, as your speaking notes. In this section, we will discuss the types and principles of outlining.

outline
A concise synopsis that displays the structure and relationship of speech ideas and concepts.

Types of Outlines

There are three types of outlines: topic, complete sentence, and key word. Each form is useful at different stages of preparing your presentation. A **topic outline** uses brief phrases to summarize the major points of a presentation. The topic outline can be useful as a rough draft of your speech by helping you sort through your material and make a preliminary selection of your main points. Topic outlines also help you select your supporting or *subsidiary* points.

Once you have "roughed out" your material using simple phrases, you can move to a complete sentence outline. A **complete sentence outline** uses full sentences, including standard punctuation, such as periods, commas, and questions marks, to delineate the speaking information. A complete sentence outline enables you to select specific words and phrases. Each of your main points becomes a thesis statement for that section of the speech. Putting the outline into

topic outline
Uses brief phrases to summarize the major points of a presentation.

complete sentence outline
Uses full sentences, including standard punctuation such as periods, commas, and question marks, to delineate the speaking information.

complete sentences forces you to clarify your purpose for each section and to articulate specific words and phrases.

Once the speech is organized into a complete sentence outline, you should construct a key word outline for use in delivery. A **key word outline** uses only a few important words from each sentence to make the outline readable at a quick glance. The key word outline is used as a memory aid and therefore should be brief enough that you can find your place in your speech quickly. Use as few words as possible but as many as necessary in your outline. A single word may be all that is necessary to remind you of the material in some parts of the speech. Other parts, however, may require more words. For example, if you have a long quote that you want to read to the audience, you may include that in your key word outline, but in general, use as few words as possible.

key word outline
Uses only a few important words from each sentence of a complete sentence outline to delineate the speaking information.

The CD outline tutor can help you correctly format an outline for your speech.

Principles of Outlining

Basic principals of outlining are the same whether you are preparing a topical, complete sentence, or key word outline. Be sure to consult your instructor for specific details about your classroom assignment, but the following guidelines will help you create an outline for most speaking situations.

List the main points to be covered in your speech. The **main points** are the most important ideas to be communicated to the audience and those that lead directly to the specific purpose of the speech. Label major sections of information according to the topic area they address and group your speech materials into main categories to establish the sections of your speech. You should have between two and five major topic categories in your outline. If you have more than five, you have not adequately identified main categories and your structure will look like a list rather than topic areas. Arrange these main points in a logical order using the speech structures we discussed earlier.

main points
The most important ideas to be communicated to the audience and those that lead directly to the specific purpose of the speech.

subpoints
Ideas that amplify or develop the main points.

Place subsidiary points under the appropriate main points. Subsidiary, or **subpoints,** are those ideas that amplify or develop the main points. For example, suppose you are giving a speech about running in a marathon. The goal of your speech is to explain to first-time marathoners how to prepare for the event. Ask yourself, What three ideas would be most important for novice runners to know? One possible answer to this question would be the (1) necessary equipment, (2) proper training, and (3) race-day strategies. These would become your main points.

I. Necessary equipment
II. Proper training
III. Race-day strategies

Your subpoints would be the development of each of these main points. Under equipment, you might mention shoes, clothing, and a runner's log. Your outline would start to look like this:

I. Necessary equipment
 A. Shoes
 B. Clothing
 C. Runner's log

You could similarly subdivide each main point. Under training, you could discuss the frequency and length of training runs and divide the section into short runs, long runs, and rest days. Finally, under strategy you could discuss helpful hints like what to eat on race day, running pace, and what to do immediately after the race. Sometimes, you will want to subdivide your subpoints. For instance, you could divide your advice about shoes into three tips on selecting the right shoes: (1) purchase shoes from a specialty running store, (2) purchase the right size, and (3) replace worn-out shoes. Each of your subpoints could be similarly subdivided. The subpoints should be relevant to the main points and develop or clarify the purpose of the speech.

Use a consistent set of spaces and symbols to identify all levels of your speech. An effective outline maps the relationship of your ideas by using a conventional system of indentations and symbols. By glancing at an outline, you can easily see the main points, the chief subpoints, and the lesser subpoints by the placement of each sentence on the page. Determine your main areas before outlining your introduction and conclusion. Each point should have one sentence only. Never use a "1" without a "2" or an "A" without a "B." If you do not have enough material to break down a subpoint into pairs, then the subpoint should be included as part of a main point.

The following is a typical set of symbols. (Check with your instructors to see what system of symbols they prefer.)

I. **First level headings use roman numerals (I, II, III),**
    A. Second level uses capital letters (A, B, C),
        1. Third level uses Arabic numbers (1, 2, 3), and
            a. Fourth level uses lowercase letters (a, b, c).

Each level should have identical indentation and should be aligned vertically. A simple topic outline for the body of our speech on running a marathon might look something like this:

I. **Necessary running equipment**
    A. Shoes
        1. Specialty running shoe
        2. Right size
        3. Replace worn shoes
    B. Clothing
        1. Shirt
        2. Shorts
        3. Socks
    C. Runner's log
        1. Runs
        2. Diet
II. **Effective training schedule**
    A. Short runs
    B. Long runs
    C. Rest—days off
III. **Race-day strategies**
    A. Before the race
    B. During the race
    C. After the race

Use parallel phrasing and sentence structure. Main points should be coordinated, or approximately equal in importance and level of support. Try to use parallel construction for main points. Related material should descend in importance from more general, abstract points to more specific subpoints.

Include an introduction and conclusion in your outline. Outlining the introduction and conclusion produces the same benefits as outlining the body of a speech. Some instructors prefer that students write out the introduction and conclusion in paragraph form, while others may want you to write out these important opening and closing statements in outline form so that you can rehearse them more precisely. Some instructors may want your specific purpose included somewhere near the introduction in the outline or at the top of the page. Finally, be sure to accurately credit the sources you used in constructing the speech at the bottom of an outline in the form of a bibliography. Table 12-2 illustrates a complete sentence outline for the body of a speech on running a marathon.

Check out examples of bibliographic formats on the CD to cite your speech sources correctly.

Outlines help speakers stay organized while building connections with the audience.

TABLE 12-2 Running Your First Marathon

This complete sentence outline of the body of a speech on running a marathon illustrates the principles of outlining discussed in this section of the chapter.

Specific Purpose: I want my audience to understand that the three basics steps in preparing for and running in their first marathon are purchasing the right equipment, conducting proper training, and employing race-day strategies.

I. You should purchase the right shoes, clothing, and runner's log for your first marathon.
  A. Shoes are the most important piece of equipment for your first marathon.
    1. Purchase running shoes from a specialty running store.
      a. A specialty store has a greater variety of shoes than a general shoe store.
      b. A specialty store has experts who can match your foot to the right shoe.
    2. Purchase the right size shoe.
      a. When purchasing shoes, you should wear your training socks to the store.
      b. Allow approximately ½ inch of room between the big toe and the shoe.
    3. Replace worn-out shoes.
      a. You should replace shoes after approximately 400 miles.
      b. You should purchase a new pair of shoes 4–6 weeks before the marathon.
  B. Light, loose-fitting, synthetic blend clothing will help you train and run your first marathon.
    1. Clothes should keep you at a comfortable temperature.
      a. Running adds 10 degrees of heat to the current air temperature.
      b. Wear a light windbreaker to protect from hypothermia when running in wind.
      c. Wear a hat only if it is cold, because hats trap body heat.
    2. Clothes should be functional, not fashionable.
      a. Remember that the weight of your clothing is important in a long race.
      b. Change your socks frequently while training to avoid blisters.
      c. Wear the same training clothes in the actual marathon.
  C. A runner's log will help you keep track of your mileage and nutrition.
    1. Write down the length and time of each training run.
    2. Write down what you eat during your training.

II. For your first marathon, you should follow a 16-week training schedule composed of short runs, long runs, and rest.
  A. Short runs make up the first 7 weeks of your marathon training.
    1. Start running or walking 20 minutes each day.
      a. Consult a physician before starting your training.
      b. Run at a comfortable pace—you should be able to carry on a conversation while running.
    2. Increase your running distance by 10 percent each week.
      a. You should be able to run 6 miles a day after 7 weeks of training.
      b. You should run five days a week.
  B. Long runs for the final 9 weeks prepare you mentally and physically for the marathon.
    1. Add one long run to your weekly training 9 weeks prior to the marathon.
      a. Start with a 10-mile-long run.
      b. Increase the long run by 2 miles each week until you reach 20 miles.

TABLE 12-2

Running Your First Marathon *(continued)*

2. Prepare for your long runs.
    a. Get at least 8 hours' sleep before your run.
    b. Drink lots of water and eat a light but nutritious snack before your run.
    c. Drink lots of liquids during your run.
        (1) Drink a sports beverage for runs longer than 90 minutes.
        (2) Carry liquids with you on long runs or plan a route where you can stop briefly to drink liquids.
        (3) Drink lots of fluids and eat a nutritious meal as soon as possible after the run.

C. Rest is important in your training.
1. Do not run the day before your long runs.
2. Do some cross-training to avoid injuries.
3. Reduce the distance of your training two weeks prior to the marathon.
    a. Reduce your long runs from 18 to 15 to 12 miles.
    b. Continue to run between 8 and 6 miles on your short runs.
    c. Do not run a long run the week of the marathon.

III. You should remember a few simple race-day strategies for your first marathon.

A. Before the race, prepare mentally and physically.
1. Run parts of the racecourse prior to the marathon.
    a. Take one long run on the course if possible.
    b. Drive the entire course once before the race.
2. Prepare physically for the race.
    a. Hydrate as much as possible prior to the race.
    b. Eat lots of carbohydrates and no fats the week prior to the race.
    c. Stay off your feet as much as possible.
    d. Get plenty of sleep the week prior to the race.

B. During the race, run an easy pace.
1. Hold back at the beginning of the race.
2. Run the middle of the race at your normal pace.
    a. Remember to shake out your arms and shoulders throughout the race.
    b. Be more concerned about your physical well-being than the time.
    c. Stop at all fluid stations.
3. Finish the race loose and relaxed.

C. After the race, take precautions to avoid serious health problems.
1. Stay on your feet after the race no matter how exhausted you feel.
2. Drink plenty of fluids.
3. Get something to eat as soon as possible.

Bibliography. To learn more about running your first marathon, consult these sources.

Higdon, H. (1993). *Marathon: The ultimate training and racing guide.* Emmaus, PA: Rodale Press.

Liberman, A. (2002). State of the art marathon training. Retrieved June 15, 2002, from http://www.marathontraining.com/.

Rossi, S. (2002). Your marathon running schedule: The training starts today, retrieved June 15, 2002, from http://www.epage.com/page/marasched

Whitsett, D. A.; Kole, T. J.; Kole, T.; & Dolgener, F. A. (1998). *The non-runner's marathon trainer.* Chicago: Maters Press.

Resources for Review and Skill Building

Many of these resources are supported by the Connections CD-ROM and free Online Learning Center website.

SUMMARY

This summary is organized around the questions found at the beginning of the chapter. See if you can answer them before reading the summary paragraphs.

1. **How do I organize the main points of my speech?**

   You should select between two and five main points for your speech. These main points should express the essence of your speech. The main points should flow smoothly in a logical way that allows the audience to understand at all times during the speech where you have been, where you are, and where you are going. There are several traditional ways of organizing your main points that accomplish this goal, including time, narrative, spatial, topical, comparison, cause and effect, and problem/solution.

2. **How do I support and develop the main ideas of my speech?**

   An effective speech uses a variety of forms of support. Speeches become monotonous and less convincing when you use only one type of development. Instead, you should use a lively mix of supporting materials. You should provide enough support to be credible and interesting. Using too little support makes the ideas shallow and less acceptable. There are many different forms of support available, including testimony, examples, analogies, statistics, explanations, and definitions.

3. **What is an effective introduction to my speech?**

   An effective introduction should gain and maintain audience attention. Your speech should begin with an attention step such as an anecdote, quotation, provocative statement, or statistic that focuses the interest of the audience on your topic. A good introduction should also state the purpose of your speech, preview your main points, establish your credibility, and give the audience a good reason for listening.

4. **What is an effective conclusion to my speech?**

   An effective conclusion should summarize the key points of your speech and reinforce the purpose of the speech with a clincher. The conclusion should also be consonant with the mood of the rest of the speech. Avoid being apologetic or making excuses for your speech. Also, do not open new areas of discussion. Introducing new topics in the conclusion leaves the audience with doubts and questions rather than the main ideas you have tried to convey.

5. **How do I outline my speech?**

   An outline is a visual and verbal map of your speech. An outline helps you organize your information and deliver your speech. To make an outline, you should first group your ideas into two to five main points and then place the subpoints under the appropriate main points. Next, mark each main and subpoint with a consistent set of spaces and symbols to identify all levels of your speech. An effective outline maps the relationship of your ideas by using a conventional system of indentations and symbols. By glancing at an outline, you can easily see the main points, the chief subpoints, and the lesser subpoints by the placement of each sentence on the page. Be sure to use parallel phrasing and sentence structure. Finally, be sure your outline has an introduction and conclusion.

KEY TERMS

Test your understanding of these key terms by visiting the Connections CD-ROM and Online Learning Center website at www.mhhe.com/dobkinpace.

analogy 333
appropriate audience attention 337
attention step 337
cause and effect speech structure 329
chronological speech structure 325
comparison speech structure 328
complete sentence outline 342
credibility 339
definition 335
examples 332
explanation 334
key word outline 343
main points 343
narrative speech structure 326
outline 342
problem/solution speech structure 330
spatial speech structure 326
statistics 333
subpoints 343
testimony 331
topic outline 342
topical speech structure 328
transitions 336

FOR FURTHER REFLECTION

1. In Chapter 11, we discussed audience analysis. How would a good audience analysis help you prepare an introduction or conclusion to a speech? Also, how would it help you identify the main points of your speech or select forms of development?
2. How could you combine the cause/effect and problem/solution organizations? Identify topics that might work with a cause/problem/solution organization.

/dobkinpace

Join a conversation about chapter concepts by visiting the Online Learning Center website at www.mhhe.com/dobkinpace

BUILDING COMMUNICATION SKILLS

1. Make a key word outline from the complete sentence outline (Table 12-2) on running a marathon. Write an introduction and a conclusion to the speech.

- If this speech turned out to be too long, how would you edit it?
- Which main point would you eliminate? Why?
- Which subpoints would you eliminate? Why?

2. We said that analogies compare one unfamiliar concept or object to something that the audience already knows or understands. Complete the following statements with both a literal and figurative analogy:

   Coffee tastes like ____________________.

   Taking a final exam is like ____________________.

   Owning a pet is like ____________________.

   A sunburn feels like ____________________.

   Chatting online is like ____________________.

   Driving an unreliable car is like ____________________.

   Standing in line to buy textbooks is like____________________.

How might your analogies help an audience understand the concept?

NET WORK

Note: While all the URLs listed were current as of the printing of this book, these sites often change. Please check our website (www.mhhe.com/dobkinpace) for updates and hyperlinks to these exercises.

1. The website http://www.presidentialrhetoric.com/ has a large collection of presidential speeches. Look up the website and choose a speech for analysis.
   - What types of information does the speaker use?
   - Are there any examples of testimony, literal analogies, figurative analogies, brief examples, extended examples, hypothetical examples, statistics, explanations, or definitions?
2. The website http://www.humanity.org/voices/commencements/ has many different commencement speeches.
   - Pick a speech for analysis and examine the introduction and conclusion. Were they effective or not? Why?
   - Go through several different speeches and identify the way that each speaker gains the audience's attention.
   - Finally, go back through those same speeches and look at the last statements in the speeches. Were these conclusions effective? Memorable?
3. Numerous websites post collections of quotations, many of which you can search by key words. The following three websites have extensive collections: http://www.creativegrowth.com/qquotes.htm/; http://www.bartleby.com/100/; http://www.famous-quotations.com/. Search these sites for quotes about your speech topic.
   - Would any of the quotes you found add credibility to the speech?
   - Are any of the sources recognizable to the audience?

MEDIA MOMENTS

The movie *American President* (Reiner 1995) tells the story of a modern, but fictional, president of the United States. This movie has several scenes in which the president speaks to the country about jobs, the budget, and his personal life. Analyze the speeches for speech structure and development of main points.

- What attention steps are used in the introductions to the speeches? What clinchers are used in the conclusions?
- Do any of the speeches use a structure discussed in this chapter?
- What forms of development and support are used in the speeches?

Delivering a Confident Presentation

CHAPTER 13

Kevin, Jessica, and Robert were walking reluctantly to their introductory accounting class. Kevin complained, "I never get anything out of class. I honestly don't think I can do it today. When Professor Wright turns on that overhead, I know I'm going to fall asleep."

"If you did, he wouldn't see you," responded Robert. "All he does is stare at the overhead while he writes with his back to us."

"Remember last week?" asked Kevin. "Wright paused while he was writing a problem on the overhead, the pen kind of trailed off to the side, and he nodded his head for a few seconds. I swear he's so boring he put himself to sleep." Everyone laughed, but then Jessica tried to defend the professor. "He is really a nice guy and he knows a lot about accounting if you would give him a chance. And he is well prepared—his handouts are very detailed and clear. And he is. . . ."

"Monotone!" Kevin finished her sentence. "Have you ever heard anyone with less inflection? The only time all semester he raised his voice above a whisper was the day his overhead marker ran out of ink."

"You're too critical," said Jessica. "You'd get more out of class if you concentrated on what he's saying instead of how he's saying it."

"You're probably right," acknowledged Kevin. "I'll try harder to listen, but please don't let this be a day when he uses PowerPoint slides!"

QUESTIONS TO FOCUS YOUR READING

1. How can I feel confident and at ease while I am speaking?
2. What are four different types or modes of delivery?
3. What words should I use in the speech?
4. How can I use my voice, gestures, and speaking aids to enhance my delivery?
5. How can I deliver a responsible presentation?

Perhaps you are familiar with the agony of listening to a well-intentioned and prepared speaker whose message is lost in poor delivery. The situation is certainly familiar to your professor. Public speaking instructors have heard many well-prepared (and some not so well-prepared) student speeches that were ineffective because of poor delivery. In the previous two chapters, we discussed strategies for preparing and organizing a speech. Even if you adopt all these strategies, however, your thorough preparation will be wasted if your speech is not delivered well.

Speeches that are delivered well enhance a speaker's message without calling attention to the speaker. A metaphor from the theater might help explain the appropriate relationship between content of the speech and delivery. A set designer in the theater works to enhance the play and not detract from it. If the audience leaves the theater and remembers only the set design but not the play, then the set designer has not accomplished his or her objective. Similarly, a speaker's delivery should enhance the content without detracting from it. For example, speaking too slowly or quietly can detract from the message. Likewise, speaking too loudly and overdramatizing the material can distract attention from the content. Effective delivery is not noticeable in and of itself, but it is evident when the ideas and content of the speech come through clearly. All speakers, with sincere effort and diligent practice, can improve their delivery and learn to present their ideas effectively. After completing this chapter, you should be able to:

- Manage any feelings of anxiety you may experience when delivering a speech.
- Identify different types of delivery.
- Choose words, phrases, and nonverbal forms of communication that will effectively communicate your message.
- Deliver a responsible presentation.

Managing the Fear of Speaking

communication apprehension Fear of communication situations.

Does the thought of delivering a speech make you nervous? If so, you are not alone. Most speakers experience some level of anxiety when preparing and delivering a speech (Sprague and Stuart 2000). Such nervousness is a type of communication apprehension. **Communication apprehension** is the fear of communication situations (McCroskey 1978). Communication apprehension can occur during the actual communication situation (e.g., during a job interview), and it can occur while you are simply thinking about an upcoming communication event. Whether this fear is strong or mild, most people experience some degree of anxiety about giving a speech.

Communication apprehension occurs in other contexts as well. It occurs in interpersonal communication (most of us are nervous about asking someone out on a date), mediated communication (even some professional actors are fearful of the camera), or group communication (we might be scared to share our opinion during a group discussion). One poll indicated that approximately 60 percent of Americans feel some level of anxiety in leading a group discussion at work, raising a complaint with their boss, or trying to persuade a colleague to accept an idea. The poll indicated, however, that the situation that people seem to be the most anxious about is standing up in public and delivering a speech (Roper-Starch 2000).

Fear of speaking in public is manageable for most people (Sprague and Stuart 2000). Indeed, experienced speakers learn to use the fear of speaking to add energy to their delivery. Experience in public speaking helps speakers cope with anxiety because the more they speak, the more comfortable they become in front of an audience. Your class in communication will provide you with opportunities to practice public speaking skills in front of a sympathetic audience. Your classmates probably share your fear and misgivings, and your professor is trained to help you succeed. This section of the chapter offers strategies for giving speeches that will help ease your fears. You can reduce and manage your apprehension by preparing and practicing, relaxing, and visualizing (Ayres, Heuett, and Sonandre 1998).

"Public speaking is easier than social conversation because you can plan what you want to say and be guaranteed a specific time in which to say it without interruption. . . . In addition, you will likely be the best prepared person there."

—Gerald Phillips, communication scholar

Taking Control of Your Presentation

Sometimes we waste energy worrying about vague fears and have uneasy feelings in the pit of our stomach. One way to reduce fear is to take control of those things you can control by working on specific goals (Phillips 1993). In public speaking, one thing you can control is your preparation and practice, making thorough preparation and practice of your speech the single most important thing you can do to reduce your nervousness. If you begin to worry about your speech in a general or vague sense, use that feeling to motivate your preparation. Usually the more you prepare, the less anxious you will feel. Here are some specific fears that speakers often have and an explanation of how preparation helps to reduce those fears:

I will forget what I want to say. Forgetting what you want to say tends to occur if the ideas in your mind are already uncertain or unclear. Preparation helps you focus your ideas and makes them more stable in your memory. Practice saying your speech several times aloud until your ideas are clear, focused, and remembered.

I will lose my place in the speech. A thoroughly prepared outline is a tremendous aid in combating nervousness because it can help you track the structure of your speech. Practice using a key word outline while rehearsing your speech so that it becomes second nature and you can find your place if you need to do so. If you cannot remember what comes next in your speech, simply pause, look at your outline, collect your thoughts, and then start the next point. With practice, such a "pause and look at your outline" will not interrupt the flow of your speech.

People won't like or accept my ideas. A careful audience analysis takes most of the guesswork out of the speech outcome. You should know your audience well enough to anticipate how they will react to your ideas. If you have made a conscious and careful effort to build areas of common ground with your audience, you will have more confidence about how your audience is likely to respond to your speech.

I might freeze up or go blank at the beginning of the speech. Apprehension is often greatest at the beginning of a speech. Plan your introduction more carefully than the rest of the speech. Know exactly how you are going to begin and practice the introduction until it seems effortless. You are likely to discover your confidence building as the speech progresses. Practice can help you start your speech as strongly as you finish it.

Learning to Relax

How do you feel when you get nervous? Do your muscles tense? Does your mouth become dry? The physical symptoms of communication apprehension are probably familiar to you. They may include an uneasy feeling in the stomach, quickened pulse, shaking or trembling, moist and cool hands, tight vocal cords, and lapses of memory (Sprague and Stuart 2000). These symptoms come from a reaction in your body called the "fight/flight" response. The body recognizes your fear and physically prepares you to either stand your ground and fight or run away as fast as you can. Neither of these reactions, however, is especially helpful in delivering a speech. As a result, you need to control, at least partially, the physical symptoms of fear to deliver your speech.

One way to control these symptoms is through relaxation. You can sometimes work off nervous energy and relax your body through exercise. Although you cannot usually run a lap around a track or pump weights just before a speech, if you have a few private moments, you might be able to take a short walk. Before speech tournaments, for instance, you might see anxious contestants pacing back and forth, practicing their presentations in the halls outside their speaking rooms. These experienced speakers have learned that a little pacing will take the edge off their anxiety. If you have no opportunity to walk or do light exercise, you can relax at your seat by taking in deep breaths and letting them out slowly. As you breathe, concentrate on relaxing your neck, shoulders, and back, areas that are frequently tight during a speech. One method for relaxing these areas of your body is to perform isometric exercises by tensing muscles and then relaxing them. Start with your neck. Tense the muscles upward and relax. Next, tense the muscles in your shoulders and relax. Finally, tense the muscles in your back and relax. Slowly repeat this exercise over and over while breathing in and out. These relatively small and scarcely noticeable muscle movements will help relieve the tension in your body. Relaxing in the days or hours before the speech can also have lasting effects. In the "Applying Communication Concepts" box, a famed acting coach shares a basic relaxation exercise that actors and actresses use before they go onstage.

Visualizing a Positive Outcome

visualization
A technique used to control communication apprehension by replacing negative thoughts and images with positive ones.

A third technique used to control communication apprehension is **visualization** (Ayres and Heuett 1997). Visualization involves replacing negative thoughts and images with positive ones. For instance, if you find yourself thinking "nobody will like my speech," quickly force yourself to think of two or three interesting or funny facts from your speech that the audience will enjoy. Think: "I am well prepared and the audience will enjoy my speech." If possible, combine positive thoughts with pictures of people giving speeches (Ayres and Ayres 2003). Regulate your breathing while you form positive thoughts. As you breathe in, imagine that you are inhaling confidence and success. As you breathe out, imagine you are purging your body of anxiety and fear. Such a combination of relaxation and imagery can help you manage your fears.

You might also use visualization by thinking in specific detail about a successful speech experience and what it will look like. Sports psychologists have long found it useful for athletes to visualize success. For example, bobsled drivers in the Winter Olympic Games usually picture the race in their mind just before they get on the track; they will move their hands and bodies in coordination with the images they are visualizing. Tennis players visualize a successful backhand, basketball players picture the perfect jump shot, and field-goal kickers think of the kick that will win the game as part of their preparation. Similarly, you should pic-

Applying Communication Concepts

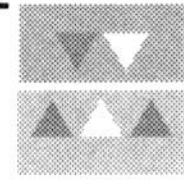

CONQUERING STAGE FRIGHT

Actors and actresses in theater often experience "stage fright," an anxiety similar to communication apprehension. To reduce this anxiety, directors and acting coaches commonly have performers do relaxation exercises before a performance. These techniques are useful for public speakers as well.

The following exercise is adapted from one that Patsy Rodenburg (2000), the renowned vocal coach of the Royal Shakespeare Company, recommends to her students. This exercise can be done just before you speak if you are backstage or out of sight of the audience, and it can be done anytime that you feel anxious in the days or hours leading up to your speech.

- Stand with your weight evenly distributed on the balls of both feet.
- Stretch your back up and make sure that your spine is straight.
- Roll your shoulders slowly up and back in a circular motion several times.
- Swing your arms.
- Stretch up and bend over at the waist. Gently shake your shoulders, neck, and head.
- Stand back up and bend your knees. While in this position, gently massage your face. Smile and open your jaw.
- Walk briskly around the room. Stop abruptly and feel the energy move in your body.
- Use your voice. Start by humming softly. Say as many words as you can think of that begin with the sounds of the letters *b* (bad, bop, and bag), *d* (dog, down, and dig), and *l* (love, lie, and like). Say each of the long vowels over and over (*aaaaa, eeeee, iiiiii, ooooo,* and *uuuuu*). Breathe in deeply. Let your breath out slowly.
- If you are backstage and about to speak to an audience, make sure that you look in a mirror—adjust your clothes and comb your hair.

ASK YOURSELF:

1. How does physical relaxation help your delivery?
2. How might a tense body hinder delivery?

ture, in some detail, a successful speech. The following narrative should help you walk through a successful visualization:

> Visualize the room in which you will give your speech. See yourself in front of the audience. You are standing tall, back straight, shoulders square. You are gesturing with your hands. You are looking at the audience. The audience is smiling and paying attention to your words. Say part of your speech in your mind. As you speak, audience members nod their heads in agreement. Think of the most important idea in your speech. Say it with confidence and force. Picture the audience enthusiastically applauding your ideas. Practice the ending of your speech. Visualize it going smoothly. See yourself returning to your seat at the end of the speech with a sense of satisfaction and pride in a job well done.

"Many of us under stress of speaking publicly . . . stop breathing just when we need it most. Frequently we try to speak on one long breath. . . . The trick is to keep breathing as you speak."

—Patsy Rodenburg, vocal coach, Royal Shakespeare Company

Learning to relax and visualizing a successful presentation are important tools in managing the apprehension that often comes with delivering public presentations.

DELIVERY STYLES

Types of Delivery

There are four main types of delivery: manuscript, memorized, impromptu, and extemporaneous. Each type of delivery can be used effectively in particular situations. For instance, you might use a manuscript delivery if the exact wording of the speech is critical, such as giving a technical report that contains many statistics and facts. Conversely, you would use an impromptu delivery when asked to speak without preparation, such as an unplanned toast or a tribute at a celebration. In this section of the chapter, we will consider the four types of delivery and how you can use them effectively.

Using a Manuscript

manuscript speaking
Delivering a speech from a script written out word for word.

In **manuscript speaking,** the speaker reads from a script that is written out word for word. Manuscript speaking is used when exact wording is necessary, when the speech might be published in written form, or when the length of the speech is precisely timed. The chair of the Federal Reserve Board, for example, almost always uses a manuscript when speaking about the nation's economy. His or her words are carefully analyzed by financial markets around the world for hints of future monetary policy, and a misspoken word can inadvertently influence the world economy. Likewise, most newscasters read from a manuscript on an unseen screen or prompter. Broadcasts are carefully timed, usually to the precise second, and journalistic accuracy is a necessity.

Although manuscripts help speakers deliver technical material and reduce the need to memorize the speech, they also limit a speaker's ability to deliver the speech effectively. Speakers who read a manuscript cannot make consistent eye contact with the audience, which can alienate audiences and give them an excuse to not listen. A manuscript delivery usually limits vocal variety and gestures. Speakers who read their speech can appear stiff and restrained instead of animated and interactive. To be sure, some speakers, like actors, can learn to read with expression and interest. But speaking from a manuscript is a difficult skill to learn and usually not advisable for beginning speakers.

If you must deliver a speech from a manuscript, keep a few simple suggestions in mind. Practice the speech so that you read with fluency, pronouncing words and names correctly and saying each word clearly. Read the speech out loud several times because extensive practice will allow you to make brief eye contact with the audience as you read. As you come to a familiar line or section of the manuscript, glance up at the audience while completing the sentence from memory. For example, suppose that you are ending a section of the manuscript like this, "You see (look up from the manuscript and make eye contact with the audience), you can go home again."

Beginning speakers often get nervous and read the words of the manuscript too quickly, so try to read somewhat more slowly than you speak. Think about the meaning of the words and sentences as you read, and concentrate on your vocal inflection and volume changes. Use pauses to your advantage by stopping briefly and looking up at the audience before important points, and pausing just before saying difficult words or combinations of words.

Delivering a Speech from Memory

memorized speaking
Delivering a speech by writing out the speech, memorizing the content, and then delivering it word for word, without the use of notes.

In **memorized speaking,** the speaker writes out the speech, memorizes the content, and then delivers the speech word for word without the use of notes. A memorized delivery allows for both precise wording and constant eye contact with the audience. In ancient Greek and Roman oratory, memorization was often the preferred method of delivery. In those times, students would sometimes practice public speaking by memorizing and delivering the exact words of speeches from their teachers. It is unlikely that your professors will ask you to memorize one of their speeches or lectures, but memorized delivery is still occasionally used in some circumstances. For example, speakers who deliver the same speech to several different audiences sometimes memorize their presentation. Also, speakers may memorize passages of a speech that they want to deliver word for word while also maintaining eye contact with the audience. One student, speaking on civil liberties, started the speech by reciting the preamble to the Constitution while looking straight at the audience. The strong eye contact gained the attention of the audience and the flawless delivery of the passage from memory established the speaker's credibility on the subject.

Speaking from memory, however, takes great skill and practice. Too often, speakers forget the exact words they want to say. It is always difficult for an audience to watch speakers start and stop several times in a speech as they search for some previously memorized words. Also, a speaker who delivers a memorized speech over and over, such as a salesperson, can begin to sound stale and flat. If you are going to deliver a speech from memory, allow enough time to memorize the speech and practice your delivery out loud. There is a fundamental difference between saying the speech in "your mind" and vocalizing it for others to hear. Find a comfortable place that you can practice the speech from beginning to end without feeling self-conscious. Memorize and practice the speech in segments. Divide the speech into meaningful parts such as introduction, first main point, second point, third point, and the conclusion. Memorize the introduction, and practice delivering it until it comes naturally. Then memorize the next segment and add it to the introduction. Practice delivering the two segments together until the words come naturally. Have a friend follow the manuscript and prompt you with words or phrases you forget. Continue this process until you have memorized each segment and can deliver the speech without mistakes. During the presentation, concentrate on vocal variety and establish eye contact with the audience. If you do have a memory lapse in the speech, simply pause and find your place before beginning again. The audience will generally be patient as you find the correct words to say.

"It usually takes more than three weeks to prepare a good impromptu speech."

—Mark Twain, author

Impromptu Delivery

Impromptu speaking means delivering the speech with little or no preparation. This often occurs when a speaker is unexpectedly asked to say something in a meeting or at a ceremony of some kind. In our opening example from Chapter 12, Esperanza was called on to give a very important but spontaneous business presentation. The spontaneous nature of impromptu speeches frequently makes the delivery energetic and enjoyable. However, an impromptu speech usually lacks structure and detail. As a result, while they are effective for very short presentations, such as toasts at a celebration, they are less effective for speeches of any length, including classroom presentations.

impromptu speaking
Delivering a speech with little or no preparation.

When speaking impromptu, remember a few basic tips:

Take what little time you have and organize your ideas. Even in the most spontaneous situation, there is usually a moment or two to prepare. Make a brief

Answering questions in public requires effective impromptu delivery skills.
© Arnold Gold/New Haven Register/ The Image Works

outline of your ideas. Organize your thoughts around one of the structures discussed in Chapter 12. For instance, you might talk about the past, present, or future of the situation or discuss its advantages and disadvantages. You might simply select one major point you want to stress and develop that point with a personal illustration, a fact, or an analogy.

vocal pauses
Sounds speakers make while stopping to think of what they are going to say next, such as "ah," "a," "and a," "um," and "uh."

As you speak, avoid vocal pauses. **Vocal pauses** are sounds speakers make while stopping to think of what they are going to say next. Many speakers fill this silence with words such as "you know," "of course," "and," "ah," "um," and "uh." Vocal pauses are distracting to the audience and are a common problem in impromptu speaking.

Be concise. The longer you speak, the more likely you are to reveal your lack of preparation. Most spontaneous speaking situations call for brief, well-organized, and cogent thoughts.

Award ceremonies are situations at which impromptu delivery is often important. A professor at our university received a teaching award at a ceremony attended by fellow colleagues. The presenter asked the professor to say a few words to the audience. Since the award was a surprise, the professor had little opportunity to prepare. The professor thanked the presenter and then related a brief story about the many mishaps that occurred during her very first semester as a teacher. The professor then concluded with the statement, "The students in that first class, twenty years ago, certainly would laugh at the thought of me receiving a teaching award. But I thank my colleagues for their patience and for this award. It means much to me. I also want to reassure each of you that if I can win this award, so can you." The impromptu acceptance speech was humorous, self-effacing, and sincere. It was organized around a single anecdote. Finally, it was brief and to the point.

Speaking Extemporaneously

extemporaneous speaking
Using a keyword outline to deliver a prepared speech.

An extemporaneous speech combines the best elements of all the other types of delivery. **Extemporaneous speaking** involves using a keyword outline to deliver a prepared speech. The speaker carefully studies and organizes the content of the presentation and, following the keyword outline, spontaneously comes up with much of the exact wording of the speech during its delivery. The speaker can establish excellent eye contact while using a keyword outline to aid her or his memory during delivery. Extemporaneous speaking is the best method of delivery for most speaking situations, because it builds connections with the audience, allows flexibility in responding to audience feedback, and lets the speaker adjust the length of the speech. An effective extemporaneous speech is lively and responsive to the audience. Table 13-1 summarizes the benefits and liabilities of each type of delivery.

TABLE 13-1

The Benefits and Liabilities of Different Types of Speech Delivery

TYPE OF DELIVERY	BENEFITS	LIABILITIES
Manuscript	Allows for precise wording and exact time limits.	Very limited eye contact and gestures.
Memorized	Allows for precise wording and exact time limits with extensive eye contact and hand gestures.	Speakers often forget what they are going to say, especially in a long speech. Memorization also limits spontaneity, and speakers cannot easily respond to changes in the situation and audience reactions. Speeches sometimes sound "canned."
Impromptu	Allows for tremendous spontaneity; speakers can respond to changes in the situation and audience reaction. The delivery is often animated and energetic. Allows for constant eye contact and extensive use of gestures.	Impromptu speeches often lack structure and detailed development. Speakers must think on their feet and come up with effective wording without preparation. Accordingly, speakers can sometimes misspeak or say inappropriate things.
Extemporaneous	Allows for careful preparation of content, including a logical structure and thorough development of main ideas. Speakers can respond to changes in the situation and audience reactions as well as establish continuous eye contact and make extensive use of gestures.	Extemporaneous speaking has slightly less precise wording than manuscript or memorized speaking. Inexperienced speakers can sometimes wander from their outline or miscalculate the length of speaking time. With practice, extemporaneous speaking has the most advantages and least disadvantages of the four types of delivery.

Selecting the Words for Your Speech

Words have great potential for both communication and miscommunication. In Chapter 5 we discussed verbal communication and observed that words have the power to influence the thoughts and actions of others. We also observed that words are often arbitrary, ambiguous, and changeable. For this reason, speakers should carefully select the actual words they will use in their speech. Often the

TABLE 13-2 Using Concrete and Simple Words and Phrases

TOO LONG OR ABSTRACT	ALTERNATIVES
In view of the fact that	Because
Adequate number of	Enough
In reference to	About
Strategize	Plan
Utilize	Use
Whether	If
Attempt	Try
Inasmuch	Since

difference between a successful speech and one that does not achieve its goal is the words the speaker uses. A large national survey asked business leaders, government employees, teachers, and others who frequently give professional presentations what public speaking skills were most important. "Choosing appropriate and effective words" was the second highest rated skill just behind "keeping your audience interested" (Engleberg 2002). As this survey suggests, a speech will succeed if the words used in the delivery are clear and motivate the audience to understand or believe. The following sections give advice on selecting words that are clear, vivid, and conversational.

Be Clear

All words have meaning, but some have more specific or concrete meanings than others. Speakers should select words that are as precise and specific as possible and avoid abstract words and long phrases that are difficult for the audience to understand. For instance, instead of saying "it is probable that," the speaker could simply say "probably." Instead of saying a word like "subsequently," the speaker could use a word more familiar to the audience, such as "later" or "afterward." Table 13-2 offers additional examples of concrete and simple words and phrases.

Be Vivid

imagery
Evoking a mental picture in the mind of the audience.

metaphor
Comparing one thing, idea, or action to another.

simile
A type of metaphor that compares two things using the words "like" or "as."

Some words create interesting mental images in the minds of the audience while others pass through without much thought or notice. Effective speakers select words that evoke **imagery,** or a mental picture, in the mind of the audience. Metaphors and similes help create imagery. A **metaphor** compares one thing, idea, or action to another. For example, we have used metaphors in the last two chapters to help explain various aspects of planning and organizing a public speech, such as, "transitions are verbal bridges that move the speech from one point or idea to the next," and "a homepage is the doorway though which additional documents or information can be accessed."

A **simile** is a type of metaphor that compares two things using the words "like" or "as." For instance, earlier we said that an "introduction to a speech is like an appetizer to a fine meal; it should be interesting, leave the audience wanting more, and set up the main course." Some similes have become **clichés** to be avoided, or worn-out phrases that are used so often that they have lost their vividness. Phrases like "time flies," "more than you can shake a stick at," "every parent's nightmare," or "cool as a cucumber" evoke very little imagery in audiences.

clichés
Worn-out phrases used so often that they have lost their vividness.

Be Conversational

Audiences like a speaker who talks "with them" instead of "to them." The speaker's words should create a sincere and trusting relationship with an audience through conversational delivery that invites the audience to listen as an equal. A conversational delivery connects the audience to the speaker and the speaker's message. Here are a few suggestions to help speakers be conversational:

Watch a video clip of a student speaker using conversational delivery (CD Clip 13.1).

- Use words that include the audience such as "we" and "our."
- Use other personal pronouns such as "she," "us," and "they."
- Use first person "I" when referring to yourself.
- Talk directly to the audience as you would in a conversation ("I know what you are thinking. You want to know if you are going to get some of this cheesecake after I show you how to make it. Am I right? Well, the answer is yes—I have enough for everyone.").
- Use rhetorical questions. A **rhetorical question** is a question you want the audience to think about but not answer vocally, such as, "How many of you would like to save money on your rent?"
- Use active verbs. Instead of saying, "The cat was sleeping," say "The cat slept."

rhetorical question
A question you want the audience to think about but not answer vocally.

Aspects of Delivery

Speakers have many resources available to help them deliver a speech, including their voice, hands, facial expressions, and speaking aids such as charts, pictures or computer slides. An effective delivery makes use of these resources by combining them into a coordinated presentation; the speaker's voice, hands, face, and speaking aids should all work together to achieve the purpose of the speech. In this section of the chapter, we will discuss the many aspects of delivery and how speakers can use them effectively.

Using Your Voice

Your voice is the most important tool you have in delivering your speech; it gives life to your presentation. Good vocal delivery depends on both loudness and clarity. First, it is vital to project your voice so that the audience can hear you. Many presentations suffer because the audience simply cannot hear what is being said. Speak loudly enough so the person farthest from you in the audience can hear you. Second, the audience must be able to understand you. Clarity in your speech is a matter of pronunciation and enunciation.

Pronunciation is saying words according to accepted standards of English and in agreement with the expectations of the audience. These standards are commonly found in dictionaries. Pay particular attention to the correct pronunciation of names and places, as mispronouncing a word or a name may offend

pronunciation
Saying words according to accepted standards of English and in accordance with the expectations of the audience.

your audience, distract from your ideas, and harm your credibility. The audience might also misunderstand what you are trying to say and be confused. Consider this example of a student who was relating an anecdote that happened in Ohio. His uncertainty about his story caused him to stumble over the word "Ohio." He blended it with "Iowa," and the place came out as "Ohiowa," leaving the audience confused and guessing about the setting for the story.

enunciation
Saying words clearly.

Enunciation is the physical production of sounds and saying words clearly. Speakers sometimes slur or distort words, such as saying, "goin' " instead of "going." Some people run words together in conversations so frequently that they start believing that two words are really one. For instance, students may write "alot," or "noone" as one word, when in reality they are two words that have been combined. Enunciation becomes an even greater problem when public speakers become nervous and speak more quickly than normal.

You can help your enunciation by slowing down your overall delivery and concentrating on each syllable of difficult words or names. Be sure that the audience understands each word you say. Practice your enunciation with vocal exercises, called tongue twisters. The "Applying Communication Concepts" box on tongue twisters contains several of these exercises.

The voice, regardless of the content of the speech, can communicate interest in the audience, enthusiasm for the topic, and commitment to the occasion. The use of the voice to communicate meaning apart from words is called vocalics and was discussed earlier in the chapter on nonverbal communication. As mentioned in that chapter, there are three qualities of vocalics that you can use in delivery: rate, volume, and inflection. A speaker with good delivery varies each of these qualities throughout the speech.

rate
How quickly or slowly a speech is delivered.

volume
How loudly a speech is delivered.

inflection
The vocal emphasis placed on each word when speaking.

- **Rate** is how quickly or slowly the speech is delivered. By varying the rate of speech, you can add meaning to the words being spoken. For example, by speaking quickly you can increase a sense of urgency or excitement. Speaking slowly communicates a need to listen carefully
- **Volume** is how loudly the speech is delivered. Again, you should alternate between soft and loud as you deliver your speech. Speaking softly can draw the audience in and compel them to listen carefully while a loud voice might communicate excitement, anger, or other strong emotions.
- **Inflection** is the vocal emphasis you place on each word. Inflection is used to highlight different meanings of words and phrases. Consider the following example. You see your friend drive to school in a new car. Later you run into this friend on campus and ask the obvious question, "You bought a new car?" While the question may be obvious, emphasizing different words in the question can change the meaning. Table 13-3 illustrates the possible meanings.

TABLE 13-3 Changes in Emphasis Create Different Meanings

You bought a new car?	Why did you buy a car when you cannot afford one?
You **bought** a new car?	Why did you buy a car when you always lease your cars?
You bought a **new** car?	Why did you buy a new car when you always buy used cars?
You bought a new **car**?	Why did you buy a car when you always buy a truck?

Applying Communication Concepts

TONGUE TWISTERS

Work on your enunciation by practicing these "tongue twisters." Say these simple phrases as fast as you can over and over again.

- Mixed biscuits.
- Greek grapes.
- Red leather, yellow leather.
- A fat free fruit float.
- Tie twine to three tree twigs.
- Freshly fried fresh fish.
- Alice asks for axes.

Tongue twisters are also a good way to "warm up" your speaking voice before delivering a presentation. Try these longer ones.

- Granny's gray goose goes last.
- She sells seashells on the seashore, the shells she sells are seashells I'm sure.
- She sifted thistles through her thistle-sifter.
- A Tudor who tooted a flute, tried to tutor two tooters to toot. Said the two to their tutor, "Is it harder to toot, or to tutor two tooters to toot?"
- If Stu chews shoes, should Stu choose the shoes he chews?
- If one doctor doctors another doctor, does the doctor who doctors the doctor, doctor the doctor the way the doctor he is doctoring doctors? Or does he doctor the doctor the way the doctor who doctors doctors?
- When does the wristwatch strap shop shut? Does the wristwatch strap shop shut soon? Which wristwatch straps are Swiss wristwatch straps?

This one, in Spanish, is called "Mi mama" (my mother):

- Mi mama me mima mucho (My mother spoils me a lot).

This one is about "Tres tristes tigres" (Three sad tigers):

- Tres tristes tigres, tragaban trigo en tres tristes trastos. En tres tristes trastos, tragaban trigo tres tristes tigres. (Three sad tigers, were gulping down wheat in three sad bowls. In three sad bowls, three sad tigers were gulping down wheat.) (Haddad 1993).

Some experts think this is the most difficult tongue twister in the English language:

- The sixth sick sheik's sixth sheep's sick (McLoone-Basta and Siegel 1987).

ASK YOURSELF:

1. Which twisters are the most difficult for you to say?
2. Which combination of syllables or words is difficult to enunciate?
3. Does speaking slowly help your enunciation?

One of the keys to effective delivery is varying the rate, volume, and inflection, often referred to as **vocal variety.** A speech is like a good symphony, with the speaker creating peaks and valleys that build towards a *crescendo.* On the other hand, a speaker who is slow and soft-spoken or continuously loud and fast soon alienates the audience. One of the hallmarks of Martin Luther King, Jr.'s "I Have a

vocal variety
Varying the rate, volume, and inflection in delivering a speech.

Dream" speech is his use of vocal variety. He started his delivery slowly, almost hesitantly, and built up the rate, volume, and inflection throughout his speech. By the time he got to the "I have a dream" refrain, he was at the peak of his vocal range and produced a stirring and emotional conclusion. Had he started speaking as fast and as loudly as he could, there would have been no place for him to "climb" vocally. Instead, both the content of his speech and his vocal variety gradually peaked to a memorable climax. Similarly, you should use vocal variety to add meaning and emphasis to your speech.

Using Your Body and Hands

Use Good Speaking Posture. Most students associate the word "posture" with a parent's admonition to "stand up straight." Maybe parents are onto something. A correct speaking posture is important to effective delivery. Standing with your back straight allows you to breathe more easily and project your voice more clearly. A good posture consists of placing both feet firmly on the floor with your weight distributed evenly between them. Your body and shoulders should be square with the center of the room so that you can easily turn and face different parts of the audience. Your chin should be raised so you can establish eye contact, and your hands should hang naturally at your side or be placed on the speaking rostrum.

An incorrect posture not only hinders delivery but also distracts the audience from the speaker's message. Too many speakers hunch over a podium, using it as a security barrier behind which they hide to cover up their nervousness. They thus create a barrier between themselves and their audience. In reality, the audience wants to see the speaker, not the podium.

Watch a video clip of a student speaker using gestures (CD Clip 13.2).

Make the Most of Your Gestures. Part of a good speaking posture means that your hands should be free from objects so you can use them to gesture and animate your ideas. Do not fidget with your hair, eyeglasses, speaking notepapers, or other objects, and do not put your hands in your pockets. Hand gestures, moreover, are an important part of delivery. In personal conversation, many speakers are natural "hand talkers" and instinctively illustrate their ideas with movement. Speech anxiety, however, makes some of these same gestures seem stiff and awkward when delivering a speech. In public, your hands can feel heavy and you may become self-conscious about even the smallest movement. Practice can help reduce much of this anxiety. Use the same hand gestures in public as you do in your conversations, only make them larger. Typical speaking gestures such as pointing can add emphasis to important ideas. Gestures can also help with the structure of a speech by indicating where you are

Animated gestures can add emphasis to and help clarify ideas.

Exploring Communication Concepts

HAND GESTURES

Research indicates that hand gestures are an intrinsic facet of human communication. Gestures are more than the random movements of nervous speakers. Rather, gestures have specific functions in most communication situations. They help speakers recall specific words and phrases and explain information more effectively, and they help listeners understand and remember information.

In one study, researchers tested the effects of hand gestures on *lexical recall*, the ability to remember a specific word (Frick-Horbury and Gettentag 1998). The subjects were students with approximately the same SAT scores and verbal ability. The researchers identified 50 common English words that were only "somewhat" familiar to the students. The researchers then read the students a definition and asked them to recall the correct term. Half of the students were allowed to use hand gestures as they tried to think of the answer. The other half, however, were asked to hold an object during the experiment, which prevented them using their hands to gesture. The students who were free to gesture recalled significantly more words than the students who were not.

In another study, students were asked to describe action scenes from a *Road Runner* cartoon to an audience. Again, half the students were allowed to use their hands to gesture while speaking and the other half was not. Those who could use gestures spoke more quickly, repeated themselves less often, and used fewer vocal pauses than those who could not gesture. The audience also rated the gesturing students as more "eloquent." The results of the study support the notion that gestures help speakers communicate. The researchers concluded that "gestures act as a mental bridge between spatial concepts and words, making it easier for us to think of the right phrase more quickly" (Doskoch and Haley 1997).

Finally, a classic study of gestures indicates that audiences comprehend more material when speakers use gestures. Researchers asked students to describe geometric shapes to an audience who could not see the diagram. The audience was asked to draw the picture as the speakers described it to them. As before, half of the speakers were permitted to use gestures and the other half was not. The audience drew significantly more accurate drawings when listening to speakers using gestures (Graham and Argyle 1975).

ASK YOURSELF:

1. Are you aware of the gestures you use when you talk in conversations? Speak before groups?
2. According to this research, what are some ways that hand gestures can help in delivering a speech?

in the speech. For instance, if you are on point number three, you can hold three fingers in the air.

Gestures can also clarify ideas. You can indicate the size and shape of objects with your hands, or *pantomime* the action you are describing. For example, when saying "It's time to tell the polluters, 'stop,' " you might put up your hand, palm forward like a traffic cop, to make the point vivid. While you don't want to be too theatrical in your delivery, you do want to energize your delivery with a variety of gestures. The "Exploring Communication Concepts" box examines several functions of hand gestures on the speaker and audience.

Using Your Face and Eyes

When audiences listen to presentations, they spend much of their listening time looking at the speaker's face. Facial expressions help set a mood and tone for the speech, so they need to match the speech content. If your speech is humorous and light, you should look happy. Conversely, if your speech is serious, you should look concerned. Sometimes speakers contradict their message with their facial gestures. Anyone who has seen a local news anchor smile through stories about war, crime, and death knows the feelings of discomfort and confusion that this contradiction can produce.

eye contact
Looking at the audience when delivering a speech.

The most important part of facial gestures is **eye contact,** or simply looking at the audience. Look at the audience 80 to 90 percent of your speaking time. By looking at the audience, you communicate your interest in them and promote a conversational style of delivery. Looking at the audience can be difficult, especially if you are anxious about your speech; some speakers prefer to stare directly at their notes as if hiding from the experience. With effort and practice, however, even the shyest speakers can learn to establish good eye contact with the audience.

When looking at the audience, do not stare at any one person. Instead, look at everyone in the audience by slowly moving your head from one side of the room to the other. Briefly establish eye contact with one member of the audience before moving to the next person. Your speaking notes should also allow you to sustain eye contact with only momentary glances at your notes. The best way to do this is with a keyword outline. A keyword outline, which we discussed in Chapter 12, is a memory guide that uses just a few words to help you deliver your speech. Typically, the keyword outline uses a single word or two for each point of the speech. Some detailed or technical information can be listed in the outline, but it should account for less than 10 to 15 percent of the actual speech. You might try printing a keyword outline in larger type so that it becomes easier to read at a glance as you are speaking. With practice, you will learn to maintain almost constant eye contact with the audience while looking only briefly at your notes.

Using Speaking Aids

speaking aids
Visual and auditory props that speakers use to develop a speech and help the audience conceptualize ideas.

Speaking aids are visual and auditory props that speakers use to develop their speeches and help the audience conceptualize ideas. There is a limitless number of possible speaking aids. Suppose you are speaking about scuba diving. During your speech, you could display a diving mask, regulator, and even an air tank to acquaint the audience with the necessary equipment. If you are talking about the changing geography of central Europe, you could display a current map to help the audience visualize the broader changes you are describing. Common speaking aids include audio and videotapes, pictures, graphs, models, objects, flip charts, chalkboards, and computer-generated graphics. Table 13-4 presents a more comprehensive list of aids.

The use of speaking aids can greatly enhance a speech. In general, aids increase the attention of the audience, help maintain interest in the subject, and increase audience recall of information once the speech is over. If speaking aids are not used properly, however, they can divert the audience's attention from your topic. Here are a few simple suggestions for making effective use of speaking aids.

TABLE 13-4

Speaking Aids

Audio Aids	Visual Aids
Tape/CD music	People
Musical instruments	Objects
Radio recordings	Models
Sound effects	Pictures/photographs
	Brochures/flyers
Computer-Projected Aids	Magazine covers/pictures
Document	Camera
Slides	Slides
Digital photographs	Maps
Computer-animated graphics	Schematic drawings
Web pages	Posters
Animated models	Chalkboard/whiteboard
Clip art	Flip chart
Sound bites	Overhead projections
	Graphs/charts
	Line drawings
	Videotape recordings

Use speaking aids that add content to the speech. Speaking aids should support the speech, not dominate it. Avoid using speaking aids that simply serve as "wallpaper." For example, one student who wanted to speak about his radio-controlled model sailboat was questioned about the purpose of the speech. He admitted that he just wanted to "show off my 'very cool' boat" and had made elaborate plans to bring a large tub of water to class so he could demonstrate how the model worked. This student's model was very impressive, but he had the wrong philosophy about speaking aids. Aids should be used to support a speech, rather than to build a speech around the aid.

Make sure the aid can be seen or heard by everyone in the audience. Practice with the aid by going to the presentation room and testing the volume or the size of the aid. Stand at the back of the room. Can you read the charts or hear the tape? Small photographs or pictures are particularly troubling. Often the first row of your audience can see these pictures, but those farthest back cannot. If an aid is not large enough to be seen by everyone in the audience, do not use it.

Use speaking aids at specific points in the speech. Use aids when they correspond with the content of the speech and remove them when they do not. If possible, hide them completely from the view of the audience. Otherwise, the attention of the audience will wander from your topic to the speaking aid. For example, suppose you are displaying beautiful travel posters of the Yucatan peninsula in Mexico on the board behind you as part of the introduction to your speech on Mayan architecture. The posters might be effective at gaining the audience's attention, but resist leaving the posters on the board for the entire speech without referring to them again or explicitly using them to illustrate any of your speaking points. Eventually, the attention of the audience will drift to the posters and away from your speech. Speaking aids should be convenient enough to display when they are needed and removed when they are not.

Effective speaking aids can enhance your delivery.
© David Young-Wolff/PhotoEdit

Avoid distributing visual aids, such as handouts, during your speech. Again, the audience's attention will be diverted to the handout rather than to what you are saying. For this reason, distribute handouts after the speech. Also, passing around a single object such as a photograph for closer observation seldom works in a short speech. Usually, only about half the audience sees the object before the speech ends.

Keep the aid simple. Edit your speaking aids as carefully as you edit your speech, and present only those details that are essential. Keep diagrams and other drawings simple. Sometimes, elaborate artwork can confuse the audience more than clarify a specific point. Audio and visual clips should be no longer than 30 seconds, and most graphs should be understandable at a single glance. Finally, do not use speaking time to set up your speaking aids. While you are setting up, the audience might lose interest in your topic.

Explain your aid to the audience. Remember that the speaking aid should be integrated into the speech. Many speakers assume that the aid is self-explanatory. Just letting the audience look at a visual aid with no explanation misses an important rhetorical opportunity. For example, interpret the figures on a graph, verbally set the scene for a video or audio clip, or use a pointer to indicate interesting parts of a picture or model. Without your explanation, the audience will seldom reach the same conclusion you had planned when preparing the aid.

Practice with the speaking aid. Many of the pitfalls of using speaking aids can be avoided with careful preparation and practice. Know how to run electronic or mechanical equipment and, if possible, practice with the actual equipment you will be using during the presentation. Plan what you are going to write on a board or flip chart before the speech and check the spelling of any difficult words. If you are going to use a volunteer from the audience, rehearse with that person the same way you would practice with other forms of speaking aids. Avoid calling someone out of the audience without prior warning, as you do not want to embarrass that person and you want to make sure that she or he will not say something to detract from your speech. They should know exactly what you expect of them.

If something goes wrong with your aid, do not panic or lose control of the situation. Often your reaction to the situation is far more important to the audience than the actual problem. If a problem arises with a speaking aid, try to solve the problem within a reasonable amount of time. If the problem persists, move on. If a picture falls off the wall, hold it while you finish speaking; if a projector doesn't work, summarize the material for your audience. Again, plan for the unexpected and have contingency plans in case of problems. For example, suppose that you are using a CD player to play the lyrics of a song. You should be prepared to read (or even sing!) the lyrics of the song to the audience in case the player malfunctions.

Most importantly, remember your audience when using a speaking aid. Speakers often forget eye contact with the audience as soon as they use a speaking aid. Talk to the audience, not the aid, and never hold anything in front of your

Think It Over

USING DRAMATIC SPEECH AIDS

Suppose one of your classmates, Gabriel, has decided to present a speech on the civil war in Sierra Leone. He opens his speech by saying, "When most of us think of 'Civil War,' we have pictures in our minds of Union and Confederate soldiers, or perhaps Abraham Lincoln giving the Gettysburg address. The current civil war in Sierra Leone stands as another of the most brutal civil wars ever fought."

As he speaks, Gabriel displays several graphic pictures of mutilated torture victims, children with amputated limbs, and decapitated corpses. How might his audience react to the pictures? Is his choice of speaking aid appropriate? Is it effective? Why or why not?

face. Even when playing an audio or video clip, remain in front of the audience and maintain as much eye contact as possible. Stand to the side of the speaking aid so that the audience can see both you and the aid at the same time.

Speakers should also think about the audience's reaction to the speaking aid. If the aid is too powerful, offensive, or controversial, it may distract the audience from the purpose of the speech. The "Think It Over" box on dramatic speech aids asks you to consider one such case.

Using Computers

The use of computer presentational packages, such as Microsoft's popular PowerPoint, is very common and almost expected in professional settings such as business briefings, sales meetings, courts of law, and even many college classrooms. Computer packages are another type of speaking aid, and the advice given in the previous section applies to their use. But the *ubiquitous* use and unique characteristics of these computer packages also warrant special consideration. Although computer packages can be a tremendous aid to speakers, they are frequently misused and often create more problems than benefits. A few simple suggestions can help you enjoy the benefits while avoiding some of the problems.

Check out PowerPoint Tutor for help in preparing slides for your speech.

Know the software thoroughly. Your credibility can be harmed easily if you show ignorance of the computer in front of the audience. There are many excellent tutorials and other sources of information accompanying each computer package; take advantage of these resources where necessary. The best way to know a presentational package is to use it often. Different packages have different technical requirements and features, and special versions of the same program are likely to have substantial differences. Find out which program and version are installed on the computer at the speaking venue. Practice your presentation in a "dress rehearsal," using the same computer, projector, and software you will use in the real presentation.

Resist the "gizmo" factor. It is easy to get caught up in the various fonts and designs graphics in a computer presentation and forget about the purpose of your speech. Select a design that enhances your message. Generally, a simple and clean design is more effective than one that has too many words or fonts. Sometimes, speakers change font size and background too frequently or add clever animated characters to impress the audience. When speakers try to get overly creative in their use of computer graphics, the audience is more likely to remember the

FIGURE 13-1 GUIDELINES FOR COMPUTER SLIDES

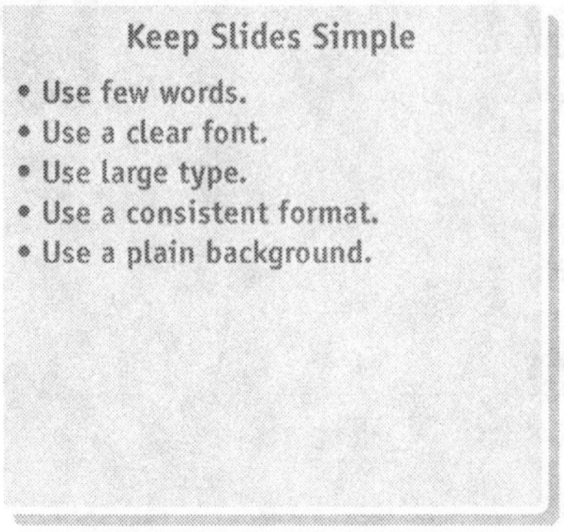

Keep Slides Simple
- Use few words.
- Use a clear font.
- Use large type.
- Use a consistent format.
- Use a plain background.

Effective:
This slide is clean and easy to read. It uses few words, a clear font in large type, consistent format, and a plain background.
This simple format will draw the audience's attention to the content of the slide.

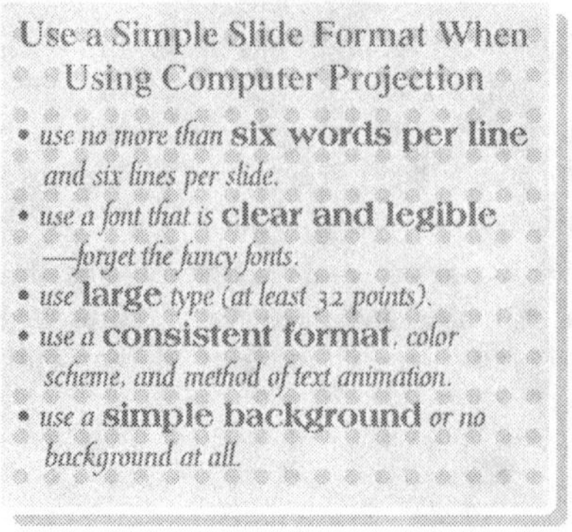

Use a Simple Slide Format When Using Computer Projection
- use no more than six words per line and six lines per slide.
- use a font that is clear and legible —forget the fancy fonts.
- use large type (at least 32 points).
- use a consistent format, color scheme, and method of text animation.
- use a simple background or no background at all.

Less Effective:
This slide is hard to read. It uses too many words and lines of text, three different fonts (some of which are too small and difficult to read), and a background that distracts the audience.
This cluttered format will draw the audience's attention away from the content of the slid.

Clean and simple computer slides are most effective

graphics than the point of the speech. For instance, one speaker presented a slide in which the text emerged or cascaded from the top of the screen, but on the next slide, the text came from the bottom or the far right. The text appeared in different font sizes and styles on each slide, and the constant change was obvious to audience members. By the end of the speech, they were talking about slide format rather than the purpose of the speech.

When preparing a slide, keep these simple guidelines in mind (Figure 13-1 also illustrates these guidelines):

- Use no more than six words per line and six lines per slide.
- Use a font that is clear and legible and forget fancy fonts with lots of scrolls and adornments.
- Use a large font size (at least 32 points) and check the size of the letters in the speaking venue to make sure that everyone can read what you have prepared.
- Use a consistent format, color scheme, and method of text animation.
- Use a plain or simple background. Detailed pictures or designs often make the slide hard to read.

Maintain your speaker's presence. Make an explicit attempt to maintain the focus of the audience on you during a computer presentation. Otherwise, the audience will focus on the projection screen (Hinman 1999). If possible, keep the lights on; even dimming the lights reduces your presence. Stand beside the projector where the audience can easily see both you and the screen. Do not turn your back on the audience. Maintain eye contact at all times and talk to the audience, not the screen. When you want the audience to focus on the screen, step to the side and gesture or point at the projected image. When you want the audience to focus on you, step in front of the projection. Sometimes placing a blank slide in strategic places during the presentation helps to reestablish your presence. Finally, some computers and many projectors make substantial noise that can interfere with your delivery. Speak up and make sure that the audience can hear you.

DILBERT reprinted by permission of United Feature Syndicate, Inc.

Use a computer presentation in the appropriate situations and places. A computer presentation is best when you have much information to communicate in a short period of time. However, the use of computer slides "locks" you into your prepared sequence and is much less flexible than other forms of speaking aids. If the situation is fluid and requires maximum flexibility, choose different speaking aids. The computer presentation should supplement your speech rather than overwhelm it, so use the computer sparingly and prepare a minimum number of slides. Otherwise, the speaking situation will be reduced to you reading the slides to the audience. If possible, turn off the projector when it is not in use and integrate other forms of speaking aids into your presentation.

Expect the unexpected and do not panic. Regardless of the care and practice that you put into your presentation, your reliance on a computer as a speaking aid might still lead to last-minute problems. Bill Gates, founder of Microsoft Corporation and the world's most famous computer expert, demonstrated his company's newest product to an estimated audience of 10,000 people when the computer he was using suddenly "crashed." Although potentially embarrassing, Gates kept his composure and simply said to the audience, "I guess we still have some bugs to work out" (Li 1998). If this can happen to Bill Gates, it can happen to you. Be prepared to do the presentation without the computer in case of technical problems. Have handouts or overheads for use in an emergency. Most of all, do not panic. Simply explain to the audience what is happening and carry on with the speech as if you didn't need the computer.

Complete the Speech Preparation Checklist to see if you've finished all the steps in preparing your speech.

Delivering a Responsible Presentation

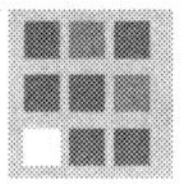

Responsible delivery should be culturally sensitive and inclusive. It should include the audience and build a relationship with them, rather than excluding or offending them. We have discussed both the responsible use of language and nonverbal communication in previous chapters, and the suggestions made there are just as applicable when delivering a presentation as when communicating in other contexts. The next two sections offer some additional suggestions for delivering a presentation that is both respectful of and responsive to your audience.

Choose Appropriate Language

Some words can offend audiences and make them feel left out of the speech. For instance, many words, phrases, or titles in English unfairly privilege males and exclude females. Referring to all mail carriers as "postmen" might offend women workers in the postal service (use "letter carriers"), and titles such as "chairman" suggest that only men are suitable for positions of leadership (use "chair"). A responsible speaker should be aware of inequities in language and select words that are neutral, both out of respect for audiences, and also because gender-neutral words are usually more accurate. The following are some guidelines to help choose responsible, inclusive language.

- Avoid *generic* use of the word "man." "Man" used to mean all humans, but it now carries a strong connotation of the "adult man," and using it in words or titles is often viewed as unfair to women. Watch out for these problems:

INSENSITIVE	BETTER
Mankind	Humanity, people, humankind
The common man	The average person
Chairman	Chair, coordinator, head
Congressman	Congressional representative
Businessman	Business executive

Avoid masculine pronouns, such as "he" or "him" to refer to everyone. This becomes a problem in speeches because English has no gender-free generic pronoun. Although many speakers have traditionally used "he" to refer to everyone, there are some remedies for this problem (Non-Sexist Language 2002), such as using plural pronouns. For example, instead of saying, "Each traveler must claim *his* own luggage," say "Travelers must claim *their* own luggage"; use "one," "you," or "he or she" instead of a masculine pronoun "Each traveler must claim *her or his* own luggage."

- Balance male and female examples, quotes, and testimony. Be sensitive to overrepresenting traditional male viewpoints and underrepresenting the viewpoints of women.

Use Appropriate Gestures

As we indicated earlier, gestures are an integral part of human communication. People who gesture freely think and convey their ideas more effectively than those who are more restrained. However, audience expectations and speaker preferences vary considerably based on the cultural context of the performance. Your nonverbal cues might be misunderstood, so try to anticipate and adjust to your audience based on the feedback they give you. For example, in many collective/high context cultures, direct eye contact might be intimidating instead of inviting. If direct eye contact seems to make an audience uncomfortable, look away or down at your notes. Similarly, adjust your delivery if your voice seems too loud, gestures too dramatic, or speaking aids too controversial.

Resources for Review and Skill Building

Many of these resources are supported by the Connections CD-ROM and free Online Learning Center website.

SUMMARY

This summary is organized around the questions found at the beginning of the chapter. See if you can answer them before reading the summary paragraphs.

1. How can I feel confident and at ease while I am speaking?

   Many people feel somewhat nervous about delivering a speech in public. This is a common and normal feeling and is called communication apprehension. Most speakers can control or manage this apprehension by preparing, relaxing, and visualizing success. Preparing and practicing your speech will help give you the necessary confidence to deliver a successful speech. Relaxing before you speak by walking, taking deep breaths, and exhaling slowly, or stretching your arms, neck, and back can also help control the symptoms of anxiety. Finally, visualize success by picturing yourself standing in front of an appreciative audience delivering a self-assured presentation.

2. What are four different types or modes of delivery?

   In manuscript speaking, the speaker reads from a script that is written out word for word. Manuscript speaking allows for precise word choice and exact time limits, but it limits the speaker's eye contact with the audience and use of gestures. In memorized speaking, the speaker writes out the speech, memorizes the content, and then delivers the speech word for word without the use of notes. Memorizing the manuscript allows speakers to establish consistent eye contact and use gestures. Memorizing a speech of any length takes a great deal of time and inexperienced speakers frequently forget what they want to say. Impromptu speaking is delivering a speech with limited preparation and notes. Impromptu speeches are often spontaneous and full of energy but often lack structure or development of main ideas. Extemporaneous speaking is the most versatile and useful mode of delivering a speech and involves careful preparation of content delivered with the help of a keyword outline. Although extemporaneous speakers practice their delivery thoroughly, they do not write the speech out word for word. Rather, they come up with the exact wording of the speech at the moment of delivery. Extemporaneous speakers can establish consistent eye contact, gesture effectively, and respond to audience reactions and situations.

3. What words should I use in the speech?

   You should use words that are clear, vivid, and conversational. Use concrete words that are simple and that the audience recognizes. Use metaphors and similes to create vivid pictures for your audience and avoid clichés. Talk directly to the audience, as if you are in a conversation, by using personal pronouns such as "we" and "I," rhetorical questions, and active verbs.

4. How can I use my voice, gestures, and speaking aids to enhance my delivery?

   Speak clearly so that the audience can understand your words and project your voice so that everyone in the audience can hear you. Vary the rate, volume, and inflection of your voice to add meaning and emphasis to your words. An effective speaking posture includes standing with both feet on the floor, squaring your body to the center of the audience, raising your head to establish eye contact, and gesturing with your hands above your waist. Look at the entire audience by constantly but slowly moving your gaze around the audience. Practice facial gestures that are consistent with the mood of the speech.

Speaking aids often help increase the audience's attention, maintain their interest in the speech, and recall ideas once the speech is over. Use speaking aids that add content to the speech. Practice using your speaking aid before the speech and if something goes wrong, don't panic. Computer presentation packages are increasingly used in professional presentations. They can be powerful speaking aids but could distract from the speech if used improperly. Be sure that you know the software thoroughly and use computer slides to enhance your message.

5. How can I deliver a responsible presentation?

   Speakers should use language and gestures that are culturally sensitive and inclusive. A responsible speaker should be aware of inequities in language and select words that are neutral. They should avoid the generic use of "man," including the general use of masculine pronouns, and balance male and female examples, quotes, and testimony. Responsible speakers adapt their gestures to the culture and feedback of the audience.

KEY TERMS

Test your understanding of these key terms by visiting the Connections CD-ROM and Online Learning Center website at www.mhhe.com/dobkinpace.

clichés 363
communication apprehension 354
enunciation 364
extemporaneous speaking 360
eye contact 368
imagery 362
impromptu speaking 359
inflection 364
manuscript speaking 358
memorized speaking 358
metaphor 362
pronunciation 363
rate 364
rhetorical question 363
simile 362
speaking aids 368
visualization 356
vocal pauses 360
vocal variety 365
volume 364

FOR FURTHER REFLECTION

/dobkinpace

Join a conversation about chapter concepts by visiting the Online Learning Center website at www.mhhe.com/dobkinpace

Earlier in the chapter, we said that varying your vocal rate and volume could be used to bring different emotions to the speaking situation. For instance, speaking quickly might indicate enthusiasm.

- How might you use your voice to communicate the following emotions: sincerity, confidentiality, urgency, annoyance, calmness, or caution?
- What possible emotions could your voice communicate with rapid but quiet delivery? Slow but loud?

BUILDING COMMUNICATION SKILLS

Practice facial gestures (with a group of friends or other members of your class) with this pantomime exercise. Write the following emotions, or others that you can think of, on small strips of paper. Write just one emotion per slip and place the folded papers in a cup or other container in the middle of the group. Members take turns selecting an emotion from the cup. They then display that emotion on their face while the other group members try to guess what is written on the paper. Here are some possible emotions (although the exercise works best if you think of additional possibilities): admiration, anxiety, awe, boredom, compassion, contempt, curiosity, defiance, desperation, determination, disappointment, disgust, eagerness, embarrassment, envy, exasperation, fascination, fear, frustration, greed, grief, guilt, hope, horror, impatience, indifference, indignation, joy, loneliness, mischief, panic, pity, pride, rage, regret, relief, respect, serenity, shock, suspicion, and sympathy.

- Which emotions were difficult to display? Why?
- How might hand gestures help you display each emotion?

NET WORK

Note: While all the URLs listed were current as of the printing of this book, these sites often change. Please check our website (www.mhhe.com/dobkinpace) for updates and hyperlinks to these exercises.

1. There are many sites on the Web that archive and display tongue twisters. Here are two additional sites that you could use to practice your enunciation and warm up for your speech: http://www.contestcen.com/tongue.htm and http://www.geocities.com/Athens/8136/tonguetwisters.html. There are also many sites on the Web that collect nursery rhymes. Here are two sites that you can access to work on vocal variety: http://www.zelo.com/family/nursery/ and http://www.nurseryrhymesonline.com/. How might saying nursery rhymes help you practice enunciation? Vocal variety? Control communication apprehension?
2. YouTube.com has many clips of people attempting tongue twisters. Watch these clips and try to say the tongue twister along with the person. Once you have mastered the twister, try to say it faster than the video clip.

MEDIA MOMENTS

In 1941 the radio was the dominant form of electronic communication, with television still some years away from mass influence. Radio broadcasts emphasized the voice as the main vehicle of communication. In 1941 the two most familiar, but distinctly different, voices on the radio were legendary CBS reporter Edward R. Murrow and President Franklin Delano Roosevelt. Murrow was head of CBS's London Bureau and reported live from the Battle of Britain twice each day. President Roosevelt was also a regular on radio with addresses to the nation and broadcasts called fireside chats. His style was conversational, intimate, and reassuring. Listen to audio samples of both Murrow and Roosevelt and analyze their delivery style. You can hear a sample of President Roosevelt's fireside chats at http://www.hpol.org/fdr/chat/. You can hear some of Murrow's newscasts at http://www.earthstation1.com/Edward R. Murrow WWII.html.

- How are these two voices different? Similar? How do the speakers use rate, volume, and inflection to communicate their personality and the meaning of their words?
- How does each speaker use pauses to add meaning to their delivery?

Speaking to Inform and Inspire

14

CHAPTER

On September 20, 2001, President George Bush addressed Congress and the American public in a televised response to the September 11 attacks on the World Trade Center in New York City and the Pentagon. President Bush had many objectives in crafting and presenting his speech: He needed to inform the American public about evidence linking Osama bin Laden to the attacks while distinguishing Muslims throughout the world from the "terrorists who are traitors to their own faith." The President also needed to announce a U.S. response to the attacks through a plan to "direct every resource at our command, every means to diplomacy, every tool of intelligence, every instrument of law enforcement, every financial influence, and every necessary weapon of war to the disruption and defeat of the global terror network." Finally, the President called the public to come together, uphold the values of America, support the victims, and continue praying: "After all that has just passed, all the lives taken, and all the possibilities and hopes that died with them, it is natural to wonder if America's future is one of fear. Some speak of an age of terror. I know that there are struggles ahead, and dangers to face. But this country will define our times, not be defined by them. As long as the United States is determined and strong, this will not be an age of terror; this will be an age of liberty, here and across the world" (Bush 2001).

QUESTIONS TO FOCUS YOUR READING

1. What are the different types of credibility, and why is credibility so important?
2. What are some types of informative speeches?
3. What are some of the most common occasions at which you might be asked to speak?
4. What are the obligations of a responsible person speaking well?

The task faced by President Bush following the terrorist attacks of September 11, 2001 was daunting. He addressed both an anxious and grieving public, and a group of political leaders ready to act. Although the situation was unique, President Bush's goals were similar to those faced by many public speakers. He needed to assess the situation and his audiences. He also needed to provide timely and reliable information. Finally, and perhaps most important for the occasion, he needed to respond to the emotions of his audiences and inspire them to have faith in their country.

As the title of this chapter suggests, public presentations can be crafted to do many things, from conveying information to raising spirits, and from increasing a speaker's social or political reputation to offering solace. Speaking in public can mean raising a hand to ask a question in class, answering questions in front of a television camera, or delivering a presentation to a large audience. You are likely to encounter a number of situations requiring an oral presentation in your career, such as giving reports to colleagues, introducing new group members or speakers, delivering executive briefings, presenting or accepting awards, explaining new procedures to other employees, answering complaints or objections, clarifying company policies, or explaining your work to a supervisor.

In all of these contexts, a few central concepts and skills apply. As previous chapters have explained, you need a clear goal, an organized presentation that moves your audience toward that goal, and a keen understanding of the situation. You now know that you need to analyze your audience, plan your presentation, organize your information, and practice delivering your speech. In this chapter we begin with the notion of speaker credibility and its importance to public speaking. We then look at informative and ceremonial speeches in specific contexts. After completing this chapter, you should be able to:

- Critically assess the credibility of others and know how to enhance your own.
- Understand and apply the distinctions between informative and persuasive speaking.
- Adapt to both formal and informal speaking situations.
- Apply public speaking skills in everyday interactions.

CREDIBILITY

Crafting a Credible Presentation

Our motivation to listen, understand, and communicate with others depends largely on how we judge people with whom we are communicating. As we noted in Chapter 12, when we perceive people as credible, or having expertise, strong character, and goodwill, we are more motivated to listen to them. Similarly, when we are giving a presentation, our words are more likely to be understood and accepted if our audience sees us as credible. We consider credible people to be knowledgeable, good-willed, and trustworthy.

> "The way to gain a good reputation is to try to be what you desire to appear."
>
> —Socrates, orator and philosopher

Trustworthiness is a critical part of credibility, and the level of trust we have in what another person says underlies all of our communication. We base trustworthiness on many things, such as our past experience with the person, the credentials the speaker appears to have, or something compelling that the speaker says. The salesperson or politician, for example, will not influence or be taken seriously by others if she or he is not believed. Similarly, students who do not respect their teacher are unlikely to learn much in the classroom. If we hear about a new medical breakthrough in curing cancer, we are more likely to believe it from a *New York Times* journalist than a supermarket tabloid writer. Credibility helps determine the degree of respect we show to others and the openness we have to new ideas.

There are many different ways to build and assess credibility. All are important to speakers and listeners, and once lost, they are difficult to regain. The following sections introduce three types of credibility: initial, derived, and enduring.

Initial Credibility

Although you cannot buy credibility or assume that you have it once you hit a magical age, there are ways to both enhance your own believability and evaluate the credibility of others. As a student, there are a few topics about which you might have **initial credibility,** or the credibility you bring to a situation by virtue of your reputation or accomplishments. Political leaders, popular professors, and many star athletes all bring a history of prior experience and knowledge with them and therefore have high initial credibility, even if their experiences do not match the topic they have been asked to address. You might be curious about hearing a celebrity such as Michael J. Fox speak on campus based primarily on his reputation as an actor, rather than any interest in the subject of Parkinson's disease with which Fox is afflicted. In your own classroom, there might be students who stand out based on the way they have handled class assignments or responded to the professor.

initial credibility
The credibility speakers bring to a situation by virtue of their reputation or accomplishments.

Initial credibility can be powerful, because it gives a speaker an advantage in gaining the attention and trust of an audience. Anything that adds to an audience's positive impression of a speaker at the outset is important. Think about your choice of topic and speech structure, your dress for the occasion, and the way you move to the front of the room. If you are wearing casual clothes, such as sweatpants and a T-shirt, and shuffle in front of people, your audience will likely see you as lacking self-confidence and interest in your speech.

The way a speaker is presented to an audience can also build or damage initial credibility. False information, hesitant delivery, or an introduction presented by someone who wants to leave the stage as soon as possible can all damage the initial credibility of a speaker. The importance and expertise of the speaker are also signaled by the amount of advance planning, the level of publicity, the way the speaker arrives at an event, and the degree of decorum surrounding the occasion. Think about the impression created when an audience is asked to rise as a speaker enters the room, such as a judge in a court of law. Audience members show respect and acknowledge a speaker's credibility by being punctual and attentive.

Derived Credibility

For the speaker who doesn't walk into a situation with fanfare and immediate audience recognition, developing credibility is particularly important. **Derived credibility** refers to the credibility created by the content of a message and the manner in which it is presented. We introduced this idea in our previous discussion of supporting materials for speeches. Ideas that are well supported and clearly presented add considerably to a speaker's credibility. Conversely, even the most popular or highly regarded individuals who give a poorly planned presentation can lose much of their initial credibility. Public figures have long been aware of the need for adequate preparation. William Manchester, a biographer of

derived credibility
The credibility, or belief, in a speaker that is created by the content of the message and the manner in which it is presented.

Winston Churchill, reported that the British prime minister and leader in World War II spent an average of seven hours to prepare a forty-minute speech. Today, the expectations are even higher. Professional speechwriters spend an average of 40 hours to prepare a twenty-minute speech, or two hours for every one minute of time spent talking (Gray 1999).

For speakers who lack status or recognition among their audience, derived credibility is particularly important. Even college students who are well known and liked by their peers enhance their credibility substantially with presentations that are thoroughly researched, clear, and adapted to their audience. For instance, one student gave an informative speech about the Grammy Awards for musical excellence just before the program aired. She previewed the better-known categories and the nominees for each award. Her mother was a successful agent for many of these same musicians, so the student showed autographed pictures of some of the stars and related personal anecdotes about others. The audience was fascinated with this inside look at the music industry and the way the speaker presented the information. For the rest of the semester, the class asked the speaker's opinion about music-related topics and inquired about the latest industry gossip. It was clear that this speaker enjoyed great credibility after giving her speech.

Think about the range of source materials and examples available to you and personal knowledge you may have about the topic, the use of a *coherent* and memorable structure, presenting your topic with your audience in mind, and polishing your delivery, all of which enhance your derived credibility.

Enduring Credibility

enduring credibility
The impression of credibility that remains with your audience.

Finally, the impression you create based on your reputation and presentation can result in **enduring credibility,** or the impression of believability that remains with your audience. When you finish speaking, people should be left with an appreciation of your ideas and high regard for you as an individual. Although we sometimes like to separate people's character from what they say, the two are intertwined. We tend to like people who are energetic, friendly, honorable, assertive, and empathetic. We also like people who like and care about us—we trust those who have our "best interests at heart." For example, whom in your life do you trust most? Your answer would probably include a mix of close friends, family members, teachers, and others who want you to succeed in life and be happy. Conversely, you probably do not trust people who have "their own interests at heart," such as telemarketers. In your speech, you can build enduring credibility by showing the audience that you are looking out for their interests, not yours. Recognize shared interests and beliefs, adapt to your audience, provide sound information, and deliver your speech with confidence. Credibility, once again, comes back to both believability and trust.

Think It Over

HOW DO YOU EVALUATE CREDIBILITY?

Which speakers do you find to be initially credible? How much does the topic of their speech matter to your perception of their credibility? Which kind of credibility is most important to you as a listener? As a speaker? If your audience doesn't know you, how might you build initial credibility? Derived? Enduring?

Charisma

John F. Kennedy is widely regarded as one of the most charismatic speakers of the past century.

Some individuals seem to possess so much credibility that no matter what they say or how they look, they will be believed and followed. Scholars have spent considerable time and effort trying to understand that "extra spark" that seems to characterize some speakers. When talking about a particularly appealing and dynamic speaker, we often use the term **charisma,** the ability to influence others in specific situations through personal dynamism, likability, and vision. Charismatic speakers are both highly credible and share a special relationship with the audience based on a social need or crisis. Public figures such as former U.S. President Bill Clinton, civil rights and spiritual leader Dr. Martin Luther King, Jr., and the British Princess Diana have all been characterized as charismatic. Even Jesse Ventura, a former professional wrestler, has been credited with winning the governor's seat of Minnesota partly due to his charisma.

charisma
The ability to influence others in specific situations through personal dynamism, likability, and vision.

Charisma, like credibility, is not a quantity of something or a quality that can be entirely learned or practiced. Many of us have some measure of *dynamism,* likability, and vision. We may become particularly animated when talking to young children, intensely motivational when addressing a team or club, or exceptionally charming when conversing with others at social events. However, charisma is more than a set of personality characteristics. It also emerges from relationships with others and arises during crises, particularly in cultures where collective identity and group action are important. For example, in the weeks after George W. Bush's inauguration as president in 2001, the tenuous conditions under which he was elected followed him into the Oval Office. After the September 11 attacks, however, some people thought President Bush showed charismatic leadership during a moment of true crisis.

Charisma attracts attention partly because of the power it brings to the individuals who possess it. Some of the most famous charismatic leaders have been capable of motivating others to commit atrocities such as mass murder, especially those who have risen to power in times of stress and have carried nationalism to extreme and disastrous ends. In the 1930s Adolf Hitler captivated his audiences with his personality and vision of a new Germany. Jim Jones, the religious leader of the People's Temple who in 1978 brought over 900 followers to their deaths in Jonestown, Guyana, has also been called charismatic. Even Yugoslav President Slobodan Milosevic, indicted by the United Nations International War Crimes Tribunal as being responsible for the rape, torture, and murder of non-Serbs, arguably possesses charisma. Each of these leaders combined personal qualities such as dynamism, attractiveness, charm, and conviction with articulate and persuasive ways of responding to crises felt by their audiences. Unfortunately, their skills and character were directed toward destroying others. Like all forms of credibility, charisma can be turned toward visions of progress that either empower or destroy.

TABLE 14-1 Cultivating Qualities of Credibility and Charisma as a Speaker

Sociability	We are attracted to optimists, to people who can look on the bright side of life. A positive, supportive, confident outlook is contagious and will help you deal successfully with others. Enhancing your sociability can be as simple as keeping an upbeat attitude about your presentation and delivering it with enthusiasm.
Competence	We appreciate people who know what they are talking about, so do your research and be proud to show that you have discovered things worth sharing with other people.
Extroversion	Credible and charismatic people are bold and assertive. In their delivery, they are powerful, confident, and dynamic. Try to exhibit good eye contact and gestures, be as fluent and eloquent as you can, and be expressive and energetic.
Composure	Enthusiastic people can get carried away; composure keeps them in balance. Do your best to maintain your poise and confidence, even if you feel uneasy or challenged by questions from the audience.
Character	Many people credit Aristotle with defining positive character as good sense, goodwill, and good morals. Others have described character more narrowly as "commitment with passion" (Weaver 1996) and the marks of community commitments that are recognizable in one's speech (Gronbeck 1997). Credible speakers demonstrate character through their commitment to succeed on behalf of others and the passion they bring to achieving their goals.

Charisma might seem easier to recognize than cultivate. There are ways, however, that you can build your own charisma and use it toward noble ends, whether to help others, provide leadership, or motivate people toward positive change. Charisma depends on context, message, and presentation, and who you are needs to shine through all of these. Table 14-1 lists some characteristics of charisma and credibility that can be cultivated (Weaver 1996). Think about which of the characteristics—sociability, competence, extroversion, composure, and character—would be easiest for you to improve, and which are most important to you as a listener.

"Knowledge is power, but enthusiasm pulls the switch."

—Richard Weaver, scholar

Types of Informative Speeches

Perhaps the most common kind of presentation you will be asked to give is one of informing the audience. Information of all kinds is readily available from many sources, such as libraries, news media, the Internet, and personal contacts, so the task of the speaker is to provide information in a way that makes it uniquely interesting and useful for the audience. There are many different types of informative speeches, and features of each type are often blended in a given presentation. We will focus on four of the most common ways to inform an audience: through speeches to describe, demonstrate, explain, and narrate.

FIGURE 14-1 CONCEPT MAP: TYPES OF INFORMATIVE SPEECHES

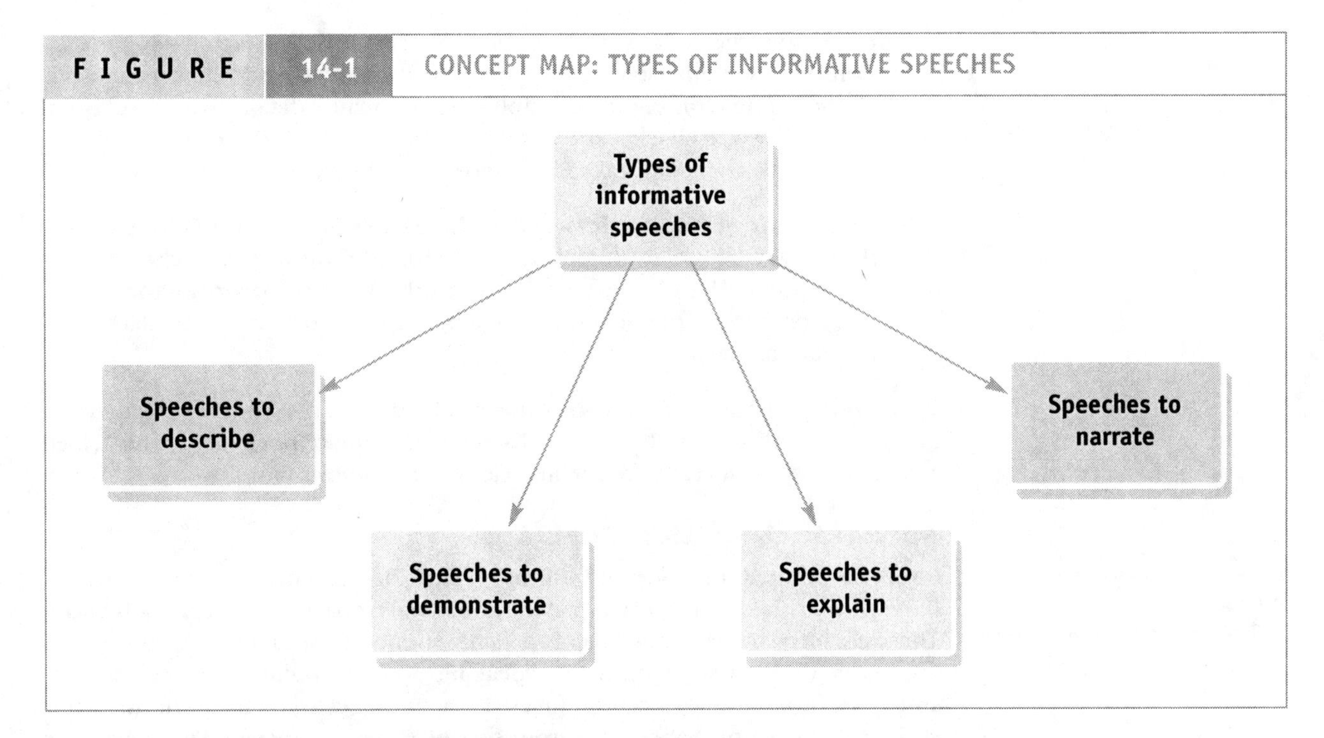

As you look at each of the following types of informative speeches, keep in mind that your general purpose in each is to offer knowledge and convey information or ideas. Conveying information clearly and in a way that is easy for audiences to understand and follow requires clear structure, ample supporting materials, and well-rehearsed and effective delivery. Good speeches often draw from elements of more than one speech type, so defining an informative speech as one of description or explanation is largely a matter of emphasis. Informative speaking is much like teaching, and the best speeches take into account the different learning styles of audience members. Some of us learn best when we hear or see information, others need an emotional or "feeling" connection to the speech, and still others grasp ideas best when they can participate in some way or act on what they have learned. For each of the speech types, we will also discuss ways that thinking, feeling, and acting can be incorporated in each of the specific purposes.

"The mediocre teacher tells. The good teacher explains. The superior teacher demonstrates. The great teacher inspires."

—William Arthur Ward, author

Speeches that Describe

This type of informative speech is arguably the most straightforward. **Speeches that describe** provide details of an object or concept. You might have had a course in composition that required you to write a paragraph about an object, such as a piece of fruit or an animal, in ways that create pictures in the minds of readers. Similarly, the speech of description provides the details that bring ideas or objects to life. A speech on travel in New England, for instance, might describe the colors of the seasons, the types of regional architecture, or the best places for fine dining. In each case, clear structure, accuracy, and vividness of language will help listeners create pictures in their minds.

speech that describes
A presentation that provides details of an object or concept.

The best speeches of description not only provide accurate and concrete information, but also help listeners form emotional connections to objects or ideas. A description of fine dining, for example, should include details that make listeners feel like they are sharing the experience of the meal. Rather than saying a restaurant serves chocolate cake, the speaker might say:

> One of the signature desserts at Mimi's Restaurant consists of a three-layer chocolate torte topped with a dollop of white chocolate mousse. The chef then drizzles raspberry puree over the torte and floats fresh berries in a surrounding moat of white and dark chocolate.

To support the learning strategies mentioned above, the speaker might even bring in a sample of food. In this way, listeners have the opportunity to think, feel, and act in ways that reinforce the main idea of the speech.

Speeches that Demonstrate

speech that demonstrates
A presentation that shows audiences how to do something.

Speeches that demonstrate inform by showing audiences how to do something, such as fold a flag, use a particular software program, or repair a bicycle. These are often the easiest kinds of speeches for novice speakers to give, because acting out a skill or working with a speaking aid helps them feel more comfortable in front of an audience and gives them an object to focus on during their speech. You have probably seen professors give demonstrations. The science or math professor who completes calculations or performs experiments in front of the class is giving a speech of demonstration, as is the instructor who edits videotape in a television production class. In each case, the speech of demonstration needs to include more than verbal instruction. Listeners must also see a process in action, understand what it feels like to participate, and, if possible, try the activity themselves. For example, a speech on bowling might not take place at a bowling alley, but even in a classroom, listeners can have the opportunity to hold a bowling ball and learn to correctly position their fingers. Be creative in ways that allow your audience to participate in your demonstration.

Speeches that Explain

speech that explains
A presentation that teaches about or clarifies an event or development.

Speeches that explain teach about or clarify an event or development. Like speeches that demonstrate, those that explain sometimes walk audiences through a process. Speeches that explain may include demonstrations, but they also offer an analysis of causes and effects. To explain something well, you need to understand your topic well enough to break it down into parts and put it into words and a sequence or structure that your audience can understand.

You might want to explain something remote from your audience, such as the causes of famine in sub-Saharan Africa or the genetic coding process that makes cloning possible, or something closer to home, such as steps in building your credit rating or your university's process of making residence hall assignments. In every case, you need to make thoughtful decisions about how much information to include and the level of technical language or jargon your audience is likely to understand. The problem of information overload is particularly common when speakers know so much about a topic that they have difficulty choosing what to emphasize for their listeners.

Consider the following opening for a speech about global warming. The speaker has gathered considerable scientific data and has recently completed a seminar on atmospheres and climate.

> Just because atmospheric greenhouse gases are natural doesn't mean they're good for you. Over the past 100 years, atmospheric concentrations of carbon dioxide have increased nearly 30 percent, methane concentrations have more than doubled, and nitrous oxide concentrations have risen by about 15 percent (Global Warming: Climate 2002, April 12). Today I want to tell you about estimates for further emissions from human activities and the effects of increasing concentrations of greenhouse gases.

This opening for a speech to explain is concise, but it assumes too much audience knowledge about global warming. Some listeners will probably wonder what greenhouse gases are, and others will be thinking about what constitutes methane and nitrous oxide. The speaker might be more effective by saying:

> If you've ever tried to grow a plant in a greenhouse, you know what happens on a sunny day. As the sun comes through the glass, it warms up the plants, and heat and moisture are trapped inside. That's just what's happening to our planet. The gases from our everyday activities, such as driving the car, heating the house, and turning computers on at the office, are acting like the glass panels of a greenhouse, trapping the heat of the earth, changing global climate patterns, and contributing to global warming.

This version provides less of the technical information that might be appropriate later in the speech and opens with the audience's previous level of knowledge in mind.

Speeches of explanation usually rely heavily on the "thinking" side of audiences, and it can be hard to incorporate "feeling" and "doing." For example, think about a speech on credit ratings. You might give a lengthy explanation about financial forms, ratings systems, and strategies for managing personal finances. However, you might also mention the anxiety produced in the credit application process or the psychological burden of carrying too much debt. You can also give your audience helpful ways to use the information, such as providing phone numbers for the major credit rating bureaus and explaining ways to correct false reports. Like other types of informative presentations, speeches that explain are best when they give audiences different ways to understand the information.

> "Tell me and I'll forget. Show me and I may not remember. Involve me and I'll understand."
>
> —Native American Proverb

Speeches that Narrate

Everyone appreciates good stories. **Speeches that narrate** use an extended story to provide information. Presenting a story in a way that makes a point can be more difficult than it sounds. Bible stories, parables, and fables all do this well; without recounting the story, you probably know the point to be learned from the "boy who cried wolf." You might have a particularly humorous or embarrassing incident in your past that you know is entertaining. Is there a lesson to be learned from your experience?

speech that narrates
A presentation that uses an extended story to make a statement.

Some companies have begun to use the narrative form as an advertisement for products. For example, the Discover card launched a 30-minute "storymercial"—"Give Me Some Credit"—about a family on vacation. This minidrama shows all of the ways that family members can use the card. Although it looks like entertainment programming, the story clearly has a message. The "storymercial" is just

Stories that make a point are among the most memorable kinds of presentations.
© Getty Images

another illustration of the ways narrative can be used to convey a message beyond the story itself (Cleland 1996). Narratives can be particularly good ways to engage the emotions of audiences; they are less effective at conveying a significant amount of new information. If you choose to use this type of informative speech, work hard to ensure that your message is clear, tied directly to the narrative, and relevant to your audience.

Many topics can be approached as speeches of narration, explanation, demonstration, or description. Table 14-2 illustrates how the same topic might look using different types of informative speaking.

Regardless of the type of informative speech, the basic rules of preparing (Chapter 11), organizing (Chapter 12), and delivery (Chapter 13) apply. The "Applying Communication Concepts" box gives an example of the way an eight-minute student speech to inform might be developed. As you read it, think about strategies that might work well and ways that the speech might be improved.

TABLE 14-2 Examples of Informative Speech Topics

TOPIC	DESCRIBE	DEMONSTRATE	EXPLAIN	NARRATE
Swimming	Types of competition, swim programs	Different strokes: freestyle, butterfly, breast, and back	The physiology of swimming	Biography of an Olympic swimmer such as Janet Evans
Dog obedience	Approaches to training	How to teach a basic trick such as "fetching"	Dog psychology	The story of rescue dogs at the World Trade Center disaster
Bilingual education	Two different approaches in bilingual education: immersion and intervention	How to adapt English-only lessons for native Spanish speakers	Advantages and disadvantages of immersion	The story of an immigrant learning to cope in U.S. schools
Genetic research	Recent advances or ethical concerns	How genes are coded	The process of cell reproduction	A dramatic reading of a section from *Brave New World* or the story of Dolly, the first cloned sheep

Applying Communication Concepts

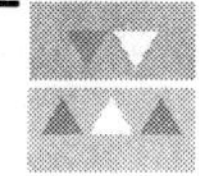

SAMPLE SPEECH TO INFORM

This student speech on windmills incorporates many of the skills presented in your text. See if you can identify the main parts of the speech (introduction, body, conclusion), the speaker's goal, and the structure of the speech.

Who is the great general standing eight faces strong in the teeth of the wild winds? He has eight masts that turn, wearing a hat at the top and standing on a needle below. His two ends can revolve at your wish, and make the waters come and go, wherever you like.

Can you guess the answers to this 13th century Chinese riddle? The windmill, that great general standing strong in the teeth of the wild winds, has battled its way into the 21st century. Though the windmill may seem to be an invention of the past, America is presently placing increasing importance on this energy source. Mark Fischetti reported in the *Scientific American* that wind turbines generate 30 percent more energy now than they did a decade ago, and federal tax credits are an incentive to citizens who want to diversify their energy sources.

For hundreds of years, humans have harnessed the wind to do their bidding. To understand the manner and devices by which the wind is captured, we can follow the development of the windmill from its origins, then discuss domestic uses of wind power, and finally explore recent innovations in wind technology.

Though the exact birth date of the windmill is unknown, scientists and historians have some specific ideas about its origin. According to Volta Torrey in his book *Wind Catchers,* the Arabs seem to have recognized the power of the wind sooner than their contemporaries.

From Persia, knowledge of the windmill spread throughout Europe and Asia. Historians such as Walter Minchinton, professor of economic history at Exeter University, explains that windmills were common in Europe and China by the beginning of the 13th century. By the 1500s, windmills had reclaimed lowlands in Holland while Don Quixote attacked mythical windmills in Spain. Don Quixote's foolishness in fighting windmills may be more understandable than most people realize, for Spanish windmills differed significantly from the friendly, picturesque Dutch windmills. The "thirty or forty monstrous giants" looked like squat stone towers, with cone-shaped roofs that resembled helmets and twirling arms that nearly touched the ground.

In contrast, Dutch windmills were more pleasing to the eye. These romantic windmills were built so the blades of the windmill would face prevailing winds. In constructing the windmills, the Dutch placed the blades in a wooden box, or "buck," which was mounted on a sturdy post. A tailpole extended to the ground, which allowed the buck to be rotated to meet the strongest winds.

By the 1600s both the Spanish and Dutch windmills appeared on America's East Coast. As with any new invention, however, Americans were not satisfied with the European model. Abandoning the short, squat types of windmills, Americans modified the blades, added many short spokes, and placed the rotor on tall, spindly legs, creating what is now called the American wind turbine.

As acceptance of the windmill grew, so did the importance of wind power to Americans. By the turn of the 20th century, wind power was second only to wood as a basic energy source. However, the perfection of the steam engine marked the decline of the windmill industry in the United States. The final blow was delivered in the mid-1930s, when the Rural Electrification Administration brought low-cost power from town and regional generators to homeowners. Only recently, as a result of skyrocketing fuel and electricity costs, Americans have turned back to the windmill as a domestic energy source. Many homeowners, especially those living in rural areas, are turning to wind power as a safe, clean, domestic energy source.

Before a household windmill is installed, three major factors must be taken into consideration: site selection, functional need, and cost. Site selection helps determine whether the strength of the winds in any given area is sufficient to generate electricity. Generally, for a home windmill, the wind must blow steadily at nine miles per hour for thirty seconds before the rotor reaches its cut-in speed—the point at which the rotor turns enough revolutions each minute to trigger a linkup with its generator. When the wind drops below nine miles per hour, the home-size machine goes out of gear.

(continued)

Applying Communication Concepts

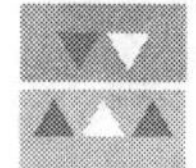

SAMPLE SPEECH TO INFORM *(continued)*

You can determine wind velocity fairly simply. Wind speed ranges from eight to twelve miles per hour if leaves and twigs are in constant motion, or the corners of a light flag are flapping. It can take up to a year of wind monitoring to gather enough data to estimate whether a windmill will work on a particular site. If a site is adequate, a second major step must be taken: a functional survey to determine the needs of the household and the best wind system to fulfill those needs. If you only want enough energy to operate a few lights and run a TV or stereo for a few hours, a homemade windmill could satisfy your needs, However, if you add a refrigerator and a washing machine to your load, you are out of the do-it-yourself category and into the commercial windmill market.

There are three basic commercial wind systems available to the homeowner. First, the windmill can work in conjunction with a utility power line. The utility power provides backup electricity when the windmill drops below the cut-in speed. Second, a battery storage system can be installed to store unused energy and provide backup electricity, as in the first system. Or third, if you live in an area with especially turbulent or high-velocity wind, you can link your windmill power to a utility grid. When the windmill produces more power than is used in the home, law requires the utility company to buy that electricity from you at the same price at which the company sells the electricity.

All three systems probably sound acceptable as home energy sources. However, one major obstacle still remains to installing a domestic windmill: the cost of current wind systems. Costs of the sleek, new wind turbines start at several thousand dollars. That cost might sound prohibitive, but if you're lucky enough to produce extra energy for a utility company, you might even make a considerable profit.

The increasing use and production of windmills has led to many recent innovations in wind power systems. A company in Vancouver, British Columbia, has started testing sites for the first offshore wind farm in North America. In our own country, wind farming is becoming a viable business. For example, Dan Juhl runs a "farm" of 17 big wind generators outside Woodstock, a town of 132 people in southwestern Minnesota. Mr. Juhl teaches others how to become wind farmers and designs self-sufficient energy projects for homes and businesses. Mr. Juhl helps farmers arrange financing, permits, and construction for their own generators and arranges contracts for power sales to utility companies. Wind farmers in his area generate enough electricity each year to replace nearly 3,800 railroad cars full of coal.

The windmill is the answer not only to a 13th-century Chinese riddle, but to some of our current energy problems. As Abraham Lincoln once stated: "Of all the forces of nature, I should think the wind contains the greatest amount of power."

ASK YOURSELF:

1. How effective is the structure of this speech?
2. How does the speaker attempt to adapt to the audience?
3. Does the speaker use adequate source material?
4. How might visual aids contribute to this speech?
5. How might the speech be more effective?

Sources: M. Fischetti, "Turn, Turn, Turn," *Scientific American*, July 2002, pp. 86–88; R. Franklin, "Woodstock Man's Wind Farm Helps Farmers, Environment," *Associated Press* newswires, July 13, 2002; M. Gulvas, "B.C. Company Propels Bid for Wind Farm: Plan Includes 50 Offshore Power-Generating Towers, Each 70 Metres High," *Delta Optimist*, July 11, 2002, p. B3; W. Minchinton, "Wind Power," *History Today*, March 1980, pp. 31–37; V. Torrey, *Wind-Catchers: American Windmills of Yesterday and Tomorrow*. (Brattleboro, VT: Stephen Greene Press, 1977).

Watch a video of a student giving a speech to inform (CD Clip 14.1).

Speaking at Special Occasions

Every culture or group has its own rituals that require its members to speak in a *patterned* way. Although these special occasions are part of our lives, we rarely consider how to treat them as communicators until we are forced into a situation where we are asked to speak. Think about graduations, weddings, award ceremonies, banquets, and funerals. Each of these events includes at least one pivotal address that brings people together and celebrates shared experiences or values. Someone will be asked to make a statement that sets the tone, addresses the occasion, and advances a central idea. There is a good chance that you will be asked to play that role at some time in the future.

> "Make sure you have finished speaking before your audience has finished listening."
>
> —Dorothy Sarnoff, author, public speaking teacher

There are at least five basic types of special occasion speeches: the speech of introduction, acceptance speech, speech of tribute, after-dinner speech, and speech of inspiration.

Speeches of Introduction

speech of introduction A presentation that gives the audience information about the key speaker.

A **speech of introduction** often opens a public presentation by giving the audience information about the key speaker. For example, suppose that your professor invites a prominent member of the business community to address the class. Since the person is a guest to your classroom, she or he requires an introduction. Your professor might introduce this guest speaker with a few brief comments about his or her qualifications and the topic of the presentation. Similarly, many of the special occasion speeches we discuss in this chapter, such as speeches of tribute, after-dinner speeches, and speeches of inspiration, are preceded by speeches of introduction. Also, when several speakers appear on the same program, short introductions of each speaker act as a transition from one person to the next. In each of these situations, a speech of introduction should facilitate the main speaker's goal by establishing the mood and expectations of the situation. When introducing a speaker, follow these simple tips:

Make it brief. Speeches of introduction should be one to three minutes in length. Most introductions can be successfully accomplished in one minute. The more important the occasion and the speaker, the longer the introduction. But remember, four or five minute introductions are too long even for important occasions.

Connect the speaker, topic, and audience. The three questions that you should answer for your audience are:

- Who is the speaker? Get to know the main speaker before the speech. Know the person's name and how to pronounce it. Ask if there is a title that you should use or qualifications you should mention to the audience.
- What is the topic? Announce the title or briefly mention the topic of the speech. Again, it is a good idea to discuss your introduction with the main speaker and ask what he or she would like said about the topic.
- Why should the audience listen? Give the audience a strong motive for listening ("Class, listen carefully to our guest today because not only is she interesting, but I am going to test you on the information") (Wallace 2002).

Applying Communication Concepts

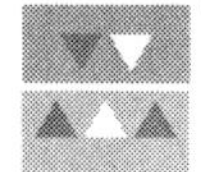

RECOGNIZING GOOD SPEECHES OF INTRODUCTION

In this example of a speech of introduction, the president of the Communication Studies Club is introducing a guest speaker to the other members at their regularly scheduled meeting:

My name is Natalia Bertsch, and I am president of the Communication Studies Club. About a month ago I went to our career development center to learn how to write a résumé. The person who helped me is tonight's guest speaker, Sue Kelly. I was so impressed with Sue's knowledge and help that I asked her to speak to the entire club. I know that you will like her as much as I do. Sue has a degree in psychology from State University and a master's degree in educational counseling from the University of the Northwest. She started working at our university 15 years ago and since then has helped thousands of graduates find employment. She tells me that she reads between 100 and 200 résumés each year and talks to about that many prospective employers. If you listen carefully, Sue can help you find a good job. Tonight, Sue will speak on the topic "Writing a Winning Résumé." Please join me in welcoming Sue Kelly [applause].

ASK YOURSELF:

1. In what ways is Natalia's speech of introduction effective?
2. Is there anything you would change about this introduction?

Keep the audience focused on the speaker, not you. Your primary objective should be to facilitate the speaker's goals rather than trying to impress the audience. Avoid clichés such as "Our speaker needs no introduction," "It gives me great pleasure to introduce," or "Without further ado." Try to be original and fresh—otherwise the audience may tune out even before the main speaker begins. Mention your name and connection to the speaker or event if the audience does not already know who you are. Speak extemporaneously. Use a keyword outline to help you remember facts and information, but do not read the speech. Establish eye contact and show enthusiasm for the speaker.

The "Applying Communication Concepts" box provides an example of a student speaker making an introduction. See if the speaker follows any of the guidelines for a good introduction.

Acceptance Speeches

acceptance speech
A brief statement made upon the receipt of an award, gift, or special honor.

The **acceptance speech** is a brief statement made upon the receipt of an award, gift, or special honor. Perhaps you can recall a film actor making a memorable statement upon receiving an Oscar (or more likely, you are familiar with the jokes about long lists of people whom the actor wishes to thank). The best acceptance speeches fulfill the following functions:

Acknowledge those who supported you. Acceptance speeches are important places for thanking those who have helped you achieve recognition. Think about people who have been instrumental in helping you become successful or have given you moral support. If you are presented an award and asked to speak, think about taking the opportunity to use your communication skills and give something back to the people who have acknowledged you.

Honor the occasion. The best acceptance speeches also honor the occasion by addressing the values for which the award stands and using language that is appropriate for the occasion. In addition to giving a sincere thank-you to those who helped you, explain how you hope to exemplify the qualities that the award seeks to honor, or how you respect the achievements of others who received the award before you.

Some acceptance speeches stand out for their sincerity and contribution to the overall purpose of the occasion without being overbearing or self-indulgent. In 2004, when Tim Robbins accepted the Best Actor Oscar for his portrayal in *Mystic River* of an adult haunted by the sexual abuse in his childhood, he ended his acceptance speech with a plea of sympathy for victims of abuse: "If you are out there and are a person who has had that tragedy befall you, there is no shame and no weakness in seeking help and counseling. It is sometimes the strongest thing you can do to stop the cycle of violence." Similarly, in receiving his Best Actor Oscar for his portrayal in *Philadelphia* (1993) of a person suffering from AIDS, Tom Hanks highlighted the plight and sacrifice of people with the illness.

> The streets of heaven are too crowded with angels. We know their names. . . . They finally rest in the warm embrace of the gracious creator of us all, a healing embrace that cools their fevers, that clears their skin, and allows their eyes to see the simple, self-evident commonsense truth that is made manifest by the benevolent creator of us all.

"It has been a long journey to this moment."

—Sidney Poitier, Academy Award Winner, Best Actor, 1964

Speeches of Tribute

speech of tribute A presentation that includes eulogies, toasts, and other speeches that commemorate special events such as national holidays.

The **speech of tribute** includes eulogies, toasts, and other speeches that commemorate special events such as weddings, birthdays, or national holidays. They are similar to introductions and presentations of awards in that they honor individuals and their accomplishments. Rather than leading to another speaker, however, these are "stand alone" speeches that recognize special events, celebrate accomplishments, and honor the enduring values exemplified by individuals. Think about someone you admire and respect, and then spend a moment considering how that person has earned your admiration. We tend to celebrate great sacrifice, overcoming hardship, perseverance, service to humanity, and purity of motives. If you think about someone who has had a substantial impact on you, that person probably exemplifies some of these characteristics. A speech of tribute develops these qualities and adds a human element, such as a personal anecdote, so that audience members can truly appreciate and honor the subject of the speech.

Toasts. The most common speech of tribute is the toast. You might be asked to give a toast for a favorite coach at an awards ceremony, a best friend at an engagement or wedding party, or a relative at an anniversary or birthday. Toasts are one of the few speech types that should be memorized. They need to be brief, inspirational, and carefully worded. The best toasts are small speeches of tribute; they refer to the occasion, honor an individual, and leave the audience in the appropriate mood for the event.

Eulogies. A far more difficult but no less common tribute is the eulogy. Eulogies have two purposes: to honor the dead and to comfort the living.

The best toasts honor an individual, refer to an occasion, and convey a mood.

"We have gathered here not merely to pay tribute, but to refresh our spirits and stir our hearts for the tasks which lie ahead."

—John F. Kennedy, former U.S. president

Although they are perhaps the most difficult speech of tribute to make, they are no less important. In reviewing a book of eulogies, David Shribman (1997) in the *Wall Street Journal* wrote that eulogies "are about life, not death, and a well-written eulogy is like a well lived life: It informs, enriches, and ennobles those of us left behind." In addition to conferring honor, they create an emotional connection with the audience that often mingles pain and grief with poetic language and inspiration. This connection is created in one sentence from W. E. B. Du Bois's eulogy to his infant son Burghardt, who died because no white doctor would treat him. Du Bois said: "I saw his breath beat quicker and quicker, pause, and then his little soul leapt like a star that travels in the night and left a world of darkness in its train" (Shribman, p. A16).

To illustrate the functions of a eulogy, consider these sections from President Bill Clinton's (1996) eulogy for former congresswoman Barbara Jordan. He began by personalizing her and introducing themes of perseverance and dignity.

> Through the sheer force of the truth she spoke, the poetry of her words, and the power of her voice, Barbara always stirred our national conscience. She did it as a legislator, a member of Congress, a teacher, a citizen.
>
> Perhaps more than anything else in the last few years, for those of us who had the privilege of being around her, she did it with the incredible grace and good humor and dignity with which she bore her physical misfortunes. No matter what, there was always the dignity. When Barbara Jordan talked, we listened.

Clinton continued to draw from Jordan's own words and those of people who had known and honored her.

> As Ann Richards said, if we're all going to tell the truth today, Barbara Jordan made every one of us stand a little straighter, speak a little clearer, and be a little stronger. She took to heart what her Grandpa Patten told her when she was a little girl. "You just trot your own horse, and don't get into the same rut as everyone else." Well, she sure trotted her own horse, and she made her own path wide and deep.

Like all good speeches of tribute, Clinton combined the commemoration of an event with recognition of a particular individual and the creation of a mood that uplifts the audience. If you are asked to give a speech of tribute, such as a toast or eulogy, consider the request an honor, and use the opportunity to give your best effort back to your audience.

After-Dinner Speeches

A fourth type of special occasion speech, the **after-dinner speech,** is far removed from the gravity of a tribute, although it also can recognize the accomplishments of an individual or group. The after-dinner speech entertains or enlightens in an amusing way. It can be given after any meal; some groups with lunch meetings like to end their meal with an address that leaves them thinking but also lighthearted. Because of its reliance on humor, this kind of speech poses its own challenges. Like a good speech of narration, the speech should have a central idea to convey, but the language, pacing, and style all need to appeal to an audience that is seated at tables, finishing a meal, engaged in casual conversation, and possibly getting sleepy. After-dinner speeches often balance humor and seriousness. One particularly difficult challenge for the after-dinner speaker is to find a way to use humor that is both funny and appropriate for the audience. The "Exploring Communication Concepts" box invites you to consider standards for using humor in public presentations.

after-dinner speech
A presentation that entertains or enlightens in an amusing way.

Speeches of Inspiration

The **inspirational speech** shares much with the persuasive speech because it aims to motivate listeners and arouse their passions. We hear inspirational

inspirational speech
A presentation that aims to motivate listeners and arouse their passions.

Exploring Communication Concepts

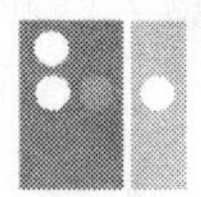

WHAT CONSTITUTES DESIRABLE HUMOR?

Audiences usually appreciate truly funny speeches. Determining what kind of humor will work, however, is not always easy. University students often find the following types of humor desirable: "uses good-natured jests to put others as ease," "uses intellectual wordplay," "prefers recounting comedic episodes from real life to telling jokes," and "finds humor in the everyday behavior of animals." Undesirable behaviors include: explaining jokes after telling them, laughing before finishing jokes, taking delight in ethnic jokes, joking about the imperfections of others, and using bathroom humor (Craik 1997).

The appropriateness of humor varies based on culture as well. For example, whereas the friendly use of "put-downs," "ranks," or "snaps" are common in African-American cultures, people from Africa or the West Indies often find such humor to be offensive. When the cultural backgrounds of speakers and their audiences differ, audiences may view the use of humor as insincere (Maples, Dupey, Torres-Rivera, Phan, Vereen, and Garrett 2001).

ASK YOURSELF:

1. What standards for the use of humor in speeches would you endorse?
2. What behaviors do you find funny that might not be appreciated by others?

speeches at staff meetings, retreats, locker room pep talks, and in more formal contexts, such as commencements and keynote addresses for conferences. Good inspirational speeches make a connection to the audience and are presented with a particularly enthusiastic speaking style. Speeches that inspire must draw on the shared values of their audience, create energy and passion, and demonstrate the speaker's own commitment to the values they endorse.

Commencement speeches are notorious for failing at the goals of inspirational speaking. Done well, however, they can make a lasting impact. Consider the following excerpts from a 1991 commencement address at Ithaca College by Charlayne Hunter-Gault, an award-winning national affairs correspondent (Hunter-Gault 1994). She began with a reference to the occasion and by establishing common ground with her audience:

> I greet you this morning, the Class of 1991, with the greatest amount of admiration and respect. . . . I have shared the experience of your parents and loved ones this morning on the occasion of my daughter's college graduation in the not too distant past; and I have just finished freshman year all over again with my son, who is now doing what he calls a "deep chill" in what we, his father and I, hope will be a brief interim before he goes out and finds a summer job. . . .
>
> So that is what you and your parents have experienced to get to this point—the highs and the lows, the joy and the pain, the bank accounts stretched to the limit, and most recently the anxiety of find-

> ing a job after graduation—all constitute one of the sources of my empathetic admiration and respect.

As her speech progressed, Hunter-Gault introduced a challenge to the new graduates.

> I think that you young people are in the vanguard of a continuing, unfinished American Revolution and I think that as with students of my generation, the nation may have abdicated to you, perhaps involuntarily, the responsibility to write this chapter of our history . . . .
>
> In my fantasy, ... I am looking at your faces and I am seeing you take your place in society, hoping that you realize all your dreams and ambitions, but also hoping that you are suitably prepared for the bad times, where some of those dreams may be deferred.

She then dramatized her call to students with a personal narrative that illustrates her own passion, commitment, and values.

> You see, when I was 12 years old, I had this fantasy that one day I would grow up to be like my comic strip role model, girl reporter, Brenda Starr. Even my high school counselor tried to bring me down to the reality of my life's chances: being black in the segregated South, where no school would prepare me and no paper would hire me, held out the hope that my fantasy would ever come true.
>
> At 16, I took the first big step, applying to the University of Georgia's Journalism School. It had never admitted a black applicant in its 175-year history. Soon, I found the entire power of the State of Georgia allayed against me and my fantasy. My dream was deferred. But I pressed on, undaunted by the obstacles and inspired by the support of people of goodwill. And we prevailed. Although I walked alone through the jeers and taunts and people telling me "nigger go home," even the tear gas from the riots outside my dormitory protesting my presence, which had been ordered by the federal court, I was not alone. And knowing that gave me the courage to continue that journey.

As she concluded her speech, Hunter-Gault extended the inspirational tone with a call to action for her audience.

> I have shared some of my fantasies with you this morning because I believe that within you lies the power to turn them into reality. I can only hope for my sake and the sake of all of us who want our lives to be productive and happy, in a country that values each of us equally, that you will act to make that so.

"Use a sweet tongue, courtesy, and gentleness, and thou mayest manage to guide an elephant with a hair."

—Sa'di, poet

Like the best special-occasion speakers, Hunter-Gault brings her audience together, builds a bond with them, celebrates shared values, and leaves them with a memorable moment. As you learn to develop your own public speaking voice and cultivate your communication skills of understanding and sharing, you will become an active creator of these special events.

The Responsible Person Speaking Well

Being a responsible, competent, and engaging speaker requires careful preparation and conscientious practice with the interests of the audience in mind. We have emphasized these skills in previous chapters, so you should be familiar with several strategies and ethical responsibilities in the planning (Chapter 11), organizing (Chapter 12), and delivering (Chapter 13) of public presentations. Speaking responsibly, however, involves more than effective use of these strategies; it also means responding to the needs of the audience, whether your goal is to inform, persuade, or entertain. Above all, the following guidelines are essential when the knowledge the audience is gaining or the feelings that go along with the occasion are important to them.

Watch a business presentation that illustrates many of the skills discussed in this chapter (CD Clip 14.2).

Treat Your Audience with Care and Respect. During times of stress or celebration, think about ways to inspire others. When you want to give a special thanks to those who are important to you, write a letter or say a few words of tribute. Above all, be sincere. In situations like these, you will be developing your skills and creating competent, responsible speech interactions. The skills you develop for informative presentations and speaking at special occasions will help you think more critically and participate more effectively and responsibly in your professional and social lives.

Use Humor Appropriately. When used well, humor can gain audience attention, establish a mood, or help the speaker make a point. Humor should be relevant, brief, and enjoyable. Consider the following tips when deciding whether the funny moments you have planned are appropriate:

- Avoid ridiculing individuals or groups. Humor at the expense of others may seem funny to a few people, but it is far more likely to offend them. Jokes aimed at groups usually draw upon stereotypes. Even if you think you are "safe" to make such jokes (e.g., making fun of disabled people because you don't see anyone with a wheelchair in the room), you will damage your credibility by demonstrating bad will toward others. A little *self-deprecating* humor is often appreciated, though, so feel free to poke a bit of fun at yourself and show that you are human.
- Steer clear of off-color humor. Jokes about taboo topics such as bodily functions rarely add to the substance of a speech and, like ridiculing others, can insult your audience and damage your credibility.
- Use material that is fresh and varied. Jokes, stories, and puns work well if they are adapted to the purpose of your speech, are new to the audience, and—like any form of supporting material—come in different forms throughout the speech. For instance, although you may be a master at puns, resist the urge to sprinkle only one form of humor throughout your speech.

Resources for Review and Skill Building

Many of these resources are supported by the Connections CD-ROM and free Online Learning Center website.

SUMMARY

This summary is organized around the questions found at the beginning of the chapter. See if you can answer them before reading the summary paragraphs.

1. What are the different types of credibility, and why is credibility so important?

   Credibility refers to the perception that a speaker is knowledgeable, believable, and trustworthy. Credibility helps to determine the success of a speech and establish the respect and acceptance the audience shows the speaker. There are three different types of credibility. Initial credibility comes from a speaker's reputation and occurs even before the speech starts. A well-known speaker or a noted expert in a field will bring more initial credibility to a speech than someone who is unknown to the audience. Derived credibility is created by the content and delivery of the speech. Ideas that are organized and well supported with convincing evidence will enhance derived credibility as will a delivery that is practiced and engaging. Enduring credibility is the impression a speaker leaves with the audience. If the audience has an enduring feeling of trust after the speech, they are more likely to believe the speaker and do what he or she has asked.

2. What are the types of informative speeches?

   The goal of an informative speech is to convey knowledge. Descriptive informative speeches provide details of an object or concept. An effective speech of description uses vivid language that creates a mental picture for the audience. Speeches that demonstrate show the audience how to do something. Demonstration speeches usually include more than verbal descriptions and perform some action for the audience, such as showing how to fly-fish. Explanatory speeches teach about or clarify an event or concept. Speeches of explanation are verbal descriptions of processes such as writing a résumé. Finally, speeches that narrate use an extended story to make a statement or clarify a concept.

3. What are some of the most common occasions at which you might be asked to speak?

   Speeches of introduction precede many public speeches and should facilitate the main speaker's goals by establishing the mood and purpose of the occasion. A speech of introduction should integrate the speaker, topic, and audience. An acceptance speech occurs when the speaker receives an award, gift, or honor. An acceptance speech should acknowledge those who sponsor the award, honor the occasion, and express appreciation for the honor. Speeches of tribute, such as toasts and eulogies, highlight the accomplishments of another person. After-dinner speeches are just that—speeches after an audience has eaten a meal. After-dinner speeches are often entertaining or at least enlighten the audience in an amusing way. Good after-dinner speeches use appropriate humor to make an inspirational point. Finally, speeches of inspiration attempt to motivate listeners and arouse their passions. Good inspirational speeches include a connection to the audience and an enthusiastic speaking style.

4. What are the obligations of a responsible person speaking well?

   Speakers have an obligation to live the values they speak about. Sincerity is a key component of credibility and audiences often label an insincere speaker as a hypocrite. Many of the special-occasion speeches discussed in this chapter focus on helping others. A responsible speaker should pay tribute to the accomplishments of others and try to inspire audiences to better themselves.

KEY TERMS

Test your understanding of these key terms by visiting the Connections CD-ROM and Online Learning Center website at www.mhhe.com/dobkinpace.

FOR FURTHER REFLECTION

Join a conversation about chapter concepts by visiting the Online Learning Center website at www.mhhe.com/dobkinpace

New York Mayor Rudy Giuliani was considered charismatic by some audiences for his public presentations shortly after the September 11, 2001 terrorist attacks on the World Trade Center. New York City needed action and leadership as it tried to cope with personal and financial devastation. In Giuliani's speeches to New York City, he combined the resolve to carry on with genuine sorrow for the victims, in what *Time* magazine called speeches of "grief and iron" ("Person of the Year," 2002). He declared, "Tomorrow, New York is going to be here . . . we're going to rebuild, and we're going to be stronger than we were before . . . . I want the people of New York to be an example to the rest of the country and the rest of the world that terrorism can't stop us." He also mourned the victims, acknowledging that "the number of casualties will be more than any of us can bear." Giuliani's tough but sympathetic leadership became a charismatic symbol of survival to the entire country.

- How important is the existence of a crisis or social problem in audience perceptions of a speaker's charisma?
- Are charismatic speakers always credible?
- Is charisma an example of initial, derived, or enduring credibility? Give some examples to support your point of view.

BUILDING COMMUNICATION SKILLS

1. Take a speech topic of your choice and show how it might be developed into a speech that describes, demonstrates, explains, or narrates.
2. Find a quote or short piece of writing to use for the basis of a speech to inspire. Write an introduction to that speech.
3. Research one or more of the following famous people and write a short speech of introduction for that person. Assume that the person you select is coming to your class as a guest speaker. Use the suggestions in this chapter to help you craft an effective introduction for one of the following:

   Diego Rivera
   John Muir
   Sacagawea
   Michael Moore
   Golda Meir
   Jane Goodall
   W. E. B. Du Bois
   Oscar Arias
   Barbara Jordan
   Hideki Matsui
4. Write a different toast for your best friend for each of the following occasions: birthday, graduation, wedding, and a wake. How would your toast change to fit each occasion?

NET WORK

Note: While all the URLs listed were current as of the printing of this book, these sites often change. Please check our website (www.mhhe.com/dobkinpace) for updates and hyperlinks to these exercises.

1. Go to YouTube and search for "Oscar Speeches." Watch several of these clips. Which ones seem memorable? Why?
2. General Douglas MacArthur's farewell speech to West Point is an oft-quoted speech ("In my dreams I hear again the crash of guns, the rattle of musketry, the strange, mournful mutter of the battlefield. But in the evening of my memory I come back to West Point. Always there echoes and re-echoes: duty, honor, country." Again search YouTube for "MacArthur's Farewell Speech." Watch the clip. Is this a speech of tribute or inspiration? Or both?

MEDIA MOMENTS

The film *Erin Brockovich,* directed by Stephen Soderbergh (2000), tells the story of Erin Brockovich (Julia Roberts), a single mother of three who talks her way into a job with her attorney Ed Masry (Albert Finney) despite her lack of experience as a lawyer, paralegal, or legal secretary. While working for Masry, she investigates a cover-up of contaminated water in a local community and helps to win one of the largest settlements in a direct-action lawsuit in U.S. history. Watch the movie, focusing on Brockovich's personal transformation and effectiveness as an advocate. Consider the following questions:

- How does Brockovich establish credibility with her audiences? Why is doing so difficult for some of the other characters?
- Identify moments of description, explanation, and narrative. How effective is Brockovich at using informative speaking?
- At what points does Brockovich need to inspire her listeners? How does she do so?

Speaking to Persuade

CHAPTER 15

When Erica started school at Cascade College, she chose to live off campus and drive to school each day. Although she liked using the travel time to listen to music and talk with friends as she shared rides, Erica also grew increasingly frustrated with the lack of parking on campus. She chose local parking issues as a presentation topic for her communication class. After conducting research for the speech, she learned that some campuses have parking spots reserved solely for people in car pools. Erica started an e-mail campaign; interviewed students, faculty, and staff; and conducted campus surveys.

In preparing for her speech, Erica learned that some people might not want to give up close and convenient parking spaces to people in car pools. She would have to convince students of the benefits of setting aside a few spots for car poolers. Erica decided to develop a speech that would get the attention of her audience with predictions of a future parking crunch on campus; point out the need for traffic congestion to be reduced; tell how her plan could improve parking, traffic flow, and air quality for everyone; show the audience where the car pool spots could be placed; and ask her audiences to support a petition that she would present to the president and board of trustees of the university.

QUESTIONS TO FOCUS YOUR READING

1. Why are speaking to inform and to persuade part of a continuum?
2. What are the types of persuasive speaking?
3. How can you distinguish between claims of fact, value, and policy?
4. How are arguments built, and what kinds of appeals can be used to support them?
5. What are some options in organizing persuasive speeches?
6. How can speakers recognize and practice ethical persuasion?

Erica gave presentations to the student government and commuter student organizations at her college. Her hard work and extensive communication efforts prompted the college administration to institute a system of special parking permits and spaces reserved for people in car pools, which not only made more efficient use of parking spaces on campus, but also relieved stress for commuter students, encouraged the development of more car pools, and raised awareness of environmental issues on campus.

Erica recognized the power of speaking persuasively to change her world. Her efforts at persuasion included talking to friends, conducting interviews, giving presentations, using e-mail, and organizing and leading meetings. Her success depended not only on her mastery of communication in different contexts, but also on her personal commitment and willingness to act on her convictions.

persuade
Influence others by reinforcing or changing their beliefs.

Erica took on one of the most difficult persuasive tasks: moving people to action. We all engage in attempts to **persuade,** or influence others by reinforcing or changing their beliefs). Our efforts range from inspiring others ("that comment made me feel really proud"), to seeking agreement ("don't you think that's a good idea?"), to changing behavior ("I volunteered at the hospital today"). Each interaction involves motivating others to change a belief or take an action and requires specific skills that are necessary for good persuasive speaking. After completing this chapter, you should be able to:

- Identify different persuasive goals and types of speeches.
- Build persuasive arguments.
- Organize a persuasive speech.
- Recognize and practice ethical persuasion.

The Informative-Persuasive Continuum

Most of our speaking in groups or public settings is done to inform or to persuade others. Think about a typical day for Dennis, a retailer of designer jewelry and precious gems. At a staff meeting, he gathers his employees and tells them of the month's performance and sales goals. He outlines a strategy for an upcoming promotion of pearls and tries to motivate the staff as they leave the meeting. As he works with customers, he explains the "C's" of diamond appraisal—clarity, cut, color, and carat—to show how his gems are rated. Dennis's day includes listening carefully to a customer's vision for a new necklace. He asks ample questions about design and comfort, and demonstrates how his on-site jeweler might craft that item. Dennis then presents one of his showcase necklaces, establishes the credibility of the designer, and talks about the investment value of precious gems. He might even elaborate with a story about his journey to find this particular, unique necklace. Finally, Dennis appeals to the customer's desire for status and esteem by letting the customer wear the necklace and commenting on the statement it makes about the wearer, thus building emotional attachment to the item.

The day of the jeweler illustrates many of the ways that informative and persuasive speaking are used. As we discussed in Chapter 14, informative speaking

Think It Over

"STEALTH SITES" ON THE WEB

Increasingly, companies that try to sell you a product or get private information about yourself sponsor websites that look educational. For instance, a site called "Circuit Breaker" advertised itself as an entertainment guide for a major city and was called a "hot site" in *USA Today*. If you logged on, you were invited to play interactive games after registering and providing information such as your name, e-mail address, age, and whether you smoke. Brown & Williamson Tobacco Corporation, the makers of Lucky Strike cigarettes, sponsored Circuit Breaker, although this was not mentioned on the site. Circuit Breaker was an attempt to see if Brown & Williamson could reach its target audience over the Web (Chapman 1997).

"Stealth sites" such as Circuit Breaker are marketing ploys disguised as unbiased content. Stealth sites include book reviews sponsored by bookstores, and medical information about infectious diseases produced by pharmaceutical companies trying to sell their drugs.

How do these sites blur the line between informational and persuasive speech?

Are they ethical?

To what extent are communicators responsible for making their purpose clear?

can have the specific purposes of description, demonstration, explanation, or narration. Although Dennis gave minipresentations that drew from informative speech types, he spent much of his day persuading people. He confirmed positive feelings and impressions with staff and customers, influenced their opinions, and closed sales with customers.

Speaking to Inform Involves an Element of Persuading. Each of the informative speech types—description, demonstration, explanation, and narration—can overlap with the persuasive speaking. Although the primary goal of informative speaking is to convey knowledge, the speaker still needs to do some convincing, even if it means only getting the audience to listen. Speakers want listeners to see them as credible and to appreciate what they are saying, and that is a process of influence. Speakers also need to persuade listeners that their informative speech topics are significant and interesting. However, the primary focus of an informative speech is to educate rather than urge listeners to change their minds and behaviors.

Sometimes speakers will present themselves as educators, while their primary objective is really a persuasive one. Often their attempts to persuade are transparent, such as the personal trainer of a fitness club offering a free training session or the owner of a craft store giving free workshops to potential customers. The personal trainer and store owner are both providing information, but they also have a persuasive goal. At other times, the attempts to persuade are less obvious. The "Think It Over" box asks you to think about the ethics of Internet websites that blur the line between information and persuasion.

Speaking to Persuade Involves an Element of Informing. Just as informative speeches must influence audiences, persuasive speeches include an element of informing. During a persuasive speech, speakers are likely to give the audience new information, convey ideas, and perhaps tell a story. However,

FIGURE 15-1 THE INFORMATIVE-PERSUASIVE CONTINUUM

INFORMATIVE			PERSUASIVE
Present data	Present opinion	Encourage acceptance of new beliefs or opinions	Encourage action
(define, explain, describe, narrate)		(reinforce, convince)	(solve problem, act)

The more change a speaker asks from an audience, the more challenging the presentation.

their topics are more likely to be controversial, and their primary goal is to change the audience's beliefs, attitudes, and possibly behavior. Think of informing and persuading as parts of a *continuum,* as shown in Figure 15-1.

The more change you want your audience to accept, the more persuasive you must be, and the more difficult the task ahead of you. Audiences are more likely to agree with you than to change their behavior. For instance, they might be perfectly willing to acknowledge the importance of breast cancer research but less likely to write a check in support of the cause. To be persuasive, you must have a vision or mental image of an idealized future, or the way you would like the world to be. Then you must be able to articulate your vision in a way that motivates others to pursue it with you.

"Give to us clear vision that we may know where to stand and what to stand for—because unless we stand for something, we shall fall for anything."
—Peter Marshall, photographer

Effective Persuasive Speakers Know Their Audiences. In Chapter 11 we discussed the importance of analyzing the audience for any public presentation. The persuasive speaker has the added challenge of knowing how audience members are likely to judge the beliefs they are being asked to accept. According to **social judgment theory** (Ramsey 1999; Sherif, Sherif, and Nebergall 1963), we evaluate persuasive messages based on the beliefs that we already hold. Those beliefs are called **anchors** and, depending on how personally involved or how deeply we hold those beliefs, we are more or less likely to listen to points of view that differ from our anchor. For example, a senior citizen is more likely to be personally interested in preserving social security benefits than a recent high school graduate. Or suppose that Melissa is listening to a speech about private school vouchers. Melissa's father went to a public high school, her mother graduated from a public university, and she opposes any program that would take funds from public schools. This is her anchor position, and she holds it strongly. Social judgment theorists suggest that there are three possible ranges, or types of responses, that Melissa will have to make about her anchor beliefs. These responses are called "latitudes." In the case of school vouchers, Melissa has a narrow **latitude of acceptance,** which means that she will consider few opposing beliefs. Melissa's **latitude of noncommitment,** or range of beliefs about which she has no opinion, is also narrow, because it is hard for her to be neutral about this topic. Finally, Melissa's **latitude of rejection,** or array of views to which she objects, is fairly wide because she is likely to discount beliefs that are not close to her own. When depicted as a model, latitudes of acceptance, noncommitment, and rejection might look something like Figure 15-2.

social judgment theory
Evaluation of persuasive messages based on the beliefs we already hold.

anchors
Attitudes or beliefs that act as a personal standard for judging other messages.

latitude of acceptance
The range of positions a listener is likely to accept or tolerate.

latitude of noncommitment
The range of positions a listener neither accepts or rejects.

latitude of rejection
The range of positions a listener is likely to reject or consider intolerable.

FIGURE 15-2

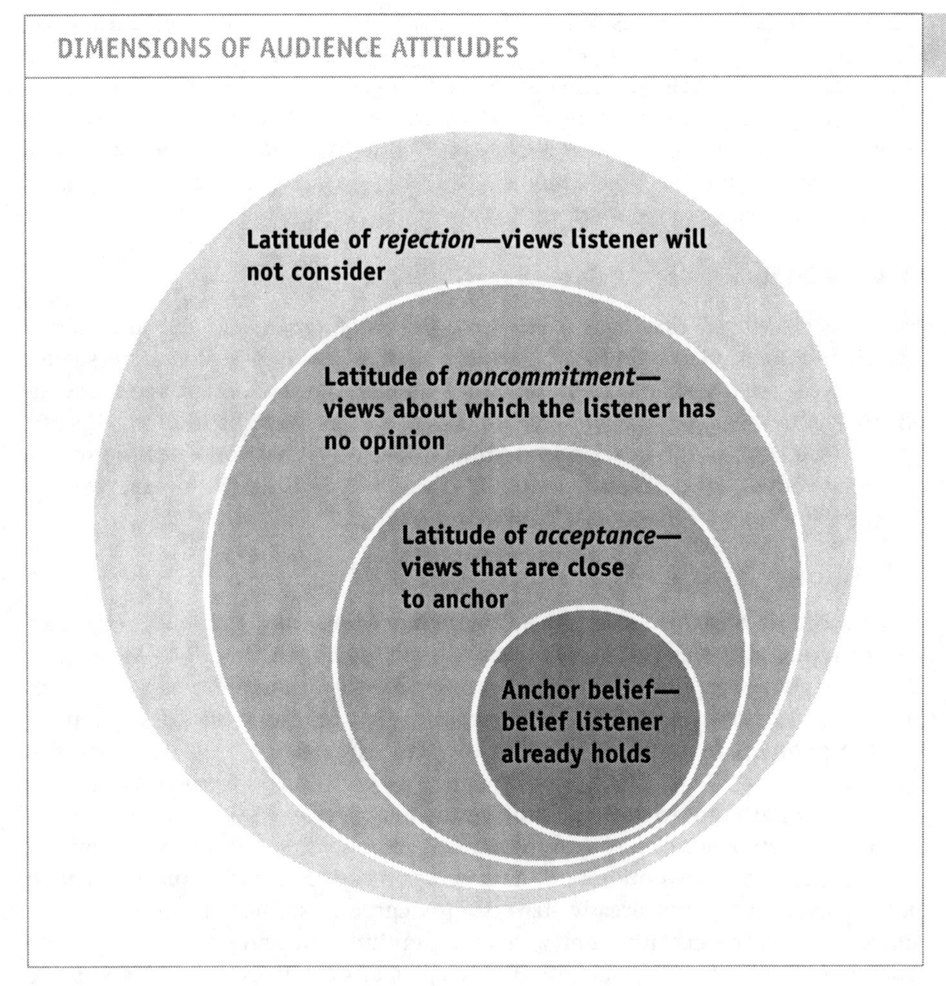

Latitudes of acceptance, noncommitment, and rejection vary based on personal investment in a belief.

Effective speakers are more likely to persuade listeners by focusing on their latitudes of acceptance and noncommitment. Consider the following statements. If you were a listener, which ones would fall in your latitude of rejection? Noncommitment? Acceptance?

- Under no circumstances should a person's race be considered for college admissions.
- In almost all circumstances, a person's race should not be considered for college admissions.
- Things are almost certainly better when race is not a consideration in college admissions.
- It is difficult to say whether a person's race should be considered for college admissions.
- Under some circumstances, it might be desirable to consider a person's race for college admission.
- In every circumstance, a person's race should be considered for college admissions.

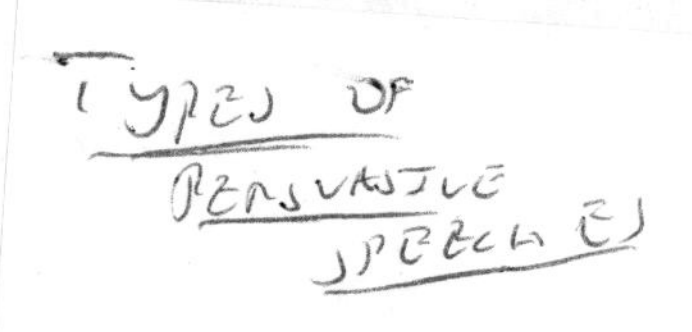

When you present a persuasive speech, be aware that your anchor belief might be different from that of your target audience. Just as persuading an audience is more challenging than offering information, moving an audience's attitudes and beliefs from one latitude to another, or from their anchor beliefs to your own, requires small steps toward realistic goals. As you read about the different types of persuasive speeches, consider which might be most appropriate based on your goals and the audience's points of view.

Types of Persuasive Speeches

Watch a video of a student speaking to persuade (Clip 15.1).

Jay Conger (1998), writing in the *Harvard Business Review,* described effective persuasion as "a negotiating and learning process through which a persuader leads colleagues to a shared solution." The following types of persuasive speeches all attempt to influence the audience to accept the speaker's attitudes or beliefs. As you read each of the descriptions, think about ways that you can account for the perspectives of others and create the common bonds that will make your attempts to influence others both honest and lasting.

Speeches that Reinforce

speech that reinforces
Persuasive speaking that attempts to strengthen existing attitudes, beliefs, or values.

A **speech that reinforces** tries to strengthen existing attitudes, beliefs, or values by bolstering attitudes and convictions that the audience already possesses. Of the several types of persuasive speeches, a speech that reinforces most closely resembles informative speaking. Since speeches that reinforce do not attempt to *change* people's thoughts or actions, they are the easiest type of persuasive speech to give (Wilcox 1986). However, they do constitute a form of persuasion because they attempt to increase motivation, bolster convictions, and put the audience in a better position to resist counterarguments. The school spirit rally and the political party convention both have this persuasive goal of reinforcement. In both cases, participants already share some degree of support; these events are aimed at renewing commitment, generating enthusiasm, and preventing people from wavering in their support. Similarly, a speaker who gives statistics about the dangers of child pornography or the importance of preventing child abuse is likely to reinforce existing beliefs among audiences who already recognize child pornography and abuse to be social problems.

Speeches that Convince

speech that convinces
Persuasive speaking that urges listeners to accept contentious facts, evaluate beliefs, or support actions.

Perhaps the most common type of persuasive speech is one that aims to convince. A **speech that convinces** urges listeners to accept *contentious* facts, evaluate beliefs, or support actions. Each of these reflects a particular kind of change in the listener that we will explore.

claims of fact
Statements about the truth or falsity of some assertion or statement.

Claims of Fact. The first part of our definition, urging listeners to accept contentious facts, refers to speeches that propose a position based on facts. We usually don't think of facts as points of argument; something is either true or false. **Claims of fact** ask listeners to accept the truth or falsity of some assertion or statement. A speaker who says, "Osama bin Laden was responsible for the September 11, 2001, attacks on the Pentagon and World Trade Center," is making a claim of fact. Although most U.S. citizens would take the statement to be true and unquestionable, some in the U.S. as well as citizens in other countries might need to have the statement proven.

Public officials spend much of their time speaking to convince others.

© Syracuse Newspapers/Gary Walts/ The Image Works

We have encyclopedias, reference libraries, and online databases to give us the answers to many of our questions about facts. Some determinations of truth, however, are more difficult to make. Entire conferences of scientists are organized around debates about the causes of diseases, weight-loss companies spend billions to convince us that their products work, stock market analysts make predictions that are treated as facts, and wars are fought over disputed boundaries between countries. In 2004, much of the news media in this country were absorbed with the question of Scott Peterson's guilt or innocence in the murder of his pregnant wife, Laci, and their unborn son, Connor. All of these topics entertain claims of fact and require speakers to convince listeners that their facts are persuasive and that they know the truth.

Claims of Value. When speakers ask us to form a judgment or evaluation, they are presenting a **claim of value.** This kind of speech can range from everyday concerns such as which dining commons serves the best food to whether capital punishment is moral. Statements of "good," "best," "right," and "moral" are all claims of value. Speeches based on determinations of worth must include a definition of the value that listeners are urged to adopt. For instance, you might argue that "football player X was the greatest running back to play the game." To support this claim, you would need to define "greatest." Does this mean highest average yards rushing per game? Per season? Over an entire career? Or is it measured by the number of championship games won? Once you have defined "greatest," you would need to show how player X meets the standard you have established.

claims of value
Statements that ask listeners to form a judgment or evaluation.

Similarly, consider a student who gets a research paper returned from a professor, sees a grade of C at the end, stuffs the paper in a backpack, and says: "This grade is unfair. I worked hard on this." The student has concluded that the grade is unfair and has created a standard for fair grades that looks something like: "any paper that takes considerable effort from a student deserves an above average grade." However, the professor is likely to have a different standard of evaluation. Her criteria might be that "student work should be graded on the criteria for academic excellence defined in the syllabus." For the student, the effort expended in creation is more important; for the professor, the final product matters more. These people are unlikely to come to a mutual agreement about "fairness" until they discuss their different standards of evaluation behind the grade.

Although speakers should always establish the criteria they are using for claims of value, they do not always do so, leaving some audience members to wonder what standards the speaker supports. Other audience members might accept the speaker's claims without questioning the standards on which they are based.

Reproduced by permission of L. J. Kopf.

claims of policy
Statements that ask listeners to consider a specific course of action.

Claims of Policy. We have seen how persuasive speeches designed to convince can target our beliefs about facts or our values. They may also try to influence our support of policies. **Claims of policy** are used when speakers ask us to consider a specific course of action. They invariably advance an argument about something we "should" do. Speakers who say we should (or should not) support clean needle exchanges for heroin addicts, limit funding of college athletic programs, or increase licensing restrictions for private pilots are all giving speeches based on claims of policy. When speakers tell listeners they ought to vote, sign something, give money or time, buy a product, or go somewhere, they are using claims of policy. Such claims require special attention to the need for change and the desirability of the action that is proposed.

A good persuasive speech can include each type of claim. For instance, a policy plan often needs to be supported by both statements of fact and value. Suppose André is giving a speech in support of paid leave for the care of dependents, such as infants or sick relatives. He might choose to support his claim with statements about the value of parenting or of caring for the elderly, and he might provide facts about the productivity of employees who are offered the opportunity to care for loved ones. André's speech will be most effective if he focuses on one claim as the thesis or central objective of the speech and use other claims to support his central idea.

"The main dangers in this life are the people who want to change everything . . . or nothing."
—Lady Nancy Astor, first woman member of the British parliament

Consider the following examples of speech topics (Table 15-1). They can be based on claims of fact, value, or policy depending on the goal of the speaker:

TABLE 15-1

Claims of fact, value, and policy

TOPIC	CLAIM
Energy Conservation	Fact: *Unless we decrease our consumption of fossil fuels, we will produce a greenhouse effect.* Value: *Limiting our consumption of fossil fuels is a worthwhile goal.* Policy: *The federal government should increase fuel taxes to discourage the consumption of fossil fuels.*
Parking on Campus	Fact: *The demand for parking spaces on campus will exceed available spaces within the next school year.* Value: *Close and accessible parking is an important part of campus life for students, faculty, and staff.* Policy: *The university's parking services should raise parking fees by 25 percent to help fund a new parking garage.*

Speeches that Call for Action

A **speech that calls for action** builds on the support a speaker has earned and moves the audience to a specific behavior. The speaker might try to get listeners to recruit volunteers for a campus organization, change their eating habits, buy a product, or vote for a person or proposal. Speeches that call for action are the most difficult kind of persuasive speech to give, because they require listeners not only to agree with the speaker, but also to *do something* based on those beliefs. You might convince your audience that a clothing company is immoral because it relies on child labor in its foreign plants. Getting listeners to boycott popular clothing lines will be more difficult to achieve. However, if the audience agrees to take even one small step in the direction of your proposal, such as buying a different brand of athletic shoes, they are more likely to agree to additional requests, such as boycotting shorts and shirts by that clothing company as well. The speaker who starts with a small request and follows later with a more substantial one is using the **"foot in the door"** technique (Freedman and Fraser 1966; Girandola 2002). Even if the action you attempt to achieve seems as minor as having your audience complete a survey or use a recycling bin, you are one step closer to making your persuasive speech have a lasting impact.

speech that calls for action
Persuasive speaking aimed to move the audience to a specific behavior.

foot in the door
The technique of starting with a small request and then following later with a more substantial one.

Building Persuasive Arguments

One of the first decisions to make in planning your persuasive speech is which type of claim—fact, value, or policy—will become the thesis for your presentation. Once you've focused on a claim, you need to build arguments in support of that claim. British philosopher Stephen Toulmin (1969) identified three parts to every **argument:** a claim, evidence, and reasoning. Evidence can come in many forms. As we discussed in Chapter 12, supporting materials can include testimony,

argument
A statement of belief, or claim, presented with evidence and reasoning.

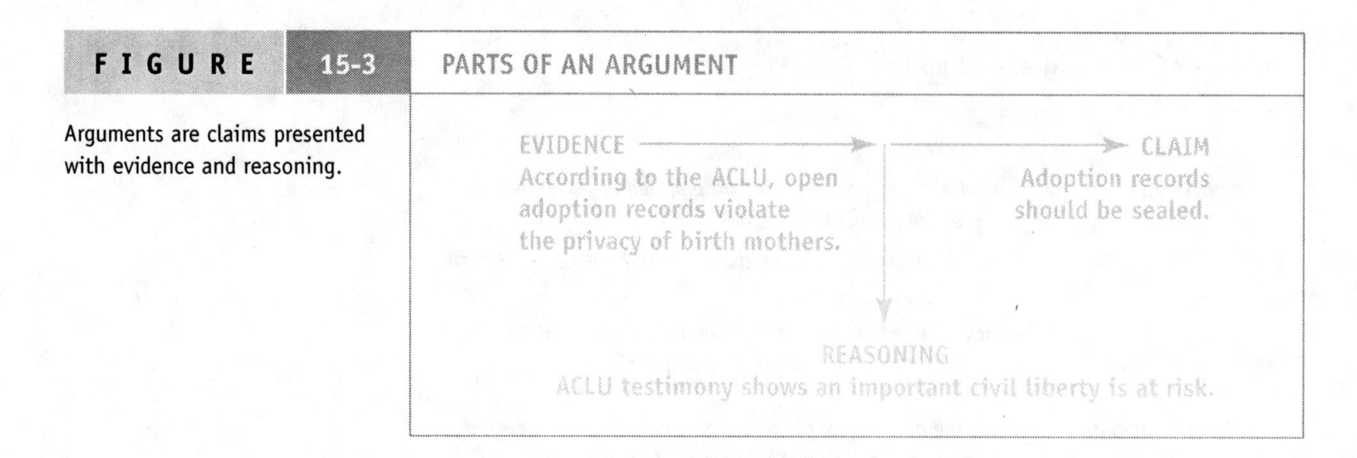
EVIDENCE
According to the ACLU, open adoption records violate the privacy of birth mothers.
CLAIM
Adoption records should be sealed.
REASONING
ACLU testimony shows an important civil liberty is at risk.

FIGURE 15-3 PARTS OF AN ARGUMENT

Arguments are claims presented with evidence and reasoning.

examples, analogies, statistics, explanations, and definitions. Arguments also consist of reasoning, or an inference that justifies the connection between the evidence and the claim the speaker wishes to make. A claim without reasoning or evidence—"Adoption records should be sealed"—might be a belief that listeners will accept, but it lacks the necessary support to constitute an argument—"The American Civil Liberties Union (ACLU) says that open adoption records violate the civil rights of birth mothers. This testimony shows that records should be sealed to protect birth mothers" (Knickerbocker 1998). Figure 15-3 illustrates the connections between claims, evidence, and reasoning.

There are different ways to interpret evidence. While we might not argue about facts, we often disagree about the implications of those facts. For instance, although the ACLU says that open adoption records violate the civil rights of birth mothers, perhaps you consider the ACLU to be a biased source. Or you might believe that the rights of adopted children are more important that those of birth mothers. However, if you agree with the ACLU, then you are likely to accept the speaker's claim. Persuasive speakers need to convince the audiences that their evidence is sufficient and their reasoning is sound. If the reasoning is solid, then the conclusion should follow.

Just as the most effective informative speeches help listeners understand by appealing to their minds, emotions, and behavior, persuasive speeches also work best when they rely on more than one type of argument and appeal to the needs and interests of the audience. The distinctions made by the Greek philosopher Aristotle over 2,000 years ago are still useful today. Aristotle wrote that there are three primary modes of persuasion: *ethos,* or persuasion based on credibility, *logos,* persuasion based on logical arguments, and *pathos,* persuasion based on appeals to emotion. Contemporary communication scholars have added a fourth type of appeal as well: *mythos,* or persuasion based on shared cultural knowledge.

Persuasion Based on Credibility

ethos
The ethics or credibility of the speaker.

In Chapters 12 and 14, we discussed the importance of a speaker's credibility for her or his effectiveness. Credibility is so important to persuasive speaking that Aristotle included it as a mode of persuasion, which he called **ethos.** Many people define ethos as an appeal based on ethics. For the persuasive speaker, ethos refers primarily to how the audience judges the ethics, or credibility, of the speaker. Think about the story of Erica at the beginning of the chapter. Although she had no particular expertise in parking management or environmental issues, she established ethos through the strength of her convictions, her careful research and audience analysis, and her dedication as a student. Erica's thorough preparation showed she had good sense, her concern for the environment demonstrated goodwill, and her tireless efforts exemplified good moral character. By the time she addressed audiences such as college administrators, she had built credibility that would help her to be particularly persuasive.

Persuasion Based on Logic

The claims a speaker makes are only as solid as the evidence and reasoning that support them. Aristotle used the term **logos** to refer to arguments based on logic or reasoning. Most audiences listen for the logic that connects a speaker's evidence and claim, particularly when they disagree with a speaker. For example, suppose audience members believe that using the dietary supplement ephedra poses no serious health risks. These listeners would probably benefit from hearing research about the way ephedra affects the body and examples of people who may have died from using the drug. In constructing your own arguments, try to identify the form of reasoning you are using and be able to assess the strength of your logic. There are two general types of reasoning: induction and deduction.

logos
Arguments based on logic or reason.

Induction. **Induction** is reasoning from a particular instance to a generalization; it requires the use of an inference. In Chapter 4 we defined "inference" as "a projection or interpretation based on facts." Inductive reasoning requires a leap of judgment that can always be questioned based on the strength of the connection between a specific case and a general condition. For example, much of our medical knowledge is based on generalizations drawn from scientific observations. We trust the conclusions of medical professionals when they are based on a sufficient number of examples and when the examples are representative. Suppose your doctor recommends a surgical procedure that has only been tried on a few dozen people. Worse yet, those dozen people were 10 years younger than you or were all members of the opposite sex. It might be hard for your doctor to persuade you that the claim, "this surgery is safe for you," is justified.

induction
Reasoning from a particular instance to a generalization.

Speakers who draw on inductive reasoning ask listeners to believe that specific instances fit a broader pattern. Consider the following argument based on an incident at the University of Montana:

> Earlier this month, a psychology professor, her female partner, and her son narrowly escaped death by crawling through an open window while their house burnt to the ground. The horrible fire was the work of an arsonist, and it came after the professor filed a lawsuit in the hopes of getting the University to provide domestic partner benefits. Sadly, this attack was not the first threat on her life, nor the only time a gay employee at the University has been harassed. We cannot let heinous attacks such as this stand unanswered. Our University has an obligation to set an example of tolerance and support of all members of our community, and we should move quickly to adopt domestic partner benefits for our employees.

Arson Follows Suit Over Domestic Partner Benefits (2002, May/June). *Academe, 88,* 3, 17–18.

The speaker in this example is asking the audience to draw a conclusion about the safety of some employees based on specific incidents of harassment. Then, as in many persuasive speeches, the speaker suggests a course of action (adopt partner benefits) based on the meaning of that conclusion (the university must address the problem of harassment).

deduction
Reasoning that starts with a general statement and draws a specific conclusion.

syllogism
A form of reasoning that draws a conclusion based on two premises.

Deduction. Instead of moving from specific instance to general conclusion, **deduction** starts with a general statement and draws a specific conclusion. Deductive reasoning has three parts: a major premise, a minor premise, and a conclusion. The classic way to put this all together is by means of the following structure, called a **syllogism.** A syllogism is a form of reasoning that draws a conclusion based on two premises. Here is an argument that has been structured as a syllogism:

Participation in organized sports teaches teamwork. (major premise)

Soccer is an organized sport. (minor premise)

Participation in soccer teaches teamwork. (conclusion)

The major premise identifies characteristics that are present in all members of a class of objects. If a single person, object, or event fits that class (minor premise), then the conclusion will necessarily follow.

The major premise is usually a generalization or definition, such as the statement, "Universities that charge high tuition are superior." The minor premise shows that a specific case fits the first part of the major premise, such as "University X charges high tuition." The final claim would be: "University X is superior." You have undoubtedly heard this kind of argument many times in its shortened form, called an enthymeme. Think about the argument that a luxury car with a high price tag is a superior vehicle. Such arguments can be challenged at the level of either major premise ("Expensive items are of high quality") or minor premise ("Luxury cars are expensive").

Deductive reasoning is compelling when speakers connect specific values or policies to major premises that are shared by the audience. As you formulate your own arguments, think about the assumptions you are making and the logical leaps that you ask your audience to take. If you know your audience well, you are more likely to appeal to the inferences and major premises that make sense to them.

Persuasion Based on Emotional Appeals

pathos
Arguments based on emotional appeals.

Although many of us like to think we are persuaded only by pure reason, emotions also play an important role in persuasion. Indeed, for some people arguments based on personal experience and passions are more compelling than the soundest statistics. Aristotle used the word **pathos** to refer to arguments based on emotional appeals. For instance, in trying to convince members of an audience to wear bicycle helmets, you might present the statistical risks of riding without one. You might also illustrate these risks with a dramatic story about an individual who suffered a traumatic head injury. The statistics provide evidence to support your argument about potential risk, and the illustration draws from human experience to appeal to emotions such as empathy and fear.

One way to generate ideas for constructing persuasive arguments based on emotional appeals is by drawing on types of human needs and desires. The psychologist Abraham Maslow (1954) identified basic needs, or things missing in our lives, and desires, the experiences and stimulation we seek (Rowan 1999). We often seek to fulfill basic, survival-oriented needs and desires before considering other ones, so these needs are sometimes listed as a hierarchy.

Basic Needs and Desires. First are basic physiological needs, such as food, water, air, and sleep. If your listeners are hungry, dehydrated, or sleep deprived, they must have these needs addressed before they can consider arguments about social needs. Issues such as water contamination, air pollution, and famine easily lend themselves to appeals to basic needs. For example, in a speech addressing world famine, you might describe the hunger and malnutrition suffered by children in impoverished or drought-stricken countries as a way to get listeners to empathize with people who are starving. Physiological desires can also motivate listeners. Some listeners might be inspired by the desire for fine food or the sensation of *luxuriating* in a bath. For some speech topics, basic needs are the most relevant to address.

Security. There are many kinds of security, including freedom from crime, job security, personal confidence, and national security. At some level, we are never completely secure; we might feel good about our jobs but fearful of personal attacks. Speakers who talk about rising crime rates, the possibilities of terrorist attacks, or potential economic collapse are all appealing to emotional insecurity. On the other hand, some people like to have their security threatened or to seek thrills, as illustrated by the popularity of extreme sports.

Belonging. The third type of need or desire, belonging, refers to the social side of humans. We all have associations with groups, whether they are our families, fellow employees, clubs, or athletic teams. Speakers can talk about the benefits of belonging to an organization or the importance of taking actions (e.g., volunteering time, giving money, recruiting new members) that are important to a group. For some people, belonging means knowing the rules, wanting to please others, and living up to the expectations of others. A speech on high school gangs, for example, could acknowledge the emotional importance of peer pressure while offering constructive ways to meet belonging needs.

Love and Esteem. Everyone wants to be appreciated and respected. Advertisers who appeal to our personal insecurities and loneliness frequently rely on the need for love and esteem: Perfume advertisements promise romance, personal hygiene products play on potential social embarrassment, and beer commercials show drinkers in settings where social fantasies are fulfilled. Love and esteem are also desires; people like to be appreciated. Some people are particularly motivated by status, and arguments that promise social advancement are important to them. A speech promoting adult education programs in prisons could include appeals based on the self-esteem that comes with acquiring a college degree.

Self-Actualization. Finally, people often want to achieve their personal best, whether from finishing an important project, creating a work of art, or raising a happy child to adulthood. Sometimes the desire for self-actualization is so strong that other needs are ignored in pursuit of it. For example, you may have participated in a particularly challenging sporting event in which you blocked out

Lawyers must often combine logical and emotional appeals in their attempts to persuade jurors.

physical pain in pursuit of winning. Some companies appeal to this desire in their advertisements. Think about Nike's "Just Do It" campaign. This slogan suggests that we should exercise for personal fulfillment as well as for general fitness.

These needs and desires represent fundamental human concerns that can be addressed by speakers who wish to convince others. When expressed in dramatic ways, these appeals can involve listeners at an emotional level, particularly when they are already predisposed to agree with the speaker. Suppose that you already run four miles a day and sometimes compete in local races. An appeal to your desire to belong to an organization and the self-actualization that comes from helping others might work well for a speaker asking you to participate in a fund-raising run for the Muscular Dystrophy Family Foundation.

When paired with logical appeals, pathos can be powerful, particularly with audiences who are skeptical or hostile. Consider the speaker who wishes to talk about *amnesty* for illegal Mexican immigrants to an audience that supports strict regulation of U.S. borders. The speaker could refer to the 3,000 Mexican emigrants who have died trying to cross the border since Operation Gatekeeper was initiated in 1994, or the thousands of farm and factory workers who support the U.S. economy (Rips 2002). This information might be more compelling, though, when combined with emotional appeals based on the physical and security needs of emigrants (e.g., stories of Mexican families living in poverty, or of emigrating families that starve, die in auto accidents, or suffer extortion and abuse at the border).

Even with friendly audiences, pairing logical and emotional appeals is a good idea because relying solely on emotional appeals to persuade puts the speaker on shaky ethical ground. Think about the feeling you get when you feel a tearjerker film has manipulated your emotions. The same resentment you might experience applies to persuasive speaking. For example, a story that details the trauma suffered by an abused child might engage audience emotions but also leave audiences too disturbed to continue listening. As the "Exploring Communication

Exploring Communication Concepts

FEAR APPEALS AND THE BOOMERANG EFFECT

You have probably been in situations where an attempt to persuade you with a threat had little effect. Perhaps you took a driver education course that showed you graphic images of highway accidents in an attempt to encourage responsible driving. These persuasive campaigns don't always produce their intended effects. For example, anti-drug advertisements intended to scare teens into believing that marijuana use leads to stronger drugs can backfire (Yzer, Capella, Fishbein, Hornik, and Ahern 2003). Another study on the effectiveness of messages about sexual violence found that some attempts to influence people not only failed to make audiences more sensitive to victims of sexual violence, but led to a "boomerang" effect and contributed to dangerous attitudes toward sexual harassment and rape.

Researchers Winkel and De Kleuver (1997) showed two videos about sexual violence to students of high school age. One video focused on a male perpetrator and the punishment he received because of his actions. The video concentrated on how the criminal justice system deals with sex offenders and the negative ways people react to them. A second video focused on the psychological trauma of female victims, their life experiences, and the effects of their abuse on their male partners. The first video seemed to do more harm than good. Researchers found that exposing boys to the threat of punishment actually reinforced sexist stereotypes. They were more likely to agree with statements such as "boys do not need to stop if they bother a girl physically and she is resisting," "girls want to be taken violently," and "under some conditions, a boy is permitted to have forced sex." Possibly, some of the boys identified with the perpetrator and his lack of remorse, rather than fearing potential punishment for acts of sexual violence.

ASK YOURSELF:

1. Why might it be more effective to build empathy with victims than to focus on consequences for perpetrators?
2. What does this research suggest about the use of emotional appeals?

Concepts" box suggests, emotional appeals can even backfire. Emotional chords shouldn't be struck in ways that short-circuit logic and rationality. Use emotional and rational appeals together for a sound and responsible presentation.

Persuasion Based on Cultural Myths

Every culture has a set of stories that its members use to help define themselves and show how their group is unique. Some communication scholars like to refer to persuasion based on cultural stories as **mythos,** or the use of myths, legends, and folktales to guide people in their thoughts, actions, and identity (Haggins 1999; Sutton 1997; Osborn 1990). These stories are known by members in the group and convey their beliefs, values, and expectations. Think about the phrases, "cry wolf," "George Washington and the cherry tree," and "rags to riches." If you lived in the United States as a child, you probably recognize the stories and their underlying values of telling the truth and working hard. Effective speakers can draw from myths, legends, and folktales throughout their speeches. For instance, perhaps you are proposing steps to alleviate a nursing shortage. You might refer to Florence Nightingale, the founder of modern nursing.

mythos
The use of myths, legends, and folktales as persuasive appeals.

Sometimes mentioning shared stories, history, or superstition is sufficient to lay the groundwork for a persuasive argument (Podolinská and Kováč 2002). Suppose that Pixote is giving a speech about an initiative to change the college mascot from the "Chiefs" to the "Jaguars." He appeals to college traditions:

> I remember last year's homecoming game, when we beat the Central State Mavericks by one point. It was quite a game; perhaps you remember it, too. It was such a moment of pride for me until our mascot, Chief Charlie, went whooping and skipping around the field.
>
> I know Chief Charlie has been with us a long time, but our school spirit has been with us longer. It's time to adopt a mascot that honors not just our lighthearted humor and superiority on the playing field, but also our academic strength and respect for others.

"The universe is made of stories, not of atoms."

—Muriel Rukeyser, poet

Like credibility, logic, and emotional appeals, shared stories can be used in persuasive speeches to connect with the audience and support persuasive arguments.

Putting It All Together

Once you have determined your central thesis and the types of appeals that might be most effective, you need to choose an organizational structure for the speech. In Chapter 12, we identified several ways to organize speeches. To reinforce existing views, a topical or chronological pattern might be sufficient, as this persuasive speech type is closest to an informative one. For speeches to convince or call to action, cause-and-effect or problem-solution patterns might be most appropriate.

motivated sequence
A persuasive speech structure designed to move audiences toward taking immediate action.

Perhaps the most common types of organization for persuasive speakers are problem-solution and the **motivated sequence,** developed by Alan Monroe in the 1930s as a persuasive speech structure designed to move audiences toward taking immediate action (Monroe 1935). As we discussed in Chapter 2, problem-solution speeches require an explanation of the problem or existing condition, the standards for evaluating it, and the consequences or course of action to be adopted. The motivated sequence is particularly useful for speeches that call for action, because it adds the step of encouraging audience behavior.

The persuasive speech using a motivated sequence has five stages: attention, need, satisfaction, visualization, and action. In practice, the motivated sequence looks like this:

1. *Attention.* As we discussed in Chapter 13, the first task of any good speech is to get the attention of the audience. You can do this with a startling statistic, an anecdote, a compelling quote, or a rhetorical question. Introduce your speech topic in a way that creates interest and motivates the audience to listen further.
2. *Need.* Depending on the existing beliefs and attitudes of your audience, this could be the most important section of your speech. This step answers the question, Why should I care? Show that the problem you are addressing affects the audience personally and has broad implications. Demonstrate how existing conditions are costing money, health, lives, national security, and/or

Getting listeners to take action is one of the most challenging goals for a persuasive speaker.

quality of life. This is a good time to combine logos and pathos, as you want to give your audience solid evidence while also appealing to their personal interests.

3. *Satisfaction.* Once you have created a need for a solution, you must satisfy that need by providing a plan that solves the problem. Explain how your plan can be implemented and find examples of places where your plan has been tried successfully.
4. *Visualization.* This step calls for creativity. Try to create a mental image of what the world would look like once your plan is in place. Show your audience how they will benefit and how they will feel once they take action. Or, show them what the world will look like if they don't adopt your plan.
5. *Action.* By this point, you will have created a desire on the part of your audience to take specific action. Tell your audience exactly what you would like them to do, whether it involves signing a petition, writing a letter, investing their money, or volunteering their time.

Use the motivated sequence with the same thought and care that you would for any of the speech structures identified in previous chapters. It provides a clear map for a speech urging action that goes beyond the other patterns; for that reason alone, many students choose to use it. You can also note the popularity of this structure by looking for it in other popular speeches and advertisements. Think about the barrage of ads for cold medications during the winter. In a shortened form, advertisers will get your attention with a key character such as a suffering child, identify needs by showing miserable people during "flu season," show the product and how happy the child is after taking it, and then tell you to buy the product. Table 15-2 outlines a speech using the motivated sequence to further illustrate this type of speech structure.

TABLE 15-2 Outline for a Speech Using the Motivated Sequence

Topic: Make National Service Mandatory

Structure: Motivated Sequence

I. In his 2002 State of the Union Address, President George W. Bush called on all Americans to spend two years serving their country. (Attention)
   A. Every person has a duty to give to his or her country.
   B. I spent a year as an AmeriCorps volunteer.
   C. Service to country helps both the nation and the volunteer.
      1. I learned valuable skills.
      2. I made a difference in other people's lives.
   D. Due to the increasing needs of the country, a year of national service should be required for every American citizen between the ages of 18 and 25.
      1. The United States faces increasing threats to the security of the country.
      2. The United States lacks people who are trained to respond to crises and natural disasters.
      3. Mandatory national service would be an effective way to meet our civic obligations, enhance our skills and education, and help preserve our nation's security.

II. U.S. military preparedness is declining. (Need)
   A. Military recruitment is in a state of crisis.
   B. Military training has become less rigorous so that more people will stay in the armed service.

III. The United States lacks people who are trained to respond to crises and natural disasters. (Need)
   A. Infantry troops are increasingly asked to perform humanitarian and social duties.
   B. Domestic aid organizations are asked to address a growing range of social problems.

IV. Mandatory national service would be an effective way to meet our civic obligations, enhance our skills and education, and help preserve our nation's security. (Satisfaction)
   A. We could be given an option of military or civilian service.
      1. Our armed forces would no longer have to rely exclusively on recruiting volunteers.
      2. We could join programs such as Learn and Serve America, Senior Corps, or AmeriCorps and help improve schools, provide disaster relief, educate communities, rehabilitate neighborhoods, and build homes.
   B. We would learn new skills, enhance our self-esteem, and earn money toward our education.
      1. Military training often provides useful skills for civilian life.
      2. Service organizations teach trade skills and present leadership opportunities.
      3. Service comes with stipends to support additional education.
   C. Countries around the world, such as France, have benefited from mandatory national service.

TABLE 15-2

Outline for a Speech Using the Motivated Sequence *(continued)*
V. Picture yourself after college, during that time of choice before you launch a career. (Visualization) A. You could be learning how to fly jets or test software programs. B. You could be cultivating a community garden and helping people grow their own food. C. You could be building a house for a poor, rural family. D. You could be teaching a child to read.
VI. You have the power to transform yourself, help others, and serve your country. (Action) A. Check out the USA FreedomCorps website to find a short-term service opportunity in your neighborhood. B. Volunteer for the AmeriCorps National Civilian Community Corps. C. Support initiatives for mandatory national service.

No matter how engaging, well researched, organized, and polished your speech, some listeners will disagree with you. Think about the thesis of the speech presented in Table 15-2. What objections might listeners have to mandatory national service? What might the speaker do to address these objections? If you have gotten the most resistant speakers to understand your point of view, you should consider your effort a success. The "Applying Communication Concepts" box gives suggestions for adapting your speech to a possibly hostile audience.

Applying Communication Concepts

SPEAKING TO A TOUGH CROWD

Any good speech begins by establishing common ground between the speaker and the audience. When the audience disagrees with or is hostile to you, creating shared understanding and persuading them can be particularly difficult. Try to keep the following strategies in mind:

- *Start with shared beliefs or values.* An audience needs to know that its concerns or priorities are also embraced by the speaker. A speech on increasing federal funding for defense could start by emphasizing the value of preserving U.S. security.
- *Present their point of view.* Show that you understand the audience's objections and are willing to respond to them. If you address their point of view early in your speech, the audience can relax more easily and listen to your presentation.
- *Respect their right to disagree.* Even if your audience appears unfriendly, try to maintain your composure and show that you are willing to consider a different point of view.
- *Practice good listening.* As we suggested in Chapter 4, listening involves more than your ears. Listen with your eyes; watch how your audience is responding to you. Try to engage them with your delivery and be prepared to answer questions at the end of your speech.

ASK YOURSELF:

1. Which of your own beliefs might evoke hostility from your classmates?
2. How might you invite them to share your point of view?

Recognizing and Practicing Ethical Persuasion

We engage in persuasive speaking all the time, whether in convincing a friend to do a favor or launching a campaign to change campus parking. When we begin the persuasive process, we are asking listeners to trust the soundness of our arguments and the motives behind our presentation. In addition to constructing our own presentations responsibly, we need to think critically about the persuasive attempts of other speakers. This final section offers guidelines for practicing ethical persuasion, as well as evaluating the ethics of persuasive speakers and checking for fallacies in their reasoning.

Demonstrating Your Integrity

Throughout this text, we have emphasized the importance of establishing your credibility by doing thorough research, carefully scrutinizing the sources you use, and building common ground with your audience. There a number of other ways to demonstrate your personal integrity as a speaker.

1. Show respect for opposing points of view. Even if you do not agree with other ways of looking at your topic, acknowledge that other points of view exist and deserve consideration.
2. Keep the interests of the audience in mind, rather than acting out of self-promotion. Are you asking your audience to do something that might make them uncomfortable or put them at risk? Think carefully before asking listeners to take actions which might seem unethical or be illegal.
3. Welcome listeners to verify your information. If your information is accurate and you have represented your sources fairly, then you should be able to invite listeners to check your information with confidence. If something is true, there is probably more than one person who supports or says it, and you should be confident that other credible people can be found who share your views.
4. Avoid coercion. We introduced coercion as a conflict management style in Chapter 9, and just as coercion is inappropriate in interpersonal interactions, it should also be avoided in public presentations. Threats, blame, and ridicule may seem like effective tactics of persuasion but, in addition to being unethical, they rarely work and can often backfire.
5. Consider your own feelings and values. Are you too emotionally invested in the topic to be objective? Be sure that the topic is not so close to home that your effectiveness as a speaker will be compromised.

Use the speech critique to evaluate both your own speeches and those of your classmates (Clip 15.2).

The same skills used in crafting a sound and responsible persuasive speech should help you in recognizing and resisting unethical persuasion. The easiest way to resist unethical speakers is to avoid those you know are suspect, whether they are media personalities who distort information or charismatic individuals who are motivated only by self-interest. Beyond avoidance, do your own research and think about the implications of the speaker's suggestions based on your own knowledge and values. Finally, when you trust the speaker or the information confirms your existing beliefs, be careful not to suspend your critical listening skills. As you read this final

> "Blessed is the influence of one true, loving human soul on another."
>
> —George Eliot, novelist

section, think about ways to check your own reasoning and that of the persuasive speakers around you.

Checking for Fallacies

When speaking to others, we don't always think carefully about the reasoning we are asking listeners to accept, particularly when we think our arguments are based on common sense. If we are not careful, our logic can be susceptible to one of many fallacies. A **fallacy,** or error in reasoning, can be seductive; at face value, it often makes sense. However, a speaker who relies on fallacies is usually trying to compensate for insufficient evidence or poor reasoning. Here are some of the more common fallacies.

fallacy
An error in reasoning.

Name-Calling.

Name-calling consists of personal attacks on others based on their physical appearance, character traits, or affiliations rather than the content of their arguments. Suppose you are arguing with a friend about the way she voted in a recent election. You tell her, "I'd expect you to vote that way. Both of your parents worked on that candidate's campaign." You are arguing that she voted based on her association with her parents rather than her own reasons. Personal attacks can be subtle, such as judging a politician on her hairstyle rather than her policy recommendations. Name-calling distracts our attention from issues and can prompt us to dismiss what a speaker is saying before we have fully attended to his or her words. The speaker who challenges a woman talking about military strategy based on her sex ("What can a woman know about combat?") or man arguing for the rights of gun owners based on his dress ("What do you expect from a cowboy?") is committing the fallacy of name-calling.

name-calling
A fallacy based on attacking a speaker's physical or character traits rather than the content of his or her argument.

Appeal to Popular Opinion.

The **appeal to popular opinion,** also called the bandwagon fallacy, argues that a substantial group of people think or act the same way. Like most fallacies, there can be a glimmer of truth to these arguments. If several of your friends like a movie and you share their tastes, then the assertion that you would like the same movie could be a sound one. But even this argument is based on implicit comparisons of taste rather than the empty statement that you will like the movie because it is popular. Advertising campaigns often ask us to be part of a popular group by buying a particular product; some sports teams gain a greater following when they are doing well, and "fair-weather" fans join the bandwagon. The fallacy of appealing to popular opinion draws on our need to be accepted and belong to a group, even when doing so might not be in our best interests.

appeal to popular opinion
A fallacy based on the premise that the listener should think or act the same way as a substantial group of people.

False Cause.

The **false cause** implies a cause-and-effect relationship where none exists. We are often asked to assume that two events occurring at the same time have a causal connection, or that one event will inevitably lead to another. These are the assumptions that speakers make when they argue that corporations who sponsor credit card promotions for college students are responsible for the high debt of some students. Although attaching blame to corporations is popular with many audiences, other factors, such as a lack of personal responsibility, contribute to high credit card debt. There are often multiple causes behind any event, yet we sometimes assume a connection and assign blame rather than evaluating our reasoning.

false cause
A fallacy that implies a cause-and-effect relationship where none exists.

False Choice.

In a **false choice** fallacy, the speaker presents the audience with two choices, claiming they are mutually exclusive. For example, a speaker

false choice
A fallacy in which the speaker presents a false dichotomy between two choices.

might argue that either new parking lots must be built or congestion will cripple transportation on campus. The friend who says you don't like professional baseball because you dislike a star player such as Mark McGwire might be using a false choice fallacy. Finally, the speaker who argues "either you accept my view, or you're my enemy" is using a fallacy of false choice in a way that often ends discussion and intimidates listeners. These dichotomies are divisive, and speakers who don't wish to consider alternatives to their own points of view often use them.

appeal to authority
A fallacy in which someone serves as a spokesperson outside his or her area of expertise.

Appeal to Authority. Persuasive speakers sometime use an **appeal to authority,** or rely on someone serving as a spokesperson outside his or her area of expertise. Celebrity endorsements commonly rely on this fallacy. In the "Got Milk and Milk Mustache" campaign, the International Dairy Foods Association featured a series of actors, athletes, and politicians with milk mustaches. Although the ads were clever and popular, milk consumption did not increase noticeably (Pollack and Teinowitz 1998), perhaps because consumers realized that expertise in sports or politics doesn't necessarily indicate authority on the advantages of drinking milk. Similarly, the actress Candice Bergen served for many years as a spokesperson for a telephone company. The appeal to authority often attempts to trade star status for legitimacy about a product or service.

hasty generalization
A fallacy in which the speaker draws a conclusion about a group or general condition based on limited examples.

Hasty Generalization. In a **hasty generalization,** the speaker draws a conclusion about a group or general condition based on limited examples. We use inductive reasoning all the time, so checking the validity of our generalizations is particularly important. For instance, a speaker might say that going "cold turkey" is the best way to quit smoking, because that's how her mother did it. Her sample size, a group of one to support her claim, is clearly inadequate. When listening for evaluation, be sure to question whether the instances used to justify generalizations are sufficient and credible.

slippery slope
A fallacy based on the assumption that once a single step is taken, many other destructive ones are sure to follow.

Slippery Slope. The **slippery slope** assumes that once a single step is taken, many other destructive ones are sure to follow. This fallacy inspires fear and is commonly used by people concerned that their rights will be eroded. Some gun control opponents, for instance, argue that any restrictions on gun ownership will lead to the total abolition of Second Amendment gun rights. As with the other fallacies, there can be an element of legitimacy to the argument, so careful evaluative listening is necessary to decide if the fear is warranted or being exaggerated for persuasive purposes.

All fallacies in reasoning compromise the strength of the inference, that vital connection between evidence and conclusion. Identifying standards for evaluation and recognizing fallacies as you listen helps you form thoughtful opinions and beliefs about what you hear.

When misused, persuasive speaking can certainly be devious and manipulative. For instance, most of us dread shopping for motor vehicles. After all, some of the most distasteful forms of persuasion are equated with car salespeople. Politicians and lawyers also tend to fall toward the bottom of lists of trusted people as these occupations are often associated with manipulation, cajoling, begging, and applying pressure in ways that sometimes damage others. At its worst, persuasion turns into propaganda—distorted, emotional messages that lead you to a simplistic conclusion, rather than a thoughtful one (Pratkanis 1992). Good persuasion does none of this. Speakers who understand their audience's points of view and incorporate their ideas into a shared solution create the most persuasive presentations.

Resources for Review and Skill Building

Many of these resources are supported by the Connections CD-ROM and free Online Learning Center website at www.mhhe.com/dobkinpace.

SUMMARY

This summary is organized around the questions found at the beginning of the chapter. See if you can answer them before reading the summary paragraphs.

1. Why are informative speaking and persuasive speaking part of a continuum?

   Persuasive speeches share much with informative ones. The primary goal of informative speaking is to convey knowledge, but the speaker must convince the audience to listen. Persuasive speakers often need to educate listeners, but their main objective is to change the attitudes, beliefs, and possibly behaviors of their audience. According to social judgment theory, speakers need to identify the audience's anchor beliefs and try to influence attitudes that fall within their latitudes of acceptance or noncommitment.

2. What are the types of persuasive speaking?

   There are three types of persuasive speaking: speeches that reinforce, convince, or call for action. Speeches to reinforce attempt to strengthen existing attitudes and beliefs. Speeches to convince urge listeners to accept contentious facts, evaluate beliefs, or support actions. Speeches that call for action build on the support a speaker has earned to move the audience to a specific behavior.

3. How can you distinguish between claims of fact, value, and policy?

   Claims of fact, value, and policy each reflect a different goal of the speaker and desired response from listeners. Claims of fact make claims about the truth or falsity of a statement. Claims of value ask listeners to form a judgment or evaluation. Claims of policy ask listeners to consider a specific course of action.

4. How are arguments built and what kinds of appeals can be used to support them?

   Arguments consist of claims, evidence, and reasoning. Even if an argument makes sense, audiences will not necessarily accept it, so speakers must rely on persuasive appeals to support their arguments. Persuasive appeals can be based on credibility, reasoning, emotion, or cultural myths. Speakers establish credibility by demonstrating good sense, goodwill, and good moral character. Appeals based on reasoning demonstrate a clear and justifiable connection between the evidence provided and the conclusion drawn. They can be based on either inductive or deductive reasoning. Speakers can appeal to emotions by referring to the physical needs for food and water and to human needs and desires for security, belonging, love and esteem, and self-actualization. Myths, legends, and shared stories can also form the basis of persuasive appeals.

5. What are some options in organizing persuasive speeches?

   Speeches to reinforce often use topical or chronological patterns. Cause-and-effect and problem-solution patterns are often appropriate for speeches to convince. One of the most common organizations for speeches that call for action is the motivated sequence. The motivated sequence has five stages: attention, need, satisfaction, visualization, and action.

6. How can speakers recognize and practice ethical persuasion?

   In addition to demonstrating credibility by thorough and careful preparation, speaking responsibly requires showing respect for opposing points of view, keeping the interests of the audience in mind, welcoming listeners to verify your information, avoiding coercion, and considering your own feelings and interests. Speakers also need to check their own reasoning and avoid common fallacies such as name-calling, appeals to popular opinion, false cause, appeal to authority, hasty generalization, and the slippery slope.

KEY TERMS

Test your understanding of these key terms by visiting the Connections CD-ROM and the Online Learning Center website at www.mhhe.com/dobkinpace.

anchors 406
appeal to authority 424
appeal to popular opinion 423
argument 411
claims of fact 408
claims of policy 410
claims of value 409
deduction 414
ethos 412
fallacy 423
false cause 423
false choice 423
foot in the door 411
hasty generalization 424
induction 413
latitude of acceptance 406
latitude of noncommitment 406
latitude of rejection 406
logos 413
motivated sequence 418
mythos 417
name-calling 423
pathos 414
persuade 404
slippery slope 424
social judgment theory 406
speech that calls for action 411
speech that convinces 408
speech that reinforces 408
syllogism 414

FOR FURTHER REFLECTION

Join a conversation about chapter concepts by visiting the Online Learning Center website at www.mhhe.com/dobkinpace

1. Claims of value are common but often escape our attention. At some time, for instance, you have probably been convinced by a friend to see a movie on the basis of a favorable review. Your friend might have said something like, "We've got to see it—*Entertainment Weekly* says it's a great movie." Did you stop to ask what makes the movie great or what standards the reviewer used to evaluate it? These questions are the kind that you should ask whenever you hear a proposition of value, such as the statement that a movie is great.

   In a survey of leading movie critics, Kimberly Conniff found that most of their movie reviews are favorable. In a three-month period, Gene Shalit *(Today)* gave a "thumbs-up" to 84 percent of the movies he reviewed; Richard Corliss *(Time)* gave positive reviews to 75 percent. The top 12 reviewers, including Peter Travers *(Rolling Stone)*, Janet Maslin *(New York Times)*, Roger Ebert *(Chicago Sun-Times)*, and Kenneth Turan *(Los Angeles Times)* all gave movies a positive review more than 50 percent of the time (Conniff 1999).

   Are movies really this "good?" What does this suggest about the ways that movie critics define a good movie? What might be the motives of some of the critics for giving positive reviews? How persuasive do you consider movie critics to be?

2. This chapter has presented many different types of appeals for persuasive speaking.

- Which ones are you most comfortable using?
- How much are you willing to adapt your speaking when faced with a tough audience?

BUILDING COMMUNICATION SKILLS

Sometimes it's difficult to distinguish inferences from facts and opinions. See if you can identify the types of claims made below.

1. Robert is calling to see which auto parts store has replacement sunroofs, so his must have broken.
2. Brand X is the best sport nutrition bar because it has the most vitamins and minerals in it.
3. Dr. Sampson gives the highest grades in the department.
4. Candidate G is most likely to win the upcoming election.
5. That driver is shaking his fist at the car in front of him; the driver must be pretty angry.

(Answers: 1—inference; 2—opinion; 3—if true, a fact; 4—inference; 5—inference)

NET WORK

Note: While all the URLs listed were current as of the printing of this book, these sites often change. Please check our website (www.mhhe.com/dobkinpace) for updates and hyperlinks to these exercises.

1. One website on propaganda, www.propagandacritic.com lists several examples of common fallacies used by politicians and pubic organizations. Check out some of the examples on this website. Which fallacies are easiest to identify? What separates bad logic from propaganda?
2. Go to the Online Speech Bank where you will find links to thousands of public speeches: http://www.americanrhetoric.com/speechbank.htm. See if you can find a speech that effectively integrates appeals to credibility, logic, emotion, and cultural myths.

MEDIA MOMENTS

In *Remember the Titans* (Yakin 2000), set in the early 1980s, Coach Boone (Denzel Washington) is hired as a new head football coach at a recently integrated high school in Virginia. He replaces Coach Yoast (Will Patton), who is demoted and expected to be Boone's assistant. Upon his arrival, Boone faces the hostility of Yoast and the white football players and heightened expectations from the local black community. Above all, Boone needs to build common ground among teammates and lead his team to victory. In watching *Remember the Titans,* consider the following questions:

- How does Coach Boone establish his credibility with both hostile and sympathetic audiences?
- What kinds of persuasive appeals does Boone use, and how do they vary based on his audience?
- How does Boone draw on specific contexts (e.g., the football field, Gettysburg) to build appeals based on shared cultural knowledge?
- How does the movie itself use emotional appeals to deal with issues of racial tension?

A Brief Guide to Interviewing

APPENDIX

An interview is a unique communication situation composed almost entirely of asking and answering questions. Two common interviewing situations that you may encounter in college are asking questions (to gather information in a probing interview) or answering questions (in a selection process to get a job or win an award). The asking and answering of questions is a communication skill that can be improved with practice. The following sections offer suggestions for asking questions in an informational interview and answering questions in a selection interview.

Conducting an Effective Informational Interview

The goal of an informational interview is to gather information. You might conduct one to gather information about a possible career, write a story for your campus newspaper, or collect information for a speech. The following are a few strategies for conducting an effective informational interview.

Be prepared. Research the person you are interviewing and the topic for discussion before the interview. Thorough research enables you to prepare intelligent and relevant questions and to spontaneously probe the interviewee's answers. Also, the interviewee will be more open and forthcoming if he or she thinks you are prepared and knowledgeable. Without proper background information, your questions might sound uninformed. Such questions often discourage interviewees and make their responses superficial. For example, suppose that you were interviewing a practicing attorney about her or his profession. Before the interview you should learn something about the profession, the qualifications for entering it, and some challenges in practicing law. This knowledge would enable you to ask interesting questions that build on your research. For further illustration, compare the following uninformed questions with those that demonstrate some prior knowledge of the topic. Which questions do you think the attorney would be more interested in answering?

UNINFORMED	INFORMED
How do you like being an attorney?	Why do you practice civil law instead of criminal law?
Is getting into law school hard?	When applying to law school, is it more important to have a good grade point average or a high score on the LSAT?
Do you make a lot of money?	What are the advantages of requiring a retainer before you take a case compared to working off a commission?

Organize your questions. Structure the interview just as you would organize a speech, with an introduction, body, and conclusion. The introduction should be brief and to the point. Often the introduction is more conversational than a list of formal questions. The best introduction establishes rapport between the communicators and previews the body of the interview. Small talk is one way to put both parties at ease and establish the relationship for the rest of the interview. Find out something interesting about the interviewee and come prepared with two or three questions about his or her life ("I hear you are writing a book. How is it going?"). But do not prolong the small talk. Look for an early opportunity to begin the interview ("As you know, I am here to ask you questions about your career") and then preview the topics ("I would like to discuss your preparation for your career, what your job responsibilities are, and what qualities you think are necessary to be successful").

The body should flow logically so that the interviewer and the interviewee both know where the discussion is going. One structure that works well for an informational interview is to divide the interview into topics. Your background research should provide you with three or four appropriate topics. Introduce each topic with a general, introductory question and then follow up with increasingly specific questions. For a 20- to 30-minute interview, you should plan approximately four questions on three or four topics. You will also be asking spontaneous probes that you do not prepare ahead of time. Often you will prepare more questions than you ask. You should mark some of your questions or even topics as "ITP" (if time permits). If you have plenty of time, you can ask the ITP questions. But if you ask a lot of spontaneous probes or if the interviewee is very talkative, then you should skip the ITP questions.

The conclusion should clearly signal the end of the interview. Signal a desire to finish nonverbally by leaning forward and making direct eye contact with the interviewee. Verbally, use a closing question to signal the end of the interview ("Is there anything else that you would like to say?"). Once you have completed asking questions, express gratitude to your interviewee for his or her participation in the interview. If you are going to write an article or paper based on the interview, you might offer to send a copy to the interviewee. You might also engage in additional small talk, but do not prolong the ending. Be brief and appreciative.

Ask open questions. Open questions are general questions that allow the interviewee to determine the amount and kind of information (Stewart and Cash 2000). Closed questions ask for specific comments on narrow subjects and are often called yes/no questions. Closed questions restrict the interviewee's responses. Some closed questions can be useful in an interview to set up open questions or clarify information. (Q: Did you study at Oxford University? A: Yes. Q: What do you see as the major difference between the British and American systems of higher education?) Open questions provide a greater opportunity for the exchange of information and should be used frequently in an informational interview. For example, compare these closed and open questions.

CLOSED	OPEN
Did you think you were going to win the race?	What were you thinking just before the race started?
Are you patriotic?	How do you show patriotism in your life?
Are the Beatles the greatest rock band of all time?	Why are the Beatles your favorite band?
Should I ask open-ended questions in my informational interview?	How do open-ended questions encourage more detailed responses in an informational interview?

A Brief Guide to Interviewing

APPENDIX

Carefully phrase your questions. Your questions should be clear and concise so that the interviewee can easily and quickly grasp your meaning. In an informational interview, you should talk only about 30 percent of the time (Stewart and Cash 2000). If you talk more than this, the respondent might become confused by the lengthy questions or will not have sufficient time to answer. Beginning interviewers, in their nervousness, sometimes talk too much. They talk around an issue, searching for just the right combination of words. For instance, consider this question: "What do you think is the reason why animals have no rights—do you think they need some government agency or something like the humane society to help protect them?" A more precise question might be: "How can the government protect animals against unethical treatment?" Problems of phrasing can cause confusion. Here are some tips for asking clear and concise questions.

- Ask one question at a time. Sometimes interviewers unintentionally ask two or three questions at the same time. These double-barreled questions sometimes confuse interviewees, leaving them wondering which question to answer.

DOUBLE-BARRELED QUESTION	ONE QUESTION AT A TIME
Do you think the country is heading into a recession and should the federal government lower the interest rate to help the downturn in the economy?	How does lowering the interest rate help prevent a recession?
Do you think the university should offer a major in ethnic studies, because doesn't such a major help people understand each other better?	How would a major in ethnic studies benefit the university?

- Ask objective questions. Objective questions are impartial and allow the interviewee to decide how to respond. The opposite of objective questions are leading questions, which suggest or imply a proper response. Leading questions sometimes restrict answers and limit the exchange of information. Interviewees will sometimes say what they think you want to hear rather than what they really think. Strong leading questions, called loaded questions, can create an atmosphere where the respondent feels compelled to answer a certain way. Instead, phrase the question so that it allows interviewees to speak their minds freely.

LEADING	OBJECTIVE
Most students dislike the university's pass/fail policy. What do you think?	What do you think of the university's pass/fail policy?
The new fall fashions seem so bulky and uncomfortable. Do you like them?	What is your opinion of the new fall fashions?
We have such a parking problem on campus. Don't you think we should build a new parking garage?	What are the advantages of building a new parking garage on campus?

- Use language that is easily understood by the interviewee. Translate or define any difficult phrases or specialized vocabulary. Avoid jargon. Try to translate technical words so that the interviewee will understand your meaning. Similarly, try not to use acronyms or abbreviations that may not be familiar to the interviewee.

HARD TO UNDERSTAND VOCABULARY	MORE ACCESSIBLE LANGUAGE
How often do you watch **CMT?**	How often do you watch the Country Music Channel?
Do you agree with the **new law** on child safety seats?	How do you feel about the new law that requires children under the age of four to be restrained in a safety seat?

Probe the answers to your questions. Some of the most interesting information in an interview comes from spontaneous follow-up probes to your main questions. Such spontaneous exchanges often encourage interviewees to go beyond their initial response and provide more detail and insight. Here are four different types of probes that you can use to follow up your main questions.

- Nudging probes (Stewart and Cash 2000). Nudging probes are simple verbal or nonverbal actions that encourage an interviewee to keep talking. Vocalizations like, "yes," "I see," "really," or "then what happened?" encourage interviewees to extend their answers. Nonverbally, you can gently nudge the interviewee to keep talking by nodding your head. A silent probe is also sometimes effective. If an interviewee seems to be struggling for the right words or thinking of what to say next, simply wait in silence until he or she starts speaking again. If you jump in too quickly with your own words, you might disrupt the interviewee's thoughts and cut short an answer.
- Informational probe. An informational probe follows up on specific words, phrases, or concepts in an answer. Listen carefully to the respondent and develop a new question based on his or her answer. Use informational probes to clarify answers, probe unstated feelings and opinions, or to simply seek more information about the topic. For instance, if the interviewee admits, "I drink too much coffee," you could probe, "How much is too much?" Or perhaps the interviewee says, "It was very difficult to leave Missouri for New York." You could probe, "What do you miss about Missouri?" or "Why was it difficult to leave Missouri?"
- Restatement probe. A restatement probe repeats the main question in a new way or with different words. Use a restatement probe when the interviewee does not understand or does not answer the main questions you asked. For example, consider this exchange:

  Q: What is it like to be a professor?

  A: Well, most people think you are absent-minded.

  Q: I mean, what are your research responsibilities as a professor?

- Paraphrasing probe. A paraphrasing probe repeats the interviewee's answer or series of answers in your own words. Use a paraphrasing probe to check the accuracy of your perceptions and understanding. "It seems you are saying that educational reforms, such as mandatory testing and smaller classrooms, are not working. If these current reforms are not working, what would you suggest we try next?"

Participating in a Selection Interview

You might participate in a selection interview to obtain a job, to get into a club or organization, to win an award, or to be promoted. Participating in selection interviews reverses your role from asking questions to answering them. You will often be selected based on how you answer these questions. Here are a few tips to participating in a selection interview.

Be prepared. Many interviewees in a selection process fail because they do not properly prepare for the encounter. Their lack of preparation is often revealed in the interviewing process, and interviewers are likely to think that they are not serious about being selected. In one recent example from our career development center, a company mailed information about the company and the job to all potential interviewees. The first questions the interviewer asked were about this information. If the interviewee admitted not reading the material or seemed uninformed about it, the interviewer ended the interview abruptly. The company was not interested in talking with anyone who was unprepared.

Watch a video about how to participate effectively in selection interviews (Clip A.1).

Know as much as possible about the company or organization. Locate the company website and read about its history, performance, and other background information. Research the company in an index of printed or Internet resources. Two excellent sources of such information are the career journal index from *The Wall Street Journal* (http://www.careerjournal.com) and the company directory for the national Association of Colleges and Employers (http://www.jobweb.com). Finally, ask the career development center at your university for information about the company. Most career centers have a library of material on companies that recruit on campus.

You should also read the selection announcement, such as a job description, carefully. Ask yourself what kind of person are they looking for? You might also contact the organization and ask if a more detailed description is available, or you might try to speak to someone involved in the selection process. Ask this person the same question: "What kind of person are they looking for?" After carefully considering the answers to this question, write each of the qualifications for the job or award vertically down one side of a piece of paper. On the other side, write your characteristics that match those qualifications. Think of specific examples that demonstrate your qualifications. For instance, if the description says the organization is looking for an independent worker, think about a project at school that you initiated and conducted on your own. Continue the process until you have a comprehensive list of your qualifications with examples that pertain to the job.

Create a favorable first impression. The old adage, "You don't get a second chance to make a first impression," is especially true in a selection interview. A favorable first impression establishes your initial credibility and provides a favorable beginning to the selection process. There are a few simple things you can do to create a favorable first impression. These are not substitutes for effective answers to the interviewer's questions and will not get you the award or the job by themselves, but they do set the stage for effective answers.

APPENDIX | A Brief Guide to Interviewing

- Dress appropriately. Ask about the appropriate dress and conform to those expectations. Unless otherwise specified, dress professionally. This usually means a dark suit of some type for both men and women. Dressing professionally will not only impress the interviewer but will also increase your own confidence.
- Arrive early. Be at the interview at least 10 minutes early. Promptness is a quality that most employers are seeking, and arriving early demonstrates your strong interest in the job or award. Arriving late, on the other hand, is one mistake that may be difficult to overcome. Locate the address ahead of time and obtain clear directions. If you are unsure of the location, you may want to arrive early to check the location.
- Be aware of your nonverbal communication. When the interviewer approaches you, make direct eye contact and smile. Use a firm but not overpowering handshake. When entering the interview room, wait for an invitation to be seated. Sit with an open posture (do not cross your arms) and face the interviewer. Lean slightly forward and use a confident but not overpowering voice. Again, remember to smile.

Anticipate and practice common questions. There are standard questions that apply to most selection interviews. Rehearse answers to these questions before you get to the interview. Some common questions include:

1. Tell me about yourself.
2. What motivates you to put forth your greatest effort?
3. Why do you want to work for us? (or win this award?)
4. What are your short-term career goals?
5. Where do you see yourself five years from now?
6. How do you handle conflict?
7. What type of boss do you like to work for?
8. What is your greatest strength?
9. What is your greatest weakness?
10. Tell me about a mistake you made recently and how you corrected it.

Many websites contain even longer lists of common questions used in selection interviews. Two good ones are http://www.job-interview.net/ and www.nextsteps.org/interview/intques.html. Preparing answers to these questions will be useful even if the interviewer does not ask them. For instance, even if the exact question is not asked, many of your prepared answers will be appropriate for different questions. Practicing answers to these questions will give you the chance to rehearse your confident delivery.

Sell yourself. You should never exaggerate your qualifications on your résumé or in an interview, but you should present yourself in the most positive way possible. Every question in the interview basically asks the question, Why should I select you? You want to answer this question positively. Many first-time interviewees feel awkward talking about themselves. They feel as if they are boasting or bragging too much. In a selection interview, you need to overcome these feelings and be assertive in selling yourself. Speak confidently and succinctly about your accomplishments and qualifications. Your answers should be between 30 seconds and two minutes long. If an answer takes longer than two minutes, the interviewer will often becomes restless and stop listening.

Answer questions with specific examples. One key to a successful interview is answering questions with specific examples. Specific examples illustrate your qualifications in a memorable way by helping the interviewer remember your answer and distinguishes you from other candidates. It is easy to say you work well with people, but a specific example of working with people provides some tangible evidence to support your statement. When giving a specific example, remember the *acronym* CAR, which stands for *c*ontext, *a*ction, and *r*esults. Provide context for your example with a few brief comments about the situation. Next, explain specific actions you performed in the situation. Finally, describe tangible results that occurred from your actions. Below are three examples of CARs.

STATEMENT OF PERSONAL QUALIFICATION	I AM VERY ORGANIZED
Context	This semester I carried 18 units, wrote for the campus newspaper, and worked 20 hours a week at a part-time job.
Action	Using a daily planner, I scheduled my time carefully, including reserving blocks of hours for study and tracking my assignments on a project manager.
Results	Even though this was my hardest semester, I earned my highest grade point average ever and was selected to the dean's honor roll.

STATEMENT OF PERSONAL QUALIFICATION	I AM GOOD AT DELEGATING RESPONSIBILITY
Context	I work at a large department store, and I was in charge of our United Way giving campaign last year. We have over 300 employees. I couldn't talk with each one individually, and an announcement in the employee newsletter seemed too impersonal.
Action	I sought out reliable volunteers from each department within the store to be group leaders. I held two training sessions where I reviewed the value of the program and taught the group leaders how to approach colleagues for donations. I made two follow-up phone calls during the campaign to each group leader to offer encouragement and to check the status of the campaign.
Results	With very little investment of my own time, we had the most successful campaign in recent years.

APPENDIX | A Brief Guide to Interviewing

STATEMENT OF PERSONAL QUALIFICATION	I TAKE INITIATIVE IN SOLVING PROBLEMS
Context	Last year I noticed that our campus did not have a recycling program for classroom buildings and offices. Students were throwing aluminum cans and glass bottles into the regular trash.
Action	I approached the student senate with a plan that called for a recycling canister to be placed in every classroom building. I estimated the cost of the program and arranged for a local company to collect the items to be recycled and share the profits. The senate approved the plan and budgeted enough money for a trial program in the largest buildings.
Results	We made enough money on the trial program to expand the effort to every building on campus.

Follow up the interview with a thank-you note. Finally, follow up the interview with a thank-you note. Experts estimate that less than 10 percent of employment applicants send thank-you notes (Banis 2002). Sending a thank-you note is not only polite and thoughtful, but it sets you apart from 90 percent of the other candidates.

GLOSSARY

Abstract words that refer to thoughts, ideas, or theories.

Accent a nonverbal function that highlights, accentuates, or emphasizes verbal messages.

Acceptance speech a brief statement made upon the receipt of an award, gift, or special honor.

Accommodation sacrificing, in whole or in part, your own preferences and points of view.

Acronyms a word or name formed out of the first letter of words in a series (such as PUSH, for People United to Save Humanity).

Active listeners people who focus on the moment, are aware of interactions as they unfold, respond appropriately, and are aware of distractions.

Ad hoc groups temporary groups created for the purpose of making a specific decision or solving a unique problem.

Adaptors nonverbal gestures that we use to adapt to our environment, such as fanning ourselves when we are hot.

Adept skilled.

Affective emotional or sentimental.

After-dinner speech a presentation that entertains or enlightens in an amusing way.

Agenda a written guide that lists the order of tasks to be accomplished and topics to be discussed by the group.

Agenda-setting the process by which media identify and structure important and meaningful issues for audiences.

Alienation to be unfriendly or hostile—to isolate someone from the group.

Allness the use of one aspect of our identity to describe our whole self.

Ambient sounds background noise in a particular context, such as the clatter of plates and murmur of people talking in a busy restaurant.

Ambiguous words that do not have a clear meaning.

Ambushing a barrier to listening by which listeners seek ways to respond to or attack the speaker.

Amnesty an official pardon or forgiveness for wrongdoing.

Analogy compares or contrasts one unfamiliar concept or object with something that the audience already knows or understands.

Anchors attitudes or beliefs that act as a personal standard for judging other messages.

Anecdote a brief story.

Appeal to authority a fallacy in which someone serves as a spokesperson outside his or her area of expertise.

Appeal to popular opinion a fallacy based on the premise that the listener should think or act the same way as a substantial group of people.

Appreciation the goal of listening for pleasure or enjoyment.

Appropriate audience attention focuses the audience's thoughts on the topic and purpose of the speech.

Appropriated take for one's own use.

Appropriateness responding in ways that fit the communication context.

Arbitrary words that have no direct connection to the objects they represent.

Argot the specialized language of a coculture.

Argument a statement of belief, or claim, presented with evidence and reasoning.

Artifactics the use of objects to communicate nonverbally.

Attending the first stage in the listening process involves making the conscious choice to listen.

Attention step an explicit attempt by the speaker to gain the audience's interest.

Attractiveness what we visualize as the "perfect look" or idealized physical attributes.

Attractiveness bias the tendency to think better of attractive people than unattractive people and to make positive attributions about their behavior.

Attribution in the context of preparing and delivering a speech, crediting or referencing the sources of information.

Attribution in the context of perception, the assignment of meaning to the actions of ourselves and others.

Audience centered speakers adapt the speech to the audience's needs, level of knowledge, background, and interests.

Audience expectations what the audience believes is going to happen during the speech.

Authoritarian leadership the leader of the group makes all decisions for the group.

Autonomy the desire to retain independence.

Avoidance attempting to evade conflict.

Back context a private environment that requires a less conscious effort to manage the impression you project to others.

Banal dull or commonplace.

Biorhythms recurring cycles of biological processes, such as alertness or hunger that peak at a regular time each day.

Blind quadrant the part of yourself that others know but you do not.

Breadth the number of contexts in which communicators interact in a relationship.

Brief example an illustration familiar to the audience, which therefore requires very little detail.

Cause and effect speech structure divides the speech into the causes of some phenomenon and the effects that result from it.

Change the need for novelty and new experiences.

Changeable words based on social, political, and cultural contexts, and the historical time in which they are located.

Channels the mediums that carry messages between communicators.

Charisma the ability to influence others in specific situations through personal dynamism, likability, and vision.

Chronemics the use of time to communicate nonverbally.

Chronological speech structure organizes a speech around segments or sequences of time.

Civic engagement participating to create change, organizing others who share a common vision, and working to improve communities and organizations.

Civility accepting others as equal partners in reaching common goals.

Claims of fact statements about the truth or falsity of some assertion or statement.

Claims of policy statements that ask listeners to consider a specific course of action.

Claims of value statements that ask listeners to form a judgment or evaluation.

Clichés worn-out phrases used so often that they have lost their vividness.

Co-culture cultures within a culture.

Code a set of conventions or rules shared by members of a culture and which governs the use of words and symbols.

Code-switching the ability to adopt a preferred code based on the group with which you are interacting.

Coercion psychologically or physically forcing the other person to accept your point of view.

Cognitive dissonance the uncomfortable tension listeners experience when two ideas, concepts, or things that they believe, value, or do are related but contradictory.

Coherence the standard of evaluating narratives that asks whether a story makes sense based on the details, order of events, credibility of the storyteller, behaviors of the characters, and comparisons with similar accounts.

Coherent easy to follow; logical and consistent.

Cohesion a sense of attachment, solidarity, and camaraderie that binds a group together.

Collaboration working together to reach consensus.

Collectivism emphasis on the importance of group obligations, needs, and identity.

Colloquial informal language.

Communal relating to a community or group of people who share interests.

GLOSSARY

Communication the process of creating and sharing meaning through the use of symbols.

Communication apprehension fear of communication situations.

Communication climate the way people feel about their interactions with others, either in relationships or in groups.

Comparison speech structure organizes information around distinct points of similarity or difference.

Complement a nonverbal function that adds meaning to verbal messages.

Complete sentence outline uses full sentences, including standard punctuation such as periods, commas, and question marks, to delineate the speaking information.

Comprehension the goal of listening for understanding.

Compromise giving up something in order to find an acceptable solution to the problem.

Concrete words that come as close as possible to an objective description of reality.

Confirmation when others accept our presentation of self and act in harmony with the image we are displaying.

Conflict a condition of disharmony and disagreement that exists when people who depend on one another see their needs, beliefs and values, or goals as incompatible.

Connection the need to be included in a relationship.

Connotation the meaning of words based on individual or cultural experiences or values.

Construct an idea or category of meaning.

Constructive responses to conflict communication characterized by cooperation, shared interests, flexibility, open discussion, and support of differences.

Constructivism a theory that people interpret and act on experience based on a mental system of organizing knowledge.

Contempt disdain, scorn, or disapproval.

Contentious controversial or debatable.

Continuous a characteristic of nonverbal communication that indicates that nonverbal messages are streams of cues.

Continuum an uninterrupted range or field.

Contradict a nonverbal function that opposes, denies, or disagrees with a verbal message.

Credibility the audience's perception of the speaker's expertise, character, and goodwill.

Crescendo building toward a climax or highest point.

Cultivation theory an approach to media research which argues that media consumption has a cumulative influence in promoting a shared worldview.

Cultural sensitivity possessing the knowledge, awareness, and skills to communicate effectively and appropriately with diverse people.

Culture everything that makes up our way of life, including shared values, knowledge, behaviors, and symbolic expression.

Curriculum a set of courses in a college or other school.

Dating a process that places observations in a specific time frame to suggest that change is possible.

Decoding the interpretation of a message by deciphering symbols into understandable and meaningful ideas, thoughts, and feelings.

Deduction reasoning that starts with a general statement and draws a specific conclusion.

Defensiveness acting protectively or as if one has been attacked.

Deference high esteem or respect.

Definition establishes the meanings of words or concepts.

Demeanor one's outward behavior or way of carrying oneself.

Democratic leadership The leader of the group allows all members to participate fully in the decision-making process.

Demographic characteristics the age, sex, socioeconomic status, ethnicity or nationality, level of education, and professional interests of the audience.

Denotation the most concrete, specific, and objective meaning of a word.

Depth the amount of time communicators interact and the personal level of information they exchange in a relationship.

Derived credibility the credibility, or belief, in a speaker that is created by the content of the message and the manner in which it is presented.

Despotic a cruel and repressive leader.

Destructive responses to conflict communication characterized by competition, self-centeredness, hostility, and defensiveness.

Dialectical tensions ongoing, changing needs that are often opposite or contradictory.

Disconfirmation when others ignore our presentation of self and act indifferent to the image we are displaying.

Discrete separate and distinct.

Disfluencies vocal pauses such as "um," "aaa," and "and a."

Disfranchised alienated or excluded.

Display rules cultural expectations about the public display of emotions.

Disruptive roles satisfy member's needs at the expense of the group.

Diversity valuing the process by which difference becomes meaningful and developing the competence to live, learn, and work within many cultures.

Dogmatic rigid and inflexible.

Doublespeak the use of language to intentionally obscure, confuse, equivocate, or deceive.

Dyads consist of two people communicating.

Dynamism energy and drive.

Electronic society the stage at which all forms of communication have been influenced, either directly or indirectly, by electronic media.

Emblems nonverbal gestures with specific and definitive meanings, often substituting for explicit verbal words.

Empathetic echo a listening or response technique that paraphrases or repeats a message.

Empathetic listening establishes common ground between people by acknowledging the legitimacy of feelings and giving support to others.

Empathy the ability to accurately perceive the experience and behavior of another person.

Encoding the initiation and creation of a message as a communicator translates ideas, thoughts, and feelings into symbols.

Enduring credibility the impression of credibility that remains with your audience.

Entertainment the form of gratification we get when media function as a form of wish fulfillment, providing satisfying images and stimulating emotions.

Enunciation saying words clearly.

Epithet a negative label used to describe a person.

Equivocate use of ambiguous words to deceive.

Estranged no longer close or affectionate; unfriendly or hostile.

Ethics the principles that guide our decisions about what is good or bad, right or wrong.

Ethos the ethics or credibility of the speaker.

Euphemism a socially accepted word or phrase substituted for an uncomfortable or unacceptable one.

Evaluation the goal of listening to render an opinion or judgment.

Examples illustrations or stories that explicate a particular point.

Explanation clarifies some concept or idea by further identifying its source, explaining how it works, or relating it to other concepts.

Expression the need to be or have others be open, candid, and confiding.

Expressive communication verbally acknowledging how others feel and sharing experiences.

Extemporaneous speaking using a keyword outline to deliver a prepared speech.

GLOSSARY

Extended example a single illustration retold with detail and context.

Eye contact looking at the audience when delivering a speech.

Facework the act of presenting the self.

Fallacy an error in reasoning.

False cause a fallacy that implies a cause-and-effect relationship where none exists.

False choice a fallacy in which the speaker presents a false dichotomy between two choices.

Feedback a response or reaction to a message.

Femininity an emphasis on interdependence, quality of life, and variability in the roles that females and males are expected to perform.

Fester annoy, irritate, or aggravate to make something worse.

Fidelity the standard of evaluating narratives that refers to the truthfulness of a story based on the facts and relevance to personal experience or values.

Figurative analogy compares two or more concepts, objects, people, or places from different classes or categories.

Flaming impolite outbursts.

Fluctuates changes, varies, alternatives, swings back and forth, ebbs and flows.

Foot in the door the technique of starting with a small request and then following later with a more substantial one.

Front context a public setting where you actively manage the impression you project to others.

Fundamental attribution error the overestimation of the degree to which other people's behaviors are due to internal factors and underestimation of the significance of external forces.

Gatekeepers editors, producers, webmasters, and other media managers who decide which messages will get produced.

Gender identity the conception you have of yourself as a male or female, masculine or feminine.

General speech purpose the overall objective of the speech, such as to inform, to persuade, or to entertain.

Generalized other a composite view of society's reflection of yourself.

Generic general, standard.

Gestures significant body movements that convey a message.

Gossip talk about an absent third party.

Gratification function the active use of media to fulfill needs and desires.

Group charge the overall or main objective of the group.

Group norms expectations, established through interaction, about how members should behave.

Group synergy group members combine their abilities to produce an outcome greater than the sum of their individual abilities.

Haptics the use of touch to communicate nonverbally.

Hasty generalization a fallacy in which the speaker draws a conclusion about a group or general condition based on limited examples.

Hearing the act of perceiving sounds or other related stimuli.

Hidden quadrant those things that you know about yourself but others do not.

High context an interaction style in which people expect others to figure out implicit meanings based on the situation or the relationship between communicators.

Homepage the first document posted on a website and the doorway through which additional documents or information can be accessed.

Homophobic possessing irrational fear and/or hatred of homosexuality.

Hypodermic needle model explains direct media effects by suggesting that a specific message can be "shot" into an unsuspecting audience.

Hypothetical example an illustration that is not real, but imaginary.

Identity the conception of yourself as a member of a group or category.

Idiosyncratic personal, unique, individual, all your own.

Illustrators nonverbal gestures that accent or clarify verbal messages.

Imagery evoking a mental picture in the mind of the audience.

Imaginary audience syndrome tendency of teenage girls to think that other people are preoccupied with their appearance and behaviors.

Imbue invest with or permeate.

Impervious unresponsive to or incapable of being affected by what someone says or means.

Impromptu speaking delivering a speech with little or no preparation.

Inclusive language verbal communication that demonstrates respect for others by using language that values them as individuals.

Indexing a process that ties evaluations to a specific circumstance to make them unique.

Indifference a lack of interest in listening.

Individualism emphasis on the importance of individual rights over group rights, individual needs over group needs, and individual identity over group identity.

Induction reasoning from a particular instance to a generalization.

Inference a conclusion, projection, or interpretation based on facts.

Inflection the vocal emphasis placed on each word when speaking.

Information when discussing media gratification, the desire for knowledge based on curiosity, personal investment, or need.

Initial credibility the credibility speakers bring to a situation by virtue of their reputation or accomplishments.

Initiator one who begins or advances the communication process by generating a message.

Inspirational speech a presentation that aims to motivate listeners and arouse their passions.

Instrumental communication listening or responding to help others solve problems or accomplish goals.

Integrating topics areas of common interest that members of a relationship enjoy discussing.

Interim an intervening or temporary step.

Internal summary reviews concepts or ideas to help remind the audience of key points and to move the speech to the next important point.

Interpersonal communication interaction among a small number of people; occurs when individuals treat each other as unique and interact in an individual or customized way.

Interpersonal similarity occurs when we share common attitudes, values, habits, and communication styles with other members of a relationship.

Interpretation stage of perception in which we determine the meaning of an event or interaction.

Interpreter one who perceives and attempts to understand a message.

Interpreting the second stage in the listening process involves giving meaning to sounds or related stimuli.

Intimate interpersonal relationships characterized by high levels of trust, warmth, and affection; nonintimate relationships are more impersonal, distant, and formal.

Intrapersonal communication an internal dialogue with ourselves

Intrinsic a characteristic of nonverbal communication indicating that nonverbal messages are inherently connected to our emotions and mental states.

Intrinsically inherently or fundamentally connected to something.

Jargon a technical language often associated with a particular profession.

Johari Window a model depicting an individual's degree of self-awareness.

Key word outline uses only a few important words from each sentence of a complete sentence outline to delineate the speaking information.

Kinesics the use of body motion to communicate nonverbally.

Laissez-faire leadership the leader of the group gives minimal guidance and allows group members to work with little or no structure.

GLOSSARY

Latitude of acceptance the range of positions a listener is likely to accept or tolerate.

Latitude of noncommitment the range of positions a listener neither accepts or rejects.

Latitude of rejection the range of positions a listener is likely to reject or consider intolerable.

Lavish plentiful or extravagant.

Lay people individuals who are not part of the clergy.

Leadership the process of exerting positive influence over other group members.

Leakage a nonverbal cue that reveals emotions we are trying to conceal.

Lexical recall ability to remember a specific word.

Linguistic relativity hypothesis the idea that our thoughts are influenced by the words we know and the patterns of language that dominate our culture.

Listening the process of perceiving, constructing meaning from, and responding to spoken or nonverbal messages.

Literacy ability to comprehend and use written symbols.

Literal analogy compares two concepts, objects, people, or places that are inherently similar to each other.

Logos arguments based on logic or reason.

Low context an interaction style in which communicators expect information to be direct and explicit.

Luxuriating to indulge oneself in a lavish or extremely comfortable manner.

Main points the most important ideas to be communicated to the audience and those that lead directly to the specific purpose of the speech.

Maintenance roles serve to build relationships within the group and to create a sense of teamwork.

Manuscript speaking delivering a speech from a script written out word for word.

Masculinity emphasis on power, assertiveness, independence, materialism, and rigid distinctions between expectations of males and females.

Mass communication the creation of meaning through messages sent to a large, unseen, and anonymous audience.

Media the vehicles that carry messages.

Media literacy ability to understand the language of media and critically assess the contribution of media to society.

Media synergy the use by media conglomerates of as many channels of delivery as possible for similar content.

Mediated communication occurs when communicators use some form of technology, including television, radio, film, newspapers, and the Internet.

Memorized speaking delivering a speech by writing out the speech, memorizing the content, and then delivering it word for word, without the use of notes.

Message a symbolic expression of ideas, thoughts, and feelings.

Message overload occurs when communicators are overwhelmed with the number of messages; communicators who experience overload stop attending to or comprehending some or most of the messages they perceive.

Metacommunication communication about communication; discussing the relationship dimension of messages is one type of metacommunication.

Metaphor comparing one thing, idea, or action to another.

Misnomer misnamed or inappropriate use of a name, label, or title.

Monochronic cultures cultures that view time as linear rather than circular.

Moral relativism the idea that there are no absolute moral standards.

Motivated sequence a persuasive speech structure designed to move audiences toward taking immediate action.

Mundane ordinary, routine, or unexceptional.

Mythos the use of myths, legends, and folktales as persuasive appeals.

Name-calling a fallacy based on attacking a speaker's physical or character traits rather than the content of his or her argument.

Narrative speech structure organizes a speech around one or more stories.

Network society the integration of several communication technologies into a new social system.

Noise anything that interferes with the creation of shared meaning between or among communicators.

Nonlinguistic a characteristic of nonverbal communication indicating that nonverbal messages are outside languages.

Nonverbal communication messages expressed through symbols other than words, including hand gestures, facial expressions, touching, vocal inflection, and clothing.

Occasion the time, mood, and setting of the speech.

Olfactory the use of smell to communicate nonverbally.

Open quadrant the part of yourself that is known both to you and to others.

Oral cultures cultures in which speaking and hearing are the dominant forms of communication.

Organization placing stimuli in a knowledge structure or category to give them meaning and aid retention.

Outline a concise synopsis that displays the structure and relationship of speech ideas and concepts.

Pantomime to act out or demonstrate without saying any words.

Paradox an apparent contradiction or inconsistency.

Paraphrasing listeners summarize messages in their own words.

Participation the level of communication where we accept others who are different as unique, valuable, and integrated into our lives.

Passive aggression indirect expression of hostility, often through the use of humor, guilt, or inconsiderate behavior.

Passive listeners people who expend little or no energy in the listening process.

Pathos arguments based on emotional appeals.

Patterned follows a regular order.

Peer reviewed experts in the discipline select only the best articles to publish in a journal.

Penny press inexpensive, mass-produced newspapers designed to appeal to the growing immigrant population in the United States.

Perception process of assigning meaning to sensory information and experiences.

Perception check a tool that gauges the accuracy of your perceptions by engaging in conversations with others.

Perception shifts strategies for thinking creatively and managing different perspectives.

Perceptual constancy the tendency to maintain the same perception of people and events over time.

Perceptual field the range of stimuli that the mind can apprehend.

Personal constructs categories by which people and events can be differentiated.

Perspective taking the ability to consider behavior from someone else's point of view.

Persuade influence others by reinforcing or changing their beliefs.

Physical attraction occurs when we are attracted to someone's appearance through such attributes as facial features, height, body type, and hair color.

Pithy clever or noteworthy.

Plagiarism using other people's ideas, methods, or words without proper acknowledgment.

Polychronic cultures that view time as circular rather than linear.

Power distance the relative value that cultures place on status and power in relationships.

Predisposition a tendency or inclination to think or behave in a particular way.

Preliterate the state of a people before acquiring the ability to read and write.

Primary source firsthand knowledge, testimony, or direct evidence from authors who created the information.

GLOSSARY

Priming audience use of conceptual categories that have been emphasized in the media.

Privacy the need to be or have others be restrained, circumspect, and distant.

Problem/solution speech structure organizes information in a speech around one or more problems and one or more solutions to those problems.

Problem-solving agenda (PSA) a standard approach to group problem solving that maximizes critical thinking while minimizing rash or impulsive decisions.

Process speech describes how to make or do something by listing the essential steps of the process in time order from the earliest to the latest.

Pronunciation saying words according to accepted standards of English and in accordance with the expectations of the audience.

Prototype a specific person, personality, or phenomenon that exemplifies a set of characteristics.

Proverbial having the characteristic of a well-known story or proverb.

Proxemics the use of space to communicate nonverbally.

Proximity the equality of being close to something, an object, person, or event.

Pseudolistening pretending to listen.

Public communication interaction with large numbers of people.

Rate how quickly or slowly a speech is delivered.

Reciprocity taking turns, responding in kind.

Reconnaissance to scout out a location beforehand.

Recrimination to seek revenge or punishment.

Reference groups groups with which we most strongly identify.

Referential meaning a meaning that can be indicated by pointing to an object.

Regulate a function of nonverbal communication that controls, adjusts, or alters the flow of verbal messages.

Rejection when others contradict the presentation of ourself and act inconsistently with the image we are displaying.

Remembering the final stage in the listening process involves the retention and recall of the messages.

Repeat a function of nonverbal communication that reiterates verbal messages.

Repertoire a range of effective and ethical communication behaviors from which to choose.

Repugnant extremely distasteful.

Resilient strong; able to recover quickly from injury, either mental or physical.

Resistance the level of communication where we judge others who are different and avoid or reject them.

Respect the level of communication where we begin to see value in the ways that others are different.

Responding the third stage in the listening process involves any discernable reaction including both verbal and nonverbal feedback.

Rhetorical question a question you want the audience to think about but not answer vocally.

Role taking the act of understanding the motives, interests, and actions of other people and adopting those actions, at least temporarily.

Ruminating mull over, ponder, and think about over and over.

Salience personal relevance or interest.

Scripts guides to actions and expectations based on the categorization of perceptions.

Secondary source information based on other people's observation or research.

Selection focusing on some sensory stimuli rather than others.

Selective exposure people choose to watch or listen to media messages that confirm existing beliefs.

Selective retention people choose to remember media messages that confirm existing beliefs.

Self the total composite of a person's personality, experiences, and identity.

Self-awareness the consciousness of our existence and degree to which we understand ourselves.

Self-concept a relatively consistent image or set of perceptions that you have about yourself.

Self-deprecating criticizing or making fun of oneself.

Self-disclosure the intentional revelation of personal aspects of your self, including thoughts, preferences, feelings, and experiences, to another person within the context of an interpersonal relationship.

Self-esteem the value you attach to your self-concept.

Self-fulfilling prophecy the tendency to live up to the expectations created for us.

Self-monitoring the ability to see, think about, and act based on the consequences of your behavior.

Self-serving bias the tendency to attribute external causes to our own misfortunes, but not to those of others.

Semantic noise a barrier to listening triggered by a particular word or phrase used by a speaker.

Sensations perceptions of the body's condition.

Shock talk words or statements designed to horrify, outrage, or otherwise offend listeners.

Significant others people who are particularly important to you and with whom you share a close relationship.

Signpost tell an audience where they are and where they are going in a speech.

Similarity bias the attribution of our own motivations to someone else's behaviors.

Simile a type of metaphor that compares two things using the words "like" or "as."

Simultaneous occurring at the same time.

Slippery slope a fallacy based on the assumption that once a single step is taken, many other destructive ones are sure to follow.

Small group a limited number of individuals who communicate interdependently to achieve a common goal.

Small group communication interaction among three to seven people who communicate over time to accomplish some goal or purpose.

Social comparison when we understand our self by comparing it to others.

Social identity theory our identification with social groups is important for our self-concept, and the relative salience of a given identity depends on social context.

Social judgment theory evaluation of persuasive messages based on the beliefs we already hold.

Social learning the general theory that we learn new behaviors, customs, and routines by watching others.

Social penetration theory we disclose increasingly personal information about ourselves as the relationship develops, and we reserve discussion about our most private thoughts for our most intimate relationships.

Social proximity refers to "social closeness"; and we are often attracted to people who live near us, belong to the same groups or organizations, or attend the same school.

Social utility the function media serve when they provide common topics about social relationships and models for behavior.

Socially ascribed having characteristics attributed by others.

Spatial speech structure organizes a speech around familiar relationships in the environment, such as near and far, up and down, right and left, or east and west.

Speaking aids visual and auditory props that speakers use to develop a speech and help the audience conceptualize ideas.

Specific speech purpose the precise goal the speaker wants to achieve with the audience.

Speech of introduction a presentation that gives the audience information about the key speaker.

Speech of tribute a presentation that includes eulogies, toasts, and other speeches that commemorate special events such as national holidays.

GLOSSARY

Speech that calls for action persuasive speaking aimed to move the audience to a specific behavior.

Speech that convinces persuasive speaking that urges listeners to accept contentious facts, evaluate beliefs, or support actions.

Speech that demonstrates a presentation that shows audiences how to do something.

Speech that describes a presentation that provides details of an object or concept.

Speech that explains a presentation that teaches about or clarifies an event or development.

Speech that narrates a presentation that uses an extended story to make a statement.

Speech that reinforces persuasive speaking that attempts to strengthen existing attitudes, beliefs, or values.

Speech to entertain a speech whose overall objective is to amuse, enthrall, cheer, charm, or otherwise please an audience.

Speech to inform a speech whose overall objective is to explain a concept, idea, or process to an audience.

Speech to persuade a speech whose overall objective is to influence an audience to accept a belief, agree with a value, or take an action.

Stability the need to control our environment through safe and conventional routines.

Stages of relationship development patterns or life cycles that relationships pass through as they develop or deteriorate. Relationships have a beginning (or birth), middle (coming of age), and an end (death).

Standing group a group that has a broad mandate and works continuously on a variety of related problems.

Statistics numerical representations used to quantify ideas or concepts.

Stereotypes specific kinds of labels that characterize people based on the assumed traits of others in their group.

Stimuli things that evoke a reaction.

Stonewalling attempt to avoid or postpone discussion.

Subpoints ideas that amplify or develop the main points.

Subsidiary secondary or lesser importance.

Substitute a function of nonverbal communication that takes the place of verbal messages.

Surveillance the function of media to keep the public informed about social and political events.

Syllogism a form of reasoning that draws a conclusion based on two premises.

Symbolic the property of words that allows us to talk about things without being the things themselves.

Symbols the words, images, gestures, and expressions that we use to represent our thoughts, ideas, beliefs, and feelings.

Sympathy showing compassion for another person's feelings or situation.

Synchronize to coordinate activities and behaviors.

Syntax a characteristic of languages that prescribes a certain word order.

Taboos prohibited words or the behaviors that those words describe.

Tangential off the subject and unrelated to the main discussion.

Task roles facilitate the group goal or purpose.

Task-avoidance engaging in excessive socialization to postpone or forestall working on the group project.

Technological convergence the union of different, specialized media to meet the individual needs of users.

Territoriality the tendency of humans to mark and defend a particular space.

Testimony stated opinion in support of an idea.

Third person effect the belief that media influence others more than ourselves.

Tolerance the level of communication where we are willing to acknowledge that differences exist.

Topic outline uses brief phrases to summarize the major points of a presentation.

Topical speech structure organizes a speech around types or categories.

Toxic noise excessive environmental sound that distracts or pollutes the quality of life.

Transactional communication messages that communicators initiate and interpret simultaneously.

Transcendent surpassing human experience or beyond the material world.

Transitions verbal bridges that move the speech from one point or idea to the next.

Trash talk words or statements designed to insult perceived adversaries, usually involving name-calling or threats.

Trite worn out, clichéd, or trivial.

Turning points particular events, feelings, or interactions that change the direction or intensity of a relationship.

Ubiquitous everywhere, ever present.

Uncertainty avoidance the degree of uncertainty tolerated by members of a culture or group.

Unknown quadrant the category of things that neither you nor others know about yourself.

Urban legend an outrageous story that circulates in the tabloid press or on the Internet, such as stories of travelers who enjoy a drink in a lounge and awaken to find that their kidneys have been removed by criminal organ harvesters.

Verbal communication messages expressed through a formal language, using oral, written, or signed words.

Verbal language the systematic use of words and symbols to create and convey meaning.

Visualization a technique used to control communication apprehension by replacing negative thoughts and images with positive ones.

Vividness includes all sensations that seem to stand out from their surroundings.

Vocal pauses sounds speakers make while stopping to think of what they are going to say next, such as "ah," "a," "and a," "um," and "uh."

Vocal variety varying the rate, volume, and inflection in delivering a speech.

Vocalics the use of your voice to communicate nonverbally.

Volume how loudly a speech is delivered.

Voyeurism the practice of obtaining enjoyment or sexual gratification from the observation of others in private settings.

REFERENCES

Abrams, D., & Hogg, M. (1990). *Social identity theory: Constructive and critical advances.* Hemel Hempstead, England: Harvester Wheatsheaf.

Allen, M., D'Alessio, D., & Brezel, K. (1995). A meta-analysis summarizing the effects of pornography II. *Human Communication Research, 22,* 258–83.

Allen, S. (1999). "Mad dogs and Englishmen." *Guardian Weekly,* reprinted in *News Culture.* Buckingham, Eng.: Open University Press, 178–79.

Altman, I., & Taylor, D. (1973). *Social penetration: The development of interpersonal relationships.* New York: Holt, Rinehart, & Winston.

American Association of University Professors (AAUP). (1990). *Policy documents and reports (pp. 79–80).* Washington, DC: American Association of University Professors.

American Psycho (2000). Lions Gate Films.

Amichai-Hamburger, Wainapel, G., & Fox, S. (2002). "On the Internet no one knows I'm an introvert": extroversion, neuroticism, and Internet interaction. *Cyberpsychology & Behavior,* 5, 2.

Andersen, P. A. (2008). *Nonverbal communication: Forms and function, Second Ed.* Mountain View, CA: Mayfield Publishing.

Angell, L. R. (1998). Communication comforting strategies and social bereavement: Verbal and nonverbal planning and appropriateness. *Journal of Personal and Interpersonal Loss, 3* (3), 271–84.

Arnet, R. (1986). *Communication and community.* Carbondale: Southern Illinois University Press.

Aronson, E. (1984). *The social animal* (4th ed.). New York: W. H. Freeman.

Associated Press (2010). Public Speaking. Retrieved March 15, 2010 from http://www.encyclopedia.com/doc/1P1-157446034.html.

Astin, A. W. (1993). *What matters in college? Four critical years revisited.* San Francisco: Jossey-Bass.

Awamleh, R. G. (1999). Perceptions of leader charisma and effectiveness: The effects of vision, content, delivery, and organizational performance. *Leadership Quarterly, 10,* 345–74.

Ayers, J. & Ayres, T. A. (2003). Using images to enhance the impact of visualization. *Communication Reports, 16,* 47–56.

Ayres, J., & Heuett, B. L. (1997). The relationship between visual imagery and public speaking apprehension. *Communication Reports, 10,* 87–94.

Ayres, J., Heuett, B. L., & Sonandre, D. A. (1998). Testing a refinement in an intervention for communication apprehension. *Communication Reports, 11,* 73–86.

Bachen, C. M., & McLoughlin, M. M. (1999). Assessing the role of gender in college students' evaluations of faculty. *Communication Education, 48,* 193–201.

Baker, A. (2000). Two by two in cyberspace: getting together and connecting online. *Cyberpsychology & Behavior, 3,* 2.

Balint, K. (1998, May 24). Getting personal: Research finds computers often treated like human. Copley News Service. Retrieved June 5, 1998 from http://natcom.org/NCAnews/pressclips/articles1.htm.

Balint, K. (1999, August 29). Treatment of minorities harsher, officers admit. *San Diego Union Tribune,* p. A18.

Bandura, A. (1977). *Social learning theory.* Englewood Cliffs, NJ: Prentice Hall.

Bandura, A. (1983). Psychological mechanisms of aggression. In R. C. Green and E. I. Donnerstein (Eds.). *Aggression: Theoretical and empirical reviews.* New York: Academic Press, 1983.

Banis, W. J. (2002). The art of writing job-search letters. *Planning Job Choices: A Guide to the Job Search for New College Graduates,* 45th edition, 61–67. Bethlehem, PA: National Association of Colleges and Employers.

Bank, A. L., & Hupka, R. B. (1996). Sex differences in jealousy: Evolution or social construction? *Cross-Cultural Research, 3,* 24–60.

Baran, S. J. (1999). *Introduction to mass communication: Media literacy and culture,* Mountain View, CA: Mayfield.

Barge, D., & Meredith, W. (1994, July). A causal model of adolescent depression. *Journal of Psychology Interdisciplinary and Applied, 128,* 4, 4555.

Barker, L., Edwards, C., Gaines, C., Gladney, K., & Holley, R. (1981). An investigation of proportional time spent in various communication activities by college students. *Journal of Applied Communication Research, 8,* 101–109.

Bate, B., & Bowker, J. (1997). *Communication and the sexes.* Prospect Heights, IL: Waveland Press.

Bavelas, J. B., Coates, L., & Johnson, R. (2002). Listener responses as a collaborative process: the role of gaze. *Journal of Communication, 52,* 566–581.

Baxter, L. A. (1990). Dialectical contradictions in relational development. *Journal of Social and Personal Relationships, 7,* 69–88.

Baxter, L. A., & Bullis, C. (1984). Turning points in developing romantic relationships. *Human Communication Research, 12,* 469–93.

Baxter, L. A., & Montgomery, B. M. (1996). *Relating: Dialogues and dialectics.* New York: Guilford.

Baxter, L. A., & Wilmot, W. W. (1984). "Secret tests:" Social strategies for acquiring information about the state of the relationship. *Human Communication Research, 11,* 171–201.

Beamer, L. (1998). Bridging business cultures. *China Business Review, 25,* 54–58.

Beattie, G., & Shovelton, H. (1999). Mapping the range of information contained in the iconic hand gestures that accompany spontaneous speech. *Journal of Language and Social Psychology, 18,* 438.

Beatty, M., McCroskey, J., & Heisel, A. (1998, September). Communication apprehension as tempermental expression: A communibiological paradigm. *Communication Monographs, 65,* 197–220.

Beddingfield, K. T. (2002). Sharing a dorm room with a total stranger. Retrieved April 21, 2002, from www.usnews.com/usnews/edu/college/articles/devroom1.htm.

Benne, K. D. & Sheats, P. (1948). Functional roles of group members. *Journal of Social Issues, 4* (2), 41–49.

Benoit, W. L. & Benoit, P. J. (1995, Winter). Participants' and observers' memory for conversational behavior. *Southern Communication Journal, 61,* 139–55.

Benson, T. W. (1996). Rhetoric, civility, and community: Political debate on computer bulletin boards. *Communication Quarterly, 44,* 359–79.

Bentley, S. (1998, February). Listening better. *Nursing Homes and Long Term Care Management, 47,* 56–59.

Berlo, D. K. (1960). *The process of communication.* New York: Holt, Rinehart & Winston.

Billboard (2004). A free and open dialogue. *Billboard, 116,* 10.

Billboard (2004). The Billboard 200. Retrieved June 19, 2004 from http://www.billboard.com.

Bobo, K., Kendall, J., & Max, S. (1996). *Organizing for social change: A manual for activists in the 1990's.* Santa Ana, CA: Seven Locks Press.

Bonebrake, K. (2002). College students' Internet use, relationship formation, and personality correlates. *Cyberpsychology & Behavior, 5,* 6.

Brage, D., & Meredith, W. (1993, Fall). Correlates of loneliness among midwestern adolescents. *Adolescence, 28,* 685.

———. (1994, July). A causal model of adolescent depression. *Journal of Psychology Interdisciplinary and Applied, 128,* 4, 4555.

Brantley, A., Knox, D., & Zusman, M. E. (2002). When and why gender differences in saying 'I love you' among college students. *College Student Journal, 36,* 614–616.

Brinkert, R. (2010). "A literature review of conflict communication causes costs, benefits, and interventions in nursing." *Journal of Nursing Management* 18 (2), 145.

Brookfield, S. (1997). *Developing critical thinkers.* San Francisco: Jossey-Bass.

Brown, D., producer. (1982). *The verdict* [Videotape]. Los Angeles: CBS/FOX.

Browning, G. (1999, April 18). Office politics: Communication—the number one problem. *The New Straits Times,* pp. 2–27.

Brummet, B. (1991). *Rhetorical dimensions of popular culture.* Tuscaloosa: University of Alabama Press.

Burgher, V. (1995, April 18). Signing on. *Village Voice,* pp. 4–6.

Burgoon, J. K. (2000, February 16). Another take on time. *Communication Research and Theory Network.* Retrieved on March 9, 2001 from http://lists1.cac.psu.edu/cgi-bin/wa?A0=CRTNET.

Burke, K. (1966). *Language as symbolic action.* Berkeley: University of California Press, pp. 44–62.

Bush, G. W. (2001). President Bush's address to a Joint Session of Congress and the American people (9-20-01). Retrieved March 7, 2002, from http://www.americanrhetoric.com/speeches/gwbushjointsessionspeech9-20-01.htm.

Bushman, B. (1998, May). Priming effects of media violence on the accessibility of aggressive constructs in memory. *Personality and Social Psychology Bulletin, 24,* 537–53.

REFERENCES

Bushman, B., & Green, R. (1990). Role of cognitive-motional mediators and individual differences in the effects of media violence on aggression. *Journal of Personality and Social Psychology, 58,* 156–63.

Calvert, C. (1997). Hate speech and its harms. *Journal of Communication, 47,* 4–19.

Campbell, R. C. (2000). *Media and culture,* 2nd ed. Boston: Bedford/St. Martin's Press.

Cantor, H. K. (1997). The relationship between media consumption and eating disorders. *Journal of Communication, 47,* 40–69.

Carbaugh, D. (1991). Communication and cultural interpretation. *Quarterly Journal of Speech, 77,* 336–42.

Carterette, E., & Friedman, M. (1978). *Handbook of perception.* New York: Academic Press.

Carvajal, D. (2000, September 27). Major studies used children to test-market violent films. *New York Times,*. Retrieved May 25, 2002, from http://www.nytimes.com/2000/09/27/arts/27VIOL.html.

Castellano, G, Villalba, S. D., and Camurri, A. (2007). *Affective Computing and Intelligent Interaction.* Berlin: Springer.

Castro opens party congress with speech lambasting U.S. (1997, October 9). *San Diego Union Tribune,* p. A22.

Chapman, F. S. (1997, August). Web of deceit. *PC World,* pp. 145–51.

Choo, V. (1994, October 1). Music for surgeons. *Lancet, 344,* 947–53.

Clark, M. L., & Ayers, M. (1992). Friendship similarity during early adolescence: Gender and racial patterns. *Journal of Psychology: Interdisciplinary & Applied, 126* (4), 393.

Clark, N., Lee, S. & Boyer, L. (2007). A place of their own: An exploratory study of college students' uses of Facebook. A paper presented at the annual conference of the International Communication Association.

Cleland, K. (1996, 4 November). Discover takes to long from with "storymercial." *Advertising Age,* pp. 3–4.

Clinton, B. (1996, 29 January). Remarks at the funeral service for Barbara Jordan in Houston, Texas. *Weekly Compilation of Presidential Documents, 32,* 85–87.

Cohen, B. (1996). *The press and foreign policy.* Princeton, NJ: Princeton University Press.

Cohen, J. R. (1998). *Communication criticism: Developing your critical powers.* Thousand Oaks, CA: Sage.

Collins, E. (2001). From space: A world of shared dreams. Address delivered to Syracuse University commencement, Syracuse, NY. May 13. Reprinted in *Vital Speeches of the Day, 1018*(17), 538–42.

Collins, P. (1986). Learning from the outsider within. *Social Problems, 33,* 514–32.

Conger, J. (1998). The necessary art of persuasion. *Harvard Business Review, 76* (3), 84.

Conniff, K. (1999, April). We loved it! How critical are Hollywood critics? *Brill's Content,* p. 100.

Cooley, C. H. (1964). *Human nature and the social order.* New York: Schocken Books.

Cooper, P. (1993). Communication and gender in the classroom. In L. Arliss & D. Borisoff (Eds.), *Women and men communicating: Challenges and changes* (pp. 122–41). Fort Worth, TX: Harcourt Brace Jovanovich.

Coping. (1998, June 29). *People,* p. 74.

Cornell Library (2001). Evaluating information from the World Wide Web. Retrieved November 12, 2001, from http://www.library.ucla.edu/libraries/college/help/critical/index.htm.

Court, R. (1998, Feb. 10). TV ads tailored to you. *Wired News.* Retrieved: August 10, 2000. http://www.wired.com/news/news/business/story/10198.html.

Craik, K. H. (1997, March). The laughter curve. *Harper's Magazine,* pp. 27–28.

Cuvelier, M. I. (2002). Cringe factor: Your body betrays embarrassment. *Psychology Today,* p. 21.

Davidson, L. R., & Duberman, L. (1982). Friendship: Communication and interactional patterns in same-sex dyads. *Sex Roles, 8,* 802–22.

Delia, J., O'Keefe, B., & O'Keefe, D. (1982). The contructivist approach to communication. In F. Dance (Ed.), *Human Communication Theory: Comparative Essays* (147–91). New York: Harper and Row.

Diamond, R. (1997, August). Curriculum reform needed if students are to master core skills. *Chronicle of Higher Education,* p. B7.

Dindia, K., & Fitzpatrick, M. A. (1997). Self-disclosure in spouse and stranger interaction. *Human Communication Research, 23* (3), 388.

"Do employees believe your publication?" (1999, December). *Ragan's Strategic Employee Publications,* pp. 1–2.

Doskoch, P., & Haley, H. (1997, March/April). Let your fingers do the talking. *Psychology Today,* pp. 24–25.

Doyle, R. (2000). Women and the professions. *Scientific American,* 30–35.

Duck, S. (1984). A perspective on the repair of personal relationships: Repair of what? when? In S. W. Duck (Ed.). *Personal Relationships, 5: Repairing Personal Relationships.* London: Academic Press.

Duke Libraries (2002). Finding background information. Retrieved June 3, 2002 from www.lib.duke.edu/libruide/background.htm.

Dunn, L. J. (1998). Nonverbal communication: information conveyed through the use of body language. Retrieved June 16, 2004 from http://clearinghouse.mwsc/manuscripts/70.asp.

Eastman, P. D. (1960). *Are you my mother?* New York: Beginner Books.

Ebstein, R.P., Israel, S., Chew, S.H., Zhong, S. and Knafo, A. (2010). "Genetics of human social behavior." *Neuron* 65 (6), 831.

Edesu, A. S., & Burgoon, J. K. (1996). Nonverbal Communication. In M. B. Salwen & D. W. Stacks (Eds.). *An integrated approach to communication theory and research* (pp. 345–58). Mahwah, NJ: Lawrence Erlbaum.

Edwards, H. (1995, April). Communication predicaments of older health care consumers: What can "we" do about it? *Social Alternatives, 14,* 33.

Eisenstein, E. L. (1979). *The printing press as an agent of change: Communications and cultural transformations in early-modern Europe.* Cambridge: Cambridge University Press.

Ekman, P. (1997). Should we call it expression or communication? *Innovation: The European Journal of Social Science, 10,* 338.

Ekman, P., & Friesen, W. V. (1975). *Unmasking the face.* Englewood Cliffs, NJ: Prentice Hall.

Elgrably, J. (1998, August 20). Telemedicine in the "hood": Technology enables an historically black medical college to serve poor Los Angelenos at greatly reduced costs. *Black Issues in Higher* Education, 36.

Elshtain, J. B. (1998). Civil society. *Liberal Education, 84,* 4–9.

Engleberg, I. (2002). Presentations in everyday life: Linking audience interest and speaker eloquence, *American Communication Journal, 5.* Retrieved June 19, 2002, from http://acjournal.org/holdings/vol5/iss2/special/engleberg.htm.

Engleberg, I. N., & Wynn, D. R. (1997). *Working in groups: Communication principles and strategies.* Boston: Houghton Mifflin.

Evans, B. (1999). A gift for all of America. Address delivered to the Biennial Session, Wyoming Conservations Congress, Casper, WY. July 10. Reprinted in *Vital Speeches of the Day, 1016*(2), 54–61.

Farb, P. (1973). *Word play: What happens when people talk.* New York: Bantam.

Feldman, J. (2009). "Bayes and the simplicity principle in perception." *Psychological Review,* 116 (4), 875.

Festinger, L. (1954). A theory of social comparison processes. *Human Relations, 7,* 117–40.

Festinger, L. (1957). *A theory of cognitive dissonance.* Evanston, IL: Row, Peterson.

Fisher, R., & Brown, S. (1988). *Getting together: Building a relationship that gets to yes.* Boston: Houghton Mifflin.

Fisher, R., & Ury, W. (1981). *Getting to yes: Negotiating agreement without giving in.* New York: Penguin Books.

Fisher, W. R. (1989). *Human communication as narration: Toward a philosophy of reason, value, and action.* Columbia: University of South Carolina Press.

Fiske, J. (1987). *Television culture.* London: Methuen.

Floyd, J. F. (1985). *Listening: A practical approach.* Glenview, IL: Scott, Foresman.

Folkerts, J. (1996, September 1). The ethics of questionable advertising campaigns. *The World & I 11,* 310.

Fox, V. (2001). Mexico-U.S. relations based on trust. Address delivered to the House of Representatives Joint Session of Congress, Washington, DC. Sept. 6. Reprinted in *Vital Speeches of the Day, 1017*(23), 706–709.

REFERENCES

Freedman, J. L., & Fraser, S. C. (1966). Compliance without pressure: The foot-in-the-door technique. *Journal of Personality and Social Psychology, 4,* 195–202.

Frick-Horbury, D., & Gettentag, R. E. (1998). The effects of restricting hand gesture production on lexical retrieval and free recall. *American Journal of Psychology, 111,* 43–63.

Frohnmayer, J. (1994). *Out of tune: Listening to the First Amendment.* Nashville: Freedom Forum.

Galanes, G. J., Adams, K., & Brillhart, J. K. (2000). *Communicating in groups: Applications and skills* (4th ed.). New York: McGraw-Hill.

Garrigan, P & Kellman, P. J. (2008). "Perceptual learning depends on perceuptual constancy." *Proceedings of the National Academy of Sciences of the United States of America,* 105 (6), 2248.

Garten, J. E. (1998, November 30). "Cultural imperialism" is no joke. *Business Week,* pp. 26–27.

Gerbner, G. (1994, Spring). Reclaiming our cultural mythology. *In Context, 38,* 40.

Gerbner, G., Gross, L., Morgan, M., & Signorielli, N. (1994). Growing up with television: The cultivation perspective. In J. Bryant & D. Zillmann (Eds.), *Media effects: Advances in theory and research* (pp. 17–42). Hillsdale, NJ: Erlbaum.

Gergen, K. J. (1971). *The concept of the self.* NY: Holt, Rinehart and Winston.

Girandola, F. (2002). Sequential requests and organ donation. *Journal of Social Psychology, 142* (2), 171–79.

Givens, D. B. (2008). Nonverbal dictionary. Retrieved May 5, 2008, from http://members.aol.com/nonverbal2/aromacve.htm.

Glaman, J. M., & Jones, A. P. (1996). The effects of co-workers similarity on the emergence of affect in work teams. *Group & Organization Management, 21* (2), 192.

Goffman, E. (1959). *The presentation of self in everyday life.* Garden City, NY: Doubleday Anchor Books.

———. (1967). *Interaction ritual: Essays on face-to-face behavior.* Garden City, NY: Anchor Books.

Goizueta, R. (1996). The real essence of business. Speech delivered to the Executive Club of Chicago, Chicago, IL. Nov. 20. Reprinted in *Vital Speeches of the Day, 1018*(7), 199–201.

Gottman, J. M. (1999). *The marriage clinic: A scientifically based marital therapy.* New York: W. W. Norton.

Grabe, M. E., Lombard, M., Reich, R., Bracken, C. C., & Campanella, T. B. (1999, April). The role of screen size in viewer experiences of media content. *News Photographer, 54,* 4–10.

Graf, F. (1991). Gestures and conventions: The gestures of Roman actors and orators. In K. Thomas (Ed.) *A cultural history of gesture.* Ithaca, NY: Cornell University Press.

Graham, J. A., & Argyle, M. (1975). A cross-cultural study of the communication of extra-verbal meaning by gestures. *International Journal of Psychology, 10,* 57–67.

Granatstein, L. (2004). Indecent exposure. *Media Week, 14,* 43–45.

Granito Jr., V. J. (2002). Psychological response to athletic injury: gender differences. *Journal of Sport Behavior, 25,* 243–260.

Gray, E. (1999, February–March). Talk tips: Start brain before wagging tongue. *Executive Speeches, 13* (4), 25–30.

Gregory, H. (2002). *Public speaking for college and career.* New York: McGraw-Hill.

Grindstaff, L. (1997). Producing class, trash, and the money shot. In J. Lull & S. Hinerman (Eds.), *Media scandals.* NY: Columbia University Press (pp. 164–202).

Gronbeck, B. E. (1997). Character, celebrity, and sexual innuendo in the mass-mediated presidency. In J. Lull & S. Hinerman (Eds.). *Media Scandals* (pp. 122–42). New York: Columbia University Press.

Guerrero, L. K., & Afifi, W. A. (1998, Summer). Communicative responses to jealousy as a function of self-esteem and relationship maintenance goals: A test of Bryson's Dual Motivation Model. *Communication Reports, 11* (2), 111.

Gundykunst, W. B. (1994). *Bridging differences* (2nd ed.). Thousand Oaks, CA: Sage.

Gundykunst, W. B., & Kim, Y. K. (1997). *Communicating with strangers: An approach to intercultural communication* (3rd ed.). New York: McGraw-Hill.

Gusfield, J. (1981). *The culture of public problems: Drinking, driving, and the symbolic order.* Chicago: University of Chicago Press.

Haddad, R. J. (1993). Trabalenguas Mexicanos. Tempe, AZ: Editorial Bilingüe.

Haggins, B. L. (1999). Translating the mythos: homefront viewers rethink the American dream. *Journal for the Study of Media & Composite Cultures, 9,* 117–130

Hall, E. T. (1966). *The hidden dimension.* Garden City, NY: Doubleday.

Hall, E. T. (1977). *Beyond culture.* New York: Anchor.

Halstead T., & Lind, M. (2002). Unity and community in the twenty-first century. *National Civic Review, 91,* 95–115.

Hanks, T. (1993). Oscar acceptance speech. Retrieved March 7, 2002 from http://www.oscarworld.net/oscarspeeches.asp.

Hanson, T. L. (2000). So what if you found it on the Internet: An exercise in evaluating web-based information. *Communication Teacher, 14*(2), 6–7.

Harris, J. H. (1994). Do speech courses serve the business student? *Journal of Education for Business, 70,* 30–33.

Harris, T. E. & Sherblom, J. C. (2002). *Small group and team communication* (2nd ed.). Boston: Allyn & Bacon.

Harwood, J. (1997, Spring). Viewing age: Lifespan identity and television viewing choices. *Journal of Broadcasting and Electronic Media, 41,* 203–14.

Hayakawa, S. I. (1964). *Language in thought and action.* New York: Harcourt Brace Jovanovich, p. 179.

Henderson A. (1994). *Gods of Our Fathers.* Reading, PA: Bullfrog Films.

Henderson, S. (1997, March 5). Style and substance: "Mode" magazine figures it has what plus-size women want. *Dallas Morning News,* p. 5E.

Herr, N. (2004). Television statistics. Retrieved October 28, 2004, from http://www.csun.edu/~vceedooz/health/docs/tv&health.html.

Hinman, L. A. (1999). Using computers in the classroom. Retrieved March 27, 2002, from http://ethics.acusd.edu/Images/Updates2.gif.

Hirokawa, R. Y. (1982). Group communication and problem-solving effectiveness I: A critical review of inconsistent findings. *Communication Quarterly 30* (2), 134–41.

———. (1983). Group communication and problem-solving effectives II: An exploratory investigation of procedural functions. *Western Journal of Speech Communication 47*(1), 59–74.

Hirokawa, R. Y., & Pace, R. C. (1983). A descriptive investigation of the possible communication-based reasons for effective and ineffective group decision making. *Communication Monographs 50* (4), 363–79.

Ho, R. (1999, June 14). Only extra nice will suffice: Service-call satisfaction means happy customers. *The Wall Street Journal,* p. B16.

Hoffman, D. (1979). Oscar acceptance speech. Retrieved March 7, 2002, from http://www.oscarworld.net/oscarspeeches.asp.

Hoffner, C. (1997). Children's emotional reactions to a scary film: The role of prior outcome information on coping style. *Human Communication Research, 23,* 323–41.

Hofstede, G. (1997). *Cultures and organizations: Software of the mind.* New York: McGraw-Hill.

Hofstede, G., & Bond, M. (1984). Hofstede's cultural dimensions. *Journal of Cross-Cultural Psychology, 15,* 417–33.

Holton, S. A. (1998). *Mending the cracks in the ivory tower: Strategies for conflict management in higher education.* Boston: Anker.

Homepage. (2000). International Listening Association. Retrieved July 31, 2000 from http://listen.org.

Hones, D. F. (1999). Making peace: A narrative study of a bilingual liaison, a school, and a community. *Teachers College Record, 101,* 106–45.

How much television does the average American watch a month? (2002). infoplease.com. Retrieved from www.infoplease.com on 15 June 2002. Other sources vary: David Poltrack, (1999, July 26). "Stat's don't lie; people do," *Media Week 9,* 30; 12–15, reports average daily viewing at three to four hours.

Howes, D. & Weber, J. (Directors) (2008). *Project Listening.* Minneapolis, MN: [motion picture] Rikshaw Films.

Hughes, L. (1951). A dreamed deferred. In L. Hughes and A. Rampersad (Ed.), *The Collected Works of Langston Hughes* (2001). Columbia: U. of Missouri Press.

Hunter-Gault, C. (1994). Commencement address, Ithaca College, New York, 1991. In DeFrancisco, V. L. & Jensen, M. D. (Eds.). *Women's voices in our time: Statements by American leaders* (pp. 139–146). Prospect Heights, IL: Waveland.

Hutton, F. (1993). The ideological origins of the black press in America. In Biagi, S.

REFERENCES

(Ed.), *Media/Reader,* 2nd ed., (p. 34). Belmont, CA: Wadsworth.

If the shoe doesn't fit. (1994, June 1). *Contemporary Women's Issues Database,* 3, 11. Retrieved June 26, 1998 from http://www.elibrary.com.

Imai, G. (2001). Gestures: Body language and nonverbal communication. Retrieved July 9, 2001 from thehttp://www.csupomona.edu/~tassi/gestures.htm.

Interpersonal relationships—close bonds promote health. (2000, May). Bryan LGH Medical Center. Retrieved March 30, 2002 from http://www.bryan.org/healthyliving/Apr99MindBodyInterpersonal.htm.

Iyengar, S., & Kinder, D. (1988). *News that matters: Agenda-setting and priming in a television age.* Chicago: University of Chicago Press.

Janis, I. L. (1983). *Groupthink: Psychological studies of policy decisions and fiascoes.* Boston: Houghton Mifflin.

Job market. Job Outlook 2010. Retrieved March 15, 2010 from: http://www.careerjournal.com/en/mediathek/223.html?infoView=24750.

Johnson, 5. (2004). The art of googlebombing. *Discover, 25,* 22–24.

Jourard, S. M. (1964). *The transparent self.* Princeton, NJ: D. Van Nostrand.

Karlsberg, J. A., & Karlsberg, R. C. (1994). The affectionate bond: The goal of couple-centered therapy. *Journal of Humanistic Psychology, 34* (1), 132.

Kay, S. W., & Lindgren, M. (1999, May 10). Skinny models in ads cause immediate anger, depression in women. *Women's Health Weekly,* p. 11.

Kelly, G. A. (1955). *The psychology of personal constructs.* New York: W. W. Norton.

Kennedy, G. A. (1980). *Classical rhetoric and its Christian and secular tradition from ancient to modern times.* Chapel Hill: University of North Carolina Press.

Kimmel, M. S. (2000). *The gendered society.* New York: Oxford University Press.

Klapper, J. T. (1960). The effects of mass communication. New York: Free Press.

Klohnen, B. C. and Shanhong Luo, B. C. (2003). Interpersonal attraction and personality: What is attractive: self similarity, ideal similarity, complementarity, or attachment security? *Journal of Personality and Social Psychology, 85,* 4, 709–813.

Klohnen, E. C. & Shanhong, L. E. (2003). Interpersonal attraction and personality: what is attractive—self similarity, ideal similarity, complementarity, or attachment security? *Journal of Personality and Social Psychology, 85,* 709–723.

Knapp, M. L. (1978). *Nonverbal communication in human interaction* (2nd ed.). New York: Holt, Rinehart and Winston.

Knapp, M. L., & Hall, J. A. (1997). *Nonverbal communication in human interaction* (3rd ed.). Fort Worth, TX: Harcourt Brace.

Knapp, M. L., & Vangelisti, A. L. (1996). *Interpersonal communication,* 3rd ed. Boston: Allyn and Bacon.

Knickerbocker, B. (1998, December 16). Birth mothers battle to keep records closed. *Christian Science Monitor,* p. 1.

Knight, Z. G. (2009). "Conceptual considerations regarding self-disclosure: a relational psychoanalytic perspective." *South African Journal of Psychology, 39* (1) 75.

Kolb, J. A. (1999). A project in small-group decision making. *Journal of Management Education, 23* (1), 71.

Kollack, P., & O'Brien, J. (1994). *The production of reality: Essays and readings in social psychology.* Thousand Oaks, CA: Pine Forge Press, p. 138.

Koudsi, S. (1999, July 19). Workplace anxieties. *Fortune,* p. 38.

Kuhn, M., & McPartland, T. (1954). An empirical investigation of self-attitudes. *American Sociological Review, 19,* 68.

Kyratzis, A. (2000). Tactical uses of narratives in nursery school same-sex groups. *Discourse Processes, 29,* 269–300.

LaFrance, M., & Mayo, C. (1976). Racial differences in gaze behavior during conversations: Two systematic observational studies. *Journal of Personality and Social Psychology, 33,* 547–52.

Lasswell, H. (1948). The structure and function of communication in society. In L. Bryson (Ed.). *The communication of ideas* (p. 37). New York: Institute for Religious and Social Studies.

Lawson, J. K. (1998). Promising prospect: Why U.S. farming will prosper. Address delivered to the Association of Illinois Soil and Water Conservation Districts Annual Meeting, Springfield, IL, July 28. Reprinted in *Vital Speeches of the Day, 1015*(1), 19.

Leas, S. (1984). *Discover your conflict management style.* Washington, DC: The Alban Institute.

LeBlanc, A. (2001). Racial profiling mediation. *National Public Radio.* Retrieved June 25, 2001, from http://www.npr.org.

Lee, L. (2000). Old flames flicker brightly, electronically. *New York Times,* vol. *149,* Issue 51458, Section 9, p. 1, Op, lc, lbw.

Letters. (1998, June–July). *Young and Modern,* p. 38.

Levine, S. (1999, February 8). Again, listening to the sounds of silence: Younger generations can't hear well. *Washington Post National Weekly Edition,* p. 32.

Li, K. (1998, April 21). A pitch by Gates brings broken window. *New York Daily News,* p. 5.

Light, R. J. (2001). *Making the most of college: Students speak their mind.* Cambridge: Harvard University Press.

Lippman, W. (1921). *Public opinion.* New York: Macmillan.

Listening factoids. (2000). International Listening Association. Retrieved July 31, 2000 from http://listen.org/pages/factoids.html.

Living to age 100 is becoming more common. (1999, July 20). *Gannett News Service.*

Luft, J. (1984). *Group processes: An introduction to group dynamics,* (3rd ed.). Palo Alto, CA: Mayfield.

Lundin, S. C., Paul, H., & Christensen, J. (2000). *Fish! A remarkable way to boost morale and improve results.* New York: Hyperion.

Lustig, M. W., & Koester, J. (1999). *Intercultural competence: Interpersonal communication across cultures* (3rd ed.). New York: Longman.

Ly-Phin Pan, P. (1998, December 1). To look the other way: Chinese-American girls confront a cultural tug-of-war. *The World and I,* 222.

MacGeorge, B. L, Gillihan, S. J., Samter, W., & Clark, R. A. N. N. B. (2003). Skill deficit or differential motivation?: testing alternative explanations of gender differences in the provision of emotional support. *Communication Research, 30,* 272–303.

Macy, J., Gomes, M. E., & Kremer, J. (2000). The wisdom of uncertainty: Living with the Shambala. *ReVision, 23,* 19–24.

Maples, M. F., Dupey, P. Torres-Rivera, E., Phan, L. T., Vereen, L., & Garrett, M. T. (2001). Ethnic diversity and the use of humor in counseling: appropriate or inappropriate? *Journal of Counseling & Development,* 79, 53–61.

Marsh, A. A. (2010). "Nonverbal accents: cultural differences in facial expressions of emotion." *Psychological Science, 14* (4), 373.

Martin, M. M., Anderson, C. M., & Mottet, T. P. (1999). Perceived understanding and self-disclosure in the stepparent-stepchild relationship. *Journal of Psychology Interdisciplinary & Applied, 133* (3), 281.

Maslow, A. H. (1954). *Motivation and personality.* New York: Harper and Row.

Mathers, M., Bass, M, & Bass, J. (1999). Just don't give a f***. *The slim shady LP.* UNI/Interscope.

McCabe, D. L. (2002). The Center for Academic Integrity: Research. Retrieved August 5, 2002 from http://www.academicintegrity.orglcai_research.asp.

McCombs, M., & Shaw, D. (1972). The agenda setting function of mass media. *Public Opinion Quarterly, 36,* 176–87.

McCroskey, J. (1978). Validity of the PRCA as an index of oral communication apprehension. *Communication Monographs, 45,* 192–203.

McGrath, J. E. (1984). *Groups: Interaction and performance.* Englewood Cliffs, NJ: Prentice Hall.

McLoone-Basta, M., & Siegel, A. (1987). *The second kids' world almanac of records and facts.* New York: Pharos Books.

McLuhan, M. (1964). *Understanding media.* New York: McGraw-Hill.

Mead, G. H. (1934). *Mind, self, & society.* Chicago: University of Chicago Press.

Mercer, J. (1994, August 3). Native Hawaiians push to extend and deepen university's diversity. *Chronicle of Higher Education,* p. A28.

Milius S. (1999, November 6). Each nostril smells the world differently. *Science News,* p. 293.

REFERENCES

Miller, M. C. (2002, January 7). What's wrong with this picture? *The Nation.* Retrieved January 12, 2002, http://www.thenation.com/special/bigten.html.

Mind/body flash. (1998, March). *Self,* p. 73.

Monroe, A. H. (1935). *Principles and types of speech.* Chicago: Scott, Foresman.

Morgan, M., Shanahan, J., & Harris, C. (1990). VCRs and the effects of television: New diversity or more of the same? In J. R. Dobrow (Ed.). *Social and cultural aspects of VCR use* (pp. 107–23). Hillsdale, NJ: Erlbaum.

Moss, F. (1985). Perceptions of communication in the corporate community. *Journal of Business and Technical Communication, 9,* 63–77.

Motley, M. T. (1990). On whether one can(not) not communicate: An examination via traditional communication postulates. *Western Journal of Speech Communication,* 54, 1–20.

Motley, M. T., & Reeder, H. M. (1995, December). Unwanted escalation of sexual intimacy: Male and female perceptions of connotations and relational consequences of resistance messages. *Communication Monographs, 62,* 355–82.

Mudore, C. F. (2002). Are you an introvert? Current Health, *29,* 17–20.

Mulrine, Anna & Hsu, C. (2003). LOVE.com. *U.S. News & World Report, 135,* 52–59.

Murane, R. & Levy, F. (1996). *Teaching the new basic skills.* New York: Free Press.

Murray, E,, Burns, J., See, T. S., Lai, R., and Nazarth, I. (2005). "Interactive health communication applications for people with chronic disease." *Cochrane Database of Systematic Reviews* 4, Art. No.:CD004274.DOI:10.1002.

Murray, T. (1999, June–July). In "What's in a (last) name?" *Parenting,* p. 28.

Nader, L. (2001, July 13). Harmony coerced is freedom denied. *Chronicle of Higher Education,* p. B13.

National Communication Association. (1998). *Competent communicators: K-12 speaking, listening, and media literacy standards and competency statements.* Annandale, VA: National Communication Association.

National Film Board of Canada. *Gods of Our Fathers.* (1994). Reading, PA: Bullfrog Films.

National Public Radio (2010). *How to overcome the fear of public speaking.* Retrieved March 15, 2010 from http://www.pbs.org/standarddeviantstv/episode_res_public.html.

"New words and phrases" (2001, March 17). *The Encarta World Dictionary.* Retrieved March 17, 2001 from http://www.worldenglishdictionary.com/Features/New_words.html.

Newhart, B. (1997). Humor makes us free. Address delivered to the Catholic University of America commencement, May 17. Washington, DC. Reprinted in *Vital Speeches of the Day, 1013*(19), 607–609.

Nichols, M. P. (1995). *The lost art of listening.* New York: Guilford.

Nichols, R. (1969). Listening is a 10-part skill. In R. C. Hussman (Ed.), *Readings in interpersonal and organizational communication* (pp. 472–79). Boston: Holbrook Press.

Nielsen. (2010). *Television Ratings.* Retrieved May 15, 2010 from http://nielson.com.

Non-Sexist Language. (2002). Non-sexist language. Retrieved June 17, 2002, from http://owl.english.purdue.edu/handouts/print/general/gl_nonsex.html.

Noonan, P. (1999, Spring). The culture of death. *Human Life Review, 25,* 109.

Norell, B. (1999, January 25). Prime time TV only wants white faces. *Lakota Times,* p. A6.

Notebaert, R. (1998). Leveraging diversity: Adding value to the bottom line. Address delivered to the National Black MBA Association, Detroit, MI. Sept. 17. Reprinted in *Vital Speeches of the Day, 1015*(2), 47.

Ong, W. J. (1991). Print, space, and closure. In Crowley, D., & Heyer, P. (Eds.). *Communication history: Technology, culture, society* (pp. 102–13). New York: Longman.

———. (1998). *Orality and literacy: The technologizing of the world.* London: Routledge.

Osborn, M. (1990). In defense of broad mythic criticism—a reply to Rowland. *Communication Studies, 41,* 121–27.

Oser, K. (2004). Snapple effort finds women as they browse. *Advertising Age, 75,* 22.

Osmond, H., Osmundsen, J., & Agel, J. (1974). *Understanding understanding.* New York: Harper and Row.

Ouellette, P. M., Lazear, K., & Chambers, K. (1999). Action leadership: The development of an approach to leadership enhancement for grassroots community leaders in children's mental heath. *Journal of Behavioral Health Services and Research, 26* (2), 171.

Page, B. I. (1996). *Who deliberates? Mass media in American democracy.* Chicago: University of Chicago Press.

Palomares, N. A. (2008). "Explaining gender-based language use: effects of gender identity salience on references to emotion and tentative language in intra- and intergroup contexts." *Human Communication Research* 34 (2),263.

Paterson, M., & Kraut, R. (1998). Internet paradox: A social technology that reduces social involvement and psychological well being. *American Psychologist, 3* (9), 1017.

Pearce, W. B., & Littlejohn, S. W. (1997). *Moral conflict: When social worlds collide.* Thousand Oaks, CA: Sage.

Pearson, J. C., West, R. L., & Turner, L. H. (1994). *Gender and communication,* (3rd ed.) New York: McGraw-Hill.

Pells, R. (2002, April 12). American culture goes global, or does it? *Chronicle of Higher Education,* p. B7–10.

Penn, S. (Director) (2007). *Into the wild.* Los Angeles, CA: [motion picture] Paramount Vantage.

Penn State Center for Public Speaking and Civic Engagement (2002). Center aims to involve students in public dialogue. Retrieved May 30, 2002, from www.psu.edu/ur/2002/centerpublicspeaking.html.

Perry, J. T., & Schneider, G. (1999). *New perspectives on the Internet.* Cambridge, MA: Course Technology.

Person of the year. (2002, January 7). *Time,* p. 34.

Petrie, D. (Director) (2003). *How to lose a guy in 10 days.* Los Angeles, CA: [motion picture] Paramount Vantage.

Phillips, G. (1993). *Help for shy people.* New York: Barnes and Noble.

Phillips, R. (1996). Jessie's glove. In J. Canfield, (Ed.), *Chicken soup for the soul at work.* New York: Health Communications.

Pines, A. M., & Friedman, A. (1998). Gender differences in romantic jealousy. *Journal of Social Psychology, 138,* 54–76.

Pipher, M. (1994). *Reviving Ophelia: Saving the selves of adolescent girls.* New York: Ballantine.

Podolinska, T. & Kovac, M. (2002). 'Mythos' versus 'logos.' *Dialogue & Universalism, 12,* 85–100.

Pollack, J., & Teinowitz, I. (1998, November 2). Milk mustache ads, Bozells come under fire. *Advertising Age,* p. 2.

Postman, N. (1985). *Amusing ourselves to death: Public discourse in the age of show business.* New York: Viking Penguin.

Pratkanis, A. (1992, October 31). Propaganda flying in blitz of advertising: Warning signs of manipulation. *New York Times,* p. A1.

Preczewski P. (1999). You do not have to sit outside in the dark. Retrieved March 7, 2002, from http://honors.syr.edu/messenger/old/99-00/stories/speeches.htm.

Priest, P. (1995). *Public intimacies: Talk show participants and tell-all TV.* Creskill, NJ: Hampton Press.

Radford, M. L. (1998). Approach or avoidance? The role of nonverbal communication in the academic library user's decision to initiate a reference encounter. *Library Trends, 46,* 699.

Ramsey, G. (1999). Communication theories on trail: can the scales of justice by swayed by the application of communication theories? *Communications & the Law, 21,* 31–45.

Ranganathan, K. (2001). How to make software peer reviews work. Quality Progress, *34,* 69–73.

Reagan, R. (1986). President Reagan's Speech on the Challenger disaster. Retrieved March 7, 2002, from http://reagan.webteamone.com/speeches/challenger.html.

Reeves, R. (2001, April 2). We bowl alone, but work together. *New Statesman,* pp. 23–25.

Reiner, R. (Producer). (1995). *The American President* [Videotape]. Los Angeles: Warner Home Video.

Retrieved July 8, 2002 from http://www.library.yale.edu/ref/err/primsrcs.htm#PRIMD-EF.

Rich, W. C. (1998). Spontaneous talk, linguistic capital, and diversity. *Administration and Society, 30,* 315–330.

REFERENCES

Richards, I. A., & Ogden, C. K. (1923). *The meaning of meaning.* London: Kegan, Paul, Trench, Trubner.

Rierdan, J., & Koff, E. (1997, September 22). Weight, weight-related aspects of body image, and depression in early adolescent girls. *Adolescence, 32,* 615–25.

Rips, G. (2002, January 28). Getting by. *American Prospect,* pp. 41–43.

Reitman, J. (Directory). (2007). *Juno.* Los Angeles, CA: [motion picture] Fox Searchlight.

Roa, N. (2009). Perception. Retrieved April 15, 2010 from: http://knol.google.com/k/perception#.

Rodenburg, P. (2000). *The actor speaks: Voice and performer.* New York: St. Martin's Press.

Roefs, W. (1998, Fall). Better together. *Teaching tolerance,* pp. 35–40.

Roper-Starch. (2000). How Americans communicate: A public opinion poll. Washington, DC: National Communication Association. Retrieved June 19, 2002, from http://www.natcom.org/research/Poll/how americans communicate.htm.

Rose, F. (1999, November 8). Think globally, script locally. *Fortune,* pp. 156–60.

Rosenblatt, S. (1998, December 21). The color of my world. *Newsweek,* p. 14.

Rosenzweig, J. (1999, July–August). Can TV improve us? *American Prospect,* pp. 58–64.

Rothwell, J. D. (1998). *In mixed company: Small group communication* (3rd ed.). New York: Harcourt Brace.

Rowan, J. (1999). Ascent and descent in Maslow's theory. *Journal of Humanistic Psychology, 39,* 125–34.

Rupley, S. (2004). Will Google read your email? *PCMagazine, 23,* 21.

Salibrici, M. M. (1999, May). Dissonance and rhetorical inquiry: A Burkean model for critical reading and writing. *Journal of Adolescent and Adult Literacy, 42,* 628–38.

Salwen, M. B., & Dupagne, M. (1999). The third person effect: Perceptions of media's influence and immoral consequences. *Communication Research, 26,* 523–50.

Samovar, L., & Porter, R. (Eds.) (1994). *Intercultural communication: A reader.* Belmont, CA: Wadsworth.

Sandhu, D. S., & Reeves, G. T. (1993). Cross-cultural counseling and neurolinguistic mirroring with Native American adolescents. *Journal of Multicultural Counseling and Development, 21,* 106.

Sanneh, K. (2001, February 9). Hearing the voices of hip-hop. *New York Times,* p. A23.

Sapir, E. (1921). *Language: An introduction to the study of speech.* New York: Classic Books.

Scheidel, T. M., and Crowell, L (1979). *Discussing and deciding: A desk book for group leaders and members.* New York: Macmillan.

Schudson, M. (1991). Trout or hamburger: Politics and telemythology. *Tikkun, 6,* 2, 47–54.

Sears, P. A. (1994). "Some thoughts on changing paradigms in management education: The role of production and operations research faculties in the educational outcomes movement." In *The Educational and Research Foundation Program Proceedings* (pp. 33–35). Falls Church, VA: American Production and Inventory Control Society.

Senna, D. (1998, December 31). Passing and the Problematic of Multiracial Pride. *Black Renaissance/Renaissance Noire,* p. 76.

Sherif, M., Sherif, K., & Nebergall, R. (1963). *Attitude and attitude change: The social judgment-involvement approach.* Philadelphia: W. B. Saunders.

Shribman, D. M. (1997, 23 July). Grave eloquence. *The Wall Street Journal,* p. A16.

Siegert, J. R., & Stamp, G. H. (1994). "Our first big fight" as a milestone in the development of close relationships. *Communication Monographs, 61,* 345–60.

Signorielli, N. (2001). Television's world of work in the nineties. *Journal of Broadcasting and Electronic Media, 45,* 4–23.

Signorielli, N., & Morgan, M. (1990). *Cultivation analysis: New directions in media effects research.* Newbury Park, CA: Sage.

Simon, S. (1997, September 20). The new doublespeak. National Public Radio. Retrieved July 27, 1998 from http://www.elibrary.com.

Skinner, C. (1999, June 24). Class journal for Communication Studies 198, B. Dobkin, University of San Diego.

Skinner, D. (2000, Winter). McLuhan's world—and ours. *Public Interest, 138,* 52–65.

Smith, J. (2009). College Students Facebook Use. Retrieved June 4, 2010 from http://www.insidefacebook.com.

Socializing elderly live longer. (1999, July 24). *The Globe and Mail,* p. C5.

Sourcebook (2004). Television. Retrieved June 19, 2004 from http://www.csun.edu/~vceed002/health/docs/tv&health.html.

Span of Control (2004). Retrieved June 21, 2004 from http://www.theworkingmanager.com/articles/detail.asp?ArticleNo=219.

Speight, S., & Vera, E. M. (1997). Similarity and difference in multicultural counseling: Considering the attraction and repulsion hypotheses. *Counseling Psychologist, 25* (2), 280.

Spence, G. (1995, November–December). Lessons from lawyers. *Psychology Today,* pp. 22–25.

Sprague, J., & Stuart, D. (2000). *The speaker's handbook,* 5th ed. New York: Harcourt Brace.

Staiano, M. (2006). The importance of listening in communication. Retrieved June 7, 2010, from http://ezinearticles.com/?The-Importance-Of-Listening-In-Communication&id=210731.

Stanley, S. M, Markman, H. J., & Whitton, S. W. (2002). Communication, conflict, and commitment: insights on the foundations of relationship success from a national survey. *Family Process,* 41, 659–676.

Stein, M. (1995, Fall). Discovering a language. *Parabola, 20,* 76–79.

Stephens, M. (1991, September 22). The death of reading. *Los Angeles Times Magazine,* p. 42.

Stewart, C. J., & Cash, W. B. (2000). *Interviewing: Principles and practices* (9th ed.). New York: McGraw-Hill.

Stewart, J., & Logan, C. E. (1998). *Together: communicating interpersonally.* New York: McGraw-Hill.

Stossel, S. (1997, May). The man who counts the killings. *Atlantic Monthly,* pp. 86–104.

Sutton, D. (1997). On mythic criticism: A proposed compromise. *Communication Reports, 10,* 211–18.

Swan, S., & Wyer, R. (1997). Gender stereotypes and social identity: How being in the minority affects judgments of self and others. *Personality and Social Psychology Bulletin, 23,* 1265–77.

Sweet, L., & Wisby, G. (1998, June 25). From A's to Z's: Later school start, fresher pupils sought. *Chicago Sun-Times,* p. 4.

Swirsky, J. (1999, April 25). Treating the doctor's bedside manner. *New York Times,* p. A2.

Tajfel, H., & Turner, J. (1979). An integrative theory of intergroup conflict. In W. Austin & S. Worchel (Eds.). *The social psychology of intergroup relations* (pp. 33–53). Monterey, CA: Brooks/Cole.

Talwar, V. and Lee, K. (2002). Development of lying to conceal a transgression: children's control of expressive behavior during verbal deception *International Journal of Behavioral Development,* 26, 436–445.

Tannen, D. (1990). *You just don't understand: Women and men in conversation.* New York: William Morrow.

———. (1998). *The argument culture: Moving from debate to dialogue.* New York: Random House.

Tavris, C. (1992). *The mismeasure of woman.* New York: Simon & Schuster.

The Word Tree: Ethnic Americanisms. (1998). NY: U.S. Department of the Interior.

Thomas, K. (1991). *A cultural history of gesture.* Ithaca, NY: Cornell University Press.

Thompson, J. (1999). Second kind of mind. In J. Canfield, M. V. Hansen, K. Kirberger, & D. Clark (Eds.), *Chicken soup for the college soul* (pp. 163–5). Deerfield Beach, FL: Health Communications.

Thornton, K., McKinnie, R., & Stetz, M. (1999, August 29). Treatment of minorities harsher, officers admit. *San Diego Union Tribune,* p. Al., A18.

Ting-Toomey, S. (2000). Managing intercultural conflicts effectively. In L. A. Samovar & R. E. Porter (Eds.), *Intercultural communication: A reader* (pp. 388–99). Belmont, CA: Wadsworth.

Toch, H., & Smith, H. (Eds.), (1968). *Social perception.* Princeton, NJ: D. Van Nostrand.

REFERENCES

Tolson, J. (1999, March 1). Can the quietest war be brought to an end? *U.S. News and World Report,* pp. 58–60.

Toulmin, S. (1969). *The uses of argument.* Cambridge: Cambridge University Press.

Tracy, J. and Matsumoto, D. (2008). "The spontaneous expression of pride and shame." Proceedings of the National Academy of Sciences of the United States of American, 105 (33), 11660.

Triadis, H. C. (1995). *Individualism and collectivism.* Boulder, CO: Westview.

Trosset, C. (1998, September–October). Obstacles to open discussion and critical thinking. *Change,* pp. 44–50.

Turner, S., Hamilton, H., Jacobs, M., Angood, L., & Dwyer, D. H. (1997, September). The influence of fashion magazines on the body image satisfaction of college women: An exploratory analysis. *Adolescence, 32,* 603–15.

Ulinski, M. & O'Callaghan (2002). A comparison of MBA students' and employers' perceptions of the value of oral communication skills for employment. *Journal of Education for Business, 78,* 193–197.

UNESCO. (1997). Body language. *UNESCO Courier, 50,* 35.

Vale, L. (1995, December). The imaging of the city: Public housing and communication. *Communication Research, 22,* 646–64.

Valian, V. (1998, September–October). Sex, schemas, and success: What's keeping women back. *Academe,* 50–55.

Van Benschoten, E. (2000). Youth-led civic organizing: Countering perceptions of apathy and redefining civic engagement (a conversation with Joel Spoonheim of the Active Citizens school). *National Civic Review, 89,* 301–308.

Van Den Buick, J. (2004). The relationship between television fiction and fear of crime: an empirical comparison of three causal explanations. *European Journal of Communication, 19,* 238–249.

Van Dijk, J. (2000). *The network society: An introduction to the social aspects of new media.* Newbury Park, CA: Sage.

Vanlear, C. A. (1991). Testing a cyclical model of communicative openness in relationship development: Two longitudinal studies. *Communication Monographs, 58.* 337–61.

Wachs, F. L., & Dworkin, S. (1997, November). There's no such thing as a gay hero. *Journal of Sports and Social Issues,* 21, 329–50.

Walker, L. (2002). Unpublished student journal. University of San Diego: Communication Studies 100.

Wallace, M. (2002). How to introduce speakers: Tips and templates. Retrieved March 7, 2002, from http://www.11rx.com/columns/guide8.htm.

Watzlawick, P., Beavelas, J. B., & Jackson, D. D. (1967). *Pragmatics of human communication: A study of interaction patterns, pathologies, and paradoxes.* New York: W. W. Norton.

Weaver, R. L. (1996, August–September). Motivating the motivators: Eight characteristics for empowering those who empower others. *Executive Speeches, 11* 1, 35–38.

Weimann, G. (2000). *Communicating unreality: Modern media and the reconstruction of reality.* Newbury Park, CA: Sage.

Weisfeld, C. C. & Stack, M. A. (2002). When I look into your eyes. *Psychology, Evolution, & Gender, 4,* 125–148.

Wenger, C. B., & Jerome, D. (1999). Change and stability in confident relationships: Findings from the Bangor longitudinal study of aging. *Journal of Aging Studies, 13* (3), 269.

Westen, R. (1996, July 17). The real slant on gossip. *Psychology Today,* p. 44.

Wheeler, D. L. (1999, June 25). With ingenious experiments, a psychologist studies the mental lives of chimps. *The Chronicle of Higher Education,* p. B2.

Whitaker, R. (2002, March 17). We've come too far to be reduced to the small screen. *Washington Post,* p. B1.

Weisfeld, C. C. & Stack, M. A. (2002). When I look into your eyes. *Psychology, Evolution & Gender, 4,* 125–148.

White, C. (2004). HD for the masses: more affordable HD production moves downmarket. Retrieved June 19, 2004 from http://www.digitalproducer.com/articles/viewarticle.jsp?id=25392-0.

Whorf, B. (1956). *Language, thought, and reality.* New York: John Wiley.

Wicks, R. H. (1996). Joseph Klapper and the effects of mass communication: A retrospective. *Journal of Broadcasting and Mass Communication, 40,* 563–70.

Wilcox, D. L., Ault, P. H., and Agree, W. K. (1986). *Public relations: Strategies and tactics.* New York: Harper and Row.

Wilmot, W. W., & Hocker, J. L. (2001). *Interpersonal Conflict* (6th ed.). New York: McGraw-Hill.

Wilson-Smith, A. (2000, February 28). Playing for the cameras. *Macleans,* p. 12.

Winkel, F. W. W., & De Kleuver, E. (1997). Communication aimed at changing conditions about sexual intimidation. *Journal of Interpersonal Violence, 12* (4), 513–30.

Wolak, J., Mitchell, K. J., & Finkelhor, D. (2002). Close online relationships in a national sample of adolescents. *Adolescence, 37,* 441–456.

Wolff, F. I., & Marsnik, N. C. (1992). *Perceptive Listening* (2nd ed.). Fort Worth, TX: Harcourt Brace Jovanovich.

Wood, J. T. (1994). *Gendered lives: Communication, gender, and culture.* Belmont, CA: Wadsworth.

———. (1997). *Communication theories in action: An introduction.* Belmont, CA: Wadsworth.

———. (1998). *Communication mosaics,* Belmont, CA: Wadsworth.

Worldwide Boxoffice (2004). Retrieved June 19, 2004 from http://worldwideboxoffice.com.

Wycoff, E. (1994, April). The language of listening. *Internal Auditor, 51,* 26–29.

Yale University Library (1996). Yale University library primary sources research. Retrieved July 8, 2002 from http://www.library.yale.edu/ref/err/primsrcs.htm PRIMDEF.

Yam, P. (1999, February). In brief: Violently forgetting. *Scientific American,* pp. 26–29.

Yzer, M. C., Capplelia, J. N., Fishbein, M., Hornik, R., & Ahern, R. K. (2003). The effectiveness of gateway communications in anti-marijuana campaigns. *Journal of Health Communication, 8,* 129–143.

NAME INDEX

SUBJECT INDEX

PHOTO CREDITS

Ch. 1, p. 2, © Jeff Greenberg/PhotoEdit; Ch. 2, p. 36, © Michael Prince/Corbis; Ch. 3, p. 64, © Gale Zucker/Stock Boston; Ch. 4, p. 90, © Bob Daemmrich; Ch. 5, p. 120, © Jeff Greenberg/PhotoEdit; Ch. 6, p. 148, © Hideo Haga/HAGA/The Image Works; Ch. 7, p. 178, © Sonda Dawes/The Image Works; Ch. 8, p. 208, © Dwayne Newton/PhotoEdit; Ch. 9, p. 236, © Myrleen Ferguson Cate/PhotoEdit; Ch. 10, p. 268, © David Young-Wolff/PhotoEdit; Ch. 11, p. 296, © Cindy Charles/PhotoEdit; Ch. 12, p. 322, © David Young-Wolff/PhotoEdit; Ch. 13, p. 352, © Bettmann/Corbis; Ch. 14, p. 378, © Spencer Grant/PhotoEdit; Ch. 15, p. 402, © Syracuse Newspapers/Dick Blume/The Image Works